Social Development

Social Development

David G. Perry
Florida Atlantic University

Kay Bussey
Macquarie University

Prentice-Hall, Inc., Englewood Cliffs, New Jersey 07632

Library of Congress Cataloging in Publication Data

PERRY, DAVID G.
    Social development.

    Bibliography: p.
    Includes index.
    1. Child psychology.   2. Social interaction
in children.   I. Bussey, Kay.   II. Title.
BF721.P4153 1984   155.4′18   83–13933
ISBN 0-13-816034-1

Editorial/production supervision
    and interior design: Dee Amir Josephson
Cover design: George Cornell
Manufacturing buyer: Ron Chapman

Prentice-Hall Series in Social Learning Theory
    Albert Bandura, Editor

Printed in the United States of America

10   9   8   7   6   5

ISBN 0-13-816034-1

Prentice-Hall International, Inc., *London*
Prentice-Hall of Australia Pty. Limited, *Sydney*
Editora Prentice-Hall do Brasil, Ltda., *Rio de Janeiro*
Prentice-Hall Canada Inc., *Toronto*
Prentice-Hall of India Private Limited, *New Delhi*
Prentice-Hall of Japan, Inc., *Tokyo*
Prentice-Hall of Southeast Asia Pte. Ltd., *Singapore*
Whitehall Books Limited, *Wellington, New Zealand*

Contents

Preface

Research on social and personality development has exploded in the past two decades, and many universities now offer specialized child development courses on topics such as social development, personality development, socialization, and parent-child relations. Unfortunately, though scores of textbooks continue to be available for use in general child development courses, only a handful of books are devoted primarily to a coverage of the major issues in social development, such as infant attachments, moral development, aggression, and sex typing. Furthermore, most of these books suffer from deficiencies in either breadth (perhaps the book concentrates on the contribution of the family to social development and ignores other important influences such as the school, the peer group, and the television set) or depth (the book may con-stitute an adequate introduction to social development for undergraduate students, but be too superficial for use at the graduate level).

Kay Bussey and I have tried to correct these deficiencies by putting together a textbook that covers the major aspects of social development, as well as the major influences on social development, at a level that challenges not only the intelligent undergraduate student but also the beginning graduate student. Although we suspect that many students opting for a course in social or personality development will have previously taken a course in general child development, we have used a jargon-free writing style that does not presuppose the student's having had prior coursework in child psychology.

This book is organized by topic (aggression,

moral development, etc.), but books on development also can be organized by age (infancy, early childhood, etc.). The difficulty with a chronological organization is that redundancy results when the development of the same child behaviors is discussed at each of several age levels. For example, many of the processes governing aggressive development in early childhood are still important in aggressive development in later years, and reminding the reader of this fact at several points in the book can prove tedious. Moreover, it is simply much easier to grasp the development of a behavior by reading about how that behavior develops from birth to maturity within a single chapter.

The first five chapters are concerned mainly with theories and processes of development. We begin with a critical discussion and comparison of several theories of social development. This first chapter also includes a review of the contemporary methods researchers use to evaluate hypotheses empirically. The next chapter depicts how social relationships and social habits become established in infancy. Chapters 3 and 4 deal with two major processes of social learning: The third chapter is concerned with how children learn directly from the instruction and discipline they experience at the hands of their parents and other socializing agents, and the fourth with how children learn vicariously by observing the actions of their parents, peers, television characters, and other classes of models. In Chapter 5 the child's social-cognitive development is described. Because social cognitions may be considered mediating links between children's social learning experiences and their social behavior, this chapter provides a transition from the earlier ones on social learning to the subsequent chapters, which discuss selected aspects of children's overt social behavior. Separate chapters are devoted to moral development, aggression, prosocial behavior, sex-role development, and peer relations.

Throughout the book several themes are stressed. First, the field of social development today is generating a great deal of theoretical controversy; we have tried to communicate this by stressing, whenever possible, how different theories compete for explanation of a developmental phenomenon and by highlighting studies that help shed light on the relative merits of various theoretical positions. We try never to lose sight of the fact that psychology is a science, and that our goal is to come up with a set of theory-derived principles that help us describe, explain, and guide human social development. Second, many of our discussions reflect our belief that a research result merits our greatest confidence when the same result is reached independently by several studies employing different methodologies. Thus we do not favor studies using a particular methodology but rather report the results of field studies as well as laboratory studies, interview as well as observational studies, experimental as well as correlational investigations, cross-sectional as well as longitudinal projects, and so on, all the while looking for convergences of evidence. Third, our book acknowledges that children are active contributors to their own development. It has become a hackneyed truism of late to mention that development is a function of person-environment interaction, but recent data allow us actually to chart some of the crucial sequences of organism-environment interplay that are associated with certain developmental outcomes. For example, the likelihood of child abuse increases when a parent with certain qualities (of temperament, childhood experience, social stress, etc.) is forced to accommodate to an infant with certain qualities (of temperament, birth weight, physical appearance, rate of development, etc.). Whenever possible, we provide illustrative data that help us appreciate the nature of the reciprocal influence between the developing child and his or her social environment. Fourth, although the principal purpose of our book is to review basic processes of personality and social development, whenever possible we point out when research findings suggest a practical application for parents or teachers in child-rearing or educational contexts. Thus our chapter on infancy reviews ways to promote healthy, secure attachments; our chapter on child-rearing practices compares the effectiveness of various disciplinary tactics; our chapter on modeling discusses the dangers and benefits of various sorts of television fare; and so on. It is hoped, then, that the book will have appeal not only as a core text in university courses but also as a volume of practical interest to parents and educators.

Many people helped us in the preparation of the book. We wish to thank John Isley, psychology editor at Prentice-Hall, for his continued encouragement of a project that took far longer than promised to complete. We are especially grateful to Al Bandura for his interest in our work and for his thoughtful, detailed reviews of early drafts. All the following individuals either provided a review of one or more of the chapters or contributed to our endeavor in some other significant way: Ed Cornell, Len Eron, Mark Greenberg, Joan Grusec, Mavis Hetherington, William Kurtines, Marsha Liss, Ross Parke, Brendan Rule, Kathleen Senior, Ron Slaby, and Wes Snyder. The Departments of Psychology at the University of Alberta and Florida Atlantic University generously provided resources that helped with manuscript preparation. Many typists worked on the project but Sylvia Friedman, Susan McDonough, and Ruth Murray deserve special thanks for their efforts. I would like to thank Dee Josephson and Carey Perry for their superb editorial work. Most important, I am grateful to my wife Louise for her emotional support and intellectual input throughout the writing of the book and to my children, Elizabeth and Michael, who doubled and tripled in age during the project, and who are my very special tutors of development.

David G. Perry
Boca Raton, Florida

To Louise, Elizabeth, and Michael

1 Theories and Research Methods

The primary goal of this book is to evaluate how far the science of psychology has progressed in formulating a set of principles that help us to describe, explain, predict, and guide human social development. Thus one of our main concerns will be with how well social developmentalists have fared as theorists. What are the major theories of social development? Are some theorists better than others at developing a neat set of principles to explain empirical research findings, at generating novel research that extends our understanding of development, and at offering guidelines for practical intervention? In this chapter, we present an overview of several influential theories. Later, in topic chapters, we review in detail the research that supports or refutes the various theories.

Adequate evaluation of theory rests on sound research methods. In a second major section of this chapter, we review some of the tools psychologists use to study development, especially those used to evaluate theory-relevant hypotheses.

THEORETICAL PERSPECTIVES

A psychological theory is a system of interrelated rules and principles (including assumptions and derivations) designed to explain and predict behavior. A good theory has several characteristics. First and foremost, it must generate predictions and propositions ("If _____, then _____" statements) about events, which are verified when the relevant data are collected. Because almost any theory can explain events after they have occurred, the current tendency in evaluating a theory is to concentrate on its potential for making accurate predictions (Baldwin, 1967; Bandura, 1977). Of utmost importance to theory building is specifying the *causes* of behavior; if we know the necessary and sufficient causes of a behavior, we are in a better position to guide and alter human behavior.

By noting that good theories make accurate predictions, we do not mean that they will always predict what is going to occur in real life in a soothsayer or fortune-teller fashion. Theories are designed only to make predictions about what will happen *if* certain conditions are met. For example, a theorist might say that a child will behave aggressively *if* the child is frustrated. Once such a propositional statement is generated, researchers attempt to determine the theory's validity, here perhaps by subjecting groups of children to frustrating or nonfrustrating experiences and then measuring their level of aggression.

A second characteristic of a good theory is public verifiability or "repeatability." This means that the theory is communicated in such clear and explicit language that other psychologists are able to set up the conditions for the predicted event and can recognize the predicted event when it happens (Baldwin, 1967). A theory that specifies that frustration leads to aggression must indicate the conditions and operations necessary for producing frustration and also for measuring aggression. Theories should be presented with such logic and clarity that they are testable, or capable of disproof.

A good theory not only generates new predictions but can also accommodate or "handle" known empirical findings. The broader the range of empirical phenomena the theory can deal with, or the more comprehensive the theory, the better. However, a good theory accounts for a given range of events with the fewest number of principles, variables, or constructs possible. This is the rule of parsimony, or simplicity.

We begin our survey of the major theories of social and personality development with Freud's colorful *psychoanalytic theory*. Freud viewed personality as the product of dynamic clashes among various forces acting within the individual. Though his theory is guiding little research today, it has influenced the direction that theory and research have taken. It is important to grasp the basics of Freudian theory and the reasons for its disfavor among contemporary researchers.

We then summarize *trait theory*. Trait theorists conceptualize personality as the individual's location on a set of personality dimensions, such as honesty, aggressiveness, intelligence, and so on. They have had little to say about how children's personalities develop, but they have influenced how psychologists conceptualize and measure aspects of the personality.

Next we turn to *social learning theory*. Social learning theorists regard personality as the product of the individual's transactions with his or her social environment. According to this theory, as children get older they develop and continuously refine their conceptions of what society deems to be appropriate and inappropriate conduct for people like themselves. Children are thought to base these notions on a variety of social learning experiences, including the discipline they receive at the hands of their parents, observations of how their peers are treated for their actions, and direct verbal instruction from adults and peers. While children are developing these conceptions of desirable and undesirable conduct, they presumably are learning to regulate their own behavior to conform to these conceptions.

According to *cognitive-developmental theory*, personality and social behavior are strongly influenced by the individual's underlying level of intellectual (or "cognitive") maturity. In fact, cognitive-developmental theorists believe that social behavior proceeds in a fixed sequence of stages, each stage characterized by basic defining thought structures (ways of processing information) that strictly determine the level of sophistication of both the child's thinking abilities and social behavior. Although both the cognitive-developmental theorists and the social learning theorists believe that social behavior is influenced by mental activity on the part of the child, the two sorts of theorists differ dramatically in the exact role assigned to cognition in the social development process.

Finally, we review the *ethological perspective*. Ethologists suggest that certain crucial patterns of social behavior develop because they have survival value for the species. Consequently, ethologists stress that certain patterns of behavior are under the control of inherited instincts.

One of the exciting things about current theoretical development in the field is that most theories are in a state of constant flux and revision, adding or dropping concepts or principles as the incoming data dictate. Furthermore, no single theory has a monopoly on interpreting all the facts or generating testable new hypotheses.

Freudian Theory

The Structure of Personality   Sigmund Freud (1964) defined personality as the *ego's* attempts to satisfy the desires of the *id* while dealing with opposition from both the *superego* and the real world. According to Freud, children are born with only the most primitive element of psychic structure—the *id*. The id may be thought of as inherited instincts, which consist chiefly of sexual and aggressive drives. Freud believed that all psychological functioning and behavior require energy, and the id was considered to be the primary source of such energy. He further theorized that the id is the only aspect of psychic structure possessed by children for roughly the first year of their lives and that the id operates strictly according to the *pleasure principle*, or the hedonistic tendency to seek pleasure and avoid pain. Thus Freud viewed young infants as wildly unsocialized creatures who seek immediate gratification whenever their sexual and aggressive urges are aroused.

The id is incapable of postponing gratification, and cannot instruct a child to delay expressing an impulse until environmental circumstances favor it. Thus even if a young child is likely to be punished for displaying aggression, he or she may not be able to inhibit the impulse to behave aggressively when the id presses for hostile expression. Freud believed that the particular conditions causing the sexual and aggressive drives to become aroused changed with age, but in infancy stimulation of the oral cavity (mouth, lips, tongue, etc.) was thought to arouse the infant's sexual drive, and frustrating delays of gratification were thought to arouse the aggressive drive. Though more mature aspects of the personality gradually emerge, the id is never lost. In fact, more mature aspects of personality emerge precisely because they are needed to control the id.

Because the human organism could hardly survive without the ability to regulate its behavior to conform to the demands of external reality, the child also develops an *ego*, or the rational, planful component of personality. The ego is capable of dealing appropriately with the objective world of reality and operates by the *reality principle*—it can plan, delay gratification, and block irrational choices of the id, waiting until the time is ripe for a reality-oriented solution. The toddler whose aggressive drive has been aroused by frustration now waits until the parent is out of sight before attacking a sibling or throwing a tantrum. The ego is thus the "executive" of the personality. It is crucial to remember, though, that the ego is still primarily in the service of the id. In other words, the ego develops and persists because it helps the child satisfy the desires of the id in the face of opposition from the real world.

The third aspect of the personality, the *superego*, is acquired toward the end of the age period that includes years 3 to 5. Freud believed that during this age period children experience the Oedipal crisis, which they resolve by identifying with the same-sex parent, thereby acquiring a conscience or an internal representation of the values and sanctions of society. We shall describe the Oedipal crisis and how it is thought to lead to superego development more fully in a later section of this chapter. Clearly, many of the values of the superego are in direct opposition to the desires of the id, and especially the id's strivings for immediate sexual and aggressive gratification. The ego now has the problem of trying to satisfy the moral goals of the superego as well as the id's more primitive desires. Thus the stage is set for complex battles among the aspects of the personality, the outcomes of which make a lasting imprint on the child's personality development.

Personality Dynamics Freud believed that personality functioning was fueled by a fixed amount of psychic energy that originated with the id, but that eventually became distributed among the id, ego, and superego in varying proportions. If, for example, a person's Oedipal identification and superego development were weak, the id would retain control over a large share of energy and the person's behavior would be impulsive and primitive. On the other hand, if superego development was intense, the personality would be dominated by moralistic concerns.

Equally important in personality dynamics, however, were the conflicts experienced among components of the psychic structure. If the ego could successfully satisfy the id without upsetting the superego, conflict was minimal. This was thought to be the case among most normal people, who were able to express their sexual and aggressive urges within socially and personally acceptable limits. But when this balance was upset by a strong id or an unusually repressive superego, conflicts followed. For example, a young woman who has identified with her mother's restrictive attitudes toward sex may experience conflict upon entering adolescence, when hormonal changes reawaken her id and sensitize her to sexual stimuli.

The important thing about conflicts is that they give rise to feelings of intense anxiety.

And the important thing about anxiety is that it is an extremely unpleasant sensation and hence people (their egos) are motivated to avoid it or escape it—at any cost. There are a number of ways the ego can reduce anxiety intrapsychically. These are called *defense mechanisms*. In Freudian theory, a person's system of defenses essentially defines that person's personality.

Defenses are varied and colorful. *Repression*, a basic defense, involves the expulsion from consciousness of any thoughts related to a conflict. The sexually conflicted girl may simply stop thinking about sex. *Projection* is the attribution of one's own unacceptable impulses to another. Saying "He hates me" allows a person to express a hostile impulse under the guise of defending oneself against an enemy. *Reaction formation* occurs when an unacceptable and anxiety-provoking thought is replaced with its opposite. A mother may mask rejection of a child by smothering the child with affection and attention. *Identification*, or making oneself more similar to another person, is thought to occur when the child is threatened by someone. Presumably the ego reasons that becoming similar to someone else reduces the chance of that person harming you. *Displacement* is the substitution of an original object choice with a less threatening, socially acceptable one. Leonardo da Vinci presumably satisfied his longing for intimacy with his mother by painting madonnas. Surgeons and dentists were also said to be practicing societally-sanctioned actions that would satisfy their aggressive impulses. In fact, Freud argued that most human interests, values, and attachments represented displacements. These and other defenses, then, represented unconscious attempts by the ego to effect compromises between the id and superego.

Psychosexual Stages Freud hypothesized that development proceeds in stages, each stage involving unique frustrations and anxieties. If too much energy was invested in wrestling with a conflict at a particular stage, the child might develop a "fixation" at that stage and the personality would be irrevocably scarred by the concerns of that stage. Freud in fact believed that people's basic personality cores were fixed for life from such early experiences and fixations.

Freud proposed five developmental stages. The stages differ in terms of the region of the child's body that is thought to offer sexual pleasure. The first is the *oral stage*, which lasts about 1 year. During the oral stage, sexual pleasure is thought to result from stimulation of the lips and oral cavity. Frustrations at this stage could lead to the development of certain personality traits, such as a strong dependency on other people or a tendency toward being bitingly sarcastic, which would surface in adulthood. In the second year the child is in the *anal stage*. Now pleasure is derived from controlling the bowel muscles. Depending on how parents handle toilet training, a child can develop lasting traits of rebelliousness, hostility, wastefulness, stinginess, or even generosity.

The all-important *Oedipal*, or *phallic, stage* lasts roughly from ages 3 to 5. This stage differs somewhat for boys and girls. According to Freud, the boy desires sexual intercourse with his mother, but, fearing retaliation in the form of castration from his father, resolves the crisis by defensively identifying with his father. Freud believed that the girl begins her Oedipal crisis by noticing she lacks a penis. She blames her mother for this lack and desires sexual contact with him who possesses the desired organ—her father. The girl fears, however, that her mother will be jealous of such desires and will somehow symbolically reenact the violent act that made her a female in the first place. This fear causes the girl to identify with her mother. Through identification with the parent of the same sex, the child is believed to acquire the values, beliefs, motives, morals, attitudes, and masculine or feminine sex-role identity of that parent.

The phallic stage is followed by a *latency period*. During this stage, which lasts until ad-

olescence, the sexual instincts lie dormant and the child is calmly absorbed in play and schoolwork. It has been suggested that this stage is useful in that it enables the child to organize the defenses he or she has acquired in previous stages.

In adolescence, the sexual instincts are reawakened, and the *genital stage* begins. Freud believed that in the healthy person (i.e., the person lacking serious conflicts), sexual energy now becomes focused on a loved person of the opposite sex.

Critique of Freudian Theory As a scientific theory, Freudian theory is seriously deficient. First, there are shortcomings in the methods Freud used to validate his hypotheses. Freud's primary data were the verbal reports of neurotic patients who were asked to *free associate* (say whatever came to mind) and to recount their dreams. Freud believed that free associations and dreams were windows to unconscious conflicts. One problem with this research method is that patients' verbal reports may not be reliable indicators of the patients' real thoughts and conflicts. Also, Freud's interpretations were subjective and may not have been confirmed by others.

A second problem is that Freud's concepts are not defined in ways that make them amenable to concrete behavioral assessment. In other words, it is difficult, if not impossible, to know precisely which of the child's behaviors should be taken as measures of Freud's internal concepts. How do we measure a child's level of psychic energy? How do we measure the strength of a child's ego or superego?

A third criticism is that although Freudian theory can explain just about anything and everything after it happens, it predicts very little. It is extremely difficult to predict, for example, what defenses a person's ego will adopt given certain antecedent conditions. In general, "Freudian theory is markedly deficient in providing a set of relational rules by which we can arrive at any precise expectations of what will happen if certain events take place" (Hall & Lindzey, 1970, p. 71).

A final criticism is that Freud places too much emphasis on intrapsychic determinants of behavior, paying too little attention to environmental influences. Although Freud acknowledged that parent-child interaction influences development, he believed that the intrapsychic conflicts and defenses the child develops are ultimately responsible for the formation of the child's personality. Furthermore, he believed that these conflicts and defenses tend to function and persist with little interference from environmental influences.

Freud's Legacy Because Freud's theory is so "unscientific" and leads to so few clear-cut empirically testable propositions, it is guiding little research in social development today. Nevertheless, psychoanalytic theory has, over the years, had a tremendous impact on many research directions and issues. For instance, Freud hypothesized that infants become attached to the mother because she satisfies their oral needs by providing a breast to suck. Though this belief is shared by few psychologists today, it did lead early students of the mother-infant relationship to focus their research on effects of specific maternal caregiving practices, such as breast versus bottle feeding and demand versus schedule feeding. Furthermore, many psychologists still believe that infants become attached to the mother because she satisfies their biological drives in one way or another. In later chapters we shall see how Freudian theory not only influenced early research on infant development but also influenced early research on the development of other behaviors such as aggression and morality.

Many modern theorists share Freud's view that the early years are important and formative. However, most contemporary psychologists give more credit to the child's transactions with the social environment in influencing development than did Freud, and they are more optimistic that personality and social habits can continue to be modified in important ways beyond early childhood.

Trait Theory

The Basics of Trait Theory Trait theorists conceptualize personality in terms of how much an individual possesses each of several behavioral dispositions or *traits*, such as intelligence, aggressiveness, conscientiousness, and achievement motivation (e.g., Allport, 1966; Cattell, 1957; Eysenck, 1957; Guilford, 1959). Although trait theorists disagree on the number of basic traits needed to structure personality, each theorist defines personality in terms of a person's location in an *n*-dimensional space, with *n* referring to the number of independent personality dimensions or traits that the theorist considers necessary to account for most of the variability in social behavior.

Trait theory is closely associated with the psychometric movement in psychology. This is because trait theorists favor statistical techniques (e.g., factor analysis), which help them select items for paper-and-pencil personality inventories designed to assess people's locations on personality traits. The objective has been to develop tests that permit comparisons of an individual's position on trait dimensions with those of other persons tested under comparable, standardized conditions. By establishing group norms, it is possible to chart individual *personality profiles* (e.g., "So-and-so is well above average for his or her sex and age on extraversion, about average in dependency," etc.).

Most trait theorists use traits as explanations of behavior. That is, they regard traits as tendencies within people that account for their unique but relatively stable reactions to stimuli. Thus traits are viewed as relatively stable and enduring predispositions that exert fairly generalized effects on behavior.

Trait theorists have paid little attention to how children develop greater or lesser amounts of various traits. Considerable controversy has developed concerning this theory, as we review below.

A Problem for Trait Theory According to trait theory, traits are internal qualities that cause people to behave consistently across diverse situations. Thus trait theorists expect *cross-situational consistency* in social behavior: A boy who is noted for being highly aggressive should, compared to his peers, behave in a relatively aggressive fashion across all situations—at home as well as at school, toward his parents and teachers as well as his playmates, and so on; a girl who is low on the trait of dependency should behave in a relatively nondependent manner across many situations; and a child who is moderately extraverted should display average amounts of friendliness across all situations.

Research in this area has not supported such consistency, however (Mischel, 1968; 1979). For example, in a classic study on the "generality of honesty," Hartshorne and May (1929) found little evidence supporting a consistent pattern of moral character in school children across situations. Children were observed for the degree of deception, helpfulness, cooperativeness, self-control, persistence, and cheating that they displayed in different situations, which included sports events and classroom activities. Results revealed considerable *situational specificity* in moral behavior, meaning that the degree to which a given child behaved morally fluctuated markedly from situation to situation. It is true that some children showed some consistency in moral character (tending to score consistently above or below average on the morality scale across situations), but overall the contribution of situational influences was stronger (Burton, 1963). Mischel (1968) reviewed numerous studies revealing similar findings for other traits. An exception holds for traits related to intellectual functioning. People who behave intelligently in one situation are likely to behave intelligently in other situations.

The fact that people are variable in their standing on most behavioral dimensions across situations has led many psychologists to conclude that behavior cannot be predicted from a knowledge of a person's standing on a trait measure, and therefore traits are figments of our imagination rather than behavioral realities. These critics argue that we have clung strongly to trait constructs because it is intuitively appealing to do so. Psychologists, like laypeople, seem to have a need to assign trait labels to people—we like to believe that people behave consistently across situations. The amount of information we can process and remember about the idiosyncrasies of any individual's behavior is limited, and we simply find it more convenient, more efficient, and easier to describe someone's personality in terms of where that person falls on a few global trait dimensions.

New Directions in Trait Theory But are traits really nothing more than figments of our imaginations? A number of psychologists believe that the rejection of traits as realities is premature. Several theorists have suggested that some people may be fairly consistent on most personality traits across situations, whereas other people may be relatively inconsistent (Snyder, 1979; Underwood & Moore, 1981). According to this view, people who are introspective and self-reflective are more consistent across situations because they are not giving their full attention to changes in their external environment as they move from one situation to the next. In contrast, there are other people who have developed the habit of attending to and relying on external cues as guides to the appropriateness of their behavior. For these people, behavior varies considerably from situation to situation because they are constantly concerned with adjusting their behaviors, attitudes, opinions, and so on to be what they deem appropriate to each new social situation encountered. Snyder (1979) developed a questionnaire aimed at identifying people who tend to monitor their behavior in terms of external cues. For example, subjects are presented with the statement, "When I am uncertain how to act in a social situation, I look to the behavior of others for cues." Adults who endorse such statements actually do reveal more situational specificity in their expression of such behaviors as generosity, honesty, and hostility. In essence, then, people differ in the constancy of their social behaviors.

Other researchers propose that different traits assume different degrees of significance, and hence consistency, in different people (Bem and Allen, 1974). One man may be concerned with preserving his masculinity, thus displaying a high degree of masculinity across situations, but be relatively unconcerned with friendliness, honesty, and generosity, therefore revealing a high degree of situational specificity on these latter dimensions. This man's high score on the trait of masculinity is meaningful, but it would be senseless to attach much meaning to his average scores on the other traits since he reveals a high degree of situational variability on these traits. Another man, a priest perhaps, may be more concerned with displaying consistent degrees of honesty and generosity than the other behaviors. These examples illustrate that people differ in the traits that are of importance in describing their personalities. A trait will be useful for describing a person only to the extent that the person shows low cross-situational variability for the behavior in question. A number of studies have shown that people do vary in terms of the traits for which they display consistency (Bem & Allen, 1974; Kenrick & Stringfield, 1980; Pervin, 1976).

Monson (1982), offering another perspective on traits, has proposed that a trait should be conceptualized not as a person's average intensity of a behavior across situations but rather as a person's stable disposition to seek or avoid situations that provoke the behavior. Consider the behavior of extraverts and introverts. When observed in a given social situation, both types of individuals may display roughly the same degree of sociability and friendliness. But when they are allowed to select their social conditions, extraverts may more often spontaneously choose situations conducive to socializing. While extroverts may spend more time "shooting the breeze" with dormmates, introverts may choose to spend more time alone in the library. In a study of elementary school boys, Bullock and Merrill (1980) found that some boys report a stable preference for situations conducive to aggression, whereas other boys shun these situations.

The possibilities that people vary in their overall level of behavioral consistency (e.g., Snyder's view), that people differ in terms of the traits on which they are consistent and inconsistent (Bem and Allen's view), and that people differ in their dispositions to seek out certain sorts of situations (Monson's view) raise interesting questions for developmental psychologists. What causes children to develop a sensitivity to external cues that renders their social behavior situationally specific? How do children develop particular concerns for maintaining consistency on some trait dimensions but not on others? How do children develop preferences for certain kinds of situations? The trait theorists themselves have not tried to answer these questions, but we shall see that some of the other theorists do address them.

Regardless of how one tries to resolve the trait issue, the research on cross-situational consistency of behavior has left us with one inescapable conclusion: Situations exert powerful influences on behavior. In most cases it would be futile to try to predict a person's behavior solely from an "average" score on a trait measure simply because the person's behavior on any one particular dimension is likely to vary markedly from situation to situation. Some situations elicit a similar reaction from all people. For example, most people will try swimming if thrown into the ocean. However, many situations allow for a wider range of reaction and elicit different responses from different people. For example, frustration can provoke aggression in one child, but withdrawal in another.

Thus it seems increasingly clear that human social behavior can reliably be predicted only from knowing how a particular person tends to respond in a particular situation. Considering social behavior to be a joint function of person and environment variables has been called an *interactionist* view of personality (Bowers, 1973; Ekehammar, 1974; Endler & Magnusson, 1976). One implication of the person-situation interaction view is that psychologists need to study what causes different children to react differently to the same situation. This issue has been explored extensively by the learning theorists, who are discussed in the following section.

Social Learning Theory

The Fundamentals of Social Learning Theory According to social learning theorists such as Bandura (1977; Bandura & Walters, 1963b) and Mischel (1973, 1979), as children develop they continuously refine their conceptions of the sorts of behavior society considers appropriate or inappropriate for people like themselves to perform in various situations. Children base these conceptions on a variety of social learning experiences: the direct rewards and punishments they experience at the hands of their parents; the consequences they see others receive for performing various responses to certain situations; and the verbal instructions they receive from teachers, parents, peers, and other socializing agents. Children integrate the information they receive from these diverse social learning experiences to formulate *response-outcome contingency rules*. For example, by seeing what happens to themselves and others for impulsively aggressing toward parents and other adults, most children eventually conclude that aggressing against authority figures leads to negative outcomes and that self-control in such situ-

ations is expected and praiseworthy. These cognitive representations of social experiences, which differ from child to child depending on each child's unique social learning history, are thought to serve a motivational function: Children seek to perform behaviors for which they expect to be rewarded, and they strive to avoid behaviors that they know are inappropriate and blameworthy. Although much of social behavior is thought to be under the control of anticipated external consequences, such as praise or criticism from adults, social learning theorists also believe that behavior is often influenced by anticipated self-evaluations. This refers to the child's expectation of feeling proud and satisfied or guilty and upset for performing various acts. We shall elaborate these points below.

Social learning is strongly influenced by the direct disciplinary experiences children encounter at the hands of their parents and other socializing agents. By punishing, rewarding, instructing, and reasoning with children, adults provide them with enormous amounts of information about the sorts of behavior that are desirable or undesirable to perform in various circumstances. Chapter 3 evaluates many of the methods used by adults to teach children appropriate behavior through discipline. Some techniques are more effective than others: Many child-rearing techniques are effective in getting children to perform desirable behavior and inhibit undesirable conduct, but some, unfortunately, lead to results opposite to those intended. For example, parents who use severe physical punishment to control their children's aggression may be unwittingly communicating the lesson that control through physical force really is all right, thereby nullifying the intended effect of the disciplinary method.

Another major way that children learn about response-outcome relationships is through observational learning. When children see other children—especially children who are similar to themselves—being rewarded or punished for displaying various responses in certain situations, they infer that they too might incur positive or negative treatment for performing such behaviors under similar circumstances. As we detail in Chapter 4, observation of the actions of others and the consequences of those actions is an extraordinarily powerful and efficient mechanism of social learning.

Social learning theorists emphasize that because different children experience different social learning experiences, they are likely to form different rules linking a behavior to its consequences. Some parents are permissive of aggression in the home; some are intolerant of aggression. In some homes children are allowed to watch television programs displaying rewards for violent behavior; in other homes, children are not. Children coming from these different family environments will probably generate different rules about the acceptability of aggression. Social learning theorists, then, expect individual differences in social behavior as a function of child-rearing climate, social class, and other variables predictive of behavior-consequence rule learning.

Social learning theorists stress that in generating response-outcome rules, children display discrimination learning. If a child is consistently rewarded for a response when it is performed in one situation, but punished for the same behavior when it occurs under other circumstances, the child is likely to discriminate between the different contingencies, learning to perform the behavior in the first situation but not in the others. Social learning theorists take issue with the trait theorists' prediction of cross-situational consistency in behavior, arguing that consistency across situations is very unlikely because environments frequently reward behavior in certain situations, but frown on the very same behavior under other circumstances. For instance, it is all right to kick and shout on the soccer field, but not in church. Thus social learning theorists are inclined to take a situational specificity perspective on behavior.

The fact that social learning theorists favor the situational specificity perspective does not imply, however, that they believe that all children come to react in the same way to a given situation. One child may be punished for aggression at home, for example, but be able to get away with it on the playground. Another child, however, may be punished for attempts at peer-directed aggression, but may learn to react with aggression to frustrations encountered in the home environment; parents who maintain an indulgent and permissive attitude toward aggression may encourage this. The discriminative stimuli for aggression differ for these two children, but in each case there is situational specificity in behavior. Predicting behavior, then, depends on knowing each individual's unique history of reinforcing and punishing consequences for a behavior within particular situations.

Although social learning theorists tend to regard most social behavior as being situationally specific rather than characterized by broad traitlike predispositions, they do not deny that some people may develop cross-situational consistency on some behavioral dimensions. If, for example, a boy's parents consistently reward him for masculine behaviors and punish him for feminine behaviors and also make a point of labeling toys and activities as "only for boys" or "only for girls," then presumably the child will find it to his advantage to start monitoring his own behavior in accordance with such standards. The child may develop a rigid set for perceiving and classifying situations as either masculine or feminine. Furthermore, the boy may anticipate reward for performing a broad range of masculine activities and fear censure for any activity perceived as feminine. The end result of such a process is that the boy's behavior will reveal some approximation of a "masculine trait."

It should be clear that modern social learning theorists argue that it is how experiences with the environment get organized and represented in one's mind that guides subsequent social behavior. In other words, "mediating cognitions" are considered to be the prime determinants of social behavior. *Cognition* is a broad term referring generally to the higher mental processes, such as perceiving, recognizing associations, conceiving, judging, forming mental images, organizing, planning, and anticipating. Cognitions, the social learning theorists argue, should be regarded as flexible structures, not fixed ideas. For instance, children's mental representations of response-outcome contingencies are thought to change as children are exposed to new social information or learn to attach greater or lesser weight to existing pieces of information.

Social learning theorists assign importance to the self in regulating behavior. For example, when children see that a certain form of behavior reliably produces an aversive outcome (e.g., social disapproval, punishment, or failure), they are motivated to initiate the self-controlling responses that will help avoid the negative outcome. Similarly, when children see that a certain behavior produces a positive external outcome, they try to master the behavior, perhaps setting subgoals of desired behavior, and rewarding or punishing themselves for matching or falling short of these goals. Thus social learning theorists regard social behavior and development not simply as the consequence of external forces and incentives but also as a function of self-generated standards and goals and self-evaluation of progress made toward attaining these goals.

We have discussed some of the influences on development, both external (e.g., incentives in the environment) and internal (e.g., personal standards). In actuality, social learning theorists stress reciprocal causal influences among three classes of variables: person variables, situations, and behavior. Each of these three factors both influences and is influenced by the other two factors. Bandura (1978b) has termed this interacting system of causes *reciprocal determinism*. By *person variables*, the social learning theorists do not mean traitlike predispositions, but instead are referring to such factors as the person's standards, interests, goals, perceived competencies, expectancies, repertoire of behaviors acquired through observational learning, strategies for interpreting and assigning values to situations and stimuli, and self-regulatory systems and plans (Mischel, 1973).

Here is an example of reciprocal determinism: A boy who favors television programs with aggressive content (a person variable) chooses to spend his evenings in front of a television set tuned to violent programs (an environment variable). While watching attentively (a behavior variable), the boy learns new modes of aggressing toward people and also learns that aggression is usually successful in that aggressive people often get what they want. In this scenario, a person variable (the boy's preference for television violence) leads the boy to select an environment that is conducive to the learning of new aggressive habits and expectations. These newly acquired expectations (a person factor) may then lead the boy to attempt the newly acquired forms of aggressive behavior. If these behaviors are reinforced, stable tendencies toward overt aggression may result. Bandura suggests that in light of the fact that development is frequently a product of chains of events that involve reciprocal causal influences among person, behavior, and environment variables, it is foolish to try to assign primary causal status to any one of these factors over the other two. Although we began our hypothetical scenario with a person variable (the boy's program preferences), it is obvious that this person variable must have had its own antecedents.

Critique of Social Learning Theory
Social learning theory has many positive features. The theory is clear-cut and its concepts are usually simply stated in ways that permit objective measurement and empirical evaluation. Much of our knowledge about the de-

velopment of aggression, morality, altruism, and sex typing comes from work conducted within the social learning framework. In addition, learning theory has demonstrated practical utility: The success of many behavior modification techniques is due to principles formulated by learning theorists (Bandura, 1969a). Nevertheless, several criticisms have been directed toward the theory. Although some of these criticisms are myths, it is worthwhile to review them.

First, it is popularly thought that social learning theorists view children as passive beings who are simply molded by their environments. It is true that social learning theorists regard development largely as the product of the child's learning experiences rather than the result of traits residing within the individual, but this does not mean that social learning theorists take a mechanistic view of children or regard them as behaving in automatic machinelike fashion in response to environmental forces. We have already seen that social learning theorists believe that children are active contributors to their own socialization, setting goals for themselves, praising and criticizing themselves, selecting certain situations for themselves, and so on. As Bandura points out, if actions were determined solely by external rewards and punishments, people would behave like weather vanes, constantly shifting in different directions to conform to the momentary influences impinging upon them. "Anyone who has attempted to change a pacifist into an aggressor or a devout religionist into an atheist would quickly come to appreciate the existence of personal sources of control" (Bandura, 1977; pp. 128–129).

The false impression that social learning theorists regard children as passively molded by their environments probably results from confusing modern social learning theory with old-fashioned conditioning theories of social learning. When psychologists first tried to explain development in terms of learning theory, they tried to account for human social development in terms of principles of oper-

ant and classical conditioning, which were discovered in laboratory experiments with animals (Aronfreed, 1968; Bijou & Baer, 1965; Gewirtz, 1969; Skinner, 1953). These theorists believed that most social behaviors are "shaped" in children in much the same manner that rats, dogs, and pigeons are trained to respond. Clearly, modern social learning theory, with its emphasis on cognitive processing and self-direction, has come a long way beyond these primitive models of social learning.

Two other distinctions between social learning theory and conditioning theory have caused confusion and misunderstanding. First, according to conditioning theory, in order for learning to occur, a child must both perform a response and be reinforced for it. Although social learning theorists acknowledge that a child sometimes learns because of consequences experienced following certain actions, they stress that most learning occurs through observation, without the child performing a response and being reinforced for it. As we shall see in Chapter 4, children can acquire the potential to perform numerous new response patterns, as well as learn the likely consequences for enacting the responses, simply by observing the actions of others and encoding the behavior and its consequences in memory.

Another distinction between conditioning theory and social learning theory is that conditioning theory describes behavior as being controlled by its immediate consequences. According to conditioning theory, external reinforcement has the effect of directly strengthening the association between a stimulus and a response, and punishment has the effect of weakening such links. Sometimes conditioning theorists invoke notions of affective conditioning to explain these response-strengthening and response-weakening effects of reinforcement and punishment. For example, they may say that reinforcement strengthens behavior by conditioning positive feelings to the behavior and that punishment weakens behavior by conditioning anxiety to it. Modern social learning theorists, however, do not believe that most behavior is rigidly governed by its immediate consequences. They concede that immediately available situational incentives sometimes influence behavior, but they believe that most behavior is governed by mental conceptions of behavior and its consequences, which are formed gradually over months or years and are based on the child's ability to synthesize information from directly experienced consequences, observational learning, and verbal instruction. Thus in social learning theory, behavior is thought to be centrally mediated by mental rules rather than by positive or negative emotion residing in the behavior itself. Also, behavior often is thought to be motivated by incentives quite distant in time and place, but yet cognitively represented in the child's mind.

Although modern social learning theory is far more popular than its conditioning theory predecessors, we will see in later chapters that conditioning theory is still very influential in conceptualizing development in several areas. For example, learning theorists' explanations of the attachment process in infancy are strongly influenced by conditioning principles. It is important to bear in mind that conditioning theory and social learning theory are distinctly different.

Social learning theory has been criticized for not being a developmental theory. This is a valid point. Social learning theorists have been far more concerned with formulating a general set of principles and mechanisms that help explain social learning across the age span than they have been with pinpointing and explaining the specific qualitative changes in behavior that occur with age. Social learning theory does recognize, however, that people differ concerning what they teach, model, and reinforce with children of different ages (Bandura, 1977). For example, parental control is at first necessarily external. In attempting to discourage dangerous conduct in young children who haven't yet learned to talk, parents must resort to physical intervention.

Later, social sanctions replace physical ones. Eventually, of course, internalized control begins to replace external control, with the child's standards and self-evaluative processes assuming major importance. The social learning theorists have not studied the ages at which these changes occur, but they have pointed to this important sequence in social development and have offered some important principles to account for progression through the sequence.

If the learning theories can be characterized as heavy on process and light on description of age-related changes, the opposite can be said for the next theory we consider: cognitive-developmental theory.

Cognitive-Developmental Theory

Cognitive-developmental theory (Kohlberg, 1969; Piaget, 1932) is based on the premise that social development proceeds in parallel with, and as a consequence of, sequential changes in the structure and quality of children's underlying thought patterns. According to this theory, as children develop they change in the ways that they mentally represent and process information about their social worlds. Furthermore, these changes in thought patterns are believed to be associated with changes in how children interpret, understand, and react to social stimuli.

Schemas—the Building Blocks of Development According to cognitive-developmental theory, children's social responses depend on the quality and sophistication of children's *schemas*, or their mental representations of events and experiences. Broadly defined, schemas may be conceptualized as internal representations of experience. Schemas help children organize, comprehend, and react to events occurring around them. Young infants' mental representations will necessarily be few, perhaps limited to visual images (for example, visual images of their mothers' faces). As children mature, their social schemas become more diverse, integrated, and sophisticated, resulting in more complex rules for connecting events ("When I cry, mommy comes"; "Boys are laughed at if they play with dolls"); rules for organizing information ("People are divided into groups like boys and girls, grownups and children"); rules for solving problems and making judgments ("Whether someone deserves to be punished depends on the person's intentions to do harm as well as on how much damage the person has caused"); and so on.

Furthermore, children's schemas about their social worlds influence their social behavior. Infants obviously cannot display a preference for the company of their mother over other people (a sign of attachment) until they form a visual-image schema of their mother and can differentiate mother from nonmother. And young children will not show a preference for imitating same-sex playmates over opposite-sex peers unless they can tell boy from girl and know in which group they themselves belong. These are just two examples of the endless number of links that exist between social-cognitive schemas and social behavior.

Cognitive-Developmental Stage Concepts The schemas that guide social thought and action undergo qualitative changes as the child develops. In fact, the changes that take place in children's schemas are thought to conform to an orderly sequence of stages. Piaget's theory of cognitive development suggests that children progress through a series of distinct stages of development, each stage characterized by several unique underlying *thought structures*, or basic ways of processing information. At any given point in development, all of a child's schemas are believed to share certain properties or limitations that reflect the basic thought structures characterizing the child's stage of cognitive development. This is why cognitive-developmental theory is called a *structuralist theory*—it holds that mental structure or organization is the best way to explain how people think and behave.

Before we describe the cognitive-develop-

mental stages, and the schemas associated with each stage, it is instructive to review four general points about the stages. First, cognitive-developmentalists use stages to describe the qualitative differences that exist in children's modes of thinking and solving problems at different ages. Thus younger children's cognitive responses are not just less complete or less accurate than older children's, but rather are qualitatively different. Second, it is assumed that stages follow an invariant sequence, meaning that all children are believed to progress through the stages in the same order. Not all children necessarily reach the highest stages, but skipping a stage and regressing from a more advanced stage to a less advanced one are incompatible with the theory. Cultural and biological factors may change the speed, but not the sequence, with which children progress through the stages. Third, each stage is purported to be a structured whole. That is, each stage of development is considered to be a distinct, self-contained entity defined by its own special thought structures. Finally, stages are hierarchically organized. The higher stages represent displacements or reintegrations of the structures found at lower stages. Furthermore, people prefer to solve a problem by using the most sophisticated schema available to them.

What are the thought structures that characterize the cognitive-developmental stages? Jean Piaget, the Swiss psychologist, proposed that cognitive development proceeds through four major stages. Though Piaget's theory is primarily one of intellectual development, he did speculate about how children's social schemas and their social functioning change with age as a function of the child's stage of cognitive development.

Piaget's Stages Piaget called his first stage the *sensorimotor stage*. During much of this stage, which lasts from birth to about 2 years of age, infants learn to coordinate and integrate behaviors, which initially represent little more than biological reflexes, into complex and voluntary patterns. But the most important feature of this stage is the attainment of a capacity for symbolic thought. Piaget theorized that the infant's early motor and perceptual experiences provided the foundation for early symbols. He believed that when infants repeatedly played with an object such as a rattle, by dropping it to the floor to see how it looks en route, how it lands, and what sound it makes, the infants are teaching themselves important lessons about the object and its properties. By playing with numerous objects in this way, the child presumably learns several general lessons, including the knowledge that objects maintain their identities when viewed from a different angle, that objects continue to exist when out of sight (object permanence), and that motor actions have predictable consequences.

These accomplishments have ramifications for social behavior. As we noted, when children develop some internal representation of their mother, they can differentiate her from other figures. When they attain object permanence, they can search for mother in her absence. When they develop schemas of instrumentality (means-end relationships), they can call to mother with the expectation that she will respond. And when they develop the capacity to represent and store a sequence of actions performed by another person, they can imitate a model's behavior long after witnessing it.

At about 2 years children pass into the *preoperational stage,* where they remain until about age 7. At this stage, children are actively engaged in formulating relatively simple rules about the functioning of their social worlds (e.g., "Only boys can be doctors" and "Mommy spanks when something gets broken"). Many such rules get "practiced" in the form of play. Very often child's play is symbolic in the sense that the child lets one object represent another object, or one child represent another person.

Although many of the preoperational child's schemas take the form of rules and propositions ("If _____, then _____" statements), the preoperational child's schemas and logic are thought to be seriously limited by certain immature underlying thought structures. Piaget identified *centration* as the major problem characterizing the preoperational child's thinking patterns. When young children encounter a stimulus, they tend to focus their attention exclusively on only one feature of the stimulus—the most obvious or perceptually salient one. The classic example of a centration problem is seen in the preoperational child's failure to display an understanding of *conservation principles.* If a given volume of water is poured from a tall skinny container into a short stubby one, or a ball of clay is molded into a different shape, the preoperational child often believes that the amount of water (or clay) has changed. This is because the child selects only one dimension (for example, the height *or* the depth of the water in a container) to decide how much of the substance exists at a given moment. The child cannot coordinate several dimensions and has no sense of the notion that increases in one dimension can compensate for decreases in another dimension. The child does not grasp this principle concerning conservation because she has no sense of the fact that objects can have underlying invariant properties (e.g., volume) that remain unchanged despite changes in superficial appearances. Because the child's ability to solve problems is governed by the child's senses rather than by logic, the child's problem solving often seems impulsive and intuitive.

The tendency to base judgments on superficial qualities is believed to influence children's social schemas. For instance, a young girl will claim that she will become a boy if she cuts her hair and wears pants. She does not appreciate the fact that gender identity is an underlying invariant that remains unaltered across changes in superficial appearance. When they are asked to describe their friends, preoperational children tend to focus on superficial qualities (physical appearance, possessions, and so on). They do not seem to understand that people can also be described in terms of underlying psychological qualities, such as relatively enduring motives or personality dispositions. When asked to judge how good or bad someone is, they tend to focus on what meets the eye—the degree of tangible success the actor has had or the amount of material damage the actor has caused—rather than on internal motives that are hidden from view (such as the person's intent to do harm). All of these limitations of the young child's social-cognitive functioning are believed to be due to centration.

An important manifestation of centration is what Piaget called *egocentrism*. Egocentrism is the tendency to be so captivated by one's own point of view that one cannot accurately appreciate that other people have perspectives, thoughts, and feelings that are different from one's own. As a consequence of egocentrism, the social skills of young children are believed to be deficient in a number of ways: Young children presumably attribute their own opinions and wants to others, show little empathy or altruism, and are poor at communicating in ways that take the special needs of a listener into account.

At about 7 years children pass into the stage of *concrete operations*. Now children can "decenter" by breaking attention away from the most obvious feature of a stimulus to consider other relevant aspects. They can coordinate several dimensions and they have some sense of compensation. Children in this stage can classify, order, and reason transitively (i.e., if Susan is more popular than Jane, and Jane is more popular than Alice, then Susan is more popular than Alice). Above all, children at this age attain an understanding of conservation, or the knowledge that things and people have underlying invariant properties (e.g., weight, volume, or sex) that do not change, regardless of changes in superficial appearances. However, concrete operational children are capable of applying these logical mental operations only to concrete, familiar, and easily imaginable events, such as ones that they themselves have experienced. The hypothetical is beyond the realm of comprehension.

These newly attained skills of decentration and compensation permit new degrees of so-phistication in a child's social schemas. A child can evaluate people in terms of their underlying motives and intentions, can realize that one causal factor sometimes compensates for another (for example, moderate success on a task can be caused by high ability and low effort, low ability and high effort, or an equal amount of both ability and effort), and can break away from his or her own perspective to appraise and respond to the points of view and needs of others.

The final stage of *formal operations* is entered around age 11. Children can now imagine and mentally operate on the hypothetical level, thinking about how things "ought to be" and solving problems in their heads. There is a genuine understanding of the experimental method. This involves the knowledge that in order to isolate the cause of an event, it is necessary to manipulate in turn each possible causal variable while holding rival causal variables constant.

Motivational Constructs What do the cognitive-developmentalists believe motivates the child to progress through the stages? Cognitive-developmental theorists draw on concepts of intrinsic motivation to explain development. They argue that people possess an innate disposition to master or understand new experiences that are moderately discrepant from their current level of understanding. Old events bore rather than stimulate curiosity and learning, but totally novel events are also ignored because they contain no elements to which children can relate. It is moderately novel events, or blends of the familiar and the unfamiliar, that arouse children's interest, puzzlement, or, as Piaget would call it, *cognitive disequilibrium*. When children are exposed to the moderately unfamiliar, they are motivated to generate a new rule or schema to help them understand the event. For example, the young child who firmly believes that "all doctors are men" may be quite puzzled when introduced to a female doctor for the first time. The puzzlement forces the child to reexamine the initial schema and to work out a better one. Eventually the new schema may be that "most doctors are men, but some are women." Cognitive-developmentalists like to say that development is a function of "person-environment interaction" because they believe that the motivation for learning and development depends on an optimal match between the child's current level of understanding and new environmental input.

Two key concepts in Piagetian theory are assimilation and accommodation. Attempting to understand a new experience in terms of an existing schema (for example, concluding that a woman introduced as a doctor must really be a nurse masquerading as a doctor) is known as *assimilation. Accommodation* refers to the process of changing one's schemas to agree with new realities. The child who alters a schema to include female doctors is evidencing accommodation. Presumably, a number of faulty or not totally satisfying assimilations can motivate accommodation. Both processes continue throughout development.

Critique of Cognitive-Developmental Theory Cognitive-developmental theorists have a dual goal: first, to describe and explain the universal sequences in development and, second, to specify and explain the similarities among individuals of any given age. This emphasis stands in stark contrast to that of the learning theorists, who are interested in explaining individual differences among children at particular age periods (as a function of differential reinforcement histories, modeling exposures, etc.), but who pay little attention to group changes that occur with age (Bandura & Walters, 1963b). How well do the cognitive developmentalists achieve their goals? First, they must receive credit for charting typical sequences in development and for pointing out the dependence of social behavior upon underlying cognitive processing. However, a major problem with cognitive-developmental theory is that both Piaget's and Kohlberg's stages are not well-

knit "integrated wholes," as the theorists claim. Remember that cognitive-developmentalists suggest that each stage is characterized by unique underlying thought structures (for example, centration and egocentrism) that cause the child to react similarly across diverse tasks and situations. The preoperational child who cannot decenter presumably should fail to conserve volume of liquid, should fail to appreciate another's perspective, should describe others only in terms of superficial characteristics, should fail to realize that sex assignment remains invariant across changes in hair style and clothing, and should fail on any other task that requires a level of thinking more advanced than preoperational thought. The empirical evidence is rather damaging to the theory on this point. A given child usually does *not* inflexibly display the same thought structure in all instances of social-cognitive functioning. For example, when making moral judgments, most young children sometimes focus on the damage an actor causes (presumably a preoperational, centering response) and sometimes focus on an actor's intentions (presumably a concrete operational response), depending on the particular transgression being judged and the circumstances surrounding it. It is just not true that all of a child's responses can be identified with a single stage.

The cognitive-developmentalists' thesis that progression through the stages occurs in an invariant sequence also is questionable. In later chapters we shall see that children sometimes skip stages and sometimes regress from a higher stage to a lower one.

Another problem is that cognitive-developmentalists sometimes use stages as explanations. That is, they make statements like, "So-and-so did not solve the problem because he or she is functioning at stage X." This is a dangerous practice. In order to name stages as causes, one must clearly establish what causes a child to function at a particular stage. Unfortunately, cognitive-developmental theorists do not do this.

Finally, the cognitive-developmentalists'

idea that social-cognitive development is motivated by attempts to reduce cognitive disequilibrium aroused by moderately discrepant events is intuitively appealing, and in later chapters we shall see some support for it. However, cognitive-developmental theory can be criticized for placing too much emphasis on intrinsic sources of motivation and ignoring certain important environmental influences, such as parental child-rearing practices.

The Cognitive-Developmental versus the Social Learning View of Cognition It is clear that both cognitive-developmental theory and social learning theory assign a prominent role to cognition in the regulation of behavior, but the two theories' views of cognition are radically different. It is useful to compare them. The main difference is that the cognitive-developmentalists take a *typological* view of cognitive functioning, whereas the social learning theorists take a *multivariate* view of cognition (Rosenthal & Zimmerman, 1978). That is, in cognitive-developmental theory, a child's thoughts, rules, judgments, beliefs, expectations, and other cognitions are all believed to reflect a particular *type* of thinking determined by the particular thought structures that characterize the child's stage of development. All of the preoperational child's cognitions, for example, should belong to the same category of thinking because they should all be handicapped by centration problems. In social learning theory, children also develop rules and organize knowledge, but their schemas do not reflect inflexible rules based on structural limitations. The social learning theorists argue that almost any cognition, whether it be a standard of self-reinforcement, a basis for making moral judgments of other people, an anticipated consequence, or one's perception of ability to perform a task, is *multiply determined* by a host of social experiences that include verbal instruction, modeling exposures, and direct reinforcement history. This means that children are assumed to process, weigh, and integrate diverse sources of social information to arrive at rules, judgmental criteria, and other social-cognitive schemas.

To illustrate, consider how the cognitive-developmental and social learning theorists differ in their explanations of how children decide the degree of punishment a peer should receive for behaving in an aggressive manner. The cognitive-developmentalist would argue that the basis for children's moral judgments depends on their current stage. The centering, preoperational child should focus exclusively on how much obvious damage or injury the actor caused; the decentering, concrete operational child should look beneath the surface to judge on the basis of the actor's intent and motive. The structure of the child's thinking causes the child to make one type of judgment or the other.

In contrast, the social learning theorists argue that children process information from diverse social sources (their own disciplinary experiences, observation of the consequences received by others for their behavior, and so on) to arrive at conceptions of what constitutes blameworthy behavior. Putting the information together, children abstract principles about when aggression is considered acceptable or unacceptable. Gradually they learn that evaluations of aggression depend on many kinds of discriminations: Deliberate harm to someone is worse than accidental damage; aggression against one's parents and other adults is more punishable than aggression against one's playmates; and giving someone a bloody nose is worse than just making someone cry. Children's rules change as their social learning experiences change, or as they learn to assign more weight to certain sources of information. For example, if parents punish a child for causing pain to others regardless of whether the child really intended to injure, the child may come to believe that the amount of material damage is more important than the actor's intentions in making moral judgments. Children's criteria for moral evaluation are not seen as inflexibly linked to a hypothetical cognitive-structural stage.

In sum, cognitive-developmental theorists have served an important function by pointing to sequence and qualitative change in cognitive and social development. However, the notion of stages as integrated wholes that depend on underlying and inflexible cognitive structures and that unfold in fixed sequence is under attack.

Ethological Theory

Ethologists regard certain patterns of social behavior as the product of evolution. Consider the close attachment bonds mothers form with their infants. Ethologists suggest that such bonds exist because they have helped the species survive through many generations. Furthermore, ethologists argue that if certain patterns of social behavior exist because of natural selection, then it is reasonable to assume that aspects of these behavior patterns will be controlled by inherited instincts. Thus, according to ethological theory, human infants are biologically wired to emit responses that keep them close to their mothers, and mothers are programmed to love and look after their infants (Ainsworth, 1973; Bowlby, 1969). A more detailed discussion of the ethological theory of attachment can be found in Chapter 2.

Certain other patterns of social behavior are held by the ethologists to serve a survival function. Obviously many aspects of sexual behavior would be expected to be under instinctive control. Ethologists also suggest that children are inclined to form dominance hierarchies because hierarchies help reduce intragroup aggression (Blurton-Jones, 1972). It is possible that pretend play as a form of social interaction has evolved because it is a way for children to practice and prepare for adult roles (Vandenberg, 1978).

Perhaps most controversial has been the ethologists' view that human aggression has an instinctive basis (Lorenz, 1966; Tinbergen, 1972). Ethologists view aggression as an innate drive that is aroused when a person encounters specific stimuli such as threat or frustration, which automatically direct the person toward the goal of injuring or destroying the source of the irritation. Furthermore, when aggressive drive is aroused, energy is thought to be generated. This energy, which is unobservable, helps propel the person toward the aggressive goal; if the goal is not achieved, however, the energy does not dissipate. Instead, it is believed to motivate the person to engage in certain substitute activities that help reduce the drive. For example, if a person's aggressive drive is aroused but direct retaliation is not possible or is dangerous, then the person will have to seek discharge of the energy in another way, perhaps by aggressing against a scapegoat or even by engaging in a competitive sport. Many psychologists, especially learning theorists, object strongly to the ethologists' notion of aggressive drive. The learning theorists point out that it is difficult to get measures of drives that are independent of the behaviors they are supposedly motivating. Moreover, some of the predictions that stem from drive theory, such as the hypothesis that energy accumulates and must be discharged in one way or another, have not received empirical confirmation. We discuss this issue more fully in Chapter 7.

The ethologists' view that certain crucial patterns of social interaction are under the control of instincts has had a definite impact on the research methods ethologists favor. Instincts are rigid chains of behavior that are reflexively elicited by specific environmental stimuli called *releasing stimuli* or *triggering stimuli*. A major aim of ethological research is to chart the stimuli that trigger, guide, and terminate instinctive chains of behavior under natural environmental conditions. Thus ethologists spend long hours studying mother-infant interaction to determine what aspects of each member's behavior serve to attract the other member; they observe closely children at play in order to determine what events serve to trigger or inhibit attacks by one child against another; and so forth.

It seems undeniable that certain social behaviors in children are at least partly under the control of inherited instincts, especially in the early months of life. The infant's early social responses, such as smiling, looking, and vocalizing, follow a built-in timetable of responsiveness to specific cues from caregivers. As children develop and have more opportunities for social learning, however, it becomes more difficult to untangle the effects of instincts from the effects of experience. Moreover, as children develop, their cognitive capacities increasingly allow them to evaluate stimuli and various courses of action, with the result that reflexive responses become less common. Clearly, different children learn to assign different interpretations and meanings to a stimulus they encounter, leading them to react very differently from one another. One child may react to frustration with attack, for example, while another child may retreat. The ethological approach, then, may be most helpful in understanding how certain social patterns are established in the early phases of development, but the usefulness of the approach diminishes as children mature and begin to reap the benefits of learning and thinking.

RESEARCH METHODS

One feature of a good theory is that it furnishes hypotheses that can be empirically evaluated, that is, that can be confirmed or disconfirmed by observing children as they actually interact with their social and physical worlds. In this section, we take a look at some of the research designs that child psychologists employ to test the validity of theory-relevant hypotheses. First, we briefly review strategies for charting age changes in behavior. Recall that some theorists, notably the cognitive-developmentalists, specify that as children develop, their thought patterns and social behaviors undergo qualitative changes. Special research strategies exist that help us chart these changes. The emphasis in these strategies is on description rather than explanation of age changes, although occasionally these strategies can also shed light on the pos-

sible causes of development. Second, we examine techniques used to discover the determinants of development. Recall that many theories state their hypotheses in the form of "If _____, then _____" propositions. A good research design permits unequivocal evaluation of these cause-and-effect predictions.

Methods for Studying Age Changes

The Cross-Sectional Design In the cross-sectional design, the investigator samples children from several different age levels and observes the children at roughly the same point in time. For example, in order to determine whether children change in the typical number of peer friendships they form over the elementary-school years, a researcher might survey separate groups of first through sixth graders and quiz them on their friendship patterns.

The advantage of the cross-sectional method is apparent: Surveying a group of children representing a wide age span allows a researcher to collect data in a hurry. Unfortunately, the technique has several limitations. First, the design does not permit direct study of the factors that cause the age differences. One can, of course, interview the children or their parents to determine possible causal factors, but this is often an unreliable method. Second, the cross-sectional method provides no information on the shape of individual growth curves. The typical child may develop a behavior in sudden spurts rather than gradually, but a plot of group averages may obscure this fact. Third, it is impossible to estimate the stability of behavior from the cross-sectional method—one cannot answer, for example, the question of whether the child who has the most friendships in early elementary school is also the most sociable in adolescence. A final problem is that the cross-sectional method confounds age effects with time-of-birth effects. If 60-year-olds enjoy watching aggressive television programs less than 30-year-olds, is it because a preference for viewing violence decreases over middle age or is it because the child-rearing, educational, and cultural climate into which the 60-year-olds were born was less conducive to the development of such a preference than the climate experienced by more recent generations?

The Longitudinal Method   The investigator using the longitudinal method samples a single group of children, all roughly about the same age, and periodically observes the children as they pass through the age period of interest. The advantages of this technique make it an especially valuable tool for the developmental psychologist. It is possible to examine individual growth curves and to estimate behavioral stability. It is also possible to record observations on the possible causes of development and to relate these factors to children's development. For example, the aggressiveness of young men has been predicted from how much violent television the men watched as third graders (Eron, Lefkowitz, Huesmann, & Walder, 1972); the frequency of crying in 1-year-olds has been predicted from how quickly their mothers had quieted their crying in previous months (Bell & Ainsworth, 1972); and the gains children make in IQ over the grade-school years have been predicted from how much the children displayed personality traits like independence and self-initiation in previous years (Sontag, Baker, & Nelsen, 1958). It is not always possible to draw firm cause-and-effect conclusions from such findings, but the relationships are certainly suggestive.

Of course, the longitudinal method has its costs. First, it is expensive in terms of time and money. Second, many of the children may drop out of the study before it is over, and the remaining children may constitute a biased sample. A third problem is that the participants may become test conscious or bored. Fourth, the researchers may find their research methods—or even their theories—becoming outdated before the study is completed. And finally, the longitudinal method confounds age effects with time-of-measurement effects. What if a group of adults turning 30 in 1984 professed to hold fewer sex-role stereotypes than they reported 10 years earlier? Is the relaxation of sex stereotypes a function of unique developmental processes occurring between one's 20th and 30th birthdays, or could it simply reflect the fact that people's views about sex roles generally became liberalized in the 10-year period? It is obvious from this example that one cannot generalize automatically the results of a single longitudinal study to other generations.

The Cross-Sectional/Short-Term Longitudinal Design   In this combination approach, the investigator longitudinally follows the development of groups of children who were of different ages when the study began. The following example illustrates when this approach would be useful. A researcher interested in studying development between the ages of 6 and 12 wants to avoid some of the problems of the cross-sectional method, but is unable to devote 6 years to the study, which would be required if he used the longitudinal approach. The investigator could combine the approaches by taking three samples of children—one of 6-year-olds, one of 8-year-olds, and one of 10-year-olds—and following the development of each of the three groups of children for 2 years. Thus, in 2 years the investigator would have data covering a 6-year span. Several psychologists have proposed rather complicated statistical analyses that can be applied to data obtained in this manner to help sort out the independent contributions of such variables as age, time of birth and time of measurement (Baltes & Schaie, 1973).

Although the discovery of reliable age changes is a major goal in child psychology, only a very small percentage of published research studies actually report data on how children's behavior varies as a function of age. That is, use of any of the three designs we discussed above is actually quite rare. Most researchers simply examine children of a single age at a single point in their development, which indicates that the overriding concern of developmental psychologists for the last several decades has been with the explanation of the developmental process rather than with the description of age changes. Investigators have been interested in discovering the factors (parents' child-rearing practices, children's television habits, etc.) that lead to individual differences among children in the expression of a behavior. In the next section, we shall take a look at some of the strategies aimed at clarifying these cause-and-effect relationships.

Methods for Studying the Determinants of Development

A Comparison of Two Traditional Methodologies Two popular, traditional strategies used to study the factors influencing development are the field-correlational method and the laboratory-experimental method. These are not the only two strategies available to the psychologist interested in the determinants of development, but comparing them will allow us to consider a number of important methodological issues.

As the name implies, the *field-correlational method* involves observing children's behavior in a natural environment and using correlational statistics to test for relationships between the children's behavior and other variables. For example, children may be observed at home, in school, or in some other real-life setting, with each child rated on how much he or she displays certain target behaviors such as aggression, dependency, or altruism. At the same time, the investigator gathers information on a variety of possible determinants of the target behaviors. If the investigator's theory suggests that parental discipline is influential in the development of the target behavior, then detailed questions may be posed to each child's parents about the ways they attempt to control their child. If a child's television preferences are hypothesized to be important determinants, then interviews designed to elicit information

about the children's viewing habits may be given to the children or their parents. In addition, information is usually collected on a host of other variables, such as the child's intelligence, social class, and family structure (number and sex of older and younger siblings, whether the mother works outside the home, whether the father is deceased, etc.). In such projects, the children's behaviors are often labeled *dependent variables* because they are believed to depend on the operation of the various causal factors being studied. The hypothesized causal factors are called *independent variables.*

In the statistical analysis of a field-correlational study, children's scores on each dependent variable are then correlated with their scores on each independent variable. The correlation between two variables is said to be positive if children who have low scores on one variable also have low scores on the other variable, and if children who have high scores on one variable also have high scores on the other variable. For example, if a project finds that the more television violence children watch, the more aggressive they are, then the conclusion would be that viewing violence on television and aggression are positively correlated. In contrast, when high scores on one variable are associated with low scores on the other variable, the correlation is said to be negative. The finding that the more parents rely on physical punishment to discipline their children, the less the children exhibit self-control in temptation situations, is illustrative of a negative correlation. Of course, many variables are unrelated to one another; under these conditions, neither a positive nor a negative correlation will be noted.

The field-correlational technique has its advantages and disadvantages. Its chief advantage is that it allows us to estimate the direction and strength of the relationship that actually exists between two variables in natural settings. For this reason, the technique is indispensable. However, there are a number of problems with the method. The main problem is that the correlational strategy does not permit inferences about causality. Although watching violent television programs does correlate positively with aggression (Eron, 1963), does this necessarily mean that watching a lot of television violence causes the aggression? Couldn't it be that aggressive children seek out the excitement of aggressive television? We do not know. It is also possible that some third factor is causing the association between children's aggression and their television viewing. Perhaps aggressive children have fathers who discipline their children in ways that encourage aggressive behavior and who happen also to insist that the television set be tuned to violent programming when it is on. Here a third factor— the father's behavior—is responsible for the correlation between children's aggression and their television viewing habits, and the latter two variables are not causally related.

Traditionally, field-correlational studies have been associated with a number of other problems. For example, in the 1950s, when this technique was popular, investigators often collected their data through questionable means. Instead of directly observing children's social responses in real life settings, investigators frequently took shortcuts to get their data, either by interviewing subjects about their behavior or by having them complete questionnaires. Thus investigators interested in studying the effects of parental discipline on children's aggression might ask the parents to describe their customary disciplinary tactics, and they might ask the children's teachers or peers (or perhaps even their parents) to rate the aggressiveness of the children. Often, the questions call for global and impressionistic answers and are not tied very well to behavioral referents or situations (e.g., "How often do you find it necessary to punish your child physically?"). This technique raises the question of the extent to which interviews and questionnaires can reflect true behavior. Some respondents may adopt a "social desirability" response set, offering a rosier picture of themselves and their children

than actually exists. And even trained interviewers are subject to biases, perhaps by interpreting the answers of liked and unliked interviewees differently. These problems can become especially serious if information on both the dependent and independent variables is collected from the same respondents, as when the children's parents are asked to report on both their children's behavior and their own disciplinary practices. Significant correlations emerging from studies with this flaw may, in fact, reveal more about what variables the respondents believe should be correlated than about what variables really do go together. Finally, data from interview and questionnaire studies are especially suspect if respondents are asked to give retrospective reports, meaning that they are asked to report on events or behaviors that occurred years earlier.

Of course, interviews and questionnaires are entirely appropriate means for collecting data if the investigator is interested in studying respondents' *perceptions* of their experiences or of people. A boy who believes his father is rejecting him may be adversely affected regardless of his father's actual behavior. But when intended as a shortcut to information about real behavior, interviews and questionnaires often lead to problems.

Because of these problems, investigators turned increasingly in the 1960s to direct behavioral observation, (for reviews of these trends, see Lytton, 1971; and Martin, 1975). Research workers took their clipboards and stop watches into the school and home and worked hard at developing reliable and valid systems for observing and coding the behaviors of children and adults in specific situations (e.g., during aggressive episodes on the playground, or during disciplinary encounters at home). Of course, direct observation does not guarantee validity; it is valid only to the extent that the presence of observers does not disrupt or distort natural interaction. To overcome this problem, some investigators have successfully taught parents how to take and record observations in the home. (See, for example, Patterson & Reid, 1970; Zahn-Waxler, Radke-Yarrow, & King, 1979.) A limitation of this type of method is that the investigator must sometimes wait long hours for instances of the target interactions to occur. Bear in mind, however, that information about a wide range of behaviors across a wide range of situations can be obtained very quickly using interviews and questionnaires.

There are also a number of problems direct observation researchers must face when deciding how to break up the flow of natural interaction for analysis purposes: How large or how small should the categories be that describe behaviors? Should behavior be coded strictly in terms of its observable properties or should behavior be categorized in terms of its underlying motivational properties (e.g., in terms of what the participants are intending to do)? In spite of these problems, direct observation techniques have brought us many steps closer to understanding naturalistic interaction. An excellent example of the development and application of a direct observation coding scheme of parent-child behavior can be found in Patterson and Cobb (1971).

Because many of the early interview and questionnaire studies produced data of dubious validity, and because correlational analysis does not permit inferences about causality, many investigators turned to the radically different *laboratory-experimental method*. In the field-correlational method, the investigator merely observes the associations that exist between variables in the natural environment. In the experimental method, the investigator introduces some change in the child's environment (i.e., the investigator manipulates the independent variable) and then observes the effect of this change on the child's subsequent behavior (the dependent variable). In the laboratory experiment, both the manipulation of the independent variable and measurement of the dependent variable occur in the laboratory. For example, to test the hypothesis that exposure to violence on television causes children to become more aggressive, children might first be randomly assigned to one of two groups: an experimental group who watch an aggressive program and a control group who watch an equally exciting but nonaggressive program. Thereafter, the children are tested for aggression, perhaps by measuring the intensity and duration of obnoxious noises the children choose as punishment for another child's errors on a learning task. The average levels of aggression shown by the two groups are then compared. In the experimental method, it is possible to conclude that the independent variable is *causally responsible* for between-group differences in the behavior of the children, because (a) the time order of the manipulation of the independent variable and measurement of the dependent variable is known, and (b) the experimental treatments are identical in every respect save the crucial independent variable.

The laboratory experiment has some obvious advantages. Since the research is conducted in the investigator's specially created environment, it is possible for the investigator to exert a high degree of control over the stimuli that influence the subject. By systematically varying possible causal factors, either singly or in combination with one another, the experimenter can reach fairly precise and sometimes complex conclusions about the causes of behavior. Furthermore, by issuing explicit instructions to the subject and by structuring the situation, the investigator can readily elicit and reliably measure the behavior under study (e.g., by requesting children to punish a learner's errors by pushing buttons that will deliver noise).

Despite its advantages, the laboratory experiment does not escape criticism. First of all, it is important to keep in mind that when a cause of behavior is discovered in the lab, one cannot automatically assume that this same cause is actually an important determinant of the behavior in real-life settings. Just because A can cause B, it cannot be concluded that all, or even very many, instances of B are caused by A. The discovery in the laboratory, for example, that exposure to aggressive television programming can cause aggression does not necessarily mean that children who behave aggressively in real-life settings are doing so because they have watched lots of, or even any, violence on television. Other factors may be much more important. This is one reason why field-correlational studies, which permit an estimate of the actual covariation between variables in the natural context, will always be an important companion strategy for experimental psychologists.

A second criticism that is sometimes directed against laboratory experiments is that they are "artificial." It is true that many of the ways in which an independent variable is manipulated or a dependent variable is assessed represent totally novel and unrealistic experiences for children. Children do not usually aggress against peers by delivering noise stimuli, for example. Is it legitimate to assume, then, that noise aggression in the lab functions according to the same laws as other, more natural expressions of aggression in the field? Several psychologists have stressed that we ought to enhance the "ecological validity" of our research by designing projects that involve settings, occasions, roles, and activities that resemble real life in its naturally occurring state (Bronfenbrenner, 1977, 1979; Cochran & Brassard, 1979; Weisz, 1978). Without question, developmental psychologists want to uncover principles that apply in the real-life setting as well as the lab, but critics who suggest that researchers abandon the laboratory experiment because of its "artificiality" may be doing the science of psychology a disservice. As Bandura (1978a) has noted, experiments are not intended to duplicate all aspects of events as they occur in everyday life, and they would lose their value if they did. Experiments should be judged, not in terms of physical resemblance to situations in everyday life, but on the degree to which they identify the important determinants and processes of change. Bandura (1978a) has argued that:

This view of experimentation is taken for granted in all other branches of science. Airliners are built on aerodynamic principles developed largely in artificial wind tunnels; bridges and skyscrapers are erected on structural principles derived from experiments that bear little resemblance to the actual constructions; and knowledge about physiological functioning is principally gained from artificially induced changes, often in animals. Indeed, preoccupation with mimicking things as they occur naturally can retard advancement of knowledge—witness the demise of venturesome fliers who tried to remain airborne by flapping wings strapped to their arms in the likeness of soaring birds.

In the final analysis, experiments are judged not on artificiality criteria, but in terms of the explanatory and predictive power of the principles they yield. (p. 89)

Throughout this book, we shall offer numerous examples of how our understanding of the determinants and processes of social development has been elucidated through the use of carefully controlled laboratory experiments.

We have now reviewed the advantages and disadvantages of both the field-correlational and laboratory-experimental techniques. It should be apparent that neither method is "better" than the other. Instead of relying on one as the method of choice, it is more sensible to employ a "strategy of converging operations" when evaluating a psychological hypothesis (McCall, 1977). Our confidence in an hypothesis being true should depend on the degree to which the hypothesis receives confirmation by different methods. Consider the following case history of an hypothesis. An early field-correlational study by Eron (1963) showed that aggression and viewing violent television shows were positively correlated in the natural environment. In subsequent laboratory experiments (e.g., Bandura, 1965), researchers confirmed that viewing violence on television was one possible cause of aggression. More recently, experiments have been designed to reveal exactly what variables enhance or diminish aggressive modeling effects. Researchers ask questions such as, What happens if the aggressive characters are rewarded or punished?; Does it matter what the aggressive character's motives are?; and, Does it matter if the television aggression is in cartoon or real-life format? Finally, a longitudinal study by Eron and his associates (1972) was also helpful by revealing that boys with strong violent television preferences grew up to become aggressive adults even if they weren't aggressive as children. Certainly, the presentation of the results from the different studies gives strength to the hypothesis that exposure to aggressive models causes aggression in real-life settings.

New Research Designs: Breaking Traditional Boundaries   The field-correlational and laboratory-experimental methods are the extreme opposites of one another, differing in nearly every way conceivable. In a thoughtful essay on research designs, Parke (1979) points out that a large number of potentially useful designs can be arrived at by combining certain elements of the field-correlational and laboratory-experimental designs in novel ways. To understand how this can be done, it is first necessary to realize that the field-correlational and laboratory-experimental designs differ from one another in four independent ways.

First is the context in which the independent variable is assessed or manipulated. In the field-correlational study the independent variable is studied in the field; in the laboratory experiment it is studied in the laboratory. The second way in which the two methods differ is according to the locus of assessment of the dependent variable. Here again, of course, the dependent variable is measured in the field in the field-correlational study and in the laboratory in the laboratory experiment. Third, the degree of structure in the way that the dependent variable is assessed is dissimilar in the two meth-

ods. In many field-correlational studies, the situation in which observations are collected is unstructured; the investigator must wait for the target responses to occur naturally. In laboratory experiments, the situation is designed so that the responses of interest are readily elicited. Fourth is the research design, or the method chosen for relating the independent and dependent variables. In the field-correlational study, the design is nonmanipulative and conclusions about relationships between independent and dependent variables are restricted to statements about covariation, not causality. In contrast, the logic of the interventive experimental method permits causal conclusions.

The field-correlational and laboratory-experimental designs represent two combinations of these factors, but these combinations are not the only ones possible. In fact, if one considers that each of the four factors has two levels (field vs. lab locus of independent variable, field vs. lab locus of dependent variable, structured vs. unstructured assessment of dependent variable, and correlational vs. experimental design), then it is logically possible to combine the factors to form a total of 16 research strategies ($2 \times 2 \times 2 \times 2$). Which level of each factor an investigator employs should depend on the focus of the particular study. Some breaks across traditional boundaries may be useful in helping investigators reach their particular objectives. For example, if a researcher wishes to study in the field a behavior that has a low base rate of occurrence, the researcher may introduce structure into the natural environment in order to increase the frequency of the target responses. Yarrow, Waxler, Barrett, Darby, King, Pickett, and Smith (1976) used this technique to determine levels of altruism in nursery-school children. An adult who behaved in ways designed to increase the children's opportunities for prosocial behavior was introduced into the classroom environment. The adult behaved as if he or she were deprived of play materials that the children were using, evidenced emotional distress, and so on, and the children's spontaneous helping responses were recorded.

Other nontraditional examples help clarify the possibilities. To test the hypothesis that watching a lot of aggression on television deadens one's emotional responses to violence, Cline, Croft, and Courrier (1973) conducted a study in the laboratory in which children who watched either a lot or very little television at home were compared for heart rate and palmar sweating responses while they viewed a movie featuring aggressive scenes. Here the independent variable (amount of home television viewing) is field-assessed, but the dependent variable is assessed in a structured, laboratory setting. The design is correlational because the investigators merely observed, but did not manipulate, the children's viewing habits.

O'Connor (1969) tested the hypothesis that social participation could be increased in withdrawn nursery-school children by showing them a competent peer model. Isolated children were randomly assigned to watch either a film of a child learning to enjoy social interaction or a control film. Later the children were observed in their classrooms and compared for rates of social interaction. Here the independent variable was manipulated in the laboratory, but the dependent variable was assessed in an unstructured way in the field; the design was experimental. For an excellent discussion of issues involved in the choice of a design, see Parke (1979).

Some Other Designs Actually, not all research designs fit into the above classification scheme. Four other methods deserve brief mention. The first of these is the *natural experiment*. Here the investigator does not personally manipulate the independent variable for research purposes, but nonetheless the independent variable gets manipulated and the researcher takes advantage of it. Examples would include studying the effects of racial integration in the schools, natural disasters such as flooding, and airliner highjackings.

A second method is the *cross-cultural approach*, in which patterns of development are compared across two or more cultures (e.g., American children are compared with Japanese children). Theorists who subscribe to the view that there exist universal sequences in development, such as the cognitive-developmental theorists, sometimes employ the cross-cultural method with the expectation that it will reveal similarities in the paths of development across cultures. Of course, learning theorists can use the method too. Children coming from societies with divergent child-rearing practices, for example, should develop in different ways.

Third, the *comparative approach*, which studies processes across species (e.g., mice vs. chimps vs. human beings), provides another way of improving our understanding of developmental issues. As an example, if observational learning depends on cognitive mediation, one would expect an increasing capacity for delayed imitation (i.e., imitating a model's response long after seeing the model perform it) as one moves up the phylogenetic scale because of the increasing capacity to represent in symbolic form the observed experiences.

Finally, we should mention *twin studies*. If members of monozygotic, or identical, twin pairs are more similar to one another on some attribute than are members of dizygotic, or fraternal, twin pairs, then there is reason to believe that genetic factors play at least some role in the development of the attribute. This is because the genetic make-up of identical twins is the same, whereas fraternal twins are no more genetically alike than any two non-twin siblings. Of course, one problem with this method is that parents may treat identical twins more similarly than they treat fraternal twins, which would result in the child-rearing environment being more alike for identical than for fraternal twins. Parents probably do treat identical twins more alike than fraternal twins, but the more similar treatment received by identical twins may very well be prompted by their greater genetic similarity! (See Lytton, 1977.) This brings us to our next topic—the issue of how child characteristics and adult reactions interact to influence development.

Recognizing the Child's Contribution to Development

From Unidirectional to Interactional Models of Development Traditionally, most theories of child development have assumed a unidirectional model of socialization. In the *unidirectional model*, the direction of social influence was believed to flow in only one direction—from the environment to the child. The child was viewed simply as the passive recipient of socialization influences. Because parents and their child-rearing techniques figure prominently among the child's environmental experiences, these models of socialization are sometimes called "parent-as-cause, child-as-effect" viewpoints. The unidirectional perspective to socialization may have had its origin with Freud, but it was amply reinforced by subsequent theories of socialization, and especially by the early learning theories. The unidirectional theme also found its way into the research vocabulary of the child psychologist: Child behaviors were designated "dependent" variables, and parental practices and other environmental factors "independent" variables.

In 1968, Richard Bell published a classic article, entitled "A Reinterpretation of the Direction of Effects in Studies of Socialization," that dramatically altered both thinking and research on the socialization process. In his article, Bell argued that many research findings that are usually linked to a parent-as-cause, child-as-effect model may just as easily be taken to support a child-as-cause, parent-as-effect model. Specifically, Bell claimed that many of the parental behaviors that are usually interpreted as the causes of correlated child behaviors may just be reactions on the part of parents to constitutionally (i.e., genetically) based traits in their children. He argued, for example, that aggressive children have physically punitive parents not because the children are frustrated by such parents or because the children are imitating their parents' aggression, but rather because aggressive children are born with certain social traits, such as a high activity level, that provoke the parents into using harsh methods of discipline. Bell reviewed convincing evidence (mainly from twin studies) to support his claim that there exist genetic variations among children in certain traits, and he presented a provocative theory regarding the predictable reactions produced by parents depending on the strength of these traits in an infant.

Few psychologists have been willing to take Bell's extreme position that the effects of children on adults are more powerful or significant than adult effects on children, but most—even the learning theorists—have conceded that because of their differing constitutional endowments, children produce different reactions from their social environments, which then feed back upon the children to help shape their personalities in different ways. Children with congenitally high activity levels, for example, may in fact elicit the kinds of disciplinary reactions from adults that serve to socialize them toward high levels of aggression. Social development is an interactive process, the product of continuous reciprocal influences between children and their environments.

An outstanding longitudinal study by Thomas, Chess, and Birch (1968) of a large group of children observed from birth illustrates how hereditary traits and social learning experiences interact to influence development. Before the children reached 2 years of age, the researchers had identified a subgroup of children whom they labeled "difficult" children. The difficult children showed the following symptoms: biological irregularity, especially with respect to sleeping, feeding, and elimination cycles; withdrawal and distress reactions to new stimuli, such as the first bath, new foods, or strange people; slow adaptability to change; and a general tendency for displaying negative moods. The investigators surmised that most of these traits were biological in origin.

The interesting point is that some of the difficult children went on to develop character disorders, with the crucial factor being the nature of the reactions the children's problems elicited from the social environment. The parents of the difficult children did not differ as a group from the parents of normal children in the early years. But as the difficult children grew older, disturbances in parent-child interactions emerged that appeared to be reactive to the special characteristics of the children. Some parents reacted with self-blame, some with patience, and some with resentment and punitive treatment of the child. The authors describe two difficult children that were very similar in temperamental make-up in the first few years of life. The two sets of parents, however, reacted very differently to the children's problems. One child, a girl, had by elementary school developed a marked behavioral disturbance characterized by episodes of explosive anger, negativeness, thumb sucking, fear of the dark, defecating in her clothes, poor peer relations, and protective lying. The other child, a boy, developed no symptoms of behavior disorder. The father of the girl was intolerant of her difficulties, disciplined her harshly for them, and spent little or no recreational time with her. The mother was more understanding and permissive, but quite inconsistent. Parents of the boy, on the other hand, were patient and tolerant of his slowness to adapt to new situations and other difficulties.

Thomas and his colleagues also note how quiet, reflective children may elicit different reactions from different parents. The parents of one temperamentally calm and self-reliant girl were delighted by their daughter's per-sistence and nondistractibility. They appreciated the girl's ability to amuse herself, though they did occasionally try to draw her attention away from a deep preoccupation if they deemed it inappropriate. In contrast, the parents of another reflective girl were frustrated and overconcerned about her lack of emotion and interpersonal responsiveness, thinking she should be more relaxed and joyful. They interpreted this to mean she was unsatisfied with things they did for her. The parents reacted by shifting their attention to her brothers, and she became a rejected child.

These case histories illustrate that children are the architects as well as the victims of their environments. The age-old debate over whether heredity or environment is the major contributor to development has been dropped, and theorists have turned to developing models to describe *interaction processes*. In a moment, we shall discuss some of the research methods psychologists have developed to explore interaction processes.

We should point out that in the studies cited above (Bell, 1968; Thomas et al., 1968), children's effects on their parents were constitutionally, or genetically, based. But children also learn patterns of behavior that influence how parents behave. The manner in which children sometimes learn to display temper tantrums, for example, illustrates a chain of events in which children first learn one behavior, the parents react to it, and the children then go on to develop a behavioral problem. The following illustrates how this sequence sometimes works. When a child is ill, parents tend to be attentive, building up strong dependency habits in the child. When the child recovers from the illness, the parents may attempt to withdraw some of their attention. The child, in turn, may respond with intense temper tantrums. Depending on how the parents then react to the tantrums, the child may go on to develop intense, coercive, aggressive habits. The main point of this discussion is that children's behaviors and attributes—whether innate or learned—provoke reactions from their parents that then shape their destinies still further. Figure 1–1 illustrates how development involves a sequence of reciprocal influence between the child and his or her social environment.

Interactional Research Designs The realization that social development is a process of reciprocal influences has implications for research methods. Longitudinal investigations in which researchers monitor the continuous interplay of child and adult variables, as in the study by Thomas and his colleagues (1968), are clearly necessary. The technique of "regression analysis" should prove to be a useful tool in such studies. Here the researcher assesses numerous variables (e.g., child behaviors, parent behaviors, and environmental factors) at several points in time and analyzes the data to see what *combinations* of variables at one time predict target child behaviors at later times. For example, low-birthweight infants with difficult temperaments born into lower-class homes where one or both parents are prone to react punitively to irritations may be found to constitute a population at risk for developing later disturbances in parent-child relations.

Another trend in research methods is the analysis of sequences in social interaction, with family researchers developing techniques for coding episodes of family interaction into sequences. These researchers recognize that responses of one member of an interacting dyad are not only reactive to the previous behavior of the other member but also serve as stimuli for future behavior by the other member (Cairns, 1979a; Gottman, 1979; Patterson & Cobb, 1971; Rausch, 1965). In the study by Patterson and Cobb (1971) of behavior sequences, certain crucial and repetitive chains of parent-child interactions were shown to play a major role in the development of childhood aggression.

Current Research on "Child Effects" The recognition that children contribute to their own socialization has excited a large number of child psychologists, many of whom are actively engaged in research designed to show the importance of "child effects" in socialization. At present, research interest seems focused on three issues. First, psychologists have become increasingly interested in identifying early aspects of children's temperaments and personalities that may play

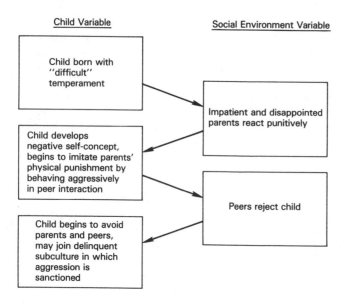

Figure 1–1 A hypothetical sequence of development as a function of reciprocal influences between the child and the social environment.

a role in eliciting varying responses from caregivers. Many of these early sources of individual differences will be determined at least partly by constitutional factors. We know that attributes such as sex, race, hair and eye color, physical attractiveness, and body build are genetically influenced. But there are a number of behavioral characteristics that also seem to be at least partly influenced by constitution. These attributes include fussiness, activity level, the time of onset and frequency of smiling, laughing, making eye contact, the tendency to stiffen or to relax when picked up, the preference for orienting to people rather than to inanimate objects, the tendency to persevere when frustrated, soothability, fear, rhythmicity of sleep and hunger cycles, and distractibility (Bates, Freeland, & Lounsbury, 1979; Buss & Plomin, 1975; Rothbart, 1981). Can we really expect children who differ tremendously on some of these characteristics to elicit identical responses from their social environments?

A second concern of child-effects researchers involves specifying the exact impact of various child behaviors and attributes (whether innate or acquired) on their caregivers and other people (cf. Bell, 1979; Bell & Harper, 1977). Since later chapters are replete with illustrations of child effects, we will not exhaustively review the findings here, but a few examples may well be helpful in demonstrating what psychologists are discovering. Perhaps the most potent of all child factors is sex: Sex has been found to determine the clothes, toys, and activities adults choose for children; the expectations parents have for their children's academic and career achievement; the motives adults ascribe to children; and the kinds of sanctions children receive for engaging in various sex-typed activities. Child variables also influence the kinds of discipline children receive. Children who have high activity levels or who display defiant reactions to punishment, for example, provoke sterner discipline; children who are physically attractive prompt positive evaluations from adults as well as from their

peers; and aggressive children tend to be rejected. Of course, the kinds of reactions we are talking about here—rejection or acceptance by one's peers, the kind of discipline one's parents favor—also significantly influence the child's subsequent development. The fact that social development involves circular processes of reciprocal influence should by now be obvious.

An interesting point is that many of these studies of child effects have employed experimental research designs—but with a new twist. The subjects are usually adults rather than children, although children participate as accomplices of the experimenter. The adult subjects are randomly assigned to one of several treatment conditions, each of which involves interacting with a child who has been "programmed" by the experimenter to display certain responses (e.g., a high or low activity level, or a high or low dependency on the adult). The adults' responses to the child are then measured. In this experimental design, the tables of tradition have been turned: The child responses are now the independent variables and the adult reactions, the dependent variables.

A third issue intriguing researchers is the question of why adults often differ in their reactions to a given child characteristic. We learned earlier, for example, that some, but not all, parents react punitively to temperamental irritability in an infant (Thomas et al., 1968). Can we predict which adults will react to a given child characteristic in a particular way? This important question has received relatively little attention. It is likely that adults' social class, education, own child-rearing experiences, familiarity with child-rearing literature, and personality will influence the reactions they have to their children's attributes. Probably, cognitive factors will prove to be important, along with the parents' expectations, aspirations, and perceptions. Some parents are more concerned than others with questions like, "What should my child be doing?" and "Is my child's behavior up to the standard level?" Consider, too, the expectant father who is hoping that his "bundle of joy" will be a robust boy who will play hockey by the time he is old enough to walk. This father may very possibly display signs of hostility and rejection if instead his newborn is a premature, scrawny infant girl who is slow to smile and make eye contact and has an irritable disposition. It is likely that a number of researchers will begin a serious examination of the variables that cause one person to react one way to a child and another person to react another way. Once child psychologists can pinpoint which adults will more than likely react to certain child characteristics in certain ways, they obviously will have a lot more to offer the field of parent education.

SUMMARY

There are several theories of social development. A good scientific theory leads to a precise set of "If _____, then _____" predictions that are verified repeatedly by data. In addition, there are a number of major research methods used by psychologists to evaluate these theories.

Freud regarded personality as the way the individual resolves various conflicts that arise among the id, ego, and superego at different stages in the person's psychosexual development. Though influential in guiding early research in a number of areas of social development, Freud's theory is regarded by many today as unscientific, and hence is not referred to in current studies nearly as often as it once was.

Trait theorists believe that behavior is caused by internal predispositions that lead one to display consistent degrees of various social behaviors across situations. Trait theory is not a theory of development, but it has been influential in conceptualizing and measuring personality. However, the discovery that social behavior is more situation specific than trait theorists would have us believe has sparked several revisions in original trait theory.

Social learning theorists believe that personality results from the child's transactions with the social environment. On the basis of diverse social learning experiences—including the discipline they receive from their parents, observation of the consequences others receive for their behavior, and verbal instruction—children are thought to formulate rules of appropriate conduct for people like themselves. They then regulate their own behavior to conform to these standards. In contrast to conditioning theories of learning, modern social learning theory holds that behavior is centrally mediated through cognitive representations of social experiences (especially response-outcome contingency relationships) and assigns a major role to the self in guiding behavior and development. The theory is popular because its concepts are stated clearly and are testable and because so many of the theory's hypotheses turn out to be verified when the relevant data are collected.

According to cognitive-developmental theory, children's social behavior changes with age because their underlying thought structures change with age. This view suggests that development occurs via an invariant sequence of stages, each stage characterized by one or more unique cognitive-structural properties that broadly influence the child's intellectual and social functioning. For instance, the thinking of children younger than 7 years is believed to be characterized by the tendency to base judgments only on superficial, perceptually salient variables (centration). Young children react to others, then, more on the basis of their appearance, possessions, and observable effects on the environment than on the basis of their motives and other hidden factors. Children progress through the stages of development because moderately new experiences arouse a curiosity that motivates them to generate new rules to account for events in their physical or social world. While the cognitive-developmentalists have pointed to important sequences in development, their view that development proceeds via discrete stages, each with its own broadly influential thought structures, has been criticized. This criticism stems from the finding that, at any given point in their development, most children do not inflexibly apply a single set of thought structures to all aspects of their social-cognitive functioning.

Ethologists are concerned with the naturalistic study of the behavior systems that a species has developed for survival purposes. They suggest that members of many species are instinctually wired to display certain behaviors when they encounter certain environmental releasing stimuli. For example, intense novel stimuli reflexively elicit the infant's crying, which, in turn, reflexively elicits maternal caregiving. The ethologists' belief that many behaviors reflect biological drives has been criticized, but their stress on observing behavior as it occurs under natural conditions has been well appreciated.

A theory is only as good as the quality of the empirical relationships it predicts. Similarly, an empirical relationship discovered by a researcher is only as good as the quality of the investigator's research design and procedures. The methods generally used in discovering relationships between age and behavior are the cross-sectional, longitudinal, and cross-sectional/short-term longitudinal designs. Methods that concentrate on elucidating relationships between child behavior and its possible determinants differ in terms of where the independent variable is manipulated, where the dependent variable is assessed, whether the dependent variable is assessed in a structured or an unstructured setting, and whether the research design is correlational or experimental. The choice of which method to use depends on a researcher's purposes. Confidence in the validity of a cause- and-effect relationship is strongest when the relationship is confirmed by a variety of research methods.

Although children are influenced by their environments, they also influence their environments. For example, children's behaviors and attributes (temperament, activity level, person orientation, and so on) cause parents, peers, and teachers to react to children in particular ways, and these reactions then help children develop in different ways. Researchers are asking a number of crucial questions about "child effects." What aspects of early child behavior are constitutionally based? What effects do different child behaviors have on adults? Why do adults differ in the way they react to a given child trait? Indeed, social development is a process of reciprocal influence between the child and his or her environment.

2
Social Relationships in Infancy

From birth, the human infant is a social crea-
ture. In fact, some of the newborn's responses seem explicitly designed to ensure
that the infant will fall into crucial patterns
of interaction with other people. Consider the
newborn's crying response. Hardly anything
is more aversive to parents than the sound of
their baby crying. Hence, when infants cry,
they tend to be fed or comforted. But the
young infant's social capabilities are limited.
Foremost among these limitations is an in-
discriminateness in neonates' social reactions: They do not adjust their social behavior according to the identity of the person
with whom they are interacting. Most 1- and
2-month-old babies are just as easily soothed
by a stranger as by their mother, for example,
and they babble and smile at a stranger as
much as at their father.

As infants move closer to the middle of
their first year, they become more discriminating in their social responsiveness. Advances in their perceptual and cognitive
apparatus allow them to differentiate among
people on the basis of voice, facial features,
and so on. Even more important is that infants develop different styles of interacting
with different people, and people come to
hold different meanings for them. Mother
may become the one to turn to in times of
distress; father may become a preferred partner for play; and strangers with certain characteristics may be treated with uncertainty
and wariness.

This chapter describes the emergence of
these early relationships, the factors responsible for them, and their significance for the
child's social development. Certainly the most

striking of the infant's social relationships is the emotional attachment the infant forms to its primary caregivers. Virtually all infants, somewhere in the middle of their first year, reveal that they have come to form a special bond with their mother, their father, and perhaps one or two other special people. Much of this chapter is devoted to the nature and significance of these special relationships.

The infant also develops styles of interacting with other groups of people, such as siblings, babysitters, day-care workers, and unfamiliar persons. We describe these relationships and their importance for the child's development. (Infants' relationships with their peers are discussed in Chapter 10.)

A central theme underlying the work on infant social behavior is that infancy provides young children with opportunities for learning important lessons about themselves and other people, lessons that influence the direction the children's development will take in later years. Through interaction with a sensitive and responsive caregiver, for example, it is thought that infants develop a conception of themselves as effective, competent, and valued people, as well as a conception of others as reliable and trustworthy. We shall see support for the notion that infancy is a time when children acquire habits of action, thought, and feeling that influence the ease with which they form satisfactory social relationships in later years.

THE CONSTRUCT OF ATTACHMENT

Somewhere around their sixth month most infants begin to show clear evidence that they have become attached, or have formed relatively enduring emotional ties to at least one other specific person. Infants reveal this attachment in a number of ways: by seeking to be near their attachment figures, especially in times of distress; by showing pleasure (e.g., smiling, babbling) when in the company of their attachment figures; by protesting (e.g.,

crying) when their attachment figures leave them; by expressing joy or relief when reunited with their attachment figures; and by using their attachment figures as "secure bases" from which to explore novel environments (moving away from their attachment figures to explore intriguing people or things, but periodically checking back with the attachment figures for reassurance when frightened or overwhelmed). In this section, we raise issues related to the definition and assessment of attachment relationships. Later sections deal with theories of attachment development, the causes of attachment, individual differences in attachment, and the consequences of early attachment for the child's adjustment in later years.

Definition of Attachment

Emotional relationships are difficult to define and assess, and *attachment* is no exception. Probably most students of attachment would agree, though, that it is the stable disposition to seek the proximity of a specific other. Thus, to be considered attached, an infant must satisfy three criteria: (a) the infant must display responses that bring it closer to other people; (b) the infant must direct its proximity seeking with greater frequency or intensity toward one or more specific others; (c) the infant's preference for the proximity of the specific other(s) should be stable over time (Hay, 1980). We shall briefly discuss each of these three points.

The Measurement of Proximity Seeking

What Infant Behaviors Qualify as "Attachment"?   Despite their relatively limited behavioral repertoires, infants can achieve proximity to other people in a startlingly large number of ways. Some psychologists (notably the ethologists, whose theory of attachment we discuss later) consider it fruitful to differentiate between two classes of attachment responses: signal and executive. *Signal responses* are the more distal varieties of social responses and include crying, smiling, making eye contact, vocalizing, and calling. These are called signal attachment responses because they presumably serve as signals to the caregiver that the infant needs or wants social contact.

Executive attachment responses are characterized by the infant directly taking the initiative to achieve proximity. The more important varieties include: turning one's head or body toward the attachment figure; crawling, walking, or running toward the attachment figure; and following, clambering up, embracing, and clinging to the attachment figure.

The measurement of infants' proximity seeking can take place through questionnaires or interviews that are given to the parents or, preferably, through direct observation of infants interacting with their caregivers at home or in the laboratory. One standardized laboratory technique that has achieved widespread popularity for assessing attachment is the Strange Situation Test developed by Mary Ainsworth. This procedure, summarized in Table 2–1, consists of a series of eight episodes designed to create a situation of gradually escalating stress for the baby (Ainsworth & Wittig, 1969). The assessment takes place in an unfamiliar room (usually a research laboratory at a university) that is furnished with two chairs, magazines for the mother, and a variety of toys for the infant. Sessions are usually videotaped and later scored by trained observers. The conditions of the test are intended to be comparable to the brief, everyday experiences infants have in our culture, but the situation is somewhat more stressful because it includes leaving the infant with a stranger in an unfamiliar environment. Throughout the episodes, observers record a variety of infant behaviors: proximity and contact seeking; distance interaction (signal responses); use of the mother as a secure base from which to explore the environment; distress upon separation; search behavior during separation; quality of the child's greeting to an entering or returning figure; avoidance of or resistance to interaction; and willingness to be comforted by the strange adult. Because so much information about the infant can be gleaned in a relatively short time, the Strange Situation

Table 2–1   Ainsworth's Strange Situation Test

Episode	Time	Content
1	1 min.	Mother and infant enter room; mother interests infant in toys.
2	3 min.	Mother sits and allows infant to explore and play freely.
3	3 min.	Stranger enters; sits silently for 1 min.; talks to the mother for 1 min.; engages infant in interaction or play for 1 min.
4	3 min.	Mother leaves; stranger allows infant to play alone, but is responsive to interaction bids; if the baby cries, the stranger tries to comfort him or her.
5	3 min.	Mother calls to infant from outside the door; steps in and pauses at doorway to greet infant and offer contact; stranger leaves; if necessary, mother comforts baby and reinterests baby in the toys; mother remains responsive to infant, but does not intrude on current activity.
6	3 min.	Mother leaves the infant alone.
7	3 min.	Stranger returns; sits, and, if the infant is distressed, offers comfort.
8	3 min.	Procedure for reunion Episode 5 is repeated.

Test has become an extremely popular technique for assessing infants' attachment behavior.

How are the Various Attachment Responses Related to One Another? We have seen that infants can achieve proximity to their caregiver in a variety of ways, but a question of considerable interest involves the relationships among the various measures of attachment. Do the measures of attachment intercorrelate with one another? In other words, is attachment a unidimensional trait? The answer is no: When infants are tested on several measures of attachment and their scores on the various measures are intercorrelated, the correlation coefficients tend to hover around the zero point (Coates, Anderson, & Hartup, 1972; Masters & Wellman, 1974).

What does this mean? Does it make sense to speak of an infant "being attached" if the various measures of proximity seeking do not hang together? The key to resolving this dilemma lies in a simple point: Each infant develops its own pattern of proximity-seeking responses. Two infants may be equally attached, but may express their desire to be close in different ways. One may prefer distal means of regulating proximity (e.g., looking and smiling at the mother, crying when she departs) and rarely seek physical means of comfort and contact, whereas a second may express attachment in quite a different style. Infants' patterns of proximity seeking are also bound up with situational factors. One infant's attachment responses may be strongly activated only when the infant is stressed or placed in a novel setting; another's proximity seeking may show up under quite different circumstances. Clearly it does not make sense to regard attachment as a unidimensional trait that has the same behavioral referents for all infants. Instead, it makes more sense to consider attachment as a *behavioral system,* or a set of interchangeable, functionally equivalent behaviors that have the same predictable outcome (promoting proximity to the care-

giver), but that are not necessarily organized in the same way for all infants.

Satisfying the Specificity Criterion

One cannot assume that an infant is attached to his or her mother just because the infant smiles at her and protests her departure; he or she may behave this way toward all adults (Cohen, 1974). Thus the assessment of attachment necessitates comparing the offspring's proximity seeking toward the primary caregivers (e.g., the mother and father) to the infant's proximity seeking toward comparison persons (e.g., unfamiliar adults).

Ainsworth's Strange Situation Test allows for the assessment of selective responding. Does the infant explore as much in the presence of the stranger as in the presence of the mother? Is the infant as easily comforted by the stranger as by the mother? An advantage to Ainsworth's test is that it allows for multiple measures of the infant's proximity seeking. Remember that an infant may score as attached on some measures but not on others.

Stability of Attachment Relationships

Do attachment relationships endure over time? Does the 6-month-old who clearly prefers his mother to all others still do so the next month, or the next year? Actually, few data speak directly to this issue, but several longitudinal studies confirm what most parents already know: Infants usually do enter into attachment relationships with their caregivers that endure for months and even years (Schaffer & Emerson, 1964; Stayton et al., 1973).

Perhaps a more interesting question is whether the *quality* of infants' attachments to their caregivers remains stable over time. Is the infant who smiles a lot at her mother at 9 months still smiling a lot at 1 year? Does the 6-month-old who refuses to let his mother comfort him in times of distress still seem unappreciative and resistant a year later? Research on the stability of attachment behavior yields the following generalization: Specific social responses (e.g., frequency of smiling or looking) show little stability over time, but when several infant behaviors that serve a common psychological function are combined into broader "behavior categories," stability is considerably enhanced (Clarke-Stewart & Hevey, 1981; Waters, 1978). For example, Waters (1978) observed infants with their mothers at 12 months of age and again at 18 months. Individual differences in specific responses (looking, vocalizing, smiling, gesturing, approaching, touching, holding on, etc.) were not stable over this time interval. However, Waters also combined certain infant responses into broader behavior categories, such as "proximity seeking," "proximity avoiding," and "proximity maintaining." For instance, infants' scores on the proximity-avoiding dimension were determined by how often the infants displayed any (or all) of the following responses: turning the face away, pouting, aborted approaches on reunion (starting toward the mother but then turning away), and refusal to make eye contact. Infants' positions on these relatively broad behavioral dimensions showed a respectable degree of stability over the 6-month period.

These findings illustrate an important point about continuity in development: Stable individual differences in behavior are in part a function of the level of organization at which behavior is assessed (Sroufe, 1979; Waters, 1978). If we search for stability in discrete bits of behavior without regard for the meaning the behavior holds for the infant, we are likely to be disappointed. It is important to bear in mind that as children develop, they can continue to possess the same underlying motive, attitude, style of adaptation, or competency, and yet change dramatically in the way that they express the underlying construct.

Today psychologists are actively involved in identifying the important underlying motives, styles of adaptation, and so on that may

have their roots in the infancy period and may evolve from the infant's interactions with its attachment figure. Ainsworth (1979) and Sroufe (1979), for example, believe that through interaction with a warm, sensitive, and responsive caregiver, infants develop a basic security in their attachment relationships. Secure infants are ones who can count on receiving mother's help and comfort, if needed. One-year-olds demonstrate this security by being able to tolerate brief separations from mother without extreme distress (they know mother will come back if called) and by using the mother as a secure base from which to explore novel people and objects. Older infants reveal their security in different ways, perhaps by showing an interest in playing with their peers or by an eagerness to tackle challenging new problems outside the home. Presumably, these infants are secure in their knowledge that if they were to encounter difficulties, they could look to home for comfort and assistance. This knowledge gives them the peace of mind necessary to test their independence beyond the home. We describe the course of secure and insecure attachments in detail later in this chapter. The important point here is that a psychological construct (such as security of attachment) can have different behavioral referents at different points in development. Therefore, if we are to succeed in finding stable individual differences in children's behavior, it becomes necessary to search for continuity in the *meaning* of behavior over time rather than in exact behavioral identities (Sroufe, 1979).

THEORIES OF ATTACHMENT FORMATION

The work on attachment provides a good opportunity to contrast several of the major theories of social development. Freudians believe that infants become attached to the mother because, by providing food for the infant, the mother satisfies the infant's need for oral sexual stimulation. Cognitive-developmental theorists believe that the infant's attachment behavior reflects changes in the child's underlying thought structures and processes. The ethologists point out that attachment is a behavior system that has evolved because it helps ensure the survival of the species: The attachment figure furnishes protection, food, shelter, and a secure base from which the young can explore and learn autonomy. Thus the ethologists argue that certain crucial aspects of the attachment process are probably governed by inherited instincts. The learning theorists regard attachment as the product of learning experiences: Caregivers acquire conditioned (secondary) reward value for the infant because caregivers are associated with a variety of unconditioned (primary) biological reinforcers, such as relief from hunger, thirst, and distress, and with the provision of pleasurable sensory stimulation. All the theories emphasize that early attachments provide opportunities for the child to develop a basic trust and security in his or her social environment—the feeling that social interaction can be benign, predictable, and partly under one's own control. We shall now elaborate on four theories of attachment formation.

Freudian Theory

Freud believed that infants derive sexual pleasure from stimulation of the oral *erogenous zone*—the mouth, lips, oral cavity, tongue, and cheeks. And because the mother, by providing her breast or a bottle to feed the infant, is the one who usually furnishes oral stimulation, she becomes the infant's first love object. Few psychologists today agree with Freud's emphasis on sexual bonding as the key to attachment, but many do agree that the mother's role in regulating the infant's biological needs is important in the establishment of a healthy attachment. One neo-Freudian, Erikson (1959), for example, argues that it is through interaction with a sensitive and affectionate caregiver that the infant develops a sense of "basic trust"—a trust not only in the predictability and kindness of others but also in one's own ability to cope with one's bodily and psychological urges.

Though Freud's theory has little evidence to support it, it has been responsible for several important trends in subsequent theory and research on attachment. First, Freud's emphasis on the mother as the infant's primary object of attachment led for many years to an exclusive focus on mother-infant relations. Researchers ignored the impact of fathers, day-care workers, and other groups on the infant's development. Contemporary research is correcting for this deficiency.

Second, although few subsequent theorists agreed with Freud that the mother becomes the attachment figure because she satisfies the infant's sexual drives, many did agree that the mother acquires value because she satisfies the infant's biological needs. For example, early learning theorists retained Freud's notion that satisfaction of unconditioned (biological) drives is essential for attachment formation. However, we shall see that this early learning-theory view has also fallen into disrepute.

Third, Freud believed that the specific caregiving practices parents use have lasting effects on the child's personality. Freud was especially concerned with how mothers handled their baby's oral sexual needs in the feeding situation. He claimed that either severe frustration or severe indulgence of the infant's oral drive, for example, could lead to a *fixation* at the oral stage (a continued preoccupation with oral activities past the oral stage and a tendency to regress under stress to oral and dependent behaviors). Oral indulgence, for example, was hypothesized to lead to qualities such as optimism, a need to be ministered to, attempts to recapture the blissful state of passive dependency, talking, singing, drinking, chewing, craving to receive affection, and needing protection. Excessive oral frustration was thought to produce pessimism, depression, dissatisfaction, a feeling of being cheated, and, if the frustration occurred after the infant had started to teethe, an aggressive demandingness and a biting sarcasm. Freud's hypotheses led researchers to study the effects of specific feeding practices, such as whether infants should be fed on a fixed schedule or on demand, whether it is better to feed infants by breast or by bottle, and whether early weaning is better or worse than late weaning. In fact, little evidence for relationships between specific caregiving practices and enduring personality traits in children was found (Caldwell, 1964).

Finally, Freud suggested that attachments make children more susceptible to parental discipline and more likely to identify with their parents' value systems. In Chapters 3 and 4, we shall see support for these suggestions.

Cognitive-Developmental Theory

Cognitive-developmental theorists (Kagan, 1971a, 1971b; Kohlberg, 1969; Piaget, 1951) emphasize that attachment is related to the infant's underlying cognitive apparatus. Certain relationships are obvious. Infants clearly cannot form specific attachments until they are capable of perceptually discriminating among various people. But other links that the cognitive-developmentalists posit between cognition and attachment are less self-evident. For example, some cognitive-developmentalists suggest that infants cannot form an attachment until they have attained *person permanence*, or the knowledge that other people continue to exist even when they are out of sight (Bell, 1970; Schaffer & Emerson, 1964). The supporting argument is that infants cannot seek to be near an absent figure unless they know that this person exists. Although the hypothesis seems reasonable, it has been difficult to confirm (Bell, 1970; Cook, 1972, cited in Flavell, 1977). For one thing, person permanence is not an all-or-nothing accomplishment, but develops in stages. It may ultimately turn out that attainment of certain facets of person permanence are required for certain manifestations of at-

tachment, but as yet the links are not at all clear.

Some theorists with a cognitive-developmental orientation, notably Kagan (1971), propose that infant smiling, crying, and exploring are responses that represent certain forms of underlying cognitive activity on the part of the infant. Remember from Chapter 1 that cognitive-developmentalists believe that children are constantly engaged in the process of trying to understand experiences that initially seem puzzling or a bit unusual to them. In the language of cognitive-developmental theory, the children are trying to assimilate perceptually discrepant events to their existing schemas, or to their mental representations of previous experiences. Smiling, crying, and exploring are all thought to begin with the infant's attempt to fit incongruent events to existing schemas, but which of these three responses results depends on how successfully the infant accomplishes its information-processing task.

Smiling, according to Kagan, indicates that the infant has successfully assimilated a stimulus, meaning that he or she has finally recognized as familiar something that at first seemed an odd blend of the familiar and the unfamiliar. Watching infants smile, it is often difficult to escape Kagan's conclusion that smiling reflects an assimilation process. For example, when infants are presented with a face they have seen several times before, they tend to spend several sober seconds scrutinizing the face and then they suddenly break into a smile, as if finally having found a familiar mental pigeonhole into which to place the face. A smile, then, may mean a mental "Aha! I know what that is!"

Crying, on the other hand, more likely represents a failure to assimilate. Kagan proposes that distress reactions occur when the infant experiences perceptual incongruity, but cannot find a suitable mental response to make. Distress is likely to occur if the discrepant stimulus is very intense, in part because the infant may not know what kind of response is appropriate. If a total stranger suddenly looms toward the infant, for example, the infant may feel compelled to respond, but, not knowing the person and his or her habits, may not be able to generate a response that will allow it confidently to control and pace the stranger's actions. Thus, when the infant is aroused, but cannot find a response that makes incoming stimulation more predictable and controllable, the infant becomes distressed.

Exploratory responses (e.g., cautiously but intently examining novel objects or people) may also be sparked by perceptual incongruity. The infant is fascinated by combinations of the familiar and the unfamiliar and is trying, as always, to assimilate the new experience to see if it matches up to some stored representation of a similar experience. As long as the novel stimuli are not too arousing or threatening, and as long as the infant is not far from an attachment figure who can provide reassurance if needed, the infant continues its exploration. Exploration frequently leads to accommodation, or the formation of new schemas. For example, if the infant has extensive experience exploring a friendly stranger, the infant may eventually form a mental image of the stranger's face, a small but significant act of creation. Furthermore, the next time the infant sees the stranger and recognizes him or her, the infant may smile, revealing an assimilation process. Recall that assimilation and accommodation are considered to be the two main processes of cognitive growth in cognitive-developmental theory.

Here we have characterized smiling as successful assimilation, crying as failed assimilation, and exploration as attempted assimilation turned accommodation. Throughout this chapter we shall see considerable support for the notion that infant social behavior rests upon underlying cognitive processing.

Ethological Theory

Ethologists point out that without mechanisms to keep infants close to adults and to motivate adults to care for and protect their offspring, our species (and many others) would never have survived. Attachment bonds ensure that the infant will turn to a caregiver in times of hunger, distress, or danger. They ensure also that infants will have a base from which they can gradually venture out to explore their environments and to learn new competencies, secure in the knowledge that they can return home for reassurance and "recharging" if the novelty becomes overwhelming. By ensuring proximity of the young to mature members of the species, attachments also help the young acquire the skills of the more competent members of the species.

Ethologists recognize that attachments are reciprocal bonds, involving not only the infant's proximity seeking toward a caregiver but also the caregiver's proximity seeking toward (and attending to the needs of) the offspring. Thus caregivers are just as motivated to provide food, comfort, shelter, a secure base for exploration, and a model of competence for their infants as their infants are motivated to seek these qualities in their caregivers.

Ethologists contend that if attachment bonds represent the products of evolutionary adaptation, then it is reasonable to expect that certain aspects of attachment formation and responding are under the control of inherited instincts. Instincts may be considered to be relatively rigid chains of behavior that are triggered by specific external events, known as releasing stimuli, whose power to trigger the behavior is biologically programmed in the organism. Ethologists have found it fruitful to take a comparative approach to the study of attachment. Comparative research involves comparing the processes governing attachment across different species. One general conclusion is that bonding in lower species is indeed often under the rigid control of instincts, but as one climbs the phylogenetic scale, instincts increasingly interact with learning experiences to influence attachment (though instincts probably still play some role).

To better understand the ethologists' notion of attachment as instinctive behavior released by specific environmental eliciting stimuli, we shall examine some examples of the ethologists' discoveries. (For an extended discussion, see Maccoby, 1980.) In several species of birds and ducks, bonding results from the offspring imprinting on any large moving object to which they are exposed during a critical period, which is usually a certain number of hours after birth (Hess, 1959).

Leon's (1977) work with attachment in rat pups illustrates how instinctual responses in both the mother and offspring involve synchronized, mutual adaptation. Rat mothers emit an odor that the pups find attractive. When the pups become mobile, but are still unable to feed and protect themselves, the mother secretes strong doses of the odor and the young rats' sensitivity to the odor increases as well. This helps to keep the pups "tied to their mother's apron strings," ensuring that they don't become lost or endangered. But once the pups can fend for themselves, there is a decline in both the mother's secretion of the odor and the attractiveness of it to the pups.

Observations of attachment in monkeys illustrate how infants and mothers regulate the distance between them on the basis of such factors as the degree of threat, the infant's age, and the strength of competing curiosity motives in the infant. Young monkeys cling to their mother's fur as soon as they are born and spend most of their infancy in direct contact with the mother's body. As they grow older, an ever-increasing amount of time is spent away from the mother. But if the separation is of too great a distance or if the infant is stressed by threat or novelty, then the infant and mother quickly reestablish contact. The infant's curiosity about objects and places and the desire for play with peers help pull the infant away from the mother, but hunger and the need to be soothed when alarmed serve as magnets that keep the infant in periodic touch with the maternal base. Eventually the mother plays an active role in

weakening the attachment relationship—she refuses to carry or nurse the infant, pushes the infant away, and perhaps even bites or slaps her offspring. In baboons, this happens around 6 months of age, when the infant's fur changes from black to the normal adult color.

What about human attachments? Psychologists who apply principles of ethology to human development (Ainsworth, 1973; Bowlby, 1969) suggest that genetic programming causes the human mother and infant to respond immediately to one another after birth and eventually to establish a pattern of mutual attachment. Infants are believed to be genetically wired with an early social signaling system that causes them to smile, cry, look, vocalize, and suck in response to certain critical releasing stimuli from their caregivers. For instance, the touch of the mother's breast against the infant's cheek causes reflexive sucking, and the mother's high-pitched voice triggers vocalizing and smiling. Similarly, mothers are programmed with a reciprocal set of caregiving responses that are elicited by the infant's signals. The infant's cry prompts the mother to soothe the infant and the infant's smile elicits reciprocal smiling and vocalizing from the mother. Ethologists maintain that the mother's hormonal state at birth renders her especially sensitive to the infant's signals.

According to ethologists, an important function of the attachment relationship is helping the child explore and master novel environments. Ethologists point out that the attachment figure provides a reassuring base that children can turn to when they become frightened or overwhelmed in the course of exploration. When 1-year-olds are placed with their mothers in a strange environment (e.g., a laboratory room with novel toys), the infants usually, at first, stay close to their mothers, but they gradually venture out to engage the environment. However, maintaining periodic contact with the mother is essential for smooth exploration. Young infants return physically to the mother every so often, but with age infants begin to maintain contact distally—they glance back at mother or listen for her voice every now and then. Ethologists contend that without an attachment figure to use as home base, infants would never overcome their fear of the novel and would remain seriously frightened of unfamiliar settings. As infants get older and become more used to novel environments, fears decrease, exploratory drives become more powerful, and the intensity and frequency of attachment wane. The infant, with the blessing of his or her caregivers, spends more time away from home base and in the company of other people, such as the peer group.

Learning Theory

The underlying theme of the learning theory of attachment is that infants are attracted to people because people are the most important and reliable sources of stimulation. Since specific individuals regularly provide this stimulation, these individuals are valued by the infant and become the objects of attachment (Bijou & Baer, 1965; Gewirtz, 1969). In Chapter 1 we noted that it is important to distinguish between two brands of learning theory: conditioning theory and cognitive social learning theory. To date, most of the theorizing about attachment by learning theorists has been done by conditioning theorists; social learning theorists, such as Bandura, have had little to say about the attachment process.

The conditioning theorists believe that it is possible to account for most of the important facts about attachment development in terms of three basic principles of conditioning. First, the mother is believed to acquire conditioned or secondary reward value because she provides unconditioned (unlearned) primary reinforcers. Different learning theorists have stressed different primary reinforcers as crucial. Among the primary reinforcers suggested to be important are the giving of food and water, the provision of tactile stimulation and contact comfort, the furnishing of exciting visual and auditory stimulation, the relief from distress, and the regulation of temperature. According to learning theory, when a formerly neutral stimulus (e.g., the mother) is paired with a primary reward, the neutral stimulus acquires some positive value all its own; it will now be sought out for its own sake.

A second tenet of learning theory is that the primary caregiver acquires discriminative stimulus properties. A discriminative stimulus is a stimulus that lets an organism know when it will be rewarded for performing a response. If a rat is rewarded with food for pressing a lever only when a red light is turned on in its cage, it will soon learn to restrict its lever pressing to times when the red light is on; the red light is a discriminative stimulus. Presumably, infants learn that they are more likely to be rewarded for smiling, vocalizing, bidding for attention, and so on if they emit these responses in the presence of their caregivers than if they emit the responses in the presence of unfamiliar others. Thus infants learn to direct their social responses more to their specific caregivers than to less familiar people. The mother is to the infant what the red light is to the rat.

A third principle is that an infant's unique pattern of proximity-seeking responses will depend on the schedule of rewards and punishments that its caregivers have dispensed for the responses. For example, if a mother contingently responds to crying with attention, but ignores smiling, the child presumably will be more likely to become a crier than a smiler.

We shall see that infancy is indeed a period when the child engages in much learning. But it is not clear that the nature of the infant's learning is accurately described by the conditioning principles we have just reviewed. For example, the third principle we mentioned above—the hypothesis that infant responses are subject to simple laws of reinforcement—has come under considerable attack, notably by Ainsworth, (e.g., Bell & Ainsworth, 1972). Ainsworth, a psychologist who explains attachment in terms of a blend of ethological and cognitive concepts, argues that learning theorists are making a mistake when they treat the infant's social responses as subject to the same laws of learning as the rat's lever pressing or the pigeon's key pecking. In fact, she believes that when caregivers respond promptly to an infant's cries, smiles, and other social signals, the caregivers are not strengthening the specific infant responses being attended to, but rather are strengthening the infant's underlying belief in his or her ability to predict and control the caregiver. In other words, contingent caregiver responsiveness teaches the infant that the caregiver is accessible and will come if signaled. Thus contingent responsiveness to the infant's cries and other signals is thought not to increase the infant's crying, but rather to *reduce* the frequency of crying, because the contingent reactions give the infant a sense of security ("Mother will come if I call her") that helps the infant handle minor stresses without distress.

In sum, Ainsworth charges that contingent responsiveness does not serve simply to reinforce the surface behaviors it follows, but rather teaches the infant basic lessons about his or her effects on other people. It is these lessons that then influence how the child behaves. Ainsworth's hypothesis is an important one, and we shall see some preliminary evidence that supports it.

Most conditioning theorists, as we have noted, believe that the mother becomes valuable to the infant because she is associated with unconditioned primary reinforcers. One prominent conditioning theorist's version of attachment formation, however, departs from this traditional view (Cairns, 1966). According to Cairns, any salient stimulus that is consistently present in the infant's environment and accompanies many of the responses that the infant makes will in time become an object of attachment. The idea is that if a salient stimulus is consistently present when a behavior is performed, it eventually becomes necessary for the response to be performed

smoothly, without disruption and distress. Applied to attachment, Cairns sees the mother as a perceptually vivid and salient stimulus who accompanies many of the infant's responses (e.g., feeding and being put to sleep). Thus her presence becomes necessary for the smooth performance of a wide range of infant behaviors. When she departs, the infant's behavior is disrupted and distress results. To understand this theory of attachment, it may be helpful to draw a parallel with the smoker who can not perform certain tasks effectively without a cigarette. We shall see considerable support for Cairns's view that attachment rests upon the infant's having learned to organize many of its responses around a salient and familiar stimulus—the primary caregiver.

THE DEVELOPMENTAL COURSE OF ATTACHMENT

Early Steps in the Bonding Process

Attachments develop much more gradually in human infants than in the young of lower primates. Human infants cannot cling or crawl to adults, and initially they cannot even distinguish their own caregiver from other figures. Nonetheless, almost immediately from birth human infants and their caregiver (usually the mother) enter into certain predictable patterns of mutual adaptation that ultimately lead to the formation of a close, reciprocal attachment.

The Contexts for Early Interaction There are several contexts in which crucial initial patterns of caregiver-infant interaction become established. One of the most obvious is the feeding situation. The sucking reflex, which causes the infant to suck when something is placed in his or her mouth or when someone strokes a cheek, literally binds the infant to the caregiver. Sucking also stimulates the mother's nipples, which activates a hormone that produces yet more milk. Though we shall see later that the actual provision of food is probably not terribly important in attachment formation, feeding sessions clearly do provide the infant with a chance to grow familiar with the caregiver's face, voice, and other unique qualities and to develop confidence in the caregiver's ability and willingness to adjust his or her behavior to the infant's states and needs.

Another important context for early interaction is the distress-relief situation. When an infant cries, adults become aroused and experience a mixture of aversion and empathy that propels them to try to stop the infant's cry (Murray, 1979). Thus when they hear an infant cry, most adults rush to soothe the infant. They may pick the infant up to hold, cuddle, or rock; change a diaper; or comfort in some other way. Infants usually do calm down when picked up, rocked, warmed, or swaddled. Thus the distress-relief cycle provides highly predictable outcomes for both members of the mother-infant dyad: The infant can predict someone will respond to distress signals, and the mother can predict that her infant will calm down when she intervenes. In this way, mother and infant establish a pattern of mutually reinforcing behavior. Furthermore, it may be in the context of distress-relief interactions that infants eventually learn important lessons like "My behavior has an effect on other people" and "When I'm in trouble, I can count on Mom to help."

A third important context for the roots of mutual adaptation and regulation is affectionate play. Stern (1974) filmed face-to-face interactions between 3-month-old infants and their mothers. The playful interactions were not disorganized, but instead were highly orchestrated interchanges, with mother and infant stimulating each other in ways that maintained an optimally pleasurable level of input for the infant. The mothers constantly shifted their behavior to elicit and maintain the baby's attention. They exaggerated their speech, talking loudly and slowly, and elongating their vowels. They exaggerated their facial expressions, forming their expressions

slowly and holding them for long periods of time. The infants contributed to the regulation of interaction largely by controlling their gaze. When the stimulation became too much, the infants looked away; in turn, the mothers reduced their input.

Subsequent studies have found that infants (even newborns) contribute to the regulation of dyadic interaction not only through gaze aversion but also through vocalization (Bateson, 1975; Rosenthal, 1982), head turning (Peery, 1980), and facial expressions (DeBoer & Boxer, 1979). For example, infants take turns vocalizing with their mother, and they move their heads backward or forward depending on whether their mother's head moves toward or away from them. Possibly, some of the important lessons of reciprocity in social interaction—that people are supposed to take turns holding center stage while interacting, that it is appropriate to match the emotional tone of one's responses to a partner's, and so on—are learned in part during early playful interactions.

If early caregiver-infant interaction lays the foundation for reciprocal attachments, then one might wonder whether mother-infant pairs who are denied opportunities for early interaction are at risk for breakdowns in the attachment process. Some pediatricians claim that the typical routine in most hospitals impedes the bonding process meant to begin immediately at birth (Klaus & Kennell, 1976). In the typical hospital, the mother usually gets a quick peek at her baby after delivery, but then is separated from her infant for several hours before regular visits and feedings begin. In an intriguing experiment, Klaus and Kennell (1976) compared the development of two groups of newborns and their mothers. One group was subjected to the usual hospital routine after birth (control group). In an experimental group, however, the infant and mother were placed in a warm, quiet room where they could lie together unclothed for an hour after the birth. In addition, these pairs were together five hours on each of the first 3 days after delivery.

The investigators concluded that contact immediately after birth may be especially important for bonding. The infants in the extended-contact group spent about 40 minutes of their first hour on earth in a state of rapt attention, and they were capable of fixating on and slowly tracking their mothers' moving faces with their eyes. For their part, the mothers shifted around to arrange themselves in a face-to-face position with their infants. The mothers spent a good deal of time touching and massaging their infants. The opportunity for early communication with their infants seemed to produce something close to a state of ecstasy in the mothers.

Klaus and Kennell claimed that benefits of the extended contact were still evident months later. When the mothers and infants were observed 1 year later, the extended-contact mothers displayed more physical affection during feeding, they were more likely to soothe their infants if they were distressed, they engaged in more eye-to-eye contact, and they were more concerned about leaving their offspring in someone else's care. Subsequent studies have not always produced results as dramatic as these (Grossman, Thane, & Grossman, 1981; Svejda, Campos, & Emde, 1980), but the findings have prompted some pediatricians to arrange greater opportunity for mother-infant interaction in the period immediately following birth.

The Klaus and Kennell findings do not imply that early mother-infant separation will inevitably lead to breakdown in attachment, nor do they imply that any difficulties that result from early separation are irreversible (Bakeman & Brown, 1980; Rode, Chang, Fisch, & Sroufe, 1981). What the findings do show is that bonding is a sensitive process that begins in the early weeks of life.

The Interaction of Biology, Cognition, and Social Learning in Early Social Responsiveness It is difficult to escape the conclusion that many of an infant's earliest social responses—sucking, crying, smiling, vocalizing, and looking—constitute instinctive reactions to specific environmental releasing stimuli. Consider the smiling response. For the first week or two, smiles represent reactions to patterns of internal tension, arousal, and discharge in the central nervous system, but thereafter they come increasingly under the control of external eliciting stimuli. During the latter part of the first month, smiling is elicited by gentle tactile and auditory stimulation (especially a high-pitched tone or voice); in the second month, a nodding head or a face with a wagging tongue is an excellent elicitor, especially if accompanied by a voice; and in the third month, static faces (of either familiar or unfamiliar people) evoke smiles (Sroufe & Waters, 1976; Wolff, 1963).

The looking response is another example of how early responding follows a built-in timetable of responsiveness to external stimuli. Young infants prefer patterns with contours; as they get older, they show a preference for more complex patterns, and especially those with a concentric quality (e.g., a pattern with a small circle embedded within a larger one); and by the time they are 2 months old, infants respond to the eyes of faces presented to them (Fantz, Fagan, & Miranda, 1975; Maurer & Salapatek, 1976). One wonders whether the young infant's preference for concentric patterns is an inborn precursor of the infant's eventual preference for eye-to-eye contact with other human beings.

Crying also has its natural elicitors. Early crying occurs mainly in response to discomfort and hunger, but by the second month infants cry when interesting things are removed from their field of vision, and they cry louder if a person leaves than if an object is removed (Schaffer, 1971; Wolff, 1969).

Note a common theme in many of these observations: As the infant matures, stimuli eliciting the infant's responses become progressively more social in nature. Also, with age the infant's responses become decreasingly dependent on tactile stimulation and increasingly regulated by distance receptor stimulation—auditory and visual stimuli (Walters & Parke, 1965).

Innate reflexes may play a crucial role in initiating the infant's social responses, but as the child gains in cognitive maturity and experience, the child's social reactions become increasingly mediated by internal cognitive processes. Changes with age in the stimuli that provoke smiling, for instance, confirm the cognitive-developmental theorists' hunch that smiling signifies "effortful assimilation," or successful matching of an initially puzzling stimulus to a stored schema (e.g., Kagan, 1971a). At what age does this begin? Sroufe and Waters (1976) propose that a major landmark is reached when infants begin to smile at a static face, which usually occurs around 8 to 10 weeks of age. They suggest that this represents the infant's first visual image—an idealized or prototypic mental picture capturing the essential features of all faces. At this early stage, infants smile as much at unfamiliar faces as at familiar ones, presumably because they have only a single general face schema into which to assimilate all the faces they see. In other words, at this early stage, infants are capable only of recognizing a face as a face. However, as infants mature they form separate schemas for the faces of specific familiar others. They no longer take pleasure in matching just any face to their general face schema (they have done this so often that it is boring), and they become more discriminating in their smiles, restricting them to times when they recognize the faces of selected familiar people.

Infants' social behavior is influenced not only by biology and cognition but also by social learning experiences. Infants begin to learn at a surprisingly early age. In a study by Thoman, Korner, and Beason-Williams (1977), newborn infants (12 hours old) heard a woman's voice when they were picked up for soothing. After 100 pairings of the voice and being held, the voice alone acquired some capacity to calm the infants. This did not

happen to infants for whom the voice and being held had not been paired.

Some psychologists suggest that infants are born biologically prepared to learn certain stimulus-response associations—especially those with adaptive significance—more rapidly than other sorts of associations. For example, it may be easier for young infants to learn to suck at the sight of the breast, to cry when they see their caregivers prepare to leave, or to calm down at the sight or sound of their caregivers than it is for infants to learn other sorts of associations (Hinde & Stevenson-Hinde, 1973; Sameroff & Cavanaugh, 1979; Seligman, 1970). The dependence of early learning on biological preparedness is a good example of how biology and learning interact to influence early development.

When discussing the learning theory of attachment, we noted that there is a controversy over whether contingently responding to an infant's social responses (smiles, cries, vocalizations, etc.) always functions to strengthen, or *reinforce*, the infant behavior. Evidence for a reinforcing effect of contingent responsiveness is stronger for smiling and vocalizing responses than for the crying response. When adults deliberately reinforce an infant's smiling or vocalizing, perhaps by tickling the baby's tummy or by vocalizing each time the infant emits the target response, the response increases in frequency (Brackbill, 1958; Millar, 1976; Rheingold, Gewirtz, & Ross, 1959; Weisberg, 1963). Some critics (e.g., Bloom, 1979) claim that such effects cannot confidently be attributed to conditioning processes, because the reinforcers (the tickles, reciprocal vocalizations, etc.) may be the natural elicitors of the infant's responses. That is, the stimulation the researchers are using as reinforcers may trigger the infant's innate reflexes rather than create learned associations. Regardless of which explanation one accepts, it is clear that stimulating and responsive caregivers are likely to promote more socially responsive infants. Gewirtz (1965), for example, showed that infants reared at home or in Israeli kibbutzim were quicker to develop the smiling response than infants reared in a less stimulating orphanage environment.

But does contingent responsiveness increase infant crying? A provocative longitudinal study by Bell and Ainsworth (1972) suggests not. In this study, infants and their mothers were observed at home every few weeks for the first year of the infants' lives. Measures of the frequency of infant crying and of the mothers' latency to respond to their infants' cries were taken during each observation period. Mothers who consistently responded promptly to their infants' cries in the early months had infants who cried the least by their first birthday. Bell and Ainsworth argued that quick maternal responsiveness does not "spoil the baby," but instead teaches the infant that the caregiver is retrievable if necessary; this feeling of security increases the infant's threshold for distress, rendering crying less likely. Not all theorists are in agreement with the Bell and Ainsworth analysis (e.g., Gewirtz & Boyd, 1977). Nevertheless, the evidence suggests that contingent responsiveness does more than strengthen the specific infant responses it follows; it also teaches infants general lessons about their control over the environment and about the accessibility of their caregivers in times of need.

The Gradual Emergence of Discriminated Attachments

For most infants, the first 2 or 3 months of life are marked by indiscriminate social responsiveness: Newborns react similarly to familiar and unfamiliar people. But by their fourth month, infants usually show that they can distinguish their caregivers (or at least their mothers) from other people, and they start to direct some of their social signals more often to their mothers than to unfamiliar people. Three-month-olds prefer to look at their mother's face rather than at a stranger's (Barrera & Maurer, 1981), and they smile at their

mothers (Watson, Hayes, Vietze, & Becker, 1979) and coo to them (Roe, 1978) more than to a stranger.

But the 3-month-old's attachment is primitive and bears little resemblance to the intense emotional preference the infant comes to display for the attachment figure over the next several months. Three- and four-month-olds are still fairly friendly to strangers, and though they may show signs of not wanting to be left alone, they usually do not protest the departure of familiar caregivers any more than they do the departure of strangers (Maccoby, 1980). By 6 or 7 months, however, this changes. Infants obviously enjoy staying close to specific people, and particularly mothers and/or fathers. Separations from familiar caregivers become particularly distressing (Schaffer & Emerson, 1964), and infants show more pleasure when reunited with their mothers (positive vocalizing and putting their arms out to be picked up) than when they greet other people (Stayton, Ainsworth, & Main, 1973). Nobody can comfort a distressed infant as well as his or her attachment figure. It is hard to escape the conclusion that specific others now serve as a source of emotional security. Figure 2-1 illustrates how one index of attachment—separation protest—becomes increasingly differential as the infant moves into the second half of the first year of life.

In review, three phases in the emergence of discriminated attachments can be identified (Bowlby, 1969). In the first phase (lasting for roughly 8 to 12 weeks), infants orient themselves and direct their social signals (smiles, looks, and vocalizations) more to people than to inanimate objects, but they respond alike to familiar and unfamiliar people. In the second phase (3 to 6 months), infants intensify their signals and emit them more to their caregivers than to others, but they are still relatively friendly to strangers. Finally, in the third phase (6 months to 2½ years) infants take a more active role in promoting proximity to their caregivers (crawling and following), they use their mothers as secure

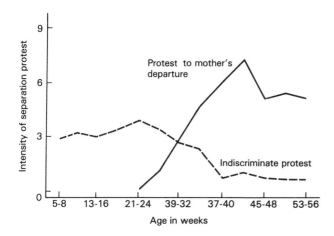

Figure 2-1 The developmental course of separation protest. Young infants protest the departure of anyone, but with age, infants come to reserve vigorous protests for separation from their attachment figures (adapted from Schaffer & Emerson, 1964).

bases for exploration, and they show an intense preference for their mothers over strangers, especially when distressed.

To Whom (and to What) Do Infants Become Attached?

Traditionally it was believed, especially by Freudians and ethologists (cf. Bowlby, 1969), that there was an innate bias for the infant to become attached to a single figure—the mother. The theory was that only after establishing a foundation of affection and trust with a single "primary" attachment figure could the infant branch out to form secondary attachments to other specific individuals. Recent evidence challenges this view. Instead, it seems that as soon as the infant emerges from the phase of indiscriminate social responsiveness (around the third or fourth month), the infant begins to establish attachments with several figures (mother, father, sibling, grandparent, babysitter, etc.) simultaneously. However, the infant is still fairly selective in his or her choice of attachment figures. Furthermore, the fact that a baby may have several attachment figures does not imply that they are all equally important—an infant's attachment relationships may be hierarchically arranged. A baby may enjoy and derive some security from all of his or her

attachment figures, but yet, under certain circumstances (e.g., illness, fatigue, or stress), show a decided preference for one figure over another (Ainsworth, 1979).

The comparison of children's attachments to their mothers and fathers illustrates the above conclusions. Infants begin to show a clear-cut preference for their fathers over strangers at just about the same time they come to prefer their mothers over strangers—about 6 months of age (Lamb, 1977b). However, the quality of the infants' attachment to their fathers differs from their attachment to their mothers. Interestingly, when the three are observed in a relaxed, nonstressful environment (e.g., no strangers present), infants actually prefer to affiliate with their fathers more than with their mothers: The infants do not show greater physical approach to their fathers, but they do send more distal signals to them—they smile, vocalize, and look more toward their fathers than their mothers. However, when threat or stress is introduced into the scene (e.g., a stranger enters), the infants show a decided preference for mothers over fathers, approaching and staying close to their mothers (Lamb, 1976a, 1976b).

What accounts for this pattern? Perhaps the father is more often the target of the infant's distal signals because the infant is "exploring" him or cautiously inviting him to interact. Fathers are familiar to infants, so they do not frighten them, yet they are more novel than mothers and hence a cause for curiosity. Fathers also spend a good deal of their time with infants in play, and the infants may be looking for this. Fathers do have a more engaging style of stimulating their infants than mothers, and this may help explain why fathers attract and hold their infants' attention more than mothers (Belsky, 1979; Clarke-Stewart, 1978). Perhaps mothers are a preferred source of solace when stress arises because they typically have been the ones to comfort their children in times of stress in the past.

Infants can become attached to their siblings. Samuels (1980) observed 23-month-old infants twice in the back yard of a home. He observed each infant with both his or her mother and an older sibling present and once with only the mother. Siblings facilitated infant exploration: When siblings were present, the infants ventured farther away from their mothers, inspected and manipulated objects in far corners, and less often cried and begged to go home.

Is it possible to become attached to inanimate objects, such as a favorite stuffed animal or a "security blanket"? Research with animals certainly indicates attachments to inanimate objects are possible. Later in this chapter, we shall see that lambs can become intensely attached to television sets, and monkeys to poles covered with comfortable terry cloth. Children also sometimes become attached to something soft and comfortable. In one study, a group of 2-year-olds who had become attached to a blanket were identified through interviews with their mothers (Passman & Weisberg, 1975). The children were then observed in a novel laboratory setting either alone, with their mothers, or with their blankets. Having their blankets present was just as effective at preventing distress and facilitating exploration as having their mothers present! However, when the novel setting was made more threatening (by dimming the lights and making eerie noises), only the

mothers functioned to quell distress (Passman, 1976).

Situational Influences on Attachment

Ethologists stress that two sorts of stimuli are especially effective in activating or intensifying the infant's proximity seeking to a caregiver: novelty and separation. Presumably, in generations past, infants who knew how to retrieve their caregivers when a strange and potentially dangerous situation arose, or when they became separated from their caregivers, were more likely to survive. There is considerable evidence that both novelty and separation do instigate attachment behavior.

Novelty   Novelty serves a dual purpose: It arouses the infant's curiosity and therefore attracts the infant, yet it makes the offspring wary and hence motivates the infant to stay close to his or her mother. We have remarked that the infant's gradual engagement of novel environments from a secure maternal base is adaptive for the child's development. Young infants seem to require periodic *physical* contact with their mothers in order to explore novel items or surroundings. For instance, 1-year-olds often return to their mothers to cling, but after a brief contact, they continue their exploration (Ainsworth & Bell, 1970; Rheingold & Eckerman, 1970). As infants mature, physical contact with their mothers becomes less essential, but *distance receptor* contact with them continues to be important for exploration into the toddler years. When 2-year-olds are placed with their mothers in a novel playroom, they position themselves so that face-to-face contact with their mothers is possible. If a mother moves out of sight (hides behind a screen, for example), exploration is reduced (Carr, Dabbs, & Carr, 1975; Corter, 1976). A mother's willingness to attend to her infant influences the infant's exploration, too. In one study, infants were less likely to explore a novel environment if their mothers were busy reading a newspaper than if they were attentive and eager to respond to their infants' attempts to "check back" with them (Sorce & Emde, 1981).

By the time children reach 3 or 4 years of age, symbolic representation of the mother is sometimes all that is needed to allow the infant to explore without distress. In fact, simply hearing a recording of the mother's voice or seeing her image on a television or film screen is sometimes just as effective in promoting exploration as the presence of mother herself (Adams & Passman, 1979; Passman & Erck, 1978). One suspects that as children mature still further, they can play away from their mothers for increasingly long durations without distress because they are able to represent their mothers cognitively in a way that is reassuring (e.g., "I know I *could* contact mom if I needed to").

Separation   We noted that from 6 months of age infants protest the departure of their caregivers (especially if they are left in a strange setting) and that such protests are still common in some infants as long as 2 years later. Ethologists stress the adaptive significance of such protests, but cognitive-developmental theorists claim that the infant's cries upon separation signify that the infant is experiencing a discrepant event that he or she is having trouble assimilating. Some interesting observations support this suggestion. For example, 15-month-old infants cry more when they see their mothers leave through an infrequently used door (e.g., a door to the attic or to a closet) than through a door that their mothers customarily use (Littenberg, Tulkin, & Kagan, 1971). Presumably, the infants are puzzled by such behavior and cannot "act cognitively" on the departure, as by imagining their mothers close by in the next room, ready to return if called. Also, the more control infants have over a separation, the less they protest: Infants cry less when their mothers leave the door open than when they close it after they leave (Rinkoff & Corter, 1980).

These observations mesh with Bell and Ainsworth's (1972) view that frequent infant crying reflects infant insecurity about the mother's accessibility. Infants who enjoy a responsive caregiving environment presumably find separation less a cause for concern than infants who feel helpless in the face of separations (Bell & Ainsworth, 1972; Spelke, Zelazo, Kagan, & Kotelchuck, 1973).

Possibly, separation protest implies different things about the infant's underlying psychological health and cognitive maturity at different points in development. For young, 4- or 5-month-old infants, separation protest may index a fairly advanced intelligence. At this age, separation protest may mean the infant has just learned that the mother continues to exist when out of sight, although the infant may yet be uncertain about her whereabouts or whether she will return. At 1 year or later, however, infants who still frequently protest their mothers' departures in common everyday situations (e.g., the mother leaves the infant in the living room to go into the kitchen) may be the less bright or the less secure infants. By this age, infants should have had ample opportunity to learn that their mothers usually do come back, especially if summoned. In fact, brighter 2-year-olds do show less distress when separated from their mothers than less intelligent children of the same age (Weinraub & Lewis, 1977).

As children become older, separation fears wane. The environment becomes less novel and fear provoking. Children learn how to react to and control more situations and can accomplish more on their own (Maccoby, 1980). The development of communication skills means that children can keep others informed of their needs and can do so at greater and greater distances (especially with the help of the telephone). Still, a great deal has yet to be learned about what is going on in children's minds as they separate themselves from their caregivers. When 4-year-olds are playing at a neighbor's house, do they think of their mothers who are at home? If so, what, in particular, are they thinking? What makes them periodically want to check back home? What might children be thinking about when their parents drop them off at day care or pre-school? Are all 5-year-olds confident that their parents will pick them up when their school day is over, or does some insecurity persist even at this age?

THE CAUSES OF ATTACHMENT

What exactly is it about caregivers that en-dears them to their offspring? In our section on theories of attachment, we reviewed sev-eral suggestions, ranging from Freud's view that the mother acquires value because she provides the infant with oral sexual gratifi-cation to Cairns's view that the mother is a salient, familiar stimulus that becomes a con-ditioned cue necessary for smooth perfor-mance of many of the infant's response systems. Does the research show that certain quantities or qualities of caregiving are re-quired for attachment formation?

The Quantity of Caregiving

Some minimum quantity of caregiver-infant interaction is obviously necessary for attachment to occur, but the exact lower limit has been hard to determine. Even infants who are placed from an early age in day care and who see their mothers only on weekends and for brief periods in the early morning and late afternoon during the week develop at-tachments to their mothers on schedule (Schwarz, 1975). Apparently, the minimum amount of mother-infant contact necessary for attachment is lower than what most work-ing mothers provide.

The Quality of Caregiving

Providing Food and Comfort   Taking a lead from Freud's view that mothers acquire value because they satisfy their infants' bio-logical needs, early learning theorists put forth a *drive reduction* hypothesis on attach-ment formation. According to this view,

mothers acquire value because they alleviate infants' drive states, such as hunger, thirst, and pain.

Classic research by Harlow and Zimmer-man (1959) challenged the view that mothers acquire value by virtue of their association with hunger reduction. In this research, in-fant monkeys were reared on surrogate in-animate "mothers"—erect posts, each topped with a head made to resemble the head of a monkey, that the infants could climb and hold onto. Infants who were reared on a surrogate "mother" that had nipples and lactated showed no more attachment to their "mother" than infants who were fed by the experimenter. This finding casts doubt on the hunger-reduction explanation of attachment.

From his experiments with monkeys, Har-low concluded that the provision of *contact comfort* is far more important than hunger re-duction in attachment formation. Infant monkeys reared on a surrogate "mother" covered in comfortable terry cloth (a surface supportive of clinging and snuggling) showed more signs of attachment than infants reared on a "mother" covered only by wire screen-ing. The former infants clearly derived solace from their "mother" when frightened by toy constructions resembling bugs. They first ran to the "mother" to cling, but then gradually ventured out to explore the object, periodi-cally running back to the "mother" as if for reassurance. In other words, they showed the normal pattern of using the mother as a se-cure base from which to adapt to novelty. In-fants reared on bare wire froze, rocked and huddled, lost control of their bladders and bowels, and failed to adapt to the fear stim-ulus.

Lacking fur, human mothers of course do not provide a surface as supportive of cling-ing and comfort as do monkey mothers. Nevertheless, it is possible that contact com-fort plays a role in human attachments as well as in monkey attachments. Remember that the most reliable way of soothing distressed infants is by comforting physically—by pick-ing them up, holding them to the shoulder, and rocking, warming, or swaddling them. Caregivers who reliably relieve their infants of pain, fear, fatigue, illness, or discomfort by providing contact comfort may be especially targeted for attachment. In other words, tactile comfort may play a role in attachment in so far as it contributes to soothing in distress-relief interactions.

Even if contact comfort contributes to the selection of an attachment figure, it would not appear to be a necessary condition. Schaffer and Emerson (1964) found that Scottish infants formed attachments to some individuals, such as fathers and relatives, who played little or no role in routine child-care activities like feeding or changing diapers. In the next section, we see too that animals can form attachments without ever having physical contact with their attachment object.

Distance Receptor Stimulation   Walters and Parke (1965) suggest that visual and auditory stimulation of the infant is more important in attachment formation than is proximal, contact stimulation. We have seen that distance receptor stimuli (e.g., high-pitched voices and facelike visual patterns) play a crucial role in eliciting many of the infant's social responses (e.g., smiling, looking, vocalizing, and crying) that eventually become part of the infant's attachment system. The sheer entertainment value of the sights and sounds produced by the caregiver, such as peek-a-boo games, nursery rhymes, and changes in facial expression, may also help attract the infant to the caregiver. Even 3-month-olds appear to be pleasurably engrossed when their mothers entertain them in face-to-face play (Arco & McCluskey, 1981); on the other hand, if mothers are instructed to remain nonresponsive during face-to-face interaction, infants appear to resent the passivity, expressing this by averting their gaze and withdrawing (Tronick, Als, Adamson, Wise, & Brazelton, 1978). Another observation supporting the idea that infants appreciate distance stimulation is the finding by Haugan & McIntire (1972) that an adult's

vocal imitation is a more effective reinforcer of infants' vocalization than either tactile stimulation or food. Perhaps caregivers are targeted for attachment simply because infants enjoy hearing and seeing them.

An experiment by Roedell and Slaby (1977) illustrates how young infants can develop a preference for caregivers who stimulate them distally. Five-month-old infants became acquainted with three adult women (previously unknown to the infants) over a 3-week period. The infants participated in a series of interaction sessions with the women, each of whom interacted with the infant in a different way. One woman smiled and talked to the infants, but avoided physical contact; a second rocked and patted the babies, but avoided visual and auditory stimulation; and the third sat by the infants without responding in any way. The infants were given periodic tests of preference for the adults—each infant was placed in a specially designed walker and the researchers measured the infant's moves toward or away from the adults. As can be seen in Figure 2–2, infants increased their preference for the distal interactor over the 3-week period.

Figure 2–2   Mean percentage of trial that infants spent near each interactor during each week in the Roedell and Slaby (1977) study (adapted from Roedell & Slaby, 1977). Copyright 1977 by the American Psychological Association. Adapted by permission of the author.

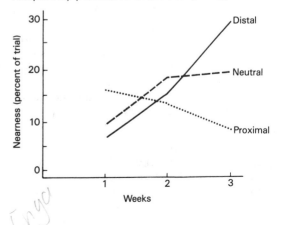

Infants develop attachment to those which have developed a predictable... out.

More evidence for the importance of the distance receptors in attachment comes from animal studies. Cairns (1966) found that when a lamb was reared in a cage next to a ewe (a wire fence permitted visual and auditory but not physical contact), the lamb formed a close attachment to the ewe. The lamb moved back and forth along the fence as the ewe moved and even became distressed when the ewe was taken away. Cairns also found that lambs reared with a constantly-playing television set vigorously protested whenever the set was removed, but quickly calmed down whenever the set was reinstated.

The fact that distance receptor stimulation figures in attachment is evidence for Cairns's theory that children form attachments to objects that become familiar to them through their eyes and ears. However, we might wonder whether distance receptor stimulation is a necessary condition for attachment. Infants who are born either blind or deaf, for example, eventually form attachments, though they are usually slower to do so than normal infants (Fraiberg, 1981; Schlesinger, 1980). It appears that infants lacking one sensory modality develop attachment through an unusual reliance on the sensory capabilities available to them. Blind infants, for example, make extraordinary use of hearing and touch in developing their attachments. It almost seems that human infants are programmed to become attached, and if they lack the normal means for accomplishing this, they will find an alternative route to the same goal. We do not have evidence on attachment in infants born both blind and deaf, but we suspect that they too find ways of becoming attached. In sum, distance receptor stimulation typically plays a powerful role in attachment, though infants lacking one or the other (and perhaps both) distal modalities form attachments, too.

Mutual Synchrony and Accommodation   We saw that by their sixth month, infants have developed unique styles of synchronous interaction with their mothers.

Patterns of mutual synchrony promote predictability and inspire confidence in the infant that chains of behavior (e.g., feeding, getting dressed, and changing of diapers) will be carried out smoothly. As Maccoby (1980) puts it, "The participants know their own moves and they know the other's moves. It is as though each member of the pair possessed one-half of the same habit" (p. 66). If an unfamiliar person tries to help out, the infant doesn't know what to do, how to adapt, how to predict the other member's behavior; feelings of immobilization and distress ensue. Thus, Maccoby suggests that attachments reflect the infant's wanting to be near others with whom dependable interaction patterns have been established. Maccoby's hypothesis is appealing, but we should bear in mind that attachments can develop, at least in animals, even when "mother" is nonresponsive and cannot integrate her responses with the infant's (Cairns, 1966; Harlow & Zimmerman, 1959).

Giving the Infant a Sense of Control
Piaget observed that infants often take great delight in noting that their behavior has an effect on the environment. Six-month-olds appear pleased when they hear the noise produced by shaking a rattle, and they think it great fun to push food off their highchair tray and watch it spill to the floor. Furthermore, the pleasure seems to be derived more from the knowledge that one is making the environment change than from just the change alone. To examine the effects of giving infants control over a stimulus, Watson and Ramey (1972) suspended a brightly colored mobile above the cribs of infants. Some infants were equipped with a special pressure-sensitive pillow that caused the mobile to turn whenever the infants moved their heads. For other infants, the mobile was programmed to turn independently of the infants' behavior. Infants who controlled the movement of the mobile smiled and cooed more, apparently delighted at their control of the situation.

It is possible that mothers acquire value

because they are a reliable source of contingent stimulation and hence impart to infants a pleasurable sense of mastery and control over the environment (Martin, 1975). Furthermore, if infants know how to signal distress and can count on their caregivers' protective response, then they may not feel so helpless in the face of novel situations (Maccoby, 1980). It is indisputable that caregivers are a salient and reliable source of contingent responsiveness. We have frequently commented on the mother's quick response to infant distress, for example. Yet we must again remind ourselves that attachments can and do develop to objects that do not respond to the infant: Cairns's television sets and Harlow's surrogate "mothers" did not respond contingently to the infants' signals.

Conclusion   We have reviewed several possible contributing factors to attachment formation. Can we identify the necessary and sufficient conditions for attachment?

Although it is obvious that some minimum amount of caregiver-infant familiarization is needed for attachment to develop, we appear to have failed in specifying the minimum amount of caregiver-infant contact that is required. Furthermore, we seem to have failed in identifying any single quality of caregiving that is absolutely essential for attachment to occur. Offspring have been known to form attachments to caregivers who do not feed them, who do not provide them with contact comfort or relief from distress, whom they cannot see, whom they cannot hear, who do not synchronize their responses with the infants', and who fail to respond contingently to the offspring's bids for attention. Admittedly, some of these findings come from work with animals, but it has not yet been demonstrated that any of the foregoing qualities is necessary for human attachment.

The human infant is remarkably flexible and adaptable, and we suspect that the caregiving qualities we have outlined above may properly be conceptualized as alternative routes to the same end. Although for the vast majority of human infants, all of the above qualities may contribute to attachment, it is clear that when one caregiving quality is not available, the infant exploits other avenues to reach its goal of forming an attachment. Of course, some caregiving qualities may produce attachment more efficiently or effectively than others. At present, for example, the evidence suggests that distance receptor stimulation typically makes a considerable contribution to attachment, whereas pairing of the caregiver with food does not.

Thus far we have no evidence that attachment rests on having a "good" mother—one who is warm, sensitive, and responsive. Indeed, infants become attached even when their mothers are openly hostile, insensitive, and rejecting. But the fact that maternal attitudes do not influence whether an infant becomes attached does not imply that mother love does not affect the *quality* of the child's attachment. Maternal affection, sensitivity, and responsiveness do affect attachment, as we will explain in the next section.

INDIVIDUAL DIFFERENCES IN ATTACHMENT: SECURE AND INSECURE ATTACHMENTS

Ainsworth has proposed that infants develop different styles of relating to their caregivers and that these different styles reflect the degree of underlying *security* the infant feels in its attachment relationship. One infant may be happy and contented in her attachment relationship, secure in the knowledge that her mother is accessible and will come if needed; another infant may also be attached (i.e., seek his mother in preference to other people), yet feel helpless and anxious, perhaps because his mother ignores many of his bids for attention or has a style of interaction that is abrasive and unsettling rather than comforting and soothing. Here we review the assessment, causes, and consequences of secure and insecure attachments.

Assessment of Secure and Insecure Attachments

On the basis of her observations of infants in her Strange Situation Test, which we reviewed earlier, Ainsworth has developed standardized criteria for classifying a baby as securely or insecurely attached. Furthermore, she has identified two subgroups of insecurely, or anxiously, attached infants: anxious/avoidant and anxious/resistant subgroups. Thus a baby is categorized as having one of three types of attachments: secure, anxious/avoidant, or anxious/resistant. What behavioral criteria are used to determine an infant's classification?

Recall that Ainsworth's Strange Situation Test is a cumulative stress situation that involves two separations from and reunions with the mother. In the first separation the child is left with a stranger and in the second the child is left entirely alone. Attachment classifications reflect patterns of behavior across all the episodes of the Strange Situation Test, but are heavily weighted by the infant's behavior during reunion episodes. Most infants become distressed at separation, but secure infants derive comfort and pleasure from their mothers when reunited with them and they are soon able to resume exploration, using their mothers as home base. Anxiously attached infants fail to show the smooth balance between attachment and exploration that securely attached infants show. In more detail, here is how the three sorts of infants behave:

Secure Infants   These infants explore actively in the preseparation episodes. As long as their mothers are in the room, they play comfortably with the toys, react positively toward the stranger (while still preferring their caregivers), and use their mothers as a base for exploration. They are affectively in tune with their mothers, smiling, vocalizing, and

sharing emotional experiences with them (Waters, Wippman, & Sroufe, 1979). When a mother leaves, play is reduced and distress is obvious. When a mother returns, her infant actively greets her and seeks contact or interaction with her. The contact is effective in terminating the distress and in promoting the return to absorbed play. For these infants, then, the attachment and exploratory systems are in healthy balance.

Anxious/Avoidant Infants   These infants fail to use their mothers as a base for exploration. In the preseparation episodes, they do explore, but they do so without checking back with their caregivers. They behave similarly toward their mothers and the stranger, and they are not particularly distressed by separation. At reunion they turn away, avoid contact with their mothers, and refuse interaction. Their avoidance is especially strong during the second reunion, even though stress is usually considered to be greater here. It would be tempting to conclude that these infants are emotionally uninvolved with their mothers were it not for the fact that these infants show accelerated heart rates during reunion (Sroufe & Waters, 1977). These infants, then, can separate themselves from their mothers, but they fail to seek comfort when one might think they need it. In sum, for anxious/avoidant infants, exploration is ascendant over attachment.

Anxious/Resistant Infants   These infants are anxious and fussy even during preseparation. They are distressed by the unfamiliar room and the stranger, even in their mothers' presence. They explore very little and stay close to their caregivers. They are intensely distressed by separation. They have difficulty settling down upon reunion and may reveal ambivalence in their feelings toward their mothers by mixing contact seeking with proximity avoiding. They may put out their arms to be picked up, but then stiffen, squirm, and cry to be put back down, only to repeat the cycle when they are put down. They may show anger by hitting, kicking, or batting away toys that their mothers offer. Thus, in anxious/resistant infants, intense attachment behavior preempts exploration.

In most samples, about two-thirds of the infants score as secure, with the remaining infants split between the two insecure categories. Not all infants fit neatly into one of the three, but investigators usually agree on whether an infant should be judged secure or insecure. Most studies have focused exclusively on infants' attachments with their mothers, but Main and Weston (1981) included an extra session of this test to assess infants' attachments to their fathers. They found that the quality of the infant's attachment to his or her father was independent of the quality of the infant's attachment to the mother: An infant could be securely attached to both parents, insecurely attached to both, or securely attached to one but insecurely attached to the other. Thus it is less accurate to refer to an infant as basically "secure" or "avoidant" than to refer to the infant as "secure with mother," "avoidant with father," and so on.

How stable is an infant's attachment classification? In several studies, infants have been observed twice, first at 12 months and then a second time at around 18 months. Among middle-class samples, where there is considerable stability in the quality of the caregiving environment, there is remarkable stability in infant attachment classification. Waters (1978), for example, found that 48 out of 50 infants in a middle-class sample received the same classification on the two testing occasions. Main and Weston (1981) discovered that classifications of father-infant attachments were just as stable as classifications of mother-infant attachments. However, attachment relationships are not fixed. Insecure attachments can be transformed into secure ones, especially if a previously chaotic home environment becomes stabilized. And secure attachments can deteriorate into insecure ones, especially if new stresses are introduced into the family's social environment; such stresses may include a

mother returning to work or increased financial pressures (Thompson, Lamb, & Estes, 1982; Vaughn, Egeland, Sroufe, & Waters, 1979). These changes in life circumstances may lead to changes in parent-infant interaction, which may then result in changes in the attachment relationship. Next we take a closer look at how caregiver-infant interaction affects the quality of an infant's attachment.

Causes of Secure and Insecure Attachments

Quality of Child Care Ainsworth (1979) hypothesizes that attachment security is determined primarily by the quality of care the infant receives. When mothers are observed interacting with their infants at home or in the laboratory, mothers of secure infants do in fact differ from mothers of insecure infants. (In many studies, the subtypes of anxious infants are lumped together, so comparisons are drawn only between secure and insecure groups.) Mothers of secure infants differ from those of anxious infants in at least four important ways.

First, mothers of secure infants respond more reliably and quickly to their infants' bids for attention, and especially to their infants' distress signals (Ainsworth, Bell, & Stayton, 1972; Bell & Ainsworth, 1972). Ainsworth suggests that infants whose attachment figures are not readily accessible must devote a good deal of attention to monitoring and worrying about where their caregivers are, and thus can afford little time for exploring or affiliating with others. Presumably, responsive mothers let their infants know that they are accessible, and this mental comfort reduces the infants' feelings of distress.

Second, mothers of secure infants show more sensitivity in interpreting and responding to their infants' signals than do the mothers of infants classified as insecure (Ainsworth, 1973; Blehar, Lieberman, & Ainsworth, 1977). Mothers of secure infants are concerned about carrying out feeding, diaper changing, playful exchanges, and other care-giving functions in a way that is comfortable for the infant. They are on the lookout for signs from their offspring that the interaction is progressing smoothly, and they alter their behavior to maintain or restore their infants' comfort. They let the infants be active partners in pacing interactions. Consider the feeding situation. Mothers of secure infants exhibit greater sensitivity in initiating, pacing, and terminating feedings: They are less likely to try to force their infants to take food, they pause when it looks as if the infant needs burping, they let their infants reject a food, and so on. These mothers do not try to impose their own feelings or will on their infants; they make their responses contingent on the babies' signals rather than on their own moods, wishes, and activities.

The greater sensitivity displayed by mothers of secure infants continues to be apparent after the child enters the toddler years. In one study, mothers of 2-year-olds who had been classified as either secure or insecure at 18 months of age were observed while they helped their children solve some problems. For example, the children had to figure out what tools to use to remove some candy from a plexiglass box. Mothers of children who had been labeled secure at 18 months provided a more supportive environment for their children's problem solving: They were more attentive, made themselves available without being pushy or taking the initiative away from their children, and they more often helped their children take credit for their own efforts (Matas, Arend, & Sroufe, 1978).

Third, mothers of secure infants express their affection for their infants more consistently and in somewhat different ways than do mothers of insecure infants. Mothers of securely attached babies engage in more affectionate touching, smiling, and verbal communication with their infants (Clarke-Stewart, 1973). Mothers of insecure infants are sometimes openly rejecting of their children: They may seem angry at their children and more often mock them and show disgust

concerning them (Main, Tomasini, & Tolan, 1979). Mothers of insecure infants often have an aversion to close bodily contact with their offspring. They sometimes show an unusually high frequency of kissing their infants, but they tend to avoid picking them up and hugging them. Since close bodily contact is an effective way to calm distressed infants, these mothers may not be fulfilling their half of the bargain in distress-relief interactions (Tracy & Ainsworth, 1981). We ought to note that mothers of insecure infants are not totally lacking in loving, affectionate feelings for their infants. It seems that they sometimes become so overwhelmed by irritation and resentment at their infants' interference with their other interests and activities that they end up intermingling their expressions of affection with signs of rejection.

Interestingly, a pattern of inconsistent parental response to children's bids for affection is also associated with intense, anxious attention-seeking in older, preschool-age children. Some nursery schoolers have a penchant for "bugging" their parents, teachers, and even playmates, for attention in a way that is aggressive and irritating. These immature children tend to have parents who display inconsistent reactions to their children's bids for dependency, on some occasions giving them the desired levels of affection and attention, but on other occasions reacting with resentment, impatience, rejection, and perhaps even physical punishment (Becker, 1964; Martin, 1975; Sears, Maccoby, & Levin, 1957). It is noteworthy that parental inconsistency in responding to children's bids for attention is associated with exaggerated, frenzied proximity seeking in children across a rather broad age span (Maccoby, 1980).

Finally, mothers of securely attached infants are more concerned about maintaining high standards of physical care for their infants. Egeland and Sroufe (1981) studied a sample of economically deprived mothers and their infants. The more a mother showed signs of neglect in her treatment of her infant (e.g., grossly unsanitary conditions in the home, untreated wounds on the child, leaving the child without arranging for proper care, and persistent failure to change diapers), the more likely the infant was to be classified anxious/resistant.

Infant Temperament There are indications that infant temperament can contribute to the quality of infant attachment. Infants who are temperamentally more "difficult" (i.e., irritable, irregular in body cycles, slow to adapt to changes in routine, and given to negative moods) may "turn off" their mothers somewhat, causing their mothers to be less responsive, sensitive, and affectionate (Crockenberg, 1981; Milliones, 1978). This may impede the establishment of a secure attachment. Indeed, Waters, Vaughn, and Egeland (1980) found that 10-day-old infants who possessed qualities that made it difficult for their mothers to coordinate their behavior with their infants' (e.g., motor immaturity, problems with physiological regulation, and unresponsiveness) were more likely to have developed insecure attachments by their first birthdays than were infants who were not born with these problems. Not all difficult infants will develop problems with attachment, however. In a study illustrating how biological and environmental factors interact, Crockenberg (1981) found that infant irritability reduced maternal responsiveness and the baby's chances of developing a secure attachment only if the mother lacked a social support system, such as a network of helpful family or friends, that could buffer the effects of having a difficult child. At present, it seems best to conclude that infant temperament, family circumstances, and maternal caregiving practices all combine to influence attachment security.

Consequences of Secure and Insecure Attachments

According to Ainsworth (1979) and Sroufe (1979), the factors that make infants feel secure in their attachments—caregiver sensitivity and contingent responsiveness—help infants develop conceptions of themselves as competent and effective organisms as well as conceptions of other people as trustworthy, reliable, and available for assistance, if needed. These underlying cognitions about the self and others should have significant consequences in the infants' social behavior, both within the family and beyond. Indeed, here we see that securely attached infants are more competent at establishing harmonious relationships with peers and new adults and that they approach challenging new problems more eagerly than their less secure counterparts.

In a longitudinal study of the relationship between the child's security of attachment and the child's competence in the peer group, Waters, Wippman, and Sroufe (1979) assessed infants' attachment in the Strange Situation Test at 15 months and then took measures of their competence in preschool play groups at 3½ years. Children who had tested as secure at 15 months showed greater leadership qualities and skill in social interaction as toddlers. They more often suggested activities to other children, were more sought out by other children, and showed more sympathy when other children were distressed. Lieberman (1977) found that the peer interactions of securely attached children were more often characterized by reciprocity (sharing and giving) and less often by negative behaviors (crying, physical aggression, and verbal threat). Securely attached children are also better at forming possible solutions to an interpersonal problem (e.g., "What could kids do if they both wanted to play with the same toy?") than are insecurely attached children (Arend, Gove, & Sroufe, 1979). When they do get into squabbles, securely attached children are more apt to redirect themselves into another activity (Pastor, 1981). It is tempting to conclude that securely attached children learn patterns of positive, reciprocal interaction at home with their caregivers and that they generalize these habits to interaction with the peer group.

To compare securely and insecurely at-

test

④ tached infants' reactions to an unfamiliar adult, Main and Weston (1981) introduced infants of each type to an adult dressed in a clown costume who attempted to attract their attention. Infants who were securely attached to both of their parents showed the highest degree of involved, positive interest in the adult by making eye contact and expressing delight more often. Infants who were insecurely attached to both parents exhibited the most signs of conflict: They more often alternated approach and avoidance responses, froze, rocked back and forth, assumed odd postures, or emitted unusual vocalizations (e.g., sudden empty laughter). Infants who were securely attached to one parent and insecurely attached to the other showed responses that fell somewhere in between these two extremes. It seems clear that attachment security is related to infants' responses to new people.

As securely attached children advance in age, they show less of a need for physical contact with their mothers and a greater interest in exploration and the peer group. Insecurely attached infants, however, have difficulty making this shift. Paradoxically, it is the insecurely attached child who appears to be the most closely bound to its parents in the post-infancy period. In their study of infants from 12 to 30 months, Clarke-Stewart and Hevey (1981) charted changes in percentages of time securely and insecurely attached children spent in physical contact with their mothers during home observations. Their data are cited in Figure 2–3. Notice how the developmental patterns for the two groups are almost mirror images of each other. Of special interest is the fact that physical contact between mother and child decreases for secure infants after 24 months, but increases for insecure infants after that time. As the authors put it, "Insecure children started out initiating more physical contact with mother than securely attached children did and then—insecurely—could not let go" (p. 143).

Anxious attachments may be associated with an increased risk for developing a be-

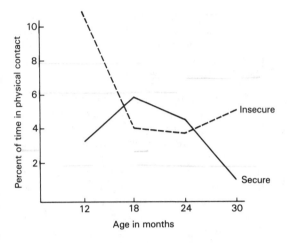

Figure 2–3   Changes with age in the percentage of time that secure and insecure infants spend in physical contact with their mothers (from Clarke-Stewart and Hevey, 1981. Copyright 1981 by the American Psychological Association. Adapted by permission of the author).

havior disorder. Insecurely attached infants are less cooperative and compliant with their mothers as well as with other adults, and they whine more and are more prone to temper tantrums (Londerville & Main, 1981; Matas et al., 1978). These findings are important because children who have a history of early oppositional and noncompliant behavior at home stand an increased risk of developing serious behavioral problems, and especially problems controlling aggression, later on.

Although we have outlined some of the negative consequences sometimes associated with insecure attachments, we must reemphasize that insecure attachments are not irreversible: Insecure children can become secure.

ATTACHMENT FAILURE AND LOSS

Some infants are denied the opportunity to form an attachment to a specific caregiver. They may be given up by their mothers at birth and, until adopted by foster parents, placed in an institution where caregiving is administered by an ever-changing staff of nurses and attendants. If children do not form a specific attachment by a particular age, are their chances of ever forming satisfying emotional relationships with other people damaged? Are infants who fail to form attachments at risk for psychological problems in later life? There is also concern about children who manage to form attachments only to lose their attachment figures—a parent may die or be lost through divorce, or the child may be hospitalized for an illness and separated from family members for days, weeks, or even months. What are the consequences of such losses? We shall review research on attachment failure and loss in the following sections.

Effects of Attachment Failure

Two broad hypotheses have been suggested regarding the effects of failing to form an attachment in early childhood (Bowlby, 1969). The first is that children who fail to form an attachment will be unable to form close relationships in later life. According to this theory, early attachments are necessary because they teach children that human beings can be predictable and trustworthy, that social relationships can be mutually satisfying, and that the self can play an active role in initiating, shaping, and sustaining such relationships. If children are deprived of learning this lesson, they may be afraid of, or not know how to form, close relationships in later years.

The second hypothesis is that children who fail to become attached will lack a secure base from which to explore the world. Not being able to desensitize themselves to frightening and novel stimuli, they will remain characteristically fearful and withdrawn, perhaps for life.

Evidence bearing on these hypotheses comes from two kinds of studies: research with human children who have suffered some

variety of maternal deprivation and experimental studies with animals who have been prevented from forming attachments in infancy.

Studies of Maternal Deprivation in Human Children   Are children who have spent their first months or years in an orphanage—without the opportunity to form a special, sustained relationship with a single caregiver—unable to form close emotional relationships in later years? It is true that the longer an infant remains in an institution without forming an attachment, the more difficult it is for the infant to form close emotional relationships with adoptive parents when transferred to a foster home. If infants are transferred by their first birthdays, for example, they tend to have little difficulty forming attachments (Rheingold & Bayley, 1959), but if transferred at 3½ years, they sometimes show considerable resistance (Goldfarb, 1943).

A famous longitudinal study by Skeels (1966) demonstrates that early attachment failure is not necessarily associated with long-term, irreversible maladjustment. Skeels followed a group of children who at 19 months had been transferred out of a multiple-caregiver institution and eventually placed in permanent adoptive homes. As adults, these individuals were indistinguishable from the normal population in terms of education, marriage, number of children, intelligence, income, and occupation. Longstreth (1981) points out that the infants that Skeels observed may have been the brighter, hardier, more attractive, and better-behaved infants at the institution, but the study nonetheless demonstrates that spending the first 19 months of life without an attachment figure does not place the infant on a one-way road toward gross maladjustment. Of course, if the infants had been much older than 19 months when transferred, it may have been considerably more difficult for them to have made the adjustment as well as they did.

Does the failure to have a specific attach-

[handwritten: Reversal possible but require right social situations]

ment figure serving as a secure base from which to explore the environment render a child fearful and withdrawn? The evidence suggests not. If anything, early attachment failure seems to fuel exaggerated attention-seeking and aggressive behavior in children. Rutter (1979) reviewed the results of two on-going longitudinal projects (by P. Dixon and B. Tizard) with English children reared in institutions with multiple caregivers. As toddlers and preschoolers, the children clung excessively to their housemothers. They were also overly friendly toward strangers, displaying an almost insatiable need for attention. Even at 8 years, most of the children had still not formed a close, preferential relationship with their housemothers, yet they continued to seek affection more than other children. At school, they tended to be restless, disruptive, disobedient, and unpopular. Though they made many social approaches, other children didn't reciprocate their overtures because their behavior was inappropriate and not pleasing. If the children were adopted into private homes, they did eventually develop deep bonds with their adoptive parents (even if they were not adopted until 4 years of age), but their social and attentional difficulties at school continued. In several respects, the behavior of these children resembles that of insecurely attached children, described earlier. Their tendency to show intense attention seeking beyond infancy and their uncooperative and noncompliant style of interaction are examples. It will be necessary to await the completion of these longitudinal projects to determine if these signs of insecurity are still evident when the children reach adulthood.

Experiments with Monkeys   In several studies by Harlow and his colleagues, infant monkeys have been separated from their mothers at birth and reared in total isolation for 6 months to 1 year (Suomi & Harlow, 1978). The infants never see, hear, or touch another monkey and their cages are bare. When they emerge from isolation and are placed with normal monkeys, the isolates reveal a range of bizarre behaviors, including extreme withdrawal and self-stimulation (rocking, self-clasping, sucking their own fur, and even biting themselves). As they develop, their misfit qualities persist. They remain fearful, play little, and aggress inappropriately, attacking much larger monkeys, for example, or picking on young, defenseless ones. Suomi and Harlow (1978) suggest that the isolates cannot cope because they have developed without the normal means of overcoming fears—attachment figures. They also suggest that the self-stimulating behavior exhibited by the isolates reflects the absence of maternal soothing: lacking mothers who can calm them, the isolates try to be their own social partners.

[handwritten: Sum] The consequences of attachment failure in human infants and monkey infants are somewhat different. As we saw, children reared in institutions tend to be rather attention-seeking and aggressive, whereas isolated monkeys tend more toward the withdrawn, fearful end of the scale. However, there is one important point on which the human and monkey data agree: Early maternal deprivation is not inevitably associated with irreversible damage. Given the right sort of social retraining, isolated monkeys can eventually become very much like their normal counterparts (Novak, 1979). We shall see in Chapter 10 that one of the more successful techniques for rehabilitating deprived monkeys involves caging them on a one-to-one basis with nonthreatening, younger peers, who slowly draw the isolates out of their withdrawn state and teach them social skills.

Effects of Attachment Loss

How damaging is it, once a child has formed an attachment, to separate the child from its attachment figure? Sometimes the breaking of an attachment bond is unavoidable, as when the attachment figure dies. But child welfare workers need answers to questions like these: Are there psychological costs to the infant when an attachment is broken? When an infant is institutionalized at birth, is it better to foster an attachment to a temporary caregiver (pending adoption), or is it better to avoid letting the infant develop a specific attachment until placed with permanent adoptive parents, so that the infant doesn't undergo a painful separation? Does forming one attachment and then losing it foster or impede the establishment of later relationships? Unfortunately we do not have answers to these questions. However, we can review some preliminary studies on the reactions of animals and children to the loss of their caregivers.

Monkeys who are separated from their mothers for several days or weeks after they have formed attachments show severe disruptions initially, but they eventually recover, especially if left with other familiar animals (Kaufman & Rosenblum, 1967; Spencer-Booth & Hinde, 1971). If the monkeys are reunited with their mothers, their everyday functioning with familiar others may return to normal, but, compared to monkeys who were never separated, they may continue to have unusually debilitating reactions to stress. For example, they may show exaggerated fright when a human being approaches or when they have to get food that is out of reach. The effects of early separation in monkeys, then, may take the form of a greater vulnerability to stress (Maccoby, 1980).

Sometimes human infants are placed from birth in temporary foster homes where they stay until permanently adopted. Naturally such an arrangement provides an opportunity for the infants to form attachments to the foster parents, which we might expect them to do by around 6 months of age. Yarrow conducted a long-term comparison of two groups of infants: Infants in one group were transferred to permanent adoptive homes before 6 months of age, while those in the second group were transferred after 6 months. Immediate distress reactions to the separation were much more severe in the latter group (Yarrow & Goodwin, 1973), but 10

years later the investigators could find no crucial differences between the two groups in personality, adjustment, and competence (Yarrow, Goodwin, Manheimer, & Milowe, 1973). Furthermore, there was no relationship between intensity of separation distress in infancy and adjustment 10 years later. From such findings, we may conclude that the child's later adjustment is determined mainly by the quality of the child's relationship with the new caregiver rather than by the separation experience itself (Maccoby, 1980).

We should note too that separations may sometimes be beneficial, especially if they furnish children with opportunities to practice coping responses (Maccoby, 1980). Stacy, Dearden, Pill, and Robinson (1970) studied the reactions of 4-year-olds who were hospitalized for tonsillectomies. Parents could visit, but not stay overnight. Some children were extremely frightened and distressed, but those who weren't often had had some separation experience before, perhaps visiting grandparents for a few days or staying overnight with a friend.

For some children, of course, separation is not unusual because they are used to spending time in day-care centers. Do these everyday separations pose a threat to the infants' social development? In the next section we examine some of the findings from the growing literature on the effects of infant day care.

EFFECTS OF INFANT DAY CARE

Mothers are entering the work force in increasing numbers. One-third of mothers who have children under 3 years of age and who live with their husbands are employed; the figure increases to 50 percent for mothers who have children under 6 years of age. The work rate is even higher for mothers who are single parents (Hoffman, 1979).

How are the infants of working mothers cared for? Most mothers who work arrange for a babysitter to come into their homes; the next most popular practice is "family day care," in which mothers place their babies in the home of a woman who minds several children in her home; finally, a minority of mothers place their infants in a nursery or day-care center. Despite the relatively infrequent use of day-care centers, most of our knowledge about day care comes from comparisons of center-reared children with children reared at home with their mothers. Of course, day-care centers differ on so many dimensions (e.g., caregiver/child ratio, training and experience of staff, space, hygiene, equipment, social stimulation, and stability of staff and children) that it is impossible to talk about the general effects of day care. Furthermore, most centers that have been studied are high-quality centers, often sponsored by universities for research purposes, so one cannot generalize on the sort of care most of the nation's children are receiving (Belsky & Steinberg, 1978).

It is important to bear in mind that comparisons of children reared in centers with those raised at home are not based on random assignment of infants to conditions. Mothers who work do so because they want to or have to. Thus differences found between center- and home-reared children may be due as much to differences in parental attitudes and life conditions as to differences in day-care versus home experiences.

This point is an important one, for working and nonworking mothers do differ in attitudes, and these attitudes may affect the child's development. As a group, working mothers are less anxious about their infants' development and are more content with their role than nonworking mothers (Hock, 1978; Hoffman, 1979). Mothers who want to work, but do not, seem to be the least satisfied group of all, and their frustration may negatively influence their children's development. Farel (1980) found that preschoolers who received the lowest ratings on social adjustment and academic competence were those whose mothers wanted to work but did not.

We will now examine more closely the effects of day care on the mother-infant relationship and on the infant's relationship with his or her peers.

Day Care and the Mother-Infant Relationship

Some psychologists, particularly those of the ethological persuasion (Bowlby, 1969), have argued that any arrangement that deprives the infant of continuous access to the mother impairs attachment and undermines the infant's emotional security. How can a mother be contingently responsive, affectionate, sensitive, and teach her child she is accessible if she habitually separates herself from her infant for long periods of time?

To be sure, some infants and young children show signs of alarm when they begin day care, especially if they have entered the stage of discriminated attachments and know that they are being separated from their mothers. They may cry and their exploration of the new day-care environment may be limited during their first visits to the center. But typically, infants adapt very quickly. In one study, by 3 months after they had begun day care, infants cried very little and cheerfully separated themselves from their mothers to join an appropriate activity (Ragozin, 1980).

But do the daily separations take their toll on the mother-infant relationship? One way to answer this question is by comparing day-care and home-reared infants for signs of insecurity in attachment, perhaps by comparing their behavior in Ainsworth's Strange Situation Test. Signs of insecurity (e.g., avoidance of the mother in reunion episodes) are sometimes found among infants who have averaged only a few months in day care (Blehar, 1974), but the longer the child has been in day care, the less likely are signs of insecurity in the mother-infant relationship (Blanchard & Main, 1979). In fact, in the vast majority of studies of children attending high-quality centers, the proportions of day-care and home-reared children diagnosed as secure or insecure do not differ (Belsky & Steinberg, 1978; Moskowitz, Schwarz, & Corsini, 1977; Portnoy & Simmons, 1978; Ragozin, 1980). This does not mean that day care is never associated with an increased risk of insecure attachment. In a study of severely economically disadvantaged women and their infants, Vaughn, Gove, & Egeland (1980) found that infants whose mothers went to work before the infants' first birthdays stood a considerably enhanced chance of developing anxious/avoidant attachments. The authors suggested that during the first year, when the attachment bond is being formed and consolidated, separations and stresses may hurt. But it should be emphasized that the mothers observed were poor and uneducated, and experienced much stress associated with their return to work. Moreover, the substitute care the infants received was unstable and may have been of poor quality since it was chosen by the mothers for convenience rather than excellence. In sum, high-quality care is not associated with an increased risk of insecure attachment, but low-quality care sometimes is.

One concern sometimes expressed by adversaries of day care is that infants will develop attachments to substitute caregivers that weaken or even supplant their attachments to their parents. There is no evidence for this. It is true that infants frequently do develop attachments to their day-care instructors, especially if these people are highly involved with them. For example, when a responsive and involved day-care worker is substituted for the mother in the Strange Situation Test, infants often show evidence of an attachment—in fact, a secure attachment—to the caregiver. Under these circumstances, the infants prefer the caregiver to the stranger, and they use the caregiver as a secure base while they explore (Anderson, Nagle, Roberts, & Smith, 1981). However, attachments to substitute caregivers typically do not replace or supersede attachments to the mother. When infants' reactions to their mothers and to substitute caregivers are compared, most infants clearly prefer their mothers (Ragozin, 1980), and they are especially likely to prefer their mothers if they are frightened or distressed (Cummings, 1980; Farran & Ramey, 1977). In sum, children can form stable, secondary attachments to substitute caregivers without threatening the integrity of the mother-infant bond.

In some respects day care may even be a boon to the mother-infant relationship. Many working mothers are careful to compensate for their lack of contact with their infants by making sure that the contacts they do share are of high quality. Indeed, working mothers have been found to be more demonstrative and vocal when communicating with their infants than mothers who are with their infants all day (Schubert, Bradley-Johnson, & Nuttal, 1980).

Rubenstein and Howes (1979) compared the stimulation day-care infants received from their substitute caregivers at day care with the stimulation infants of nonworking mothers received from their mothers at home. There was no indication that the day-care group experienced less contingent responsiveness, affection, or sensitive caregiving than the home infants. In fact, positively toned affective exchanges were more frequent in the day-care setting than in the home: Day-care workers and their charges engaged in more reciprocal smiling, more mutual play, and more holding and hugging than did mothers and their infants at home. Interactions at home between nonworking mothers and their infants were more often negatively toned. The researchers reported that the home infants cried more than the infants in day care, they were reprimanded more often, and the nonworking mothers were generally more irritable than the day-care workers. Clearly, full-time mothering may strain the mother-infant relationship (Vandell, 1979).

Families may discover other advantages of day care. For example, day care may allow a mother time to further her education; it may contribute to the improvement of marital relations; it may allow parents to pursue stimulating adult friendships, and it may prevent a mother from overinvesting in the mother role in a way that might lead her to discourage self-sufficiency in her child (Belsky & Steinberg, 1978; Hoffman, 1979). In sum, maternal employment and day care may foster harmony rather than discord between mothers and infants.

Day Care and Peer Relations

Children with substantial experience in day care are more peer-oriented. That is, they take a greater interest in their peers than do home-reared children. Ricciuti (1974) compared the reactions of day-care and home-reared infants to an unfamiliar peer. Infant-mother pairs were instructed to spend time in a room with another infant who was similar to the young subjects in age. Day-care infants ventured farther away from their mothers to explore and interact with the peer than did the home-reared children. Although day care appears to make infants more interested in their peers, this seems to come at the expense of interest in new adults: Day-care children actually show more reluctance to interact with a strange adult than do home-reared children (Belsky & Steinberg, 1978; Ragozin, 1980; Schachter, 1981). Thus one consequence of day care may be a swing in children's interest away from adults and toward the peer group.

Children learn both positive and negative behaviors from their peers at day care. For example, day-care children know more sophisticated ways of manipulating and playing with toys and objects (Rubenstein & Howes, 1979). Unfortunately, not all that children learn at day care would be regarded as desirable by most adults. Children in nursery school with day-care backgrounds are more aggressive toward their peers and adults, are more impulsive, have higher activity levels, are more egocentric and self-assertive, are less

cooperative, and are less impressed by punishment than home-reared children (Belsky & Steinberg, 1978).

PARENTS' ATTACHMENTS TO THEIR OFFSPRING

We have seen that responsiveness, sensitivity, and affection are good for the infant, but not all parents possess these qualities. What determines whether a parent will be a good caregiver? Here we examine several influences on parents' attachments to their offspring. We shall see that "mother love" does not come automatically or inevitably. On the contrary, it develops gradually and depends on many factors. Interestingly, the personalities of the mother and father, as measured by standard personality tests, do not predict their degree of affection for their infant. Instead, the infant is the main determinant of parental attachment—the appearance, health, and social responsiveness of the infant are crucial. Most parents develop strong ties to their infant, but occasionally there are disappointments, and these can tax the parent-infant relationship.

The Infant's Contribution to Parental Affection

Perhaps the single most powerful influence on the development of parental attachment is an infant's ability to emit the social responses that enchant the eager parents. The more infants smile, look, vocalize, and respond, the more affection and interest they get from their caregivers. Infants can be trained to respond socially, too, with the result that their caregivers become more affectionate. Rosenfield (1980) discovered that providing an experimental group of premature infants, who are typically less socially responsive than full-term infants, with extra stimulation (a program of stretching, rocking, and stroking) made the infants more alert, wakeful (eyes open), and responsive. The improved state of the infants in turn caused their parents to visit them more often in the intensive care nursery. Even parents who give birth to normal, full-term babies, however, sometimes have difficulty developing feelings of attachment for the newborn. For example, some mothers express immediate delight with their newborns, but many experience some initial feelings of distance and strangeness with their babies. These feelings may lead to depression and anxiety that continue, or even intensify, after the mother and infant leave the hospital. A mother may report that it was easier to enjoy the baby in the hospital, where most of the caregiving was accomplished by others. Luckily, most of these mothers eventually develop strong, affectionate feelings for their infants—What causes them to change? In a longitudinal study of mothers and their first-born infants, Robson and Moss (1970) found that mothers' affection toward their babies often emerged rather suddenly once the infants began emitting specific social signals, and especially when they began smiling and making eye-to-eye contact.

Infants who are born fussy, irritable, and impassive may retard maternal responsiveness (Crockenberg, 1981; Milliones, 1978). Furthermore, mothers who feel that their mothering is not having the desired impact on their infants may lose some interest in their babies. Donovan (1981) suggests that when an infant does not respond in the intended way to a mother's overtures (e.g., the baby does not stop crying when the mother tries to soothe him or her), the mother comes to feel helpless, and her confidence in her caregiving and her interest in her baby are undermined. Clearly, a strong mother-infant bond is unlikely to develop if the infant's behaviors do not facilitate reciprocity in the caregiver-child dyad.

Does an infant's appearance influence the degree of parental affection expressed? Parke and Sawin (1975) found that it did: Compared to mothers of babies rated as unattractive, mothers of attractive infants made more eye contact with their infants, maintained closer body contact with them, and kissed them more often; fathers of attractive infants more often stimulated their infants by touching, moving, and kissing them.

Ethologists propose that the young of many species share certain physical features that act to stimulate maternal affection and interest in caregiving. These features, collectively referred to as "babyishness," include a head that is large in proportion to the body; a protruding forehead that is large in relation to the rest of the face; large eyes below the midline of the head; and round, protruding cheeks (Lorenz, 1943). It is because these qualities presumably make the young look "cute" and "irresistible" that manufacturers of dolls and stuffed animals design their products to conform to these standards. Do people really prefer animals and people who look babyish? Fullard and Reiling (1976) showed second-grade through adult subjects slides of faces. Each slide depicted a babyish face paired with an adult face. Subjects had to tell which face they preferred in each slide. Up to puberty, subjects of both sexes preferred adult faces, but thereafter there was a marked switch—especially for females—to a preference for babyish faces. At this point it is debatable whether the shift to an interest in infants is due to hormonal changes at puberty (as ethologists maintain) or to learning that a preference for babyishness is expected.

Premature Infants as a High-Risk Group for Breakdowns in Parental Affection

Some infants are born lacking in the qualities that facilitate maternal bonding. As a group, for example, premature infants possess qualities of appearance and behavior that place them at risk for breakdowns in parent-infant attachment. Premature infants are scrawny; their skin is wrinkled and transparent, often making their veins visible; their bodies may be marked by bruises or other marks occurring as a result of various hospital tests and procedures; their heads are disproportionately large; feeding them is often difficult; their cries tend to be high-pitched and irritating; and they are late to smile.

Adults react less positively toward premature infants than full-term infants. In a revealing experiment, Frodi, Lamb, Leavitt, Donovan, Neff, and Sherry (1978) asked adults to view videotapes depicting an infant who was first quiet, then crying, and finally quiet again. Half of the adults viewed a normal (full-term) infant, while the remaining subjects viewed a premature infant. Sound tracks were dubbed so that half of the infants in each group emitted the cry of a normal infant, while the others emitted the cry of a premature baby. The cry of the premature infant, especially when paired with the face of a premature infant, elicited greater autonomic arousal (exhibited by increased blood pressure and perspiring hands) and was perceived as more aversive than the cry of the normal infant.

The prevention of early mother-infant interaction due to the incubation of the premature infant for several weeks has also been found to carry risks for mother-infant bonding. In some hospitals, mothers are not allowed to participate in feeding, diaper changing, affectionate touching, or other physical contact with babies in incubators: They can look but not touch. Such lengthy periods of frustrated parenting can cause the mother to lose self-esteem and confidence in her ability to care for her infant, especially if the infant is her first, and can engender feelings of guilt, failure, and alienation (Seashore, Leifer, Barnett, & Leiderman, 1973). Even after their infants have been at home for several weeks, mothers of infants who have been incubated in the hospital sometimes display less affectionate touching, caressing, smiling, and holding of their infants than do mothers of full-term infants (Karger, 1979; Leifer, Leiderman, Barnett, & Williams, 1972).

Having a premature infant places an added burden on the household and is associated with increased probabilities of several unfortunate outcomes, including child abuse, relinquishing custody of the child, and even divorce (Parke & Collmer, 1975). Sometimes, signs of the strain that a premature infant places on the family are visible before the infant even leaves the hospital. Rosenfield (1980) found that the parents of some premature infants developed atypical patterns of visiting their infants in the intensive care nursery. For example, the mother visited but the father never did, or the mother did not visit but the father would come to the hospital. These atypical patterns of visitation were associated with an increased chance that the parents would develop serious marital problems centering on the infant and his or her difficulties. Of course, not all parents react negatively to disappointing qualities in their infants (Donovan & Leavitt, 1978; Frodi & Lamb, 1978), but the potential for trouble is high enough to have prompted several investigators to design intervention programs to educate and assist parents of infants at risk (e.g., Field, Widmayer, Stringer, & Ignatoff, 1980).

Parents' Upbringing as a Factor in Their Affection for Their Infant

The way a parent reacts to offspring is in part determined by the way the parent was treated by his or her own parents as a child. Even the likelihood of having an illegitimate child is affected by one's own childhood circumstances. In a study of Scottish women having their first baby, it was found that women who themselves had been illegitimate or whose parents had been divorced or separated were twice as likely as other women to have an illegitimate child or to "have to get married" (Rutter, 1979). Also, women who were reared in broken homes were more apt to prop up their babies so they could feed themselves and interacted less with their infants than women not coming from disadvantaged backgrounds (Frommer & O'Shea, 1973; Wolkind, Hall, & Pawlby, 1977).

Maternal Fear of Separation

A caregiver's protection and affection are essential for successful adaptation in the young. But competent mothers must balance their wish to stay close to their infants with encouragement of the infants' independence and self-sufficiency. Occasionally mothers do not want, or are not able, to help their children explore their environments or establish independence outside the home. In such cases, we might expect the children to experience excessive separation anxiety and fear of the novel.

Martin (1975) suggests that some mothers develop intense fears of separation from their infants, which cause the children to display *school phobia* when beginning nursery or grade school. School phobia is a dread of attending school that is often accompanied by stomach upset, inability to eat, and psychosomatic symptoms. Although school phobia is typically conceptualized as the child's problem, Martin points out that school phobias may actually originate in the mother's fear of separating herself from her child. The mother's anxiety may be communicated to and internalized by the child. Indeed, mothers of school phobics are often more alarmed than their children when therapists try to implement a program of therapy that involves gradual separations (Eisenberg, 1958; Waldfogel, 1957).

The causes of a mother's fear of separation from her child are not known. Perhaps the children of some mothers who develop separation fears suffered severe early illness that led their mothers to become oversolicitous, or perhaps mothers who have separation anxieties substitute close relationships with their children for unsatisfactory marital relationships. At any rate, some mother-child pairs develop mutual patterns of interaction with the result that separation is experienced as aversive, and reunion as reinforcing, to both members. This kind of theorizing suggests that we must study not only the roots of ma-ternal affection but also determinants of mothers' willingness to "let go" of their infants at the appropriate times.

FATHER-INFANT INTERACTION

Although fathers typically participate in routine caregiving far less than mothers, they tend to offer unique varieties of stimulation to their infants. Thus fathers may teach their infants different things than mothers do. Here we will examine the nature and significance of the father-infant relationship.

Fathers' Participation in Caregiving

Despite the recent rhetoric and ideology in favor of egalitarian sex roles, fathers continue to spend far less time than mothers in routine caregiving activities, such as feeding, bathing, checking or changing diapers, and wiping the baby's face. In fact, fathers spend less time overall interacting with their infants as compared to mothers (Parke, 1978). In part, lower levels of father interaction are due to fathers not being home as much as mothers, but even when fathers are home, they interact less with their infants than mothers; in fact, even when both parents are in the same room with their offspring, fathers spend less time interacting with their babies than mothers. As infants get older, however, differences in the amount of time fathers and mothers spend with their infants diminish (Clarke-Stewart, 1978).

Although fathers interact less with their infants than mothers do, fathers are not less skilled or less sensitive when they do participate in caregiving. Parke and Sawin (1975) observed infants with their mothers and fathers during feeding and found that fathers were just as successful as mothers in getting their infants to finish a bottle and were just as skilled at holding babies comfortably and reading their signals. For example, when the infants signaled distress by spitting up, coughing, or sneezing, fathers were just as likely as mothers to cease feeding and to try to determine the reason for the distress. In sum, fathers are just as contingently responsive to infants as mothers are, and are not rated by observers as less stimulating, less affectionate, or less effective in their caregiving than mothers (Clarke-Stewart, 1973).

Though fathers as a group interact less than mothers with their infants, there are vast individual differences among fathers in involvement with their babies. Some fathers hardly ever see their infants, whereas others are highly involved in caregiving and other forms of interaction. Research reveals that high father involvement is beneficial to the infant's social and cognitive development. For example, compared to infants of uninvolved fathers, infants of involved fathers develop greeting behavior earlier (Pederson & Robson, 1969), are less distressed by separations (Spelke et al., 1973), and score higher on tests of intelligence (Clarke-Stewart, 1978).

Some fathers do assume the primary caregiving role with their infants, although this is still rare. Perhaps parents have decided on a division of labor that assigns the father this role, or perhaps the father has received custody of his infant following divorce or the death of his wife. Fathers who accept this role are not deficient caregivers (Field, 1978; Lamb, Frodi, Hwang, Frodi, & Steinberg, 1982). In fact, Lamb (1979) speculates that fathers may typically have better success functioning as a single parent than mothers, primarily because single fathers are a highly selected and self-motivated group.

Stylistic Differences in Mother-Infant and Father-Infant Interaction

Though fathers interact less with their infants than mothers, fathers rival mothers in the degree to which they engage their infants in play. Fathers spend a much higher percentage of their time with their infants in play than mothers do (Clarke-Stewart, 1978; Parke, 1978).

Furthermore, mothers and fathers differ in the *styles* of play they adopt with their infants (Clarke-Stewart, 1978; Lamb, 1979; Parke, 1978). Fathers' play tends to be much more vigorous and physical than mothers' play. Fathers may pick their babies up, toss them a few inches in the air and then catch them, or they may get down on the floor with their infants, chase them, roll them over while tickling them, and so on. Rarely do fathers use toys to get their infants' attention. The social-physical games fathers play with their infants tend to involve unpredictable and idiosyncratic sequences. Mothers' play is often more intellectually oriented, often involving verbalization (e.g., nursery rhymes and repetitive bursts of talking) and conventional games (e.g., pat-a-cake and peek-a-boo). Mothers are more likely to stimulate their infants with toys.

Whom does the infant enjoy playing with more, mother or father? Judging from the available research data, the answer would be the father. We have seen that infants prefer to affiliate with their fathers under relaxed circumstances (Lamb, 1976a, 1976b). Furthermore, when 18-month-olds are given a choice of play partners, they more often choose their fathers over their mothers (Clarke-Stewart, 1978).

There is an interesting sex effect in parent-infant interaction: Parents attend to, stimulate, and interact with infants of their own sex more than infants of the opposite sex (Parke, 1978). This is especially true for fathers. Fathers make more trips to visit their newborns in the hospital if they are males; they engage their sons in more play, and especially physical play, than they do their daughters; and they hug, kiss, and imitate their infant sons more than their infant daughters (Belsky, 1979; Field, 1978; Lamb, 1979; Weinraub & Frankel, 1977).

The extra stimulation that boys get from their fathers may have important consequences for male development. First, boys may reciprocate their fathers' interest and affection. Indeed, by their second birthday, boys typically show a preference for interaction with their fathers over their mothers (Belsky, 1979; Lamb, 1979). Fathers who imitate and behave affectionately toward their sons may be increasing the chances that their sons will imitate them in return, for, as we shall see in later chapters, imitation is often a reciprocal affair between two people. Second, the special sorts of stimulation that fathers provide for their sons may teach them competencies that the boys are unlikely to learn from others. Parke (1978), for example, reported that infant boys who had lost their fathers through death or divorce showed less interest in manipulating novel objects than boys from intact families. In later chapters we will see that father absence is associated with a variety of other outcomes for male children, including reduced interest in traditionally masculine activities, poorer moral internalization, lowered intelligence, and a reversal in the usual male pattern of higher performance IQ than verbal IQ. The earlier in life a boy loses his father, the more severe these effects usually are.

Girls also benefit from interaction with their fathers, but father absence is typically associated with more negative consequences in male children than in female children. We might add that the adverse outcomes associated with father absence in male children may not always be due to the absence of the father per se. For example, mothers who are rearing children without the benefit of a supportive husband may encounter more difficulty consistently enforcing discipline with their male children than mothers in intact homes, and the inconsistency of the maternal discipline may be at least partially responsible for some of the unfortunate outcomes seen in boys from homes where the father is absent.

INFANTS' REACTIONS TO STRANGERS

Children do not live in the confines of the family all their lives; they must learn to establish new friendships and relationships beyond the home. Of special interest to researchers are the anxiety reactions experienced by some infants in the presence of strangers. What makes infants sometimes fear a stranger and how do infants gradually make friends with people who initially are strange and anxiety-arousing?

Age Changes in Infants' Reactions to Strangers

Infants' reactions to strangers follow a developmental timetable that parallels, in part, phases in the development of attachment. Remember that for the first 3 months, infants typically react no differently toward strangers than they do toward their primary caregivers: They look at, smile at, and vocalize to strangers just as much as to their caregivers; they are just as easily comforted by strangers as by their caregivers; and so on. By 3 months, infants usually prefer their caregivers, but they are still fairly friendly toward strangers. Once infants have become attached, however, which occurs at about 6 months of age, they are decidedly less appreciative of strangers. They direct fewer affiliative signals (looks, smiles, and vocalizations) toward strangers, they fail to protest the departures of strangers, and they do not allow strangers to comfort them in times of distress. Still, until this age, the most we can say is that infants' reactions to strangers have grown less positive; they are rarely characterized by overt withdrawal or fear.

When infants are about 7 or 8 months old, they begin *occasionally* to express overt signs of wariness, fear, and avoidance when confronted by a stranger. They may stare soberly, take on a disturbed facial expression, and glance away, and their hearts may pound faster. Sometimes their distress is severe: Their faces redden and express panic, and they cry loudly (Campos, Emde, Gaensbauer, & Henderson, 1975; Schaffer, Greenwood, & Parry, 1972; Sroufe, Waters, & Matas, 1974; Waters, Matas, & Sroufe, 1975). Such anxiety reactions increase in intensity and frequency as infants near their first birthday and, for some infants, these reactions remain fairly common throughout the second year (Bronson, 1978; Greenberg, Hillman, & Grice, 1973; Lewis & Brooks-Gunn, 1981; Morgan & Ricciuti, 1969).

The nature of the fear-of-stranger response depends on the infant's age. When 1-year-olds have an attack of stranger anxiety, they engage in intense attachment responses that inhibit exploration and affiliation with the stranger: The infants rush to their mothers, give up exploring the room, and direct few smiles, looks, and vocalizations toward the stranger. They may eventually venture away from their mothers to resume exploring the inanimate environment (e.g., toys in the room), but they tend still to ignore the stranger (Bretherton & Ainsworth, 1974). Two-year-olds rarely react to strangers with all-out distress, but signs of wariness—a sober expression or gaze aversion—are still common. At this age, wariness is still accompanied by heightened attachment and decreased exploration and affiliation, but the activation of attachment is more temporary, and the infants usually warm up to the stranger for brief periods of distal affiliation. By the time children are 3, wariness of a stranger is only fleetingly associated with attachment responses. Instead, along with being a bit wary of the stranger, toddlers also show signs of interest and affiliation, coyly smiling, looking, and perhaps saying a word or two to the stranger, but periodically sobering and looking away when wanting to "cool things" (Greenberg & Marvin, 1982). This behavior is actually rather adultlike: Adults also combine their smiles and looks with gaze aversion when trying to regulate the pace of interaction with a stranger (Kaltenbach, Weinraub, & Fullard, 1980).

Explanations of Stranger Anxiety

The Ethological/Biological View Ethologists claim that infants are biologically wired to respond to strangers with fear. They suggest that crying in response to strangers attracts the mother and therefore has facilitated survival of the species. Some observations support this notion. The fact that infants are most afraid of figures who are large and powerful (Lewis & Brooks-Gunn, 1981; Weinraub & Putney, 1978)—qualities that might once have been possessed by predators —fits with the conception of stranger anxiety as an instinct with survival value. Whether or not stranger anxiety evolved because it has survival value, there is evidence that genetics do contribute to stranger anxiety. Plomin and Rowe (1979) found that identical twins are more alike in their reactions to strangers than are fraternal twins. Thus we must conclude that biological factors do play a role in fear of strangers.

Cognitive-Developmental Factors Typically, infants spend several seconds gravely scrutinizing a stranger before showing a fear response. During this prefear interval, the infant's heart rate may temporarily slow down (Campos et al., 1975). Heart rate deceleration is usually taken as a sign that an infant is making an "orienting response" or is cognitively evaluating a stimulus (Graham & Clifton, 1966). After a brief period of intense evaluation, the infant's heart rate may suddenly accelerate, and, if it remains accelerated, a fear reaction may ensue.

It is difficult to escape the conclusion that the fear reaction is the product of some sort of cognitive processing on the part of the infant. Some writers, notably Hebb (1946), argue that fear is produced when a new event is perceived as incongruous or discrepant with some internal referent or schema. The infant may perceive, for example, that a stranger resembles his or her mother in some ways (perhaps she has the same color hair), but is dissimilar in other respects (the stranger may have a distinctly different face). The failure to fit a new stimulus to a stored image of the familiar may be disturbing (see also Schaffer et al., 1972). Kagan (1976) proposes that fear occurs when the infant experiences perceptual incongruity, becomes aroused, feels compelled to make a response, but cannot find a satisfactory mental response to make to the situation. If an odd-acting stranger looms toward an infant, the infant may be struggling to match the stranger's face to a stored schema and at the same time be trying to come up with a response that will help slow the ongoing interaction to a more comfortable pace. In trying to do too much too quickly, the infant's information-processing capacities become overloaded, and all-out distress ensues. In line with Kagan's theory is the fact that intense fear reactions to strangers are most likely when strangers approach in an unnatural way (e.g., with a blank stare) and interact without allowing the infant to predict and pace the interaction (Greenberg et al., 1973; Morgan & Ricciuti, 1969; Ross & Goldman, 1977). On the other hand, Kagan suggests that when infants are confronted by a playful stranger slowly approaching from a distance, they may be only mildly aroused and may have the presence of mind to remember that mother is nearby and will come if needed or that unfamiliar people can sometimes be fun. In sum, Kagan argues, whether an infant's reaction to perceptual incongruity is one of fear or pleasure depends on whether the infant can mentally determine a satisfactory, reassuring solution to the discrepant event.

Some infants seem better able than others to pace their exposure to an approaching stranger, and these infants are more likely to keep their distress from getting out of hand (Sroufe, 1977; Waters, Matas, & Sroufe, 1975). When meeting a stranger, these infants may initially be aroused (as indexed by accelerated heart rate), but then the infants avert their gaze or briefly glance away from the stranger. At this point, their heart rates decelerate. The infants seem to be taking a breather while they recover from the "shock" of seeing a stranger. Importantly, these infants are usually able to reengage the stranger without fear. That is, their gaze aversion calms them down enough so that they can eventually engage the stranger in positive, distal-affiliative interactions. If they get overaroused again, they avert their gaze once more and wait until they are calm before they try interacting again. In this way the infants habituate themselves to the stranger. On the other hand, some infants proceed directly to intense distress reactions upon seeing a stranger. Usually these are infants who fail to show any signs of wariness (e.g., sobering, gaze aversion) when they see a stranger. Their heart rates accelerate, but instead of alleviating the pressure by momentarily looking away, the infants just continue staring. The result is that the infants are overwhelmed, and they panic. We do not know the roots of these different styles of regulating arousal to strangers, but the ability to pace exposure may contribute to the infant's ability to befriend new people.

Social Learning Experiences Learning theorists suggest that infants' reactions to strangers represent generalizations from the infants' prior experiences with people similar to the stranger. For example, infants who have had negative interactions with male adults should be afraid of new men. Similarly, if the arrival of a particular babysitter reliably signals a distressing separation from mother, then infants should cry when individuals resembling the babysitter appear.

Learned aversions do seem to account for some instances of stranger anxiety. Bronson (1978) discovered that infants who reacted negatively to a stranger were ones who had had prior unpleasant experiences with another stranger.

Do infants generalize the experiences they have with their mothers to strangers? One might think that infants who enjoy a secure attachment with a sensitive and responsive caregiver might bring expectations of positive, enjoyable interaction to encounters with strangers and therefore exhibit little fear. Clarke-Stewart has found that infants who have the most positive experiences with their mothers do indeed react the most positively toward strangers (Clarke-Stewart, Umeh, Snow, & Pederson, 1980; Clarke-Stewart, VanderStoep, & Killian, 1979).

How a Stranger Becomes a Friend

Even infants who react initially with fear to a stranger can eventually establish a close, trusting, and affectionate relationship with the person, although the process may take several hours, or even days or weeks. How do strangers become friends?

Infants often require the presence of a reassuring secure base—their mother or father, for example—to explore comfortably and eventually befriend a stranger. Two-year-olds can make friends with a stranger rather quickly. Greenberg and Marvin (1982) found that when 2-year-olds were allowed to affiliate and play with a stranger for several minutes in their mothers' presence, the infants continued to interact comfortably with the stranger even after their mothers left the room. It usually takes 1-year-olds longer to learn to enjoy and derive a sense of security from unfamiliar people (Feldman & Ingham, 1975; Fleener, 1973).

Even young infants can overcome their fears of novel people and things rather quickly, however, if they are given a *sense of control* over the frightening event. Gunnar-Vongnechten (1978) exposed 1-year-old infants to a toy that tends to scare young infants—a mechanical monkey that clashes cymbals together loudly. One group of infants was given control over the toy: The monkey clashed its cymbals only when the infants hit a panel. For a second group, the toy was activated just as often as in the first group, but the infants had no control over activation. Infants who had control over the toy moved closer to it, touched it, and laughed and smiled at it more. Noncontrolling infants fussed and cried more, stayed closer to their mothers, and more often froze.

Why does giving the infant control reduce fear? One possibility is that having control allows the infant to predict the occurrence of the aversive event, and predictability may be the critical factor in fear reduction. A subsequent study by Gunnar (1980), however, indicates that predictability alone does not reduce fear. In this study, infants in one condition had no control over activation of the monkey, and yet they could predict when the monkey was going to clash the cymbals because the cymbal clashing was always preceded by an auditory warning stimulus—a tone. Fear was not reduced in this condition. Infants must actually be able to control the occurrence of the stimulus in order for their fear to be reduced. Gunnar suggests that overcoming the fear of a stimulus involves realizing not only that one can activate the stimulus but also that one can avoid the stimulus altogether by inhibiting the response that activates it.

Levitt (1980) showed how 10-month-old infants could develop positive feelings toward a strange person if given control over the stranger's actions. In an initial phase of Levitt's experiment, a female stranger engaged infants in a variation of the game peek-a-boo. For some infants, the stranger appeared from behind a curtain to smile and exclaim, "Hi,_____ (baby's name)!" whenever the infant touched a plastic cylinder. For others, appearance of the stranger was independent of the infants' actions. Later, in a session with both mother and stranger present, infants who had had control over the appearance of the stranger displayed less fear when the stranger approached. They moved closer to the stranger, imitated the stranger more, and played more happily than the noncontrolling infants. Children do not fear, and may learn to enjoy, what they can control.

SUMMARY

Most striking of the infant's social relationships are the intense emotional attachments infants form to specific others, and particularly to their primary caregivers. Attachments develop gradually in a series of three phases.

For roughly their first 3 months, infants tend to respond the same way to all people. At around 3 months, they begin to direct their social signals (looks, smiles, vocalizations) to their caregivers more than to others, but they are still fairly friendly toward strangers. Infants begin to show an intense preference for their caregivers at about 6 months that exposes a strong underlying emotional tie. Different infants develop different styles of expressing their attachment bond; therefore, we conceptualize attachment as a behavior system rather than a unidimensional trait having the same behavioral referents for all infants.

Infancy and the attachment relationship furnish a context for infants to learn basic lessons about themselves and other people (e.g., "Mother comes if summoned"; "I am effective at influencing others"; and "I can count on emotional support if I run into trouble"). These lessons lend continuity to the way children adapt to their social environments as they move from infancy into the toddler years.

The theories of attachment receive varying degrees of support. The Freudian hypothesis that infants become attached to their mothers because mothers provide infants with oral sexual gratification has little direct evidence to support it. Freud erred when he claimed that the mother is the infant's exclusive attachment object, and he overestimated the contribution of the mother's association with feeding as a factor in attachment formation.

Cognitive-developmental theorists claim that the infant's social behavior reflects underlying cognitive processing. For example, smiling is thought to represent effortful assimilation-to-schema, or successful matching of an event to a stored mental representation of similar events based on previous experience. The cognitive-developmentalists have taught us that infants constantly strive to impose meaning on the events they experience (e.g., "That face looks a little familiar; I wonder if I can recognize it"; or "Mom has left,

but I know she's close and will come if I call, so I won't get upset"). These interpretations of everyday events guide the infants' choice of response.

Ethologists emphasize that reciprocal attachment bonds between mothers and infants have helped the species survive and therefore that certain crucial aspects of the bonding process are probably under the control of inherited instincts. For example, infants are believed to be genetically wired to emit smiling, crying, sucking, looking, and vocalizing responses reflexively in response to certain patterns of social stimulation. Many of the infant's early social responses do follow a built-in timetable of responsiveness to external eliciting stimuli, but it is clear that cognitive and social learning factors gradually assume ascendance over innate reflexes in regulating the infant's social behavior.

Learning theorists suggest that mothers acquire conditioned (secondary) reward value because they provide unconditioned positive reinforcers (e.g., food, contact comfort, entertaining distance receptor stimulation, and relief from distress). There is little evidence that mothers acquire value because they provide food, but their provision of distance receptor stimulation and relief from distress may be important to attachment formation. However, the usefulness of simple conditioning principles to explain social responding is increasingly being called into question. One issue under debate is whether contingent responsiveness serves automatically to strengthen the specific responses it follows or whether contingent responsiveness teaches infants more general lessons about their effects on the environment and about the accessibility of their caregivers. There is some evidence to suggest, for example, that mothers who respond quickly to their infants' cries have infants who decrease rather than increase their frequency of crying. Presumably, infants whose mothers respond quickly come to believe that mother is available if needed, and this gives them a sense of security that reduces their need to cry.

In fact, most infants probably form attachments through a variety of complementary avenues. Most mothers not only feed their infants but also provide them with exciting distance receptor stimulation, relief from distress, contact comfort, and a sense of control. All these factors may contribute to attachment, although with varying degrees of efficiency. For example, the caregiver's association with distance receptor stimulation may typically make a stronger contribution to attachment than the caregiver's provision of food. Infants, however, seem so determined to become attached that when one or more of the usual avenues to attachment are unavailable, the infant exploits other routes to attachment (e.g., blind infants develop attachments through auditory and tactile contact with the caregiver). Perhaps the caregiving qualities that facilitate attachment should be conceptualized as alternative routes to the same end.

Ainsworth proposes a distinction between secure and insecure attachments. Securely attached infants are those who trust their caregivers to be available in times of need. Presumably through interaction with an affectionate, sensitive, and responsive caregiver, these infants have learned that mother (and/or father) is available to give aid and comfort if required. Ainsworth has proposed behavioral criteria to differentiate securely and insecurely attached children. Infants and toddlers identified as securely attached make an easier adjustment to the peer group and display more competence in problem-solving situations beyond the home. Perhaps the knowledge that a caregiver is accessible if required gives these children the courage and confidence to test new activities and relationships.

With maternal employment on the rise, more and more infants are being placed in day care. High-quality day care does not harm the infant's tie to his or her mother or other important aspects of the infant's social and emotional development, and it may even benefit the child's development, especially if the child's mother would be dissatisfied not working. Low-quality day care has sometimes been found to be associated with an increased risk of the child developing an insecure attachment with the caregiver.

Because parental sensitivity and responsiveness benefit the child's attachment, researchers are studying the factors that lead parents to develop affectionate feelings for their offspring. Infants themselves seem to play a major role. Infants who smile and make eye contact at the expected times, who are attractive, and who are responsive to their caregivers' attempts to soothe and comfort them tend to elicit affection from their parents.

Father-infant interaction has been the focus of much recent research. Infants form attachments with their fathers at about the same time that they are forming them with their mothers, but the attachments differ. In relaxed circumstances, infants often prefer to affiliate with their fathers rather than with their mothers. This may be because fathers spend a high proportion of time with their infants in play and have an engaging style of attracting and maintaining their infants' attention. Fathers' play is more physical and unpredictable than mothers' play. Furthermore, fathers may teach their infants things that mothers do not. Infants whose fathers are not active caregivers, for example, are less competent at manipulating objects than children with involved fathers.

Because children must learn to establish relationships beyond the home, their reactions to strangers are of interest. As infants become attached to their caregivers, their responses toward strange adults become less positive, more wary, and tentative. Beginning around 8 or 9 months of age, infants in fact occasionally react with fear and withdrawal when confronted by a stranger. Biological, cognitive, social learning, and situational factors all contribute to the anxiety experienced by infants in the presence of a stranger. Even infants who are initially frightened by a stranger can eventually grow fond of the stranger if the person is careful to make his or her behavior contingent on the infant's actions, thereby giving the infant a sense of control over the interaction.

3 Social Learning: Child-Rearing Practices and Their Effects

This chapter and the next are devoted to discussions of the two major ways children learn from their social environment, or the people around them. In this chapter we will concentrate on how children learn from the discipline and instruction they directly experience at the hands of their parents, teachers, and other socializing agents. The following chapter deals with vicarious social learning, or how children learn by observing the actions of other people. These two varieties of social learning are powerful influences on the child's social behavior and development.

The process of direct instruction and discipline begins in infancy. Almost from the very moment they bring their infant home from the hospital, parents are faced with a number of difficult questions about how to control, teach, and guide their child's behav-

ior and development. At first, parents use discipline mainly to ensure their child's safety. Many situations are exceedingly hazardous, and infants and toddlers must be taught not to touch hot stoves, put dirty objects in their mouths, and cross busy streets. Young children cannot anticipate the consequences of their actions and cannot organize and plan their daily activities. Parents must give structure to their child's environment, establish routines, and serve as the child's anticipation center until the child can achieve this alone (Maccoby, 1980).

Gradually, parents become explicitly concerned with transferring the locus of control from themselves to the child. They search for disciplinary strategies that will help the child display self-control, show empathy and altruism, inhibit aggression, and behave in other desirable ways—even when not under the watchful eyes of adults. In other words, parents strive to instill some degree of "internalization" in their offspring.

The choices of child-rearing practices are many, but sound answers about their relative effectiveness are few. Parents differ widely in the tactics they use to control their children's behavior. Some subscribe to a philosophy of permissiveness, swearing never to interfere with their offspring's activities unless absolutely necessary. Others have long lists of house rules that they ardently enforce. The use of physical punishment is abhorred by some caregivers, while others find forceful discipline a legitimate and expedient way to get results. And some maintain an even tempo in their discipline by consistently reacting to a given misdemeanor with the same sanction, while other parents ignore a deviant act on one occasion, but explode with anger and spank the child for the same act at another time. How do these various styles of discipline affect the developing child?

This chapter surveys the various techniques of socialization and the mechanisms underlying their effects. Our aim is to abstract a set of principles of social learning that will provide a foundation for understanding the socialization process.

THEORIES ABOUT CHILD-REARING PRACTICES

Social Learning Theory

According to social learning theory (e.g., Bandura, 1977), discipline is important because it provides children with information regarding the consequences that their behavior is likely to incur under various circumstances. Essentially, discipline helps children acquire response-outcome contingency rules that they can use to guide their behavior. Disciplinary action is not the only method to use in teaching children standards of appropriate conduct. Observing the consequences similar others receive for their actions (e.g., seeing a classmate get criticized for misbehavior) and simply being told what is likely to happen if they do certain things (e.g., "If you do that, you'll go to your room!") are other important influences on children's response-outcome rules. But the direct rewards and punishments children receive are important sources of social learning.

Disciplinary experiences help motivate and sustain processes of self-regulation in children. Understandably, once children learn that a particular behavior reliably brings reward in a situation or that a certain behavior consistently brings punishment in a situation, they are motivated to regulate their behavior so that it brings the desired outcome. For example, children who learn that aggression toward a playmate is punishable are likely to resist behaving aggressively toward their peers, especially if they perceive that the contingency of punishment is operating in the situations in which they are tempted to aggress. Children in this situation may try to talk themselves out of deviating and they may deliberately suppress the motor components of behaving aggressively. Also, children who know that they will be rewarded by their parents for receiving an "A" in spelling on their report card may arrange study sessions for themselves, perhaps even depriving themselves of desirable activities, such as watching television, until they master their spelling words. Once children begin the process of self-regulation and find that successful self-regulation brings them personal and social rewards, they are motivated to continue practicing self-regulation in the future. They set goals of desirable conduct for themselves, monitor their behavior more closely, chastise themselves when they fall short of their standards, and praise themselves when they match or exceed their standards for appropriate conduct. Child-rearing practices are important because they tell children what behaviors are essential to self-regulate and they provide the necessary support system to sustain children's efforts at self-regulation.

Much self-regulation, especially in young children, is motivated by immediate external incentives, such as fears of parental punishment or expectations of material reward. But with age and experience, self-regulation becomes less dependent on immediate external incentives and rests more upon internal, self-generated, symbolic incentives, such as self-critical and self-praising comments. In Chapter 6, we discuss the processes involved in self-control in more detail. The point to be made here is that discipline informs children of what society deems desirable and undesirable behavior and motivates children to initiate self-regulation to conform to these standards.

According to social learning theory, several factors should enhance the effectiveness of child-rearing practices. First, discipline should be designed in such a way that it helps children grasp and appreciate the link between behavior and its consequences. Second, parents should accompany their discipline with verbal reasoning that clarifies to children exactly what aspects of their behavior are desirable or undesirable and why. Third, discipline should be applied consistently. This means that parents should consistently respond negatively to an unwanted behavior and consistently reward a desired action. Erratic discipline confuses and frustrates children. Fourth, unnecessarily harsh discipline is to be avoided. It may be so upsetting that it distracts children from learning and remembering the association between a deviant act and its consequences, and it may cause children to learn and imitate aggressive means of interpersonal control. Fifth, in order to give children practice in self-regulation, age-appropriate demands for mature behavior should be made of children. Sixth, these demands should be firmly enforced, and the children should be given suggestions for effective self-regulation. Seventh, when children successfully execute self-regulation, they should be praised.

In social learning theory, child-rearing practices are important not only because they aid in the establishment of self-regulation but also because they help children develop new skills and competencies. Bandura (1981) points out that children are constantly appraising their abilities to perform various behaviors. Furthermore, children's perceptions of their competencies (or their "perceptions of self-efficacy," to use Bandura's term) influence the activities children undertake and avoid. Regardless of their true capabilities, if children do not believe that they are capable of solving algebra problems, of petting a dog without experiencing intense fear, or of making a friend at school, they are unlikely to attempt these behaviors. Children's perceptions of their competency at an activity are influenced by many factors, but one important factor is the degree to which children have observed themselves succeed at the activity in the past. In other words, authentic mastery experiences contribute greatly to self-efficacy perceptions. Thus parents should arrange for children to master challenging or threatening experiences by encouraging participation and facilitating gradual success experiences.

Attribution Theory: A Provocative New Perspective

Much of our understanding of the effects of child-rearing practices is based on research carried out by social learning theorists. Over the last few years, however, psychologists working within the framework of *causal attribution theory* have presented an alternative conceptualization of the effects of discipline on the child's development (e.g., Lepper, 1981). Attribution theorists believe that children are constantly striving to perceive the causes of their own and other people's behaviors. These theorists suggest that when children are persuaded by parental discipline to comply with an adult request, the children ask themselves, "Why did I go along with that?" Furthermore, the attribution theorists propose that the particular explanation or causal attribution children generate to explain their compliance influences whether or not they internalize the desired behavior, or their willingness to perform the behavior at another time without adult surveillance. We shall elaborate on this interesting viewpoint and outline its implications for child-rearing practices.

To understand the attribution perspective, first consider how an act of good behavior by a child (e.g., an act of kindness, honesty, generosity, or delay of gratification) can be motivated by any one of many possible causes. Perhaps the child has performed the behavior only because his or her mother has threatened the child with punishment for not doing it or has promised a reward, such as an ice cream cone, for doing it—rather externally based motivations for the good behavior. Or maybe the child perceives the act to be an inherently nice thing to do and simply *wants* to do it—an intrinsic source of motivation. Naturally one goal of socialization is to instill in children intrinsic motives for being good. We want them to understand why some actions are inherently desirable and others intrinsically bad; for example, helping someone else is good because it makes the other person happy; aggression is bad because it causes suffering to another person. We also want children to believe that they are by nature the kinds of people who desire to perform good behavior and refrain from performing bad behavior.

Lepper (1981) argues that it is unlikely that children will learn to think of themselves as intrinsically motivated to perform good behaviors (and avoid bad ones) if their parents rely on "external" disciplinary tactics—ones that draw children's attention to the fact that their behavior is under external control, such as threats of punishment or bribes of material reward. He believes that when people can explain their behavior in terms of some external cause, they tend to ignore or discount intrinsic sources of motivation. In fact, perceiving that they have been externally pressured into certain behaviors is thought to prevent people from believing that intrinsic factors could have contributed, too. The argument is that children will conclude that they are in-

trinsically motivated to be good (e.g., "I am the kind of person who likes to share my toys") only if they have seen themselves performing the good behavior, but have not had their arms twisted into doing so (see also Bem, 1972).

This theory raises some interesting implications for child-rearing practice. It suggests that socializing agents should take pains to avoid using "heavy" disciplinary techniques that rely on forceful external incentives; children who comply under these pressures cannot infer they have been good because they really wanted to. Furthermore, children who have been extensively subjected to external control tactics may become dependent on them: They may perform desired behaviors as long as the threats, bribes, and external surveillance are operating, but when faced with a temptation situation and little chance of getting caught for deviating, they may very well succumb to the temptation. In contrast, when children who attribute their compliance to internal factors are confronted with the temptation to break the rule in the absence of adult supervision, they should not be able to do so without violating their own self-image of being a "good person." The prospect of guilt or dashed self-esteem for misbehaving should motivate them to conform.

It is instructive to highlight some points of difference between the attribution and the social learning perspectives. First, attribution theorists stress the *negative* role that external controls and incentives, such as external punishments and rewards, play in the socialization process. In fact, some attribution researchers (e.g., Lepper, 1981) suggest that parents should do whatever they can to eliminate external incentives and substitute more subtle ways of inducing compliance in children. Lepper, for example, suggests that a major goal of research should be the discovery of new socialization techniques that allow adults to manipulate children into displaying desired behaviors without the children realizing that they are being externally pressured (Lepper, 1981; Lepper & Gilovich, 1982). In contrast, social learning theorists see a positive, constructive role for external incentives in the establishment and maintenance of self-regulation. In social learning theory, contingent external outcomes serve to inform children about the sorts of behavior that are important to self-regulate. For example, when children see that a certain form of behavior reliably produces an aversive outcome (e.g., social disapproval, punishment, or failure), they are motivated to initiate the self-controlling responses that will help them avoid the negative outcome. Social learning theorists are doubtful, too, that it is always possible to motivate children to engage in self-control without sometimes using forceful external incentives.

A related point is that social learning theorists do not make the same distinction between perceptions of internal causation and perceptions of external causation that attribution theorists do. Attributionists often express the opinion that perceived internal motivation and perceived external motivation for a behavior are mutually exclusive. In contrast, social learning theorists stress that self-regulation is often in the service of an external end. This implies that children can fuse internal and external attributions into a single self-statement that motivates self-regulation (e.g., "I am a good boy because I made my bed every morning this week, which means I can have my allowance;" or, "I am a good girl—I managed to go a whole week without disrupting the class so the teacher wouldn't send me to the principal's office"). In the social learning analysis, external and internal attributions can be compatible, and even mutually reinforcing, making it difficult to say that one sort of attribution is more important than the other in sparking and maintaining self-control. It is partly for this reason that social learning theorists prefer to speak of "self-regulation" rather than "internalization."

In this chapter, we shall see some evidence supporting the social learning view as well as some evidence supporting the attribution theory. Our belief is that a better understanding of the socialization process can be reached by combining some of the principles of social learning theory with some of the principles of attribution theory, which we attempt to do toward the end of the chapter.

Other Theories of Discipline

Most of the other theories of social development that we reviewed in Chapter 1 have little to say about child-rearing practices and their effects. Trait theorists, cognitive-developmental theorists, and ethologists are largely unconcerned with the effects of various techniques of discipline.

Freud was against the use of punishment as a means of discipline. He believed that punishing children for yielding to their natural impulses could produce serious conflicts and generate neurotic anxiety, with debilitating effects. His argument was that children develop internalized controls not through disciplinary experiences but by identifying with the same-sex parent.

Freud's unfavorable view of punishment helped produce a swing toward permissive child-rearing in the 1940s and 1950s. Interestingly, today the pendulum is swinging back in the direction of a somewhat greater restrictiveness and punitiveness (Walters & Grusec, 1977). In this chapter, we will document recent research that justifies this trend: Firm control is an indispensable part of successful child-rearing.

Another Warning About the Child-as-Effect Model

In Chapter 1, we discussed how socialization is no longer viewed as a unidirectional (parent-as-cause, child-as-effect) process, but rather is conceptualized as a process that involves reciprocal influences between children and their caregivers. In this chapter, we focus on the parent variables affecting child behavior, but we will note some recent attempts made to determine the ways in which children influence their disciplinarians as well.

APPRAISING THE TECHNIQUES OF SOCIALIZATION

We will begin our appraisal with a discussion of the techniques used to eliminate behavior, and then we will turn to the techniques used to strengthen behavior. Theory and research will be presented for each technique. At a later point in the chapter, we summarize the results of field studies that have assessed the effects of different combinations of parenting qualities on the child's development.

Techniques for Eliminating Behavior

Physical Punishment: When is it Effective? Physical punishment may be considered a consequence intended by a socializing agent to be physically aversive and to reduce future occurrences of the behavior it follows.

Some startling statistics reveal this technique to be much more common than probably is realized by critics who claim that contemporary parents are too lenient: It has been reported that 25 percent of infants under 6 months and 50 percent of adolescents in their last year of high school experience actual or threatened punishment. And at some point in their development, over 90 percent of all children are physically punished (Parke & Collmer, 1975). Is physical punishment effective? Does it have unwanted side effects? Should it be used? Evaluating this common but controversial tactic is an important task.

Research indicates that physical punishment can, under certain circumstances, be quite effective in teaching children to avoid unwanted forms of behavior (Parke, 1970, 1974; Walters & Grusec, 1977). Evidence from both laboratory and field studies contributes to this conclusion. The story of laboratory research on physical punishment is an interesting one, because it illustrates how conceptualizations of punishment, which were originally based on relatively simple conditioning principles, gradually had to be modified to incorporate cognitive variables.

The typical laboratory study consists of a training phase and a test phase (e.g., Parke, 1969). During training, the child is presented with attractive toys, two at a time, with instructions to reach for whichever toy he or she prefers. The experimenter explains that the child is not to touch or play with some of the toys, but that the experimenter will teach the child which ones are in this group. On certain trials, the experimenter punishes the child for his or her choice (regardless of which toy the child chooses), usually by sounding a startling and irritating buzzer. During the test period that follows, the adult leaves the child alone with the prohibited toys and observes him or her through a one-way mirror.

Many of the early experiments carried out within this model were designed to test hypotheses stemming from conditioning theory. According to conditioning theory (e.g., Aronfreed, 1968), if a child is punished for deviant behavior, then anxiety becomes associated with the deviant act, at least when it is performed in situations similar to the one in which it was originally punished. This means that when children are tempted to perform the behavior on subsequent occasions, they should experience anxiety. If intense enough, the anxiety should forestall the deviant action. Furthermore, the moment children hesitate or shift their plans away from deviating, their anxiety subsides. Hence, avoiding the punished behavior becomes reinforced by anxiety reduction. In the future, then, when children are tempted, they are likely to make the avoidance response even sooner. Thus punishment causes children to avoid behavior via a two-step process: first, the classical conditioning of anxiety to behavior and, second, the instrumental conditioning of avoidance responses that are reinforced by anxiety reduction. This is called the *dual-process theory of anxiety*.

Some early experiments on punishment produced results consistent with this conditioning interpretation. For example, the more intense the punishment (the louder the buzzer), and the more quickly the punishment was administered following an attempt to touch a toy, the less the children touched the prohibited toys during the test phase (Parke & Walters, 1967; Walters & Demkow, 1963). However, it soon became apparent that cognitive factors play a central role in mediating the effects of punishment. In a landmark experiment, Parke (1969) discovered that if the experimenter accompanied the punishing buzzer with a verbal rationale explaining why the children should refrain from playing with certain toys (e.g., "You shouldn't touch that because it might break" or "That one belongs to other children and they don't want you to touch it"), then the children displayed extremely high resistance to temptation in the test phase. In fact, when the experimenter provided the children with a reason, performance of the punished behavior fell to such low levels that there was little room for factors previously found to influence punishment effectiveness (e.g., punishment intensity and timing) to contribute. The message from this research is clear: By appealing to children's cognitive faculties, adults can often achieve better results than by relying solely on the anxiety-arousing qualities of punishment.

The results of field studies also indicate that physical punishment—if used judiciously—can benefit the socialization process. Several field investigators have explored the effects of "power assertive" discipline on children's behavior. Power assertion is a term used to refer to any discipline that involves the parent using his or her superior strength and power to achieve compliance from the child (Hoffman, 1977a). Physical punishment and the threat of physical punishment are two major types of power assertive discipline, although some researchers include certain other tactics, such as deprivation of privileges. To determine parents' use of power assertive discipline, parents are usually interviewed or asked to fill out questionnaires about their child-rearing practices. In addition, some researchers directly observe parents and children during disciplinary encounters in the home.

Research on the effects of power assertive discipline yields two conclusions. First, when parents want to teach their children to avoid undesirable conduct—and it is clear that force is the only means of achieving this—then they are better off using force (in the ways specified below) rather than giving up on their attempts to teach their children the desired conduct. In other words, measured use of power assertion to ensure compliance is more conducive to positive socialization than is permitting children to behave in ways that violate norms of desirable conduct. Second, the use of extreme forms of power assertion, such as harsh physical punishment, or a reliance on power assertion to the exclusion of other valuable forms of discipline is associated with a variety of undesirable outcomes in children. We shall consider each of these points in turn.

Several field studies indicate that parents who exercise "firm control" over their children—who make age-appropriate demands of their children for moral and prosocial action and strictly enforce these requests (with external sanctions, if necessary)—have children who score high on indices of morality and altruism and low on measures of antisocial behaviors such as aggression. For example, Baumrind (1973) found that competent preschoolers (children who show a combination of friendliness, assertiveness without aggression, self-control, and goal-directedness) have parents who make a habit of strictly enforcing their requests for mature behavior *and* are willing to use force when necessary. In other words, when they ask their children to change their ongoing behavior, these parents follow through on their requests, making sure that the children comply. Even the use of physical punishment was found to be associated with child competence, as long as it was no more intense than necessary to gain compliance, was accompanied with reasoning, and was given by a parent who was generally affectionate and encouraging of the child's display of initiative. Hoffman (1970b) also reports that mild physical punishment may be necessary when children are unreasonably defiant and inattentive. In such cases, physical punishment can be used to gain the child's attention so that the parent can then reason with the child. Note a common theme to these observations: Physical punishment is most effective and advisable when administered in conjunction with reasoning—a finding reminiscent of the laboratory research.

How do the two major theories of child-rearing practices—social learning theory and attribution theory—handle the finding that physical punishment, when used in the ways described, benefits the child's socialization?

According to social learning theory, effective socialization begins by imparting to children a clear understanding of proper and improper behavior and by requiring them to conform behaviorally to these standards. If children are allowed to behave in ways that violate a social norm, they are hardly likely to realize that society genuinely considers the norm important, and they will probably not regulate their own behavior to agree with the norm. Furthermore, as any parent knows, simply asking children to perform desired behaviors is not always enough; a degree of force, such as physical punishment or its threat, is often required to ensure compliance. Thus social learning theorists would predict that physical punishment, when used in measured fashion and only in the intensity necessary to gain compliance with requests for mature behavior, can aid the socialization process.

From the standpoint of attribution theory, however, the finding that power assertion can be associated with desirable socialization poses a problem. Because physical punishment involves the use of force by an external agent, it should cause children to generate external attributions for conformity. Remember, children who believe external incentives are the only reasons for conforming to a rule should cease conforming as soon as they perceive that the external contingency is no longer operative.

In addresssing this issue, Lepper (1981) proposes that parents who have been identified in field studies as successfully using firm control to achieve internalization of desirable behaviors in their children are parents who are skilled in eliciting such behavior without making their children aware of the fact that their behavior is externally coerced. Lepper points out that although parents who exercise firm control frequently do use power assertion, they are careful to combine their use of force with auxiliary techniques that help downplay the significance of external control. For example, such parents tend not to enforce sanctions arbitrarily and erratically, they justify their disciplinary action with reasoning, they engage their children in verbal give-and-take, and they are willing to modify their disciplinary action when their children's arguments merit it (Baumrind, 1973). In a study directly relevant to Lepper's argument, Dix and Grusec (1982) found that when parents use a combination of power assertion and reasoning to elicit compliance from children, as opposed to using power assertion alone, children are less likely to view the compliance as externally forced. In sum, attribution theorists believe that power assertion is not harmful to the internalization of social norms, and may even facilitate it, if the power assertion (a) is of the lowest intensity sufficient to ensure compliance and (b) is embedded in a context that minimizes perceptions of external control.

Physical Punishment: Some Dangers
The use of force as a means of making children observe certain rules may sometimes benefit children's socialization. However, numerous field studies attest that parents who favor severe power assertive discipline (e.g., physical beatings) or who rely on power assertive techniques to the exclusion of other techniques (e.g., reasoning or praise for good behavior) have children who score low on several indices of internalization—especially resistance to deviation, remorse following transgression, and inhibitions against express-

ing aggression outside the home (see reviews, Hoffman, 1977a; and Martin, 1975). Investigators have suggested that the negative outcomes may be the result of several unintended side effects of using harsh power assertive discipline. Let us review some of the possible negative side effects of physical punishment.

First, there is an imitation-of-aggression hypothesis: Children subjected to physical punishment may practice on others the physical aggression they have experienced at home at the hands of their parents. Indeed, many aggressive infants (George & Main, 1979), delinquent adolescents (Bandura & Walters, 1959), and criminal adults (McCord, 1979) share a history of being erratically and brutally disciplined by their parents.

Second, excessively punished children may begin to avoid their parents and thus receive less instruction in desirable forms of behavior. Physically abused infants have been found to avoid the overtures of their caregivers. They also sometimes show signs of conflict when approaching their caregivers. For example, they turn about and backstep or approach the caregivers with an averted head (George & Main, 1979). Of course, battered children represent extreme cases, but normal children also sometimes avoid adults who interact with them punitively (Redd, Morris, & Martin, 1975). It should be noted, though, that children are less likely to avoid punitive adults if the adults balance their punishment of deviant behavior with reward for positive behavior (Morris & Redd, 1975).

Third, physical punishment may sometimes interfere with learning and remembering rules of appropriate conduct. Intense punishment that elicits strong startle and anxiety reactions may prevent children from cognitively associating a deviant action with its consequences (Walters & Parke, 1967). Children do, in fact, frequently fail to recall why they were punished (Maurer, 1974). Very intense punishment may also interfere with the child's ability to listen to or remember any verbal reasoning the adult may be providing

at the time of punishment (Cheyne, Goyeche, & Walters, 1969).

A fourth problem with forceful discipline is that it sensitizes children to the fact that their behavior is under the control of external factors. According to attribution theory, severe punishment may be effective in getting children to obey, at least as long as the threat of punishment looms, but at the same time it may reduce their belief that they complied because they wanted to, because by nature they are the sort of people who want to be good (Bem, 1972; Lepper, 1981). Instead, children subjected to severe physical punishment may conclude that since others see fit to control them with drastic means, they must be very bad indeed. Such self-perceptions of badness may actually encourage unacceptable behavior in children. Furthermore, if children attribute their good behavior to external factors, they may limit their performance of good behavior to occasions when they believe that the external contingency is in effect. When external surveillance is suspended, thereby alleviating the fear of being caught and punished, deviant behavior may occur. Therefore, attribution theorists strongly urge parents not to apply more external pressure than is necessary to achieve compliance from their children. Lepper (1981) has called this the "principle of minimal sufficiency."

An intriguing experiment by Lepper (1973) illustrates, from the standpoint of attribution theory, some of the potential dangers in eliciting compliance from children through a show of force greater than that actually needed to achieve control. Second-grade children were asked to resist the temptation to play with an attractive toy while the experimenter ran an errand. Before leaving the children, however, the experimenter threatened the children with either mild or severe punishment for deviating. To children in the mild-threat group, the experimenter remarked that she would be a little annoyed if the children played with the toy; to those in the severe-threat group, she remarked that she would be extremely angry and might "have to do something about it" if the children deviated. Both the mild and severe threat were sufficient to prevent children from deviating. However, Lepper hypothesized that the two groups of children would reach rather different conclusions about the reasons for their willingness to avoid playing with the toy. Children who were mildly threatened, lacking a strong external justification for their avoidance of the toy, should generate internal attributions for their conformity. That is, they should come to believe that they resisted playing with the toy because they are inherently trustworthy and good children. In contrast, those who were severely threatened should view their obedience as externally governed. When Lepper asked the two groups of children to rate themselves on adjectives chosen to reflect an honesty-dishonesty dimension, mildly threatened children's self-perceptions were indeed more positive than those of children who had complied after receiving severe threats.

Furthermore, Lepper reasoned that because mildly threatened children form more positive self-perceptions, they should behave more morally in a new situation than severely threatened children. Thus all of the children were tested for honesty in a second situation: They were given an opportunity to falsify their scores secretly on a game in order to win a prize. As predicted, mildly threatened children cheated less than severely threatened children, despite the fact that the test for cheating followed the initial compliance by several weeks and was conducted by a different adult in a different room of the children's school. This experiment is an important one, for it suggests that the ways adults solicit initial compliance from children can influence how the children will behave in the future.

In sum, although firm enforcement of requests for mature behavior is essential for successful socialization, using more force than necessary may undermine the socialization process.

Verbal Punishment   Verbal punishment can range from simple, unemotional indications to children that their behavior is undesirable to derogatory and insulting criticism. This broad definition makes it difficult to generalize about the effects of verbal punishment. Few investigations of the effects of extremely harsh verbal punishment (name-calling, ridiculing, etc.) have been carried out, but one might expect unnecessarily cruel verbal criticism to offer the same bad side effects as unnecessarily harsh physical punishment. Indeed, parents who frequently engage their children in unpleasant verbal interactions (by ridiculing them, teasing them, shouting orders at them, etc.) are likely to have aggressive children (Patterson & Cobb, 1971).

On the other hand, informative feedback regarding inappropriate behavior can sometimes be an extremely powerful tool of behavior change. A number of experiments reveal that verbally informing children when they make incorrect responses can be an effective means of changing their behavior. Suppose children are shown a wooden box with two holes in the top. Each child is given a bag of marbles and is asked to drop the marbles, one at a time, into the box through the holes. Unknown to the children, one hole has been designated the "correct" hole and the other one the "incorrect" hole. The experimenter wishes to compare the effectiveness of two different strategies for teaching children to drop the marbles into the correct hole. In one group, the experimenter punishes the children when they make incorrect responses by saying "No" or "Wrong" each time they drop a marble into the incorrect hole, but remains silent whenever they drop a marble into the correct hole; in the second group, the experimenter rewards children by saying "Yes" or "Good" when they make correct responses, but ignores incorrect marble drops. Most child psychology students, believing in the "power of reward," would expect the reward-only approach to be the more effective. However, the truth is that learning in the punishment-only condition is far superior (see Cairns, 1967, 1970; Paris and Cairns, 1972; and Spence, 1970). Of course, these findings do not mean that positive social reinforcement is unimportant to the socialization process; it is extremely important, as we will see later. But a child-rearing program that ignores letting children know when they have performed undesirable behavior is unlikely to result in a substantial amount of learning.

Although verbally informing children when they have made a mistake provides valuable information to children that can help them change their behavior, some children react maladaptively to critical feedback from adults. In research of substantial social significance, Dweck and her associates have discovered that when adults tell children that they have done poorly or failed in a problem-solving situation, some children "go to pieces": They become upset, they want to withdraw from the situation, and they fail to solve similar problems even when the problems have been modified to be easily within their grasp (e.g., Dweck & Reppucci,1973). Other children, when criticized, have the opposite reaction: They eagerly ask for the opportunity to attempt similar problems, as if they are trying to prove their competence. Dweck reports a notable sex difference in the kind of reaction children are likely to experience. She found that girls are considerably more likely than boys to have the former debilitating sort of reaction. Furthermore, by the later elementary-school years, girls are far more likely than boys to develop an aversion to achievement situations altogether. That is, when given the choice, girls are more likely than boys to avoid participating in academic situations in which failure is a possible outcome. Perhaps girls' aversion to achievement settings reflects their fear of the upset they would experience if they did poorly.

What causes boys and girls to have these divergent reactions to criticism from adults for poor performance in a problem-solving situation? Dweck proposes an attributional analysis of the sex difference. Specifically, she suggests that boys and girls develop different styles of explaining the failure feedback they receive from adults. Furthermore, Dweck proposes that boys and girls learn these different ways of interpreting verbal criticism from the interactions they have with their teachers in the classroom. Dweck has conducted observational studies of classroom interaction and discovered that teachers tend to use verbal punishment, or criticism, in different ways with girls and boys (Dweck & Bush, 1976; Dweck, Davidson, Nelson, & Enna, 1978). In the classroom, teachers tend not to criticize girls nearly as often as boys, but when they do criticize a girl it is usually to inform her that she has made an academic or intellectual error (e.g., "You got that one wrong—I guess you don't know how to do it"). In contrast, teachers criticize boys far more frequently than girls, but most boy-directed criticism is for sloppiness, for not trying hard enough, or for misbehaving (e.g., "You got that wrong, Billy—you're being lazy again"). Only rarely is boy-directed criticism delivered for intellectual incompetence. As a consequence, girls learn to fear and react disruptively to criticism, because they think it means that they *lack ability*; in contrast, boys learn to brush aside criticism, taking it to mean only that they *lack effort* and are just not living up to their potential. Dweck likens the giving-up behavior of girls to the "learned helplessness" syndrome observed by Maier, Seligman, and Solomon (1969) in animals who are given experience with unavoidable and inescapable shock. Learned helplessness is a debilitating state presumed to result from an individual's perception that environmental outcomes (rewards and punishments) are not under his or her control.

The research indicates that verbal criticism may be essential for helping children learn what is inappropriate or incorrect behavior, but it is clear that adults should be careful not to use it in ways that cause children to develop debilitating self-perceptions.

Extinction Many parents, and particularly those who believe in a permissive child-rearing philosophy, try to eliminate behavior by ignoring it. This process, sometimes called *extinction*, has several limitations (Walters & Grusec, 1977). One limitation is that it is a slow and tedious process. Furthermore, sometimes when parents start to ignore a behavior, the child suddenly increases the intensity or frequency of the behavior, as if trying to provoke some reaction from the parents. The parents may be able to stand this for a limited amount of time, but eventually they may "erupt" and punish the child. The overall result, then, is inconsistent treatment.

It is largely for this reason that some psychologists suggest that there may be some danger in a child-rearing philosophy that prohibits any physical punishment (Baumrind, 1973; Parke & Collmer, 1975). These psychologists propose that when the use of moderate physical punishment is consistent with one's child-rearing values, it is more likely to be used in a controlled and measured fashion than if one has sworn never to use it at all. Indeed, Baumrind (1973) found that parents who subscribe to a theory of total permissiveness in child-rearing admit to explosive attacks of rage during which they inflict severe pain or injury on their children.

Another difficulty with extinction is that children sometimes interpret nonreaction from an adult as implicit approval, and the children may never realize that the ignored behavior is considered unacceptable. Finally, there is the problem of "spontaneous recovery": Even if extinction succeeds in reducing a response for a period of time, the response may reappear if sufficient time elapses between one extinction session and the next.

Still, extinction may sometimes be worth trying, though it should probably only be used in combination with strategies aimed at strengthening desirable behavior that will compete with the unwanted behavior. And, if the parent or teacher attempting extinction does find that a problem of inconsistent treatment is developing, it is probably wise to switch immediately to a program based on the consistent application of an aversive consequence, such as time-out.

Time-out One form of punishment, known as *time-out*, has been used with wide success in behavior modification programs and avoids some of the problems associated with physical punishment. Time-out procedures involve removing the child to a quiet room, such as a bathroom, for brief periods of time (e.g., 15 minutes) following wrong doings. The time-out contingency, and the reasons for it, are clearly explained to the child. This procedure teaches the child that deviant behavior will not be rewarded or tolerated and that one is not allowed to enjoy the company of others unless one behaves acceptably.

Withdrawal of Love Occasionally parents discipline their children by withdrawing their affection from them. Examples of love-withdrawal techniques are turning one's back on the child, isolating or ignoring the child for long periods of time, stating that one is disappointed in or dislikes the child, and threatening to leave the child or send the child away. Although not physically painful, love-withdrawal often lasts a long time and can arouse intense anxiety, especially when the child is young and lacks the time perspective necessary to realize the temporary nature of the parent's action.

Most parents use love-withdrawal at least occasionally, but parents who rely on love-withdrawal as their main technique of discipline may cause their children to develop exaggerated anxieties over behaving aggressively and about losing the affection of others (Hoffman, 1970b). It is probably safe to conclude that brief periods of removal of affection can be used advantageously. For example, withdrawal of attention increases children's attempts to gain adult approval, making it easier to influence their subsequent behavior (Gewirtz & Baer, 1958a, 1958b; Hartup, 1958). However, the extended use of love-withdrawal is probably ill-advised.

Reasoning The use of verbal reasoning by parents to justify their disciplinary actions contributes to the successful socialization of their children. Reasoning is associated with low aggression, honesty, acceptance of responsibility for one's transgressions, and competence in the peer group (Aronfreed, 1968; Baumrind, 1973; Hoffman, 1977b).

Hoffman (1977) emphasizes that the sort of reasoning found to correlate most consistently with desirable social behavior in children is *other-oriented induction*, or reasoning in which the parent explains to the child the causal relationship between the child's behavior and positive or negative consequences for other people (e.g., "You can see Paul is sad; you can make him feel better by letting him play with your toy"). A recent study by Perry, Bussey, and Freiberg (1981) offers experimental evidence that such reasoning facilitates internalization. In this study, 7-to 8-year-old children were first asked to share half of their winnings from a bowling game with children who would not get a chance to play. For one-third of the children, the request to share was accompanied by a short inductive appeal in which the experimenter emphasized that sharing makes other people happy and also makes oneself feel good for having caused happiness for others. A second group heard a power assertive appeal emphasizing that sharing is necessary because adults expect it and get angry when they find out children have failed to practice it. A third (control) group was asked to share, but was not given any accompanying rationale. As requested, children in all three groups shared half their winnings. However, in a second phase of the experiment, children were given a further opportunity to share without adult supervision and without receiving direct instructions to share. In this phase, children who had initially shared in compliance with the inductive appeal were roughly three times as generous as children in either of the other two conditions.

Why is inductive reasoning so effective? A first possibility is Hoffman's suggestion that inductive reasoning helps children learn to anticipate guilt for failing to inhibit undesirable behavior. In Hoffman's view, guilt is an empathic response to another's distress coupled with the belief that oneself is responsible for initiating or prolonging the distressed other's state. When children who have experienced inductive reasoning are tempted to misbehave, they presumably think of the possible negative consequences their behavior might have for others. Realizing they would be to blame for the negative consequences, they begin to feel guilty. The guilt lasts until they stop contemplating the deviation.

Induction does seem to make children more aware of the feelings and thoughts of other people. Bearison and Cassel (1975) report that parents who justify their disciplinary actions with statements that focus on the intentions and feelings of others (e.g., "Your teacher will feel sad if you . . . "; "You could make her feel better if you . . . ") rather than with statements that focus on the power of the parents, status factors, or appeals for conformity (e.g., "Do it because I said so!" "All children should . . . ";) have children who are skilled at role taking (deciphering the private experiences of others). It seems reasonable to expect that such children would anticipate more guilt for transgressing against others.

Second, reasoning can teach children general principles of appropriate and inappropriate conduct, which they can use to guide their behavior in new situations (Walters & Grusec, 1977). A parent who punishes a child for hitting her sister but fails to accompany the disciplinary action with reasoning may succeed in getting the child to inhibit future attacks against her sister, but the addition of inductive reasoning (e.g., "It's always wrong to hurt other people") may help the child inhibit aggression in new situations and toward other targets as well.

Hoffman (1977) offers a third reason for the effectiveness of reasoning. He speculates that when children who have experienced inductive discipline are confronted with a later opportunity to deviate, they may recall the inductive message, but dissociate the message from its original external source, the parent. In other words, when children try to talk themselves out of deviating (e.g., "Don't do it—if you hurt him you'll have no one to blame but yourself"), they may perceive the message to have originated within themselves. Hoffman cites evidence that such dissociation of the semantic content of a message from its original context would be consistent with memory theory (e.g., Tulving, 1972). Of course, according to attribution theory, if children adopt a social value without apparent external pressure, they can be considered intrinsically disposed to adhere to the standard.

Attribution theorists Dienstbier, Hillman, Lehnhoff, Hillman, and Valkenaar (1975) proposed that the way parents reason with their children when punishing them influences whether children will deviate when later faced with the temptation to perform a similar behavior. To understand their conclusions regarding reasoning, it is first necessary to explain what these authors believe is responsible for children's behavior when tempted to deviate. They propose that resistance to temptation is a function of the causal attributions children generate to explain the emotional arousal they experience when faced with the temptation to do something they have previously been punished for doing. Dienstbier et al. believe that all children become aroused, or anxious, when faced with an opportunity to break a prohibition. Such anxiety may stem from a conditioning process (prior association of deviation with punishment), from the approach-avoidance conflict the children face, from their uncertainty over the outcome of deviating, or from something else. The researchers stress that it is the children's perception of the cause of their anxiety that determines whether they will deviate or not. Specifically, if children believe that they feel anxious because they are worried about getting caught and punished (an external attribution), then the chance of deviation in the absence of external surveillance is high. Presumably, such children reason like this: "The only reason to fear deviating is the possibility of being found out

and punished; I know nobody is watching right now, so I may as well deviate." In contrast, children who believe that their anxieties are due to an understanding that something is inherently wrong or who are afraid of violating their self-images of being good people probably would not deviate even in the absence of adult surveillance.

Dienstbier and his associates proposed that the way parents reason with their children at the time they punish them for transgressing can influence the children's causal attributions for the arousal they experience during subsequent temptations. To gather support for this position, these researchers conducted an experiment in which children were first induced to break a prohibition, then were scolded for their misbehavior by an adult who reasoned with the children in one of two ways, and finally were given a test of their willingness to break the prohibition again. First, each child was asked to perform a tedious and boring task while the experimenter went on an errand. Soon after the experimenter was gone, some very attractive mechanical toys in the room were activated by remote control. The toys were enticing enough to cause the children to misbehave, that is, to leave the boring job they had promised to do in order to play with the toys. The experimenter then returned and confronted the children with their deviation, but phrased his criticism differently for two groups of children. To one group, he remarked that the children were probably feeling upset because they had done something they had known to be wrong (internal attribution condition). To the other group, he remarked that the children were probably feeling upset because they had been caught deviating by the experimenter (external attribution condition). Finally, both groups were given another chance to perform the boring task with the mechanical toys still present. The children were told that no one would be able to tell if they deviated or not, although they were observed. Children in the internal attribution condition group deviated only half as much as the subjects in the external attribution condition group, supporting the researchers' hypothesis. In sum, how parents reason with their children influences the causal attributions children make in temptation situations, which, in turn, influence the probability that they will resist temptation.

We should also note that in order to be effective, reasoning should probably be geared to the child's level of cognitive development. Infants will obviously not profit much from reasoning. Some research suggests that for reasoning to promote resistance to deviation in preschool children, it must specify concretely the objective consequences of deviation. For example, a concrete rationale ("You should not touch that toy because it might break") is effective for both 4- and 7-year-olds. However, when a more abstract property rule is used ("You should not play with the toy because it belongs to somebody else"), only the older children benefit (Parke, 1974). LaVoie (1974) found that 11-year-olds are better able than 7-year-olds to utilize an abstract rationale that focuses on their intentions ("It is wrong to want to play with or to think about playing with that toy") or a rationale that draws on their empathic skills ("Think about how the other children would feel if they discovered that you broke the rule"). These studies illustrate how the effectiveness of particular reasoning tactics changes with age, but much more research is needed on this topic.

To have a philosophy of discipline that is based on appeals to the child's sense of reason sounds so civilized. But can reasoning really work alone? Or does it need to be backed up with enforcement that may sometimes have to be physical? It is unlikely that reasoning will be very effective unless parents teach children that they "mean business" when reasoning with them. Research confirms that parents who are the most effective "reasoners" are those who back up their words with action and firm enforcement— even physical punishment, if necessary (Baumrind, 1973; Hoffman, 1970a; Lytton & Zwirner, 1975; Walters & Grusec, 1977). This does not imply that reasoning should always be accompanied by power assertion. On the contrary, if reasoning will succeed alone, it probably should be used alone. However, if children begin to drift toward noncompliance when reasoned requests have been made, power assertive discipline may be necessary. We should note also that, to be effective, reasoning should not be delivered in a totally calm, emotionally flat way. Parents who display emotional distress (e.g., indignation or disappointment) when they are reasoning with their children are more effective in promoting altruism and signs of conscience in them (Zahn-Waxler, Radke-Yarrow, & King, 1979). Without fortification by punishment or indignation, reasoning may do little more than call attention to the deviant behavior, thereby reinforcing it.

Reinforcement of Alternative, Desirable Behavior   Last but not least, one of the most effective ways to eliminate an undesirable response—and perhaps *the* most effective—is to cultivate and reward prosocial behavior that is incompatible with the unwanted behavior (Perry & Parke, 1975). If parents, for example, concentrate on teaching empathic, altruistic, and cooperative solutions to conflict, they should have less occasion to have to punish aggression. Unwanted behavior can also be reduced by "omission training," in which children are given a reward if they can resist displaying the unwanted behavior for an amount of time specified by the caregiver (see Walters & Grusec, 1977). We shall now examine the ways that socializing agents can promote desirable behavior.

Techniques for Strengthening Behavior

Material Reward   Parents and teachers sometimes promise money, toys, gold stars, privileges, and even food to children for performing desired behavior. The best-documented attempts to shape children's behavior through material reward can be found in the work of behavior modifiers who use principles of operant conditioning to replace undesirable behavior with prosocial behavior. It is clear from this literature that when material reinforcers, such as chocolate candy or tokens exchangeable for more substantial rewards, are dispensed each time the desired behavior is performed, the desired behavior is performed with greater frequency and unwanted behavior is less commonly acted out (Bandura, 1969a; Krasner & Ullmann, 1965; O'Leary & Drabman, 1971). Behavior modifiers recognize that behavior change instigated through rewards does not automatically generalize to times and places when the rewards are no longer available. Thus deliberate attempts to ensure generalization of the treatment effects to posttreatment periods must be made. This may be done by continuing the extrinsic reinforcement on an intermittent basis, teaching parents, teachers, siblings, and peers to dispense social rewards contingent upon the desired behavior, or even transferring the role of reinforcing agent to the child.

A convincing demonstration of transferring the role of reinforcing agent to the child is illustrated by a study in which highly disruptive boys were taught to reward themselves for behaving nondisruptively (Drabman, Spitalnik, & O'Leary, 1973). This is an example of omission training, which we mentioned earlier. During an initial phase of the program, a disruptive boy and his teacher were separately required to make ratings (on a 0–5 scale) of how well the child had behaved during certain times of the school day. After both teacher and child had completed their ratings, the child's was checked against the teacher's, and if the child's was accurate (within a point of the teacher's), he earned one or more points that could later be exchanged for money and goods. The number of points the boy received depended on his self-rating: The higher the boy's self-rating, the more points he earned. This strategy quickly taught the children to be accurate in their self-evaluations and was also accompanied by a decline in disruptiveness. Gradually, checking the child's evaluation against

his teacher's to determine its accuracy was discontinued. Even after this process was totally phased out, the boy's self-evaluations remained accurate and improvement in classroom behavior was sustained. In this study, the material rewards were never completely curtailed, but the study indicates that children may be taught to control their behavior through self-reinforcement.

Despite the acclaimed success of many behavior modification programs, the use of material rewards to change children's behavior has recently come under vigorous attack—especially from attribution theorists. Attribution theorists warn that when salient extrinsic rewards are promised and given to children for engaging in an activity, the children may decide that the reward is all that is motivating them to engage in the activity. Thus the children lose whatever intrinsic interest they have in the activity, and they come to perform the behavior only when they expect a reward. According to this view, when children engage in activities (such as solving math problems, doing puzzles, or reading books), *without* any obvious external incentive, they are likely to believe that they are engaging in the behavior because they are intrinsically interested in it ("This must be fun, because I am doing this even though I don't have to"). However, once external rewards (e.g., gold stars, money, or toys) are offered for the behavior, children completely reattribute their motivation for performing the response to the reward and thereby lose intrinsic interest in it ("I only perform this activity to get a reward"). The prediction, then, is that children who are promised and given a reward for performing an activity will shun the activity later when rewards are no longer available.

In an initial experiment on this issue, Lepper, Greene, and Nisbett (1973) promised a prize to one group of nursery-school children for drawing pictures with felt pens—an activity of much interest to most preschoolers. Compared to control groups of children who were not promised any reward for drawing, the "bribed" children later avoided drawing during play periods when no rewards were available. The researchers labeled the reduced interest on the part of the previously rewarded children the *overjustification effect*: By adding unnecessary external motivation, the reward undermined the children's intrinsic interest.

Numerous subsequent studies have confirmed that material rewards sometimes undermine children's interest in an activity. The effect has been revealed for a variety of activities (solving puzzles and mazes, playing musical instruments, and working on arithmetic problems) and for a variety of rewards (money, pretzels, and toys). Reduced interest is not the only ill effect produced by introducing external rewards. Rewarded children frequently perform an activity in a sloppy, hurried fashion. Furthermore, children who have been rewarded for problem-solving activities (puzzles, math problems, etc.) sometimes lower their achievement aspirations—when given a free choice of problems to solve, they choose the easier ones (Condry, 1977; Condry & Chambers, 1982; Harter, 1978).

Not all psychologists agree that the detrimental effects of rewards are due to attribution processes. A number of alternative interpretations have been offered (Feingold & Mahoney, 1975; Karniol & Ross, 1979; Perry, Bussey, & Redman, 1977; Ransen, 1980; Reiss & Sushinsky, 1975; Smith & Pittman, 1978). Nevertheless, the effects are worrisome enough to have caused some psychologists to conclude that material rewards are the "enemies of exploration" (Condry, 1977) and that behavior modification programs based on rewards are inadvisable because "token rewards may lead to token learning" (Levine & Fasnacht, 1974).

We must be cautious in applying these findings to real-life child-rearing and educational settings, however. In most of the studies, material rewards have been offered to children who would have cheerfully consented to perform the target behavior without the promise of a reward. The results, then, may caution against using material re-

wards when they are not needed, but in many behavior modification programs, rewards may be necessary to get children even to try a desirable activity. Rewards can be indispensable when motivating people to engage in new activities so that new competencies can be developed. For example, a child may refuse to attend a swimming class or study her spelling lists unless promised a reward. But once the child enjoys some success at the activity, the child's perception of her skill at the task is likely to improve. Remember that according to social learning theory (Bandura, 1981), children's perceptions of self-efficacy are major determinants of the activities they will attempt or shun when left to their own devices. Thus, although unnecessary material bribes may occasionally undermine interest in an activity, rewards can also promote competencies and interests.

In addition, there are at least three other important circumstances when rewards do not undermine, and may in fact enhance, intrinsic interest in an activity. First, although material rewards (e.g., candy or money) sometimes undermine intrinsic interest, social rewards (e.g., praise or compliments) do not. In fact, social rewards often increase the motivation for performing an activity when no adults are present, possibly because social rewards engender feelings of competence and pride in performing the activity (Anderson, Manoogian, & Reznick, 1976; Dollinger & Thelen, 1978). Second, reward does not undermine intrinsic interest if it lets children know that they are competent at the activity. Indeed, when children are told that receiving a material reward signifies that they are doing a competent and successful job, the reward may enhance children's tendencies to engage in the activity when rewards are withdrawn (Boggiano & Ruble, 1979; Karniol & Ross, 1977). Third, rewards do not undermine intrinsic interest if children participate in determining the contingencies of reward delivery (Bandura & Perloff, 1967; Enzle & Look, 1980; Weiner & Dubanoski, 1975).

In sum, the research suggests that material

rewards, like other external motivators, should not be used if some less extrinsic and less manipulative technique will suffice. If rewards are used, they should be used cautiously and in such a way that they impart information to the child that will create rather than reduce competencies and interests.

Social Reward Social rewards are verbal expressions of approval and praise ("That's good," "Yes," "Right," and so on), as well as nonverbal expressions of affection, such as hugs, smiles, and kisses. Certain of these reactions, such as physical expressions of affection, may have a positively reinforcing basis that is partly innate. However, the power of social rewards can also be enhanced or diminished through learning experiences. One way of strengthening social rewards is by pairing them with "primary" or "unconditioned" positive reinforcers (Warren & Cairns, 1972). In the last chapter, for example, we noted that, according to learning theory, a mother's physical characteristics and expressions of affection can acquire secondary reinforcing properties if the mother is associated with a variety of unconditioned positive reinforcers, such as food, relief from distress, contact comfort, and exciting sensory stimulation.

As the child matures, judicious timing of verbal approval can increase the approval's effectiveness. For example, it is obvious that children often experience pride and pleasure when they master a new developmental task, such as pronouncing a new word correctly, learning to walk, or solving a problem (Harter, 1974, 1977). If at these times the parents verbally reward the child, it is likely that the association of the positive verbal comments with the child's exhilaration will help strengthen the approval comment's reinforcing power.

Some important observational research by Patterson and Reid (1970) reveals that one key to a happy and healthy family life is a mutual exchange of positive social reinforcers among family members. The investigators counted the frequency with which parents and children rewarded each other with praise, attention, smiles, encouragement, and so on, during home observations. Some of the homes contained a child previously judged to have a serious problem controlling aggression, whereas other homes contained normal children. In homes containing normal, well-adjusted children, family members tended to interact with each other frequently and positively. In contrast, family members in homes containing a delinquent/aggressive boy rarely engaged in pleasant interaction. When they did interact, they attempted to influence and control each other through aversive means—nagging, whining, teasing, scolding, and bossing each other around. A home atmosphere that is barren in positive social stimuli may prompt children to try out intense and obnoxious behavior in a desperate attempt to win recognition and attention from uncaring or hostile family members. In our chapter on aggression, Chapter 7, we shall see that one ingredient of a home environment conducive to aggressive development is a dearth of reciprocal positive social reinforcers among the family members.

The importance of receiving (and giving) social reinforcement is not limited to the family situation. Teachers, peers, and other people use social rewards to influence one another, too. Furthermore, a child's ability to reward his or her peers (to smile, approve, praise, give affection, show interest, and share) is an important determinant of the child's popularity with the peer group. Reciprocity in the exchange of social reinforcers is just as important to harmonious peer group functioning as it is to the happy family.

Social reinforcement is a highly useful tool in behavior modification programs. Aggressive behavior in nursery-school children can often be reduced if teachers make their attention contingent upon prosocial, cooperative behavior and ignore instances of disruptive aggression (Brown & Elliot, 1965; Slaby & Crowley, 1977). Equally important, improvements in children's behavior that are initially established through material reinforcement in a behavior modification program stand a better chance of being maintained after the material rewards are eliminated if the target children's siblings, parents, and teachers are taught how to praise and socially reward the desired behaviors (Patterson & Reid, 1970). Furthermore, as we noted in the last section, social reward does not produce the drops in intrinsic interest that material reward sometimes does.

Some of the observations we are making here about social reinforcement may seem to conflict with something we said earlier in the discussion on verbal punishment. There we noted that in simple laboratory learning tasks (e.g., the marble-dropping studies), social reinforcement does not seem to be very powerful. Remember, for example, that verbal punishment for incorrect responses often encourages learning when verbal reward for correct choices does not. One explanation of this result is that social reinforcement may not automatically be interpreted by the child to indicate a correct response. Adults—and especially teachers—tend to use approval comments such as "Good," "Okay," and "Right" frequently, but their use is not dependent on the children's behavior. This may cause words otherwise intended as approval comments to lose some of their value as reinforcers (Paris & Cairns, 1972).

Research certainly indicates that the *perceived contingency* of a social reward is a critical determinant of its effectiveness. In other words, in order to be effective in shaping children's behavior, approval comments must be perceived by the children to be informative, or relate to the degree of correctness or appropriateness of the children's actions (Babad, 1972, 1973; Babad & Weisz, 1977; Eisenberger, Kaplan, & Singer, 1974; Moore, Baron, & Byrne, 1980; Perry & Garrow, 1975). In one study, Perry and Garrow arranged for some children to interact with an adult who uttered the word "Good" frequently, but not in response to the children's behavior; other

children interacted with an adult who uttered the word "Good" immediately after the children performed specific acts (a condition designed to enhance the informativeness of the adult's reinforcers). Later, the adults tried to teach each group a new task by rewarding correct responses with the word "Good." Children who had perceived the adult's approval to be contingent on their behavior in the first phase were more responsive to the adult's reinforcers (i.e., learned the new task better) in the second phase.

Making social reinforcement clearly contingent upon behavior not only increases the later effectiveness of the reinforcement, but it also enhances the child's sense of security in interpersonal relationships, aids the child's cognitive development, and engenders in the child a sense of mastery and control over the environment. A number of research findings, some of which we have touched on in earlier chapters, support this statement. In the last chapter, we saw that infants whose bids for attention are quickly met by their mothers develop feelings of security concerning the mothers' whereabouts and availability (Ainsworth, 1979). Lewis and Goldberg (1969) report that infants of mothers who respond contingently score high on tests of cognitive maturity. Noncontingent scheduling of social rewards may promote symptoms of learned helplessness: Children without control over the rewards they receive may give up trying to influence other people (Eisenberger at al., 1974). In her observational study of preschool children and their parents, Baumrind (1967) observed that the parents of mature, competent children (children who are friendly, assertive, popular, and goal-directed) did not use praise more frequently than parents of less mature children, but they did more often make their praise contingent upon identifiable actions of the children. The importance of the contingency of reinforcement in the socialization process should be clear.

In sum, social reinforcement is a major avenue through which socialization occurs. Its exchange among members of families and peer groups is essential to harmonious functioning. It is most useful for controlling children's behavior (as well as for teaching children that they can control their own social environments) when it is used contingently as approval for desirable behavior.

Verbal Attributions One surprisingly powerful technique for eliciting a desirable behavior from children is simply to tell them that they possess the motivation and ability to perform the behavior in question. For instance, children who are told by their teachers that they are exceptionally neat thereafter become more tidy, and children told that aptitude tests reveal them to be promising mathematicians actually show gains on standardized tests of arithmetic achievement (Miller, Brickman, & Bolen, 1975). Likewise, children told that they are friendly and cooperative—that they get along well with other children, like to play fairly, are willing to share, and are not pushy—later cooperate more with their peers and show less jealousy and interference with coworkers (Jensen & Moore, 1977). As a final example, children who are told that they are the kind of children who like to help others in any way they can are more likely to seize the opportunity to come to the aid of others than children who have not been given verbal attributions of altruistic motivation (Grusec & Redler, 1980).

Why do children display the positive behaviors attributed to them? One possibility is that children endeavor to display attributed characteristics because they expect criticism from others for failing to do so. Another possibility is that when children are told that they possess desirable attributes they believe the information, and this leads them to anticipate self-dissatisfaction for failing to live up to their expectations (Perry, Perry, Bussey, English, & Arnold, 1980). This is quite possible, since children often show desirable behavior that has been attributed to them even when not

in the presence of those who have made the attributions.

Regardless of the exact mechanism involved, parents should seize whatever opportunities present themselves to tell children that they are intrinsically motivated to perform socially valued behavior. When a child chooses to tell the truth rather than lie about her misbehavior, the parent can respond, "See how you told the truth? I know you're the kind of girl who is always honest and knows that telling the truth is important for getting people to trust you"; and when a child spontaneously shares a possession with another, the parent can compliment, "That was nice of you to want to share. I know you're the kind of boy who always tries to make other people happy." In other words, it is a good idea to use social reinforcement of desirable behavior along with statements that lead the child to believe that it was his or her own enduring internal disposition to perform the behavior that caused it. We should add, however, that when a child performs an undesirable behavior, parents must avoid accompanying their criticism of the behavior with negative comments about the child's character. Comments like, "You sure like to hurt people," and "You're a bad boy," may very well do more harm than good.

Direct Instructions and Maturity Demands Parents who insist that their children keep their rooms tidy, clean up after playing, show consideration for others, play cooperatively, share their belongings with other children, say "Thank you," and so on are indeed helping to establish habits of competent, prosocial behavior. Much of the evidence for this conclusion comes from studies of altruism. Adults who insist on children sharing their possessions and who use discipline not just to stamp out unwanted behavior but also to make sure that their children actively perform in desirable, prosocial ways have children who take the initiative to share with other children even when adults are not around (Israel & Brown, 1979; Olejnik & McKinney, 1973; White, 1972; White & Burnam, 1975).

Recently, a number of psychologists have tried to determine how parents might best phrase requests they make to children in order to get maximum compliance and internalization of prosocial values. Some studies have involved the direct observation of parents and young children interacting at home. When parents present their requests as *suggestions* ("You don't have to, but you may want to . . . ") rather than as stern *commands* ("You have to . . . "), they often are more successful at soliciting compliance (Lytton & Zwirner, 1975). Parents who issue numerous brief commands may create negative reactions (Forehand & Scarboro, 1975). Parents should make sure they have their children's undivided attention before making a request of them (Schaffer & Crook, 1979, 1980). Also, preceding one's requests to a child with some positively toned action (e.g., an expression of love or approval, a hug, or a smile) often seems to help; physical controls like slapping or grabbing the child by the wrist decrease a parent's chances of gaining compliance (Lytton, 1979). Although requests should be worded politely, accompanied with reasoning, and given in a positive atmosphere, it is important, as we have noted before, that parents back up their requests with firm enforcement: They must make sure that their children do perform the desired target responses, even if it means tightening their control so that it is a little "less positive" (Baumrind, 1973).

GLOBAL STYLES OF PARENTING AND THEIR EFFECTS

Thus far we have surveyed the disciplinary tactics of child-rearing one at a time. Many psychologists point out, however, that in real life certain parental attitudes and behaviors tend to combine, forming more global "styles" of parenting. For example, parents who favor inductive reasoning tend also to be warm and responsive to their children's point of view; on the other hand, parents who rely on power assertion tend not to engage their children in verbal give-and-take and sometimes show signs of rejecting their children. We now will discuss how psychologists have tried to determine the more common styles of parenting and review how these styles influence the development of children.

The Factor-Analytic Approach

Outline of the Factor-Analytic Approach A traditional way of conceptualizing parental behavior is to treat child-rearing attitudes and habits as if they reflect a smaller set of underlying *dimensions*. To discover the basic dimensions of child-rearing, the investigator's first step is to compile a list of questions for parents about their disciplinary practices. Questions might range from inquiring about how favorably a mother felt about her pregnancy to questions about her use of specific child-rearing practices, such as whether she breast- or bottle-fed her baby, how severely she toilet-trained her child, how she currently tries to induce compliance from her child, and how much she employs each of several disciplinary tactics. Trained interviewers present the questions to the parents, scoring each parent on a variety of scales when the interviews are completed. They estimate how much the parent seems to enjoy the child, employs physical punishment, uses verbal reasoning to justify disciplinary actions, and so on.

The interviewer's ratings are then subjected to factor analysis, a statistical technique that identifies subsets of rating scales that intercorrelate with one another, but do not intercorrelate with items from other subsets. The number of subsets is taken to reflect the number of basic parent behavior dimensions. These are arbitrarily assigned labels by the investigator after inspecting the items constituting the subset or factor. To illustrate, consider a factor analysis that reveals parents' scores on all the following items to be highly intercorrelated: enjoys the company of the child; avoids the use of physical punishment; frequently displays affection for the child; refrains from calling the child names and using other harsh criticism; uses frequent praise; often arranges to do things with the child. After examining the content of these items, the investigator might decide that the items measure a single underlying dimension of parenting that is characterized by warmth at one end and hostility at the other. Additional items may cluster to form other factor dimensions. A parent's score on each dimension is found by adding his or her scores for the items tied to the dimension. The parent's score on each dimension can then be correlated with selected aspects of the child's behavior.

Most factor analyses of parent behavior yield two major dimensions—indeed, one is usually labeled *warmth-hostility* and the other, *permissiveness-restrictiveness* (Becker, 1964; Schaefer, 1959). Warmth in the first dimension is characterized by the provision of positive reinforcement, such as praise and affectionate expression; sensitivity to the child's needs and viewpoints; enjoyment of the child's company; and low use of physical punishment, criticism, and derogatory comment. The hostile end of the dimension is characterized by opposite kinds of behavior. The permissiveness-restrictiveness dimension is harder to define, because different studies use different kinds of items to measure it. In one study, the dimension may refer to how much the parent restricts the child's freedom; in another study, the dimension may tap the parent's inclination to demand a high level of responsibility from the child by assigning duties and insisting on mature behavior.

Some investigators, who believe that parental behavior may be reduced to the two dimensions of warmth-hostility and permissiveness-restrictiveness, have assigned labels to parents who fall at different points in the two-dimensional space. For example, the parent who is moderately loving and permissive may be considered to be the "democratic" parent, and the moderately hostile and permissive parent may be called the "indifferent" parent (Schaefer, 1959). Figure 3–1 depicts the relationship believed to exist between the two dimensions and includes the labels Schaefer suggests for parents who fall at different places in the scheme.

Correlates of Parental Love (Warmth-Hostility) and Control (Permissiveness-Restrictiveness) We must remember that when a correlation between a parental dimension and child behavior is found, it is impossible to know which specific aspect or aspects of parental behavior are responsible for the association, because parents' scores on the dimensions represent composites of the parents' behavior across many aspects.

Generally speaking, parental warmth is "good" in its effects, and hostility is "bad." Children whose parents are warm and loving are more securely attached, are more responsive to the parents' instruction and discipline, are more likely to imitate their parents, are less likely to avoid their parents, are less aggressive, are more compliant, have more self-esteem, are more considerate and altruistic, have stronger moral internalization (especially in terms of displaying guilt reactions after transgressions), and accept responsibility for misbehaving more readily than children whose parents are hostile. The finding that warm parents have less aggressive children suggests that hostile parents have highly aggressive children. This is so. In fact, perhaps the most consistent relationship found in the child-rearing literature is the strong association between parental hostility—particularly the use of severe physical punishment—and aggressive-delinquent behavior in children (Becker, 1964; Hetherington & Martin, 1972; Maccoby, 1980; Martin, 1975).

The effects of the permissiveness-restrictiveness dimension are not as clear-cut as those identified for the warmth-hostility di-

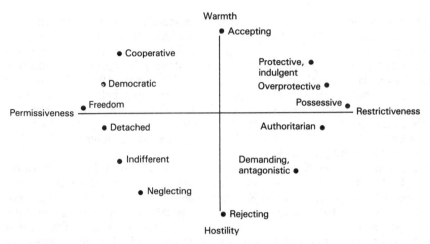

Figure 3–1   Hypothetical model of parental behavior based on
dimensions derived from factor analysis. Adapted from E. S. Schaefer,
"A Circumplex Model for Maternal Behavior," *Journal of Abnormal and
Social Psychology*, 1959, *59,* 226–235. Copyright 1959 by the American
Psychological Association. Adapted by permission of the author.

mension. As we noted earlier, one problem is
that different investigators have conceptualized the control dimension in different ways.
If restrictiveness is conceptualized as setting
narrow limits on the child's behavior, as an
overprotective parent might, or as intrusively
interfering with the child's plans and relationships, then restrictiveness is not ordinarily associated with desirable outcomes in the
child. If, on the other hand, restrictiveness is
conceptualized as demanding a high level of
responsibility from the child by assigning duties, insisting on mature, prosocial behavior,
and consistently enforcing these demands (a
style of parenting we referred to earlier as firm
control), then it is associated with a variety of
positive outcomes in the child: helpfulness,
cooperation, altruism, friendliness, independence, leadership, self-confidence, and self-
control (Maccoby, 1980).

We should note that some of the effects of
parental control are modified by where the
parents fall on the warmth-hostility dimension. In general, the positive effects of the
control dimensions are magnified by parental
warmth. In other words, the benefits of a de-

manding, strict, and nonintrusive parenting
style are magnified if the parent is also affectionate. Hostility, however, can be harmful:
Demandingness and strictness in a hostile
context may produce withdrawal and emotionality (Baumrind, 1967), and combinations
of permissiveness and hostility are especially
conducive to aggression (Becker, 1964; Martin, 1975).

Baumrind's Typology of Parenting Styles

Outline of Baumrind's Scheme   Baumrind (1967, 1973) has conducted several di-
rect-observational studies of parent-child interaction and has found that many parents
can be classified into one of three types, each
type defined by the presence of a certain
combination of disciplinary practices and attitudes. The three types of parents are defined as follows:

1. *Authoritarian.* These parents control their
children by enforcing an absolute set of standards, which they rarely justify to the children

or let the children challenge. They favor power assertion, discourage verbal give-and-take, and sometimes reject their children.

2. *Authoritative.* These parents score high on four dimensions. First, they exercise firm control by consistently enforcing directives and resisting counter-pressures from their children (even if this sometimes means using physical punishment). Second, authoritative parents make demands for maturity by pressuring their children to perform according to their abilities, socially and intellectually, and by encouraging independence and decision making. Third, they offer reasons to justify their requests for compliance, solicit their children's opinions, and allow themselves to be influenced by their children's arguments. Finally, they provide discipline in the context of a warm, emotionally supportive home environment.

3. *Permissive.* These parents act in an accepting, positive way toward their children's impulses and actions, avoid exercising control, use little punishment, make few maturity demands for household responsibility and order, and generally allow the children to regulate their own activities.

Correlates of Baumrind's Typology The clearest finding from Baumrind's own studies (1967, 1973) is that authoritative parents have socially competent preschoolers. Baumrind describes "competent" children as friendly, happy, independent, bold in approaching new people and situations, self-reliant, self-controlling, socially responsible, and well-adjusted with their peers. Children of authoritarian and permissive parents are less competent, less self-confident, and more immature. Both of these latter styles of child-rearing are associated with more overt aggression and negativism in the children (especially boys) than is authoritative parenting.

INFLUENCES ON PARENTS' BEHAVIOR

Thus far we have discussed parental influences on the child. It is time now to examine factors influencing the parent's choice of disciplinary tactics. Why, despite its ill effects, is

brutal and erratic physical punishment employed by some parents? What makes other parents favor more "psychological" techniques such as inductive reasoning or love-withdrawal?

Interestingly, parents' personalities, as assessed from their scores on personality inventories, are not good predictors of their favored disciplinary tactics. In fact, parents do not exhibit much traitlike consistency in their use of a particular strategy, and most reveal much situational specificity in their choice of a tactic. Parents generally prefer certain techniques, and they switch back and forth among them in response to a host of other variables, including their mood, the nature of the children's transgressions, and the economic and social stresses from which they are suffering (Grusec & Kuczynski, 1980).

We shall discuss two classes of influences on parent behavior: (a) the child's characteristics and behaviors, and (b) the family's social position and the social and economic stresses to which the family is subjected. We shall also consider factors contributing to child abuse.

Child Effects

Child variables that influence adult disciplinary methods include the child's sex, temperament, physical attractiveness, age, and birth order. How the child misbehaves and reacts to discipline are also important. We will consider these factors individually.

Sex Are boys treated more harshly than girls? Overall, boys receive more power assertive discipline, and especially physical punishment, than girls. Parents use inductive reasoning more frequently with girls (Zussman, 1978). Even though most parents regard aggression as more appropriate for boys than for girls, they punish aggression more harshly in boys (Maccoby & Jacklin, 1974). Earlier we pointed out that boys are criticized by their teachers more than girls, but the criticism is structured in such a way that boys interpret it to mean they just are not trying hard enough, whereas girls take it to mean they are incompetent (Dweck & Reppucci, 1973; Yarrow, Waxler, & Scott, 1971).

Findings such as these have implications for the development of sex differences in a variety of social behaviors, such as aggression and academic achievement. But little is known regarding the causes for the sex differences in discipline. Are there differences in the ways boys and girls behave that elicit their different treatments by adults? Are adults more afraid of hurting girls than boys? Do parents and teachers hold different expectations for girls and boys that influence the discipline they receive? At this point, we do not know.

Temperament   The main principle underlying adult reactions to children's temperaments is one of reciprocity: Adults respond negatively to obnoxious children and positively to satisfying children. "Difficult" infants (those who have irregular cycles of sleeping, eating, and eliminating; are slow to adapt to change; are fussy and prone to withdrawal; and are given to bad moods) have mothers who take less pleasure in talking to, holding, or playing games with their babies (Milliones, 1978). Children who are loving, warm, responsive, and socially involved elicit more interest and affection from adults, and adults favor reasoning and love-oriented tactics when disciplining such children (Cantor & Gelfand, 1977; Keller & Bell, 1979; Teyber, Messe, & Stollak, 1977). Impatient, competitive and hyperactive children elicit more intrusive attempts at control, more criticism, more power assertion, less praise, and less interest in their play and work activities (Cunningham & Barkley, 1979; Matthews, 1977; Stevens-Long, 1973). Adult men seem particularly annoyed by rudeness and angry defiance in boys and are likely to react to such behavior with power assertive discipline (Teyber et al., 1977). Parents should be wary of impulsively or habitually using a possibly undesirable technique of discipline simply because some aspect of a child's behavior invites it.

Physical Attractiveness   The sheer physical attractiveness of children may be an important determinant of discipline. Dion (1972) discovered that transgressions by a physically attractive child were evaluated less negatively than identical transgressions by a less attractive child. Adults were also less likely to attribute dishonesty and delinquency to a more attractive child.

Age and Birth Order   Few studies have examined how parents change their control tactics as children grow older, though it is obvious that parents do adjust their discipline to their children's ages. Because of the experience they gain with their first-born child, parents are usually less anxious with their later-borns. They improve in their understanding of what is expected of children. Still, extra children put an added strain on a household. Zussman (1978) reports that as family size increases, parents use more power assertion and less induction with their sons. However, an opposite relationship holds for girls: As family size grows, parents use less power assertion and more induction when disciplining their daughters. The reason for the sex difference is unclear. In a comparison of child-rearing practices used with male twins versus those used with males who were only children, Lytton, Conway, and Sauve (1977) found that the parents of twins were less controlling, used less reasoning, showed less praise, approval, and affection, and were more inconsistent in their enforcement of directives. The twins showed less internalization of standards. Thus it appears that as family size increases, boys become less likely to experience "good" methods of discipline. The findings for girls are not as clear-cut or understandable.

The Child's Misdeed and Reaction to Discipline   Parents fit the punishment to the crime. Misdemeanors that involve psychological harm to others elicit reasoning, but many other transgressions (e.g., ignoring a request, breaking a valuable object, or fighting) provoke power assertive discipline (Grusec &

Kuczynski, 1980). How children react to discipline is important, too. Children who react defiantly to their parents' attempts to control them elicit more punishment than children who, for example, show remorse by offering to repair the damage they have caused (Parke, Sawin, & Kreling, 1974). Parents repeat tactics that are successful, but they drop those that are not. In addition, they are likely to escalate punishment to a high intensity and maintain it there if they find it to be an effective way to control their children (Mulhern & Passman, 1979; Parke & Collmer, 1975).

The Family's Social Position and Stresses on the Family Unit

Social Class Lower- and middle-class parents stress different values and utilize certain disciplinary practices to different degrees. Lower-class parents stress "surface appearance" values such as obedience, neatness, and staying out of trouble; middle-class parents are more concerned with engendering happiness, independence, curiosity, and self-control. Lower-class parents use more power assertion and are more authoritarian and arbitrary; their middle-class counterparts are more often permissive or authoritative, use induction more often, and are more responsive to their children's point of view (Maccoby, 1980; Zussman, 1978).

What accounts for the social-class differences? There are several possibilities. Perhaps parents are imitating the techniques their own parents used on them. Or, perhaps lower-class parents are less able to defend their demands with reasoning, and so have to rely more on power assertion (Zussman, 1978). The greater economic and social stress in lower-class homes may reduce parents' self-esteem as well as lower their level of communication with others (Hess & Shipman, 1967). Middle-class parents may strive to foster initiative and may use reasoning and negotiation when they discipline because they

found these strategies necessary for career success (Maccoby, 1980). It is possible, too, that lower-class parents are more inclined to perceive social relationships in power terms. As Hoffman (1970b) points out, internalization is really only the worry of the middle class, and hence it is only middle-class parents who are concerned about employing the kinds of discipline that will promote internalized control in their children. Lower-class parents, because they do not always feel that they have control of their own lives, may forecast that their children will always be under the control and direction of other people and environmental circumstances, so they may be less concerned with teaching internal standards for self-direction.

Divorce How divorced parents deal with the task of raising young children was studied in a longitudinal project by Hetherington, Cox, and Cox (1977). Parent-child relations in homes headed by divorced mothers are definitely strained. The first year following the divorce is the worst, with mother-child disharmony and disorganization peaking toward the end of the year. During this first year, the divorced mother reports feeling "trapped" by her custody responsibilities and limited social life. Compared to parents in intact families, she makes fewer maturity demands of her children, communicates less well, shows less affection, and uses discipline more inconsistently. She tries to control her children by becoming more restrictive and by giving more commands, but the children tend to ignore or resist these attempts at control. Over the second year, things get better. The divorced mother generally decreases her futile attempts at authoritarian control and becomes more effective.

Divorced fathers with visiting rights at first tend to adopt an "Every day is Christmas" attitude by being permissive and indulgent. As time passes, however, the father often becomes more detached, visits less often, and shows less affection and attention when available. These disruptions in normal parenting are associated with a variety of social and cognitive problems in children, such as poor impulse control, more aggression, reduced symbolic play, poor school achievement, and lowered scores on performance subtests of IQ evaluations. These problems are usually much more severe for boys than for girls (Hetherington, 1979).

Child Abuse

What pushes some parents to carry "discipline" to the extreme and inflict serious injury on their children? The causes and correlates of child abuse are numerous, and both psychological and social in nature. When several contributing factors occur together, the probability of abuse is dramatically increased. We will briefly mention four classes of variables that are implicated in child abuse situations. (For excellent reviews of the important issues involved in conceptualizing and researching child abuse, see Belsky, 1980, and Parke & Collmer, 1975).

First is the parents' personality and upbringing. Parents' scores on personality tests are not strong predictors of abuse, but parents who score high on a paper-and-pencil test of Authoritarianism (who perceive the world in terms of power relationships, who divide people into the strong versus the weak, etc.) and who have difficulty controlling aggression do run a greater risk of coming into contact with child welfare authorities for abusing their children. It has also been shown that many abusive parents were themselves abused or neglected, physically or emotionally, when they were children.

Second, a parent-child pair may establish patterns of interaction that lead to abuse (or may fail to establish patterns of interaction that help prevent abuse). Abuse-prone interactions can be established as early as the infancy period. Low birth-weight and premature infants constitute a high-risk population for abuse. Premature infants tend to have unattractive facial features and body proportions; their veins may be visible beneath skin that is transparent and bears the scars of var-

ious hospital tests and procedures; their cry is often high-pitched and obnoxious; and they are slow to smile and make eye contact. These infants are at risk for interaction problems with their parents, especially if they have been separated from their mothers at birth and placed in incubators for several weeks. It seems that prevention of early mother-infant interaction reduces the mother's affectionate interaction with her baby and undermines her confidence in caring for the newborn (Leifer, Leiderman, Barnett, & Williams, 1972; Seashore, Leifer, Barnett, & Leiderman, 1973). Infants who are irritable, whose distress cries are difficult to soothe, and whose motor and cognitive skills are sluggish are often overrepresented in abused samples.

But, of course, not all parents react to irritating or disappointing qualities in their infants with abuse. In an interesting study, Frodi and Lamb (1980) monitored abusive mothers' and nonabusive mothers' reactions to a baby who was displaying various behaviors on videotape. The abusive mothers reported feeling more annoyed and less sympathetic when the baby cried. Furthermore, they reported feeling more indifferent when the infant smiled. Thus it seems that certain combinations of infant and parental characteristics may increase the probability of abuse. Further research aimed at identifying the combinations of child, parent, and situational factors conducive to abuse should be of great value to parent education programs.

A third variable influencing abuse is the family's relationship to society. Economic stress, such as that brought about by loss of employment, seems to contribute to abuse. Another striking feature of many families in which children are abused is their social isolation: Family members usually have few friends, such families appear to be cut off from the rest of the community, and they are not part of an extended family network. Garbarino and Sherman (1980) have reported that neighborhoods with certain characteristics—those with a run-down appearance, limited community resources, and populated by people with an "all take and no give" attitude—are at risk for child maltreatment.

Finally, there is the likelihood that the broader norms and values held in a society influence the incidence of abuse. The American acceptance of violence as a means of settling disputes and the attitude that children are the property of their parents may foster an atmosphere conducive to abuse. The fact that many parents take a "me first" approach to life in which child-rearing is regarded not as a delightful and satisfying responsibility but as an impediment to self-indulgence may also contribute to the serious problem of child abuse (Belsky, 1980).

IS THERE A RECIPE FOR SUCCESSFUL CHILD-REARING?

We have reviewed the effects of various child-rearing practices on the child's development and also some of the factors that lead parents to employ the tactics they do. On the basis of the literature we have discussed, is it possible to suggest a set of concrete guidelines for parents to follow in child-rearing? To some degree, parenting is an art, requiring sensitivity and creativity, but several principles derived from the findings we have reviewed may be worthwhile for parents to remember.

First, parents should foster an atmosphere of warmth, happiness, and mutual support and interest among family members. Affection tends to be reciprocated among family members and renders deviant behavior less likely. Parental love and interest facilitate positive moods in children, and children who are happy and contented behave more altruistically, display more self-control when tempted to misbehave, and generally behave in more mature and prosocial ways. Warmth also enhances the effectiveness of parental discipline. Parents should strive to develop some compatibility of goals with their children. Joining children in activities and pointing out the importance of each family member's behavior for the welfare of the whole family should be helpful. Overall, the fostering of warmth and joint values binds children to their families in a positive way, making the children more willing to accept guidance while enabling the parents to exercise what control is needed without having to apply heavy disciplinary pressure.

A second guideline is that parents ought to concentrate their disciplinary efforts on promoting desirable behaviors rather than on eliminating undesirable behaviors. It is true, as we have noted, that children are unlikely to learn that society frowns on certain behaviors unless the children are discouraged or punished for performing them. However, focusing one's disciplinary efforts on attempting to eliminate unwanted behavior is a deficient strategy for socialization. Parents must balance their attempts to eliminate the undesirable with deliberate, concerted efforts to establish habits of mature, desirable, prosocial behavior. In fact, when parents focus on strengthening the positive, the negative behaviors often have a way of taking care of themselves. Remember that parents who take pains to establish habits of considerateness, sympathy, and helpfulness in their children succeed not only in implanting these habits but also in reducing their children's expression of negative behaviors like aggression. Thus parents must consciously decide on the characteristics they would like their children to display and then go about the business of promoting the appropriate behaviors. They must request, insist on, and praise positive, age-appropriate forms of behavior. They should facilitate the child's development of prosocial self-perceptions by directly attributing prosocial qualities to the children (e.g., "I'll bet you shared your doll with Susie because you're the kind of girl who likes to make other people feel happy").

Third, parents should firmly enforce the demands they make on children, both when trying to elicit desirable behavior and when trying to eliminate unwanted behavior. Too many parents have the unfortunate habit of making a request and then not backing it up if the child ignores it or balks at it. Firm enforcement, of course, will sometimes necessitate the use of power assertion—a parent may use the time-out method, for example, or physical punishment.

Our fourth principle, however, stresses that parents should avoid unnecessary use of power assertion. Aversive consequences should be used only to help children understand that certain behaviors will not be tolerated, to gain compliance, or to capture their attention so that reasoning can be administered. Other techniques of eliminating behavior should be tried before resorting to physical discipline.

Fifth, parents should justify their disciplinary actions through inductive reasoning. This method highlights the inherently good or bad qualities of certain behaviors and emphasizes to children the causal role they can play in producing or preventing certain outcomes and emotions for other people. Reasoning in this manner should promote in children a sense of responsibility for their actions. Adults should listen to children, give them a chance to explain their actions, and, when appropriate, even alter their discipline in response to the children's arguments.

This brings us to the sixth point: Parents should strive to give children feelings of control over their environments. Allowing children to participate in family decision making, encouraging them to solve their own problems, and making social rewards and other consequences clearly contingent upon their behavior ought to help. Encouraging children to attempt new skills and structuring success experiences should support their self-perceptions of competence.

Earlier we remarked that an important part of successful child-rearing involves firm control, or making requests for mature behavior of children and strictly enforcing these requests—with power assertion, if necessary. But this raises a perplexing question: Do parents who are demanding and strict have children who also feel in control? Commenting on this, Maccoby (1980, p. 387) states, "Perhaps the dilemma is more apparent than real. Perhaps when the parent sets consistent and age-appropriate requirements for the child's

behavior and rewards the child for compliance, the child comes to know what to do to satisfy the parents and how to get the reward. Thus, the child is in control of the outcome and at the same time meets parental demands; parent and child are simultaneously in control." Viewed from this perspective, parents who exert firm control encourage children to develop a sense of control over their lives.

Seventh, parents must be consistent in their approach to discipline. This does not mean that parents must employ the same tactic regardless of the nature and the degree of the child's transgression, nor does it mean that parents should not maintain an open mind and experiment to see which tactics work best. It does mean, however, that parents must be consistent in their discouragement or encouragement of particular responses. Consistent reactions help the child predict, control, and develop a sense of trust in the social environment. Furthermore, numerous studies show that children who suffer sudden, arbitrary punishment for misbehaving on some occasions, but who are allowed to get away with, or are even rewarded for, similar behavior at other times, are especially likely to develop patterns of aggressive and delinquent behavior (Martin, 1975).

Finally, parents should be models of controlled, planned behavior. They should be careful to practice what they preach. In the next chapter we shall examine in detail the tremendous influence of modeling on social development.

TOWARD A DEVELOPMENTAL MODEL OF SOCIALIZATION: INTEGRATING PRINCIPLES OF SOCIAL LEARNING AND CAUSAL ATTRIBUTION

Thus far we have paid little attention to developmental factors in child-rearing. We have said little about whether children change in the way they interpret and react to various disciplinary tactics as they develop, and we have not discussed whether parents should vary their child-rearing goals as their children mature. Here we offer some speculations about developmental factors in child-rearing and socialization.

In our view, successful socialization is a gradual developmental process that can best be understood and facilitated by appealing to principles of both social learning and causal attribution. We suspect that effective child-rearing typically originates by implanting in children habits of desirable conduct that are at first clearly externally motivated. However, as children mature, internal attributions, such as a belief that the self is intrinsically motivated to do good deeds, increasingly contribute to children's motivation to perform desirable conduct in the absence of external controls.

We have already cited evidence that desirable development depends upon firm control, or parents' unwavering enforcement of demands for prosocial behavior in the early years of their children's lives. Attribution theorists (e.g., Lepper, 1981) believe that it is essential for parents to enforce these early demands for prosocial conduct in ways that prevent children from perceiving that others are forcing them to perform the desired behavior. We question whether it is possible, or even particularly desirable, for parents always to induce prosocial conduct in children without the children realizing that they are being externally forced. True, it may sometimes be possible for parents to reduce children's perceptions of external control by accompanying forceful discipline with inductive reasoning, as we discussed earlier, but there are many occasions when parents are simply unable to hide from children the fact that they are being externally forced into compliance.

Furthermore, results of the field studies suggest that when children clearly realize that a behavior is externally demanded, they are more apt to begin self-regulation of the behavior. In the field studies we cited, parents who were effective at teaching their children desirable conduct seemed to be communicating to their children, in one way or another, the following message: "You have no choice but to comply with my request for ma-

ture behavior. It is very important behavior. Noncompliance is not an option and will not be tolerated." In many cases, in order to achieve compliance, parents had to resort to various degrees of power assertion, which almost certainly caused children to realize that their compliance was externally forced. Our interpretation of these findings is that forceful commands to children to engage in prosocial behavior facilitate rather than undermine internalization of the behavior—even though the commands may (initially, at least) elicit attributions of external motivation.

This analysis suggests that social learning theory may more accurately account for the origins of effective socialization than attribution theory. By issuing and enforcing directives for desirable conduct, parents are emphasizing the importance of the behavior and are motivating children to regulate their behavior to conform to externally imposed realities.

Although children's initial motivation for conforming to parental requests may typically be external, as children develop, internal sources of motivation may also assume importance in mediating desirable conduct. Suppose a parent has succeeded in teaching his daughter always to share with a friend in need. The parent may have had to rely on forceful discipline to achieve this result, so the girl may initially believe that her main reason for helping others is to avoid getting punished—a rather external attribution. However, as the girl gets older it is likely that she will sometimes share even when no authority figure is watching, simply from force of habit. Now is the time for the child to update her attributions, making them more internal (e.g., "If I am doing this even though I don't have to, then I must want to do it"). In sum, we imagine internal attributions probably assume importance in socialized behavior primarily after habits of moral conduct have been implanted by external means.

We do not mean to imply that as children get older, principles of social learning no longer apply and that principles of causal attribution completely take over in mediating the effects of child-rearing. Even among older children, external sanctions and incentives continue to provide information about the sorts of behaviors children should learn to regulate. It is just that as children develop, perceived internal motivations for performing desirable acts become an additional factor motivating children to conform to society's rules.

The notion that socialized behavior often has its roots in externally implanted habits does not mean that parents should focus exclusively on external incentives to obtain compliance in the early years of their children's lives. Numerous field studies reveal that forceful insistence on prosocial and moral behavior is effective only if the parents generally maintain an atmosphere of warmth and respect for the child, justify their disciplinary actions with inductive reasoning, encourage verbal give-and-take with the child, and are responsive to the child's point of view (e.g., Baumrind, 1973). And the ills of using certain varieties of unnecessarily harsh discipline (e.g., severe physical punishment) have been amply demonstrated. We have also seen that there is a considerable amount that parents can and should do to help their children eventually develop internal attributions for performing desirable behaviors. For example, once children do spontaneously perform desirable behaviors, parents can offer social reinforcement and verbal attributions of prosocial dispositions— "Did you see how you helped Tom without anyone telling you to? I know you like to make your friends feel better whenever they are unhappy."

In sum, effective socialization may originate in habits of self-regulation that are externally motivated, but as children develop, their internal motivation for desirable conduct also begins to assume importance.

SUMMARY

Children learn from their social environments (family members, teachers, peers,

television characters, and other people) in two ways—directly and vicariously. Children learn directly through the personal interactions they have with other people, such as through the instruction and discipline they receive from their parents at home. Vicarious learning involves observing the actions of others. In this chapter we presented the processes involved in direct learning; the following chapter discusses processes of vicarious learning.

Two theories figure prominently in contemporary theory and research about child-rearing practices and their effects: social learning theory and causal attribution theory.

According to social learning theory, children are constantly forming and refining their conceptions of the sorts of behavior that society deems desirable or undesirable for people like themselves. The discipline children experience at home is a major contributor to their conceptions of praiseworthy and blameworthy behavior, or their "response-outcome contingency rules." Presumably, once children know what society does or does not want from them, they begin to regulate their behavior to conform to these expectations. Social learning theorists suggest that successful socialization rests upon parents instructing their children to perform in desirable ways and to inhibit undesirable behavior. These requests should be firmly enforced, with external sanctions, if necessary. Parental "firm control"—firm and consistent enforcement of demands for mature behavior—is indeed associated with desirable socialization outcomes in children, especially if parents are also warm, justify their discipline with verbal reasoning, and avoid using more force than is necessary to achieve compliance.

According to attribution theory, parents who rely on powerful external incentives, such as the threat of severe punishment or a promise of an attractive material reward, are sensitizing children to the fact that their behavior is under the control of external contingencies. If this is so, children may not engage in the desired activity when the external contingency is discontinued. In contrast, if parents can manage to elicit desirable behavior from children in subtle ways, preventing them from realizing that they were externally coerced, then presumably the children will conclude that they are intrinsically disposed to perform the behavior and will continue to do so when they are not under the watchful eyes of adults. There is evidence that excessively harsh punishment and unnecessary, manipulative use of material rewards may sometimes undermine adults' efforts at socialization, as this theory suggests.

A model of effective socialization may involve principles of both social learning and causal attribution. We proposed that in the early years of the child's life parents should, as the social learning theorists suggest, strive to establish habits of desirable conduct in their children. At first, children may perceive their motivation for conforming to their parents' demands as external (e.g., fear of punishment). As children mature, however, and begin occasionally to observe themselves performing desirable conduct in the absence of external surveillance, it should be possible for them to update their attributions to become more internal, thus producing a more mature basis for adhering to society's values.

There are some recurring trends in the literature that suggest guidelines for child-rearing. By fostering an atmosphere of warmth and mutual interest among family members, parents increase the chances that their children will display prosocial behavior, increase the likelihood that their children will

remain in their sphere of influence, and enhance the effectiveness of their disciplinary efforts. Parents should concentrate their efforts on promoting positive behavior, not only because positive behavior is itself desirable but also because prosocial habits compete with and reduce undesirable behavior. Parents should make age-appropriate demands for maturity and firmly enforce them. Because physical punishment and other power assertive techniques are associated with several negative side effects (e.g., imitation of parental aggression, attribution of one's good behavior to external rather than internal factors, and avoidance of the punitive agents), parents should limit the use of power assertion to the minimum amount necessary to get children to listen to the parents' reasoning and to let them know that requests for maturity are important enough to be enforced. Parents should justify their demands through reasoning and be responsive to their children's point of view. Children should be encouraged to engage in activities and decisions that foster feelings of independence, control, and self-efficacy. Parents must be consistent in their enforcement of sanctions, but they should appreciate that different tactics may be required for different transgressions and that the same tactic may have quite different effects on children with different temperaments and of different ages. Finally, parents should take pains to guarantee that their children are exposed to models of prosocial, competent behavior.

4 Social Learning: The Role of Modeling

This chapter deals with how children learn by observing the actions of others. Can you imagine how impossibly tedious the socialization process would be if children could not learn by example? The capacity to learn by observation enables children to acquire large, integrated patterns of behavior without having to form them gradually through direct experience. In fact, the prospects for our very survival would be slim indeed if human beings could learn only by suffering the consequences of trial-and-error actions: Imagine teaching children to swim, adolescents to drive cars, or medical students to perform surgery by having them discover the appropriate behavior through the consequences of their own successes and failures (Bandura, 1977). By observing the actions of influential social models—parents, brothers, sisters, playmates, teachers, and even television characters—children's personalities, competencies, social behaviors, and even their conceptions of how their social world functions are dramatically shaped and transformed.

Modern interest in the influence of social models can be traced to Freud. Psychoanalytic theory stressed the process of *identification*, or the idea that children's personalities are strongly influenced by their desire to take on the motives, attitudes, morals, and behaviors of their like-sex parent. Parents do, of course, serve as important models for their children. But subsequent theorists soon recognized that the influence of social models was not restricted to that of children's same-sex parent. Partly to get away from the Freudian connotations of the term *identification*, many psychologists opted for the more general term *imitation,* using it to refer to any occasion when a child matches his or her overt behavior to that of a model. An important part of this chapter involves explaining how Freudian theory originally inspired much of the work on children's imitation, but eventually lost popularity as alternative conceptualizations of the role of modeling in social learning were proposed.

Much of the early work on children's imitation focused on factors that cause children to adopt specific actions they have seen displayed by a model. What makes a girl scold or nurture her doll in ways that resemble how her mother has treated her? Why does a boy imitate aggressive acts he has seen in a television cartoon? But focusing on children's imitation of specific acts was soon recognized to be an insufficient approach to the study of modeling influences. Children learn far more than specific actions through modeling. Consider some of the other, more abstract products of children's observational learning.

Children learn important rules about the appropriateness of various forms of conduct from observing models. By detecting regularities in the consequences of other people's actions, children can abstract the common features of blameworthy and praiseworthy behavior. If children see that other children are regularly discouraged or punished for aggression, for example, they can form the rule that deliberate acts that lead to the injury of another person are inappropriate, and they should be more likely to inhibit acting aggressively themselves when opportunities arise. Thus modeling exposures can teach children not only what to imitate but also what not to imitate. This is why it is often said that modeling helps children take shortcuts through the socialization process, allowing them to learn important response-outcome contingencies vicariously that they might otherwise have had to "learn the hard way" through direct experience.

Children also acquire general rules of speech and language through observational learning. After hearing enough people add the letter "s" to form the plural of a noun, most children will eventually grasp the rule, sometimes so well that they make up new words like "sheeps" and "mouses," though they eventually learn the exceptions to this rule. In addition, children impose structure on the behaviors they observe in others, organizing the information in memory in particular ways. For instance, children encode responses they see performed more often by girls than by boys as "girl-appropriate," and girls will strive to imitate this class of behavior, while boys avoid it. Observational learning, then, involves more than motor mimicry and is an active, constructive enterprise rather than a passive, receptive process (Bandura, 1977).

This chapter begins with a survey of theories of modeling: Freud's original theory (and other views inspired by Freudian thinking), cognitive-developmental theory, conditioning theory, and social learning theory. After evaluating these theories, we discuss in detail the processes underlying children's observational learning and imitation. We consider the cognitive processes involved in acquiring and remembering a model's actions, and how children learn mental rules that cause them to limit their imitation to certain models, responses, and situations. One of the most powerful influences on children's observational learning is the television set. Therefore, we evaluate the impact this "early window" to the world has on children. Finally, we look at modeling as a tool of behavior modification. Can therapists and educators help children overcome irrational fears or learn new social and cognitive skills by exposing them to the right kinds of models?

THEORIES OF MODELING

The story of how theories of modeling have evolved is a fascinating one, beautifully illustrating how psychological theories are constantly engaged in a battle for survival of the fittest. Freud believed that children imitated their parents for one of two reasons: to become more similar to a parent for whom they had developed a sexual attachment, or to defend against their fear of being rejected or physically harmed by a hostile and threatening parent. Many psychologists saw some truth to Freud's ideas, but they found his formulations difficult to test empirically, and they were put off by his emphasis on sexual motivation and his view that imitation sometimes reflects the operation of a defense mechanism. Several early learning theorists tried to "translate" some of Freud's hypotheses into the language of learning theory, and a number of experiments were conducted to see which of these translations had merit. Other theorists found it more useful to scrap psychoanalytic theory altogether and proposed comprehensive new theories to account for observational learning and imitation. Perhaps the most influential and widely accepted of these is Bandura's social learning theory. We shall examine the major theories of modeling, beginning with Freud's theory and those that developed from it, and ending with Bandura's social learning model.

Freudian Theory and its Derivatives

Original Psychoanalytic Theory Freud distinguished between two sorts of identification, both of which were believed to operate within the family. The first, *primary identification,* was thought to occur as early as the first few months of an infant's life and to be motivated by the id's attempts to maintain contact with someone to whom the infant had become sexually attached. Remember that because infants find oral stimulation sexually gratifying, they form an attachment to the person who feeds them, usually the mother. To Freud, many of the infant's earliest vocalizations, smiles, and facial expressions represented attempts to imitate aspects of a sexually attached person in order to intensify and sustain a close rela-

tionship with this person. In many respects, early imitations were regarded as similar to the infant's sucking response: Both were interpreted as attempts to incorporate into one's own personality aspects of a sexually attached figure.

Freud did not believe that children were capable of his second type of imitation, called *secondary identification,* until they developed their ego. This type of identification represents an ego defense mechanism and is sometimes called *defensive identification.* Freud believed that when a child is threatened in some fashion by a parent, he or she becomes anxious; the ego then reduces this anxiety by directing the child to adopt the attitudes, values, behaviors, and emotional reactions of the threatening person. The premise behind this is that by becoming more similar to the enemy, a person can reduce the likelihood of attack.

Freud distinguished between two varieties of secondary identification, though both were considered to reflect the ego's attempts to deal with real or imaginary threats from parents. The first subtype is called *anaclitic identification* (deriving from the Greek word meaning "dependent") and is motivated by the child's fear of losing parental love. As infants mature, it frequently is necessary for parents to discipline them and to temporarily suspend affectionate interaction with them in order to enforce mature behavior. When this occurs, children may fear that their parents don't love them anymore. This, of course, is anxiety-arousing and motivates the ego to try to identify with the parent. It is as if the ego reasons that by becoming a little like the parent, it can hang on to the parent's love.

Freud is most famous for his second variety of defensive identification, known as *Oedipal* or *aggressive identification.* Beginning at about age 3, children are believed to develop a strong, conscious desire to have sexual relations with the opposite-sex parent. However, they refrain from acting on their impulses because they fear retaliation from the jealous same-sex parent: Boys are afraid that their fathers will castrate them, and girls fear that their mothers will do something resembling the violent act that made them females in the first place.

The conflict between the child's sexual urges and feared retaliation from the parent arouses intense anxiety, motivating the child's ego to identify with the threatening same-sex parent. Through identification, the child can reduce the likelihood of attack from the parent while at the same time vicariously achieve some sexual gratification with the opposite-sex parent. Freud believed that by identifying with the same-sex parent, the child acquires the culturally valued motives, attitudes, beliefs, conscience, and sex-role behaviors that his or her parent presumably had acquired through parental identification a generation earlier. Eventually, after identification is complete, the normal child represses the entire Oedipal experience. This supposedly is why we don't remember it as adults.

Interestingly, Freud believed that the process of parental identification was not as complete or as strong in girls as in boys: Since girls lack external genitals, their fears about what their mothers could do to punish them for their sexual advances toward their fathers were more vague than the fears of boys. Hence the motivation for parental identification was weaker in girls, and Freud believed girls were less likely than boys to develop strong moral ideals or adopt societally prescribed sex roles.

To review, Freud hypothesized three variables to motivate identification: sexual attachment to a caretaker, fear of losing a beloved parent's affection, and fear of aggression from a parent whom the child viewed as a sexual rival. These variables were believed to motivate, respectively, primary, anaclitic, and Oedipal identification. There is actually little direct evidence to support Freud's hypotheses as they were originally stated. However, each of Freud's three types of imitation

has been reformulated by some other theorist to make it more testable. Let's briefly examine the results of this work.

Primary Identification Translated: Mowrer's Secondary Reinforcement Theory of Imitation O. H. Mowrer (1950), an early learning theorist concerned with applying conditioning principles to social development, agreed with Freud that children often imitate the actions of people they love. Mowrer denied the importance of sexual attachment, but he argued that because caregivers provide the child with food, comfort, attention, affection, and other positive reinforcers, the behaviors of the caregiver (e.g., facial expressions, smiles, vocalizations, and gestures) acquire conditioned or secondary reinforcing value. These actions thus acquire some intrinsic reinforcing properties of their own. Children imitate the responses simply because it makes them feel good.

In support of Mowrer's prediction, there is abundant evidence (from both the laboratory and the field) that children are more likely to imitate the actions of warm and affectionate models than they are the actions of cold, rejecting, or indifferent models. In a typical laboratory study, one group of children spent 15 minutes interacting with an adult model who behaved attentively and affectionately toward them, whereas a second group interacted with a cold and abrupt model (Bandura & Huston, 1961). Subsequently the model displayed a variety of novel behaviors in front of the child (e.g., playing with toys in unique ways, uttering unusual verbalizations). The children were then observed in play, with special attention given to how much the children imitated the adult's behaviors. It was discovered that children who had interacted with the nurturant model showed more imitation. In a field study examining the relationship between parental warmth and children's imitation, Hetherington (1967) first interviewed parents and then divided them up into those who expressed very warm attitudes toward their children versus those who seemed relatively aloof or indifferent about their children. Children of the former group of parents were more likely to imitate their parents when later observed in a gamelike situation in the home.

Though Mowrer's theory thus receives some support, it can hardly be considered a complete account of children's imitative tendencies. Children clearly do not imitate everything they see a warm model do, and they sometimes imitate models with whom they have had no nurturant interaction. Furthermore, warmth and reward from a model sometimes undermine children's later imitation of the model, at least for certain kinds of behaviors. For instance, an adult who noncontingently indulges a child with favors and attention can place the child in a self-indulgent mood, making the child *less* likely to imitate self-sacrificing responses (such as altruistic sharing) that the adult later displays (Bryan, 1975; Grusec, 1971). "Warmth theory" also ignores the role of cognition in children's imitation. We shall see that much of children's imitation is governed by the mental rules they formulate about the appropriateness or correctness of imitating certain actions of certain models under certain circumstances. The relative warmth of a model to whom a child has been exposed may not really be of much help in predicting the particular responses of the model that the child will choose to imitate.

Love Withdrawal as a Factor in Imitation Several writers (Hartup, 1958; Sears, Maccoby, & Levin, 1957) have proposed a "nurturance withdrawal" account of imitation. According to this view, adults who are continuously nurturant toward children are not as effective in eliciting imitation as adults who are customarily highly affectionate but occasionally abruptly withdraw their affection (as when disciplining the child). The idea is that nurturance withdrawal arouses a "dependency drive," which motivates the child to adopt aspects of the adult's actions in order to win back the adult's favor.

There is some support for this hypothesis, but research on the topic was never pursued far enough for us to evaluate the hypothesis thoroughly. In the 1960s, psychologists became wary of the notion of social drives (for an explanation, see Chapter 7), and hypotheses in which drive constructs figured prominently were ignored. However, there would seem to be many of the same problems with the nurturance-withdrawal hypothesis that exist with the warmth theory of imitation.

Revisions in Aggressive Identification Theory A number of psychologists agree with Freud that children sometimes imitate people they perceive as threatening or powerful. Sarnoff (1951), a neo-Freudian, dispensed with Freud's view that aggressive identification is necessarily motivated by threats over sexual rivalry, but he suggested that identification is one defense mechanism an individual sometimes employs when he or she is victimized by, totally dependent upon, and cannot escape from a hostile and aggressive captor.

Evidence supporting Sarnoff's view of identification is scanty and mainly anecdotal, but it is provocative nonetheless. Sarnoff points to the fact that inmates of Nazi concentration camps sometimes assumed the role of the aggressive Nazi guards by wearing swastika armbands and behaving aggressively themselves when in charge of other prisoners (Bettelheim, 1943). There are several modern cases in which victims of kidnappings, such as Patty Hearst, have adopted the values of their captors. Finally, in one of the few studies to investigate systematically Sarnoff's theory with children, researchers found that nursery-school children growing up in hostile homes (where both parents reject the child and fight frequently between themselves) have a preference for imitating whichever parent assumes the dominant role in the household (Hetherington and Frankie, 1967).

These observations confirm that children sometimes imitate threatening adults, at least under extremely hostile conditions from which there is no escape. But is it really necessary to invoke the concept of ego defense mechanism to explain this? Children may imitate threatening people because doing so realistically reduces their chances of being harmed by these people. We should also bear in mind that the conditions under which aggressive identification occurs are extreme and rare. When children have a choice of imitating an affectionate adult versus a punitive one, they prefer the former (Chartier & Weiss, 1974).

Two other theories of imitation have been derived, at least indirectly, from Freud's notion of aggressive identification. One is Whiting's (1960) *envy theory*, which holds that children imitate people whom they perceive to be jealous rivals for desired resources. Presumably, rivalry arouses the feeling of being threatened, which the ego defensively strives to reduce through identification. A second is Maccoby's (1959) and Parsons's (1955) *social power theory*, which holds that children imitate people whom they perceive to be the controllers of resources they desire. Presumably, children imitate powerful controllers in the belief that they might gain some of the prestige or resources of the controller if they follow in his or her footsteps.

An early study by Bandura, Ross, and Ross (1963a) provided a comparative test of the envy and social power theories. To see whether children are more likely to imitate rivals for desired resources or controllers of the resources, Bandura and his associates had nursery-school children interact in a playroom with two adults. One adult was introduced to the children as the owner of all the toys, orange juice, and other resources in the room; the other adult pretended to be competing with the child for the available resources. Later, both adults displayed novel behaviors before the children, and the children's imitations of each adult were assessed.

Children imitated the controller far more than the rival, supporting the social power theory rather than the envy theory.

Field studies confirm the importance of models' social power in determining whom children imitate. In a fascinating study, Hetherington (1967) tape-recorded arguments between the parents of young children and then classified each parent as either dominant or submissive (using such objective measures as which parent spoke first, who got the last word in, who interrupted whom, whose opinions prevailed, and so on). The parents were instructed to play with a set of toys in novel ways, after which the children were given an opportunity to imitate their parents. Children imitated parents classified as dominant (controlling) more than those classified as submissive, with boys showing an especially strong preference to imitate whichever parent was dominant.

Summary of Freud-Inspired Theories
We have seen that children's imitations sometimes grow out of their affection for other people, sometimes out of their fear of losing this affection, and sometimes out of their desire to become like powerful or prestigious others. But we have hinted at some problems with these views. First, children do not blindly imitate every action made by warm, threatening, or powerful models. Second, children often imitate the actions of models who possess none of these characteristics. Third, even when children do imitate models possessing these qualities, it is unnecessary to invoke Freud's original defense-mechanism interpretation. Fourth, the Freud-inspired theories neglect how children learn cognitive rules that help them decide which of the myriad of models and responses they have witnessed (acted out by parents, peers, television characters, etc.) are appropriate for them to imitate.

A fifth criticism can be directed more specifically toward Oedipal identification. Freud believed that it was mainly through identification with the same-sex parent that the child acquired culturally prescribed values, morals, and sex-appropriate behaviors. Although we shall see in later chapters that children's altruism, aggression, morality, and sex roles are indeed influenced by how much they see their parents display these behaviors, Freud simply went overboard. It is not true that children develop a generalized motive propelling them to emulate their same-sex parent in virtually all respects. Furthermore, parental identification is just one of many factors that influence the development of children's social behaviors.

Cognitive-Developmental Theory

Cognitive-developmental theorists (Kohlberg, 1969; Piaget, 1951) see children's imitative tendencies as developing in a sequence of stages, each stage depending on the degree of sophistication the child has attained in basic cognitive development. Piaget focused on describing changes in imitation in infancy and tried to relate these changes to growth in the child's cognitive apparatus. He examined, for example, the child's ability to encode a model's actions into covert visual images. Kohlberg has focused on imitation in toddlers and older children, emphasizing how children shift in their choices of models as they develop increasingly firm conceptions of their own identities, of their group memberships, and of the sorts of people they want to be like.

Both Piaget and Kohlberg see progression in children's imitation processes as intrinsically motivated. Children imitate progressively more complex, difficult, and challenging patterns of action simply because it is fun and because it makes them feel more competent. They are excited by the challenge of trying to master action patterns they see displayed by others, and their feelings of self-esteem are bolstered when they finally succeed. There is an innate drive toward mastery. Presumably, children are always disposed to try to conquer behavior patterns that are slightly different from or more advanced than their current level of mastery, so there is always a pull in the direction of imitating progressively more mature modes of behavior. Thus the process of imitative development is fairly automatic and self-propelling; it does not depend on any obvious external motivators, such as the expectation of approval or praise from family or peers for taking on the characteristics of certain models.

Piaget's Stages   From observing the early imitations of his own three children, Piaget (1951) painted a detailed picture of some early developments in infant imitation. Piaget concluded that for the first 3 or 4 months, the infant will copy an adult only if the adult has just copied something the infant has done. If an infant shakes a rattle and then an adult shakes a rattle, the infant may shake the rattle again. Piaget believed that infants of this age are capable of sustaining only those actions that they had begun themselves. In addition, he thought that they were not able to differentiate actions of others from their own and that, for them, copying a model really amounted to copying themselves. It is as if infants, having started something interesting, just want to keep the interesting spectacle going.

Piaget observed that at around 4 months, infants begin to imitate without first being mimicked. They may copy an adult shaking a rattle, for instance, without first shaking the rattle themselves. Again it looks as though infants hope that by imitating the adult, the adult will continue making the interesting response. However, at this age infants can only imitate responses they can see themselves make (they cannot imitate facial expressions, for example), and they cannot imitate responses they have never performed before.

Piaget believed that a third stage starts at around 8 months of age and is marked by the ability of infants to imitate responses that they cannot see themselves make (e.g., grimaces). In the fourth stage, beginning at around 1 year, infants for the first time can imitate new responses, ones they have never made.

Finally, at about 16 to 18 months, infants show deferred imitation: They can imitate new actions in the model's absence, long after having seen the model display the behavior. Obviously this requires a capacity for imaginal representation. At this point, imitation plays a significant role in the children's social development. They begin to imitate increasingly complex sequences of action patterns displayed by parents, siblings, television characters, and so on, and they begin to use these action sequences in social ways (e.g., communicating with parents or playing with peers). Piaget regarded imitation as a major form of accommodation: By imitating others, children are restructuring their understanding of the social world and developing new ways of relating to it.

Critique of Piaget's View We must bear in mind that Piaget's stages, though based on observation of his own children, are purely hypothetical. Recent data suggest that Piaget may have been right on some points, but wrong on others.

Some researchers question whether Piaget underestimated the imitative capacities of the very young infant. Piaget had said infants cannot imitate responses they cannot see themselves make until they are about 8 months old. However, Meltzoff and Moore (1977) found that infants as young as 2 weeks imitated a model's lip movement, mouth opening, tongue protrusion, and finger flexion. The infants imitated the responses even though the model had initiated them (i.e., the model was not imitating the infant) and some of the responses were obviously ones the infants could not see themselves make. Hayes and Watson (1981) failed to confirm Meltzoff and Moore's findings, however, so the issue remains open.

In a study of older infants, McCall, Parke, and Kavanaugh (1977) concluded that Piaget was probably correct in suggesting that infants cannot imitate novel responses, ones

they have never made before, until late in the first year. These researchers also found, in agreement with Piaget, that children do not display much deferred imitation until close to their second birthday.

Piaget's view that infants' imitative skills appear in stages also has been challenged. After scrutinizing studies of infant imitation, Parton (1976) concluded that the various imitative capacities of infants do not unfold in a fixed sequence of stages. Instead, certain skills develop simultaneously, but they mature at different ages.

In addition to the hypotheses we have reviewed thus far, we must credit Piaget with another interesting hypothesis about imitation in infancy. According to Piaget, infants may be motivated to imitate because of their expectations that the people being imitated will imitate in return. Infants certainly are frequently imitated by their caregivers and they clearly delight in being the object of their caregivers' imitations. When imitated, infants often smile broadly and repeat the imitated response or try something else to get the adult to imitate them again (Haugan & McIntire, 1972; McCall et al., 1977; Piaget, 1951). Maybe infants enjoy being imitated because it leads to the cognition of "I have an influence" (McCall et al., 1977). In any case, infants work hard to get people to imitate them. Furthermore, because a caregiver is most likely to imitate an infant if the infant has imitated something the caregiver has done (Papousek & Papousek, 1977), infants may learn that it pays to imitate their caregivers first. Thus parents' playful imitation of their infants may help establish imitative tendencies in their infants.

Kohlberg's Stages Kohlberg (1969) continued the study of imitation, focusing on changes in imitation in the toddler and older child. According to Kohlberg, children imitate in order to feel more competent. Presumably, children notice that certain other people are, in some important respects, more competent than they are, and they try to imitate these models so that they can feel competent and masterful, too. However, as children grow older, they change their conceptions of what sorts of models are "competent," and hence they change the kinds of models they imitate.

Young children (2 to 5 years) equate competence with superficial qualities of models— especially their size, strength, and ownership of material goods. Thus young children are particularly likely to imitate their parents, whom they revere as godlike, superior, and virtuous. By age 2, children have developed enough of an understanding of physical causality to realize that adults can make interesting and important things happen. To assure themselves that they too can generate these consequences and operate effectively in various situations, young children insist on the right to imitate actions they have seen their parents perform: They want to feed themselves, dress themselves, and so on, often becoming extremely negativistic when their parents intervene to help them or to hurry them along. Much of the imitation during this period also involves fantasy play, such as acting out the roles of powerful creatures like monsters and robots. This early stage of imitation is thought to occur while the child is functioning at Piaget's preoperational stage of cognitive development. Remember that a major feature of preoperational thought is centration, or the tendency to focus attention on surface aspects of a stimulus. Centration is presumably why young children equate competence with salient superficial characteristics of models, such as size and strength.

As children head into the later nursery-school and early elementary-school years, their choices of models for imitation undergo changes. Many of these changes result from the fact that children are firming up their conceptions of their own identities. Most important, as children pass into Piaget's stage of concrete operations and acquire notions of class membership, they begin to conceive of themselves as belonging to certain social groups or playing certain roles. A little girl, for example, may begin to realize that she is just one girl among many girls, just one Girl Scout among many Girl Scouts, just one member of a neighborhood treehouse club, and so on. As children develop conceptions of their reference groups, they presumably develop prototypic or ideal images of what the "perfect" member of each of their reference groups does and is like. They then search for models who best exemplify these roles and begin to imitate them.

Children's motivation for imitation continues to be the striving for competence, but now "competent" models are individuals perceived by the children to be exemplars of the social roles to which they aspire. Girls may perceive feminine competence and status to be based on such attributes as being "attractive" and "nice"; boys may see masculine status in terms of being "powerful," "aggressive," and "fearless." Hence, girls will imitate females that to them have the feminine attributes, and boys will imitate males that project the masculine image. A major influence on children's motivation to imitate a model, then, is the degree to which the children perceive the model as being a competent member of a social group to which children themselves aspire.

Critique of Kohlberg's View   Kohlberg's theory is sometimes called a theory of *self-socialization,* for it stresses how children's internal cognitive advances cause children to seek out certain sorts of models and thus determine for themselves the direction their social learning will take. The theory is quite popular, and it has led to several predictions that have been confirmed. Children clearly do aspire to certain social roles, and they prefer to imitate models that to them are good examples of these roles. For instance, boys imitate men they perceive to be masculine more than men who behave like women (Perry & Bussey, 1979). Kohlberg's hunch that children's conceptions of their own gender identities influence their selective preference for same-sex models is also confirmed

(Slaby & Frey, 1975). But Kohlberg's theory is not complete. It fails to specify why children do not imitate *everything* they see competent and similar models do.

As we have seen, the cognitive-developmentalists stress the importance of intrinsic motivation—the drive for competence—in fueling children's imitation processes. The next theory we discuss, in contrast, takes the view that external reinforcement is essential for fostering children's imitative tendencies.

Contemporary Conditioning Theory (or Response-Reinforcement Theory)

Earlier in this chapter we considered one conditioning-theory account of imitation, Mowrer's translation of the Freudian notion of primary identification into the language of learning theory. Most contemporary conditioning theorists, however, have not based their work on Freudian theory. The most influential of these theorists is Baer (see also Gewirtz & Stingle, 1968).

Baer's Conditioning View: A Generalized Tendency to Imitate is Established Through Reinforcement   Baer's basic idea (Baer & Sherman, 1964; Baer, Peterson, & Sherman, 1967) is quite simple: Children's tendencies to imitate are established through direct external reinforcement. First imitations may occur by chance, or because children are directly instructed to imitate ("Do what daddy does!") or are physically prompted. If adults reward and praise these imitations, then the particular responses the child has imitated will be strengthened; what is more important, however, is that the child learns a generalized *tendency to imitate.* In other words, when children are externally rewarded for imitating *some* of a model's responses, they become motivated to imitate other responses, even responses that bear little resemblance to those they have been rewarded for imitating. Thus the little girl who is rewarded for imitating her mother's vocalizations should start to imitate some of her mother's other behaviors—her

mother's gestures, facial expressions, style of dress, and so on—even though the little girl is never directly rewarded for imitating these latter responses. Baer calls children's tendency to imitate responses they have never before been rewarded for imitating *generalized imitation.*

How does generalized imitation develop? Why should reinforcement for a few imitations lead children to imitate new responses? Baer proposes that when children are externally rewarded for imitating a model, they learn to take pleasure in perceiving themselves as similar to the model. He suggests that when children imitate, they notice they have become more similar to the model ("I'm like mommy"). If the children are rewarded for their imitation, then their perceptions of similarity to the model will also be rewarded. The association between external reward and the perception of similarity to the model causes this perception to acquire conditioned (secondary) reinforcing value. In other words, because of this association, perceptions of similarity become intrinsically pleasurable.

Once perceptions of similarity to a model become intrinsically reinforcing, children should imitate new responses the model makes simply to experience the pleasure associated with perceiving themselves to be similar to the model. Thus the little girl strives to imitate *any* response that will allow her to say to herself, "I'm like mommy," because making this observation is now sufficiently pleasurable in its own right. This is presumably why children will imitate new responses of a model even when there is no external reinforcement available. Of course, intermittent external reinforcement for imitation should provide "booster shots" for the conditioned reinforcement value of perceptions of similarity, keeping the child motivated to display generalized imitation.

The Classic Experiment on Generalized Imitation   Baer and Sherman (1964) claim to have demonstrated how generalized imitation develops. Initially, children were instructed to imitate three classes of responses modeled by a clown puppet: head nodding, mouthing, and the verbalizing of nonsense statements (e.g., "Glub-flub-bug"). The children were externally rewarded (with praise) every time they imitated one of these kinds of responses. Naturally, the children soon were imitating all three kinds of responses at a high rate. After this pattern had been established, the puppet occasionally would reach over and press a bar that was located between him and the children. The question was: Would the children imitate the puppet's bar-pressing responses even though they had never been instructed to, and even though they were never rewarded for it?

Many children did indeed imitate the interspersed, nonreinforced bar-pressing responses. Baer interpreted this to mean that the adult's praise had conditioned intrinsic reinforcement value to the children's perceptions of similarity to the puppet, and that the children imitated the bar pressing because this was simply another way they could perceive themselves as similar to the puppet.

Problems with the Conditioning Viewpoint Baer's theory offers an intriguing perspective on how children's tendencies to imitate are established, but it has been criticized on two major grounds. First, it is difficult to believe that perceptions of similarity acquire intrinsic reinforcing properties. In experimental studies of generalized imitation, if the experimenter stops rewarding the children for imitating certain behaviors, the children usually abruptly cease imitating anything the model does. This is not what one would predict from Baer's theory: If perceptions of similarity were intrinsically reinforcing, imitation should persist, at least for a while, after external reinforcement is withdrawn. It also seems likely that children in the Baer and Sherman study were practicing generalized imitation (i.e., pressing the bar) not because they were taking pleasure in seeing themselves as similar to the puppet, but because they simply thought that the adult who

was present expected them to copy everything the puppet did (Bufford, 1971; Martin, 1971; Oliver, Acker, & Oliver, 1977; Peterson, Merwin, Moyer, & Whitehurst, 1971; Peterson & Whitehurst, 1971; Steinman, 1970; Steinman & Boyce, 1971).

A second problem with Baer's theory is one we have seen with most of the other theories we have reviewed, namely that it does not account for the fact that children are selective in their imitation. According to Baer's formulation, once children are externally rewarded for imitating some of a model's responses, they should indiscriminately start imitating everything the model does so that they can maximize their pleasurable perceptions of similarity. But children do not imitate every action. The next theory we discuss, social learning theory, is very much concerned with how children learn to restrict their imitation to certain models, responses, and circumstances.

Bandura's Social Learning Theory

Albert Bandura (1969b, 1977) has proposed a comprehensive and powerful theory of modeling. It is probably fair to say that Bandura's theory stands as the most popular theory of modeling today. One of the reasons his theory is so popular is that it explicitly recognizes that children imitate only a small fraction of all the responses they learn through observation. According to Bandura, children learn a multitude of brand new social responses simply by observing the actions of salient models around them—their parents, siblings, teachers, playmates, television heroes, and even storybook characters—and by storing these responses in their memories in the form of mental images and other symbolic representations. Bandura calls this process *observational learning* and he believes that this is the major way children acquire new patterns of social behavior. However, children obviously do not imitate, or perform, everything they learn through observation.

They know that some responses are appropriate for them to perform, whereas others are not. Most boys, for example, know how to apply lipstick and put on a dress, presumably from observing female models, yet boys rarely perform these responses. This distinction between observational learning (sometimes called *acquisition*) and performance is an important one. In an early experiment, Bandura demonstrated the difference between acquisition and performance.

An Experiment to Distinguish Observational Learning from Performance In a study conducted in 1965, Bandura showed young children a film in which a woman directed a variety of novel aggressive acts toward an inflated clown doll called "Bobo" (e.g., she hit Bobo with a wooden mallet, laid him on the floor to straddle and punch him, and kicked him; see Figure 4-1). For one group of children, toward the end of the film the woman was praised and rewarded by another adult for her aggressive behavior; a second group saw the model being scolded and punished for her aggression; and a final group saw the model neither rewarded nor punished for the aggression. Subsequently, the children were left with Bobo and other toys, told they could do what they liked, and were observed for imitative aggression. This "free play" period may be considered a *test for imitative performance*. Not surprisingly, children who had seen the model punished displayed less aggression than children in the other groups. Bandura then asked the children to show him everything they had seen the model do, promising them small prizes for each action they could recall. This recall test with incentives offered for correct responses may be considered a *test of observational learning*. Children in all three groups showed excellent and roughly equal recall of the model's actions. Bandura interpreted this to mean that children in all groups had acquired or learned the model's actions equally well through observation, but that children in the model-punished group had simply chosen not to perform

the aggression during the free play period, perhaps because they feared punishment for doing so.

This study clearly reveals that it is sensible to differentiate observational learning (or original acquisition) from performance. The study also hints that one factor influencing children's imitative performance is the outcome they have seen a model receive for performing a response. Next we shall evaluate some of the processes Bandura sees as underlying observational learning and imitative performance.

Processes in Observational Learning Bandura contends that much observational learning occurs at a covert, cognitive level. By paying close attention to a model's actions and by forming mental representations of the model's behavior (such as mental images or covert verbal descriptions), children can learn and retain a vast repertoire of complicated new response patterns. Of course, observational learning will not occur if the child is too young to possess the cognitive skills necessary to encode a model's actions, or if the child for some reason is not motivated to remember the modeled activities. Furthermore, the child must possess the motor capabilities necessary to reproduce a model's response before one can say that he or she has truly acquired it.

Because most observational learning takes place without the child overtly performing the modeled action at the time it is modeled, Bandura has termed his theory of observational learning a theory of *no trial learning*. Bandura's theory of social learning obviously represents a radical departure from the viewpoint of the conditioning theorists, who insist that children must both perform and be reinforced for a response before it can be learned.

Although children can and do acquire new patterns of motor activity through observational learning, they also acquire more abstract sorts of knowledge from observing models. Often this knowledge takes the form

Figure 4–1 Aggressive Modeling and Imitation. In top row, an adult models aggressive responses toward Bobo. Lower rows depict children's imitative aggression. (Photo courtesy of Albert Bandura.)

of response-outcome contingency rules. For example, if children consistently see others rewarded for behaving altruistically, they may abstract the general rule that helping other people is praiseworthy. Presumably, children taking part in Bandura's (1965) experiment who saw the model punished for behaving aggressively concluded that aggression in that situation was blameworthy. As far as Bandura is concerned, then, social learning is largely an information-processing activity in which information about response patterns and environmental contingencies is transformed into symbolic representations that serve as guides for behavior.

Here we have briefly sketched some of the central points of Bandura's theory of observational learning. Because Bandura's theory has stimulated a tremendous amount of research, we will devote a later section to exploring in greater depth the details of the component processes in observational learning.

Determinants of Imitative Performance

We have noted that children actually perform only a small subset of the responses they have learned from observing models. Bandura suggests that imitative performance is largely under the control of *anticipated consequences* or the outcomes children expect for imitating. Imitation is most likely to occur when children expect positive consequences and least likely when they expect negative outcomes. Notice that by placing emphasis on the outcomes the children anticipate, Bandura is again assigning importance to the child's cognitions. He believes that both observational learning and performance are under the control of cognitive processes.

How do children learn the outcomes they are likely to receive from performing various responses? There are three main ways children learn response-outcome expectations. First, they learn through verbal instruction. Parents who make remarks like, "Don't ever let me catch *you* doing that!" or "I'd sure like it if you'd keep your room as neat as your sis-

ter's!" are helping their children learn to expect certain social reactions for certain behaviors.

A second way children learn outcome expectations is through the direct rewards and punishments they receive for imitating. Bandura gives children full credit for their capacities for discrimination learning, pointing out that children can rapidly learn to restrict their imitation to certain responses, models, and situations, depending on the pattern of consequences they have experienced for imitating. Consider that most children are rewarded for imitating their parents' altruism, but not their martini drinking; they are praised for imitating others of their own sex, but criticized for behaving like members of the opposite sex; and they are cheered for executing expert soccer plays in the field, but scolded for kicking balls in the house. Children definitely do learn to determine on which occasions reward is likely to be given for imitating, and they limit their imitation to these occasions (see Bandura & Barab, 1971, for an excellent demonstration of this point).

The third, and perhaps most powerful, way in which children learn to anticipate the consequences for imitation is by observing the outcomes that others receive for their actions (*vicarious consequences*). The fact that children who saw the model punished for behaving aggressively in Bandura's (1965) experiment inhibited performing the aggression themselves (though they had learned it) illustrates the power of vicarious consequences. By seeing what happens to their siblings, their classmates, their parents, and other people for performing or failing to perform certain responses, children rapidly expand their knowledge of outcome expectations.

Although children learn that some responses are clearly blameworthy and others are clearly praiseworthy, they also learn that the outcomes accorded some responses depend on who performs them: Children see, for example, that boys are sometimes laughed at for playing with dolls, whereas girls are encouraged for this behavior. When a response leads to a positive outcome for some people and to a negative outcome for other people, how do children know whether to imitate it or inhibit it? Children's imitation is most influenced by the consequences they see received by other children who are *similar* to themselves. Boys' imitation is more influenced by the consequences they see other boys receive for their behavior, for example, than by the outcomes they see girls experience. This is because children learn that society expects them to behave the same way as other children who are similar to them in terms of sex, age, and other role memberships (Bandura, 1969b; Bussey & Perry, 1976). Like Kohlberg, Bandura believes that children often strive to perform behaviors they perceive to be appropriate for others of their reference groups, but Bandura stresses outcome expectations rather than innate strivings for competence as the main motivating factor.

Children's imitative performance is also influenced by the children's anticipated self-evaluations. As we shall see in Chapter 6, once children realize that certain behaviors are considered worthy of praise and others worthy of blame, they often internalize the contingencies: They begin to expect internal feelings of pride for performing the praise-worthy behaviors and internal feelings of guilt for engaging in disapproved activities. Thus a girl may begin to take intrinsic pleasure in copying actions she has learned are girl-appropriate and may fear some discomfort for acting like a boy. In summary, then, performance of observationally learned behavior is influenced by three sources of incentives: direct, vicarious, and self-produced.

In stark contrast to Freud, who claimed that the mature child's imitation focused exclusively on the same-sex parent, Bandura emphasizes that children learn from a variety of models, picking and choosing behaviors to imitate on the basis of their usefulness and appropriateness for the situation at hand. Children's personalities are not exact duplicates of a single figure with whom they have identified.

Critique of Social Learning Theory Bandura's theory of modeling has led to a large number of precise and testable hypotheses, many of which have been amply confirmed. Like Kohlberg's theory, social learning theory assigns major importance to children's cognitive processes and regards children as active contributors to their own socialization. Children select certain models to attend to; they mentally transform what they have witnessed into symbolic representations and rules, which they can later use as guides to behavior; they deliberate over whether it would be appropriate or worthwhile to perform an action they have learned through observation; and so on. A major appeal of Bandura's theory is his distinction between observational learning and performance. The other theories we have reviewed focus exclusively on factors affecting imitative performance. This is an insufficient approach to the study of modeling influences.

Social learning theory is sometimes criticized for not being a "developmental" theory, for not paying enough attention to how children's observational learning and performance undergo changes as children develop. It is true that social learning theory does not view children's observational learning and imitation as progressing in a series of discrete stages. But this does not mean that Bandura's theory ignores developmental factors. Bandura recognizes that as children develop, they change in their capacities to attend to models, to encode and remember what models do, to reproduce the motor activities of models, to abstract rules and principles linking certain actions to certain consequences, and to monitor their own behavior in accord with such rules. In the following section, we discuss the component processes in observational learning in more detail, and how the various aspects of observational learning change with development.

COMPONENT PROCESSES
IN OBSERVATIONAL LEARNING

This section considers the development of four component processes in observational learning: attention, retention, motor reproduction, and motivation. Bandura (1977) suggests that children simultaneously mature in all four domains as they grow. In his view, adeptness in observational learning stems from acquiring skills in discriminative (selective) observation, in memory encoding, in coordinating sensorimotor and conceptual-motor systems, and in processing information about the probable consequences of matching another's behavior.

Before we discuss developmental changes in observational learning, we need to dispel a common misunderstanding about the changing role of modeling in child development. Some writers have concluded that as children age, imitation plays a lesser and lesser role in their social development. Indeed, as children get older, they become less likely to engage in the immediate, spontaneous, "copycat" type of behavior that one sees so often in infants interacting with their parents or toddlers playing with their peers (Abramovitch & Grusec, 1978; Fein, 1973; Fouts & Liikanen, 1975; Kohlberg & Zigler, 1967). But the fact that instant mimicry declines over the years ignores the fact that observational learning is increasing. As they develop, children are cognitively encoding more action sequences than they actually imitate, they are abstracting rules about how their worlds operate, and they are refining their notions about which models and responses are appropriate for them to imitate. Overt imitation is just the "tip of the iceberg" of what children learn through observation. As children mature, then, they rely to a greater extent on observational learning in developing their motor, social, and cognitive competencies (Bandura, 1977). Thus the fact that children display less imitative mimicry as they get older should not be taken to mean that the importance of modeling in the socialization process declines with age.

Attentional Processes

Children can't learn a response unless they pay attention to it. Young children are relatively distractible and are deficient in attentional skills. Yussen (1974) monitored children's eye movements as they watched an adult indicate which items in a set of stimuli he liked and disliked. Young children attended inefficiently, often glancing away just as the adult indicated a choice. In contrast, older children paid closer attention at crucial moments. Auditory attention may also be more erratic in young children, who sometimes fail to listen to a model's words. In a study of children's recall of television material, Hayes and Birnbaum (1980) found that preschoolers tended to "look but not listen" when watching television.

Several characteristics of modeled events influence whether children will attend to them. Activities that are conspicuous, accompanied by lively soundtracks (like cartoons), and intrinsically interesting (such as novel toy play or aggressive actions) are likely to command attention.

Because children are more attracted to some people than to others, they will spend more time with these people and learn more from them. Infants are especially attracted to their caregivers, so they will learn most from them, although they can also learn from other people, and even the television set when given the opportunity (Eckerman, Whatley, & Kutz, 1975; McCall et al., 1977). Preschoolers tend to segregate themselves by sex (Jacklin & Maccoby, 1978), so it is not surprising that children tend to learn behaviors appropriate for their own sex before they learn behaviors appropriate for members of the opposite sex (Edelbrock & Sugawara, 1978). Children also tend to pay closer attention to, and hence learn more about, models who are warm, powerful, or perceived as similar to themselves (Grusec & Mischel, 1966; Perry & Perry, 1975; Slaby & Frey, 1975; Yussen & Levy, 1975).

Representation and Retention Processes

Attention to a model is necessary, but it does not guarantee that a child will learn a model's response. The modeled information must be represented in memory in a succinct, symbolic form that can be retrieved by the child to guide performance. Symbolic mediators may take many forms, including vivid visual images, covert verbal descriptions, concise summary labels, and even rules and propositions (e.g., "If people do such-and-such, then they receive such-and-such in return"). Infants may be limited to imaginal forms of representation, and at first these forms probably represent only the salient physical properties of actions. The study by McCall and his associates (1977) suggested that it is not until infants are 2 that they can store a sequence of modeled events. Before that age, infants can imitate single-unit motor and social behaviors (e.g., gestures and vocalizations), but not coordinated sequences.

With age, representation of modeled events becomes increasingly verbal. In one study, first graders were shown a movie of a model performing novel play activities (Bandura, Grusec, & Menlove, 1966). Some children were asked to count backwards while viewing the film—a procedure designed to prevent the children from verbally encoding the modeled activities. Other children watched the film, but were not given any instructions to say anything out loud (a "passive observation" group). Children in the first group were able to recall fewer of the model's responses. Presumably the counting had prevented the children from using their normal means of verbally encoding the model's actions.

Children increase their spontaneous verbal encoding of a model's actions as they get older. This is illustrated in a study by Coates

and Hartup (1969) with 5- and 7-year-old children. The children were asked to watch a model display novel play responses. Some of the children at each age level were instructed to verbalize aloud the model's actions while they watched; others watched passively. The children were then tested for recall of the modeled behavior. The older children remembered as many of the model's responses in the passive observation condition as they did in the verbalization condition, presumably because children in the passive observation condition were covertly verbalizing the model's actions without any explicit instructions to do so. In contrast, the 5-year-olds remembered fewer of the model's actions in the passive observation condition than in the verbalization condition, supposedly because children of this young age do not spontaneously verbalize a model's actions if nobody tells them to. Verbal encoding becomes more spontaneous or self-initiated as children get older and realize its benefits. Symbolically rehearsing, or going over in one's head, a modeled action also aids retention (Bandura & Jeffery, 1973; Gerst, 1971). When observers are prevented from rehearsing a model's actions after witnessing them, the recall deteriorates.

Many modeled activities are learned and retained in symbolic codes that bear little resemblance to the observed activities. Observers can encode a model's sequence of turns to the left and the right, for example, in summary verbal form (e.g., RLRLL . . .) rather than by forming a mental picture of the entire sequence. Even when symbolic representations involve images, they are rarely photocopies or "internal movie reels" of a model's actions. Instead, observers extract the distinctive features of a modeled activity to form an abbreviated representation capturing the critical features. An aspiring tennis player who observes 100 serves by a professional does not encode each serve as a separate image, but extracts the essential features to form an image of a "prototypic" or idealized serve. Observational learning, then, involves "reductive memory codes" that may be verbal or imaginal, or, more likely, may represent some combination of the two (Bandura, 1977).

Much of the child's knowledge about human behavior is learned through a process known as *abstract modeling* (Bandura, 1977; Rosenthal & Zimmerman, 1978). Children frequently observe other people performing responses that embody a more general rule or principle. If children are capable of extracting the crucial properties shared by diverse examples of a principle, they may integrate the information into a rule and even use the rule to produce new instances of the behavior themselves.

Abstract modeling is well illustrated in a study by Harvey and Liebert (1979). Children listened to a model give her opinions about what courses of action several story characters should take. Some children heard the model always recommend an action that showed concern on the part of the story character for a distressed other person; other children heard the model consistently suggest action that was motivated by the story character's desire to avoid harm to the self. When children were asked to give their own opinions for a new set of stories, they tended to imitate whichever style of reasoning they had been exposed to in the experiment. By detecting a common thread that runs through diverse behaviors of a model, children probably recognize and adopt a variety of generalized motives and attitudes, such as prejudice, friendliness, helpfulness, selfishness, aggressiveness, and the like.

Abstract modeling probably plays a major role in language development, despite the fact that for many years some linguists disavowed the importance of modeling for children's language development. Particularly skeptical of the contribution of modeling to language development were the "structural nativists" (e.g., Chomsky, 1968), who argued that children are innately endowed or preprogrammed with a system of rules underlying language use and understanding. These the-

orists argued that modeling could hardly play a role in children's acquisition of language rules because so much of what children say they have never heard modeled. They pointed out that much of children's language is creative or "generative" in that children come up with brand new examples to fit language rules. Children also "overregularize" by making remarks like "He gaved me candy" or "The mouses eat cheese." Critics of the modeling position argued that children could never have imitated these utterances because adults don't model them, and hence modeling could not play a role in the acquisition of rules of language. Their reasoning was flawed. The critics failed to realize that observational learning goes deeper than simple mimicry. As we now know, through the process of abstract modeling children can learn a set of rules that enables them to generate an almost infinite variety of new sentences and utterances that they have never heard (Rosenthal & Zimmerman, 1978).

In sum, as a function of observing models, children retain new information in the form of concise images and verbal codes, they learn new ways of integrating and organizing behavior, they acquire a wide variety of highly discriminative rules relating actions and consequences (e.g., "When model-type A performs response X in situation 1 the outcome is reward, but when model-type B performs the same response in that situation the outcome is punishment"), and they abstract rules for generating new instances of a class of behavior.

Behavioral Production Processes

No matter how well aspiring Little Leaguers symbolically encode their baseball heroes' pitches, it is unlikely they will become good pitchers themselves without practice and corrective feedback followed by more practice. In order to match a model's actions correctly, observers must convert their symbolic conceptions into appropriate actions. This involves a *conception matching process*, in which observers monitor their actions, compare their enactments to the desired symbolic conception, and correct their subsequent performances for any mismatches. When sensory feedback from performance consistently indicates that a person's behavior is falling short of the action plan, the observer may attend anew to the model, trying to come up with a better cognitive representation of the essential motor components. A good deal of learning involves continuously monitoring and refining one's actions to fit one's plans (Bandura, 1977).

Practicing a skill to the point where one's performance satisfactorily matches a desired self-conception is often essential in fostering *perceptions of self-efficacy,* or people's feelings of confidence in their abilities to perform an activity competently (Bandura, 1977; Rosenthal & Bandura, 1978). Children tend to fear and avoid activities that they feel they can't master or perform satisfactorily. Children will avoid swimming, playing the piano, or ice skating if they don't perceive themselves capable of performing the responses involved. An excellent way of promoting children's perceptions of efficacy at an activity is having the children observe a model performing the motor components of the activity and then having them practice the behavioral components. The process is continued until the children's skills improve *and* they report more confidence in their ability to execute the desired responses. Later, when we discuss the role of modeling in behavior modification, we will see that one excellent way of reducing children's fears and phobias involves showing them a model making progressively closer approach responses to the feared stimulus, and at the same time getting children to imitate and practice the approach behavior. Children who successfully complete such a program both report improvement in their perceived efficacy at coping with the feared stimulus and are more likely to attempt to interact with the stimulus in the future. There is no surer way of convincing children that they are capable of doing something than by getting them to do it.

Motivational Processes

In social learning theory, motivational processes play a role in both observational learning and performance. If children feel that learning a model's actions will be useful for them in some way, they naturally will be more inclined to attend to, symbolize, and rehearse what the model does. We have noted that reinforcement of either the observer or the model is not a necessary component for observational learning—children are going to learn some responses, whether they want to or not, just because they look at the model at the right time. Nevertheless, both direct and vicarious reinforcement can certainly affect how motivated children will be to learn a model's actions. If children are praised for imitating a particular model (or class of model), they are more likely to encode and remember behaviors performed by that model (Grusec & Brinker, 1972; Perry & Perry, 1975).

Vicarious consequences can also influence children's abilities to learn by observing. In fact, when children see a model either rewarded or punished for displaying responses, they are more likely to remember the responses than when they see a model display the responses without being rewarded or punished (Cheyne, 1971; Liebert & Fernandez, 1970; Yussen, 1974). This makes sense. When children see a model responded to negatively or positively, they want to remember what the model did so that they can maximize their own rewards and minimize their own punishments. We did note earlier in the chapter that in one experiment children recalled an equal number of their model's aggressive responses, regardless of whether the model was rewarded, punished, or received no consequence (Bandura, 1965). This would seem to contradict the argument that vicarious consequences increase observational learning. However, in Bandura's experiment the novel aggressive responses were so captivating that children probably were motivated to remember them regardless of the consequences to the model. When less inherently interesting responses are displayed by a model, vicarious consequences usually do facilitate acquisition.

Motivational processes are basic to children's decisions about whether to perform responses they have learned. We have already discussed some important motivational influences on imitative performance. Infants, remember, may be motivated to imitate by the hope that they will be imitated back and will thereby derive some feelings of control over their environment. As children mature, they improve in their abilities to link certain actions with certain consequences and to monitor their behavior to agree with such action-outcome rules (Collins, 1973; Collins, Berndt, & Hess, 1974; Leifer, Collins, Gross, Taylor, Andrews, & Blackmer, 1971). Because young children sometimes dissociate an action from its consequence, they may imitate negatively sanctioned actions more often than older persons.

There are other motives for imitation. Children, and even adults, sometimes imitate other people because it helps bind those other people to them and even helps bring those other people under their sphere of influence. Parents may enjoy imitating their infants in part because they see how much their infant enjoys it, but also because they hope it will somehow strengthen their infant's feelings of affection for them. Infants, children, and adults all do display pleasure at being imitated—especially if they regard their imitators as being of higher status or more competent than themselves—and in fact become more attracted to those who imitate them (Bates, 1975; Fouts, Waldner, & Watson, 1976; Haugan & McIntire, 1972; Miller & Morris, 1974; Mueller & Lucas, 1975; Thelen, Dollinger, & Roberts, 1975; Thelen & Kirkland, 1976). Furthermore, people who have been imitated tend to return the favor

by imitating the person who has imitated them (Thelen et al., 1975; Thelen & Kirkland, 1976). This has been called *reciprocal imitation*.

An interesting possibility is that if children realize that imitating another will attract the other to them and will lead the person to imitate them in return, they may deliberately imitate someone to ingratiate the person, hoping the flattered person will someday repay the social "debt." Research suggests that children as young as the preschool years may sometimes use imitation to influence others. Children who are the leaders and the most dominant members of their peer groups, for example, not only are the most frequently imitated members of their peer groups but also do the most imitating of their peers (Abramovitch & Grusec, 1978; Thelen, Paul, & Dollinger, 1978). Perhaps these socially intelligent, leader-type children imitate other children in part because they have seen that it leads to reciprocal imitation from their peers.

By the time children reach the mid-elementary school years, they seem well aware of the rule that "If I imitate X, then X will be more likely to imitate me later." In some interesting research, Thelen and his colleagues told one group of fifth and sixth graders that they could earn some money if they could persuade a peer to eat some terrible-tasting "health crackers." Before being given the opportunity to persuade the peer to eat the crackers, the children played several games with the peer, structured to provide opportunities for the children to imitate the peer. Children who were promised money for persuading the peer to eat the crackers imitated and smiled at the peer more often than a group of control children who were not promised rewards for successful persuasion (Thelen, Frautschi, Fehrenbach, & Kirkland, 1978; Thelen, Miller, Fehrenbach, Frautschi, & Fishbein, 1980). Imitation, then, sometimes occurs because one person is trying to bring another person under control.

TELEVISION AND SOCIAL LEARNING

Television is more than entertainment. It is a major source of information for children about what life is like, about what sorts of people exist in their world, and about what these people do and what happens to them for doing it. But television does not necessarily accurately reflect real life. In fact, it distorts it. Content analyses of television programs reveal that commercial television presents children with a highly biased slice of life, emphasizing certain kinds of models and certain forms of behaviors. Let's have a look at children's television viewing habits and see how these habits influence the children's social and cognitive development.

Television Viewing Patterns

Parents position infants as young as 6 months in a place that allows them to view the television set for an average of between 1 and 2 hours per day (Hollenbeck & Slaby, 1979). Of course, infants do not attend closely, and they do not imitate what they see. It is hard to determine whether or not infants are learning anything from viewing television at this early age.

Television viewing increases rapidly over the months, and by 2 years of age children are even imitating acts performed by television models (McCall et al., 1977). Children between the ages of 2 and 12 are watching television for nearly 4 hours per day, indicating that during a year's time children spend more time in front of a television set than in front of a teacher! Average daily viewing time drops to 3 hours between the ages of 12 and 18, but increases in adulthood to reach 4.5 hours by age 55 (Slaby & Quarfoth, 1980; Stein & Friedrich, 1975). Of course, averages hide individual differences. Some children hardly ever watch television, whereas others are virtually slaves to their sets.

Researchers have found sex, social class, race, and IQ differences in studies of television viewing habits (Slaby & Quarfoth, 1980; Stein & Friedrich, 1975). Females watch more television than males, and lower-class children watch more television and show a stronger preference for violent programs than children in middle-class homes. Black children also watch more television and prefer more violent television programs than white children. Children with low IQs or poor academic achievement tend to be overrepresented in populations of heavy television users. Parents' viewing habits and the degree of freedom they give their children to watch television probably contribute to children's viewing patterns, but more research is needed to examine the factors that contribute to children's decisions to turn on and shut off the television set.

Effects of Television Viewing

Effects of Violent Televison Commercial television is replete with violence. Cartoons have the highest concentration of aggression. As children get older they watch fewer cartoons, but the proportion of their favored television programs that do contain violence increases through adolescence. It has been estimated that by the age of 14 the average child has witnessed more than 11,000 murders on television (Slaby & Quarfoth, 1980).

Television depicts violence as a highly successful technique for getting what one wants. Although television producers insist that their programs emphasize that "crime does not pay," analyses reveal that televised violence is rewarded as often as it is punished. Furthermore, the "good guys" (e.g., police, other heroes) are as violent as the "bad guys," often breaking the law in the service of supposedly good ends. When aggression does lead to negative consequences (e.g., pain for the victim, punishment for the aggressor), the consequences usually either are not depicted at all or else are shown long after the violence occurred, and hence it is difficult for the child to connect aggression with negative consequences (Slaby & Quarfoth, 1980; Stein &

Friedrich, 1975). In sum, television depicts aggression as a common and acceptable way of resolving disputes and obtaining goals.

A variety of ill effects results from watching television violence; we review this issue more fully in Chapter 7. TV teaches children new ways of injuring, threatening, and destroying; it increases the likelihood that observers will behave aggressively themselves; it makes children more afraid that they will be violently harmed; it makes children less likely to follow responsible rules of conduct in the absence of adult supervision; and it gradually erodes children's emotional sensitivity to acts of violence and suffering, making them less likely to come to the aid of or offer support to distressed others. The effects are cumulative, so that children who steadily prefer violent television over the years turn out to be more aggressive as adults (Eron, Lefkowitz, Huesmann, & Walder, 1972). Most of these conclusions are supported by experimental evidence that allows firm statements of cause and effect as well as by correlational field findings.

In light of these conclusions, what can be done to control the development of aggressive attitudes encouraged by television programs that promote violence? Data reveal that the adverse effects of viewing television are less for children who hold negative attitudes about aggression (Hicks, 1971), suggesting that adults should try to instill anti-aggression attitudes in children, perhaps by explicitly pointing out to children that television often depicts undesirable behavior. Indeed, if adults criticize aggressive episodes as children view them, the children are less likely to imitate the aggression later (Grusec, 1973; Hicks, 1968). Parents can restrict their children's viewing, but they must find alternative activities that are equally exciting and engrossing for their children to participate in. If they do not offer alternatives, children may become frustrated by the deprivation, which may lead to increased aggression (Stein & Friedrich, 1975). Parents and teachers can band together and boycott the products of

sponsors of aggressive programming, and they can also try to educate the networks about the positive benefits of producing programs that illustrate prosocial themes.

Effects of Educational and Prosocial Television Television can help as well as hurt. It can teach children about places and peoples far removed from their own existence. It can help bring education into the home. Programs like "Sesame Street" and "The Electric Company" have been successful in attracting audiences and in teaching them while they are being entertained. "Sesame Street" was designed to teach children cognitive skills such as symbolic representation (e.g., recognition of letters and numbers), to teach them methods of problem solving and reasoning (e.g., classification, perceptual discrimination, and causal inference), and to encourage their understanding of their physical and social environments (e.g., identifying and distinguishing elements of natural and human-made environments). Frequent viewers of the program do better on tests of vocabulary, counting, and shape and letter identification, are ranked higher in classroom performance by their first-grade teachers, and have a more positive attitude toward school (Ball & Bogatz, 1972). Middle-class children benefit from the program even if they view it infrequently, but disadvantaged youngsters tend to benefit only if they view it regularly. "The Electric Company" was designed to teach elementary reading skills. Children who regularly view the program along with their teachers at school do show improvements in reading (Ball & Bogatz, 1973).

Prosocial programs are designed to teach children positive attitudes and ways of interacting with others. Programs such as "Mr. Rogers' Neighborhood" and "Fat Albert and the Cosby Kids" contain segments depicting such themes as helping a friend, valuing a person for inner qualities rather than appearance, trying to understand another's feelings, and paying attention to safety rules and signs. Children who regularly view the programs show improvements on a long list of attributes: cooperation, sharing, understanding others' feelings, verbalizing one's own feelings, delay of gratification, persisting at a difficult task in order to do it well, acceptance of rules, and the tendency to engage in imaginative play (Slaby & Quarfoth, 1980; Stein & Friedrich, 1975). Thus television clearly can foster children's cognitive and prosocial competencies. Unfortunately, only a tiny fraction of children's programming is as yet devoted to this effort.

Effects of Television on Social Knowledge and Stereotypes What television depicts is an exaggeration of dominant American values with little recognition of the diversity in our culture (Slaby & Quarfoth, 1980). Middle-class white male adults are portrayed as the most powerful and important members. Women, minority group members, and lower-class men are relatively ignored. Male characters engage in a wide variety of interesting and exciting activities, while females are usually restricted to family and romantic contexts with less interesting and important options. Men are shown as more aggressive, more constructive, and more often rewarded for what they do; females are more often subservient, passive, and likely to fail at activities they initiate (Sternglanz & Serbin, 1974). Females are less often involved in television violence than men, but when they are, they are usually the victims rather than the aggressors (Gerbner & Gross, 1976). The vast majority of television characters are young or middle-aged adults, with little attention given to elderly people.

Given the distorted picture of the world that television portrays, it is not surprising that people who spend a great deal of time watching television hold different attitudes and beliefs about the world and the people in it than people who watch it less often. Heavy viewers are also more likely to report that they consider television to be a realistic portrayal of life.

Effects of Television Commercials The average child observes over 20,000 commercials per year. Most children's commercials are for high-calorie and high-carbohydrate cereals, snacks, desserts, and drinks—obviously not the best foods for children. Children who watch a great deal of television tend to believe what commercials say about a product, they pester their parents to buy advertised items (especially cereals and candy) at the supermarket, they ask for more presents at Christmas, and they hold exaggerated beliefs about the likelihood of becoming ill and the likelihood that drugs will cure them (Slaby & Quarfoth, 1980).

Although it is rarely tried, commercials can be constructed to send desirable messages to children. In one study (Galst, 1980), preschoolers who saw commercials advocating nutritional nonsugar snacks (e.g., apples, oranges, and milk) and who heard an adult comment favorably on the commercials' message tended to select the promoted snacks during choice tests. It is clear that television can affect children in positive ways.

Television is a special medium of modeling that warrants our increasing attention. Of course, the "real-life" models children are in contact with daily (parents, siblings, peers, teachers, and even strangers) also play major roles in social learning. We shall be discussing in detail the impact of these real-life models on the child's moral development, displays of aggression, prosocial development, and adoption of sex-linked activities in later chapters.

MODELING AS A TOOL OF BEHAVIOR MODIFICATION

Clinical psychologists have reasoned that if modeling is such a powerful vehicle of social learning, then it might be beneficial to use it in behavior modification programs. Modeling techniques can indeed be used to help children overcome a wide variety of social and cognitive deficiencies, and especially to help children overcome unrealistic fears and to teach them new competencies. We shall briefly illustrate some of the techniques and benefits of therapeutic modeling.

Reducing Fears Through Modeling

Many children hold irrational and exaggerated fears of certain objects and activities. Phobias of dogs, snakes, the dark, and going to the dentist or doctor are particularly common. Showing children a model who is coping effectively with the feared stimulus can help reduce the children's fear as well as avoidance of the stimulus.

Bandura, Grusec, and Menlove (1967) conducted a study on the *vicarious extinction* of extreme fear responses in young children. Young children who were terrified of dogs participated in eight sessions during which a peer model displayed progressively more fear-provoking interactions with a dog. Following the treatment series, children were given an avoidance test in which they were asked, for example, to approach and pet the dog, to feed her biscuits, and even to climb into the playpen with her. Compared to the control group who was not given a vicarious desensitization treatment, the treated children did better on the avoidance test. The beneficial effects generalized to the children's interaction with an unfamiliar dog, and the effects were still apparent during a follow-up test 1 month later. For a look at some of the responses dog-phobic children can execute after witnessing therapeutic modeling, see Figure 4–2.

Children who are afraid of dentists and doctors can also benefit from observing a successfully coping model. In one study, youngsters facing surgery were shown films of a peer model coping with circumstances similar to their own (Melamed & Siegel, 1975). The children showed reduced fear arousal both before and after the surgical operations, and they had fewer adjustment problems at home than the children who did not see the films.

The essence of vicarious extinction, then, involves exposure to a model who is gradually coping with the feared stimulus. Presumably, this procedure allows the observing child to progressively redefine the threatening stimulus as harmless (Rosenthal & Bandura, 1978). The effectiveness of vicarious extinction procedures can be enhanced, however, in several ways. One way is by exposing the phobic child to several models who are coping with the feared stimulus rather than to only a single model (Bandura & Menlove, 1968). Second, vicarious extinction is more effective if the model starts out by being afraid of the feared stimulus, but gradually develops poise and confidence, rather than if the model appears highly competent and confident right from the start. Children sometimes consider the actions of an exceedingly competent model to be hopelessly beyond their reach (Brown & Inouye, 1978). Third, the model's actions should appear realistic. In one study, children who saw a model give a slight wince when receiving a shot later showed less distress when getting a shot themselves than children who saw a model receive a shot without displaying any sign of pain or who saw no model at all (Vernon, 1974). Fourth, models who verbalize their feelings, reactions, and plans for future action are often more effective than silent models (Jakibchuk & Smeriglio, 1976; Meichenbaum, 1971). The verbalization process helps observers symbolically represent the model's actions and provides them with mental coping responses that help counteract debilitating thoughts.

Fifth, and possibly most important, vicarious extinction is especially effective when the phobic individual behaviorally practices the successive coping responses as they are modeled. In this technique, sometimes called *participant modeling,* the phobic child first observes and then practices each step in the graded hierarchy of coping responses until he or she gains enough skill and self-assurance to progress to the next step. Bandura (1977) stresses that such performance-based treat-

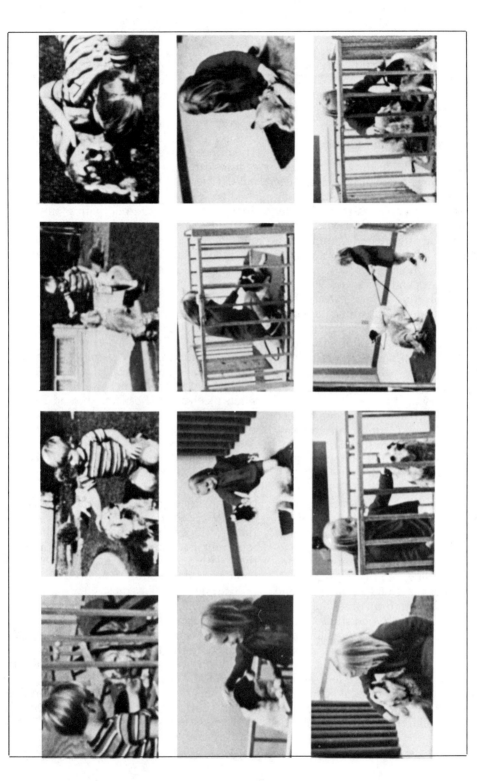

Figure 4–2 Vicarious Extinction of Fear Responses. Dog phobic children interact successfully with a dog after witnessing a peer model display progressively more threatening interactions with a dog. (Photo courtesy of Albert Bandura).

ments are especially effective in improving children's perceptions of self-efficacy, or the confidence children have in their ability to cope with a feared stimulus. According to Bandura, anxiety is most often experienced when a person feels that he or she is unable to manage a potentially aversive event. Therefore any therapy that succeeds in bolstering a person's perception of self-efficacy in managing a stimulus will reduce his or her fear of the stimulus. Participant modeling, which involves active mastery by the phobic person, is especially effective in improving perceptions of self-efficacy and reducing fear: There simply is no better way of convincing children that they are capable of coping with a threatening stimulus than by getting them to try it and proving to them that the outcome is not hazardous.

Teaching New Skills Through Modeling

Modeling is an excellent device for correcting a wide range of social and cognitive deficits in children. Children who are extremely shy, who isolate themselves from their peers, or who lack specific social skills necessary for effective peer interaction can sometimes overcome their difficulties by observing peer models who are depicted as gradually mastering the skills in question. Among the social skills that have been transmitted via therapeutic modeling are approaching other children and initiating positive interaction with them, communication skills such as listening to a speaker and asking questions at appropriate times, and exchanging positive social reinforcers (smiles, praise, etc.) with one's playmates. In Chapter 10, we more extensively review the skills necessary for acceptance by the peer group and show how these skills can be acquired through modeling.

Children can acquire a vast range of cognitive competencies through modeling. Through abstract modeling, in which children observe a model performing diverse responses that conform to some underlying principle or rule, children can learn new grammatical structures, new cognitive styles (e.g., a reflective rather than an impulsive approach to problem solving), new rules for solving problems, new action strategies, new motives and attitudes, and new standards for judging the actions of others and themselves. An outstanding review of this work can be found in Rosenthal and Zimmerman (1978).

SUMMARY

Children learn by observing the actions of others. Children imitate some of the actions they see others display, but much of what children learn through observation is not revealed in overt imitation. For example, children abstract important mental rules about how their worlds operate through watching the actions of other people and seeing what happens to people for their behavior.

Much of the early research on modeling was inspired by Freud's hypotheses about the kinds of people children choose to imitate. There is little support for Freud's hypotheses as he originally stated them, but researchers testing hypotheses that derived from Freud's theory have made some interesting discoveries. For example, children are more likely to imitate affectionate adults rather than cold adults, and they are more likely to imitate adults perceived to be of high status and in control of desirable resources than they are to imitate adults perceived as weak.

Cognitive-developmentalists, such as Piaget and Kohlberg, believe that imitation is motivated by children's innate strivings for competence and mastery. Piaget proposed that imitation in infancy follows a fixed series of stages, and Kohlberg speculated about imitation in older children. Kohlberg suggests that children imitate models whom they perceive as being competent and masterful so that they can feel that they, too, are competent and effective. Young, preoperational children equate competence with superficial characteristics of a model, such as size and strength. Thus they strive to be like adults and fanciful, powerful creatures such as monsters. Once children pass into the concrete operational stage, they begin to classify themselves and other people into various social roles (e.g., boy, girl, Cub Scout, or Brownie). Once they do this, the children try to emulate individuals who are competent exemplars, from their standpoint, of the social roles to which they aspire. Kohlberg's prediction that children tend to emulate models whose social roles are similar to their own receives support, but his theory is deficient in that it fails to explain why children don't copy everything they see competent and similar models do.

Contemporary conditioning theorists, such as Baer and Gewirtz, propose that children's imitative tendencies are established through external reinforcement to the children for imitation. Baer proposes that once a child has been externally reinforced for imitating some of a model's responses, the child's perceptions of similarity to the model acquire secondary (conditioned) reinforcement value. Hence the child begins imitating new responses (ones he or she has never before been rewarded for imitating) because these new imitations also lead to the perception of similarity to the model, which is now pleasurable in its own right. One problem with this theory is that it does not explain why, once the child has been reinforced for imitating some of a model's responses, the child does not indiscriminately imitate everything the model does in order to maximize perceptions of similarity.

In his social learning theory, Bandura has proposed a comprehensive and powerful theory of modeling. By observing the actions of the many people around them and by mentally storing these actions (in the form of vis-ual images, covert verbal descriptions, rules linking actions to outcomes, and other symbolic representations), children are thought to acquire a broad variety of novel patterns of social behavior and rules of conduct. This process is called observational learning. However, children choose to perform only a small subset of the countless number of behaviors they acquire through observation. The main influences on children's decisions about whether or not to imitate what they have learned are the consequences children anticipate for displaying the responses. By seeing what happens to people when they display various responses in various situations, children form mental rules that link certain model characteristics, social contexts, and behaviors with certain outcomes (e.g., "When this response is performed by this kind of person under these circumstances it usually gets criticized"). These rules then guide the children's imitative performance.

Much contemporary research focuses on the effects of television viewing on children's social learning. Television programs and commercials portray a highly biased perspective of life (e.g., much violence, few minority group characters, and stereotyped sex roles), and children who spend much of their time watching television may acquire distorted views of life. Educational and prosocial television can have beneficial effects, but such programming typically constitutes only a small fraction of most children's viewing time.

Modeling can be successful as a tool of behavior modification. Showing phobic children models who are progressively coping with the feared stimulus can be an effective means of vicarious extinction, especially if the children are also given guidance in practicing the models' actions. A wide variety of social and cognitive skills can be taught through modeling.

5

Social Cognition:
Understanding the Self and Others

This chapter deals with social cognition, or with how children mentally represent and process information about their social worlds. We are particularly concerned with how children develop an understanding of themselves, how they come to understand the personalities and psychological functioning of other people, and how their conceptions of themselves and other people influence their overt social behavior.

As children gain in cognitive maturity and social experience, they undergo changes in self-concept: They develop firmer notions of themselves as distinct individuals, as people who possess unique personality dispositions, thoughts, motives, plans for action, viewpoints, skills, and shortcomings. Children stabilize their assessments of their individual worth, of their ability to control the impor-

tant events in their lives, and of the sorts of people they would someday like to be, as well as who they are right now. It is clear that children have a great deal to learn about themselves.

As they grow, children also become more skilled at assessing and interpreting the personalities and actions of other people. They come to conceptualize other people's personalities in increasingly complex ways. They generate rules to help them explain and anticipate the actions of significant people around them. They become "social detectives," delving beneath the surface of a person's physical appearance, actions, and words in order to understand that person's hidden motives, thoughts, and feelings. They learn to separate their own viewpoints and opinions from those of other people, and they learn that social interaction involves coordinating and integrating their own plans and intentions with those of others.

It is not surprising that children's understanding of themselves and other people's psychological functioning influences their overt social behavior. Children who believe that they are in control of the pleasant and unpleasant experiences in life, for example, exert more effort to achieve scholastically (and socially) than children who believe that successes and failures are due to fate or something else beyond their control. Children who are skilled at inferring the nature of other people's private thoughts and feelings tend to react more sympathetically to a person in distress and are more likely to attempt some action to alleviate that person's distress than children less skilled in taking the role of another. There are numerous important links between social cognition and social behavior.

The two chapters preceding this one were concerned with how children learn from their social environment, especially from their own child-rearing experiences ("direct" instruction) and from their observation of other people ("vicarious" learning). In large part, social cognitions represent the *cognitive products* of the child's direct and vicarious transactions with the social environment. Children's understanding of themselves, for example, rests heavily on the nature of the discipline, praise, criticism, and other varieties of direct instruction that children experience at home and in school. Children learn much about others through observational learning. Social cognitions, then, may be conceptualized as intervening or *mediating links* between children's social learning experiences and their subsequent overt social behaviors.

This chapter begins with a review of theoretical perspectives on social-cognitive development. We then turn to the topic of how children acquire a sense of self. Third, we discuss person perception, or how children organize and process information about other people's personalities. A fourth section is devoted to causal attribution. Children, like adults, are motivated to explain salient events occurring around them. If someone makes life miserable for them, they wonder why. When people go out of their way to help them, they wonder if the people are selflessly trying to help or are trying to buy a later favor. In this section, we trace how children's abilities to detect the causes underlying someone's behavior change with age. We next examine developmental trends in children's role taking skills, or their ability to break away from their own egocentric view of a situation to appreciate the independent viewpoint of another person. Finally, we discuss some factors underlying children's development of a sense of humor. Once children develop expectancies about how things are supposed to operate in their social world, they find certain violations of these expectations uproariously funny. The research on humor illustrates how social-cognitive activity can often be amusing.

THEORIES OF SOCIAL-COGNITIVE DEVELOPMENT

The search for cognitive influences on social development has been inspired primarily by three theories: cognitive-developmental theory, social learning theory, and attribution theory. We shall elaborate on each of these viewpoints.

Cognitive-Developmental Theory

In cognitive-developmental theory, the building blocks of social-cognitive functioning are *social schemas*, the internal representations of social experiences. Some of the child's schemas are very simple (such as an image of a familiar face or event), whereas other schemas are more complex or abstract (such as a conception of a friend as "someone who likes to help others in any way he can"). A child's social schemas become more numerous and sophisticated as the child matures, but at any given point in development the schemas will share certain features and limitations that are dictated by the child's underlying thought structures, or more basic ways of processing and organizing information. Let's review Piaget's stages, indicating the sorts of social schemas the child is likely to generate at each stage.

By the end of the sensorimotor stage, which lasts roughly for the first two years of life, children can use symbols to represent familiar social objects and simple action sequences. They possess a schema of themselves as distinct individuals. In addition, they have formed images of familiar others and are aware that people continue to exist when out of sight (person permanence). They possess a basic understanding of instrumentality, or means-ends relationships. Thus they know that people can operate on the environment to achieve outcomes. Although by the end of this stage children can symbolically represent and store sequences of actions, their schemas are limited to representations of specific sensorimotor events; schemas do not yet take the form of general rules or laws.

Preoperational children (from 2 to 7 years) are capable of formulating simple rules to help them explain and predict their social world (e.g., "People are divided into boys and girls"; "Hammers and trucks are boy things, but dolls and telephones are girl things"; and "If a boy does a girl thing, he gets into trouble"). But preoperational children's thought structures are seriously limited by their problem with *centration*, which is the tendency to focus attention exclusively on a single superficial aspect of a stimulus, a situation, or a person. This prevents children from looking beneath the surface of a person's appearance and behavior to infer the person's hidden motives, intentions, and other aspects of private psychological functioning. Preoperational children also lack an understanding of *conservation*, which is the knowledge that people can possess stable underlying attributes (such as enduring personality traits or dispositions) that remain relatively stable across moment-to-moment changes in their surface behavior

or appearance. For example, preoperational children fail to realize that a man may be basically mean and aggressive even if at the moment he happens to be smiling at you. Another aspect of the preoperational child's thinking is *egocentrism*: Preoperational children are so captivated by their own point of view and opinion that they cannot contemplate what another person's perspective on a situation might be.

At around age 7 children pass into the concrete operational stage, where they remain until roughly age 11. Concrete operational children can decenter, or look beneath the surface of things to detect and abstract underlying regularities. This allows them to conserve the underlying qualities of objects and people by conceiving of them in terms of more basic, invariant qualities. For example, children now understand gender constancy, or the idea that a person's sex is an invariant attribute that cannot be changed by altering hair length or by dressing the person in pants rather than a skirt. And they know that a person can be basically intelligent, mean, or altruistic, even if he or she sometimes does things that indicate otherwise. Concrete operational children also understand *compensation*, or the idea that changes in one variable can compensate for changes in a second variable. For example, they realize that a moderate degree of success can be caused by high ability and low effort, low ability and high effort, or some other combination of the interacting factors of ability and effort. The stage of concrete operations is also characterized by a *loss of egocentrism*. Children now appreciate that other people have perspectives and feelings that differ from their own and they can simultaneously consider and switch back and forth between the distinct viewpoints of several different people.

The social schemas of concrete operational children, however, are limited to people and events that are familiar to the children or are easily imaginable. It is not until children pass into the stage of formal operations (around age 11) that they can appreciate schemas that pertain to the unfamiliar or the hypothetical. Adults can learn about and understand a system of social roles in a foreign country, such as India, by hearing or reading about it. Concrete operational children, however, experience much difficulty grasping something with which they do not have first-hand experience.

What motivates children to progress through the various stages of social-cognitive development? Piaget (1926) and Kohlberg (1969) emphasize the role of *cognitive disequilibrium* in fueling mental growth. When children who possess a certain social schema encounter a new event that is somewhat discrepant with their schema, they become puzzled, or experience cognitive conflict. This motivates them to try to come up with a new, more sophisticated schema to explain the new event as well as the old. For example, the boy who believes that "My daddy is the boss of the whole world" may be appalled when he sees his father stopped by a police officer and given a stern lecture (as well as a ticket) for speeding. The boy's disequilibrium may motivate him to rethink his hierarchy of social roles and to redefine his father's position within it. It is the constant interplay between children's current level of understanding about social events and the exposure to discrepant new events that motivates social-cognitive development.

Piaget also speculated that a major source of the cognitive conflict necessary for growth is *peer interaction.* He believed that young children view their parents as superior, god-like beings whose authority, opinions, and sanctions may not be challenged. When disputes and differences of opinion arise, young children tend simply to accept their parents' viewpoints and decisions at face value: Whatever parents say must be right. But when children begin to interact with their peers, they find themselves having disputes with *equals.* Not being able to settle disagreements by resorting to a superior authority, the children have to try to resolve their misunderstandings and differences of opinion by working

things out by themselves. One consequence of this is that children—if they want to remain friends—will have to find solutions that respect the opinions, attitudes, and viewpoints of each other. In this way, children sharpen their skills at deciphering others' intentions and perspectives, and they gradually abandon their egocentrism. Peer interactions, then, are thought to be an especially fertile source of cognitive conflict that helps children move from the preoperational to the concrete operational level.

In this chapter, we shall see support for the cognitive-developmental view that systematic changes in children's social thinking occur with age. As children get older, for example, they do conceptualize people less in terms of surface characteristics and begin to "conserve" people's underlying psychological qualities. It has been hard to prove, however, that social-cognitive development proceeds via a sequence of well-knit stages. For example, children's skills at physical conservation, at social conservation, and at role taking do not develop at the same pace, despite the fact that all these skills theoretically depend on the same underlying thought structures (e.g., the ability to decenter).

Social Learning Theory

According to social learning theory (Bandura, 1977; Mischel, 1973), children learn about themselves, other people, and social relationships through both the direct and vicarious transactions they have with their social environment. To the social learning theorists, one of the most important aspects of social-cognitive development involves the learning of *contingency relationships,* or behavior-outcome rules ("If ____, then ____" relationships). Children are constantly striving to impose order on and make sense out of their worlds by generating contingency principles that will help them predict the social consequences (e.g., praise or criticism) that they and other people typically receive for performing certain responses in certain situations. Once children cognitively represent the contingencies governing human behavior, they are able not only to anticipate the behavior of other people but also to regulate their own behavior by deliberately performing behaviors that lead to positive social payoffs and by avoiding actions they know will get them into trouble. Thus social cognitions serve a major *motivational function*.

How do children learn contingency rules? Primarily by synthesizing information from three sources: (1) direct social consequences, or the outcomes the children themselves receive for performing various responses in various situations (e.g., parental discipline for misbehavior; evaluative feedback from peers, teachers, etc.); (2) vicarious experience, or observation of what others do and what happens to them for doing it; and (3) verbal instruction (e.g., a parent warns, "Don't do that! You'll get into trouble if you do"). Children's social cognitions are flexible, changing as their social learning experiences change.

Many of the contingency relationships that children learn specify the *external* consequences that a response is likely to receive (e.g., "If I make sister cry, mommy is likely to punish me"). However, standards for self-evaluation constitute another important class of social cognitions. A critical feature of social learning theory is that once children form associations between behavior and its consequences, they tend to internalize the contingency in the form of personal standards, or criteria for self-evaluation. In other words, once children form conceptions of praiseworthy and blameworthy behavior, they set performance goals and they react to their own behavior with self-criticism or self-satisfaction, depending on how well their behavior compares to their expectations and criteria. These standards for self-reinforcement, or internalized response-outcome contingencies, also serve an important motivational function (e.g., children strive to avoid behaviors that they think will make them feel guilty). The development of standards for self-evaluation

will be taken up in detail in the next chapter when processes of self-regulation are discussed.

Social learning theorists recognize that as children grow, they are also constantly forming and revising their conceptions of themselves—notions about their personality, dispositions, interests, competencies, and shortcomings. Children base these self-perceptions on several sources of information. Adults and peers may aid this process by verbally attributing qualities to children (e.g., "Boy, you sure are smart"; or "You're a very selfish young lady"). But what may be of greater importance is the fact that children observe their own behavior and draw conclusions from it. A child who consistently sees herself coping well in situations where many others are afraid—perhaps she does not mind handling bugs—may draw the conclusion that "I'm not a scaredy-cat; in fact, I'm rather interested in insects." Children, then, can abstract the common elements of their behavior (as well as other people's behavior) over time and across settings. As children get older, they also are more apt to use principles of logical inference when forming conclusions about people. For example, children are less likely to use their behavior as a clue to the sort of people they are if their behavior was forced on them by external factors. A girl who cleans up her room because her mother has threatened to "ground" her for a week if she doesn't do it will be less likely to conclude "I am the kind of girl who likes to keep things tidy" than a child who cleans up her room without external pressures. The notion that children's social cognitions are influenced by the factors that they perceive to be the cause of their behavior is also a main point of attribution theory, which is discussed later.

The fact that the social learning theorists regard social cognitions as fluid entities that are directly influenced by children's social learning experiences indicates that their view of social cognition is very different from that of the cognitive-developmental theorists. Recall that the latter theorists argue that children's social schemas are strictly tied or "fixed" to the underlying thought structures that characterize a child's particular stage of cognitive development. Social learning theorists do not believe that children possess underlying thought structures, such as centration and conservation, which pervasively influence the children's schemas. They argue that children of different ages *and* different children of the same age will have different cognitive representations of social experiences simply because they will have had different social experiences. As we learned in the last chapter, children who watch a lot of television develop biased and distorted views of the world, becoming less trustful of others and exaggerating their chances of being victimized by crime, probably because television is heavily populated with evil characters. Thus, according to the social learning view, children's social cognitions are flexible, forever changing as children's direct and vicarious transactions with their social environments change (e.g., as the punishments and rewards a child experiences change, or as the sorts of models to whom the child is exposed change).

Attribution Theory

A main premise of attribution theory is that people are constantly striving to seek explanations, or causal attributions, for both their own behavior and that of other people. If we know the factors that cause people to behave the way they do, we feel the world is a more stable, predictable, and controllable place in which to live (Heider, 1958). Furthermore, the causal attributions we make for behaviors significantly influence our subsequent social behavior. For example, if we decide that someone has stepped on our toes by accident, we are less likely to respond with anger than if we deem the act deliberate. Or, if we judge our success at some task to be due to our own hard work or high ability, we are more likely to reward ourselves for our achievement than if we believe our success is

attributable to some external factor, such as good luck or an easy task.

Attribution theorists (e.g., Bem, 1972; Heider, 1958; Jones & Nisbett, 1972; Kelley, 1973; Weiner, 1979) point out that people tend to follow certain rules when they are trying to figure out the causes of someone's behavior. These rules are called *causal attribution schemas*. For example, when looking for the cause of an event, people tend to look for a stimulus that preceded rather than followed the event (e.g., "Tom was noticed at the scene of the crime before the crime occurred, so he's a more likely suspect than Susan, who was not at the scene until afterwards"). This is called the *temporal contiguity schema*. As another example, people tend not to believe that an actor was intrinsically motivated to perform a behavior if they know some external incentive could have accounted for the actor's behavior (e.g., "Bobby shared his toys with a friend, but since his mother was watching with a stern look, I doubt if Bobby's sharing was motivated by an intrinsic desire to be altruistic"). This is known as the *discounting schema*.

A major goal of research conducted by attribution theorists is the charting of developmental trends in the use of causal attribution schemas. Results show that young children are not just less skilled than older children at inferring causality, but actually use qualitatively different schemas for deciding on the cause(s) of an event. In our section on the development of causal attribution, we describe the major schemas for inferring causality and discuss how children's use of the schemas changes with age.

ACQUIRING A SENSE OF SELF

Perhaps the most important achievement in the area of social-cognitive development is coming to understand one's own personality and psychological functioning. In this section the major steps in self-concept development are outlined, the more important dimensions of the mature self-concept are described, and influences on individual differences in children's self-concept development are discussed.

Steps in Self-Concept Development

Recognizing the Physical Self Perhaps the earliest step in self-concept development occurs when the infant learns to differentiate him- or herself from the environment and gradually realizes that he or she exists as a separate and distinct physical entity. During this process the infant forms an internal visual image of his or her own body and face. To determine the age at which infants first know what they look like, psychologists have observed infants' reactions to their reflections in a mirror. Although infants as young as 6 weeks gaze at themselves and try to touch themselves when placed before a mirror, it seems that most children do not form a clear mental image of their face until they are about 18 months old. This conclusion comes from studies in which investigators first unobtrusively apply a dot of rouge to the infants' noses and then watch them react to their altered images in a mirror. Only infants 18 months or older show surprise at the dot, try to touch it, or reveal in some other way that the dot is an unexpected addition (Bertenthal & Fischer, 1978; Lewis & Brooks, 1974).

Perceiving the Self in Terms of Surface Attributes Once children acquire language, they can be asked to describe themselves. In their self-descriptions, children younger than 8 or 9 tend to emphasize physical and observable qualities, such as their appearance, possessions, house, family and friends, and favorite activities (Livesley & Bromley, 1973; Peevers & Secord, 1973). The children may also indicate their simple likes and dislikes, but they make no other reference to psychological factors.

Emergence of the Psychological Self Psychological factors rarely figure in the self-descriptions of children younger than 8 or 9, but it is clear that children much younger than this are at least aware that they possess a private, psychological self in addition to the physical self. Three-year-olds, for example, will point to their heads when asked "Where is the part of you that knows your name and thinks about things?"; they will also answer "No" when someone stares directly into their eyes and asks "Can I see you thinking in there?" (Maccoby, 1980). Thus, by age 3 children have begun distinguishing the outer, physical self that is visible to others from the inner, thinking self that is not.

But it is not until well into the elementary-school years that children describe themselves in terms of stable personality dispositions and other underlying psychological dimensions that organize their personalities and behaviors. In one study, Livesley and Bromley (1973) asked English children of varying ages to describe themselves. Here is how two children, ages 7 and 9, replied. Notice how the 9-year-old's self-description makes more references to enduring psychological dispositions:

(Seven-year-old.) I am seven years old. I have one sister. Next year I will be 8. I like colouring. The game I like is hide the thimble. I go riding every Wednesday. I have lots of toys. My flowers is a rose, and a buttercup and a daisy. I love milk to drink and lemon. I like meat to eat and potatoes as well as meat. Sometimes I like jelly and soup as well.

(Nine-year-old.) I have dark brown hair, brown eyes, and a fair face. I am a quick worker but often lazy. I am good but often cheeky and naughty. My character is sometimes funny and sometimes serious. My behaviour is sometimes silly and stupid and often good it is often funny my daddy thinks. (pp. 237–238)

The fact that children do not apply trait labels to themselves until they are 8 or 9 years old agrees with Piaget's view that children must be in the concrete operational stage before they can conserve psychological attributes. However, to date, no evidence has been collected to show that dispositional attributions actually do depend on concrete operational thought structures.

Emergence of the "Social Selves"   Much of self-concept development involves recognizing the psychological dimensions on which one *differs* from other people. But, as Maccoby (1980) points out, "a parallel process is also taking place, and it is the opposite of differentiation. Increasingly the self is invested in or extended to other individuals and groups of people. The self comes to be defined in terms of the groups or individuals with whom the person's fate has become intertwined" (p. 267). In other words, as children develop, their self-concepts become extended to include the social roles and groups to which they belong or aspire. As they get older, their self-descriptions increasingly include such comments as, "I am a boy"; "I am a Girl Scout"; "I am Paul's friend"; "I am a Democrat"; and so on (Kuhn, 1960).

At the same time, as children expand their list of so-called "social selves" (James, 1896), they are learning that different social groups and roles place different demands on them and expect different things from them, and they learn to tailor their actions and presentations of the self to specific audiences. An adolescent boy will strive to present different images of himself to his girlfriend, his teachers, his fellow baseball-team members, his prospective employers, and so on. Perhaps one sign of maturity is the ability to juggle one's social selves while at the same time maintaining allegiance to a consistent core of goals, values, and standards that define the private self.

Dimensions of Self-Concept

The mature self-concept is not a single global entity but instead is comprised of several independent dimensions. Here we briefly describe these dimensions, indicating how they are measured and commenting on their importance for the child's adjustment.

The Real Self versus the Ideal Self   As children grow, they not only develop conceptions of what their personalities are presently like (their "real selves") but they also form notions of the sort of people they ideally would someday like to be (their "ideal selves"). Some children's real selves are very much like their ideal selves, but for other children, the real self falls far short of the ideal self. The difference between a child's real self and ideal self is called *self-image disparity*. To determine self-image disparity, children are first asked to rate themselves (using a 6-point scale) on items such as "When I try my best, I usually do a good job," and "It is hard for me to make friends." The scores are then averaged, giving an estimate of each child's real self. The children take the test again, but this time they rate the items according to how much they would like each comment to be true of them. Children's self-image disparity scores are determined by subtracting their score on the first testing from their score on the second testing (Katz & Zigler, 1967).

For most children, self-image disparity increases over the elementary-school years. This is partly because children's requirements for their ideal selves become more demanding as they get older and partly because their assessments of their real selves become less positive (Katz & Zigler, 1967). The self-image disparity scores of lower-class boys, however, tend to lessen over the school years. Also, black children tend to have lower disparity scores than white children. This is mainly because black children's ideal-self scores are depressed (Phillips & Zigler, 1980).

Contrary to what one might expect, children exhibiting high self-image disparity do not show more signs of anxiety, depression, or other behavioral disturbances than children with low self-image disparity. In fact, if anything, children with high self-image disparity test as socially more mature than children who perceive themselves as already meeting their ideals (Katz, Zigler, & Zalk, 1975).

Self-Esteem   Self-esteem is the evaluative component of the self-concept: If children are pleased with what they see in themselves, they are said to have high self-esteem. In one measure of self-esteem, children answer true or false to items such as "I'm proud of my schoolwork," "I'm popular with kids my own age," and "Kids usually follow my ideas" (Coopersmith, 1967). Coopersmith's longitudinal research suggests that by the end of the elementary-school years, most children have formed a rather stable estimate of their self-worth.

To see if self-esteem is related to social behavior, Coopersmith (1967) compared the behavior of high and low self-esteem children across a number of social situations. The advantages of high self-esteem were apparent. High self-esteem children were participants rather than passive listeners; they were assertive, confidently expressing their opinions even when they expected criticism; they were unlikely to bend to irrational peer pressures for conformity; they approached new tasks with confidence; they made friends easily; and they were not preoccupied with personal problems. Of course, since the study was correlational, all these desirable attributes could have been causes rather than consequences of self-esteem.

Locus of Control   Some children develop a pervasive sense that they are in control of their behavior and its outcomes—that they can choose their own activities and friends, that they have nobody to blame but themselves for their failings, that they can prevent unpleasant things from happening to themselves, that they can succeed in school if they try hard enough, and so on. Rotter (1966) has said that such children possess an *internal locus of control*. Other children have an opposite belief—that their behavior and its outcomes are at the mercy of luck, fate, or other circumstances beyond their control. In Rotter's terms, these children possess an *external locus of control*.

Several tests have been devised to assess where children fall along the locus-of-control dimension. One by Bialer (1961) asks children to respond to items such as, "When somebody gets mad at you, do you usually feel there is nothing you can do about it?" Another test, developed by Crandall, Katkovsky, and Crandall (1965), is designed to tap children's locus of control in achievement settings. Here is a sample item: "When you have trouble understanding something in school, is it usually (a) because the teacher didn't explain it clearly, or (b) because you didn't listen carefully?" Research shows that a child's global locus of control is usually pretty well established by the time the child reaches the third grade (Crandall et al., 1965; Nowicki & Strickland, 1973).

Locus of control is highly related to scholastic achievement, with internal locus-of-control children getting better grades and doing better on standardized achievement tests (Stipek & Weisz, 1981). Children who believe that control is out of their hands take more of a "Why bother?" attitude. They are also more likely to have learning problems.

Perceptions of Self-Efficacy   People are most likely to undertake and persist at activities they believe they are capable of performing competently, and they avoid and give up on activities they do not believe they can execute effectively. A boy will avoid enrolling in an algebra class if he does not believe that he can do arithmetic problems; a girl will avoid going swimming if she does not believe that she can stay afloat. Bandura (1977, 1981) refers to people's beliefs about their abilities to execute the actions that are necessary to produce and regulate the important events in their lives as their "perceptions of self-efficacy." Each individual is thought to possess a unique pattern of self-perceived competencies that influence which activities the individual will seek out or avoid.

Perceptions of self-efficacy should be distinguished from the other aspects of self-concept that we have discussed, such as locus of control. For example, a boy may firmly believe that success at an activity is dependent on personal qualities like ability and effort (i.e., has an internal locus of control), and yet avoid the activity because he does not believe that he is capable of performing the necessary responses. Most of us know that winning the Wimbledon tennis tournament results from talent and years of personal dedication and hard work, yet we do not enter the tournament because a realistic assessment of our own competencies recommends against it.

Determinants of Self-Concept

Thus far we have reviewed some universal steps in self-concept development and outlined some of the more important dimensions of the mature individual's self-understanding. Here we review some of the processes influencing the specific conclusions children draw about themselves, paying special attention to the issue of why different children come to develop different self-concepts.

The "Looking-Glass Self"   Children's self-concepts, in part, are reflections of the way they are viewed by others. It is hard for parents, teachers, siblings, and playmates to hide from children the love, the pride, the optimism, the disappointment, the rejection, and the other feelings they have for the children. The reactions people have to children serve as a sort of social mirror for children, and children incorporate what they see in this mirror into their self-concepts. The result is what has been called the *looking-glass self* (Cooley, 1902; Mead, 1934).

Evidence for the operation of the looking-glass self comes from Coopersmith's (1967) study of the parents of boys who display varying degrees of self-esteem. Coopersmith discovered that the parents of boys with high self-esteem showed more approval, affection, appreciation, and respect toward their sons than did the parents of boys with low self-esteem. Parents of the high self-esteem group avoided the use of power assertive discipline,

and they more often allowed their sons to participate in family decisions and plans. Though the direction of causality is undetermined, it seems likely that high self-esteem in part results from feeling approved of by one's parents.

In Chapter 3, we noted that when adults verbally attribute positive qualities such as honesty, altruism, and achievement motivation to children (e.g., "I know that you're very bright"), the children frequently endeavor to display the attributed characteristics, even when the adults are not in their presence. In other words, verbal attributions may influence the degree to which children perceive themselves as possessing a trait. However, earlier in this chapter we also noted that children do not usually think of themselves as possessing traits or dispositions that produce consistency in their behavior across time and situations until they approach their eighth birthday. This raises an interesting point: If children are incapable of thinking of themselves as possessing traits until they are 8 or 9, then perhaps telling children younger than this that they possess a trait will have relatively limited effects on their behavior. Grusec and Redler (1980) conducted research to address this issue.

In their study, Grusec and Redler first asked 5- and 8-year-old children to donate to a child a portion of their winnings from a game they had played. Afterwards, some of the children of each age level were told: "You know, you certainly are a nice person; I bet you're someone who is helpful whenever possible." Later all the children were tested on a measure of altruism in a new situation—the children were given an opportunity to collect craft materials for hospitalized children, and their efforts to do so were measured. The main finding was that the verbal attribution of an altruistic trait increased altruistic behavior in the new situation for the 8-year-olds, but not for the 5-year-olds. This finding does not mean that adults should refrain from making prosocial attributions until children reach age 8, but it does suggest that children become increasingly likely to see the relevance of a trait attribution for new situations as they get older. The study also illustrates how children's level of social-cognitive functioning can influence their reactions to an adult's socialization tactics.

Are some children better skilled than others at deciphering others' opinions of them? Leahy and Huard (1976) suggested that children who are skilled in role taking, or the ability to put oneself in another's shoes and imagine what that person is thinking or feeling, should be more sensitive to other people's attitudes toward them and thus be more inclined to incorporate others' attitudes into their self-concepts. These authors found that children who scored high on a test of role taking (by doing a good job of retelling a story from the point of view of one of its characters) had higher self-image disparity scores than children who performed more poorly on the perspective-taking test. Possibly, children who are good at reading others' attitudes evaluate their "real selves" more realistically, but they may also have stricter guidelines for their "ideal selves" because they are better able to infer what other people want and expect from them.

Self-Observation   A child reaches decisions about the type of person he or she is partly by observing his or her own behavior. For example, a boy who rides dirt bikes, reads Hardy Boys mysteries, and plays baseball, but avoids playing with dolls, reading Nancy Drew books, and playing hopscotch may conclude that he is "masculine." And a girl who finds herself cheating on spelling tests and telling white lies to her mother may decide she is perhaps a little "dishonest." Numerous personality traits are probably inferred through self-observation, which is the abstraction of common elements running through one's behavior over time and place, assigning trait labels for the common threads.

A child's locus of control may result from observing his or her own behavior, its outcomes, and correlations between the two; and

the process may begin as early as infancy. Recall from Chapter 2 that infants whose mothers respond quickly to their bids for attention become more secure in their belief that mother is controllable, and that infants who have learned to control the operation of toys and mobiles show more motivation to master new and challenging learning situations than infants who have learned that they are helpless at influencing outcomes. As children get older, they encounter more and more opportunities for learning that they do or do not control important events: Playmates can follow (or refuse to follow) their suggestions for play; daddy can spank predictably whenever they misbehave (or only when the mood strikes him); and scholastic success can come only after hard work (or without even trying).

Children's assessment of their competencies—their self-efficacy perceptions—also results in part from children reflecting on their actual history of successful and unsuccessful performances. Bandura's (1981) studies, for example, show that there is no better way of convincing people that they have become capable of coping with a feared stimulus than by getting them to practice and master effective coping responses in the presence of the stimulus.

Causal Attribution of Behavior   Children draw conclusions about themselves not just from observing their past behavior but also from observing what has caused them to behave the way they have. For example, a girl who receives a prize in an essay contest will be less likely to conclude that she is a competent young author if her mother helped her write the essay than if she wrote it herself. In addition, a boy who refrains from "clobbering" a bothersome sister only because his mother has threatened him with punishment if he hits her is less likely to conclude that he is by nature a "good boy" than if he spontaneously chooses to avoid aggression without external coercion. These examples illustrate an important principle of self-understanding: Children are most likely to use their behavior to draw a conclusion about the kind of person they are when they cannot attribute their behavior to some external cause. This principle in fact is so important that it forms the cornerstone of Bem's *self-perception theory*, an influential attribution-theory view of self-cognition.

A study by Smith, Gelfand, Hartmann, and Partlow (1979) illustrates Bem's principle. Initially, children were asked to donate to charity some of their earnings from a game. Some children were promised monetary rewards for complying with the request to share, while other children were threatened with punishment for *not* sharing. Still another group was gently asked to share—the experimenter did not "twist their arms" by threatening to punish, nor were they bribed. All the children complied with the request to share, but when the children were later asked to give reasons why they shared, it was only the latter, noncoerced children who explained their sharing in terms of a personal disposition to be altruistic (e.g., "I didn't want to be selfish"; "I guess I just like to share"). When children perceive their behavior to be caused by external motivators, then, they do not conclude that they are intrinsically motivated to perform the behavior. This is one reason why we concluded in Chapter 3 that parents should avoid the use of power assertive discipline, whenever possible, when looking for ways to motivate their children to perform desirable behaviors.

Parents who are bossy, intrusive, and who insist on solving their children's problems for them may be preventing their children from concluding that they are in control of the important events in their lives. In a revealing study, Loeb (1975) asked boys with either an internal or an external locus of control to build a tower out of irregularly shaped blocks while their parents looked on. The parents were told that they could help their sons as much or as little as they liked. Parents of boys displaying an external locus of control more often gave direct orders without first allowing the boys to attempt solutions by themselves.

Parents of boys who appeared to have an internal locus of control more often left the actual solution finding to the boys, and their comments more often were of a suggestive rather than a directive nature (e.g., "Why don't you try this square piece?").

Social Comparison   One of the ways that children decide what kind of people they are is by comparing their behavior to that of other people. A child thinks she is smart if she does better than everyone else on an exam, and she may believe that she is stingy if she finds out that she gave a smaller birthday gift at a party than anyone else. The process of comparing one's actions to those of others is known as *social comparison* (Festinger, 1954).

When searching for clues to determine the sort of people they are, both children and adults tend to compare their actions to those of other people who are *similar* to themselves. To determine their competencies, for example, adults usually compare their accomplishments to those of other adults, not to the skills of children much younger than themselves. Likewise, children tend to turn to their peer reference group (i.e., others of their sex, age, etc.) to see how they compare (Brittain, 1963).

Children engage in social comparison from a surprisingly early age. In one field study, 3- and 4-year-olds were observed while they interacted with playmates in a nursery school (Mosatche and Bragonier, 1981). The children frequently made verbalizations that reflected social comparison (e.g., "My spaceship is higher than yours"; "I hope I'm ahead of you"; "I'm 4½; you're 4"). However, it is unlikely that children use social comparison to reach decisions about their *generalized underlying traits* (enduring competencies and dispositions) until several years later. Ruble, Boggiano, Feldman, and Loebl (1980), for example, found that children's estimates of their underlying abilities were not influenced by their knowledge of how their performance in achievement contexts compared with the performance of other children until the children turned 7 or 8—the typical age for the onset of self-attribution of stable traits.

PERSON PERCEPTION

At about the same time that they are refining their self-concepts, children are also becoming better skilled at processing information about others. Here we deal with the topic of person perception, or with how children perceive and organize information about others. Our discussion focuses on two questions. First, how do the dimensions in which children perceive others change with age? Second, what leads children to develop racial stereotypes?

Age Changes in Children's Perceptions of Others

The fact that infants only a few months old can recognize and selectively seek out certain people, preferring them to others (Brooks-Gunn & Lewis, 1981; see also Chapter 2), suggests that the process of building up visual-image schemas to represent specific others starts very early in life. As infants get older, they probably also begin to associate certain behaviors and events with their schemas of specific people. For example, an infant may associate his mother with relief from distress, playing peek-a-boo, and getting fed, and his father with a deep voice, a scratchy beard, and playing physical-interactive games. In Chapter 2 we discussed some of the qualities of people that seem to "matter" in one way or another to infants (e.g., whether a person is predictable and responsive, whether a person provides the child with playful distance receptor stimulation). Perhaps infants integrate certain of these social-interactive dimensions into their schemas of familiar others.

Once children acquire language, we can ask them how they perceive people. This is precisely what a number of researchers have done (Barenboim, 1977, 1981; Livesley &

Bromley, 1973; Peevers & Secord, 1973; Yarrow & Campbell, 1963). In a typical study, children of different ages are asked to pick several people whom they know well and describe them the best they can. Results reveal some striking age changes in the dimensions children use to describe other people. Some of these changes, as we shall see, parallel changes that occur in the area of self-perception.

When asked to describe people, preschoolers tend to focus on a person's superficial appearance, possessions, environment, and typical activities (e.g., "He lives in a big house"; "She has red hair"). They rarely refer to people's psychological characteristics, but when they do, their descriptors tend to be global and highly evaluative (e.g., "She is very nice"; "He is horrible"). They have difficulty thinking of people in terms of underlying, enduring personality dispositions that produce consistency in a person's behavior across time and situations. Many of the young child's comments have an egocentric flavor in that they refer to personal experiences the child has had with the person being described (e.g., "She gives me candy"; "He hits me"). The Piagetians argue that the preoperational child's problems with centration and egocentrism are responsible for the nature of these early person schemas.

Over the elementary-school years (especially the period from 7 to 10 years), children dramatically increase their use of psychological terms when describing another person. They increasingly refer to the other's inner thoughts, feelings, and intentions, and they less often talk about what the person overtly does. Egocentric references decline. At about the same time as children begin to perceive themselves in terms of underlying traits—8 or 9 years—they also begin to apply trait labels to other people (e.g., "He's stubborn"; "He's really conceited"; "She's selfish"). Again, the Piagetians believe that the use of trait labels reflects attainment of the concrete operational stage. Regardless of the merits of this claim, it would seem that the perception of traits does depend on social learning experiences. A study by Barenboim (1981), for example, shows that children begin to use trait labels to summarize people's dispositions only after years of observing people and noticing that some people consistently display greater or lesser degrees of a behavior than other people.

Some interesting developments in person perception occur as children enter adolescence. In their descriptions of others, adolescents reveal an awareness that behavior is often a function of interaction between people's personality dispositions and situational factors (e.g., "He's shy when he's around girls"; "She's usually very collected, but she can get mad if you push her"). Qualifying words like "if," "but," "because," and "when" figure prominently in their descriptions. (An exception occurs when children are asked to describe *disliked* others. In such cases, children prefer unqualified trait descriptors—the disliked person is simply "mean," "unpleasant," and "selfish," for instance, and there are no ifs, buts, or whens about it; (Leahy, 1976; Peevers & Secord, 1973; Rosenbach, Crockett, & Wapner, 1973). An interesting point— and one that is contrary to Piagetian theory— is that adolescents' descriptions of friends often contain many egocentric references. Perhaps this is because adolescent friendships tend to depend on children collaborating to satisfy each other's needs (Honess, 1980).

The Development of Racial Stereotypes

Even 2- and 3-year-old children realize that some people have dark skin and other people have light skin. Although children do not "conserve" race (or realize that it is a permanent attribute linked to underlying biological factors) until several years later (Clark, Hocevar, & Dembo, 1980), it is clear that even young preschoolers tend to associate black skin color with undesirable attributes. When children are shown pictures of black and white children and asked to select pictures of children to exemplify adjectives such as honest, smart, friendly, mean, dumb, and impolite, children of *both* races tend to choose pictures of white children to illustrate positive attributes and pictures of black children to represent negative attributes (Banks & Rompf, 1973; Cantor, 1972; Cantor & Paternite, 1973; Doke & Risley, 1972; Spencer & Horowitz, 1973; Stevenson & Stewart, 1958; Williams, Boswell, & Best, 1975). In one study, children were told stories in which the central character, who was described as being either black or white, performed acts that might have been aggressive (e.g., bumping into someone in the hallway, or using another's pencil without asking). Children of both races rated the behavior as more violent and threatening when the character was black than when he was white (Sagar & Schofield, 1980). Most of these effects do not depend on the race of the adult testing the children.

What is responsible for these findings? In large measure, children's beliefs simply mirror the oppressive and discriminative practices of American society. Children have ample opportunity for learning prejudice through direct experience and by observing the attitudes expressed by their parents, teachers, playmates, and the media. On television, for example, black people are underrepresented, tend to be assigned low-status roles, and are often made to look ridiculous when they do appear (Stein & Friedrich, 1975). Both black and white children may internalize the prejudices of the more powerful white majority, coming to believe that these prejudices are a true reflection of the black person's nature. As a consequence, black children sometimes develop symptoms of passivity, depression, fearfulness, and low self-esteem (Banks, 1976; Banks, McQuater, & Ross, 1979; Williams & Morland, 1979).

A number of lesser factors may also play a role in the development of racial stereotypes. The fact that white symbolizes goodness and black symbolizes badness in children's literature may make a contribution. Another possibility involves the young child's experiences as a diurnal, as opposed to a nocturnal, animal: Light and day are the time for happiness and social interaction with one's loved ones, whereas darkness and night signal separation and fear. This may cause lightness to take on positive qualities and darkness to assume threatening qualities. This hypothesis is supported by the finding that children who hold strong fears of the dark and of thunderstorms tend to hold the most negative stereotypes about black figures (Boswell & Williams, 1975).

Finally, there is Katz's "perceptual discrimination" hypothesis—children may have more difficulty discriminating among faces of another race. This may reduce their ability to predict and control the actions of individual members of another race, causing mistrust and fear. Lumping all members of a given race together in a single perceptual category may also increase the chances that one will react similarly (i.e., prejudicially) toward all members of that group (Feinman & Entwisle, 1976; Katz, 1973a, 1973b; Katz & Seavey, 1973; Katz, Sohn, & Zalk, 1975).

A major goal of much contemporary research is to discover ways of eliminating prejudice in children. Several methods of reducing prejudice have been explored. These include exposing children to other-race individuals who are displaying positive, counter-stereotype behaviors (Bogatz & Ball, 1971; Gorn, Goldberg, & Kanungo, 1976); teaching children to discriminate perceptually among other-race faces (Katz & Zalk, 1978); and providing positive contacts between children of different races (Amir, 1976; Stephan, 1978).

CAUSAL ATTRIBUTION

An important aspect of social-cognitive functioning involves causal attribution, or making decisions about what is causing people to behave the way they do. We have already touched on issues of causal attribution in this chapter in our discussion of Bem's view that children's self-perceptions depend on their perceptions of the causes of their behavior. But here we examine in greater detail how children come to perceive the causes underlying *other* people's behavior.

The importance of causal attribution to effective social interaction is obvious: We often cannot respond appropriately to someone's behavior unless we know the factors motivating that behavior. Consider some examples of the everyday attribution problems children face: "Did Paul hurt my feelings on purpose or by accident?"; "Did Susan share her allowance with me because she enjoys being generous or because she's planning to ask me for a special favor in return?"; and "Is Daddy acting mad at me because I did something to upset him or because he's in a bad mood?" Accuracy in causal attribution is clearly an adaptive skill to acquire.

In this section, we examine the development of the rules, or schemas, that children use to help them determine the causes of someone's behavior. There are several important questions to be answered about the development of causal attribution, and we shall try to answer them in turn: How do children come to know the usual causes of common events (how do they learn, for instance, that aggression is often provoked by frustration, or insult, or some other aversive stimulus)? How do children learn to distinguish accidental from intentional behavior? How do they infer an actor's motives and goals? How do children decide whether to hold an actor personally responsible for his or her behavior or to excuse the actor's behavior as due to compelling situational circumstances? When children realize that several causes could have contributed to an event, what rules of logic do they use to assign weights to the various possible causes?

Learning the Typical Causes of Everyday Events

Even infants sometimes behave as if they understand the causes of some events. In fact, it is difficult not to conclude that the 1-year-old who calls for his or her mother does not have at least some understanding of the rule that "calling makes mommy come." But without the benefit of language, infants' representation of cause-and-effect links will necessarily be limited.

By the time children are 3 or 4 years old, or old enough to be interrogated about their perceptions of causes, they can identify some of the typical causes of many common everyday events. For example, if preschoolers hear stories in which the central character experiences a common emotion, such as anger, fear, happiness, or sadness, and the children are asked to suggest a reason for the character's emotion, they do fairly well (Green, 1977).

To detect the cause of an event, people utilize certain *schemas of causal inference*. For example, people use a *covariation schema*, which is a rule specifying that a stimulus is unlikely to be the cause of an event unless it covaries with the event (i.e., is present when the event occurs and is absent when the event doesn't occur). People also use a *temporal contiguity schema*. Even preschoolers systematically employ these basic rules (although not perfectly) for inferring the cause of an event (Kuhn & Phelps, 1976; Kun, 1978; Shultz & Mendelson, 1975; Shultz & Ravinsky, 1977; Siegler, 1976; Siegler & Liebert, 1974).

As children get older, they improve their understanding of the causes of an increasingly broad array of social phenomena. They develop better understandings of why people get ill (Kister & Patterson, 1980); of what makes some people go crazy (Coie & Pennington, 1976; Maas, Marecek, & Travers, 1978); of why people die (Koocher, 1973; White, Elsom, & Prawat, 1978); and so on.

To determine changes in children's understanding of conception, Bernstein and Cowan (1975) asked children of different ages where they thought babies come from. The children's replies, many of which were rather amusing, could be classified into one of six

progressively more mature developmental levels. We'll briefly review these.

At Level 1, or the most primitive level of understanding, children believe that babies have always existed, preformed, inside their mothers. Most 3- and 4-year-olds fall here. At a slightly more advanced stage, Level 2, children see the baby as a manufactured object that is then implanted in the mother. Here is how one child put it:

[How does the baby get in the tummy?] Just make it first. [How?] Well, you just make it. You put some eyes on it . . . Put the head on, and hair, some hair all curls. [With?] You make it with head stuff. [How?] You find it at a store that makes it . . . Well, they get it and then they put it in the tummy and then it goes quickly out. (p. 81)

At Level 3, children see babies as the product of a loving relationship between the parents and as biologically produced during sexual intercourse, but they show confusion over whether it is the parents' love or their physical union that is primarily responsible. As one 8-year-old put it:

It's like when people are naked, and they're together, and they just lie together, I guess. Like they're hugging. Some men give hickies, except my Dad don't. They're just . . . together [What does that have to do with getting babies?] I don't know. I guess it's like mothers and fathers are related, and their loving each other forms a baby, I guess. [How?] I don't know. It's just there's love and I guess it just forms a baby, like I said before . . . (p. 88)

Level 4 children more definitely realize the importance of sexual intercourse and that it takes something from the father (usually the "seed") and something from the mother (the "egg") to produce a baby, but they do not realize that the sperm and ovum contain the genetic material that programs growth. By Level 5, children are familiar with genetic transmission, but they tend to be either *ov-*

ists, who believe that the child grows from the egg (the father's role was just to start it growing) or *animalculists,* who believe that the baby originates from and develops out of the sperm (with the mother's egg providing food). Here is the way one animalculist put it:

> Well if they're the man that made love to your mother, then they're your father because you really originally came out of him, and then went into your mother. [More?] Well you were a sperm inside of him, there. So that you're the, you're really his daughter or son. 'Cause he was the one that really had you first. [Why must the egg be there for the sperm to develop into a baby?] 'Cause otherwise the sperm will have, uh, nothing to nourish it, or sort of keep it warm or, you know, able to move or something . . . . (p. 89)

Finally, at Level 6, children provide a reasonably sophisticated scientific theory of how people get babies. Most adolescents, for example, know that genetic material from both the mother and the father combines to produce a baby.

One finding from Bernstein and Cowan's study was that children who did not know where babies come from tended to invent their own explanations. One child at Level 2 suggested that a woman who wants a baby should go to a store and buy a duck because ducks turn into babies. Some older children believed that simply lying naked next to each other and hugging produced a baby. Such findings suggest that in the absence of accurate sex education, children may construct their own notions about where babies come from.

Cognitive-developmental theorists argue that children will not grasp the causes of some events until they are in the concrete operational stage and can conserve. For example, it has been argued that children cannot comprehend the causes of death until they can conserve life (or conceive of life as an underlying invariant property of human existence) and that they cannot explain deviant

or crazy behavior until they conserve normality (or realize that there is a fixed range of acceptable behavior that characterizes the behavior of most people). Links between Piagetian operations and causal attribution have not yet been convincingly demonstrated, however. Perhaps children's improvements in causal attribution are due more to their growing knowledge of the actual causes of specific events than to their underlying stage of cognitive development (Kister & Patterson, 1980).

Distinguishing the Accidental from the Intentional

We may know that the pain we are experiencing was caused by someone stepping on our toes, but to interpret the situation meaningfully, we must go a step further than this preliminary attribution: We must also decide whether the behavior was accidental or deliberate.

By kindergarten (and perhaps earlier), children show some accuracy in differentiating between the accidental ("She didn't mean to") and the intended ("It was on purpose"). However, young children's discriminations are not perfect. One mistake that young children frequently make is that of attributing intent to actions that are in fact accidental (Flavell, 1977; Harris, 1977; Karniol, 1978; Sedlak, 1979).

How do children tell whether an act is deliberate or accidental? People use several schemas for inferring intentionality. To be deemed intentional, actions must be *voluntary* and *their effects on the environment foreseeable.* Sneezing and hiccuping are involuntary acts and cannot be performed intentionally; kicking and bumping can be either intended or unintended; and speaking and punching can only be intentional. Young children sometimes fail to utilize these distinctions when judging intent (M. C. Smith, 1978). Another schema that helps people decide if an act was intentional or not is the *balance principle* (Heider, 1958). This principle specifies that actions that serve to produce positive outcomes for the actor and actions that serve to prevent negative outcomes for the actor are probably (but not necessarily) intentional. Use of the balance principle to distinguish between accidental and deliberate acts increases with age (Whiteman, Brook, & Gordon, 1974).

Children's improvement in telling the accidental from the intentional will depend on their social learning experiences as well as their use of *intentionality schemas*. Through observational learning and personal experience children eventually notice that certain behaviors are ordinarily preceded by certain cues, embedded in particular contexts, and followed by certain consequences. Acts of kicking are often preceded by angry facial cues and followed by expressions of pain; acts of helping are typically preceded by smiles or concerned looks and followed by signs of gratitude. Children probably build up stores of expectations of what needs to be present in order to judge an act to be intentional. Kicking without anger or helping without looking concerned is less likely to be intentional than similar behavior that includes the expected antecedents. Adults may help children abstract the cues indicating intent by judiciously labeling behaviors with comments such as "She didn't mean to" and "I could tell he did that on purpose."

Perceiving an Actor's Motive

Let's say we see one child hit another. Even though we may know that the hitting was no accident (i.e., we know it was intentional), we are unlikely to be satisfied with our interpretation of the event until we know the hitter's motive. Was the hitter angry? Was the hitter trying to take something from the other child? Was the hitter trying to teach the other child a lesson?

Preschool children show some ability to infer people's motivations (Berndt & Berndt, 1975; Shantz, 1975). For example, they can tell whether someone is trying to help or trying to hurt someone else. Kindergarteners also use information about people's motives to make moral judgments about how good or how bad a person is. In one study, they judged aggression aimed at teaching the victim a lesson as less naughty than aggression aimed simply to hurt the victim (Rule, Nesdale, & McAra, 1974). As children develop, they become increasingly aware of the tremendous diversity of goals, rewards, and other motives that can propel people to behave in certain ways. We still have much to learn about the rules or schemas children of different ages employ to infer another's motives, but it is clear that skill in this aspect of social-cognitive functioning does improve with age.

Attribution of Responsibility: Is the Person or the Situation to Blame?

If we see Susie hit Sam, and he cries, we may correctly conclude that Susie's action was intentional and furthermore that it was motivated by a wish to hurt Sam. But this does not necessarily mean that we will *blame* Susie for her action. Maybe there was something about the situation that justified Susie's action and relieves her of blame or responsibility for her action. Perhaps Sam antagonized Susie by teasing or attacking her first. An important aspect of the attribution process involves deciding whether to hold a person responsible for his or her actions or whether to conclude that environmental forces compelled the person to perform the behavior (and therefore that the person is not truly to be held responsible for his or her actions).

To understand attribution of responsibility, it is helpful to realize that most causes of behavior can be classified into one of two broad categories. These categories include "personal" causes (causes that originate within the person, such as personality dispositions, traits, intentions, motives, abilities, and other internal attributes) and "situational" causes (causes originating outside the person, such as orders from a parent, pressure from one's peers, threats of external punishment, attractive material rewards, and other external incentives). Often people do not feel that they can respond appropriately to a person's behavior until they have decided how much of that person's behavior is due to personal factors and how much of it is due to external circumstances. People are more inclined to praise someone's good behavior, for example, if they regard the behavior as personally determined rather than situationally produced.

Here we shall first consider some of the schemas children use for making personal (internal) and situational (external) attributions. We then discuss some of the biases and errors that people are prone to make when apportioning responsibility.

Schemas for Making Internal and External Attributions   Let us again assume that Susie hit Sam: Is she personally responsible for her behavior or can her aggression be attributed to situational circumstances? One way to decide involves determining whether Susie behaves aggressively toward all children or whether her aggression is limited to Sam. If Susie is aggressive toward everyone, then her behavior can be attributed to a personal disposition (e.g., "Boy, is Susie an aggressive kid!"). If her aggression is restricted to a certain target, however, her action can be identified as situational. Thus one criterion for attribution of responsibility involves the distinctiveness of an actor's behavior (or the degree to which an actor limits a behavior to particular circumstances). A *distinctiveness schema*, then, specifies that low-distinctive behaviors are personally determined (Kelley, 1973).

Another approach to deciding whether to blame Susie or the situation involves comparing Susie's behavior toward Sam with the behavior of other children toward Sam. If many other children also pick on Sam, it is more likely that Susie's behavior is situational (e.g., "Boy, Sam is so irritating—he really asks

for it!"). When a behavior is performed by most people in a given situation, the behavior is said to carry high consensus. A *consensus schema*, then, specifies that high-consensus acts are situationally determined (Kelley, 1973).

By the time children reach the first grade, they use information about both the distinctiveness and the consensus of a story character's behavior to decide whether personal qualities of the character or external circumstances are to be credited for the actor's behavior (DiVitto & McArthur, 1978; Shaklee, 1976; Shultz & Butkowsky, 1977). Further research is needed to determine just how early the use of these schemas starts and what social and cognitive experiences underlie development of the schemas.

Biases in Attribution of Responsibility   Adults are strongly biased toward explaining other people's behavior in terms of personal dispositions (Heider, 1958; Ross, 1977). This is known as the *fundamental attribution error*. Most adults who see Susie hit Sam, for example, would probably assume that Susie is an aggressive child without bothering to search for possible situational contributors.

The fundamental attribution error takes time to develop. In fact, young children possess the exact opposite kind of bias—they tend to invoke situational explanations for events. In line with Piaget's observation that young children focus their attention on perceptually salient environmental events, young children search out and seize on external factors when asked to explain people's behavior (Coie & Pennington, 1976; Whiteman, Brook, & Gordon, 1974). This does not mean that young children *never* use dispositional explanations, because sometimes they do—even when adults would not. For example, when asked why a waitress has brought a glass of milk to the table, little children may answer, "Because she is a nice lady" (Flavell, 1977). And young children more often say that people who display deviant behavior (e.g., craziness or antisocial aggression) do so because they were "born that way" rather than because of possible environmental stresses and elicitors (Maas et al., 1978). Nevertheless, younger children more often look to observable situational events as causes. Eventually their bias reverses and they come to favor dispositional attributions, revealing the fundamental attribution error.

People who explain the actions of others strictly in terms of personal dispositions are doubtless going to make some errors in attribution. However, a recent study by Cutrona and Feshbach (1979) suggests that children who make the fundamental attribution error are more likely to behave toward other children in ways that reflect a sensitivity and respect for the feelings of others. In this study, children heard stories describing characters in conflict over what course of action to take. The children were asked to predict what they thought each character would do and were also asked to give reasons for their predictions. Children who described the story characters as motivated by considerations involving other people's thoughts and feelings rather than by external situational factors were rated by their teachers as more altruistic (i.e., generous, helpful, and cooperative) and as less aggressive.

Another bias in attribution of responsibility bears mentioning. Although people are biased to explain *other people's* behavior in terms of dispositional factors, most people are biased to explain their *own* behavior in terms of situational factors (Watson, 1982). This has been called the *observer-actor difference* in attribution (Jones & Nisbett, 1972; Kelley, 1973). What might account for this difference? Perhaps actors are simply more aware of the situational factors affecting them than are observers. A difference in perspective may contribute, too: Actors look out toward the environment when searching for causes of their behavior, whereas observers are looking directly at the actor (Peevers & Secord, 1973). And there is another possibility. Actors tend to believe that other people would have be-

haved the same way they did under similar circumstances—in other words, they perceive a "false consensus" for their own behavior (Ross, 1977). Remember that people tend to conclude that high-consensus behaviors are situationally determined.

Regardless of its causes, the observer-actor difference in attribution of responsibility has important implications. We shall see in the next chapter, for example, that people are more likely to make excuses for their own immoral conduct than they are to excuse similar behavior by others.

Schemas for Inferring Multiple Causes

Adults realize that most events have several possible causes and, furthermore, that two or more causes can combine to produce an effect. If, for example, a young man, John, scores high on a school exam, there are probably a number of reasons for his success (high ability, high effort, an easy test, good luck, etc.). Instead of picking out just one of these factors as *the* cause of John's success, it is possible to subjectively assign weights to the different causal factors (e.g., "It was probably mostly John's high ability that caused his success, but the test wasn't really all that hard and that may have helped too").

Preschool children show little awareness that several causes can interact in producing an effect. One way researchers have studied this is by telling children about odd or incongruous events (e.g., about a police officer who sees a man steal a car, but does nothing about it, or about a child who breaks into a smile just as a nurse sticks a needle into her arm) and then asking the children to explain the events. Preschoolers usually seize on a single possible cause—usually a situational one—to account for the behavior (Burns & Cavey, 1957; Deutsch, 1974a; Whiteman et al., 1974). As children mature, they begin to see that events can be multidetermined (Erwin & Kuhn, 1979).

When people realize that several factors

could have contributed to an event, they sometimes follow certain rules of logic in order to assign weights to the various possible causes. Earlier, when we discussed Bem's theory of how children's self-perceptions are influenced by causal attribution, we discussed one of these schemas. Specifically, we noted that when children perceive their behavior to be externally motivated (e.g., by an attractive bribe or a threat of punishment), they are unlikely to conclude that they are by nature intrinsically motivated to perform the activity.

The rule that suggests discounting intrinsic motivation when external factors can account for a behavior is called the *discounting principle*. It is one example of a more general rule called the *multiple sufficient schema*. According to the multiple sufficient schema, when people know that one cause has contributed to an event they are trying to explain, they assign less importance to other possible causes of that event. For example, John's success on his exam can be sufficiently explained by the fact that he is bright; therefore, less weight may be assigned to other possible causal factors, such as great effort or good luck (Bem, 1972; Heider, 1958; Kelley, 1973; Weiner, 1979).

By the time children enter elementary school they are using the discounting schema (Baldwin & Baldwin, 1970; Karabenick & Heller, 1976; Karniol & Ross, 1976; Kun, 1977; Leahy, 1979; Nicholls, 1978; Smith, 1975). However, younger children do not systematically employ the discounting principle. In fact, many preschoolers use a qualitatively different kind of rule when deciding what the presence of one cause implies about the contribution of other possible causes. To illustrate this, consider asking children of different ages the following question: "Who enjoys cleaning up her room: Susan, who just got up one morning and decided to clean up her room, or Alice, who cleaned up her room because her mother promised her a dollar for doing it?" School-age children will tend to answer "Susan"; they are taking the mother's

bribe as a sufficient explanation for Alice's behavior and thus are discounting intrinsic interest on Alice's part. But how will kindergarten children respond? A good number of them will answer "Alice." Curiously, they seem to be using the presence of one cause (the external bribe) to imply the *presence* rather than the absence of a second cause (the intrinsic desire to clean). These children are not just responding randomly, because they show a similar style of reasoning across other story examples. These children are said to be using an *additive principle*, because they see extrinsic inducements as adding to the strength of intrinsic factors (DiVitto & McArthur, 1978; Karniol & Ross, 1976; Kun, 1977; Leahy, 1979).

What might account for this curious feature of young children's causal attribution? According to Piaget's theory, young children believe that any behavior that is insisted on and rewarded by adults must be inherently good and desirable. Thus when little children hear that authority figures have used external incentives to encourage a child to do something, they automatically assume that the behavior is desirable and therefore that the actor must have wanted to perform it. Another possibility is that young children are relatively deficient in reading others' intentions and thus, unlike older children, they may fail to realize that adults sometimes manipulatively offer rewards to children to get them to do things that are inherently unpleasant (Karniol & Ross, 1979; Ransen, 1980). Children's immature cognitive capacities may contribute to their use of an additive principle, too. Kun (1977) suggests that young children over-apply their understanding of positive correlation: When they hear that one factor associated with an event is present, they tend to think that other factors sometimes associated with the event are also present. Thus if they hear that someone who has succeeded at a task has high ability, they tend to think that the person must have tried hard, too. An understanding of negative correlation and compensation (knowing that increases in the strength of one cause render the operation of other causes less necessary) may develop later.

Although the bulk of the research reveals that preschool children tend not to use the discounting principle, we should point out that this conclusion stems from research in which children have been asked to explain the behavior of people other than themselves. Perhaps young children do use the discounting principle when it applies to their own behavior in real-life situations (Shultz & Butkowsky, 1977; Wells & Shultz, 1980). We noted in Chapter 3, for example, that when preschool children are promised and given attractive material rewards for engaging in play activities (such as drawing pictures or playing musical instruments), they sometimes show reduced interest in the activities if the rewards are withdrawn. The usual interpretation of this result is that the children have employed the discounting principle. Presumably the bribe has led the children to view their performance of the activity to be controlled by the reward, causing them to discount intrinsic interest in the activity and stripping them of motivation to engage in the activity when external rewards are no longer offered. Clearly, more research is needed to determine under what circumstances young children favor one principle over the other (additive principle vs. discounting principle).

TAKING THE ROLE OF THE OTHER

Children who cannot put aside for the moment their own point of view in order to assume the perspective of another, which is known as *role taking*, are going to be inept socially in a number of respects. They will have trouble communicating in the many situations that require that a listener's special needs, intentions, knowledge, and perspective be taken into account. Having little cognizance of the feelings of others, they will be slow to display altruism or behave in ways that show a concern for the welfare of others. Not being able to tell what other people think of

them, they will have a hard time altering their behavior to become more acceptable to their playmates or to fit in with the plans and expectations of others. Acquiring the ability to detect what's going on in the hearts and minds of others is one of the most important aspects of social-cognitive development.

Research on role taking began with a famous experiment by Piaget. We shall first describe this experiment and the conclusions Piaget drew from it. Then we shall relate how modern researchers have found it necessary to modify Piaget's original description of role taking development.

Piaget's Classic Experiment

In a classic study, Piaget and Inhelder (1956) asked children to take a seat at a table on which were displayed three mountains made of paper-maché: One mountain had a snowcap, another had a cross on top, and the third was topped by a cottage. The children were shown photographs that depicted various perspectives on the mountains, and they were asked to select the photograph that showed the view that a doll, who was seated at a different side of the table, had of the mountains. Results were striking. Children younger than 7 attributed their own viewpoint to the dolls—they picked a photograph that depicted their own perspective on the mountain landscape. Past this age, such blatantly egocentric errors were few, but subjects were still not skilled in choosing the correct photograph until they reached roughly 10 years of age.

It was from this experiment that Piaget concluded that children younger than 7 or 8 are at a fundamentally egocentric stage of development. He concluded that young, preoperational children are so captivated by what meets their own eyes and ears (centration) that they cannot construct an image of anyone else's point of view. In fact, they seem unaware that another person can even possess a perspective that differs from their own. Piaget made another sweeping generalization from his experiment: He proclaimed ego-centrism to be such a basic deficit of early childhood that it prevents young children from appreciating and understanding *any* sort of private experience other people have, not just other people's visual perspectives. Thus young children were assumed to be incapable of assuming other people's emotions, plans, intentions, and other thoughts as well as their spatial perspectives. In essence, Piaget believed that until 7 or 8 years of age, children think other people are having the same visual, emotional, and cognitive experiences that they are having.

Next we shall see how Piaget's conclusions have been challenged by more thorough research. We shall review some modifications to Piagetian theory and summarize what more recent research proposes about role taking development.

Role Taking: One Skill or Several?

Research suggests that Piaget was wrong when he suggested that a child's success (or failure) in *all* role taking situations depends on the child's possession of (or lack of) a single underlying skill—the ability to decenter. Some evidence comes from studies in which researchers have given children "batteries" of role taking tests and then intercorrelated the children's scores to determine how their performances in different role taking situations relate to each other. Presumably, a given child should fail all tasks or pass all tasks, depending on whether or not the child still suffers from preoperational centration. In these projects, researchers have found it useful to distinguish among three varieties of role taking: *visual* or spatial role taking (inferring what other people are seeing), *affective* or emotional role taking (inferring what other people are feeling), and *cognitive* or conceptual role taking (inferring what other people are thinking, planning, or intending). Separate tests are given to children to measure their skill in each of the three domains. For example, to tap children's visual perspective taking, children

may be given Piaget's three-mountain task or a similar exercise. In a common measure of affective role taking (Borke, 1971, 1973), children hear stories that describe characters facing situations that usually produce certain emotional reactions (e.g., a girl receiving a present at a birthday party, or a boy being chased by a vicious dog). The children are shown photographs that depict various facial expressions (e.g., happiness, fear, anger, or sadness) and their job is to match the facial expressions to the characters in the stories. To measure cognitive role taking, children may hear a story and then be asked to retell the story from the point of view of one of its characters (Chandler, 1973; Feffer, 1959), or they may be asked to play a game with another child, after which they are quizzed concerning what they think their opponent's plans, intentions, and other thoughts and strategies may be (Selman, 1971).

The typical study reports low or nonsignificant correlations among the three aspects of role taking (Ford, 1979; Hudson, 1978; Kurdek 1977; Kurdek & Rodgon, 1975; Rubin, 1973; 1978). Furthermore, children's scores on several tests designed to tap a single aspect of role taking (e.g., the cognitive aspect) do not intercorrelate well either (e.g., Piche, Michlin, Rubin, & Johnson, 1975).

These findings suggest that role taking is not a global skill. Role taking probably involves several skills, and some of these subskills may be more important for one kind of role taking than for another. It is clear, for example, that spatial role taking involves the ability to make certain perceptual discriminations (e.g., knowing whether an object will appear reversed to someone else) that the other varieties of role taking do not. Even the logic underlying role taking may vary from one task to another (Salatas & Flavell, 1976). Consider, for example, that spatial and affective role taking require different forms of logic: a given spatial perspective can be experienced from only one vantage point, and all people sharing this vantage point will have the same visual experience; in contrast, a single emotion can be produced by a variety of situations, and people exposed to a single situation can each react to the situation with a different emotion. In sum, the successful study of role taking development is going to involve the study of separate component processes. Most of these subskills, however, have yet to be identified.

Developmental Trends in Role Taking

Contrary to Piaget's claims, children much younger than 7 or 8 years recognize that other people have perspectives that differ from their own. For example, 18-month-old children commonly show things to other people and try to draw other people's attention to things by pointing and gesturing (Rheingold, Hay, & West, 1976). In another study, young children shown a selection of gifts (a ball, a doll, a necktie, and a pair of stockings) and asked to choose ones for their mothers, fathers, and opposite-sex playmates, made appropriate choices rather than choosing what they would have preferred for themselves (Zahn-Waxler, Radke-Yarrow, & Brady-Smith, 1977). Finally 4-year-olds have been observed simplifying their speech when talking to 2-year-olds, revealing an appreciation of the more limited language capabilities of the younger children (Shatz & Gelman, 1973). These are hardly signs of a totally egocentric being!

Of course, these observations do not mean that preschoolers are fully-developed role takers, only that children are aware of other people's viewpoints earlier than Piaget suspected. Today, most cognitive-developmental theorists recognize that role taking development is not an all-or-nothing skill that is totally absent in the preoperational years, emerging full-blown with the introduction of concrete operations. Instead, they conceptualize role taking development as a more gradual process that involves the child progressing through a series of several stages over the childhood years. For example, after giving

children of different ages a variety of role taking tests, one neo-Piagetian (Selman, 1976) proposed that role taking development unfolds in a sequence of *five* stages over the childhood years. Because Selman's hypothesized sequence holds promise for future research, we shall briefly outline his stages here. (The ages Selman gives for each stage are approximate and will depend on cultural factors, individual intelligence levels, and social experience.)

Stage O. *Egocentric role taking* (ages 4 to 6). At this stage, children recognize that other people have thoughts, feelings, and other private experiences, but the usual way children tell the content of another's private experience is by simply remembering how they themselves have reacted under similar circumstances. In other words, role taking usually involves the simple projection of one's own past reactions onto someone else. (Occasionally children at this stage do attribute to someone else a reaction they have not previously had themselves, as when they indicate that their mothers would prefer a gift of stockings over a toy. But these are fairly stereotyped judgments that result from the children having observed other people's previous reactions to a situation.)

Stage 1. *Social information role taking* (ages 6 to 8). Children now appreciate that different people possess different psychological properties (i.e., purposes, motives, intentions, and abilities) that can lead people to have different reactions to a single situation. Thus children know that another person's reaction to a situation might be different from their own because they know that the internal psychological workings of another person are different from their own.

Stage 2. *Self-reflective role taking* (ages 8 to 10). Children begin to understand that their own private experiences can be the subject of another person's role taking efforts. Thus they can start to evaluate themselves according to how others see them. Now children can both take the role of another and imagine the role taking experiences of another. However, children can consider only one person's point of view at a time: They cannot simultaneously consider and coordinate their own perspective and another person's perspective. For example, a boy may know his own wants and may know his sister's wants, but he may not be able to consider them both at one time in order to reach a compromise.

Stage 3. *Mutual role taking* (10 to 12). Children can now consider both their own perspective and another person's perspective at the same time (e.g., "He knows part of what I know, but also some things I don't know").

Stage 4. *Social and conventional system role taking* (age 12 and up). Children begin to view the social system within which they operate as the product of shared perspectives among many members of society (e.g., "Most people abhor violence, so we shall outlaw it") and they begin to compare their own views with those of society's more "generalized other" (e.g., "Although most people around here support the draft, I'm against it").

Certain aspects of Selman's hypothesized sequence receive confirmation in research conducted by other investigators. For example, preschoolers are indeed most accurate in taking on other people's thoughts and feelings in familiar situations where their own experiences and observational learning can lead them to make reasonably accurate predictions about others (e.g., "I'm always happy when going to a birthday party, so this story character who is going to a party must be happy, too"; "I see mommy wearing stockings rather than wearing ties or playing with balls and dolls, so I'll choose stockings as a gift for her") Abramovitch, 1977; Borke, 1973; Deutsch, 1974b, 1975; Feshbach & Roe, 1968; Urberg & Docherty, 1976). These youngsters may sometimes be correct in inferring another's attitude or emotion, but they do not seem to be aware that different people possess different psychological mechanisms that can cause them to have divergent reactions to a single situation (Gove & Keating, 1979). Also, young children do, as Selman suggests, have difficulty simultaneously considering the distinctly different perspectives of two or more people. It is not until sometime during the elementary-school years, for example, that

children do well at retelling a story from the point of view of one story character without confusing that character's perspective with the perspectives of other characters in the story (Urberg & Docherty, 1976). In summary, although preschoolers are successful in some aspects of role taking, strides in role taking continue to be made well into the school years.

Egocentrism as a Response Bias, not a Basic Stage

Flavell (1977) suggests that we should consider egocentrism not as a basic stage in development but rather as a *response bias* that leads people of all developmental levels to make egocentric errors when they are faced with a very difficult role taking task. When people's own views are obvious to them and it would require a great deal of energy to reconstruct another person's point of view, it is common to avoid the task by assuming that the other person's thoughts or feelings are the same as one's own. Presumably children in Piaget's three-mountain experiment made egocentric errors because the demands of the task exceeded their capabilities. Flavell points out that even adults sometimes find themselves in a state of mind that is conducive to egocentric behavior. For instance, when people are distressed physically or psychologically, they are likely to have little mental energy left over for any sort of social-cognitive activity beyond what concerns them and their immediate problems.

In any case, egocentrism is not confined to early childhood. Looft (1972) noted that some elderly people, especially those who engage in relatively little interaction with other people, centered increasingly on their own thoughts, reacted less often to others, and showed greater rigidity in values and behavior—a syndrome sometimes characterized as *regression to egocentrism*. Egocentrism, then, is not a basic stage. It is a kind of error a person is likely to make when the demands of the role taking situation exceed the role taking capacities and energy of the role taker.

Social Influences on Role Taking Development

Peer Influences Does peer interaction really serve a special function in role taking development that other sorts of social contact cannot fulfill, as Piaget suggested? The evidence is equivocal regarding this question. Experiments do show that preschoolers who participate in sessions of constructive play (e.g., working together to build some object, such as a house or a wagon) or fantasy play (e.g., acting out make-believe themes and roles) later score higher on tests of spatial, affective, and cognitive role taking (Burns & Brainerd, 1979; Saltz & Johnson, 1974). But the question of whether peer contact is better than adult contact is not resolved. Researchers compared the role taking skills of children reared on Israeli kibbutzim, where peer contacts are unusually high, with the role taking skills of children reared at home. Although Nahir and Yussen (1977) confirmed the Piagetian hypothesis by finding better role taking among kibbutz children, West (1974) failed to find this group to be superior.

While the question of whether peer or adult contact is more important is not resolved, it is apparent that children who enjoy high amounts of social interaction with people of any age are better role takers. For example, children who are reared in European rural villages and farms, where chores prevent them from socially interacting with either adults or children, are poorer role takers than children reared in cities (Hollos, 1975).

Child-Rearing Influences Hoffman (1970) suggests that parents who make frequent use of inductive discipline, pointing out to children the harmful or beneficial psychological consequences of their actions for others, are helping their children develop skill in imagining the inner states of others. In support of this, Bearison & Cassel (1975) found that children skilled in role taking tend to have parents who justify their disciplinary actions with statements that focus on the intentions and feelings of others.

Training Children in Perspective Taking When children are given experimental sessions in which they are forced to compare others' viewpoints with their own, their role taking skills often improve. In one study, Chandler (1973) asked groups of adolescents to write skits, which they then had to act out and videotape. Each skit was reenacted and revideotaped until each participant had occupied every role. Children then viewed the videotapes and discussed the problems they had had in shifting roles. Compared to children who did not have this experience, the experimental children did better on later tests of cognitive role taking.

A study by Iannotti (1978) revealed some social benefits of training children to be able to assume the roles of others. Children who played roles in skits and then discussed the feelings, thoughts, and motives of their characters later scored higher on tests of helpfulness and cooperation—behaviors that require the ability to appreciate the thoughts and feelings of other people. In the following chapter, we shall see that role taking expertise is also associated with maturity in moral reasoning. It is understandable, then, that researchers concerned with "moral education" are especially interested in promoting children's role taking development.

Cognitive Development and Role Taking Several investigators have studied links between children's role taking skill and their attainment of Piaget's stage of concrete operations. Role taking is thought to require the Piagetian operations of conservation and reversibility because a person must conserve his or her own perspective (by storing it in memory) while temporarily shifting attention away from it to consider another person's perspective.

Sometimes children who can conserve are found to be better role takers than nonconservers (Rubin, 1973), but more often no relationship between conservation and role taking is found (Hollos, 1975; Turnure, 1975). Social experiences may be more important than general cognitive development in expediting role taking development.

Interpersonal Problem Solving: A Broader Perspective on Role Taking

Role taking is only one facet of a broader social-cognitive skill that some psychologists have labeled *Interpersonal Problem Analysis* (IPA) (Urbain & Kendall, 1980). Children must learn to recognize situations where there is the potential for a group of people to have conflicting views. They must learn to generate alternative solutions to such problems and to evaluate each alternative in terms of how it benefits or disadvantages each party involved. Furthermore, children must know how to select a solution that is based on principles of fairness and mutual benefit.

Little is known about how children develop competencies in this important area, but a study by Marsh, Serafica, and Barenboim (1980) indicates that children's skills in IPA improve if the children are trained in role taking. In this study, children were first tested for skill in IPA, and then some children were given training to improve their role taking ability, while others were not. Finally, all the children were retested for skill in IPA. To ascertain the children's initial skills in IPA, they heard several short stories (e.g., in one story a child must choose between helping a friend with an exam and living up to an honor code; in another, a child must decide which of three friends is to be excluded from a rock concert and what excuse is to be given). For each story, the children were asked to respond to the following questions:

What is the problem here?

What are all the things that need to be considered?

What are all the possible ways to solve this problem?

Now, what might happen for each of these solutions?

Considering these different solutions and their possible consequences, what solution do you think is best?

The children's answers were scored for the number of alternatives they generated as well as for the quality of the solutions they suggested. (Solutions that reflected an effort to incorporate the feelings of all the parties involved were scored as better than solutions that satisfied only one child. For example, for the rock concert problem, a solution that involved "telling all three the party is off and taking two others instead" received a lower score than "not going to the concert and selling the tickets to get money for another concert".) After taking the IPA test, the experimental group of children received role taking training in the form of enacting and videotaping skits and then viewing and discussing their roles in the skits. On the post-test of IPA, the experimental children performed significantly better than control children who were not given training in role taking.

CULTIVATING A SENSE OF HUMOR

Children are not always completely serious as they go about the business of processing information about their social worlds. Many events make them smile, laugh, or giggle—sometimes for so long that their parents find it quite exasperating. Freud hypothesized that humor often represents the aggressive and sexual urges of the id temporarily managing to break through the ego's suppressive barrier. Contemporary theories of humor do not deny that humor can sometimes spring from tension derived from "naughty" impulses, but they emphasize that most humor is the result of the child's social-cognitive activity. Specifically, most theorists today regard humor as a response children are likely to make *after they have reached certain conclusions about social stimuli that at first strike them as disturbing or puzzling.* We will briefly outline two of the more promising cognitive-processing theories of the humor response.

Humor as Tension Appraised as Safe

Rothbart (1973) suggests that children laugh when they become tense or aroused but at the same time cognitively appraise the situation as "safe" or inconsequential. She observes that a toddler will laugh when his or her father playfully threatens "I'm gonna get you!" because although the situation arouses tension, the child knows it is safe. In contrast, the same child will probably scream and cry if approached in the same manner by a strange man on the street. Thus, in Rothbart's theory, tension plus an appraisal of safety leads to laughter; tension plus an appraisal of danger leads to distress.

What kinds of events arouse tension, and what determines whether an event is appraised as safe? Tension can be triggered by a variety of things, including unexpected stimulation (such as a sudden, loud noise or the dimming of lights); stimuli that are incongruous or discrepant with present knowledge or expectations (a major feature of many jokes and riddles); anticipation of an exciting event (such as being on the verge of winning a game); and taboo subject matter. Factors that influence whether a situation is judged as safe or not include whether the stimulation occurs in a secure, familiar setting or in a novel, threatening setting; the proximity of security or attachment figures (such as the child's mother); and the general playfulness of the situation. Of course, the particular events that children find arousing, safe, or threatening change with age and experience.

MacDonald and Silverman (1978) conducted an experiment with infants to test Rothbart's hypothesis that laughter stems from tension in a safe setting. One-year-old infants interacted with an adult who played peek-a-boo while either looming toward the

child (high arousal) or receding away from the child (low arousal). The adult was either the infant's own mother (high safety) or a stranger (low safety). The results of the experiment agreed with Rothbart's model: High arousal led to smiling and laughter when the "experimenter" was the mother, but produced distress when the experimenter was a stranger.

Rothbart's theory thus receives support in research with infants. It is likely that humor in older persons also sometimes results from events that are exciting, but appraised as safe, but more research on older age groups is needed.

Humor as Incongruity and Its Resolution

QUESTION: Why does a baby pig eat so much?
ANSWER: To make a hog of himself!

What makes jokes like this one funny? To be enjoyed, many jokes and riddles require that the listener first perceive some perceptual or logical incongruity and then resolve the incongruity by rather suddenly seeing how certain aspects of the situation fit together in an unexpected way. In the above riddle, the question and answer parts of the joke seem unrelated at first (incongruity), but when the listener realizes that there is a pun involved concerning the word hog (resolution), the humor of the riddle is appreciated.

It has been suggested that even infants sometimes smile or laugh because they have successfully resolved an incongruity. When the mother of a 3-month-old appears over the infant's crib, the infant will sometimes spend several sober seconds scrutinizing the mother's face before suddenly breaking out into a wide grin. Kagan (1971a; Kagan, Kearsley, & Zelazo, 1978) suggests that the infant smiles when he or she realizes that the face is a familiar one. Presumably, when mother's face first appears over the infant's crib, the infant is not sure whether the face is familiar or unfamiliar, but if after a few seconds the infant can match the face to a stored mental representation of his or her mother, the infant has an "Aha! I know that face!" reaction—and smiles.

Of course, the sorts of events that spark humor change with age. Unlike infants, adults do not usually delight in resolving minor perceptual incongruities, such as matching a face to an existing schema (though they sometimes do). McGhee (1976) has proposed a principle to account for developmental changes in children's humor reactions. He suggests that a child takes the greatest pleasure in resolving incongruity when the resolution requires the child to exercise a *recently acquired* mental operation. Infants laugh loudly after matching their mother's face to a stored image because they have just learned to assimilate familiar faces to representations of those faces. But as children mature and become capable of more sophisticated cognitive operations, the things they find funny will change. McGhee (1976) reports an interesting study illustrating how children's humor can depend on their attainment of certain Piagetian mental operations. First, McGhee pretested children on conservation of area (understanding, for example, that the total surface area of a piece of paper remains the same regardless of whether the piece is cut into several pieces and spread out or remains intact). He then divided the children up into three groups: those who could not conserve, those who had just mastered conservation, and those who had been conserving for several years. The children then heard this joke:

Mr. Jones went into a restaurant and ordered a whole pizza pie for dinner. When the waiter asked if he wanted it cut into six or eight pieces, Mr. Jones said, "Oh, you'd better make it six! I could never eat eight!"

Children who had just learned to conserve area laughed the loudest. (For other studies linking children's humor to recently acquired mental operations, see Pien & Rothbart, 1976; Prentice & Fathman, 1975; Shultz,

1974; Shultz & Horibe, 1974; Whitt & Prentice, 1977; Yalisove, 1978; Zigler, Levine, & Gould, 1966, 1967).

To date, most research on humor has focused on pinning down the particular characteristics of stimuli (such as jokes) that make them funny, but the study of humor is broadening to encompass other interesting questions as well. One of these new directions concerns the "ecology of humor": What kinds of social contexts are conducive to laughing and joking? Sherman (1975), for example, studied the situations that produce "group glee," or joyful outbursts of contagious screaming and laughing, among preschoolers. One curious finding was that glee almost always occurred in mixed-sex groups. Could it be that a gathering of mixed-sex children provides tension that makes children more excitable? Another direction in the study of humor is the issue of how children develop the ability to *create* humor—to think up and successfully act out a prank or to create a joke with a funny punch line. One interesting (and unexplained) finding is that boys produce more jokes and humorous events than girls (Groch, 1974; McGhee, 1974).

SUMMARY

Children develop the ability to mentally represent and process information about their social world. In many respects, children's social schemas may be conceptualized as mediating links between their social learning experiences and their overt social behavior. For example, children's cognitive representations of response-outcome contingencies may be acquired through disciplinary encounters and observational learning; once acquired, these schemas serve a motivational function by guiding the children's choices of responses in social interactions.

Research on social-cognitive development has been inspired mainly by three theories: cognitive-developmental theory, social learning theory, and attribution theory. The cognitive-developmentalists propose that children's social schemas are strictly tied to their underlying stage of cognitive development. For example, the schemas of preoperational children (2 to 7 years) are presumed to reflect the tendency of young children to focus attention exclusively on superficial qualities of a stimulus. Indeed, young children do tend to perceive people (both themselves and others) in terms of their surface appearance, possessions, and activities; it is not until several years later that children "conserve" underlying, relatively invariant psychological properties of people (or perceive people in terms of stable but hidden personality dispositions and motives). It has been hard to prove, however, that children's social schemas are strictly tied to underlying thought structures associated with their Piagetian stage of development.

The social learning theorists, such as Bandura and Mischel, believe that children synthesize social information from many sources (e.g., direct disciplinary experiences, observational learning, and verbal instruction) to formulate rules and propositions about the functioning of their social worlds. For example, children generate rules linking behavior to its consequences. In contrast to the cognitive-developmentalists, the social learning theorists view children's social schemas as determined directly by their unique social experiences, not by basic thought structures that define their underlying stage of cognitive development. Research reviewed in this chapter (as well as in other chapters) reveals that children do draw conclusions about social phenomena by integrating information from diverse social sources. Children learn to estimate their own strengths and weaknesses (perceptions of "self-efficacy"), for example, partly by observing their past successes and failures, partly by believing verbal information supplied by others (e.g., "You sure are good at that"), and partly by observing how well other children similar to themselves perform under similar circumstances. Thus, according to social learning theory, social cognitions result from an integration of diverse forms of social information, not from underlying thought structures.

Attribution theorists point out that people are motivated to understand the causes of behavior, because doing so helps make the world seem a more predictable and controllable place to live. Researchers working on the development of causal attribution have discovered that children develop more sophisticated rules for inferring the causes of someone's behavior as they get older.

There are five domains of social-cognitive functioning: self-concept formation, person perception, causal attribution, role taking, and humor. Self-concept development is a gradual process. In young children, self-concept is closely tied to tangible and observable qualities of their existence—their physical appearance, possessions, environment, and favorite activities. Though children as young as age 3 know that they possess a private, psychological self, it is not until they are 8 or 9 that they conceive of themselves as possessing stable personality traits and dispositions. Psychologists have researched several distinct components of self-concept: self-image disparity, self-esteem, locus of control, and perceptions of self-efficacy. Development in all aspects of self-concept is influenced by several factors, including incorporation of the opinions of other people about the self, self-observation, causal attribution for one's own behavior, and social comparison.

The study of person perception is concerned with how people perceive and organize information about other people. Certain developments in person perception parallel developments in self-perception. For example, preschool children tend to perceive other people in terms of their surface appearance, possessions, and activities, whereas older children are more likely to think of people in terms of their psychological functioning and enduring dispositions.

In relation to the development of causal attribution, children acquire schemas that help them to detect the causes of events, to differentiate between accidental and intentional acts, to distinguish among intentional actions on the basis of the actor's motive (e.g., to tell a well-intentioned act from an ill-intentioned act), and to decide whether to hold an actor or the situation responsible for an actor's behavior.

As they mature, children become more skilled at role taking, or putting aside their own perspectives on a situation in order to imagine another person's point of view. Piaget believed that children younger than 7 or 8 years, being at a fundamentally egocentric stage of development, were incapable of any form of role taking. His view was criticized, however, when researchers found that even young children are capable of some simple forms of role taking. Furthermore, recent research suggests that role taking is not totally absent before the school years, emerging only after attainment of concrete operations.

Instead, there are several varieties of role taking that develop gradually over the childhood years. Certain kinds of social experiences, especially those in which children are confronted with perspectives and opinions that conflict with their own, are conducive to role taking development.

A final facet of social-cognitive functioning in children is the development of a sense of humor. There are two cognitive theories of humor. The first suggests that laughter stems from tension that is experienced in a situation cognitively appraised as safe or inconsequential. The second theory is based on the proposal that humor results from the ability of children to perceive perceptual or logical incongruities and to understand that the incongruities can be cognitively resolved in unusual or unexpected ways.

6 The Development of Morality and Self-Control

This chapter is concerned with the moral development of the child: How do children develop conceptions of right and wrong, and how do they come to regulate their own behavior to conform to these standards?

From the time they can walk or crawl, children find themselves in a constant struggle between the urge to satisfy their own egotistical needs and the demands and restrictions placed on them by their parents and others in society. At first, society's demands are comparatively modest and involve requests for fairly specific motor and verbal controls: Children are not to touch certain possessions of their parents, they must withhold toilet activities until appropriate times and places, they are expected to say "please" and "thank you," and so on. Within a few years, however, children are introduced to a wider and more abstract set of rules. They generally learn that it is wrong to steal, to tell

lies, to break promises, and to endanger another person's health, property, or well-being. Children are expected to exercise control over their own behavior by adopting standards of exemplary conduct for themselves, punishing themselves with guilt when they break these standards, and reserving self-rewards for occasions when they fulfill their goals and obligations. They are supposed to inhibit impulses to be selfish and also to endure frustrating periods when gratification must be postponed. Eventually, children are expected to appreciate the logic behind society's rules, to understand the need for these rules, and to know that good rules are not arbitrarily imposed by authority figures but are based on considerations of mutual respect and reciprocity among human beings.

The amazing thing is that this happens! Most children do feel guilty when they think about telling a lie, and as adults, most will stop their cars at red lights late at night when no other cars and no police officers are in sight. Psychologists apply the term *internalization* to refer to the process by which children come to adhere to society's rules even when they are free of external surveillance or the expectation of rewards and punishments from socializing agents.

Understanding this process is the goal of this chapter. In fact, internalization may be considered a cornerstone process of socialization. We will see in later chapters that certain processes implicated in the internalization of moral values also apply to the self-regulation of aggressive urges, the disposition to behave altruistically, and even to the adoption of societally prescribed sex roles.

This chapter begins with a discussion of the construct of morality. How do we measure children's understanding of society's rules and their tendencies to adhere to these rules? How do we tell if a child is morally mature or immature? Is morality best conceptualized as a single entity or as comprised of several dimensions? Taking the view that morality is indeed comprised of several dimensions, we then consider factors influencing development along each of these dimensions. First, we consider *moral reasoning*: How do children of different ages decide whether an action is right or wrong, and how do children learn to make increasingly sophisticated judgments as they age? Second, we consider the development of *self-evaluations*: What causes children to experience guilt for transgression and pride for moral conscientiousness? Third, we review factors that influence *resistance to deviation*, which refers to the ability and willingness of children to withstand temptations to engage in attractive but prohibited activities.

THE CONSTRUCT OF MORALITY

Are There Varieties of Morality?

Sometimes psychologists refer to the three aspects of morality—moral reasoning, moral self-evaluation, and resistance to deviation—as, respectively, the cognitive, the affective, and the behavioral components. This is because moral reasoning is concerned with children's understanding of the difference between right and wrong, because self-evaluations often involve emotions such as guilt following transgressions, and because resistance to deviation is concerned with the child's overt behavior when faced with temptation. Of course, this is a gross oversimplification. Self-evaluations are not limited to emotional reactions, and whether a child resists a temptation depends on the child's emotions and thoughts in a particular situation. But let us see how psychologists attempt to measure children's development along each of these lines.

Moral Reasoning Although several children may all know that it is wrong to steal, they may have very different understandings of why this is so. One may say stealing is wrong because "you'll go to jail for it" or because "your parents will punish you for it." Another may say stealing is wrong because "it makes the other person feel bad" or because "people shouldn't do to others what they wouldn't want done to themselves." Thus, although several children may be equally aware of society's rules, they can clearly differ in their underlying moral reasoning.

To measure the level of maturity of children's moral reasoning, researchers usually read stories to them describing someone misbehaving or facing some temptation or moral dilemma. The children are asked not only to tell how good or how naughty the character is for his or her actions, or contemplated actions, but also to give the *reasons* for their moral judgments. It is not surprising that young children tend to focus on external considerations in making their moral judgments—to them, an act is deemed blameworthy in proportion to the amount of objective damage or external punishment it incurs, regardless of the actor's intentions or inner motives. Somewhat older children are often concerned with not hurting other people's feelings and with upholding society's laws. And still older children may apply more abstract rules or universal moral principles such as the golden rule.

Moral Self-Evaluation   As they grow, children acquire personal standards for self-evaluation. When morally mature children violate their moral standards by doing something that they know is wrong, they tend to experience guilt and self-criticism. In addition to punishing themselves for transgressions, morally mature children restrict their feelings of pride and self-rewards to occasions when they deserve them. Children who reward themselves with a glass of juice, a peek at television, or just the thought that "I am a good person" after every hour of homework completed have a more exacting standard of self-reinforcement than children who reward themselves without regard for whether their behavior has reached some criterion level. Mature children, then, not only chastise themselves for their shortcomings but limit their self-rewards for commendable performances.

How do psychologists measure children's self-evaluative habits? One popular way of assessing children's reactions to transgressions is with projective tests. Children are read a set of stories, each depicting misbehavior on the part of the central character. For each story, the children are to tell how the story hero feels and behaves following his or her transgression. It is assumed that the children project the reactions they themselves experience after misbehaving onto the story character. When children say that the hero lies, runs away to avoid punishment, or reveals a fear of external punishment in some other way, their responses are scored as "external" (and morally immature). Children's scores for moral internalization increase as they describe the hero as feeling guilty, confessing, offering to repair the damage, apologizing, or otherwise accepting responsibility for the misbehavior.

Sometimes behavioral measures of self-evaluation are employed. Children are lured or tricked into deviating, and then their reactions are observed. In one study, children, who were individually tested, were requested to keep a hamster in its cage by holding the lid down while the experimenter went on an errand (Sears, Rau, and Alpert, 1965). During the absence of the experimenter, a record playing on a phonograph in the room came to an end, and the needle remained on the record, making an obnoxious scratching sound. Unable to bear the sound, the children soon left the hamster cage to take the needle off the record. When they did, the experimenter, who had been observing them through a one-way mirror, activated by remote control a trap door in the floor of the hamster's cage, making it seem as if the hamster had escaped! When the children realized their "transgression," the adult returned and questioned the children to see if they took responsibility for their behavior, lied about their actions, and so on. Researchers sometimes employ an objective measure of acceptance of blame by asking children who have transgressed to give up tokens or pennies as an act of self-punishment. The more tokens a child relinquishes, the greater his or her remorse is assumed to be.

To test children's standards for positive self-evaluation, researchers first prompt children to perform various moral actions (e.g., resisting some temptation or performing some altruistic act) that require varying degrees of self-sacrifice or self-control. Following each action, the experimenter presents the children with a reward supply (e.g., a bucket of pennies or tokens exchangeable for prizes), but asks them to take only as many rewards as they think they deserve for their behavior. Children who reward themselves lavishly regardless of how much self-control or self-sacrifice they exercised are considered to have relatively low or indiscriminate standards of self-reinforcement. Children who restrict their self-rewards to occasions when they have exercised considerable self-control have higher moral standards. Obviously, self-evaluations rest in part on moral reasoning: As they grow up, children must learn increasingly sophisticated criteria for deciding whether a self-reward is deserved or not.

Resistance to Deviation   To assess the overt behavioral aspect of morality, children are placed in a real temptation situation and their tendency to withstand or yield to the pressures to deviate is assessed. Commonly, the children are prohibited from playing with a set of attractive toys, then left alone with the toys. The delay to the child's first touch of a forbidden toy and the frequency and duration of toy touching are observed from behind a one-way vision screen. Sometimes children are tested for cheating by being given opportunities to falsify their scores on a game or test in order to win a prize. Occasionally, parents, teachers, or peers are asked to rate children's tendencies to obey prohibitions and sanctions when the children think that they are not being watched.

Relationships Among the Varieties: A General Conscience or Specificity?

Is the child who shows moral maturity on one aspect also likely to reveal maturity on the other two dimensions? To answer the question of whether the three aspects of morality intercorrelate to reflect a single personality trait that we might call *general conscience*, researchers take a large sample of children, measure each child on all three aspects, and intercorrelate the children's scores on the dimensions. Though results vary (for a review, see Hoffman, 1977), the typical finding is low or zero-order correlation coefficients: A girl who usually shows high resistance to deviation does not necessarily display strong guilt reactions when she does deviate; a boy who bases his moral reasoning on sophisticated criteria does not usually reveal especially strong resistance to deviation; and so on. One interpretation of this lack of inter-

correlation is that the three aspects of morality develop independently of each other, as separate processes.

But it may be premature to accept the conclusion that the different aspects of morality are totally unrelated to one another. One possibility the previous research ignores is that the three aspects of morality may be significantly correlated when they are assessed with respect to a single situation involving a single moral standard (Dienstbier, Hillman, Lehnhoff, Hillman, & Valkenaar, 1975; Hoffman, 1977a). To date, researchers exploring correlations among the moral indices have assessed children's development in the three aspects in entirely different situations. For example, moral reasoning may be assessed by asking children to explain why they judged as naughty a child who beat up a playmate; reactions to transgression may be measured by observing children's guilt when they are caught touching a forbidden toy; and resistance to deviation may be tapped by how much the children yield to the temptation to steal some loose change. Aggression, touching prohibited toys, and stealing involve quite different moral standards. If children were tested for moral reasoning, self-evaluation, and resistance to deviation with respect to a single moral standard in a single situation, then perhaps significant correlations would emerge.

This has not been done, but there exist some data to support the prediction. For example, Perry and Bussey (1977) found that boys who cannot resist the temptation to aggress against their playmates also experience the least remorse when they do deliberately injure their peers. Also, Eisenberg-Berg and Hand (1979) found that children who reason about the appropriateness of helping others by focusing on the other's need state, rather than on their own hedonistic desires, are the most likely actually to share and sacrifice on a peer's behalf.

It is also likely that correlations among the aspects of morality exist only among children who have achieved a certain level of cognitive maturity. Most studies that report a lack of relationship among the aspects have utilized samples of nursery schoolers. These children may be too young to control their resistance to temptation by anticipating negative self-reactions or by reasoning about the rightness or wrongness of their contemplated actions. In support of this, Henshel (1971) found that girls' verbal reports of how they would *like* to behave in a temptation situation do not actually predict the girls' cheating behavior until adolescence, when a marked relationship is evidenced.

Thus, while the evidence for interrelationships among the components of morality is generally negative, there is some indication of positive associations when the components are assessed within particular settings and when the components are assessed in samples of older children.

Nevertheless, it is clear that morality cannot be considered a unidimensional trait along which people can be ordered in terms of how much or how little they possess an overall tendency to display morality in diverse ways and in diverse situations. Furthermore, within each of the three varieties of morality there is considerable *situational specificity* in children's behavior. Children who cheat freely in one situation, as during sports on the playground, are not particularly likely to cheat in other situations, such as on arithmetic tests in the classroom (Hartshorne & May, 1929). Children who experience remorse following one kind of transgression, as after injuring another child, are not especially likely to feel guilty after misbehaving in another situation, as when stealing something belonging to another child (Allinsmith, 1960). And the tendency to invoke sophisticated arguments to support one's moral judgments also depends on the particular transgression being judged (Kurtines & Greif, 1974).

We do not mean to give the impression that there is absolutely no cross-situational consistency in any aspect of morality for any person. Bem and Allen (1974; see also the discussion of trait theory in Chapter 1) suggest that *some* people may show some degree of cross-situational consistency in one or more aspects of morality. Priests and delinquents, for example, may display somewhat more stable levels of honesty across situations than the average person, although the behavior of these two groups would fall at opposite ends of the spectrum. Child psychologists need to study the child-rearing factors that help children develop generalized styles of prosocial, moral conduct across situations.

We shall now discuss development within each of the three varieties of morality. For each variety we shall summarize the relevant theories and review the research evidence.

THE DEVELOPMENT OF MORAL REASONING

Almost from the time people first learn to talk, they are prone to make *moral judgments* about the actions of others around them: "That was bad!" moralizes the toddler; "Let's beat him up for that," suggests the 10-year-old; "He ought to go to jail," claims an indignant adult. Although people of different developmental levels and walks of life all evaluate others, don't they differ in what they are attending to when making the moral judgment? Don't the criteria for making moral judgments grow increasingly sophisticated with age, hopefully reflecting a maturing concern for mutual respect among members of a civilized society? Our society certainly assumes so. We do not ask toddlers to legislate our laws, and we do not allow adolescents to vote or sit on juries.

Most of the theory and research on moral reasoning is derived from a cognitive-developmental theory perspective, with the views of Piaget and Kohlberg being particularly influential. However, the social learning theorists have had their say, too, and even the attribution theorists are beginning to investigate the problem.

Piaget and Kohlberg:
Some Commonalities

Piaget is the Swiss psychologist who formulated the original cognitive-developmental theory of morality several decades ago (1932); Kohlberg is an American psychologist who borrowed heavily from basic Piagetian theory, but formulated his own, somewhat more elaborate, stage theory of moral development. Both are cognitive-developmentalists and therefore share several views. First, they both regard moral internalization as occurring in a series of fixed, qualitatively distinct stages whose end product is a universal sense of justice or concern for reciprocity among individuals. Second, they take a typological approach to moral reasoning, assuming that an individual can be categorized into one of several distinct categories depending on what underlying mental structures characterize his or her basic thinking processes (see Chapter 1 for a description of Piaget's stages of cognitive development). The individual's stage of cognitive development is believed to limit the level of moral reasoning that he or she is capable of achieving. Because each successively higher moral stage represents a transformation and displacement of its immediately preceding stage, children must pass through the stages in sequence; "skipping" one stage or "regressing" from a higher stage to a lower one is not allowed.

According to cognitive-developmental theory, stages represent children's attempts to make sense out of their own experiences and are not implanted by culture through socialization (such as parental discipline or modeling). Children are believed to be engaged constantly in a mental struggle to figure out rules that help them distinguish right from wrong. At first, as we noted, children's conceptions of morality reflect a preoccupation with external outcomes: "Bad" acts are ones that lead to punishment or damage and "good" acts are those that lead to reward for the actor. This is because young children fo-

cus their attention on external, perceptually salient events when asked to solve a problem. As children acquire concrete operations, or the ability to solve problems in terms of less visible underlying laws and operations, they can begin making moral judgments in terms of the actor's intentions and motives. However, possession of mature cognitive structures (e.g., concrete operations) does not automatically guarantee that children will start making mature moral judgments (e.g., judgments of naughtiness in terms of the actor's intent to do harm). Certain kinds of social experiences are necessary to ensure that children's moral reasoning will reach the level permitted by their cognitive structures. Piaget and Kohlberg emphasize that children will lack the motivation to refine their moral rules unless they encounter experiences that arouse what is called *cognitive conflict* or *disequilibrium*. Presumably, when children are exposed to new events that slightly violate or challenge their current understanding of what constitutes right or wrong, they become puzzled. This puzzlement motivates them to try to formulate a new and better rule that will help them account for a broader array of moral phenomena more accurately. Consider the following example:

A young girl believes that naughty acts are those causing objective damage. One day she is visiting a friend's home. Her friend spills her milk and breaks a glass, but—surprise!—her friend's mother does *not* punish her friend for the accident. This may arouse some conflict because the girl's expectation has been violated. The girl may thenceforth be on the alert for other damaging acts that go unpunished, in an effort to figure out a better rule to help predict occurrences of punishment. *If* the child has sufficient additional exposure to appropriately conflicting events and *if* she has outgrown her preoperational centration problems, then she may eventually abstract a new rule: "One does not get punished unless one *means to* do the damage." An actor's intentions then begin to figure in her moral reasoning.

Once more mature rules become substituted for less mature ones, children presumably find reasoning that they have outgrown repulsive or laughable. Many adolescents, for example, scorn moral reasoning that focuses on the consequences of an action and excludes the actor's intentions. According to cognitive-developmental theory, there is always a "push" for moral development in the direction of increasing sophistication. Let's consider Piaget's and Kohlberg's theories in more detail.

Piaget's Theory

Overview of Piaget's Theory By watching children play marbles and quizzing them about their conceptions of rules, justice, and knowledge of right and wrong, Piaget (1932) formulated a two-stage theory of moral development. Piaget called his first stage the *morality of constraint,* so named because children's earliest sense of morality is thought to be "constrained" by a belief that adults are superior and godlike beings, whose authority is unquestioned and for whom respect must be maintained at all costs. Because young children view themselves as subordinate to and dependent upon adults, they regard wrongness as whatever adults forbid or punish. Their belief that rules emanate from sources outside of themselves causes them generally to look for objective factors as the basis for their moral judgments.

Piaget believed that the morality of constraint is evidenced by young children in three ways. First is the *tendency to base moral judgments on objective consequences* rather than on subjective intentions and motives. To examine this aspect of morality, Piaget asked children to decide which of two story characters is naughtier: an ill-intentioned character who causes a small amount of damage (e.g., "Paul was stealing a biscuit from the cookie jar when he broke a cup and saucer") or a well-intentioned character who causes a large amount of damage (e.g., "Peter was

sweeping out the kitchen when he knocked over a tray and broke 15 cups and saucers"). Children who assigned more blame to the latter character were assumed to be functioning according to the morality of constraint. A second aspect of this stage is a belief in the *immutability of rules,* which means that rules and laws are divinely inspired, handed down from on high, and cannot be changed even if a majority of the players or members of society want to change them. Third is a belief in *immanent justice,* or the idea that nature punishes (the thief who is struck by lightning is "being punished" for his wrongdoing).

At around age 9 or 10 the child passes into the *morality of cooperation* stage (also called *autonomous morality*). Children in this stage base their moral judgments on intentions rather than consequences, regard rules as social conventions modifiable by majority wish, and realize the foolishness of immanent justice. Piaget believed that interactions with one's peers are critical for crossing the bridge between the stages. This is because in playing with their peers, children participate in group decisions, gain experience in appreciating the viewpoints and intentions of others, and thereby learn that the basis for social convention is mutual respect, not unquestioning reverence for adult authority. Peer interactions, then, are what challenge children's earliest moral views and provide the cognitive conflict for moral growth.

Piaget's Stages: Invariant Sequence and Integrated Wholes? It is true that within each of Piaget's three aspects of morality there are predictable age trends: As children mature, they rely less on objective consequences in their moral evaluations, and their beliefs in the immutability of rules and immanent justice weaken (Karniol, 1980; Percival & Haviland, 1978; Suls & Kalle, 1979). These age trends tend to hold up across Western cultures, but in some primitive societies adolescents and adults sometimes do regress. For example, because of their religious values, members of certain American Indian tribes revert to a belief in immanent justice when they reach adulthood (Hoffman, 1970b).

The three aspects of Piagetian morality do not intercorrelate highly and, moreover, within each area there is considerable situational specificity (Hoffman, 1970b). For example, in making moral judgments, most children sometimes rely on consequences observed and sometimes on intentions inferred, depending on the situation and the demands of the task. The basis for children's judgments depends on whether the behavior they are judging is presented verbally or visually, is hypothetical or real, and is their own behavior or someone else's. More mature judgments are given in the latter instances (Bandura & McDonald, 1963; Chandler, Greenspan, & Barenboim, 1973; Larson & Kurdek, 1979; Rybash & Roodin, 1978). In sum, children do not, at one point in their development, consistently do poorly at all three aspects of Piagetian morality and then suddenly progress to do consistently well at all three of the aspects.

Recent Research on Intentions and Consequences Piaget claimed that children under 9 or 10 years of age could not judge another in terms of his or her intentions. This has bothered a number of psychologists, who point out that even 5-year-olds are heard to say such things as, "It's okay; I know you didn't mean to do it." In the last decade, extensive research findings have led to revision in some of Piaget's theories.

Psychologists have criticized Piaget's method on two main grounds. First, when Piaget asked children to judge which story character was naughtier (the ill-intentioned one who caused little damage vs. the well-intentioned one who caused severe damage), information about the severity of consequences was always given last. Because of their limited memories, young children may simply remember the consequences better (Austin,

Ruble, & Trabasso, 1977; Feldman, Klosson, Parsons, Rholes, & Ruble, 1976; Gottlieb, Taylor, & Ruderman, 1977; Nummedal & Bass, 1976).

Second, Piaget's stories confuse information about intentions with information about consequences: Good intentions are always paired with high damage and ill intentions with low damage. Young children may be capable of judging in terms of intentions, but when they hear that someone has caused grave damage, they may focus their attention on the damage and just not take the time to reflect on whether it could have been an accident or whether the actor had really had good intentions (Armsby, 1971; Bearison & Isaacs, 1975; Buchanan & Thompson, 1973; Costanzo, Coie, Grumet, & Farnill, 1973; Ferguson & Rule, 1980, Rule & Duker, 1973; Suls, Gutkin, & Kalle, 1979). In any case, when children are asked to compare the naughtiness of two actors who cause an equal amount of damage but who clearly differ in their intent, even 5-year-olds do judge in terms of intentions (Armsby, 1971; Hebble, 1971; Imamoglu, 1975; Rule, Nesdale, & McAra, 1974).

Such data have led several contemporary Piagetians to propose a revised two-stage theory of moral judgments. We can call their first stage the *either-or stage*, and their second stage, the *simultaneous coordination stage* (Chandler et al., 1973; Elkind & Dabek, 1977; Gottlieb et al., 1977; Rybash & Roodin, 1978). In this revised first stage of moral evaluation (lasting roughly from 5 to 8 years of age), children are believed to know that both intentions and consequences are relevant to moral judgments. However, they are capable of focusing on only one of these two criteria at a time. Thus when judging an actor, young children will seize on *either* the actor's intentions *or* the consequences of the action—whichever is more obvious—in formulating their evaluations. The children are thought to be incapable of simultaneously keeping in mind and coordinating information on both dimensions. Thus they cannot, for example, see that an actor's good intentions may partially offset the damage the actor causes. Presumably, consequences are often depicted as more salient, so that is the dimension young children tend to focus on.

With the advent of concrete operations (and the ability to see that increases in one dimension can compensate for decreases in another dimension), children are believed capable of simultaneously considering and weighing both intentions and consequences. They may never completely abandon consequences, even as adults, but they gradually assign consequences less weight in their evaluative equations (Surber, 1977; Walster, 1966). There is considerable support for this revised sequence in moral judgment development.

Influences on Progression Through the Piagetian Sequence Remember that according to Piaget's original view, young children's respect for adult-delivered punishment and reward causes them to consider objective consequences to the exclusion of intentions when making moral judgments, and that it is only after extensive peer interaction that children begin to appreciate the importance of intentions. In fact, there is little support for this view. Young children do not seem to hold especially strong respect for adult evaluations (Rybash, Sewall, Roodin, & Sullivan, 1975; Suls & Kalle, 1978; Suls et al., 1979), and there is no evidence that interaction with one's peers causes intention-based judgments.

Progression from the either-or to the simultaneous coordination stage, however, is probably facilitated by the child's attainment of concrete operations (Gottlieb et al., 1977). There is evidence that when children encounter transgressions that violate their expectations, cognitive conflict is aroused, which motivates them to try to figure out new, more mature rules about right and wrong (Peterson, Peterson, & Finley, 1974). Social learning experiences (such as observational learning and direct instruction) also

influence children's growth in the area of moral judgment. We shall discuss these influences when we consider the social learning theory of moral judgments.

Kohlberg's Theory

Overview of Kohlberg's Theory On the basis of his initial interviews with American boys aged 10 to 16, Kohlberg (1969) proposed a six-stage sequence of development in moral reasoning. In his view, people progress from lower to higher stages by a series of transformations, each transformation producing a qualitative change in reasoning that reflects a movement toward more mature modes of reasoning about moral issues. There are some parallels with Piagetian theory, in that people progressively shift from external to internal criteria for moral judgments, but Kohlberg's theory is more complex.

The raw data from which Kohlberg generated his theory were the responses of the boys to nine "moral dilemma" stories that Kohlberg concocted. Each dilemma described a character in conflict: The character would be in a predicament where his own needs and desires (or those of someone close to him, such as a sibling) were in conflict with the laws, prohibitions, or formal obligations of society, and the character would be forced to choose between satisfying the self or following the law. For each dilemma, the respondents first indicated what action they believed was the morally correct one for the character. Following this, they were asked to provide *reasons* for their choices. The factors the boys took into account when justifying their choices then were analyzed, not the choices themselves. Here is a well-known example of Kohlberg's dilemmas:

> In Europe, a woman was near death from cancer. One drug might save her, a form of radium that a druggist in the same town had recently discovered. The druggist was charging $2,000, 10 times what the drug cost him to make. The sick woman's husband, Heinz, went to everyone he knew to borrow the money, but

he could only get together about half of what it cost. He told the druggist that his wife was dying and asked him to sell it cheaper or let him pay later. But the druggist said, "No." The husband got desperate and broke into the man's store to steal the drug for his wife. Should the husband have done that? Why, or why not?

Kohlberg concluded that moral reasoning could be classified into one of six progressively more mature categories and, furthermore, that these six categories could be considered stages in moral reasoning. Although relatively few individuals were observed to reach the higher stages, Kohlberg claimed that in order for children to reach any particular stage they must have progressed through all the preceding stages, and in the right order.

At the earliest stage in Kohlberg's scheme, children believe that good and correct action is any action that prevents a negative or unfavorable outcome to the self. At the second stage, children believe that good behavior is whatever leads to a rewarding outcome for the self. Children define morality at the third stage in terms of behavior that leads to approval or affection from other people. At the fourth stage, children believe that the morally correct action is whatever the laws of the land specify to be correct behavior (but the children show no appreciation of the reasons underlying the laws). Individuals who score at Stage 5 believe that in order to call an action moral, the action must exemplify some general principle that involves mutual rights and obligations among people. People who reason at Stage 6 believe that moral actions are those that involve following one's own principles of conscience.

Because children at both of the first two stages define morality solely in terms of external consequences to the self, Kohlberg proposes that children in either of these two stages are functioning at a *premoral* (or *preconventional*) *level of morality*. Children who reason at either the third or the fourth stage are said to be functioning at the *conventional level of morality*, because reasoning

at both of these stages defines morality according to whatever other people have defined to be good or bad. Kohlberg says that individuals who reason at either the fifth or the sixth stage are showing a *postconventional level of morality*, because they are concerned not just with doing something that looks good but with doing something that illustrates an underlying principle of morality. Thus moral development is seen as progressing through three broad levels, with each level consisting of two substages. Table 6–1 summarizes Kohlberg's stages and gives examples of children's reasoning ability on the "Heinz dilemma" for each stage.

North Americans tend to stabilize their levels of moral reasoning in late adolescence or early adulthood. The highest stage of moral reasoning reached by most adults is actually surprisingly low, with most females leveling off at Stage 3, and most males at Stage 4 (Haan, Smith, & Block, 1968; Holstein, 1976; Kohlberg & Kramer, 1969). Adults who continue their educations in specialities that emphasize moral thought (e.g., doctoral students in moral philosophy or political science, or seminarians) attain higher scores than the average adult (Rest, Davison, & Robbins, 1978).

Kohlberg's Stages: Invariant Sequence and Integrated Wholes? As children develop, there is an increasing use of reasoning characteristic of the higher stages and a decreasing use of reasoning typifying the lower stages. But evidence of age trends is not enough to validate Kohlberg's theory. As Bandura (1977) reminds us, stage propositions require that (a) there is uniformity of judgment at any level; (b) a person cannot evaluate conduct in terms of a given moral standard without first adopting a series of preceding stages; and (c) attainment of a given evaluative standard supplants preceding modes of thought by replacing them. Evidence on none of these points is particularly impressive.

Stages are not well-knit wholes. As individuals mature, they do not follow a clear-cut,

Table 6-1 *Kohlberg's Stages and Examples of Reasoning*

Level I. Preconventional (or Premoral)

Stage 1. *Punishment and obedience orientation.* Obeys rules to avoid punishment. Examples: "He should steal it because if he lets his wife die he will get into trouble"; "He shouldn't steal the drug because he will be caught and sent to jail if he does."

Stage 2. *Naive instrumental hedonism.* Conforms to obtain reward or to have favors returned. Examples: "It's all right to steal the drug because he wants his wife to live"; "He shouldn't steal it because the druggist is in business to make money."

Level II. Conventional (or Morality of Conventional Rule Conformity)

Stage 3. *"Good-boy" morality of maintaining good relations.* Conforms to avoid disapproval by others. Examples: "He should steal it; people would blame him if he didn't love his wife enough to save her"; "He shouldn't steal it because he will bring dishonor on his family and himself."

Stage 4. *Authority and social-order maintaining morality.* Conforms to avoid censure by legitimate authorities; belief that the social order should be maintained for its own sake. Examples: "He should steal it, but only with the idea of paying the druggist"; "It is natural for Heinz to want to save his wife, but it's still always wrong to steal."

Level III. Postconventional (or Morality of Self-Accepted Moral Principles)

Stage 5. *Morality of contract, of individual rights, and of democratically accepted law.* Assumes the role of the impartial spectator, judging in terms of community welfare. Examples: "The law wasn't set up for these circumstances—taking the drug in this situation isn't really right, but he would be justified if he did"; "You can't have everyone stealing when they get desperate. The ends may be good, but the ends don't justify the means."

Stage 6. *Morality of individual principles of conscience.* Conforms to avoid self-condemnation. Examples: "He should steal it—he has to act in terms of the principle of preserving and respecting life"; "If he stole the drug, he wouldn't be blamed by other people but he would condemn himself because he wouldn't have lived up to his own conscience and standards of honesty."

step-by-step progression, with all responses falling at a single stage; rather, they display a distribution of responses shifting to progressively more mature stages (Rest et al., 1978). The same individual may express a number of criteria in his or her judgments, depending on the particular dilemma (Eisenberg-Berg, 1979a; Larson & Kurdek, 1979; Levine, 1976; Rubin & Trotter, 1977).

It is hard to tell if Kohlberg's stages form an invariant sequence. Even longitudinal studies do not provide definitive evidence: When an interval between testing is long, it is impossible to tell if a child who seems to have skipped a stage has just passed through it unnoticed! Still, skipping does *seem* to occur. Holstein (1976), for example, found that boys are more likely than girls to skip Stage 3, but girls are more likely to skip Stage 4.

Perhaps boys perceive affection-based judgments and girls perceive authority-based judgments to be sex-inappropriate for their respective groups.

Higher stages do not displace lower ones. Regression to lower-level thinking is common, even among individuals who have attained Level III (Holstein, 1976; Kuhn, 1976). It appears that several moral structures are acquired by late adolescence; which ones are activated depends on the dilemma, the respondent's feelings about the protagonist, and other factors (Levine, 1976).

Cognitive Influences on Progression through Kohlberg's Sequence Kohlberg believes that children must attain Piaget's concrete operational stage of cognitive development before they can display conventional morality, and they must attain Piaget's stage of formal operations before they can pass into postconventional morality. It is true that children with higher IQ scores are more likely to display higher-stage reasoning. However, the close, one-to-one links between children's cognitive development and their ability to reason morally have been hard to demonstrate. There is only modest support for Kohlberg's view that concrete and formal operations are necessary, though not sufficient, for conventional and postconventional moralities, respectively (Tomlinson-Keasey & Keasey, 1974).

Not all children who have the "necessary" cognitive prerequisites actually display the most mature level of moral reasoning of which they are believed capable. What determines which children will fulfill their moral potential? Like Piaget, Kohlberg emphasizes cognitive conflict, or exposure to moral reasoning that is moderately discrepant from one's current mode of reasoning. In a popular technique of "moral education," children are first read a moral dilemma. Then they are asked to pretend that they are the central character and are instructed to ask two adults (confederates of the investigator) for "advice" on what action they should take to resolve their dilemma. The adults propose opposite courses of action, but both support their advice with moral reasoning that is one stage above each child's own dominant stage. Finally, the children are tested a second time, but on new dilemmas, to see if their moral reasoning has advanced. Children do profit from such experiences—especially those who show some beginning appreciation of the concepts of formal operations (Faust & Arbuthnot, 1978; Walker, 1980; Walker & Richards, 1979).

Does cognitive disequilibrium propel movement only in a forward direction? To test this, a child's modal stage of reasoning is first assessed. Then the child hears another person's responses to the moral dilemmas. This person's opinions are rigged to represent reasoning that is one stage above the sub-

ject's ($+1$), two stages above the subject's ($+2$), at the subject's own level (0), or one stage below the subject's own level (-1). Afterwards, the child indicates how much he or she agrees with the model's opinions or is asked for his or her own moral reasoning on a new set of dilemmas. The hypothesis is that -1 and 0 reasoning are not discrepant from the child's past or present level of understanding, and that $+2$ reasoning is too discrepant for disequilibrium to be aroused. Therefore only children exposed to $+1$ reasoning should subsequently endorse the model's reasoning, or evidence growth in their own reasoning power (Turiel, 1966). Overall, the evidence does suggest that children prefer $+1$ reasoning over $+2$ reasoning, -1 reasoning, and same-stage reasoning (Keasey, 1973, 1974; Moran & Joniak, 1979; Rest, 1973; Rest, Turiel, & Kohlberg, 1969). Experiences that are just a little more advanced than the child's current level of understanding apparently do provide "food for thought" for the child.

Social Influences on Progression through Kohlberg's Sequence Kohlberg (1969) considers role taking to be the major social-cognitive influence on moral development. Children who participate in much social interaction—with either adults or peers—should have greater opportunities for appreciating the perspectives of others. This should lead them to recognize the importance of other people's feelings and intentions and to see the necessity of rules and laws to maintain reciprocal rights and obligations.

Is there evidence that opportunities for social participation and role taking correlate with advanced moral judgments? Yes. Children who are active in clubs, organizations, politics, and group decision making are more mature moral reasoners (Keasey, 1971; Maitland & Goldman, 1974). Children in highly industrialized settings move through Kohlberg's lower stages at a more rapid rate than do individuals in less urban settings (White, Bushnell, & Regnemer, 1978). Children who do well on tests of inferring other people's perspectives also score higher on Kohlberg's stages (Moir, 1974; Selman, 1971). Of course, being a good role taker and socially perceptive does not guarantee that one will reason with moral maturity. The reasoning of some of the principals in the Watergate scandal, for example, leads one to wonder just what factors are necessary to keep bright and socially capable people exercising mature moral reasoning.

Relationship of Moral Reasoning to Moral Behavior   At the outset of this chapter, we noted that relationships between moral reasoning and moral behavior are not strong. Now we can see one reason why: A given level of moral reasoning can be used to justify either of two opposing actions! Still, there are a few indications that children who support their moral decisions with higher-level reasoning are less aggressive (Kohlberg, 1969) and more altruistic (Eisenberg-Berg, 1979b). Radical student activists have been found to shun conventional morality: The activists preferred to reason at either Level I or Level III rather than at Level II (Haan et al., 1968). People who favor conventional morality, in contrast, are the most likely to change their opinions to conform to majority opinion when pressured by peers (Saltzstein, Diamond, & Belenky, 1972).

The Social Learning Theory of Moral Judgments

Social learning theory treats moral judgments as multidimensional social decisions. From their own disciplinary experiences as well as from observing the occasions on which others are criticized or praised for their actions, children learn that a variety of considerations are relevant to judging an act as right or wrong. Included in this group of relevant factors are: the nature of the act, its motivating conditions, its consequences, characteristics of the actor, the situation in which the act occurs, the remorse of the transgressor, and the number and type of people who are victimized (Bandura, 1977). The weights

children assign the various factors in their evaluative formulas will change with age, mainly because children of different ages have different social experiences. One of the reasons young children assign greater weight to consequences than to intentions in formulating a moral judgment, for example, may be that parents punish young children primarily because of damage they cause and not so much because of their intentions.

In social learning theory, then, development of moral judgment is in terms of the child learning to recognize more and more factors as relevant to moral judgments, and learning to change the weights assigned to the various factors when synthesizing a moral judgment. Development does not occur in abrupt stages.

Social learning theorists, like the cognitive-developmentalists, view children as active information processors trying to make sense out of their experiences. Children are believed to abstract the common features of acts that society praises or blames. A great many studies have shown that children do search for features underlying blameworthy actions and adopt these features in their own evaluations (Bachrach, Huesmann, & Peterson, 1977; Bandura & McDonald, 1963; Brody & Henderson, 1977; Cowan, Langer, Heavenrich, & Nathanson, 1969; Crowley, 1968; Harvey & Liebert, 1979; Jensen & Hughston, 1971; Saltzstein, Sanvitale, & Supraner, 1978; Schleifer & Douglas, 1973). For example, if children see people consistently blame others for intentional damage, but not for accidental damage, they are indeed likely to assign more weight to intentions in their moral judgments.

The social learning view that children's evaluations depend on a variety of factors including age, child-rearing experiences, cultural factors, and the particular situation and behavior being judged is illustrated nicely in research begun by Weiner and Peter (1973). These authors found that although children's evaluations of *moral* behavior reflect a steadily decreasing use of consequences and increasing use of intentions from early childhood to adulthood, the picture is quite different when children's evaluations of *achievement* behavior are considered. In achievement evaluations, children are asked to evaluate characters who have worked to achieve a goal or solve a difficult problem. Perhaps the children are asked to decide how many gold stars the character should be awarded.

When judging heroes of achievement stories, young elementary-school children start out in the usual Piagetian fashion by basing their judgments on the degree of the actor's tangible success or failure on the task (consequences-based judgments), and they virtually ignore how much effort the actor expended (the actor's intentions). During elementary school they do reverse the size of the weights they assign to intentions and consequences so that intentions become the more important criterion. However, in adolescence the children reverse their basis for judging back to consequences! The regression seems to be due to the importance placed on objective success in American society. In cultures that place greater emphasis on rewarding effort rather than outcome, (e.g., Iran), children continue to base their achievement evaluations on effort right into adulthood (Salili, Maehr, & Gillmore, 1976).

Attribution and Moral Judgments

According to attribution theory, we are less likely to assign responsibility to an actor for his or her actions if we believe that some external factor forced the actor to behave the way he or she did. That is, people discount personal responsibility for an act when they can attribute the act to an external cause. Even children at the elementary-school level follow this rule: They credit those who achieve and succeed because of their own effort and ability more than those who succeed because they had good luck or an easy task to do (Weiner, 1979). They deem aggression that is provoked, and therefore externally justified, less blameworthy than hostility performed without provocation (Berndt, 1977; Darley, Klosson, & Zanna, 1978). They judge acts of sharing and helping to be more praiseworthy if the acts are spontaneous than if they represent returning favors (Peterson, Hartmann, & Gelfand, 1977).

Children much under 6 years, however, sometimes fail to use the discounting schema employed by older children and adults. That is, they fail to infer that the presence of an external motivator implies reduced intrinsic motivation on the part of an actor. Leahy (1979), for example, found that young children were more rather than less likely to praise an actor for helping somebody if they were told the actor was getting paid for his help. The weights children assign to evaluative criteria may depend not only on social-experiential factors but also on the child's cognitive capacities to utilize certain attributional schemas.

Attribution theorists have made the intriguing discovery that people possess biases that cause them to explain their own behavior differently from how they explain the behavior of others. When people are asked to explain their own actions, they usually justify their behavior in terms of external circumstances; when asked to explain someone else's behavior, they more commonly invoke a trait or dispositional explanation (Jones & Nisbett, 1972). Thus if children are asked why they got angry at someone, they are likely to blame their behavior on the situation ("He was rude to me first"), but if asked why somebody else has aggressed verbally, they will probably blame the actor ("He's just a hostile person").

In a provocative field study designed to examine some implications of this distinction, college students who were unaware that they were participating in a psychology experiment were confronted with an elaborate set of plans for burglarizing a local advertising firm and were asked to take part in the break-in (West, Gunn, & Chernicky, 1975). Astonishingly, in some experimental conditions nearly 50 percent of the subjects agreed to go along with the proposed crime. (Of course, the burglary was never actually executed.) The interesting point was that when the students were told that the planned break-in was a hoax and they were asked why they had been willing to go along with it, they nearly always justified their behavior in terms of situational factors. They pointed out that the plan seemed well thought-out and foolproof, that respected people had proposed the break-in, that they would receive immunity from prosecution, and so on. In contrast, when different subjects were asked what they thought had caused the potential burglars to go along with the plan, they typically accused them of weak moral character. (For an interesting commentary on some of the ethical issues involved in this study, see Cook, 1975).

There are two important implications of this research. First, people who condemn someone for his or her behavior should realize that there is a good chance that they would have behaved the same way had they been subject to the same circumstances as the accused. West and his associates (1975) suggest that many ordinary citizens who condemned the men who planned and covered up the Watergate burglary may have behaved very similarly had they been members of the Nixon administration at the time. A second implication is that in order to understand what motivates moral and immoral action, it is necessary to "see things through the child's eyes." This is exactly what we shall try to do when we discuss factors influencing resistance to deviation.

THE DEVELOPMENT OF SELF-EVALUATION

Learning to feel guilty when doing something wrong and to limit one's rewards to occasions when they are deserved are crucial aspects of successful socialization. In fact, society has a special name for people who seem never to experience guilt or shame and who impulsively and noncontingently indulge themselves with rewards: the psychopath. Of course, the other extreme is just as unfortunate. People who penalize and berate themselves severely for even little mistakes and who seem never to allow themselves rewarding and pleasurable experiences sometimes fall prey to serious depressions. Obviously the trick is to find the happy medium. Here we examine how children learn to criticize and reward themselves to an appropriate degree, and at the right times and places. We shall evaluate several theoretical perspectives on the development of self-evaluation, beginning with Freud's psychoanalytic theory and ending with Bandura's cognitive social learning viewpoint.

Freud's Theory of Conscience

Freud believed that the self-judgmental function was filled by the superego, which the child presumably acquires during the Oedipal stage as a result of identification with the same-sex parent. By identifying with a loved but feared parent, children were thought to practice on themselves the love-withdrawal disciplinary techniques their parents used when the children misbehaved.

As we saw in Chapter 4, there are difficulties with Freud's theory of identification. Children do not ordinarily choose to imitate threatening and feared adults. Hoffman and Saltzstein (1967), for example, found that parents who discipline their children by threatening to withdraw their love do not encourage their children to admire them or want to take after them.

Furthermore, it is doubtful whether identification with the same-sex parent is even the major mechanism through which children develop self-evaluative tendencies or other aspects of morality. Hoffman (1971b) found that children who consciously admire and strive to emulate their parents do not show stronger signs of morality (e.g., mature moral judgments, guilt, confession, and acceptance of responsibility) than children who do not particularly wish to be like their same-sex parent. Furthermore, boys whose fathers are absent, from death or divorce, do not usually show retarded moral development (Santrock, 1975); when they do, the best explanation is probably not the absence of the parent model but rather the nature of the discipline that a mother who lacks a husband employs, such as increased physical punishment (Hoffman, 1971a).

This does not imply that modeling is unimportant to moral development. As we shall see in this chapter, moral development *is* enhanced by observation and imitation of a variety of morally mature individuals. However, the evidence does not suggest that the same-sex parent serves a unique or exclusive function in modeling morality for his or her child.

Conditioning Views of Guilt and Self-Criticism

Like Freud, conditioning learning theorists have tended to focus on the negative side of self-evaluation; that is, they have been concerned with how children develop guilt feelings and learn to punish themselves with comments like "Bad girl!" following misbehavior.

According to conditioning viewpoints (Aronfreed, 1964, 1968; Hill, 1960), children learn to criticize themselves for transgressing via a two-step process. The first step involves the classical conditioning of anxiety reactions to misbehavior: Because misbehavior is followed by painful and frightening periods of parental punishment and love withdrawal, children come to experience conditioned anxiety, in the form of guilt, when they misbehave. The second process involves children learning to reduce posttransgression anxiety by verbalizing self-critical remarks. When children misbehave and are suffering anxiety over impending punishment, parents often scold them (e.g., "That was naughty!"). Because these critical remarks tend to occur just before the aversive period finishes and

the parent reinstates his or her affection, the remarks are associated with relief and acquire intrinsic tranquilizing effects. Later, when children deviate and feel guilty, they can give themselves doses of conditioned relief by emitting the self-critical comments.

Although children may sometimes adopt the use of self-critical comments because they provide relief from guilt (Grusec & Ezrin, 1972), the conditioning theory is dissatisfying as a complete theory of guilt and self-criticism. Conditioning theory regards negative self-evaluations as nothing more than automatic and unthinking verbal operants. Intuitively, however, people know that guilt and self-criticism often reflect more than automatic conditioned reactions. Indeed, people's sense of self-dissatisfaction often results from figuring out by applying complex, cognitive methods that they have done something to violate a moral rule that is important to them.

The conditioning view also makes a prediction that is not well supported by data. Presumably, all that parents need to do in order to establish habits of self-criticism in their children is to use the kinds of discipline thought to condition anxiety to transgression (e.g., punishment and love-withdrawal) and to be careful that they criticize the child before ending disciplinary episodes. Children whose parents rely on punishment and love-withdrawal techniques, however, do not evidence the most guilt after transgressions. Instead, it is children who are disciplined with inductive reasoning (e.g., spelling out to children the causal role they can play in producing harmful outcomes for others) that display the most guilt, apologize, confess, accept responsibility, and show other signs of internal disturbance following transgressions (Hoffman, 1970b, 1977). This suggests that we may need to look more toward cognitive factors in elucidating the development of self-evaluation. Hoffman's emotion-attribution approach to understanding guilt reactions is a step in this direction.

Hoffman's Emotion-Attribution Analysis of Guilt

According to Hoffman (1977), people experience guilt because they empathize with another's distress and also believe that they are responsible for initiating or prolonging the distressed other's state. Thus, in order for a child to feel guilty over a completed or contemplated transgression, the child must (a) have an empathic response to the plight or distress of someone who is or might be harmed by the transgression, and (b) realize that he or she is or would be the cause of the other person's negative state.

In several field projects, Hoffman has found that when children are asked to describe how a story character feels after misbehaving, children who are disciplined primarily with inductive reasoning project more guilt feelings onto the story character. In contrast, children whose parents favor power assertive discipline describe the transgressing charactor as fearing external punishment, running away or lying to avoid detection, or being concerned about external consequences in some other way (Hoffman, 1970b; Hoffman & Saltzstein, 1967). Because inductive reasoning involves both making children aware of the feelings of other people and pointing out to children the causal role they can play in producing these feelings in others, it makes sense that inductive reasoning is associated with the development of a capacity for guilt in children. Hoffman's theory, then, has substantial evidence to support it.

Bandura's Information-Processing Approach to Self-Regulation

Overview of Bandura's Theory   According to social learning theory, children synthesize information from several social sources (e.g., their own disciplinary experiences, the consequences they see similar others receive for various behaviors, and verbal instruction) to arrive at conceptions of the sorts of behaviors society deems appropriate or inappropriate for people like themselves. At the same time, as children are integrating information to arrive at these standards of blameworthy and praiseworthy behavior, they see that it would be to their advantage to regulate their own behavior to conform to these standards. Thus children strive to inhibit behaviors that lead to punishment and to perform behaviors that produce social and material reward. Well-socialized children, Bandura suggests, set subgoals for themselves (e.g., "I will try to keep from hitting Billy today," or "I will try to get an A on my next arithmetic test"), rewarding themselves when they match or exceed their standards and punishing themselves when they fall short of their standards. This is the process of self-regulation.

Children generate standards of appropriate conduct in nearly every aspect of sociopersonal functioning, not just morality. Thus, in addition to forming personal standards for moral conduct (e.g., "I will never lie to my friends"), children develop standards in achievement contexts (e.g., "I want at least a grade of B in this subject"), they guide their sex-role development in terms of personal standards (e.g., "I'm not going to play with a doll because only girls do that"), and so on.

We shall consider in more detail (a) some of the determinants of children's standards of personal conduct, (b) the cognitive processes involved in self-evaluation, and (c) the intriguing question of what motivates children to persist at self-regulation even when it seemingly requires considerable self-sacrifice.

Determinants of Personal Standards
Children's standards of appropriate conduct represent syntheses of the children's direct and vicarious social learning experiences. If children are consistently punished (or rewarded) for making a response in a certain situation, they come to infer that the act is undesirable (or desirable). In Chapter 3, we reviewed some of the ways parents can arrange their child-rearing practices so that children develop clear conceptions of what is

and is not expected of them. We noted that response-outcome rule learning is enhanced if parents make demands of children for mature, age-appropriate behavior, enforce these requests consistently and firmly (with power assertion, if necessary), and justify their disciplinary action with inductive reasoning that clearly defines what is desirable or undesirable, and why (Baumrind, 1973; Liebert & Allen, 1967).

We stressed in Chapter 4 that children also develop conceptions of appropriate and inappropriate behavior by observing the consequences other people receive for their actions. In formulating guidelines for their own behavior, children are especially impressed by the consequences they see similar others receive for their behavior: A boy will develop conceptions of what is appropriate and inappropriate for himself more from observing how people punish and reward other boys his age than from seeing how people react to girls or other dissimilar people (Bussey & Perry, 1976).

Children put together information they receive from these direct and vicarious social learning experiences to arrive at standards of how they themselves should behave. Standards are flexible, not fixed, and change as the child's social learning experiences change. Sometimes the information children receive about the appropriateness of an act is confusing or contradictory, as when two adults try to impose markedly different value systems on children or when children see a message on television that contradicts what their parents are trying to teach them. In such cases, children's standards may be weak or represent compromises of the different contingencies they have experienced or observed (Allen & Liebert, 1969; McMains & Liebert, 1968).

The more clearly children understand that certain modes of behavior are socially approved or disapproved for people like themselves, the more motivated they are to regulate their own behavior to conform to such standards. Not all children are equally

skilled in successfully regulating their behavior to meet their standards, however. Bandura proposes that effective self-regulation typically involves people setting subgoals of desirable behavior, rewarding themselves for attaining or surpassing these subgoals, and punishing themselves for falling short of these subgoals. If children know that keeping their room tidy each day will bring them a reward on Saturday, they may find that it pays to institute contingencies of self-monitoring and self-evaluation during the week. Perhaps the children leave themselves reminders to clean up each morning after school, refrain from watching the morning cartoon show until having cleaned up, and even grow anxious and irritated with themselves when they forget or violate their self-imposed subgoals.

Children can acquire strategies of self-regulation in a variety of ways. Perhaps their parents verbally tutor them in ways to self-regulate (e.g., "If you'll spend 15 minutes each night studying your spelling words, you'll get your spelling tests right"; or "If you make sure that your room is cleaned up before going to school every day this week, we'll take you to the movies on Saturday"). An experiment by Liebert and Allen (1967) revealed that when adults told children that they should reward themselves only when their behavior reached a certain level of acceptance at a task, the children did impose stringent standards of self-reinforcement when left alone to do the task.

Children are also inspired to try self-regulation if they see other people practicing contingencies of self-reward and self-punishment. Children who see a parent express self-dissatisfaction when breaking a diet, or a peer take obvious pride in mastering a new skill at a sport, are learning that self-reactions are a vital component to self-regulation. Laboratory experiments also reveal that standards of self-evaluation can be transmitted via modeling. When children see models reward themselves only for high scores at a game, the children are also likely to reward themselves only for high scores when they later play the game alone (Bandura & Kupers, 1964; Lepper, Sagotsky, & Mailer, 1975). Children will also imitate models' tendencies to punish themselves for poor behavior (Herbert, Gelfand, & Hartmann, 1969). Furthermore, children are more likely to imitate a model's contingencies of self-evaluation if the model is a prestigious or powerful person than if the model is weak or unsuccessful (Grusec, 1971). Perhaps children reason that by adopting the self-regulating strategies of a high-status person they, too, will come to possess the rewards and prestige that the powerful person possesses.

Cognitive Processes in Self-Evaluation
When engaged in self-regulation, children are constantly observing their behavior and making decisions about whether their behavior is satisfactory. As we noted, a judgment that one's behavior reaches or exceeds a desired level is occasion for self-reward. In fact, when children observe their progress to be satisfactory, they tend to adjust their standards upward, requiring a greater level of self-control before rewarding themselves the next time. When children fall short of a desired behavior, they try to improve their behavior or else lower their standards (Bandura, 1977).

In making judgments about whether their behavior has reached a satisfactory level of performance (and therefore deserves self-reward), children rely on three kinds of information: comparison of their behavior with their personal standard, social comparison, and causal attribution. Comparison with their personal standard is particularly important. Careful self-observation is an important part of self-regulation, but the particular aspects of their behavior that children must attend to in order to regulate their actions vary with specific behaviors and circumstances. In sports, children must monitor their speed and agility; in achievement situations, the quality, quantity, and originality of their work is measured; and in interpersonal situations, the sociability and morality of their conduct is vital. Children have to bear in mind their

past, present, and future levels of performance because they must judge their current accomplishments against both their previous ones and their hoped-for goals.

In judging themselves, children also compare their deeds and accomplishments to those actions of other people, especially their friends, co-workers, and heroes. This is called *social comparison.* For example, children punish themselves more severely after breaking a rule if they are led to believe that their peers behaved more morally under the same circumstances (Perry, Perry, Bussey, English, & Arnold, 1980).

Self-evaluations also depend partly on what people perceive to be the causes of their behavior. In general, self-reactions (both positive and negative) are most intense when people perceive their behavior to be caused by some internal factor (a personal motive, disposition, etc.) rather than brought about by some environmental factor beyond their control. For instance, children derive more pride and pleasure from their successes in achievement situations if they can attribute their success to some internal factor such as high ability or effort rather than to an external factor like good luck; similarly, they get more upset over failures they attribute to internal causes (Ruble, Parsons, & Ross, 1976; Weiner, 1979). Children also punish themselves more harshly for moral disobedience if they are unable to blame their misbehavior on something in the environment that "made them do it" (Perry et al., 1980).

Despite their moral standards, people sometimes fail to anticipate negative self-reactions that might deter immoral behavior. We know, for example, that Nazi war criminals, Watergate participants, and a few Vietnam soldiers perpetrated crimes that might have violated their moral standards under other circumstances. Negative self-reactions can become "disengaged" from anticipated immoral action for a number of reasons. For example, one can cognitively restructure one's immoral behavior to make it appear to serve some moral end, or one can displace or diffuse responsibility for an act that has harmful consequences. In the next chapter, in which we discuss aggression, we shall deal more fully with how people learn to shed responsibility for immoral behavior.

Supports for Self-Regulatory Systems
At first glance, it may seem that by restricting their self-rewards to times when they match their standards and by punishing themselves when they do not, children are going against a natural human instinct to maximize positive payoffs and minimize negative ones. Considering their apparent costs to children, why are self-regulatory systems adopted?

According to Bandura, children adopt self-regulatory systems because they see that self-control can, in the long run, produce positive effects. To be sure, self-deprivation and self-rebuke produce momentarily unpleasant effects, but they persist because they serve ends that are on the whole beneficial. Children can see that by exercising moment-to-moment control over their progress in an achievement situation (e.g., by restricting snacks or television until assignments are completed), they can come closer to improving the skills and competencies that will ultimately yield them larger rewards. Exercising self-control also brings the respect of others, while unmerited self-indulgence is frowned on. In short, it pays to exercise self-control (Bandura, 1977; 1978b).

THE DEVELOPMENT OF RESISTANCE TO DEVIATION

A major goal of socialization is to instill in children the ability and willingness to adhere to society's rules even when the children are free of external surveillance or the expectation of punishment or reward from socializing agents. Many psychologists refer to this process as *internalization*. Here we examine the factors that help children resist temptation when free of external surveillance. First we review two contemporary theoretical perspectives on the internalization process—so-

cial learning theory and attribution theory. Then we discuss three classes of influences on the development of resistance to temptation: child-rearing factors, cognitive factors, and situational influences. Finally, we present a developmental account of internalization that draws on principles of both social learning and attribution theories.

Theories of Resistance to Deviation

Social Learning Theory Social learning theorists (Bandura, 1977) regard resistance to deviation as a natural consequence of the processes of self-regulation that we discussed in the preceding section. Once children have formulated personal standards of appropriate conduct and have set subgoals for themselves (e.g., "I will forgo watching television each afternoon after school until I have studied my spelling list"), they should anticipate self-reward for adhering to their prescribed course of action and expect self-punishment for breaking their rules. Since, according to social learning theory, behavior is governed by its anticipated consequences, and since anticipated consequences are a function of children's personal standards of appropriate conduct, then whatever factors strengthen children's personal standards should also help children resist deviation.

Social learning theorists prefer to use the term *self-regulation* rather than internalization to describe the process by which children resist temptation in the absence of external surveillance. One reason for this is that social learning theorists believe that a great deal of what looks like internalized behavior is often at least partly in the service of an external goal. To be sure, the fact that children set goals of self-regulation, and reward and punish themselves in accordance with these goals, implies that a good deal of socialized behavior can be under internal control. However, as we pointed out in the last section, much self-regulation is guided by more distant external incentives. A child may force himself to study in order to earn an A and the praise of his parents; a girl may force herself to inhibit her aggressive impulses in order to avoid going to the principal's office. External pressures help people decide what behaviors to self-regulate and help sustain people's efforts at self-regulation.

Attribution Theory According to attribution theory (Lepper, 1981), children resist deviation if they can think of a good "internal" reason for doing so. If children believe that they are inherently good people and that good people do not engage in the kind of misbehavior they are contemplating, then they should resist the temptation to deviate. This is because such children realize that deviating would mean violating their own self-image of being a "good person" and therefore would lead to dissonance, guilt, and a loss of self-esteem. In contrast, if children who are tempted to deviate can think only of an "external" reason for not misbehaving (e.g., "You better not do this because you might get caught and be punished"), then the likelihood of the children resisting deviation is slim, at least in situations where the children are fairly confident that external authorities are not watching them.

As we discussed in Chapter 3, the kinds of discipline parents use to elicit compliance from their children influence the reasons children generate for avoiding misbehavior. Presumably, if parents are successful in gaining desirable conduct from their children in subtle ways that do not draw the children's attention to the fact that they are being externally coerced into conforming, then the children will conclude that they are by nature the kind of people who want to perform in positive ways and avoid misbehaving. In contrast, if parents rely on harsh, power assertive methods of discipline to control their children, then the children are likely to conclude that the main reason for performing desirable behavior is to gain external reward or avoid external disapproval. Subsequent resistance to deviation in the absence of external surveillance should be high for the former children, low for the latter children.

Child-Rearing Influences on Resistance to Deviation

Parental Discipline Field studies indicate that children who are most likely to show responsible, self-controlled behavior in temptation situations have parents who score high on a number of important dimensions of child-rearing. These parents insist on desirable, age-appropriate conduct from their children; they firmly and consistently enforce their requests for desirable behavior (with power assertion, if required); they are warm and genuinely interested in their children's welfare and development; they are willing to engage their children in verbal give-and-take during disciplinary encounters; and they justify their disciplinary actions with inductive reasoning. Parents who make few demands for mature behavior, who enforce their demands inconsistently, or who use unnecessarily harsh levels of power assertion to achieve compliance, have children who score low on indices of internalization (Baumrind, 1973; Hoffman, 1977; Martin, 1975).

Modeling There is ample evidence that children frequently imitate naughty behavior: They often readily copy the actions of someone behaving aggressively or breaking a rule (Rosenkoetter, 1973; Stein, 1967). Furthermore, if either or both of a child's parents have been convicted of a crime, the child stands an above-average chance of developing delinquent and antisocial behaviors (Martin, 1975).

But is it possible to get children to *inhibit* undesirable behavior through exposure to models? Research suggests that there are two ways in which children can learn resistance to deviation through modeling. One method involves allowing children to observe deviant models receive punishment for their misbehavior. The second way is to have them see people choose moral over immoral actions. We shall consider each of these ways separately.

When children see a misbehaving model (e.g., a child who is playing with forbidden toys or behaving aggressively) get scolded, they are less likely later to display the deviant behavior than if they see a model misbehave but get away with it (Bandura, 1965; Walters & Parke, 1964). Adults who consistently punish children when they transgress are helping to discourage other children who have witnessed the deviant behavior from following suit. In other words, aversive vicarious consequences help prevent imitation of deviant behavior.

This does not mean that adults should go out of their way to "make examples" of deviant children. Telling other children who have not witnessed a deviant act just what a naughty child did wrong and how he or she was punished for it is not always advisable. This is because by describing one child's deviant behavior to another, an adult may be unwittingly planting the seeds of deviant behavior in a child's mind, making the child think about the joys of deviating, which otherwise may never have occurred to the child. Overall, it may be better for children never to learn of another child's deviation than it is for them to see another child deviate and receive punishment (Hoffman, 1970b).

Children who see a model resist the temptation to break a rule become more likely to resist a similar temptation themselves (Bussey & Perry, 1977; Grusec, Kuczynski, Rushton, & Simutis, 1979; Perry, Bussey, & Perry, 1975; Rosenkoetter, 1973). Models who resist deviation are especially effective if they also display alternative, acceptable behavior that competes with deviation (Bussey & Perry, 1977), or if they verbalize self-instructions or plans for resisting temptation (Meichenbaum & Goodman, 1971).

Cognitive Factors in Resistance to Deviation

The thoughts going through children's minds at the times they are tempted to deviate influence the likelihood of their resisting deviation. Here we shall consider four cognitive influences on children's ability to resist temptation—anticipated self-evaluations, causal attributions, symbolic representations of the forbidden activity, and self-verbalizations and plans.

Anticipated Self-Evaluations When we discussed Bandura's social learning theory of self-regulation, we noted that once children formulate personal standards of appropriate and inappropriate conduct, they come to anticipate positive self-reactions (feelings of pride, self-satisfaction) for conforming to these standards and to expect negative self-reactions (guilt, self-punishment) for violating their standards. Presumably these anticipated self-evaluations actually help govern children's behavior in situations that offer temptation.

There is evidence to support Bandura's hypothesis that self-administered consequences actually do control behavior. Perry and Bussey (1977), for example, found that boys who inhibit their impulses to aggress against their peers tend to become very upset with themselves when they do think they have done something to hurt another child; extremely aggressive boys do not show this pattern of self-remorse following aggression. There is also evidence that children who withhold rewards from themselves until they attain self-prescribed levels of mastery in achievement situations exert more effort to succeed and work harder to improve the quality of their performance than children with less exacting standards of self-reinforcement (Bandura & Perloff, 1967; Kunce & Thelen, 1972; Masters, Furman, & Barden, 1977; Masters & Santrock, 1976). Self-reactions do help regulate behavior.

The more children perceive their self-regulation as voluntary and as originating within themselves, the more impact their self-evaluations have on their behavior. Children who decide for themselves how much they should be punished for transgressions are more likely to resist temptations (Grusec & Kuczynski, 1977) and also accept more responsibility when they do misbehave (Aronfreed, Cutick, & Fagen, 1963). Children who commit themselves to a rule by writing it down or by verbalizing it and recording it adhere to it more faithfully (Kanfer & Duerfeldt, 1968; Kanfer & Zich, 1974).

Although anticipated self-evaluations contribute to some children's ability to resist deviating, we should remember Bandura's warning that people sometimes "disengage" aversive consequences from immoral action, or fail to anticipate or experience negative self-reactions for behavior that would, under other circumstances, violate their personal standards. In some revealing field experiments, Diener, Fraser, Beaman, and Kelem (1976) found that Halloween trick-or-treaters were more likely to steal treats if they could hide their identities and diffuse responsibility for their actions. In this research, if children trick-or-treated alone or were asked their names and addresses, they generally did not take more goodies than offered when the adult turned her back. But children who came in groups or were not asked their names and addresses often took more than they were told they could. Furthermore, when the trick-or-treaters' self-awareness was increased by placing a large mirror behind the candy bowl—ensuring that the children would see their reflections were they to deviate—the children were less likely to steal (Beaman, Klentz, Diener, & Svanum, 1979). Like adults, children can also escape self-remorse by blaming actions on obedience to authority. In one study, school children delivered what they thought were "extremely dangerous" electric shocks to a victim when an adult directed them to do it (Shanab & Yahya, 1977).

Clearly, then, wise parents are those who try to help children generate their own standards, who nurture the qualities in children that help them expect negative internal reactions for misbehaving (e.g., by inductively reasoning with children, strengthening their empathic capacities, and sensitizing them to the causal role they can play in hurting others), and who educate children about circum-

stances likely to lead to disengagement of self-evaluative processes.

Self-Perceptions and Other Causal Attributions   There is substantial evidence, as the attribution theorists maintain, that children who conceive of themselves as honest, obedient, altruistic, or otherwise intrinsically motivated to perform desirable behavior are likely to display moral behavior even in the absence of adult supervision.

There are two major ways in which children can develop positive self-perceptions. A first way involves self-observation and logical inference. If children observe themselves performing desirable behaviors and cannot find anything in the environment that is forcing them to perform the good behaviors, then they are likely to conclude that they are the kind of children who are intrinsically motivated to perform in positive, acceptable ways (Bem, 1972). In Chapter 3, we reviewed evidence that when adults use gentle, nonforceful techniques to elicit desirable behavior from children, children sometimes do conclude that they must be the kind of people who want to perform such behaviors. In contrast, using harsh, power assertive discipline sometimes leads children to view their behavior as externally coerced (Lepper, 1973; Smith, Gelfand, Hartmann, & Partlow, 1979). In Lepper's (1973) experiment, children who resisted the temptation to touch prohibited toys because an adult threatened them with severe punishment for disobedience were more likely to cheat later to win a prize than were children who had resisted touching the toys without the severe threat. Presumably the severe threat prevented children from inferring that they were the sort of children who are intrinsically motivated to be good.

A second way children can learn positive self-perceptions is by simply being told by others that they possess desirable traits and dispositions. In fact, a broad range of prosocial and moral behaviors—including neatness, academic achievement, patience, altruism, delay of gratification, friendliness, and cooperation—can be elicited in children simply by telling them that they are intrinsically disposed to display the behaviors (e.g., "I know you're the kind of child who likes to help others.") (Grusec, Kuczynski, Rushton, & Simutis, 1978; Grusec & Redler, 1980; Jensen & Moore, 1977; Miller, Brickman, & Bolen, 1975; Toner, Moore, & Emmons, 1980).

What causes children to "live up to" prosocial qualities attributed to them by adults? One possibility is that attributions of goodness make children more aware of adults' expectations of them, and children seek to conform to these expectations in order to gain the adults' approval and to avoid their censure. But there is another possibility. Perhaps children who have been told that they are good come to believe the information. If this is so, then children who have had prosocial qualities attributed to them should come to have higher *self*-expectations for good behavior. Furthermore, children who hold higher self-expectations for moral conduct should anticipate greater dissatisfaction and self recrimination for behaving improperly than children who never particularly expected the behavior of themselves in the first place.

Perry and his associates (1980) tested the hypothesis that children who have been told that they are especially good are likely to punish themselves severely when they misbehave. One group of elementary-school children was told by an adult that they were exceptionally conscientious and obedient; a second group was not told anything. Subsequently all the children were assigned a tedious task, were prepaid a sum of 30 tokens (exchangeable for small prizes) for performing the task, and were left alone to complete it. All the children were distracted from completing the task by a television set playing a lively cartoon. A different experimenter confronted the children about their failure to finish the task and gave them an opportunity to punish themselves by letting the children de-

cide how many, if any, of their tokens they should relinquish. The main finding was that children who had received verbal attributions of goodness punished themselves substantially more than other children for their misbehavior. The results were interpreted as supporting the hypothesis that children who are told by adults that they possess desirable moral characteristics experience particularly strong remorse when they fail to exercise self-control in temptation situations. Anticipation of this remorse for misbehavior may be what motivates children with positive self-perceptions to resist deviation.

There is plentiful evidence, then, that children who believe that the main reason for resisting deviation is to avoid damaging their self-image of being a good person are indeed inclined to display moral conduct in the absence of external surveillance. In contrast, children who believe that the main reason for resisting temptation is to avoid getting caught and punished are highly likely to deviate if they are confident that no one will catch them. It is worth recalling an experiment by Dienstbier, Hillman, Lehnhoff, Hillman, and Valkenaar (1975) that we described in Chapter 3. In this study, when an adult who was scolding children for misbehaving told them that they were probably upset because they had been caught and punished—a treatment designed to make the children develop concerns about external surveillance—the children were unlikely to resist deviation later when they were sure nobody was watching.

Cognitive Representations of Prohibited Activities   Some fascinating experiments reveal that how children think about the "forbidden fruit" influences whether they will withstand or give in to the temptation to deviate. The most intriguing work on this topic comes from Mischel's (1974) studies on factors that influence children's delay of gratification. Delay of gratification involves forgoing an immediately available but small reward in order to obtain a more valuable reward later. Denying oneself the income from a job in order to pursue an education that eventually will lead to a higher paying job is one example most students are familiar with.

Mischel has studied delay of gratification mainly in preschool children. We will first describe Mischel's experimental setup and then review some of the major findings from his work. In the typical experiment, children are first offered a choice between two rewards, such as a marshmallow and a pretzel. After the child chooses, the experimenter informs the child that he is going to leave the room for a while. He goes on to explain that if the child waits until he returns (at some unspecified time in the future), the child can eat the preferred treat. On the other hand, if at any time the child gets tired of waiting, the child can summon the experimenter back by ringing a bell. If the child chooses to do this, however, he or she can eat only the less preferred treat. The length of time the child waits before ringing the bell to recall the experimenter is the measure of the child's ability to delay gratification. (If the child does not summon the experimenter, he returns after 15 minutes anyway.)

In some early experiments, Mischel (1974) tested the hypothesis that leaving the reward objects in plain sight would help the child delay better. This prediction came from Freud, who suggested that imagining wish-fulfilling situations involving desirable but temporarily unobtainable objects helps people endure frustrating delays. Contrary to this prediction, however, Mischel discovered that leaving the rewards on a table in front of the children caused them to recall the experimenter much faster than when the rewards were out of sight. Mischel concluded that drawing attention to the rewards causes considerable *frustration* and leads children to ring the bell sooner to end the unbearable conflict. His view was supported by observations of how children in the rewards-present condition behaved while waiting: They covered their eyes with their hands, rested their

heads on their arms, invented distracting little games and dances, sang songs, and sometimes even fell asleep! When they stared directly at the rewards, they seemed driven to delirium.

Mischel surmised that if frustration is a critical ingredient causing children to stop delaying gratification, then introducing factors that reduce children's frustration should help them delay longer, whereas introducing factors that intensify frustration should reduce their patience still further. To test this, he instructed one group of children to think "happy thoughts" while they waited for the experimenter to come back: They had to dwell on something that made them happy, such as getting a nice present or dining on pancakes and syrup. The idea was that the happy thoughts would help counter frustration. A second group of children had to think "sad thoughts," such as falling down and skinning a knee or not getting invited to a birthday party. A final group was not given any special "think-about" assignment. In line with Mischel's predictions, the children thinking happy thoughts waited the longest, and those dwelling on sad thoughts waited the shortest time.

On the basis of these experiments, one message seems clear: One key to successful self-control in temptation situations involves distracting oneself from thinking about the desired object. However, it is necessary to distract oneself in a way that makes oneself happy rather than sad.

But does attention to a forbidden fruit always increase frustration and decrease self-control? No. In subsequent research, Mischel and his colleagues discovered that thinking about rewards interferes with self-control mainly if people think about rewards in consummatory ways, in other words, in ways that highlight their frustration at not having the rewards. When children who are left waiting for rewards are told to fantasize about how salty and crunchy pretzels are, and how sweet and chewy marshmallows are, they break down quickly and signal for the end of the delay period (Miller, Weinstein, & Karniol, 1978; Mischel & Baker, 1975; Toner, Lewis, & Gribble, 1979; Toner & Smith, 1977). On the other hand, asking children to think about rewards in ways that deemphasize their arousing qualities can facilitate delay. Showing children picture slides of the reward objects (symbolic representations) rather than the actual items, or asking children to think about rewards in nonarousing ways—to imagine marshmallows as clouds or cotton balls, and pretzels as twisted ropes—makes them wait longer than not thinking about the rewards at all (Mischel & Baker, 1975; Moore, Mischel, & Zeiss, 1976). Also, thinking about rewards may not be frustrating to children if the reward is promised to children contingent upon their completing some concrete work activity rather than for just helplessly waiting (Patterson & Carter, 1979; see also Miller & Karniol, 1976a, 1976b).

As children develop, they become increasingly knowledgeable about ways of attending to or thinking about rewards that will help them counter frustration and endure the delay interval better. In some interesting experiments in which children were given a choice as to what they wanted to look at while they waited for a delayed reward, preschool children were found to have the self-defeating habit of wanting to focus on the reward objects. This course of action heightened their frustration and reduced their chance of getting the larger reward (Yates & Mischel, 1979). By age 7, children know that it is better to look at distracting pictures devoid of any reminders. Mischel (1979) reports that third graders utilize sensible rules: They avoid looking at the real rewards, repeat the contingency ("If I wait _____, then I get _____"), and know that it is good to hide the rewards.

Self-Verbalizations and Plans   We can all remember times when we were faced with temptation and found ourselves muttering warnings like "Don't do it—you'll be sorry!" Do such self-verbalizations really assist with resistance to deviation?

Several studies suggest that they do. When children are placed in a temptation situation but are told to repeat deviation-inhibiting instructions to themselves (e.g., "I must not turn around to look at the toy"), they often resist deviating longer than they do when they are not given any self-verbalization instructions (Hartig & Kanfer, 1973; Mischel & Patterson, 1976; Patterson & Mischel, 1976; Sawin & Parke, 1979; Toner et al., 1979). The tendency to make effective self-verbalizations *spontaneously* (without being told to by adults) increases with age. In fact, preschoolers' verbalizations tend to be self-defeating because they focus on desired qualities of what is forbidden, thereby heightening their frustration ("The candy looks yummy"). By grade school, however, children apparently do talk to themselves in temptation-inhibiting ways (Miller et al., 1978; Toner & Smith, 1977).

To date, most research has focused on how children cope with temptation once it occurs. But the question of how children learn to *predict* the occurrence of tempting and frustrating situations, so that they can avoid them altogether, also needs to be studied.

Situational Influences on Resistance to Deviation

External Incentives   It hardly comes as a surprise that the more fun, valuable, or interesting a forbidden activity or object, the more children will pursue it (Winston & Redd, 1976). Anticipated social consequences for resisting or yielding to a temptation are important, too. Most children want to behave in ways that bring them respect from their parents, teachers, and peers. Sometimes, however, children are caught in conflicts between the divergent value systems of their peers and adults. Peers occasionally tempt children to go on vandalism sprees, participate in collective cheating on exams, or break some other adult-sponsored rule. How do children decide what to do?

Bronfenbrenner has studied the impact of

cultural forces on children's decisions to join their peers in misbehavior or uphold adult values. In the United States, children show an increasing preference for going along with their peers as they get older. American children seem to grow increasingly disillusioned with adult control and values as they head into adolescence. In contrast, Soviet children relatively rarely admit to wanting to join their peers in misconduct. Perhaps this is because in Russia the peer group is taught to transmit traditional adult norms by collectively sanctioning adherence to adult standards. It is interesting also that Israeli children often proudly admit (even to adults) an intention to break adult norms if their peers want them to. This may be because Israeli society generally encourages assertiveness, independence from traditional values, and initiative (Bixenstine, DeCorte, & Bixenstine, 1976; Shouval, Kav-Venaki, Bronfenbrenner, Devereux, & Kiely, 1975).

Moods   Children who are depressed, angry, or feeling the effects of some other bad mood tend to show poorer self-control in a variety of ways. Not only are they less willing to delay gratification but they are also more likely to touch prohibited toys (Fry, 1975, 1977) and are less likely to share with other children (Moore, Underwood, & Rosenhan, 1973). In contrast, positive moods promote self-control.

It is as if happiness gives children a brighter outlook that makes them more optimistic about receiving future rewards and reduces their preoccupation with their immediate needs. In contrast, sad children tend to focus on immediately available rewards to alleviate their distress. They deviate in a "self-therapeutic" attempt to improve their spirits (Moore, Clyburn, & Underwood, 1976).

An Integrated Social Learning/Causal Attribution Model of Internalization

In Chapter 3, we sketched a model of socialization that integrated principles of both social learning and causal attribution theo-

ries. Here we shall briefly indicate how the model applies to moral internalization.

In our view, moral internalization typically originates by implanting in children firm habits of desirable behavior that at first are clearly externally motivated. We base this conclusion on the research indicating that firm parental enforcement of demands for mature behavior is associated with moral and prosocial conduct in young children. In order to achieve compliance with requests for mature behavior, parents of young children must often resort to methods of power assertion— threats of mild punishment, deprivation of privileges, promises of material reward for obedience, and so on. Because young children's behavior is so often controlled by these external incentives, it seems highly likely that young children will, initially at least, correctly perceive their motivation for performing desirable behavior to be externally based. Occasionally parents may successfully reduce their children's perception of external control by accompanying their disciplinary action with inductive reasoning, but the fact remains that much of young children's initial conformity to society's rules will be externally motivated, and probably be perceived so by the children. Thus we view learning theory as more accurately accounting for the origins of desirable behavior than attribution theory. As social learning theorists suggest, external incentives help children initiate and practice the self-controlling responses that are required for mature, socialized behavior.

Attribution theorists claim that if children perceive their motivation to perform a behavior to be external, then the children will automatically discount any possible intrinsic sources of motivation for the behavior. In other words, if children can explain their performance of desirable behavior in terms of an external incentive, they will fail to perceive themselves to be "good people" who are intrinsically disposed to perform the desired behavior. Research we reviewed in the last chapter, however, suggested that children younger than 6 years do not usually take the presence of an external incentive to imply the absence of intrinsic motivation on the part of an actor. Hence the use of extrinsic incentives to motivate young children's moral conduct may not have the predicted effect of preventing young children from believing that they are good people.

Thus the research does not suggest that the use of external incentives—so long as the incentives are no more extreme than necessary to achieve compliance and are used in the ways recommended in Chapter 3—interferes with the origins of internalization. In fact, probably a great deal of what passes for internalized behavior by young children (e.g., conformity to social norms in the absence of external surveillance) is actually motivated by external concerns, such as a fear of getting caught and punished for misbehaving. Most of us can remember incidents as children when we were absolutely convinced that nobody was watching while we did something naughty, only to be quickly discovered and punished. Such experiences may make young children think that they are never truly free of external surveillance and may help motivate firm habits of internalized behavior. However, as children grow older and improve their skills at detecting the presence or absence of real surveillance, they probably begin to see themselves performing prosocial and moral acts even when no one is watching (assuming such habits have been established). Now is the time, we believe, that children can update their attributions to be more internal (e.g., "If I am doing this even though I don't have to, then I must want to do it"), and the foundation for a more mature variety of internalization is laid. Parents can encourage this transfer of perceived control from the external to the internal mode by accompanying their discipline with verbal reasoning that points out the inherently desirable or undesirable aspects of certain behaviors and by verbally attributing prosocial and moral dispositions to children.

In sum, we imagine that moral internalization typically originates by implanting habits of moral action in children by external means, but that with age internal attributions also assume importance in facilitating desirable behavior in the absence of external control.

SUMMARY

Morality should not be considered a unitary entity or a personality trait. Instead, there are three distinct aspects of morality: moral reasoning, self-evaluation, and overt resistance to deviation. Most people display considerable situational specificity in each of these aspects of morality. In other words, a child may reason about one kind of moral dilemma at a high level of sophistication, but deal with a different moral conflict at a much lower level; a child may feel guilty following one kind of misbehavior, but not after another; and so on.

We discussed factors influencing the development of each aspect of morality, beginning with moral reasoning. Cognitive-developmental theorists, such as Piaget and Kohlberg, argue that the development of moral reasoning proceeds via an invariant sequence of stages, with each stage characterized by certain underlying thought structures that permit certain kinds of reasoning. Piaget proposed two stages in moral reasoning development; Kohlberg proposed six stages. Though both theorists are correct in suggesting that children tend to give less external and more internal reasons to support their judgments of an actor's morality as they get older, it does not appear that development proceeds via a fixed sequence of well-knit stages, nor that one type of reasoning supplants another. Instead, as children mature, they consider a wider variety of factors to be relevant to decisions about moral responsibility. Under some circumstances, even mature adults use a mode of reasoning that is usually more typical of younger children. There is some evidence that more mature styles of moral reasoning are dependent on attainment of certain Piagetian mental operations, and growth in moral reasoning is aided by encountering new perspectives on morality (from parents, peers, etc.) that conflict with personal perspectives. Much less research on moral judgments has been inspired by social learning theory, but there is support for Bandura's view that moral judgments are multidimensional social decisions that depend on synthesizing several varieties of social information to arrive at conceptions of appropriate and inappropriate behavior.

Modern interest in moral self-evaluation began with Freud, who believed that children acquire a self-punishing superego through identification with the same-sex parent; but there are problems with this view. Conditioning learning theorists regard self-critical comments to be verbal operants that are influenced by appropriate reinforcement contingencies, but conditioning theorists tend to ignore the important role that cognitions play in self-evaluation. Hoffman views guilt as empathic distress coupled with the belief that the self is responsible for a distressed other's state. As Hoffman predicts, parental use of inductive reasoning helps children learn to accept responsibility for their misbehavior. Bandura's theory of self-regulation also assigns importance to cognition. In this theory, there are a number of ways in which children develop personal standards of appropriate conduct, and children learn to guide their behavior by rewarding and punishing themselves for attaining or falling short of goals they set for themselves.

The likelihood of children deviating when faced with temptations to perform immoral behavior depends on their child-rearing experiences, their cognitions when contemplating deviation, and situational factors. Children of parents who firmly and consistently insist that their children learn and practice habits of self-regulation, who justify their disciplinary action with inductive reasoning, who are warm and communicative, who avoid the use of unnecessarily harsh power assertive discipline, and who are models of self-controlled behavior have children who are most likely to display desirable conduct when free of the watchful eyes of adults. Children who think of themselves as intrinsically motivated to behave morally, who anticipate self-recrimination for deviating, who expect pride for good behavior, who know how to talk themselves out of deviating, and who know how to avoid thinking about forbidden activities in arousing and consummatory ways are better able to resist temptations than children lacking these qualities. Situational incentives and children's moods at the times they are faced with temptations also influence their likelihood of resisting temptation.

We propose that principles of both social learning theory and causal attribution theory contribute to our understanding of moral internalization. We suggest that the process of moral internalization typically originates by implanting in children firm habits of desirable behavior that are at first clearly motivated by external concerns (e.g., fears of being caught and punished for deviating). This suggestion is consistent with the social learning view that external incentives often motivate children to initiate and sustain processes of self-regulation. However, as children develop and find themselves at least occasionally performing moral conduct without an obvious immediate external incentive, they update their attributions for good behavior to become more internal. Parents can facilitate this process of internalization by using certain disciplinary techniques, such as inductive reasoning and verbal attribution of prosocial motivation to children.

7 Aggression

The staggering problem of violence among youth requires that we devote a chapter to relating what psychologists have learned about aggression and its prevention. More than a quarter of the serious crimes committed in America today—murder, rape, aggravated assault, robbery, burglary, larceny, and car theft—are committed by youths aged 10 to 17. Since 1960, the number of juvenile crimes committed has risen at twice the rate of those committed by adults. The problem of antisocial behavior is indeed pervasive, being felt in the family and neighborhood, at school, in industry, and elsewhere in society.

What are the origins of aggressive behavior? Is aggression an innate drive or is it a learned behavior? Do certain situations, emotional states, available targets, and other environmental circumstances increase the chance that aggression will be triggered? Are some children socialized by their parents, peers, and even the media to react more swiftly with an aggressive response? Does watching violence on television and in movies make one more aggressive or does it get the hostility "out of one's system"? What can socializing agents do to try to control antisocial behavior? In this chapter we seek answers to these questions.

A chapter on aggression is imperative, not just because of the grave social concerns over increasing youth violence, but because such a chapter provides an opportunity to illustrate some key issues in developmental social psychology. For example, the aggression literature illustrates why psychologists have had a falling out with drive conceptions of motivation. The research on aggression also provides the best concrete example of the role of modeling in children's social learning. Much of the early research on observational learning happened to focus on children's imitative aggression, and hence the aggression literature has furnished general principles of social learning that are relevant to understanding children's development in many domains.

We begin this chapter with a discussion of the construct of aggression: Exactly what is aggression, and why have psychologists fought over its definition? Next, we provide an overview of several theories of aggressive development, briefly outlining the perspectives of Freud, the ethologists, the learning theorists, the social-cognitive theorists, and the psychobiologists. We then go on to evaluate several of the mechanisms psychologists have proposed to account for aggressive development. The first proposition we evaluate is the original frustration-aggression hypothesis, or the view that frustration reflexively arouses an aggressive drive that provokes children to engage in injurious and destructive acts. Disenchanted with the drive theory of aggression, many psychologists turned to learning-theory accounts of aggression. Learning theorists regard aggression as behavior that is learned from the environment rather than as an inborn energy pool of hostile impulses waiting for release by frustrating stimuli. The first learning-theory account we examine is the proposition that aggressive habits can result from the child's attempts to survive in a hostile home environment—a home in which family members tease, pester, and irritate one another and where the parents tend to engage in harsh and erratic disciplinary practices. Next, the theory that aggression can be learned and maintained by positive reinforcers from the social environment (e.g., praise and respect from one's peers) is examined. We then review the voluminous research showing that exposure to violent models, especially aggressive television characters, can cause children to develop antisocial habits and attitudes. Brief sections are then devoted to discussing the victim's role in stimulating and inhibiting aggression, the relation be-

tween moral development and aggression, and sex differences in aggression. Finally, we summarize what parents and teachers can do to prevent and modify aggressive behavior.

THE CONSTRUCT OF AGGRESSION

Just how aggression should be defined is a hotly debated issue in social psychology. Reviewing the differences of opinion is instructive, for it brings to light several general problems psychologists confront when trying to define their "fuzzy" social constructs.

A classic definition of aggression was offered by Dollard, Doob, Miller, Mowrer, and Sears (1939) in their influential book, *Frustration and Aggression*. They defined *aggression* as behavior that has as its goal the injury of the person toward whom it is directed. This definition specifies that an act cannot be labeled aggressive unless the actor *intended* to do harm. Seemingly a simple definition, it has stirred much controversy. Points of debate revolve around two issues: whether it is scientifically acceptable to insist that an act be deemed intentional before it can be labeled aggressive and whether the definition is broad enough to encompass all types of aggression.

The Problem of Intent

For several reasons, the notion that an injurious act must be judged to be intentional before it can be labeled aggressive has troubled psychologists. First, intentionality is not a property of behavior but instead refers to an antecedent condition that can only be inferred from the behavior it is presumably motivating and of which it is an essential ingredient (Bandura & Walters, 1963a). If aggressive intent can only be inferred from injurious behavior, it is questionable whether it is meaningful to assign intent independent status. Second, judging whether or not someone meant to do harm is a subjective matter and is often a difficult decision to make. For example, if a girl, Susie, scratches her friend,

John, as she takes a toy from him, can we determine that she intended to hurt him, or was the scratch simply a by-product of her actions to get the toy? Such situations make it difficult for independent observers to agree on which actions are intended and which are not. The problem in determining intent is most apparent when aggression is subconsciously motivated or when an aggressor tries to disguise the motive for a specific act.

To skirt these problems, Buss (1961) suggested that aggression be defined as the delivery of a noxious stimulus in an interpersonal context. This defines aggression solely on the basis of observable behavior. However, Buss excluded from his definition of aggression injurious behavior inflicted by individuals who are acting according to clearly defined social roles, such as the dentists who drill teeth and the parents who spank their children when necessary. This definition raises problems, too. When, for example, does a parent punishing a child cross the line between being a disciplinarian and a child abuser? It would seem that making decisions about whether an individual is acting within the limits of a social role involves making subjective decisions about intentionality. Thus the first dilemma faced by aggression theorists is clear: Removing the intentionality criterion from a definition of aggression (and defining aggression solely in terms of behavioral properties) may render aggression a more scientifically acceptable construct, but whether it is possible to do this without causing the term to lose much of its customary meaning is doubtful.

It is important to realize that most of the social psychologist's constructs, such as aggression, dependency, achievement motivation, and the like, differ radically from the constructs of biologists, physicists, and chemists, in that the psychologist's constructs cannot satisfactorily be defined solely in terms of objective, observable properties. Instead, as Bandura (1973, 1979) points out, deciding whether a behavior is aggressive, dependent,

or should be categorized according to some other construct involves a *subjective social labeling* process by an observer. It is because of this, suggests Bandura, that we will not achieve an adequate understanding of what aggression is until we know the factors that lead people to attach the label of "aggressive" to some behaviors, but not to others. Research on social judgment processes reveals that whether people are likely to label an act aggressive or not depends on a great many factors, including: the perceived antecedents of the response (e.g., whether the act is judged to be intentional); the form, intensity, and consequences of the response (e.g., whether the harmful act is verbal or physical and whether it causes little or great damage); the sex, age, attractiveness, status, socioeconomic level, and ethnic background of the performer; and the values of the labeler (e.g., whether the labeler favors or disfavors the group to which the actor belongs). Because judgments of aggression depend on subjective social decisions, Bandura (1973) has suggested that aggression be defined as "injurious and destructive behavior that is socially defined as aggressive on the basis of a variety of factors, some of which reside in the evaluator rather than in the performer" (p. 8). In essence, Bandura is saying that aggression is whatever people say it is. And since most people believe a harmful act must be intended to be called aggressive, intent should probably remain a defining criterion of the construct.

The Problem of Types of Aggression

A second objection to the 1939 definition of aggression is that it describes only one variety of aggression—that which has as its goal the injury or suffering of another person. Some authors argue that it is necessary to distinguish between two types of aggression: *hostile* and *instrumental* aggression (e.g., Buss, 1961; Feshbach, 1970; Rule, 1974). To these authors, harm-inflicting behavior should be labeled as hostile aggression when the primary goal of the act is the injury itself. However, when harmful behavior results while a nonaggressive goal, such as money, status, power, or self-esteem, is being pursued, it is labeled instrumental aggression. The hostile-instrumental distinction has been criticized (Bandura, 1973; Hartup, 1974), primarily because aggression that, on the surface, seems purely hostile is often instrumental to some other end, such as the restoration of self-esteem or attainment of respect from others. Because the hostile-instrumental distinction is not always clear, Rule and Nesdale (1976) suggest a distinction between *angry* and *nonangry* aggression.

As we shall see later in this chapter, those who support the frustration-aggression hypothesis believe that all instances of aggression arise from the arousal of aggressive drives (anger). This is why their definition of aggression recognizes only hostile (or angry) aggression. But it is clear that not all aggression is motivated by anger. A child who punches a playmate to steal his toy and the cold-blooded murderer who kills for money are examples of nonangry aggression. At present, it seems sensible to conclude, along with Rule and Nesdale (1976), that some acts of aggression are motivated by anger and some are not. Furthermore, it is conceivable that different psychological mechanisms underlie the expression of angry and nonangry aggression. For example, angry aggression may tend to occur when people are subjected to aversive stimuli (e.g., frustration or insult) and label their resultant emotional state as anger ("I'm mad!"), whereas nonangry aggression may more often result from more cool-headed attempts to obtain material rewards. In this chapter, we shall see that some theories are limited to attempts to explain angry aggression (e.g., the frustration-aggression hypothesis and Berkowitz's classical conditioning model), whereas other theories try to explain occurrences of nonangry as well as angry aggression (e.g., Bandura's social learning theory).

Anger, Hostility, and Assertiveness

For clarity, we need to distinguish among several terms. Aggression is *behavior* that injures. In contrast, hostility is conceptualized as a cognitive *attitudinal* response involving thoughts of dislike and the wish to see an enemy harmed. Anger refers to the state of *emotional* arousal that sometimes accompanies hostility and aggression.

Assertiveness refers to behaviors that serve to direct or to stop another person's activity (Barrett & Yarrow, 1977). It involves attempts to exert control, but without any intent to injure or to make the other person feel bad. In this chapter, we are primarily concerned with antisocial expressions of aggression and we will rarely discuss assertiveness. Of course, teaching children assertive rather than aggressive means of obtaining their legitimate goals should be an important aspect of socialization. Unfortunately, though, little research has looked at the development of assertiveness in children.

THEORIES OF AGGRESSION

Trait Theory

According to trait theory, there exist stable individual differences among people in their dispositions to display aggression across diverse situations and over time. Let us examine this viewpoint.

Is Aggression A Unidimensional Trait?

If aggression is a unidimensional trait, then it should be possible to order children along a single continuum in terms of how much general aggressiveness they possess. Some children should behave very aggressively across diverse situations (at home with their parents, on the playground with their peers, etc.) and in a variety of ways (by being verbally insulting, physically assaultive, etc.); other children should show consistently lower levels of aggression. In one study of preschool children, there was indeed evidence for a modest degree of consistency in aggression, especially for boys (Sears, Rau, & Alpert, 1965). Evidence for a trait, however, implies nothing about the origins of the consistency. As we shall see, both biological and social learning factors probably contribute.

Furthermore, evidence for a trait does not mean that situational influences on aggression are unimportant. There are some situations that increase the chance that almost any child will react aggressively. If children are severely frustrated and see that aggression is likely to succeed in eliminating the source of their frustration, or if children have just seen a model rewarded and praised for behaving aggressively, then most children are very likely to display aggression themselves in that situation.

Of course, different children can learn to react differently to the same situation. One boy may learn to react to threats from his peers with aggression because he has found aggression in such cases to succeed, but a second boy may find that his attempts at aggressive retaliation toward his peers fail and therefore he will learn to inhibit peer-directed aggression. The relative aggressiveness of these two boys, however, may completely reverse in a different situation—home, for example. Parents of the first boy may severely punish aggression at home, while parents of the second boy may believe in permissiveness and actually permit, and even encourage, parent-directed aggression.

Thus aggression is partly a function of the child's trait level of aggression, partly a function of the situation the child faces, and partly a function of the child's unique learning history for behaving aggressively in similar situations in the past.

Is Aggression Stable Over Time? Do aggressive toddlers become aggressive school children? Do aggressive adolescents become aggressive adults? Answering these questions is difficult because children change in the way that they express aggression as they get older. For example, between the ages of 4 and 6,

outbursts of anger and the tendency simply to seize materials from another child decline, and verbal aggression, rumination, sulking, and aggression aimed to restore one's self-esteem or to hurt someone else's feelings increase (Feshbach, 1970; Goodenough, 1931; Hartup, 1974; Muste & Sharp, 1947). Nevertheless, it is still possible to assess the extent to which individuals in a group retain their relative positions on a trait of aggression over time, even though their measures of aggression change with age.

Longitudinal research does find a fair degree of stability in aggression over time, especially for boys (see Olweus, 1979, for a review of the research). The size of the correlation between children's aggression at one time and their aggression at a later time depends largely on two factors: the age of the children when the first assessment of aggression is made (the older the children, the larger the correlation) and the length of time elapsing between the two assessments (the shorter the time, the larger the correlation). Aggressive toddlers become aggressive preschoolers (Jersild & Markey, 1935). Adolescents who pick fights with other children, who are rebellious, who talk back to their teachers, and who overreact to minor frustrations tend to have the same problems a few years later (Block, 1971; Olweus, 1977). A famous project by Kagan and Moss (1962) showed how certain forms of aggression in childhood can predict different forms of aggression in adulthood. Grade-school boys who expressed their aggression by throwing temper tantrums and aggressing against their mothers tended in adulthood to be prone to outbursts and to retaliate against someone frustrating them with direct aggression, but boys who were highly aggressive toward their peers in childhood tended to grow up to be competitive rather than overtly aggressive.

What accounts for the high degree of stability in male aggression? One possibility is that highly aggressive individuals provoke certain kinds of reactions from the social environment, which help maintain their aggressiveness. Patterson and Cobb (1971), for example, suggest that one reason boys who display extreme antisocial aggression in childhood grow up to display above-average incidences of emotional disturbance, criminal arrest, and unemployment is that aggressive boys are consistently rejected by their less aggressive peers and thus are forced to turn for companionship to children who accept, and perhaps even encourage, aggressive behavior. Another possibility is that children develop fairly stable internal mediators of aggression relatively early in life. In other words, children who learn when they are young that aggression is a successful and appropriate technique for getting what one wants may very well persist in their aggressive attempts over the years. In contrast, children with initial inhibitions against aggression will refrain from the kinds of aggressive interactions that lead to the acquisition of aggressive habits. A third possibility is that children may reveal stability in aggression because of continuity in their child-rearing environments over the years. This means that aggressive children may continue to display aggression as they mature because they continue to live in a home that is conducive to aggressive behavior. Finally, we should mention that biological factors may play a role in the stability of aggression. Children born with characteristics that are conducive to aggressive interactions (e.g., high activity level, strong muscles, low tolerance for frustration) may continue to show above-average levels of aggression throughout much of their lives. All of these possibilities have merit. Not all boys, however, maintain the same level of aggression over the years: Some initially nonaggressive children can develop habits of aggression. For example, we shall see in this chapter how the peer group can teach initially nonaggressive children to become highly aggressive.

A recent study by Bullock and Merrill (1980) suggested that it may be possible to screen elementary-school children to see which ones may be predisposed to develop aggressive habits. Children were asked about the kinds of recreational activities they preferred. It was found that third-and fourth-grade boys who stated a preference for aggressive over nonaggressive activities and games (e.g., they would rather learn karate than learn to raise garden plants, or they would rather spear fish than pick berries) were often very likely to develop aggressive habits over the next year. The authors reasoned that children's preferences partly determine how children allocate their time to situations capable of making them more or less aggressive. An important goal of future research should be the discovery of ways to determine which children are "at risk" for aggressive development.

Drive Theory: Freud and the Frustration-Aggression Hypothesis

For many years, psychologists regarded aggression as a drive—an energy force that builds up within individuals and propels them toward acts of injury. This notion originated with Freud, who believed that aggression represents the human being's efforts to deflect suicidal "death wishes" outward toward other people. Freud believed that all people are born with a death wish (Thanatos) that urges the organism to cease all stimulation to the self (i.e., to die). However, Freud also believed that people are born with self-preservative instincts that compete with the death wish and cause the death wish to be deflected away from the self toward other people. *Aggressive drive*, then, may be thought of as death wishes turned outward. Although Freud believed everyone was in possession of aggressive drive, the drive only becomes activated (or seeks expression in attempts to hurt other people) when a person becomes frustrated. Frustration was defined as any event (real or imaginary) that interferes with a person's seeking of pleasure or avoidance of pain.

Freud's drive formulation of aggression involves two other assumptions. First is the idea that when the individual is frustrated and aggressive drive is aroused, a quantity of energy is generated within, causing the person to seek an outlet for the aggression in one way or another. The thwarted person must either retaliate against his or her tormentor, displace the feelings of aggression toward a substitute target, turn the aggression inward self-destructively, or simply explode impulsively with rage. It is as if the aggressive energy were operating within a closed hydraulic system: When energy is produced, it must be expressed. Second is the idea that all acts of aggression drain the individual of aggressive energy and reduce the future likelihood of aggression. This is known as the *catharsis hypothesis.* Direct aggression against the person who has caused frustration should be most successful in reducing aggressive drive, but participating vicariously in aggressive episodes that are completely irrelevant to the immediate situation—as by watching an aggressive television show or movie—is also believed to reduce a person's inclination to act aggressively. Some drive theorists (e.g., Lorenz, 1966) have suggested that aggressive energy can also be cathartically released by participating in, or even just observing, competitive sports.

Dollard and his associates (1939) put forward a modified version of Freud's theory. They, too, conceived of aggression as a drive naturally aroused by frustration and reduced cathartically by direct, vicarious, or displaced aggression. We shall evaluate their theory later in this chapter.

The notion of aggression as a drive is unappealing to many modern psychologists, especially the learning theorists (e.g., Bandura, 1973; Berkowitz, 1973). Learning theorists note that there is no way to measure the strength of aggressive drive independent of aggressive behavior. They are also skeptical of the two main implications of the hydraulic model—that frustration-aroused aggressive drive always seeks direct or displaced expression and that direct and vicarious aggression cathartically reduces aggression. Learning theorists confine their conceptualization of

aggression to observable behavior. They agree that aggression is often a response children make when frustrated, especially if the children have found aggression to be successful at eliminating frustrations, but they do not believe that frustration automatically releases instinctive aggressive drives from an inborn energy reservoir. When we evaluate frustration-aggression theory, we shall see that the learning theorists' criticisms of drive theory are well founded.

The theory that aggression is produced by frustration really is not much of a developmental theory. It does follow from the theory that children who are subjected to numerous and severe frustrations should develop the strongest aggressive urges. However, the frustration-aggression hypothesis is primarily a theory concerned with situational determinants of aggression, not with the development of individual differences in aggressive habits.

Ethological Theory

Ethologists conceive of aggression as an instinct that has evolved because it has survival value for the species (Darwin, 1872; Lorenz, 1966; Tinbergen, 1951). They point out that many of the activities necessary for a species to survive, including hunting food, defending one's territory, selecting a mate, and protecting the young, often require aggressive interactions. Hence it makes sense to expect that forms of aggression serving these functions would have evolved, with the result that individual members of certain species are instinctively "wired" to react to certain stimuli with aggression.

The ethologists have observed aggressive exchanges in many species. Their major goal has been the discovery of specific environmental stimuli that reflexively elicit and terminate aggressive attacks among members of a species. For example, in stickle-back fish, color cues seem to control aggression; in many lower primates, infringement of territorial rights is often important. The ethologists tend to agree with Freud that among human beings, frustrations, insults, and threats are critical elicitors of aggression. However, although aggression in many lower species may be quite rigidly under the control of specific environmental releasing stimuli, it is dangerous to generalize this principle to human beings (Bandura, 1973). Human beings can think, anticipate, evaluate, distort, deny, communicate through language, and engage in other cognitive processes. Thus it is hazardous to assume that aggression at the human level can also be reduced to reflexive reactions to external eliciting stimuli. In fact, in this chapter we shall see very little support for the idea that it is possible to identify stimuli that automatically and reflexively release aggressive behavior in all members of the human species.

Nonetheless, the ethological approach is gaining popularity as a means of studying children's aggression (e.g., Ginsburg, Pollman, & Wauson, 1977). Researchers working in this tradition, for example, have observed that when interacting with their peers in naturalistic settings, children send nonverbal messages to each other that help regulate aggression. The sorts of signals children who enter into a conflict send to each other depend on the children's relative positions in the peer group dominance hierarchy. For instance, when a dispute breaks out between two children, the more dominant child may threateningly jut her chin out in a way that implies "We both know I'm the stronger, so you'd better give me what I want or I'll clobber you." The less dominant child may acquiesce with a submissive gesture, perhaps lowering her head, thereby ending the exchange before it develops into a physical battle. Ethologists refer to these dominant-submissive communications as *agonistic interactions*. Systems of agonistic communication have evolved, the ethologists contend, because they help reduce intraspecies aggression, thereby contributing to survival. How children form dominance hierarchies, how

they come to emit and to read agonistic signals, and how agonistic interactions contribute to group stability are important and intriguing issues uncovered by the ethologists.

Learning Theories

All learning theorists shun drive and instinct notions of aggression, opting instead for a view of aggression as learned behavior. However, the learning theorists are not in total agreement about the critical factors in the learning of aggression, and thus several distinct "mini-theories" of aggressive development have been proposed. In the following sections we shall distinguish conditioning theory from social learning theory.

Conditioning Views Conditioning theorists can be divided into two camps: those stressing *operant conditioning* of aggressive responses and those emphasizing *classical conditioning* of aggressive reactions.

According to operant theory, external reinforcing events strengthen associations between a response and the stimulus preceding it, making the same response more probable in the presence of the same stimulus on future occasions. Punishment weakens such associations. The application to aggression is straightforward: If hitting, punching, kicking, shouting, or other aggressive responses are successful in gaining children what they want, then these responses should become more likely when the children encounter the same circumstances again.

Initially, aggressive responses may occur by chance or may be elicited by aversive events. For example, a child who wants his diaper changed, who wants his departing mother to stay home, or who has just had a favorite toy swiped by another child may try whining, grabbing, or hitting in an attempt to end the unpleasant state. If the child's response succeeds in eliminating the aversive state, the response is reinforced and is likely to occur again. This simple principle forms the cornerstone of one leading operant theorist's view of aggression (Patterson, 1976), and we shall find substantial evidence to support it.

Conditioning theorists point out that aggressive behavior is subject to the laws of discrimination and generalization. For example, children are believed to discriminate situations in which aggression is likely to be rewarded or punished and to limit their performance of aggression to situations resembling those in which they have benefited from aggression. Most children eventually learn that kicking and shouting are expected and rewarded on the soccer field and in other field sports, but not in Sunday school or other classroom situations. However, conditioning theorists point out that aggression can generalize from one response mode to another. For example, they suggest that children who are rewarded for aggressing verbally against a target person should also become more likely to assault the person physically. We shall see support for the application of some of these "laws of learning" to aggression. However, conditioning theorists tend to ignore one important factor that influences aggression: the child's cognitions. We shall see that social learning theorists consider this.

Berkowitz (1974) takes a classical conditioning approach to understanding aggression. He argues that stimuli that have been associated with successful aggression acquire the potential to provoke impulsive, almost reflexive, aggressive outbursts. If people have seen guns successfully used for aggressive purposes, then the sheer sight of a gun in the future may help provoke a violent attack; if people have seen others successfully humiliate and aggress against certain classes of victims (e.g., minority group members), then encountering a member of such a target group may help fuel an aggressive reaction. Of course, people do not automatically react aggressively every time they encounter a stimulus they have seen associated with aggression reinforcement (a gun, a common scapegoat, etc.). Berkowitz believes that aggression-associated stimuli will trigger aggression only if the individual is angry. Thus Berkowitz is unique among the learning theorists in assigning anger an essential role in aggression.

We shall see support for Berkowitz's hypothesis that stimuli associated with reinforcement of aggression often do heighten aggressive responding. It is important to bear in mind, though, that Berkowitz's theory is really intended only to help explain acts of *impulsive aggression,* as when a person becomes so enraged that he or she acts without thinking. Like most conditioners, Berkowitz deals very little with cognitive factors.

Social Learning Theory Bandura's (1973) social learning theory of aggression assigns major importance to cognitive influences on behavior. Although Bandura concedes that aggression is sometimes directly learned by successive shaping through positive and negative outcomes, he argues that most aggression is acquired through observation. By watching the behavior of playground bullies, television cowboys and gangsters, and even their own parents acting as disciplinarians, children learn how to engage in a wide variety of destructive and harmful acts. Aggressive models not only teach children new possibilities, but can disinhibit or elicit previously learned aggressive habits, especially if the children observe that the models are enjoying their aggression, are escaping punishment for it, are gaining new privileges or status from their actions, and so on.

Although most children know how to perform a large variety of aggressive acts, they are likely to perform aggressively only when they expect a positive reward for it. Children learn the typical consequences for aggressive acts partly through observation and partly through personal experience. For example, if children see others rewarded for aggression, they may infer that they too would be rewarded for behaving similarly. Direct personal experience contributes also. For instance, children who have had repeated successes in eliminating frustration with aggression should develop more confident beliefs that aggression will be worthwhile.

A major feature of social learning theory is that aggression also comes under the control of internal self-evaluative processes. In the preceding chapter on moral development, we learned that children generate personal standards of conduct, or conceptions of appropriate and inappropriate behavior. They feel good about themselves and reward themselves when their behavior matches these standards, but they feel guilty and dissatisfied when they perform behaviors that they know are wrong. Children base their conceptions of what is praiseworthy and blameworthy partly on the basis of the direct instruction and discipline they have received from their parents, teachers, and peers (they learn, for example, that behavior producing punishment is undesirable), but vicarious experiences also influence their standards. If children see others frequently engage in a behavior, they are more likely to come to think of the behavior as appropriate, especially if they see the actions lead to praise or success, than if they see models avoid a behavior or are criticized for it. If children see that certain forms of aggression in certain situations and toward certain targets are inappropriate, they may avoid acting aggressively under those circumstances for fear of self-censure. It is important to note that not all children learn the same rules. For example, members of delinquent gangs may internalize the norm that violence and destruction are worthy of self-praise rather than self-blame. The kinds of models and social support systems that surround children influence the shape their rules for self-regulation take.

We shall see considerable support for many of the social learning theory hypotheses. Bandura's work revealing that aggressive models teach, disinhibit, and provoke violent behavior in the viewer rather than drain the viewer cathartically of aggressive energy poses one of the strongest threats to drive theory. Hypotheses that relate children's aggression to their expectations for positive payoffs and to their standards for self-evaluation are also supported.

The Social-Cognitive Perspective

Dodge (1982) has proposed a *social information processing model* of aggression that appears to hold much promise. In this view, aggression results from breakdowns or deficits in the way children process social information. Suppose a boy is jostled or is hit in the back by a ball thrown by a playmate. Even if the event is purely accidental, the boy may react aggressively if he impulsively assumes the jostler or ball-thrower was deliberately trying to hurt him, if hitting back is the only response that comes to the boy's mind, or if the boy fails to consider the negative consequences (e.g., pain to the playmate, punishment from a teacher) that might result from reacting aggressively. Dodge's model is concerned with how internal cognitive mediational processes (social judgments, attributions, consideration of response options, evaluation of response consequences, etc.) serve to regulate aggressive behavior.

Figure 7–1 depicts a hypothetical sequence of cognitive events that Dodge considers necessary for competent social responding. Aggressive boys are considered to possess deficits and biases at one or more points in the sequence that lead them to respond aggressively rather than constructively to certain social stimuli.

Dodge's model assumes that children come to a social situation with a memory store of past stimuli, events, and outcomes as well as with goals specific to the situation on hand (e.g., the desire to obtain a toy from a child or the desire to make a friend). A child's reactions to social cues arising in the situation are considered a function of the child's progression through five cognitive steps. Each step is a necessary, but insufficient part of appropriate responding.

The first step in responding competently

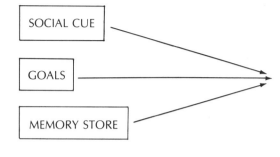

1. Decoding Process
   A. Perception of social cues
   B. Search for cues
   C. Focus (attention to cues)
2. Interpretation Process
   A. Integration of memory store, goals, and new data
   B. Search for interpretations
   C. Match of data to programmed rule structure
3. Response Search Process
   A. Search for responses
   B. Generation of potential responses
4. Response Decision Process
   A. Assessment of consequences of potential responses
   B. Evaluation of adequacy of potential responses
   C. Decision of optimal response
5. Encoding Process
   A. Behavioral repertoire search
   B. Emission of response

Figure 7-1   A Social Information Processing Model of Competence. (Dodge, 1982)

to a social cue is decoding, which involves searching for and focusing attention on relevant social information. If a child experiences pain, it makes sense for her to search for causes of the pain. Accuracy in finding relevant cues is important in this step.

After focusing on cues in the situation, children must interpret them. For example, after experiencing pain, a child must decide whether the person who caused the pain was acting deliberately or accidentally. As we discussed in Chapter 5, most children develop sensible rules for helping them decide whether someone has acted deliberately or not and for grasping what a person's motives are, but some children develop biased or inaccurate ways of interpreting experiences. For example, they may be used to aversive treatment at the hands of others and thus be biased toward interpreting pain as due to the hostility of others.

When the interpretation of a situation is complete, children must search for possible behavioral responses. This is the third step. Some children presumably search no farther than an aggressive option. When they have generated possible responses, children must weigh the likely consequences of each alternative and decide on the optimal response. Competent children think not only of the possible consequences they themselves might have to face but also of the consequences for others.

Finally, children must enact their chosen response. This is called the encoding process. Children differ in the ability to encode various behaviors. Even if a child has decided that verbal discussion is a better response to conflict than physical fighting, the child may not be able to inhibit the physical response or may lack the verbal skills necessary for discussion.

Recent studies reveal that highly aggressive children are indeed deficient in several of the skills the model depicts as necessary for peaceful, appropriate responding. For example, many highly aggressive boys do appear to have acquired a cognitive expectancy that others will behave toward them in hostile ways, and this expectancy leads them to attribute hostile intent to others when they experience aversive events that may not be hostilely motivated at all (Dodge, 1980; Dodge & Frame, 1982). Highly aggressive boys also are deficient at generating alternative solutions to interpersonal problems (Richard & Dodge, 1982; Spivack & Shure, 1974). We suspect a considerable amount of future research will be directed toward testing hypotheses that derive from Dodge's model.

We should note that this social-cognitive perspective on aggression should not be confused with cognitive-developmental theory. Dodge's five steps are not stages of development but are five steps in how a child processes a social cue. Cognitive-developmental theorists have tended not to speculate about the causes of aggression.

Biological Bases of Aggression

Enough evidence has now accumulated to conclude that biological factors play a role in aggressive development. We shall briefly review four kinds of evidence leading to this conclusion. However, it is a good idea to bear in mind from the start two important points about biology and aggression. First, it seems highly unlikely that biological factors (e.g., hormones, neurological structures, or genes) directly influence the developing child's *intent to injure*. Instead, biological factors most likely influence other aspects of the child's development and physical make-up (e.g., size, strength, activity level, and reactivity to stimulation), which affect the ease with which children will acquire aggressive habits. The second point is a corollary of the first: Even in children endowed with all the biological factors that predispose toward aggression, ag-

gressive behavior is not inevitable. Characteristics of the developing child's social setting and opportunities for learning aggression are important. Relationships between biology and aggression are not fixed or inflexible.

A first type of evidence linking biology and aggression is the relationship between *morphology*, or physical structure, and aggression. Body size and musculature are in part biologically based and these factors are associated with aggressive development (Feshbach, 1970). Boys who mature relatively early in adolescence also tend to be the more dominant and assertive in their group (Mussen & Jones, 1957). It may be that large, strong children are more often successful (i.e., are reinforced) in their forceful attempts to control other people, and this may play a role in the morphology-aggression link. Of course, superior size and strength are not necessary components for aggression: A slightly built person with a gun can do considerable damage.

Second, there is evidence that *hormones* influence aggressive development. Injecting the male hormone testosterone into pregnant rodents, dogs, and monkeys, for example, increases the probability that their offspring will display aggression. Injecting young animals with male hormones also tends to increase their aggressiveness, and castrating mature male animals sometimes renders them less aggressive (see Cairns, 1979b, for a review). However, the effects of manipulating an animal's hormones depend on several factors, including the stage of the organism's development (the aggression-enhancing effects of testosterone are usually strongest if the hormones are given when the major organ systems are developing in the fetus), the social experience and habits of the animal, and the state of the animal when injected. For example, castrating mice who have not had fighting experience reduces their inclination to attack cagemates, but castrating mice *after* they have learned to fight does not have a significant effect (Bevan, Daves, & Levy, 1960).

Third, aggression is influenced by *neurological* factors. For example, destruction or electrical stimulation of particular areas of the brain can elicit heightened aggression or docility. In an experiment with cats, Kaada (1967) found that electrical stimulation of certain loci in the hypothalamus by implanted electrodes produces patterns of attack, defense, or flight. However, the effects of brain stimulation or surgical removal are not automatic; they depend on such factors as the place of the animal in its dominance hierarchy and the nature of the potential targets (victims) that are available (Cairns, 1979b). There is evidence that children who have suffered minimal brain damage and therefore produce abnormal EEG patterns sometimes show a loss of impulse control and heightened aggressiveness (Gross, 1972). However, the relationship is not inevitable; many children who have suffered neurological damage are not aggressive.

Fourth, there is evidence that *genetic variations in temperament* play a role in aggressive development. To determine whether it is possible to inherit aggressive tendencies, Cairns (1976) performed a selective breeding experiment with mice: He bred aggressive males to aggressive females and nonaggressive males to nonaggressive females. Offspring of the former couples were more aggressive. However, Cairns (1979b) suggests that the critical factor being inherited may not be aggression per se, but rather a more mobile style of reacting to stimulation. Nonaggressive mice tend to freeze when stimulated. Obviously, it is difficult to aggress when immobile. There is also evidence at the human level that individual differences in activity level are inherited and that such differences play a role in children's aggression. Identical twins are more similar to each other in terms of activity level, for example, than are fraternal twins (Bell, 1968; Freedman & Keller, 1963), and activity level has been implicated in aggressive development (Billman & McDevitt, 1980; Buss, Block, & Block, 1980; Feshbach, 1970). However, there is not a perfect correspondence between temperamental characteristics and aggression. A lon-

gitudinal study by Thomas, Chess, and Birch (1968), for example, showed that whether children who are temperamentally disposed toward aggression go on to develop behavior problems depends on how the parents react to the children's difficulties. Children whose parents react impatiently, punitively, and are accusatory or rejecting are more likely to realize their aggressive potential.

One main point being made here is that it is practically impossible to talk of biological influences on aggression without also discussing how the biological factors *interact* with social learning experiences and other environmental variables. In fact, both learning theorists and biologists agree that aggressive development is influenced by interplays between nature and nurture issues. There are no formal theories of how biology and learning combine to affect aggressive development, but it may be useful to present some hypothetical possibilities.

Because they are biologically endowed with certain temperamental or physical characteristics, some children may elicit reactions and results from their social environment that then feed back upon the children to help them acquire aggressive habits. Children who are born with high activity levels and high thresholds for pain, for instance, may provoke from their parents the kinds of discipline (e.g., physical punishment) that help the children learn aggression. Children who are born with a low tolerance for frustration may be motivated to try to eliminate frustration, threats to their self-esteem, and other noxious states with aggressive shouting, kicking, hitting, grabbing, and so on. If these children are also endowed with physical strength, a high percentage of their forceful attempts will meet with success, and their aggressive efforts will be reinforced. Once aggressive styles are established, children may actually seek out situations and experiences that further strengthen their aggression. They may begin to instigate more fights, knowing that they are likely to win. Having associated aggression with pleasure, they may seek out the excitement of aggressive television shows and movies, thereby learning still more forms of aggression that they can try out on their next victims.

Clearly, then, aggressive development is the product of a complex interplay between the child's biological endowment, reactions and pressures from the social environment, and resulting changes in the child's behaviors and preferences for certain kinds of situations and stimulation. Pinpointing the primary cause of a child's aggressive tendencies may be an impossible task.

FRUSTRATION AND AGGRESSION

In this section, we critically examine the most influential of all drive formulations of aggression: the frustration-aggression hypothesis. As we noted, the frustration-aggression hypothesis (Dollard et al., 1939) was a reformulation of Freud's theory: Frustration automatically arouses an aggressive drive that compels the individual to perform injurious and destructive behavior. According to the frustration-aggression hypothesis, frustration always leads to aggression in some form and against some target. Furthermore, the authors of the hypothesis maintained that all instances of aggression are preceded and caused by frustration. Thus, there were two parts to the theory: Aggression is the inevitable outcome of frustration, and frustration is the inevitable antecedent to aggression.

To evaluate the theory, we shall first review research on the question of whether frustration inevitably leads to aggression. Then we shall look at the issue of whether frustration is an inevitable antecedent to aggression. Finally we shall discuss whether the catharsis hypothesis is supported.

Does Frustration Inevitably Cause Aggression?

A great many studies have demonstrated that frustration and other noxious states (e.g., being insulted, or deprived of a promised reward, or suffering physical attack) do increase the probability of aggression in both children and adults. In one study, fifth graders were promised a prize for completing a puzzle (Mallick & McCandless, 1966). Some of the children were then frustrated (by a peer who physically thwarted their efforts at solving the task while taunting them with sarcasm), but a second group was not. When the children later had an opportunity to punish the peer with electric shock, the former children elected to give more shocks than the latter.

Children aggress to prevent being frustrated, too. In one study, the degree of shoving and kicking between pairs of children who were competing for a prize increased as the size of the promised prize for the winner increased and as the resources with which to compete diminished (Rocha & Rogers, 1976).

The frustration-aggression hypothesis, however, was bolder than the simple statement that frustration increases the likelihood of aggressive reactions. It stated that frustration *always* produces aggression. Several studies have shown that aggression is not an inevitable outcome of frustration. In a classic study, Barker, Dembo, and Lewin (1941) introduced a group of nursery-school children to a handsome collection of toys. As soon as a child expressed an interest in the toys, the experimenter lowered a wire mesh screen between the child and the toys, frustrating the child's attempts to play. Although many of the children reacted aggressively by pushing, hitting, and kicking the screen (and even the experimenter), not all of the children displayed an aggressive reaction. Some of the children reacted by regressing—crying, whimpering, giving up, and withdrawing. Clearly, there are individual differences in children's reactions to frustration, and aggression is by no means an inevitable response to frustration. The first half of the frustration-aggression hypothesis then is disconfirmed.

Still, frustration frequently does produce aggression. Why? Several explanations suggest themselves. First is the Freudian hypothesis, which suggests that frustration instinctively and reflexively leads to the desire to inflict pain. This hypothesis, however, is suspect because nonaggressive reactions to frustration are common and because, as we shall see, reactions to frustration are easily modifiable by learning experiences.

A stronger possibility is that children learn aggressive responses to frustration because aggression often proves successful in eliminating frustrating conditions (Mischel, 1971). Remember that frustration is aversive and hence children are motivated to try to eliminate it. Through trial-and-error and by observing the actions of others, children may learn that forceful, aggressive responses to frustration are often very successful in alleviating unpleasant states—for instance, they may learn to attack someone who has just taken a toy from them in order to get it back. Furthermore, aggressive retaliation against frustrators may prevent future attacks from these individuals.

If this reasoning is correct, then the more successful people are in controlling unpleasant events with aggression, the more faith they should develop in their ability to counterattack successfully, and the more aggression they should display in response to frustration. It is interesting that when adults and even animals are subjected to aversive experiences that they cannot control (e.g., uncontrollable electric shock or loud noises), they subsequently display marked reductions in their aggressiveness (Dengerink & Myers, 1977; Donnerstein & Wilson, 1976; Seligman, 1975). Presumably, experience with uncontrollable noxious events makes people feel that aggression will not be beneficial in dealing with insults, threats, frustrations, and other aversive events. Thus even people subjected to intense and prolonged frustrations (e.g., ghetto dwellers) may fail to show an aggressive reaction if they have no reason to suspect their aggression will be successful.

A third explanation for the link between frustration and aggression is that children may learn a norm specifying that one is sup-

posed to aggress when insulted or frustrated, because counterattack is the culturally prescribed way to deal with such offenses (Feshbach, 1970). Individuals may retaliate to comply with this norm, fearing a loss of self-esteem or loss of respect from other people.

A fourth reason for aggressive reactions to frustrations may lie in deficient or biased social-cognitive processing on the part of the individual experiencing the frustration. Dodge (1980, 1982) has found that one characteristic of boys with reputations among their peers for being extremely aggressive is that when they are frustrated or in pain they tend to jump to the conclusion that their unpleasant state is the result of somebody else's deliberate attempt to hurt them. When they lose something, fail to achieve something they desire, or just stub a toe, they may look around for someone to blame and go after that person.

In one study, Dodge (1980) arranged for boys who had been rated by their peers as being either high- or low-aggressive to be prevented from earning a prize. Another child, acting as the researcher's accomplice, knocked over a puzzle the boys had been working on. For one-third of the boys, this was clearly made to appear accidental; for the second group, the destruction of the puzzle was made to look deliberate; and for the final third, the act appeared to be ambiguously motivated, that is, it was depicted in a way that made it unclear whether the child had knocked the puzzle over on purpose or by accident. Both high- and low-aggressive boys responded nonaggressively when the puzzle destruction was clearly accidental, and both types of boys responded aggressively when the puzzle destruction was clearly intentional. The interesting finding came when the act seemed to be ambiguously motivated. Here, low-aggressive boys reacted nonaggressively (giving the other child the benefit of the doubt), whereas high-aggressive boys reacted aggressively. It was clear that the high-aggressive children interpreted the ambiguously motivated frustration as if it had been hostilely intended. The attribution of hostile intent can clearly be a factor increasing the likelihood of aggressive reactions to frustrating events.

Aggressive reactions to frustration are also more common if people label their arousal as "anger." When depressed, disgusted, or deprived, some people are more likely than others to conclude, "Boy, am I mad!" Research confirms that when people conclude that they are upset because they are angry, the likelihood of responding aggressively increases (Dyck & Rule, 1978; Rule, Ferguson, & Nesdale, 1978). Thus highly aggressive boys may suffer deficiencies in processing information about the source of their frustration, in drawing inferences about the motives of others, and in labeling their own arousal states. These problems may cause them to react to frustration impulsively with aggression without first considering alternative courses of action (Camp, 1977).

To help children control their reactions to frustration, parents and teachers can try to teach children to be more reflective and accurate in their assessment of the causes of aversive events. But children also need to be taught more mature, prosocial, and cooperative modes of resolving conflicts and reacting to frustration. Research shows that when children have been taught to interact pleasantly with their peers, they are less likely to react to frustration with aggression. In one study, children who had been taught to cooperate with one another (by solving puzzles and assembling mosaics together) were far less likely to respond aggressively toward one another when they were subjected to a frustrating event (being deprived of watching the conclusion of an exciting movie) than were children who had not been taught prosocial ways of interacting with each other (Davitz, 1952).

In sum, frustration does not inevitably lead to aggression. And when it does produce aggression, it is unlikely that it is due to reflexive activation of an instinctive drive. In fact, most of the explanations presented for the link between frustration and aggression focused on the child's social learning experiences and cognitive reactions that come into play when frustration arises.

Is Frustration an Inevitable Antecedent to Aggression?

Studies indicate that aggression does not always have to be preceded by frustration: A number of investigators have elicited aggression without first inducing frustration in their subjects (Bandura, 1965; Mussen & Rutherford, 1961; Walters & Brown, 1963). For example, exposing children to a highly aggressive film model or rewarding children directly with marbles or chips for punching an inflated doll can cause the children to behave aggressively toward their peers in subsequent play sessions, even when the children have not first been frustrated by someone.

It is clear, then, that at least in the strict form in which it was originally stated, the frustration-aggression hypothesis is not valid. The most we can say is that sometimes frustration causes aggression, and sometimes aggression is caused by frustration.

Is the Catharsis Hypothesis Supported?

In its broadest sense, the catharsis hypothesis focuses on the idea that each time an individual either witnesses aggression (vicarious aggression) or performs an aggressive response (direct aggression), the individual's inclination to behave aggressively in the future is reduced. A revised catharsis hypothesis was offered by Feshbach (1964), who proposed that vicarious and direct aggression reduce subsequent aggression primarily in angry or frustrated people. We shall examine the relevant literature, first, with respect to vicarious aggression and, second, with respect to direct aggression.

Vicarious Aggression and the Catharsis Hypothesis   The hypothesis that viewing real-life, filmed, or televised aggression reduces the inclination to aggress is disproven. In fact, exposing either children or adults to displays of aggression increases the possibility of future aggression, whether the subjects are angry or not. In an illustrative study, Hartmann (1969) first had half of his male juvenile delinquent subjects insulted by a peer. (The boys heard a tape-recording in which the peer derisively criticized the boys' responses to a questionnaire.) The others were not angered. Subsequently, the boys saw one of three films. A third of the boys saw an aggressive film that focused on the vicious attacks that one boy directed against another. A second group also saw an aggressive film, but this version focused on the pain cues of the victim—his gestural and verbal expressions of agony. The remaining boys saw a nonaggressive control film in which two boys played basketball. Subsequently, all subjects were required to punish the peer for errors he had made on a learning task by delivering an electric shock for each error. The subjects were free to select the intensity and duration of each shock. Results showed that boys who saw either of the two aggressive films were more aggressive than boys who saw the nonaggressive film. This was true for both angry and nonangry boys. For angry delinquents, the film that drew attention to pain cues produced an especially high level of aggression; for nonangry delinquents, the film highlighting aggressive attacks produced the greatest levels of electrical punishment. Clearly, the results refute the catharsis hypothesis.

It might be argued that if angry individuals were to view someone aggressing against the specific person responsible for their misery, then their own aggression toward this person would be diminished. This possibility has not been tested with children. With adults, the evidence is equivocal (Doob & Wood, 1972; Geen & Quanty, 1977). Sometimes seeing one's tormentor get hurt reduces aggression, but at other times, it does not. Researchers have yet to discover the exact conditions that lead to increases and decreases in aggression after witnessing one's frustrator being hurt.

Direct Aggression and the Catharsis Hypothesis   There is no evidence that aggressive play produces a cathartic reduction of aggression in children. Playing with aggressive materials such as guns, listening to stories with aggressive themes, throwing darts, and other aggression-related play activities usually invite rather than decrease aggression. Again this result holds regardless of the arousal level of the subject (Feshbach, 1956; Kenny, 1952; Mallick & McCandless, 1966; Turner & Goldsmith, 1976).

There is also no support for the hypothesis that engaging in competitive activities helps drain off aggressive energy (Lorenz, 1966). A. H. Patterson (1974) found that high-school football players expressed more hostility 1 week after the football season than 1 week before it began. Furthermore, Perry and Perry (1976) found that either losing or winning in a competition against a peer who had frustrated them caused boys to increase rather than decrease the severity of punishment they later administered to the peer for making errors on a learning task. Aggressive play and competition, then, do not reduce children's aggressive inclinations.

Nevertheless, there is some evidence that when adults are angered or frustrated by someone and then aggressively retaliate against this person, their inclination to hurt the person further is reduced. For example, when adults who have been insulted are given an opportunity to punish their tormentor, they decrease the aggression they direct toward this person during a subsequent opportunity for aggression (perhaps when they are later asked to give electric shocks to their insulter for mistakes on a learning task); in contrast, the aggressive inclinations of insulted adults who are not given an opportunity to retaliate remain high (Doob & Wood, 1972; Konecni, 1975; Konecni & Ebbesen, 1976). Furthermore, aggressing against one's frustrator sometimes eases physiological tension aroused by the insulting treatment. Men who are given the opportunity to harm their adversary often show a return to base-rate blood pressure and heart rate shortly after their aggression; in contrast, cardiovascular activity takes longer to return to base rate when men are angered, but are not given an opportunity to retaliate (Geen & Quanty, 1977; Hokanson & Edelman, 1966).

Such experimental results are often taken as evidence for cathartic reduction of aggressive drive, but it is possible to explain the findings without using the drive concept. Retaliating against a frustrator may reduce a person's subsequent attacks on an adversary because retaliating has made the aggressor feel guilty (Berkowitz, 1973), because the aggressor believes in the norm that further aggression is inappropriate after the score has been evened, or possibly even because the act of retaliating has distracted the aggressor from ruminating and sulking about the original frustration (Bandura, 1973). The notion of drive reduction seems unnecessary.

Even though direct retaliation may reduce a person's inclination to hurt another further, the evidence we have reviewed advises against using cathartic techniques as a means of reducing aggression in children. Parents, teachers, and child therapists are advised not to encourage children to vent their aggressive energies in fantasy aggression, onto inanimate objects, or in competitive play. These activities invite rather than decrease aggression. Even the studies on the effects of retaliation against an agent of frustration should not be taken to mean that direct aggressive retaliation is a good way of reducing a person's long-term inclination to aggress. Even though retaliating against a frustrator may be momentarily satisfying and tension-relieving, and may alleviate the immediate need for further aggression, it may teach the lesson that aggressive retaliation is pleasurable and rewarding. This may increase the chances that a person will seek revenge in the future.

What Causes Displaced Aggression?

Irritated and frustrated individuals sometimes ventilate their hostility onto people who are not responsible for their misfortunes. Freud and other drive theorists contend that displaced aggression occurs when aggressive drive is aroused, but the frustrating person is not available as a target or that individual is too threatening to retaliate against (e.g., few people can afford to aggress against their boss). Some early learning theorists (Miller, 1948; Dollard & Miller, 1950), who were attempting to incorporate some of Freud's ideas into the concepts of learning theory, suggested that when a frustrating or tormenting person is feared, aggression is displaced to a less-feared scapegoat along a stimulus-similarity dimension. That is, the irate person chooses a victim similar to, but less threatening than, the actual frustrator.

There is some evidence that displaced aggression occasionally does occur and that it sometimes is directed, as Miller suggested, toward stimuli that are similar to, but less threatening than, the frustrating agent (e.g., Fitz, 1976). However, one limitation to Miller's model is that it is difficult to know in advance along what dimension(s) stimulus generalization will occur. Will aggression be displaced to a target of similar age? Similar race? The same sex? With the same color hair? It is hard, if not impossible, to predict the target of displaced aggression on the basis of how similar it is to the frustrator. Another deficiency in the similarity model of displacement is that similarity to a frustrator may be less influential in determining the target of displaced aggression than the angry person's history of reward and punishment for aggressing against the various alternative targets that are available (Bandura & Walters, 1963a). An angry person who fears his tormentor, for example, is likely to attack a victim who will reinforce his aggression, such as a "safe" victim, or one who is unlikely to fight back. In sum, angry people sometimes do aggress against someone other than their frustrator, although there is some question about how best to predict the exact target of a person's displaced aggression.

However, the fact that displaced aggression sometimes occurs does not necessarily support the notion of an aggressive drive that must be released in one way or another. There is no evidence that angered people who cannot retaliate against their tormentor must always take their frustration out on a substitute target or else "turn the anger inward" to become depressed, anxious, suicidal, or distressed in some other way.

Summary Evaluation
of the Drive Concept

To invoke the concept of aggressive drive to explain aggressive behavior seems both misleading and unnecessary. It is misleading because it leads to certain predictions that have not been confirmed. First, it suggests a relatively rigid relationship between frustration and aggression. The research indicates that the relationship is not fixed but rather is widely influenced by social learning and cognitive factors. Second, there is no direct evidence that thwarting events arouse a drive that always seeks expression against some target. Third, there is no evidence that vicarious aggression cathartically reduces the expression of aggression. Although there is some evidence that direct retaliation against a frustrator occasionally reduces subsequent acts of aggression and eases physiological tension, there is no convincing evidence that these effects are due to reductions in aggressive drive rather than to some alternative factor.

ACQUISITION OF AGGRESSION THROUGH AVERSIVE INTERPERSONAL CONTROL

We have seen that aggression can develop out of the child's attempts to deal with frustration and other aversive states. Here we elaborate on this theme, but the perspective will be that of learning theory rather than drive theory. We shall focus on the family situation and how children who are constantly subjected to irritating, humiliating, physically painful, and other noxious stimuli can be-

come exasperated and eventually strike back with their own brand of obnoxious, demanding, destructive, and assaultive behavior. First, we summarize the theory of G. R. Patterson (1976), who suggests that aggression in the home often represents high-powered attempts by children to "turn off" the irritations supplied by parents and siblings who are threatening, aversive, and lacking in social skills. Next, we review evidence that brutal and erratic discipline is often associated with aggressive development.

Patterson's Theory of Aggression as Coercive Behavior Elicited and Negatively Reinforced by the Family

By taking detailed observations of aggressive and delinquent boys interacting at home with their families, and by comparing the patterns of family interaction found in these homes to those found in homes of nondelinquent boys, Patterson and his colleagues have put together a provocative theory of how aggressive behavior may develop (Patterson, 1976; Patterson & Cobb, 1971; Patterson & Reid, 1970). Patterson proposes that many aggressive behaviors represent attempts by children to cope with aversive stimuli presented by siblings and parents. Many of these aversive events are seemingly trivial and mild, such as failing to give a child attention, ignoring him, commanding him to stop doing something, expressing disapproval of him, or teasing or laughing at him, but when presented in a home atmosphere that is barren of positive stimuli, these irritants may be especially aversive and provocative. Patterson views aggression as forceful attempts to turn off the noxious stimuli emanating from other people—it is used to demand attention, to stop the teasing, to stop being frustrated or, in some cases, to interrupt the boredom.

Patterson has observed that highly aggressive boys, including some who have come into contact with law enforcement agencies for delinquent behavior, come from homes where certain stereotyped patterns of family interaction predominate. In particular, the highly aggressive child is likely to live in a home where aversive stimuli constitute an unusually high proportion of the social stimuli presented to the child by other family members. Instead of simply talking, attending, expressing approval and physical affection, and generally exchanging positive reinforcers, family members are reluctant to initiate conversation, tend to ignore each other, and talk with the intent to disapprove and irritate rather than make somebody else feel good. These repeated irritations constitute a fertile breeding ground for aggression, because, being aversive, they prompt the child to eliminate them—with force, if necessary. Thus a child who is ignored by his mother may shout at her or hit her to get attention; a child who is being derided by a sibling may hit the sibling in order to stop the humiliating or teasing treatment. Thus, to begin with, the home of the very aggressive child is characterized by a high frequency of the stimuli that provoke children to attempt forceful responses to improve matters.

Furthermore, the very aggressive child is likely to have been reinforced, at least intermittently, by other family members for his aggressive retaliations—that is, when he shouts at his mother to get her attention, she attends; when he defiantly refuses to stop doing what his father asks him to, the father drops his request; when he hits his sister to make her stop teasing, she cries and leaves him alone. This type of reinforcement is called *negative reinforcement,* because it involves the withdrawal of an aversive event. (Remember that negative reinforcement serves to *strengthen* behavior.) Thus Patterson believes that acts of aggression are elicited by an aversive stimulus presented by a family member and are reinforced by the family member's withdrawal of the aversive event.

An important characteristic of many episodes of aggression by highly aggressive boys is that when a boy's initial attempt to eliminate an irritation fails, he rapidly escalates his attack. If raising his voice to get his mother's attention does not work, he curses her or pushes her; if telling the sister who is teasing to "Shut up!" does not work, he hits her. Many episodes of aggression by the problem child have a "burst" quality about them, with the intensity of aggression spiraling upward as long as the tormentor refuses to comply or continues to pester the child. In fact, Patterson calls the aggressive behavior of these children *coercive,* because in effect they are saying, "You had better stop frustrating and irritating me and give me what I want or else I will continue my attack until you do!" As we noted, highly aggressive children apparently are at least occasionally successful in getting what they want after they accelerate an attack, and it is probably the expectation of this eventual compliance that keeps such children going in the face of preliminary obstacles. In contrast, nonaggressive children enjoy family members who less often present aversive stimuli, more often present social stimuli for prosocial behavior incompatible with aggression (e.g., smiling, conversing, and approving of one another), and who refuse to reward bursts of aggression.

Patterson's finding that highly aggressive boys escalate their attacks as long as the person annoying them continues the noxious treatment by ignoring them, teasing them, fighting back, and so on is an important discovery, for it suggests several features about the causes and cures of aggressive habits. First, it suggests that aggressive boys have experienced a history of at least intermittent reinforcement for aggressing in the face of aversive stimuli. In the next section, we shall review laboratory evidence showing that when adults react to children's aggression inconsistently, sometimes reinforcing it (by giving in to the children's coercive demands) and sometimes punishing it, children learn not only to be very persistent in their attempts at aggression but also to take preliminary threats of punishment as cues for escalating their aggression. Second, aggression may simply be the only way that highly aggressive children can secure attention, compliance, indulgence, or just escape from a boring or noxious environment. Thus they desperately risk and endure aversive stimulation in order to obtain these goals. Third, the fact that aversive consequences can trigger further aggression indicates that people must be careful about how they choose to modify aggressive behavior. Punishment, the threat of punishment, and other aversive controls may increase rather than deter aggression.

Patterson's finding that highly aggressive boys escalate rather than decrease their aggression when threatened with punishment or some other aversive reaction has been confirmed in other research. Peterson (1971), for example, found that aggressive boys punished a peer for making errors on a learning task more severely if they were told the peer would later have a chance to punish them in return than when there was no threat of retaliation. For low-aggressive boys, the threat of retaliation served to reduce the punishment they gave. One major characteristic of aggressive children, then, is that they have learned to respond to real or anticipated aversive events with strong and persistent aggressive reactions.

Parental Discipline and Aggression

Child-Rearing Correlates of Aggression Studies of the child-rearing correlates of aggressive and antisocial behavior paint a consistent picture. Aggressive children tend to come from homes in which the parents are rejecting, disinterested in their children's development, are lacking in warmth and affection, are indifferent or permissive toward their children's expressions of aggression, and—when they do discipline their children—prefer power assertion, especially physical punishment, over love-oriented discipline and reasoning (Becker, 1964; Feshbach, 1970; Martin, 1975).

In an outstanding study of the antecedents of aggression in adolescent boys in Sweden,

Olweus (1980) interviewed boys' parents to obtain information on the child-rearing practices and attitudes the parents had favored when the boys were young children. He also inquired into what the boys' temperaments had been like. The aggressiveness of the adolescents was determined by ratings from their schoolmates. Olweus's results revealed four factors that contribute to children's aggression. In order of the degree to which they correlated with children's aggression (from highest to lowest), these factors were: (a) the mother's permissiveness toward aggression; (b) the mother's negative, rejecting attitude toward her son; (c) the boy's temperamental inclinations to be active, impetuous, and hot-headed; and (d) the mother's and the father's use of power assertive discipline. The general picture that emerges is that a young boy who gets too little love and interest from his parents and too much freedom and a lack of clear limits with regard to aggressive behavior is especially likely to develop into an aggressive adolescent.

Paradoxically, sometimes it is the parents' very permissiveness that makes them resort to power assertion when they do discipline their children. Permissive parents who place few maturity demands on their children, who fail to set limits on their children's aggression, who make only weak requests that they stop ongoing deviant behavior, and who fail to enforce their initial requests to children that they stop misbehaving, sometimes find themselves becoming more and more frustrated and exasperated as their children's naughty behavior continues or escalates. These parents may suddenly explode with anger, unable to control their rage (Baumrind, 1973).

One result of this chain of events is inconsistency in parental discipline. Depending on their mood and other fluctuating circumstances, parents may explode angrily and punish children for misbehaving on one occasion but let the same act go unpunished, or even reward it, on another. Numerous field studies do confirm that inconsistency in parental discipline is a major correlate of aggressive and delinquent behavior in children (for a review, see Martin, 1975).

A laboratory experiment by Katz (1971) reveals how inconsistent treatment of aggressive responding can render the aggression very difficult to eliminate. In fact, this study showed that when children are sometimes punished and sometimes rewarded for aggressive responding, subsequent attempts to control the aggression with punishment may actually accelerate rather than decrease the aggressive responding. In this study, boys were invited to punch a Bobo doll and were told that they could continue punching for as long as they wished. The boys' punches received an inconsistent schedule of rewards and punishments: Half the punches were rewarded (with a marble, a penny, or a piece of candy) and half were punished (with the sounding of an obnoxious buzzer). After 30 punches on the inconsistent schedule, one group of boys was placed on extinction—they never again got a reward or heard the buzzer. For a second group of boys, the rewards ceased, but the punches were occasionally followed by the buzzer. The main finding was that the second group of boys continued to punch for many more trials than the boys on the extinction program. Clearly, then, when punishment has been mixed with reward, it may come to promote rather than to inhibit aggression. In such cases, punishment may signal to children that if they keep aggressing, it may eventually pay off.

Reasons for the Link Between Power Assertive Discipline and Aggression The fact that physical punishment for aggression is associated with high rather than low aggression in children has intrigued many researchers, and a number of possible explanations have been suggested. One possibility is that parents who rely on physical punishment are setting examples of impulsive, antisocial behavior, and their children's aggression may reflect an imitation of the assaultive behavior they have seen in their parents. Physically punitive parents may be teaching their chil-

dren the lesson that it is acceptable to use force to influence others and to settle disputes. Parents who physically punish their children for aggression may successfully deter their children from behaving aggressively at home, but the children may practice the aggression they have learned from their parents on targets in safer settings, perhaps towards their peers at school (Bandura & Walters, 1959). We shall review this imitation-of-aggression hypothesis later in this chapter.

Second, it is likely that parents who are frequent users of physical punishment lack an appreciation of other crucial aspects of child-rearing, which may cause aggressive behavior. Parents who favor power assertion may fail to elicit and reinforce mature, prosocial behaviors that compete with aggression and may fail to use inductive reasoning, which fosters a tendency to accept responsibility and to anticipate guilt for harming others (Feshbach, 1970; Hoffman, 1970b). They may also tend to be inconsistent in their disciplining of aggression.

Third, parents who punish aggression with power assertion may cause their children to conclude that the main reason for inhibiting aggression is to avoid external punishment. According to attribution theory, once children attribute their motivation for suppressing deviant behavior to external factors, they ignore or discount other possible intrinsic motivators for good behavior—they do not learn that there is something intrinsically wrong with deliberately hurting others or that they are by nature intrinsically good people who do not want to hurt others (Bem, 1972; Dienstbier, Hillman, Lehnhoff, Hillman, & Valkenaar, 1975). Instead, their attention becomes focused on the external factors controlling their behavior. Thus physical punishment may foster a style of causal attribution that allows children to aggress when they think they can get away with it.

One implication of the causal attribution analysis, then, is that parents should strive to discipline their children for aggression in ways that promote children's beliefs that they are intrinsically motivated to behave nonaggressively. Inductive reasoning can teach children the inherently harmful aspects of aggression for other people. Direct verbal attribution of nonaggressive motivations may be useful as well (e.g., "I know you're the kind of child who doesn't like to hurt other people's feelings"). The aim is to instill in children an intrinsic dislike of aggression, so that the children will inhibit aggression even in the absence of external surveillance.

Finally, we must remember that correlations do not imply causation. The correlation between parental punishment and children's aggression may be due to the fact that boys who are congenitally high in activity level or aggressiveness are provoking their parents into using physical punishment (Bell, 1968). In one study, adults were shown a film that depicted either a hyperactive or a less active child misbehaving and were asked to prescribe a punishment for the child (Stevens-Long, 1973). The adults suggested harsher punishments for the more active child. This reveals how adults' disciplinary actions can be influenced by children's temperaments.

We have seen in this section that a variety of factors—parental permissiveness, hostility, preference for power assertion, inconsistency, and children's temperaments—conspire to produce aggressive development. Although these factors may contribute "additively" to the probability that a child will develop aggressively (in the sense that the more each of these factors is present, the more likely the child is to develop aggressive habits), we should remind ourselves that the factors contributing to aggression interact with one another, and interact in unique ways in different families. For example, one boy who is temperamentally active and impetuous may exhaust his mother, causing her to be permissive most of the time, but occasionally driving her to feel so angry that she reacts with physical punishment. In another family, a mother may react negatively to her son in part because of an unsatisfactory relationship with her husband (Olweus, 1980).

There probably does not exist a universal parent-child relationship that is invariably associated with aggressive development.

ACQUISITION OF AGGRESSION THROUGH POSITIVE REINFORCEMENT

Patterson (1976; Patterson & Cobb, 1971) has suggested that whereas aggression in the home is usually sparked by aversive stimulation and maintained by negative reinforcement, aggression in other settings, especially the school, is geared toward the attainment of positive rewards—getting a desired toy, obtaining respect from one's peers and, above all, just getting attention. Studies have shown that teachers who scold and become exasperated with children who disrupt the class are rewarding their disruptiveness. Even major acts of destruction may be maintained because the children know of no other way to gain attention. When teachers and parents fail to pay attention to desirable behavior, children often turn to antisocial behavior for recognition.

In a classic field study of aggression in nursery-school children, Patterson, Littman, and Bricker (1967) showed how aggression can be learned and maintained by positive reinforcers dispensed by the peer group. Adults observed children interacting freely in the nursery-school setting and coded each act of peer-directed aggression into one of several categories (bodily contact, attack with an object, verbal or symbolic attack, and infringement of property or territory). The observers also noted how the victim of each attack behaved and coded each victim reaction as either "positive" (passive, withdrawing, giving up a toy, crying, and assuming a defensive posture) or "negative" (telling the teacher, recovering property, and retaliating). The study lasted for several months, and the main point was to see how children's aggression changed over time as a function of the consequences provided by the victims. The main finding was that victims who provided an aggressor with a positive consequence were likely to be attacked again by that aggressor, and in the same manner as before. However, when a victim provided a negative consequence, the aggressor was more likely to change the form of attack, the victim, or both.

A second important discovery from this study was that children who were initially passive and nonaggressive learned aggressive habits if subjected to the "right" sort of interactions with their more aggressive peers. Several children who had been nonaggressive at the start of the school year were found to be frequently *initiating* aggressive interactions by spring, provided that during the year these children (a) had been frequently victimized by more aggressive children, (b) had eventually tried to defend themselves with aggressive counterattacks, and (c) had found these counterattacks to be successful (i.e., to lead to a reinforcing consequence). In other words, if initially passive children reach the point where they "aren't going to take it anymore" and attempt an aggressive countermeasure that meets with success, they may end up becoming initiators of aggressive actions themselves. Clearly, the peer group can be a potent source for the social learning of aggression, and as early as the nursery-school years.

Members of delinquent subcultures, such as gangs of delinquent boys, often reward each other for aggressive behavior and even make status in the group contingent upon adopting various injurious and destructive behaviors (Bandura, 1973). In one observational study of institutionalized delinquent girls, it was found that the girls enthusiastically reinforced acts of aggression (Buehler, Patterson, & Furniss, 1966).

Adults can also reward aggression. Bandura and Walters (1959) noted that whereas parents of highly aggressive boys harshly punished their sons for parent-directed aggression, they actively encouraged and condoned the boys' aggression toward their peers. Clearly, children are capable of discrimination learning, such that they inhibit aggression in situations where they cannot get away

with it, but freely display it where they anticipate success.

Several laboratory investigations have also examined how aggression varies as a function of its reinforcing consequences. One of the more important findings from the laboratory work is that there exists considerable *response generalization* in aggressive responding. For example, when children are rewarded for aggressing verbally, they not only increase in verbal aggression but they also increase in physical aggression. In one study (Lovaas, 1961), children were initially rewarded for making either aggressive remarks (e.g., "dirty doll"; "The doll should be spanked") or neutral remarks to a doll. Later, when children were given a choice of playing with either an aggressive toy (one in which pushing a lever made a stick hit a doll on its head) or a nonaggressive toy (one in which pushing a lever made a ping-pong ball jump up inside a cage), more of the children who had been rewarded for aggressive verbalizations chose the aggressive toy. Instead of cathartically draining children of aggressive urges, then, verbal aggression may increase tendencies toward physical aggression. Aggression also generalizes from inanimate, toy targets to real targets–people. Walters and Brown (1963), for example, found that children who were rewarded for punching a Bobo doll behaved more aggressively and competitively in subsequent play sessions with a peer. Aggression in one form begets aggression in another form.

MODELING INFLUENCES ON THE DEVELOPMENT OF AGGRESSION

Research on the effects of exposure to aggressive models provides a classic example of how investigators, after discovering a striking correlation in the field, take their research into the laboratory in order to search for cause-and-effect relationships. Early correlational research suggested the possibility that children learn aggressive habits by imitating their parents' behavior: Highly aggressive children tend to have parents who make frequent use of brutal and erratic punishment, the parents often fight between themselves, and the parents have histories of committing violent crimes (Bandura & Walters, 1959; Glueck & Glueck, 1950; McCord, 1979). The fact that boys whose fathers are absent from the home (from death or divorce) are less aggressive than boys who have fathers in the home (Bach, 1946; Sears, 1951) also hinted that the presence of an aggressive parent model may influence the development of aggression.

Intrigued with this possibility, many researchers designed experiments specifically to test the hypothesis that exposure to aggressive models causes children to become more aggressive. Early studies confirmed the prediction. Bandura, Ross, and Ross (1961) found that children who watched an adult model attack a Bobo doll subsequently tended to behave more aggressively toward the Bobo doll themselves. In another project reported around the same time, Mussen and Rutherford (1961) found that showing children an aggressive cartoon increased their inclinations to destroy a toy.

Results of early studies such as these carried several implications. First, they disconfirmed the catharsis hypothesis. Second, they lent credence to the idea that the positive relationship between parental use of physical punishment and children's aggression might at least in part be due to children's imitating their parents' power assertion. Third, they warned people about exposing children to overdoses of violence in television and the movies. But perhaps most significant, from a theoretical standpoint, was that the results prompted social learning theorists, such as Bandura, to examine more closely the mechanisms through which models contribute to social learning.

Bandura (1979) proposes that aggressive models can serve several functions. The first is an *observational learning* function. Aggressive models can teach children (and adults)

brand new ways to hurt and destroy. How many airplane hijackings would have occurred without the aid of well-publicized examples? Observing aggressive models also allows children to learn the likely consequences of practicing aggressive responses. As we learned in Chapter 4, children are much more inclined to imitate aggressive responses for which others have been rewarded than they are to imitate aggressive responses for which others have been punished. Second is a *disinhibitory function*. When children see a model act aggressively without being punished, their fears of feeling guilty over behaving aggressively themselves are reduced, and the chances that the children will imitate the aggression are increased. Also, observing a model display one form of aggression may disinhibit other forms of aggression in the child (e.g., seeing an adult aggress with a gun on television may make a child become more verbally threatening toward his peers). Third, aggressive modeling displays also serve a *stimulus enhancing function*. Aggressive models can teach children how to use certain objects, such as knives, sticks, and guns, in harmful ways. Finally, aggressive models may serve an *emotion-arousing function*. Observing aggression may promote emotional arousal that makes one respond more impulsively and aggressively than otherwise.

After the first experiments showed that violent modeling can cause aggression, work on the effects of aggressive modeling expanded rapidly. This work has refined our grasp of the conditions causing aggressive imitation and has shown that aggressive modeling increases aggression in real-life settings as well as in the laboratory. We shall now review a number of the conclusions from this work.

Witnessing Violence Increases Aggression Against Real People in Real-Life Settings

In the early studies, which found that exposure to aggressive models increases aggression, children were tested for aggression toward inanimate objects, such as the Bobo doll. Naturally, one question that arose was whether observing aggressive models increases children's aggression toward real people. To find out, Liebert and Baron (1972) showed one group of children a 3½ minute segment from the television series "The Untouchables" that contained a chase, two fistfights, two shootings, and a knifing. Other children viewed an equally long but nonaggressive sports sequence. Afterwards, all the children were given an opportunity to aggress against a peer in an adjoining room by pressing a button that presumably would cause the peer's fingers to burn while the peer worked on a task. Children in the aggressive modeling group pushed the button to hurt the peer more often and for longer durations than children in the control group.

Several excellent field studies have explored the effects of viewing violence on aggression in the natural environment. For example, when preschoolers are exposed to a daily diet of aggressive cartoons, they increase their spontaneous expressions of aggression—hitting, kicking, and throwing things—within the preschool setting (Friedrich & Stein, 1973; Steuer, Applefield, & Smith, 1971). In a series of field experiments, Parke, Berkowitz, Leyens, West, and Sebastian (1977) exposed cottages of institutionalized juvenile delinquent boys to either an aggressive movie or a nonaggressive but equally exciting movie each night for 5 nights. Boys were not allowed to watch television during that week. Boys in the cottages that were assigned the aggressive movies displayed more restlessness while watching the movies: They stamped their feet, yelled, shouted, talked, and shifted about in their seats more. Moreover, boys in these cottages behaved more violently towards one another in the hours immediately after the films. The effects of the aggressive modeling were strongest among boys who were the most dominant inhabitants of their cottage.

Sometimes the consequences of observing media violence can be extremely serious.

Rushton (1980) reviewed several case studies indicating that even violent criminal behavior can sometimes be traced to imitation of "entertainment" aggression. For example, juveniles who have been arrested for sexually molesting young children and for dousing park drunks with gasoline and setting them afire have sometimes confessed to witnessing similar acts on television or in the movies 1 or 2 days before committing the acts themselves.

Children Imitate Aggression Even When They Are the Victims

In order to argue that children imitate the aggression of physically punitive parents, one must assume that children will imitate aggression even when they are the victims. Research confirms this. In one study, an adult initially taught children a task by either punishing the children for their mistakes or rewarding them for their correct responses (Gelfand, Hartmann, Lamb, Smith, Mahan, & Paul, 1974). Subsequently, when the children were requested to teach a peer the same task, they employed with high fidelity the same punitive or rewarding strategy that had been used on them by the adult. The fact that parents who abuse their children often have a history of abusive treatment at the hands of their own parents (Chapter 3) also confirms that aversive styles of control can be transmitted from generation to generation.

The Effects of Aggressive Modeling Are Not Fleeting

Children remember aggressive acts long after seeing them. For example, Hicks (1965) found that children could recall specific aggressive and destructive acts from a movie as long as 6 months after seeing it. More frightening, a longitudinal study by Eron, Lefkowitz, Huesmann, and Walder (1972) found a positive correlation between the amount of violence in the favorite television programs of third-grade boys and how aggressive the boys were 10 years later, as young adults! The fact that the correlation between television violence in the third grade and aggression in adulthood was still significant, even when the effects of a number of other variables, including level of childhood aggression, IQ, and social class were considered, lent further support to the hypothesis that viewing violent television programs caused the aggressive development.

Characteristics of the Modeled Aggression Influence Its Effects

Children are more likely to imitate the harmful acts of models who are rewarded or who escape punishment for their aggression than they are to copy the actions of models who are punished for behaving aggressively (Bandura, 1965; Bandura, Ross, & Ross, 1963b). However, this does not mean that showing children aggressive models who are punished will guarantee that the children never imitate the aggression. Remember from Chapter 4 that even when children inhibit imitation of vicariously punished actions, the children still tend to store the modeled acts mentally. If the children later encounter a situation where they believe the aggression will yield a reward, they may go ahead and perform the response they previously suppressed.

Some skeptics of the conclusion that violence in the entertainment media increases aggression in viewers argue that aggressive after-effects of observing violence are likely only when the modeled aggression is realistic. They point out that much media violence is fictitious and unrealistic (as when it is in cartoon form) and that viewers will not see these acts as relevant to their own behavior. This argument has no merit. Numerous projects reveal that aggression is imitated regardless of whether it is depicting fictional or real-life aggression, whether it is shown in cartoon or human form, and whether it is presented in live, televised, or film format (Bandura, Ross, & Ross, 1963a; Meyer, 1972; Stein & Friedrich, 1975).

The Closer the Viewer's Predicament Matches the Model's, the Greater the Imitative Aggression

The aggressive effects of viewing violence are strongest when the observer later encounters a stimulus situation similar to that which triggered the model's aggression. For example, seeing a model violently punish someone for insulting him or her is especially likely to dispose a viewer to react aggressively to insults (e.g., Geen & Stonner, 1973).

A finding with considerable social relevance is that when people are frustrated or annoyed by someone who resembles a person they have seen victimized by others, they are especially likely to respond to that person with aggression. In several intriguing studies by Berkowitz (1970), adult men were most likely to give electric shocks to a person who had insulted them if the person bore the same last name as someone they had just seen get beaten up in a movie boxing match. Perhaps if children notice that certain other children tend to be picked on by their peers, they become more likely to bully those children themselves. Aggression toward members of minority groups may partly result from this process. If children see that members of certain minorities are frequently scapegoated or victimized, they may become more inclined to aggress against members of these minorities themselves.

When people see models use certain objects (e.g., knives, guns, or clubs) for aggressive purposes, they become more likely to use the objects for aggressive purposes themselves. In one study, a group of nursery-school children was given toy guns to play with. A control group was given toy airplanes. Children in the group given the guns not only imitated the ritualistic aggressive acts they had seen television heroes enact with firearms (e.g., pointing the gun and saying, "Bang, bang, you're dead!") but they also displayed other varieties of assaultive behavior toward their peers, including hitting, shoving, insulting, and threatening each other (Turner

& Goldsmith, 1976). In other words, furnishing children with implements they have seen used for aggressive purposes elicits and disinhibits a variety of aggressive responses in the children.

Characteristics of the Observer Influence the Effects of Media Violence

The sex of the observer influences imitative aggression: Boys usually display more imitative aggression than do girls (Bandura ct al., 1963a, 1963b). This is probably because children observe that aggression is more often displayed by males than by females and therefore that it is more appropriate for males. Although girls may not spontaneously imitate as much aggression as boys, we should not assume that they are invulnerable to aggressive models. Girls may mentally store aggressive responses for long periods of time and may choose to enact the responses when incentive conditions favor doing so.

Children with established aggressive tendencies are more likely to imitate new instances of aggression than children who are less aggressive, although the latter children are usually not totally unaffected. Also, children with positive attitudes toward aggression are more likely to imitate it than are children with negative attitudes (Hicks, 1971). Stein and Friedrich (1975) point out, however, that even if it were demonstrated that only a minority of individuals were incited to violence by media aggression, this would not necessarily constitute grounds against its regulation by society. The considerable damage that can and has been inspired by media violence (see Bandura, 1973, and Rushton, 1980, for reviews) is a grave social concern.

Given the alarming results of exposure to violent movie fare, an important research task becomes that of discovering factors that cause some people to seek out aggressive movies and television. We already have some clues. People who have just behaved aggressively themselves show a preference for viewing violence by others (Fenigstein, 1979). Also, witnessing or hearing about acts of violence can arouse people's desire to see aggression. In one field study, the number of people attending violent movies increased after a murder in the neighborhood, whereas attendance at nonviolent movies showed no change (Boyanowsky, Newtson, & Walster, 1974). Aggression begets a preference for viewing aggression, which begets further aggression.

By Disapproving of Modeled Aggression, Socializing Agents Can Reduce Its Harmful Effects

When adults who are viewing displays of aggression along with children express disapproval of the violence, the children are less likely to imitate it (Grusec, 1973; Hicks, 1968). Parents would do well to criticize instances of aggression that their children see performed on television and elsewhere, explaining why such actions are undesirable.

Viewing Violence Has Other Deleterious Consequences

Watching aggression does not just promote aggressive development; it impedes the development of prosocial behavior. Reductions in altruism are one outcome. In one study, boys who watched an aggressive cartoon were subsequently less willing to share a play activity with another child than were children who watched a nonaggressive cartoon (Hapkiewicz & Roden, 1971). In another experiment, children who had seen several gun battles, shoot-outs, and fistfights in an 8-minute film clip took longer to come to the rescue of two younger children who were in trouble than did children who had not watched a violent program (Drabman & Thomas, 1974).

Another outcome is emotional desensitization or habituation to violence. In one study, boys who had averaged either less than 4 hours or more than 25 hours of television viewing per week for the preceding 2 years were shown a segment of a movie that contained several violent boxing sequences. The low television-exposure boys showed markedly more skin conductance (sweating on the surface of the palm) and a quicker pulse during the aggressive boxing scenes than the high television-exposure boys, suggesting that the high-exposure boys' sensitivity to violence had been blunted by habitual viewing (Cline, Croft, & Courrier, 1973). Of course, this study is really correlational, and one might argue that boys with low reactivity to violence simply prefer to watch it more. However, an experiment by Thomas, Horton, Lippincott, and Drabman (1977) confirms that viewing violence can cause reduced emotional sensitivity to aggression. In this study, after subjects had viewed either an aggressive or nonaggressive television program, their physiological sensitivity to scenes of real-life aggression (a video sequence of two children fighting or police and demonstrators clashing) was measured. Subjects who saw the aggressive program showed less reactivity. The finding that watching television violence dulls one's emotional arousal to aggression does not imply a reduced tendency to act more aggressively following exposure. On the contrary, it suggests that displays of violence are less likely to arouse anxiety that might otherwise inhibit the imitation of aggression. Furthermore, people whose emotional sensitivities to violence have become deadened should be less likely to experience empathic distress for victims of aggressive attacks. This may reduce their motivation to rescue or come to the aid of a distressed person.

Finally, a steady diet of television violence changes one's views of the world. People who spend a great deal of time watching television are more likely to regard television violence as realistic, to overestimate the crime rate and the percentage of citizens employed as law-enforcement officers, and to express positive attitudes toward violence (Gross, 1974; Stein & Friedrich, 1975).

THE ROLE OF THE VICTIM

An interesting issue involves the role of the *victim* in guiding an aggressive attack. Do some victim reactions serve to anger an aggressor even further, thereby intensifying the attack? Is there something a victim can do to hasten an end to an attack that is being waged against him or her?

Most psychological investigations of the role of the victim have focused on the effects of a victim's expressions of pain on an attacker's behavior. Some theorists have argued that pain cues should lead an aggressor to continue an attack because pain cues serve as positive reinforcers. They contend that the sight of pain in a victim acquires conditioned or secondary reinforcement value because pain cues are often associated with successful aggression. For example, victims often cry or grimace as they give in to an aggressor's demands. Is there support for this view that pain cues reinforce and sustain aggressive responding?

Although Patterson and his associates (1967) found that nursery-school children were indeed likely to continue attacking a victim who cried or took a defensive posture, this apparent reinforcing effect of pain seems limited to young children. This is because a number of additional studies with older children and adults report an opposite effect: A victim's pain cues serve to reduce the intensity of an aggressor's attack, even when the aggressor is moderately angry (Baron, 1971a, 1971b; Patterson & Cobb, 1971; Perry & Bussey, 1977). For example, Perry and Perry (1974) found that fifth-grade boys reduced the intensity of noise punishment they gave a peer for making errors on arithmetic problems when the peer indicated that he was suffering (e.g., "This is hurting my ears so much that my whole head aches"), but their aggression remained high if the peer denied experiencing much pain (e.g., "This doesn't hurt my ears at all").

For the very young child, pain cues may

have an arousing and reinforcing effect that serves to sustain a burst of aggression. With development, however, the matter becomes more complex. For most older children and adults, pain cues probably help to curtail an aggressive attack, partly because pain cues arouse empathic distress and partly because the individual has learned that to prolong suffering in another person is wrong. Furthermore, as children get older, an increasing number of their aggressive acts are intended to restore their self-esteem, such as when they are trying to get even with someone who has insulted them (Feshbach, 1970; Hartup, 1974). In such cases, once children succeed in getting their target to suffer, they may feel that they have evened the score. Having attained their aggressive goal, they stop their attack. Of course, individuals who are extremely angry or who are characteristically high in aggression may be less ready to tone down their attack in the face of pain feedback (Baron, 1974; Perry & Bussey, 1977). Perhaps their empathic reaction to distress is dulled, or they are motivated to perceive a higher degree of suffering before being satisfied that adequate retribution has been made.

MORAL DEVELOPMENT AND AGGRESSION

If children believe that aggression is bad and expect self-condemnation for perpetrating harmful and destructive acts, they should strive to avoid behaving aggressively. What *do* children think about the rightness or wrongness of aggression, and do children who anticipate feeling guilty for behaving aggressively actually show less aggression than other children?

Children's Moral Judgments of Aggression

Most children learn the general rule that "aggression is bad," but children also learn that some acts of aggression are worse than others. A number of researchers have read children stories that describe the specific actions of an aggressive character and then have requested that the children evaluate the story hero by rating how good or bad they think he or she is (perhaps by deciding how large a paddle should be used to spank the character). Results reveal that even preschool children make evaluative discriminations along a number of dimensions. For example, they judge an aggressor who causes a large degree of damage or injury as worse than one who causes little harm; they judge aggression intended to teach someone a lesson or to restore justice (prosocial aggression) as less blameworthy than aggression carried out for the actor's personal gain (instrumental aggression) or to hurt the victim (hostile aggression); they judge aggression directed toward a parent as worse than that directed toward a peer or sibling; and they evaluate intentional aggression as more blameworthy than accidental injury (Rule & Duker, 1973; Rule, Nesdale, & McAra, 1974; Shantz & Pentz, 1972; Shantz & Voydanoff, 1973). An interesting question for future research is whether high- and low-aggressive children differ in their evaluative discriminations. Perhaps one problem with highly aggressive children is that they do not realize that aggression on some occasions is less permissible than on other occasions.

Self-Evaluation and Aggressive Behavior

In the last chapter we saw that children develop standards for self-evaluation, or behavioral criteria for rewarding and punishing themselves. We noted that children base these personal standards on a variety of social learning experiences. Their standards sometimes involve internalizations of the disciplinary contingencies adults practice on them (e.g., children often punish themselves for engaging in activities that their parents have punished them for performing). Children's standards are also influenced by vicarious learning. In other words, children can abstract rules about appropriate and inappropriate behavior by observing the circumstances in which other people aggress or refrain from aggressing and the social consequences other people receive for aggressing under these various circumstances. Adults can also help sharpen children's standards by verbally discussing the pros and cons of aggressive behavior, especially by using inductive reasoning that emphasizes to children the causal role they can play in producing or preventing unpleasant states in others.

Do children's standards for self-evaluation influence their overt expression of aggressive behavior? Several studies suggest that this is true. Perry and Bussey (1977), for example, found that boys rated as nonaggressive by their peers punished themselves (by voluntarily reducing the value of a prize they could have) when they were led to believe that they had hurt another child; boys rated as highly aggressive by their peers, however, failed to punish themselves for injuring another child. It is likely that the anticipation of guilt feelings helps deter the former boys from behaving aggressively in natural settings. Feshbach (1970) has reviewed evidence showing that highly aggressive children tend to focus their attention on not getting caught after they behave aggressively (e.g., they think about running away to escape punishment, telling lies, or blaming their problem on someone else), whereas less aggressive children are more concerned with accepting personal responsibility for their harmful acts. It is likely that aggressive children's concerns with external consequences in part flow from the greater use of power assertive discipline and lesser use of inductive reasoning by their parents. Aggression is also related to moral reasoning: Adults who score at the higher stages in Kohlberg's scheme of moral reasoning are less likely to penalize a partner in a game when it is of no benefit to themselves than are students whose reasoning falls at lower stages (Anchor & Cross, 1974). Perhaps the more children realize that aggression is

inherently wrong (rather than wrong just because it leads to punishment or criticism from others), the more likely they are to anticipate guilt for needless wrongdoing.

Bandura (1977) has pointed out that anticipatory self-condemning reactions are likely to be activated most strongly when the causal connection between reprehensible conduct and its injurious consequences is unambiguous. In other words, people are most likely to expect to experience guilt feelings for wrongdoing when they cannot deny that they were personally responsible for causing the pain and suffering of someone else. He notes, however, that individuals learn ways of distorting their responsibility for negative outcomes, and this allows them to dissociate anticipated guilt from their actions. For example, people may portray their aggression as serving a moral end, they may contrast their acts with more flagrant inhumanities committed by others, they may distort their contribution to a cause-and-effect relationship by diffusing decision making in collective action, they may cognitively minimize the harm they cause, and they may devalue and dehumanize their victims. How children learn these techniques for avoiding guilt, and how they might be taught to become aware of these techniques in themselves and others, are matters for future study.

SEX DIFFERENCES IN AGGRESSION

The male sex is the more aggressive. Numerous studies reveal that boys aggress more than girls in a wide variety of situations and in a wide variety of ways. It has sometimes been suggested that boys are more aggressive only in terms of physical aggression, especially aggression involving large muscle activity (Feshbach, 1970), but more recent reviews reveal that this is not so: Males surpass females in verbal aggression as well as physical aggression (Maccoby & Jacklin, 1974).

Although males usually surpass females in aggressiveness, there exist some situations in which females come close to, and even equal, males in their aggression. When females believe nobody is observing them aggress, when they can diffuse responsibility for their aggression by embedding it in group action, or when they can blame their aggression on someone else, their levels of aggression rival those of men (Brodzinsky, Messer, & Tew, 1979; Caplan, 1979; Frodi, Macaulay, & Thome, 1977). For example, when women act in a group, they prescribe levels of electric shock punishment for a target person that equal those prescribed by men. Thus sex differences diminish when aggressors can escape social censure or avoid personal responsibility for their harmful actions. This suggests that women possess a high potential for aggression, but choose to express it less often. We might add, however, that in today's society the number of situations in which women are more reluctant than men to aggress may be diminishing. The juvenile crime rate for females, for example, is increasing at a faster rate than is the rate for males.

What are the causes of the sex difference in aggression? The evidence suggests that both biological and social learning factors conspire to produce sex differences in aggression. The position that sex differences in aggression are at least partly attributable to biological factors has been championed by Maccoby and Jacklin (1974, 1980). These writers do not deny the importance of social learning experiences, but they suggest that at least four lines of evidence point to the conclusion that biological influences contribute, too. First, boys are more aggressive than girls in virtually every society that has been studied. Second, sex differences in aggression occur early in life—so early, in fact, that social learning experiences may not yet have had a chance to operate. A third sort of evidence favoring a biological contribution is that several species of subhuman primates (e.g., baboons and chimpanzees) also reveal greater male aggressiveness. Fourth, there is evidence linking aggressive behavior to sex hormones. For example, injecting mice or monkeys prenatally with the male hormone

testosterone increases the incidence of aggression in these animals after birth.

The two sexes receive different treatment at the hands of their social environment, and this is also likely to contribute to sex differences in aggression. Society expects more aggression from males than from females, and children are aware of this difference in expectation as early as 3 or 4 years of age. Furthermore, people behave toward children in ways that make such expectations come true. As we shall document in Chapter 9, adults prompt sex-appropriate behaviors from children, reward them for conforming to sex-role stereotypes, and punish them for departing from these guidelines. People are also more likely to direct remarks like "You're angry," "You're mean," or "You're a tough guy" to boys than they are to girls. Boys learn that aggressive, competitive behaviors are required of them in order to be perceived as masculine by themselves and by their peers.

Although parents usually reward sex-appropriate behavior and discourage sex-inappropriate behavior, a curious situation exists with respect to aggression: Research shows that boys are more harshly punished for aggression than girls (Maccoby & Jacklin, 1974). In other words, despite the fact that parents regard aggression as more appropriate for boys, they more often react to boys' aggression with physical punishment and other power assertive discipline. Exactly why this is the case is not known. Possibly girls' aggression is less intense or less upsetting to adults. Or perhaps boys react more defiantly to their parents' attempts to curb their aggression, causing the parents to escalate their punishment to more powerful levels. Regardless of the reason, parents' harsher treatment of boys' aggression probably has the paradoxical effect of strengthening the boys' aggressiveness. This conclusion follows from a point we made earlier that parents who employ physical punishment are teaching their children aggressive ways of influencing others. They may also be teaching their children the rule that aggression is bad because it leads to external punishment rather than because it is inherently undesirable. And remember from Chapter 3 that parents use more power assertive discipline with boys, while they use more inductive reasoning with girls. This may also contribute to sex differences in aggression.

Sex differences in aggression may also be partly due to sex differences in children's imitation of aggressive behavior. Both boys and girls cognitively acquire a vast repertoire of aggressive responses by observing the violent behavior of their playmates, parents, television characters, and other models, and they store these responses in their heads for long periods of time. However, because children see that aggression is more often performed by males than by females, they come to encode aggression as male-appropriate rather than female-appropriate. Research shows that children strive to perform responses that they have encoded as appropriate for their own sex (Perry & Bussey, 1979). Thus, in the language of the social learning theorists, the sexes may not differ terribly much in the observational learning of aggression, though they do differ in its performance.

Certain sex differences in children's interests and activity preferences (reviewed more fully in Chapter 9) may also contribute to sex differences in aggression (Tieger, 1980). Girls more frequently prefer to play alone indoors, often near adults who might discourage aggressive activity. Boys are more peer-oriented and prefer to play outdoors with other boys away from adult supervision—circumstances more conducive to aggression.

Although it is possible to list separately the various biological and experiential contributors to sex differences in aggression, in actuality the two sorts of influences probably *interact* to produce greater male aggressiveness. For example, because of their male hormones, their greater strength and muscularity, their higher activity levels, and their higher thresholds for physical pain, boys may more often be born predisposed to react to frustration and other aversive stimuli with forceful attempts to eliminate the irritant. Furthermore, a good proportion of these attempts may be successful, teaching the boys that physical force is a good way to get what they want. At the same time, parents of these children may find their children's behavior especially disturbing. They may come to perceive and label their sons as "aggressive" and they may be driven to employ power assertive discipline (perhaps on an inconsistent basis). This, of course, would just increase the children's unruly behavior. As the children get older they also come to realize that it is culturally appropriate for them to perform physically forceful responses, to copy aggressive models, to avenge insult with aggression, and so on. We believe this kind of spiraling chain of events is more likely to happen among boys than among girls.

A final point about sex differences in aggression is that boys more often serve as the victims as well as the perpetrators of aggression. Why might this be? Children may learn that it is inappropriate to aggress against girls. Possibly, signs of pain and suffering are somehow more disturbing and more likely to elicit empathic distress reactions when displayed by girls. Another possibility derives from the fact that children tend to segregate themselves by sex: Boys play with boys, and girls with girls. Since more boys are aggressors, and since boys tend to play with other boys, it would be expected that the victims of aggression would more often be male. One could use this same method of reasoning, however, to reach the conclusion that boys are more aggressive because they tend to play with the sorts of children who elicit aggression—other boys. Clearly, more research on the reasons for greater male aggression and victimization needs to be done.

METHODS USED
TO CONTROL AGGRESSION

Traditional psychoanalytic approaches to treating disturbed, hyperaggressive children often are based on a catharsis principle: Children are encouraged to express their aggressive urges, frequently in "therapeutic" doll play sessions, in the hope of draining off their excess aggressive drive. However, behaving aggressively, fantasizing about aggression, and witnessing aggression usually act to strengthen children's aggressive habits rather than to lessen aggressive urges. Thus treatment programs based on catharsis principles should not be employed.

The research literature provides a solid basis for making several recommendations for preventing and reducing children's aggression. A first recommendation involves withdrawing the stimuli that elicit aggression. A second one involves consistently demonstrating to children that their aggression will not be tolerated. A third recommendation is that people take pains to elicit and reinforce prosocial behavior that is incompatible with aggression. Finally, a fourth recommendation is that adults teach children self-control—they should learn to monitor their own aggressiveness and to reward themselves for behaving nonaggressively. We shall briefly elaborate on each of these suggestions, but bear in mind that a combination of strategies is likely to be most effective.

Remove Stimuli that Elicit Aggression

Wise parents and teachers avoid subjecting children to excessive irritation, frustration, and boredom, because these states often prompt intense coercive attempts by the children to alleviate their aversive state. Structuring play activities so that competition over resources is minimized and discouraging children from playing with guns and other objects likely to spark aggression should also help. When settling disputes and disciplining children, adults can set an example by using a controlled and reasonable approach to influencing others rather than by displaying impulsiveness and forcefulness. By restricting children's viewing of violent television and criticizing aggressive episodes they know their children have seen, parents can limit observational learning of aggression and communicate the value that aggression is repre-

hensible. In an attempt to get television networks to reduce the level of aggression in children's programs, parents can band together and boycott products of sponsors of violent television programs.

Eliminate the Payoff for Aggression

Compliance with a child's whines, demands, and other coercive behaviors may very well bring an aggressive episode to an end (because it gives the child what he or she wants), but it probably increases the child's attempts at aversive control in the future. The child must be taught that coercive behavior and its escalation into intensely obnoxious and demanding behavior will not be rewarded. Sometimes parents unwittingly contribute to their child's learning of coercive habits. Consider, for example, the parent who initially says "No" to a child's demand, but eventually gives in after the child intensifies the unpleasantness of his or her request. This unfortunate practice rewards the child's demanding response at a high intensity and teaches the child to persist in aversive attempts. Parents should develop a habit of saying to themselves whenever a child makes a demand, "If I say 'No,' am I prepared to insist on it if the child escalates the demand and keeps pestering me for it?" In her observational study of preschool children and their parents, Baumrind (1973) found that parents who enforce their initial demands on a child had children who were nonaggressive, but otherwise friendly and competent, so long as the parents were also warm and reasonable in their approach to discipline. It is hard to overemphasize the importance of setting reasonable limits on the degree of demanding-type behaviors that will be tolerated from a child, and of then firmly and consistently enforcing these limits when they are challenged.

Parents who "mean what they say" no doubt forestall the development of coercive behavior. But we have seen that refusing to give in to the aggressive demand of a child who has *already* developed a strong habit of successful coercive control may only fuel increased disagreeableness from the child. Punishment or the threat of punishment may stimulate rather than inhibit aggression from these children. What can the socializing agent do under these conditions? Extinction, or ignoring the aggression, does not always work and may in fact lead to an increase in the deviant behavior. Bandura (1973) notes that the withdrawal of reward, especially physically removing the child from the reinforcing situation and isolating the child (the time-out method) for a few minutes following each infraction, can be very effective and is unlikely to cause the bad side effects associated with physical punishment (Chapter 3). It is important, however, to make it clear to the child exactly what behaviors lead to the use of this method. This technique of removing attention from antisocial behavior is most effective when combined with a deliberate strategy of reinforcing incompatible behavior, described next.

Elicit and Reward Behavior Incompatible with Aggression

The sensible teacher or parent makes an effort to occupy children's time and attention in ways that elicit behavior that competes with aggression. Finding activities that keep children occupied and happy, responding to children's attempts to communicate, and arranging for children to participate in play activities that involve opportunities for learning and practicing cooperation and sharing should help. Parents can instruct children in peaceful means of resolving conflicts (e.g., teaching them to take turns with a toy rather than fight over it). In the next chapter we discuss in greater detail the research on how to foster the development of sharing and other forms of altruism.

Socializing agents must teach children the lesson that adult attention, approval, and affection depend on the display of acceptable behavior by the children. Numerous behavior

modification programs reveal that when parents and teachers shift their attention away from children's deviant behavior and make a concerted effort to praise children for behaving cooperatively or for just going a specified period of time without behaving aggressively or disruptively, the frequency of aggression declines (Brown & Elliot, 1965; Patterson & Reid, 1970). Sometimes, in the initial phase of a treatment program, children can accumulate tokens for good behavior and exchange these tokens for privileges or goods as they reach certain levels. Long-lasting effects are not generally noted, however, until the children learn that acceptable behavior also leads to social rewards.

A corollary of this principle is that family members who are deficient in the ability to present the positive social reinforcers—praise, approval, smiles, and mere attention—necessary to help sustain behaviors incompatible with aggression must be taught how to become more rewarding. Patterson and Reid (1970) have found that for many parents of deviant children, especially those coming from lower-class backgrounds where family members engage in little positive interaction, this is not an easy task. In fact, in order to motivate some parents to reinforce their deviant child for prosocial behavior, researchers must promise rewards to the parents—such as driving lessons or trips to the hairdresser—for keeping up a program in which they make efforts to reward their children's prosocial behaviors. In other words, many parents of delinquent children have to be trained in how to give positive attention to their children and how to praise their children's good behaviors, and they must be bribed in order to adhere to their role in a behavior modification program with their children. It has sometimes been very difficult to get parents to cooperate in such ventures, but when they can be persuaded, the results are usually well worth the efforts.

The rather simple strategy of eliminating attention for aggression (sometimes by employing the time-out procedure) and training parents, siblings, teachers, and peers to reward alternative desirable behavior may strike one as too low-keyed an approach to deal successfully with extreme antisocial behavior. This is not so, however. A wide range of antisocial behaviors—from simple outbursts of disruptiveness in the classroom to setting cars and buildings afire—has been successfully treated with this basic approach.

Teach Children to Monitor and Control Their Own Behavior

Discipline that helps children learn to accept personal responsibility for acts that cause injury to others should enhance the likelihood that the children will anticipate guilt for behaving aggressively. Inductive reasoning that highlights the negative consequences of children's acts partly fulfills this function (Hoffman, 1970b; Martin, 1975). Directly attributing nonaggressive dispositions to children (e.g., "I know you're the kind of child who hates hurting other people's feelings") may also strengthen their perceptions of themselves as nonaggressive: Children often do strive to live up to prosocial qualities attributed to them. Children who are extremely disruptive in the classroom can also be taught to monitor their own behavior and to reward themselves only for behaving nondisruptively and prosocially. In the chapter on child-rearing practices, Chapter 3, we mentioned a study by Drabman, Spitalnik, and O'Leary (1973) in which aggressive and disruptive boys were taught to make accurate assessments of their classroom disruptiveness and to reward themselves with valuable tokens only when they behaved nondisruptively. The children did learn to monitor and reward themselves accurately, and their behavior improved.

SUMMARY

The questions psychologists confront when trying to define aggression typify the problems social psychologists nearly always face when trying to conceptualize their constructs. Should an actor's motives and intentions be taken into account when trying to decide whether an act is aggressive or not? Do there exist varieties of aggression that should be distinguished from each other? Psychologists still debate these issues.

Aggression may be considered to be in part a trait because at least some children evidence rather consistent and stable predispositions to display above-average or below-average degrees of aggression. But situational influences on aggression are often very powerful, too.

Freud and the architects of the frustration-aggression hypothesis advanced a drive notion of aggression. Their main idea was that frustration arouses a hypothetical aggressive drive that compels the individual to attack his or her frustrator, to attack a substitute (displaced) target, or to turn the aggression inward. Furthermore, both vicarious and direct aggression were believed to drain the individual cathartically of aggressive drive, thus reducing subsequent aggression. It is true that frustration often elicits aggression, but frustration does not always cause aggression, and it is not necessary that it exist before aggression occurs. Reactions to frustration are strongly influenced by a variety of learning experiences. There is no evidence that frustration arouses an aggressive drive that *must* be expressed against some target. Furthermore, vicarious aggression increases rather than decreases aggression. Direct retaliation against a frustrator occasionally eases physiological tension and reduces the likelihood of immediately subsequent aggression, but these effects may be explained without the use of the drive concept. Consequently, the drive notion of aggression is considered today by many psychologists to be misleading and unnecessary.

There are a variety of themes concerning the origins of aggression that, when considered together, provide rather impressive support for the learning theories of aggressive development. People who have found aggression to be successful in eliminating frustration and who have not experienced strong reinforcement histories for performing prosocial behavior incompatible with aggression (e.g., sharing, cooperating, and talking) are most likely to react to frustration with aggression. Patterson's observations of family interaction in homes containing an aggressive child reveal that aggression is often a forceful attempt to turn off the endless irritations, annoyances, humiliation, boredom, and lack of attention provided by the other family members. Numerous studies show that aggressive children are likely to come from homes where the parents employ erratic physical punishment. This causes the children to adopt aggression as a style of personal influence, to avoid their parents, to believe that the only reason for inhibiting aggression is to avoid getting caught and punished, to become hardened to aversive stimulation, and even to take punishment and the threat of punishment as cues for further aggression.

If, for a number of years, a child dwells in a home lacking in encouragement and praise for mature social behavior, but rich in the conditions conducive to the establishment of aggressive habits, the chances of the child's eventually developing a serious conduct disorder are considerably increased. Children who have not learned how to carry on a conversation, who have few interests that overlap with their peers', who have no interest in academic or extracurricular pursuits, and so on, are likely to be rejected by those peers who do espouse these values. Instead, these children are likely to be attracted to peers who share their deficiencies in prosocial behavior as well as their proficiencies at aggression. The children fall prey to a vicious cycle of failing to learn acceptable ways to obtain desired goals while at the same time being exposed to more aggressive modeling and receiving more reinforcement for their aggressive actions.

The contribution that real-life and media models make to the development of aggression again substantiates a learning-theory viewpoint. Aggressive models can teach new modes of injury and destruction as well as disinhibit and elicit previously learned aggressive responses. The ill effects of viewing aggression can be long-lasting and are at least as strong for angered viewers as for nonaroused viewers. Observing completely fictional or make-believe aggression can be just as harmful as watching realistic aggression. Observing aggression leads not only to increases in playful aggression but also to increased injury and decreased altruism toward real people in real-life settings. The effects of viewing aggression are not confined to a given sex or age or to children with already established aggressive tendencies.

Aggression is related to moral development. Children learn that aggression under some circumstances is more justified than aggression under other circumstances, and they also learn to punish themselves with guilt when they aggress inappropriately. Children who learn to expect negative self-evaluations for behaving aggressively tend to avoid aggressive behavior.

Psychologists have found several strategies effective in controlling aggression. These include eliminating the stimuli that provoke aggression (e.g., frustrations and viewing television programs of an aggressive nature), teaching children that aggression does not pay (e.g., refusing to yield to children's attempts at coercion and employing time-out procedures), teaching children prosocial modes of interacting and resolving conflicts, and instructing children how to monitor and control their own behavior. It is important to teach children that it is mature, prosocial behavior that leads to attention, affection, and approval. Encouraging children to participate in acts of aggression, whether vicariously or directly, with the hope of cathartically draining them of their aggressive drives is a strategy of the past and is not recommended.

8 Prosocial Development

This chapter focuses on the socialization of prosocial behavior, or the ways in which children learn to benefit their fellow beings—to share their belongings with a friend in need, to come to the rescue of a distressed or endangered other, to cooperate for the common good rather than compete for personal gain, to praise and compliment others rather than brag about their own accomplishments, and to enhance the well-being of people in still other ways. The last 2 decades have seen psychologists tire of concentrating on the negative aspects of children's development, such as aggression, and turn their interest to the positive side of the nature of children. The growth of humanistic psychology, the emergence of student activism, the peace movement, the concern with civil rights, and the desire of more people for their fair share of the earth's resources have all contributed to this shift of interest (Bryan, 1975; Hoffman, 1977b).

Furthermore, cross-cultural studies that compare the altruistic tendencies of children from different societies have yielded some alarming findings. American youth have been shown to be singularly deficient in prosocial development. They measure lower in helping, sharing, and offering support and comfort than children in many African, Asian, and Western cultures (Madsen & Shapira, 1970; Whiting & Whiting, 1975). As American children get older, they develop competitive streaks that erode their cooperative tendencies (Bryan, 1975; Cook & Stingle, 1974). Many American adults also seem to have developed a concern for the self to the exclusion of a concern for the welfare of others. Their preoccupation with self-awareness, self-actualization, self-improvement, self-assertiveness, self-indulgence, and the like has gained them the reputation of the "Me generation" that lives by the motto of "I'm selfish and I'm proud" (Rushton, 1980).

Much of the current research in altruism is guided by an optimism that it is possible to correct this picture, that one can design child-rearing experiences that will promote the establishment of prosocial habits and attitudes in children. This chapter examines this literature. First we discuss what psychologists mean when they use terms such as prosocial behavior and altruism. Then we briefly outline theories of prosocial development. Next we discuss in turn three sets of factors that influence the child's prosocial development. First are socialization influences, including the kinds of disciplinary pressures for altruistic behavior that exist in the home environment and the extent to which children are exposed to altruistic examples in the media, at home, and in school. Second are situational influences, such as children's momentary mood states and whether their play and work environments are structured for cooperative or competitive interaction. Finally are social-cognitive influences: These include the child's understanding of social norms governing the appropriateness of altruistic action, the child's ability to empathize with and take the role of a distressed other, and the degree to which being altruistic is important to the child's self-image.

THE CONSTRUCT OF ALTRUISM

Definition and Measures of Altruism

Prosocial behavior refers simply to action that benefits other people. The range of actions that qualify as prosocial is broad, as we have noted, and most psychologists use the term prosocial quite loosely. In contrast, a number of psychologists have tried to define more precisely the term *altruism*. For example, some believe that the label of altruism should be reserved for prosocial action that

occurs at a net cost to the actor. Consider the definition of altruism by Bryan and London (1970): "Those behaviors intended to benefit another but which have a high cost to the actor with little possibility of material or social reward." Of course, it is often quite difficult to be sure that someone is performing a helpful response without any expectation at all of some later reward. Some apparently altruistic actions, for example, may be motivated by the knowledge that the recipient will feel obligated to repay the favor later.

Interestingly, children's conceptions of what is kind or altruistic do not always coincide with the views of adults. For instance, adults and older children consider an actor who performs a helpful act without expecting a payoff to be kinder than an actor who performs a similar act with the expectation of personal gain. However, preschool and early-elementary-school children sometimes employ a reverse logic: They believe, for example, that a boy who shares some of his lunch because the teacher promises him a dollar is nicer than a child who shares his lunch without the expectation of reward (Leahy, 1979). Remember that young children tend to define the worth of an action in terms of its material consequences (Chapter 6) and fail to use a discounting schema or the rule that the presence of an external motivator usually implies reduced intrinsic motivation for an act (Chapter 5). Children's conceptions of what is kind and good should be charted more thoroughly because they probably influence not only how children react to assistance from other people but also the likelihood of children performing helpful acts themselves.

How do psychologists measure children's altruistic tendencies? Researchers have tended to concentrate on the development of two aspects of children's altruism: sharing one's belongings with a needy other (generosity) and giving comfort and aid to a distressed person (rescue). In studies of generosity, children are first provided with valuables such as candy, money, or tokens exchangeable for prizes. They are then given an opportunity to donate or share their valuables, anonymously, with less fortunate children. No watchful adults are present, and the children are asked to donate by placing items into a special box, perhaps one decorated with a poster of a starving child. To tap children's tendencies to rescue, children may first be put to work on a task in one room. They then hear a loud crash and cries of pain from an apparently injured person in an adjoining room. Experimenters measure the children's willingness to help. In less dramatic tests, an adult who is interacting with a child suddenly feigns pain, or drops and breaks something of value, in order to see if the child will offer sympathy or help.

Of course, children display prosocial behavior in other ways, too. Investigators have looked at children's tendencies to initiate and sustain positive interactions with others, to smile at and verbally reward their playmates, and to play cooperatively rather than alone or competitively. In one popular laboratory measure of cooperation, children are tested in pairs, seated opposite each other. Each child is given a handle that can make a pointer on a board between the two children either go off to one side (in which case only the child making that response wins a prize) or to the center (in which case both children receive a prize, so long as both children move their pointers to the center). Children who try to coordinate their responses with those of their partners score high on cooperation.

Not all the measures of prosocial behavior are equally applicable to children of all ages. Most we have mentioned have been used with children of preschool age and older. Some recent studies, however, reveal that even infants are capable of rudimentary forms of altruism. For instance, children as young as 1 year try to share with others events and objects that fascinate them, by pointing to them, holding them up for others to see, and even giving them away (Rheingold, Hay, & West, 1976). They also engage in playful interactions that require cooperative turn-taking (Hay, 1979). They sometimes begin to cry when they hear another baby cry, as if reacting empathically (Hoffman, 1975b). The study of altruism in very young children is only a recent enterprise, but it seems essential if we are to isolate the early roots of altruism that need to be nurtured.

The Problem of Underlying Motivation

We have already noted that seemingly altruistic actions are not always motivated by complete self-sacrifice. Often there are hidden motives for apparently altruistic actions. Consider for a moment the wide range of possible motivations underlying helpful acts. Helpful behavior may be motivated by

1   expectations of adult approval

2   fear that failure to help would be punished

3   the expectation that to help will alleviate one's own empathic distress or anxiety caused by another's plight

4   the hope that the recipient will eventually reciprocate the favor

5   the rule that one should repay a previous favor

6   the norm that one should help the needy or the handicapped

7   the rule that it is simply good to give

8   the desire to eliminate guilt or to restore esteem in someone else's eyes

9   the expectation that one will feel pride and pleasure for having acted the way one did

Several psychologists have suggested that because the possible motivators underlying prosocial behavior are so diverse, we ought to consider a *typology* of altruistic acts that is based on what is motivating the act (e.g., Masters & Pisarowicz, 1975; Rushton, 1976; Yarrow, Scott, & Waxler, 1973; Yarrow, Waxler, Barrett, Darby, King, Pickett, & Smith, 1976). In other words, should we say there exist several distinct types of altruism, each with its own motivation? This idea is similar to that of several aggression researchers who proposed that aggressive acts should be distinguished on the basis of whether the aggression is motivated by the desire to hurt someone (hostile aggression), by the desire to attain some nonaggressive goal (instrumental aggression), or by the desire to teach someone a lesson (prosocial aggression). At present, no single typology of altruistic acts has been agreed on. However, researchers are very much aware of the diverse functions that helpful behavior can serve, and they are actively turning to the study of how children acquire the various motivations that can prompt them into acting on another person's behalf. Today, then, psychologists are not so much interested in debating exactly what should or should not be included under the label of "pure" altruism as they are in acknowledging and researching the diverse motivational bases for prosocial action.

THEORIES OF PROSOCIAL DEVELOPMENT

In many ways, altruism can be considered a form of moral behavior. Altruism, like most moral actions, involves self-control and the inhibition of self-indulgence in favor of what is good for others. Why then are we devoting a separate chapter to its development? In part, the answer is a practical one. The research on altruism has grown so voluminous that it simply is more convenient to discuss it separately. But there is another reason. Altruism involves a unique kind of self-denial, namely, self-denial in the interest of a needy *other*. Consequently the development of special other-oriented capacities, such as the ability to empathize with a suffering other and the ability to see what is causing distress in another and how that distress might be alleviated, may be especially relevant to understanding altruism, but less important for other forms of moral behavior.

In this section we shall briefly present theories of prosocial development, some of which do assign importance to the development of other-oriented capacities. Since theories of general moral development also apply to altruistic development, however, we suggest that students review the related material in Chapter 6.

Trait Theory

Trait theorists have been more concerned with the assessment of altruism than with its development. Remember that trait theorists are concerned with the measurement of stable individual differences among people in the tendency to display a particular class of behavior across diverse situations and over time. Is there a general trait associated with altruism? Are children who behave prosocially in one way likely to behave prosocially in other ways as well? Do children possess differing degrees of a predispositional "core" to behave altruistically, making them respond consistently across situations?

The answer to these questions is "Yes." When children are given a battery of tests for altruistic tendencies and their scores on the tests are intercorrelated, positive, though modest, correlations among the measures usually emerge (Bryan, 1975; Krebs, 1970; Rushton, 1976; see also Payne, 1980). Among the varieties of prosocial behavior that have been found to coexist in individuals are sharing, cooperating, giving nurturance and sympathy, thoughtfulness, helping people with their work, verbally acknowledging that concern for others is a worthwhile value, and understanding that the kindest acts are those that are voluntary rather than obligatory (Baumrind, 1973; Dlugokinski & Firestone, 1974; Friedrich & Stein, 1973; Rubin & Schneider, 1973; Rutherford & Mussen, 1968). Children acquire stable reputations for altruism among their peers and teachers, and their reputations correlate rather highly with composite behavioral altruism scores derived from direct observation in several different situations (Hartshorne & May, 1929; Rushton, 1980). In sum, many children do develop some consistency in the degree to which they display altruism across situations and response measures.

Of course, traits should not be mistaken for causes of behavior. Evidence for a trait simply means that, on a descriptive level, people show some consistency on a behavioral dimension. Traits may reflect genetic factors, social learning experiences, or more likely, some combination of the two. One goal of research on altruism is to pinpoint what is responsible for variability among people on the trait of altruism. Are some children more altruistic than others, for example, because they have stronger empathy reactions, because their parents have insisted on altruistic behavior from them, or because they are better skilled at visualizing possible ways to alleviate another's plight?

The evidence in favor of a trait of altruism does not mean that situational influences on altruism are unimportant. In fact, situational factors exert extremely powerful effects on children's prosocial tendencies. Being in a very bad mood or seeing another child punished for sharing are two situational factors, for example, that are likely to depress helpfulness in almost any child, no matter what the child's trait level of altruism. Of course, some people are more influenced by situational factors than others (cf. Bem & Allen, 1974). People for whom altruistic behavior is critical for high self-esteem (e.g., priests) may show consistently high degrees of altruism across situations. Similarly, extremely antisocial individuals may find almost any form of helpfulness distasteful, a source of shame rather than pride, and display low levels of altruism across situations. Most people, however, are probably less consistently high or low in terms of altruism; their prosocial tendencies are more heavily swayed by fluctuating situational circumstances. The questions of how people acquire varying degrees of consistency in altruism and how certain situations acquire the potential to elicit altruism

from some people but not from others are important problems to be investigated.

Learning Theories

Conditioning Theory Conditioning theorists apply principles of operant and classical conditioning to an explanation of altruistic development. Their argument is that altruistic habits are strengthened by external rewards, such as social praise or other payoffs for performing helpful acts. Of course, helpful behavior frequently occurs without any apparent external motivation. To explain this, conditioning theorists invoke the concept of affective conditioning: When a helpful act is externally rewarded, some of the pleasant emotion caused by the reward becomes associated with the helpful act and even with the thought of acting helpfully. The child may act helpfully in the future without external rewards because helping simply feels good by itself; in essence, altruism becomes intrinsically reinforcing (Aronfreed, 1968; Cialdini & Kenrick, 1976; Weiss, Buchanan, Alstatt, & Lombardo, 1971). We shall see some support for the hypothesis that rewarding children for helpfulness nurtures their altruistic dispositions.

Conditioning theorists also stress the conditioning of empathy reactions in their formulations of altruistic development (e.g., Aronfreed, 1968). They point out that if people become distressed when they see another in pain or trouble, then they should be more likely to help that person, in part because alleviating the other's distress should alleviate their own. Similarly, if people become happy when they see others happy, they should be likely to perform actions that lead to others' happiness. Conditioning theorists propose that empathic reactions are often acquired through classical conditioning processes, and especially through the sharing of emotional experiences with other people. Consider these examples: If several children are given ice cream cones at the same time, the children will both feel good and observe signs of feeling good (e.g., smiles) in others; if several children are all scolded for misbehaving, they will feel bad while simultaneously observing signs of unhappiness in others. With each of these shared emotional experiences, the mere sign of an emotional experience in another may acquire the potential to elicit a corresponding emotion in the viewer.

The conditioning theorists, then, often explain prosocial behavior in terms of conditioned emotional reactions. Little emphasis is placed on children's cognitive potential. Children are not viewed as abstracting rules of appropriate conduct or as monitoring their behavior in order to live up to internal moral standards. We turn now to a theory that assigns explicit recognition to these cognitive processes.

Social Learning Theory According to social learning theory (Bandura, 1977), children's moral and prosocial action is guided by the consequences children anticipate for their actions. Children may perform or inhibit prosocial behavior because they expect external reward or punishment, such as praise or criticism from a parent or from the recipient of their helpfulness. But the internal reactions children expect from themselves (e.g., pride, self-congratulations, self-remorse, or guilt) for behaving or failing to behave altruistically are also important. The main determinants of children's expected self-reactions are the children's internal moral standards. On the basis of a wide variety of social learning experiences, children are believed to abstract regularities concerning the occasions on which it is and is not appropriate for people like themselves to perform certain forms of prosocial action. These regularities tend to become internalized by children in the form of personal standards, with the children rewarding themselves when their behavior matches or exceeds their expectations for prosocial action, but punishing themselves when their behavior falls short of their standards.

Among the more influential social learning experiences that contribute to the children's learning of personal standards are verbal instruction (e.g., whether parents encourage and explain the value of prosocial action); modeling exposures (e.g., whether children observe significant others practicing altruism and whether children observe others receive reinforcement for behaving prosocially or for failing to do so); and direct disciplinary experiences (e.g., whether the children find their efforts at altruism rewarded or unrewarded).

The standards children formulate are flexible, changing with social learning experiences, age, and cognitive maturity. In this chapter, we shall chart some of the changes that occur with age in children's conceptions of what constitutes appropriate prosocial action.

According to social learning theory, it is important to study not only the influence of separate social learning experiences (modeling, verbal instruction, etc.) on children's standards but also how children assign weights to various kinds of social information when formulating their standards. For example, are children's standards more greatly influenced by hearing adults preach the virtues of altruism or by actually seeing adults practice altruistic acts? Children's standards, remember, represent their efforts at processing, weighing, and synthesizing diverse sorts of social information. We shall see that a great deal of our knowledge about the development of children's altruistic tendencies has stemmed from research conducted within the framework of social learning theory.

Cognitive-Developmental Theory

According to cognitive-developmental theory, moral development proceeds via a fixed sequence of stages. Each stage is believed to be characterized by unique underlying thought structures, or styles of processing information, which make that stage qualitatively distinct from preceding and subsequent ones. Cognitive-developmentalists have devoted their efforts primarily to charting developmental changes in children's moral reasoning (Kohlberg, 1969; Piaget, 1932). They suggest, for example, that young children's preoccupation with external observable events causes them to judge other people mainly in terms of the objective consequences of their actions rather than in terms of internal criteria such as their intentions and motives.

But the cognitive-developmentalists also contend that the motivational forces compelling children to act prosocially change as children progress through various stages. Prosocial development can be described as proceeding through three stages. Children younger than about 7 years (preoperational children) are considered to be egocentric, incapable of considering another's needs, and responsive only to hedonistic motives, such as the avoidance of pain and the attainment of pleasure. Children of this age should share only when it is likely to lead to one of these desired external outcomes. When children are in elementary school, most are entering the stage of concrete operations. They have had many opportunities to interact with peers (e.g., arguing with their playmates and playing games that require children to assume different roles), which should have helped them learn to separate others' viewpoints from their own. Their new-found capacity to place themselves in another's position and to detect the factors that can cause another's plight or happiness means that their prosocial behavior can be motivated by considerations of the other's welfare rather than their own. During adolescence, children enter the formal operations stage, and they begin to abstract rules based on universal principles of moral fairness (e.g., "Do unto others as you would have them do unto you"). This process should encourage altruistic behavior.

Research carried out by the cognitive-developmentalists, however, has not addressed the issue of whether children's prosocial behavior follows a series of discrete stages. Instead, research has focused on the issue of whether certain cognitive factors believed to motivate altruism actually function in this way. Many studies, for example, have tested the hypothesis that skill at assessing another's perspective and one's altruistic tendencies are positively correlated. We shall see support for the hypothesis that children who have difficulty imagining the separate needs and emotional states of other people tend to engage in few attempts to help other people.

Sociobiology

Is there a genetic basis for altruism? At first glance, a positive answer to this question would appear to contradict Darwin's theory of evolution, which suggests that organisms have survived not because of self-sacrifice but because of an egoistic motivation to outdo others in the race for survival. However, according to Hoffman (1981), who reviewed recent theory and evidence drawn largely from the emerging discipline of sociobiology (e.g., Wilson, 1975), a biological basis for an altruistic motive does seem plausible. According to sociobiologists, many of the activities that have led to reproduction of the species (e.g., hunting, agriculture, and communication) require cooperation, trust, honesty, loyalty, and a willingness to sacrifice for the group. This being the case, it may be that natural selection has favored characteristics that benefit the group or species as a whole rather than the individual.

But there may also be survival benefits to the individual in altruistic action. Trivers (1971) points out that because recipients tend to reciprocate altruistic actions, helpful acts increase the survival chances of the helper as well as the recipient. In other words, if person A rescues person B, the chances that B will someday rescue A are increased. Thus it pays for people to be disposed to helping others.

Eberhard (1975) suggests that the likelihood of a person performing an altruistic act is a direct function of the degree to which the act will help the person's genes survive. Close relations share our genes, so we are most likely to perform acts that help them survive (*kin selection*). However, we are also likely to help distantly related or even unrelated others if doing so also increases the chances of our genes surviving.

All the foregoing views argue for a genetic basis for altruistic motivation. Hoffman (1981) proposes that the specific psychological response that is inherited and that mediates altruistic behavior is empathy, or the tendency to become aroused by another person's distress. We shall see in this chapter support for a link between a person's empathic capacities and altruistic tendencies, but it remains for future research to demonstrate a clear genetic basis for empathic reactions.

SOCIALIZATION INFLUENCES ON PROSOCIAL DEVELOPMENT

What kinds of social experiences are conducive to the formation of altruistic habits? Not surprisingly, psychologists have focused on the effects of various child-rearing practices on altruistic development. How do global dimensions of child-rearing, such as parental warmth-hostility and permissiveness-restrictiveness, relate to prosocial development? How important is it for parents to prompt altruism from their offspring, to reward altruism when it occurs, to punish children when it does not occur, and to provide convincing rationales to children for insisting that they show concern for others? We shall also examine the effects of exposing children to altruistic models. Can children's altruistic habits be strengthened or undermined by how they see their parents, peers, and television heroes behave? What kinds of models influence children the most?

Child-Rearing Practices and Prosocial Development

Parental Warmth and Hostility Common sense might predict that parents who are open in their expression of affection for their children, who are responsive to their children's needs, who prefer praise and reward to criticism and physical punishment when con-

trolling their children, and who strive to provide an atmosphere of mutual interest among family members (by arranging activities the whole family can enjoy, etc.) will foster prosocial sensitivities on the part of their children. Parental warmth should relate to prosocial development for a number of reasons. Loving parents should help reduce children's preoccupations with their own needs, freeing the children to think about the problems of others. Responsive, considerate parents are also setting examples of kindness and sympathy. Parental warmth should help orient children to their parents, making the parents' deliberate attempts to discipline their children toward altruism more successful. Warmth also fosters positive moods in children, and we shall see in this chapter that children in good moods are more disposed toward behaving prosocially.

Research confirms the expected positive relationship between parental warmth and altruism. Children who perceive their parents as especially warm and loving are more generous, supportive, comforting, and cooperative (Hoffman, 1975a; Hoffman & Saltzstein, 1967; Rutherford & Mussen, 1968). We ought to add, though, that simply overindulging children noncontingently with favors is not necessarily conducive to altruistic development. When adults dispense rewards excessively and needlessly, they may create an atmosphere of self-indulgence that actually impedes consideration for others (Weissbrod, 1980). Parental warmth is most helpful in fostering prosocial development when it is dispensed in response to a child's expressed *need* of parental attention and care, as when a child cries for help (Bryant & Crockenberg, 1980).

Parental Permissiveness and Restrictiveness One of our conclusions from the chapter on child-rearing practices was that parents who place age-appropriate demands for mature behavior on their children and then firmly enforce these demands are promoting social competence in their children. It is not enough, then, for parents to limit their disciplinary efforts to the elimination of

unwanted behavior. Parents whose disciplinary approach is purely *reactive,* in that they
discipline their child only when the child does
something that irritates them or that strikes
them as immature or inappropriate, are adopting an insufficient approach to child-rearing.
It is essential that parents also actively construct mental images of the desirable, prosocial modes of behavior that they would like
to see in their children, and then deliberately
build these habits into their children's repertoires. The conclusion that parents must assume an unwavering, "hard-line" commitment to nurturing prosocial expression in
their offspring suggests that doses of parental
strictness may be more conducive to altruistic development than parental permissiveness.

A variety of field and laboratory findings
confirms that demanding prosocial action
from children strengthens their altruistic habits. Altruistic toddlers—those inclined to show
sympathy, to aid, and even to protect distressed others—tend to have mothers who
state forcefully to their children that socially
responsible behavior is expected (Zahn-Waxler, Radke-Yarrow, & King, 1979). Parents
who place demands on their preschoolers to
behave prosocially and who firmly enforce
such demands (with physical punishment,
if necessary) are promoting cooperative,
friendly dispositions in their children, so long
as the parents are also warm and accompany
their disciplinary action with reasoning
(Baumrind, 1973). Parents who use discipline
primarily to promote positive behaviors in
their children rather than to eliminate undesirable behaviors (parents who adopt a *pre-
scriptive* rather than a *proscriptive* approach to
discipline) have children who are more generous (Olejnik & McKinney, 1973).

In their important cross-cultural investigations, Whiting and Whiting (1975) compared the altruism of children from small
communities in six cultures (India, Kenya,
Mexico, Okinawa, the Philippines, and the
United States). Of all the cultures, the American children were the least altruistic, scoring
low on offering help, offering support, and
suggesting to distressed others ways in which
they could improve their situations. The
Whitings concluded that altruism is highest
among children who live in societies that *need*
and *require* altruism from the children of the
society. Specifically, altruism was highest in
cultures that assign many tasks to children
(especially tasks involving care of younger
children and production of food), where the
mothers have considerable work responsibilities outside of the home, and where the family size is large. Under such circumstances,
the children's work makes a genuine contribution to the family's welfare, and the children may see the necessity of prosocial
behavior for everyone's safety, health, and
comfort.

In laboratory experiments, directly instructing children to share leads to increases
in altruism, even after the instructions to
share are dropped. Furthermore, the more
explicit and forceful one makes a request to
share, the more effective it will be. For example, some children might be given a *command* to share some of their winnings from a
game with another child ("You must share
. . ."), whereas other children may be given a
suggestion to share ("You might want to share,
but you don't have to . . ."). Both groups of
children will usually comply with the request
to share, but the former children are more
likely to continue sharing during tests for donating after the experimenter has explicitly
said that sharing is no longer required (Israel
& Brown, 1979; White, 1972; White & Burnam, 1975).

Several studies have tried to "train" children to exhibit helpful behavior by requiring
them to participate in role playing or guided
rehearsal sessions (Friedrich & Stein, 1975;
Skarin & Moely, 1976; Staub, 1971c). In these
projects, the children are required to take
turns at acting out the roles of the helper and
the person being helped in situations calling
for rescue or consolation (e.g., a child trying
to carry a chair that is too heavy for him or
her; a child standing in the path of an oncom-

ing bike). When training sessions are carried out over a period of weeks in the child's natural surroundings (e.g., the preschool), the beneficial effects on the child's altruistic development can be dramatic, persisting for weeks or months and generalizing to new, unrehearsed opportunities for prosocial action.

Considered together, the findings indicate that directly instructing children to behave altruistically, firmly enforcing directives to behave prosocially, and drilling children in altruistic practice have beneficial effects on the child's prosocial development. These findings support a social learning theory perspective, because these strategies for eliciting altruism should make children aware that altruism is expected and is appropriate behavior. And as we saw in Chapter 6, once children formulate rules of appropriate conduct, they often internalize the rules in the form of personal standards of self-evaluation, fearing self-criticism for not performing the expected behavior and expecting self-satisfaction for matching their conceptions of appropriate conduct.

From another theoretical perspective, however, the results we reviewed here are rather startling. Causal attribution theorists, in particular, would argue that when children feel pressured into being good, they should attribute their motivation to the external forces operating on them (e.g., the threat of punishment from their parents). According to attribution theory, once children perceive their good behavior to be externally motivated, they are prevented from concluding that they are intrinsically motivated to be good and, furthermore, they will continue to behave prosocially only when they think the external motivator is still operating. Thus the attribution-theory prediction would be that obvious external pressures for altruism would undermine rather than enhance the development of enduring internalized dispositions toward altruism.

We have seen slim support for this perspective, but admittedly the research we have reviewed has focused on relatively young children. Research on older children and adults may show that attempts to induce altruism through coerced practice sometimes backfire, by generating resentment and negativism, and by preventing people from believing that by nature they are good people. Indeed, some research with adults does show that when adults feel externally coerced into performing an altruistic act, they are less likely to volunteer altruistic action in the future (Uranowitz, 1975).

Skillful parents must adjust their childrearing tactics to the developmental level of their children. Perhaps for young children external insistence on altruism is necessary to teach the children ways of helping and to establish habits of sharing. Young children may view enforced instructions from adults as legitimate expressions of adult authority and therefore experience little resentment over their use. They may also lack the cognitive skills required to realize that external coercion implies a lack of intrinsic motivation (see Chapter 5). Gradually, with age, children may discover themselves occasionally behaving altruistically even in the absence of external motivators. This may result from the force of habit, or possibly from the fact that the children have previously been caught and punished for not behaving altruistically on occasions when they thought nobody was watching, and this has shaken their belief that they are ever truly free of external surveillance. Once children do realize, however, that they are at least occasionally acting altruistically even when they do not have to, the likelihood of their developing self-perceptions of an intrinsic altruistic nature increases (e.g., "If I am performing good acts even when I don't have to, then I must *want* to be a good person"). Adults should be able to facilitate this process of internalizing an altruistic disposition by giving children convincing rationales for altruistic action and by deliberately saying things to children to make them perceive themselves as intrinsically motivated to engage in altruistic behavior. We shall now take a look at how parents can reason with and praise children in ways that bolster the children's feelings that altruism is intrinsically worthwhile behavior.

Preaching and Reasoning Adults who try to get children to share by issuing warnings that simply remind the children of norms of social responsibility (e.g., "You should give to others") are usually not very successful (Bryan & Walbek, 1970; Grusec, 1972; Grusec, Saas-Kortsaak, & Simutis, 1978; Grusec & Skubiski, 1970). To be effective, preaching usually must include some element of reasoning, some justification for recommending altruistic action. Hoffman (1970b, 1975a) emphasizes that parents who justify their requests for altruism with *inductive reasoning* are especially likely to promote altruistic dispositions. Recall (from Chapter 3) that induction involves spelling out to children the consequences of their actions for other people. *Victim-centered reasoning* is a form of induction in which parents point out to children how they have hurt another person and what they can do about repairing the damage.

Victim-centered reasoning should be effective for several reasons: It encourages children to imagine themselves in the other person's place and experience the other's feelings and thoughts; it supplies a rational basis for discipline and fosters a respect for rules; it suggests how children can make up for a wrongdoing; and it helps children learn to identify cues in others (e.g., distress signals, smiles) that should serve as guides to their behavior.

Research supports the hypothesis that induction promotes altruism. Hoffman and Saltzstein (1967) found that girls nominated by their classmates as those most likely to "care about the other children's feelings" and to "defend a child being made fun of by the group" had parents who preferred induction to power assertive discipline. In another study, parents were asked how they would handle hypothetical misbehavior by their children (e.g., how they would react if their child knocked down a friend's block tower,

teased a child, or made fun of a crippled person). Parents who indicated that they would want their children to apologize and make amends were most likely to have children rated as considerate by their peers (Hoffman, 1975a). In an enlightening observational study of toddlers and their mothers, researchers discovered that to be effective, induction should not be dispensed calmly and cooly (Zahn-Waxler et al., 1979). Mothers of highly considerate youngsters delivered their induction forcefully and sometimes harshly in a tone charged with indignation and disappointment (e.g., "Look what you did! Don't you see you hurt Amy? Don't ever pull hair!"). Their communications when their children transgressed were of high clarity and intensity, both cognitively and emotionally, and they helped to emphasize in a variety of ways exactly what is expected for socially responsible behavior.

Laboratory experiments also confirm the importance of induction. Children usually donate more following empathic preaching (e.g., "Well now, I think that people should share with the poor children. They would be so happy and excited if they could buy food and clothes. After all, poor children have almost nothing. If everyone would help these children maybe they wouldn't look so sad!") than after neutral appeals (Dlugokinski & Firestone, 1974; Eisenberg-Berg & Geisheker, 1979; Perry, Bussey, & Freiberg, 1981). In contrast, power assertive reasoning that draws children's attention to the fact that their altruism is externally coerced (e.g., "You'd better share or you'll be spanked!") is probably not a desirable or effective way to elicit long-lasting altruistic attitudes (Perry et al., 1981).

Social Reinforcement and Verbal Attribution If adults react positively when children behave altruistically, by giving the children their undivided attention and lavishly praising them, the children are more likely to act prosocially in the future (Fischer, 1963; Gelfand, Hartmann, Cromer, Smith, & Page,

1975; Grusec & Redler, 1980). In an excellent field experiment, Slaby & Crowley (1977) asked nursery-school teachers to reinforce an experimental group of children whenever the children said anything that hinted of a cooperative intent. For one week, every time a child made a cooperative verbalization (e.g., "Can I help you?"), the teacher immediately exclaimed, "_____(The child's name), you said, '(the exact phrase the child used)'!" This treatment of attending to the child and simply repeating what he or she had said had dramatic effects. Not only were there increases in cooperative verbalizations, but there were increases in physical cooperation *and* corresponding drops in both verbal and physical aggression.

Social reinforcement probably is effective in part because it helps specify expected behavior and thereby contributes to children's formation of standards for self-evaluation. It is also likely that praise for altruism helps children develop self-perceptions of an intrinsic motivation to be altruistic. After all, social reward often includes statements that directly attribute prosocial intent to the child (e.g., "That was very good of you to do that"). In one study (Smith, Gelfand, Hartmann, & Partlow, 1979), when children who had been praised for sharing were asked why they had shared, they attributed their sharing to an intrinsic desire to help or to a concern for the welfare of other children (e.g., "I guess I just like to share"). In contrast, children who had been materially bribed with penny rewards for sharing failed to give reasons for their sharing that referred to an intrinsic desire to share. Children who perceive themselves to be intrinsically altruistic people should strive to behave more prosocially, in part because they fear feeling disappointed with themselves for failing to live up to their high standards.

If social reinforcement is effective in part because it fosters self-attributions of altruistic motivation, then perhaps simply telling children that they possess prosocial attributes will help strengthen their altruistic dispositions. Such is the case. In one study (Jensen & Moore, 1977), an adult first interviewed children about their interests and habits. Then, regardless of the children's answers, the adult verbally attributed cooperative motives to one group of children and competitive motives to another group. To the former group, she remarked, "According to this test it shows you can really get along with others. It also shows that you can play fair, are willing to share, and don't get pushy with others. You work well with others." The latter group was told, "According to this test it shows that you are a real winner. You don't settle for second best but climb right to the top. You also get out and get things done. You could be the best at things you do." Later each child was observed building a block tower with another child. The first group of children cooperated more and showed less jealousy and interference with their coworker.

Adults can also strengthen children's altruistic dispositions if, each time they see a child behave altruistically, they interpret the child's altruism to him or her as a reflection of the child's internal disposition to be altruistic (e.g., "I'll bet you shared because you're the kind of person who likes to help others whenever you can") (Grusec, Kuczynski, Rushton, & Simutis, 1978; Grusec & Redler, 1980). It is difficult to overemphasize the importance of sending children the message that not only is their altruism appreciated by others but that they are by nature intrinsically motivated to perform altruistic actions.

Modeling Influences on Prosocial Development

Effects of Prosocial Models In the last chapter, we saw that aggressive models, such as parents who use brutal physical punishment and television characters who fight and shoot one another, tend to teach children to settle their own disputes aggressively. We also saw that exposure to aggressive models can reduce children's prosocial inclinations, blunting their emotional sensitivity to the suffering of others and reducing their chances of intervening to help someone in distress (Cline, Croft, & Courrier, 1973; Drabman & Thomas, 1974; Liebert & Baron, 1972; Thomas, Horton, Lippincott, & Drabman, 1977). The great number of aggressive models present in real-life situations and in the media is a serious social problem and probably contributes to the low rates of altruism among American youth (Rushton, 1980). Partly because of this, concerned social scientists have turned to the question of whether it is possible to promote prosocial development by deliberately exposing children to models who are exhibiting concern for others.

Results of research on this question, thankfully, are very encouraging. An early study by Rosenhan and White (1967) found that children who observed a model donate half of her winnings from a game she was playing to charity, subsequently donated more of their own winnings from the game than children not exposed to a donating model. Subsequent experiments have shown that a wide range of prosocial acts—expressing sympathy, rewarding others, rescuing, and sharing—is transmittable via modeling (Bryan, 1975). Altruistic models can produce effects that last for weeks, can cause children to behave altruistically even when adults are no longer watching, and can incline children to perform new, unmodeled forms of helping even in situations quite remote from that in which the original modeled acts of altruism occurred (Friedrich & Stein, 1975; Rice & Grusec, 1975; Rushton, 1975; White, 1972; Yarrow et al., 1973). Rushton (1975), for example, found that the effects of observing a generous model lasted beyond the initial experience. In an eight-week follow-up experiment, children donated anonymously not only to recipients they had seen the model donate to but also to a new class of recipients.

Research on altruism is moving out of the laboratory into the child's natural environment. Do the degrees of altruism displayed by children's parents, teachers, and television

heroes influence the children's prosocial development? It seems so. Nursery schoolers whose parents give them lots of affection frequently hug, kiss, give support, and offer friendly greetings to others (Hoffman, 1963; Hoffman & Saltzstein, 1967; Rutherford and Mussen, 1968). Children who are nominated by their peers as being highly considerate and concerned by distress in others are likely to have a same-sex parent who assigns altruism a high place in his or her hierarchy of values (Hoffman, 1975a). Rosenhan (1969) found civil rights activists to have at least one parent who had been committed to an altruistic cause for some time.

In an outstanding field experiment, Yarrow and her associates (1973) studied some of the qualities that help make adults working in nursery schools good models of altruism. They found that adults who interacted warmly with children over a period of several weeks and who periodically modeled acts of altruism for the children (by suggesting and displaying altruistic solutions to the real or the hypothetical distress of other people) were quite effective in getting the children to be more helpful and comforting to others in real-life situations.

Recent years have seen a concern with the development and evaluation of prosocial television. Do programs such as "Lassie," "Mr. Roger's Neighborhood," and "Sesame Street" foster altruism? Sprafkin, Liebert, and Poulos (1975) found that fourth graders who viewed a "Lassie" program (in which a boy risks his life by hanging over the edge of a mining shaft to save Lassie's puppy) were themselves later more likely to rescue a dog that became distressed, even though doing so meant the children had to quit a task that was earning them pennies. Control subjects who saw another "Lassie" program that lacked the prosocial theme behaved less altruistically. "Mr. Roger's Neighborhood" is a program especially designed to portray prosocial themes, including cooperation, helping, sharing, caring about others, valuing oneself and others as unique individuals, listening to others, talking about one's own feelings, using imagination and creative fantasy, and coping constructively with anger and frustration. Having entire classrooms of nursery-school children watch either "Mr. Roger's Neighborhood" or "Sesame Street" episodes daily has also been found to increase the youngsters' natural prosocial behavior in the classrooms (Coates, Pusser, & Goodman, 1976; Friedrich & Stein, 1975; Friedrich-Cofer, Huston-Stein, Kipnis, Susman, & Clewett, 1979).

Why is altruistic modeling effective? It is easy to see why aggressive models make children more aggressive—aggression is fun and thus even brief exposures to others acting aggressively are often enough to disinhibit aggressive impulses. It is more difficult to understand, however, why children also readily imitate self-sacrificing behavior. There are several factors involved. First, recall from Chapter 6 that children's standards of self-evaluation are strongly influenced by how they see models behave. If children perceive significant others behaving altruistically, they are inclined to infer that such behavior is appropriate for themselves as well. They may fear self-censure for failing to act prosocially when the situation calls for it.

Second, altruistic modeling may be effective because it dispels fears people hold about possible adverse consequences of helping others. People are often afraid of helping. Sometimes they are in conflict between the wish to help and other implicit rules of conduct that deter them from helping, such as "Mind your own business," or "Don't interfere." They may also be unsure of *how* to help without looking silly or perhaps even making matters worse. Consequently, they often look the other way or "freeze" when opportunities for altruism arise. Altruistic models can teach people how to help and can show them that helping does not produce negative consequences for the helper (Grusec & Skubiski, 1970; Staub, 1970, 1971b). This should help nudge people who are wondering "Shall I help or shall I not help?" in the direction of action.

Third, altruistic modeling can also illustrate the positive consequences of helping. By observing helpful acts, children learn that altruism produces relief and gratitude in distressed people. Altruistic modeling is especially effective if the models are praised for their altruism (Presbie & Coiteux, 1971) or if the models themselves express obvious satisfaction and pleasure with their actions (Bryan, 1971).

Finally, altruistic modeling may be effective because children are particularly impressed when they see people practice what they preach. It is easy for parents simply to preach altruism, but actually practicing altruism requires real effort and real self-sacrifice. Children apparently know that actions speak louder than words. Several studies show that children are more likely to behave altruistically if they have seen an adult display altruism than if they have merely heard the adult describe and recommend the altruistic action without actually performing it (Bryan & Walbek, 1970; Grusec, 1972; Grusec & Skubiski, 1970). It is particularly bad for adults to act hypocritically, that is, to preach altruism yet fail to show it in action when they have the chance. In fact, children are so repelled by hypocrisy that they may start ignoring the instruction of hypocritical adults (Midlarsky, Bryan, & Brickman, 1973).

Characteristics of Effective Altruistic Models We have already noted that adult attentiveness and affection are qualities that usually help the child's prosocial development. Several experiments have varied the degree to which an adult behaves warmly toward children and then tested the children for imitation of some altruistic response modeled by the adult. Results show that when the modeled altruistic act is some form of *rescue* behavior, model warmth consistently enhances imitation (Bryan, 1975; Staub, 1971a; Weissbrod, 1976; Yarrow et al., 1973). Perhaps a warm atmosphere reduces children's fears about being frowned on for "interfering" with another's situation, or perhaps happy children somehow become more empathically sensitive to the distress of others.

On the other hand, when the modeled altruism is *sharing* behavior, model warmth sometimes reduces rather than enhances imitation of the model's altruism (Grusec, 1971; Weissbrod, 1980). That is, children who see a warm model share sometimes show more stinginess than children who see a neutral, or cold, model share. However, this seems to occur mainly when model warmth has been created by a brief experimental session in which the model noncontingently indulges the children with rewards. This may have the effect of making children feel free to be self-indulgent. In real life, when a model's warmth is established over a long period of time and in the context of contingently responding to the children's needs, warmth may facilitate imitation of the model's sharing. One field study did find that children were especially likely to imitate the generosity of a peer with whom they had enjoyed a long history of friendly interaction at school (Hartup & Coates, 1967). In sum, the modeling of either rescue or sharing in the context of an enduring relationship in which participants care warmly for one another is probably conducive to altruistic development.

Children are especially likely to imitate the altruism of models perceived to hold influence or power over them (Bryan, 1975; Grusec, 1971). They are also likely to adopt the actions of altruistic models if they are given practice in rehearsing or role playing what the prosocial models did. In one study, preschoolers who not only viewed a series of "Mr. Roger's Neighborhood" episodes but also took turns acting out the roles of helper and the person being helped from the episodes later behaved more prosocially in their natural interactions with their peers (Friedrich & Stein, 1975).

In sum, socializing agents who are warmly responsive to children's needs, who set and enforce exacting standards of prosocial conduct for children, who justify their demands for altruism with victim-centered reasoning, who praise children's altruism in ways that promote the children's self-perception of an intrinsic altruistic motivation, and who set a conscientious example of altruism themselves are likely to foster the development of prosocial tendencies.

SITUATIONAL INFLUENCES ON PROSOCIAL BEHAVIOR

Children reared in environments high on all the dimensions we found to promote altruism should have learned a broader variety of ways to help others and have become convinced of the necessity and desirability of showing concern for others whenever and in any way they can. Thus they should score high on trait assessments of altruism—they should be inclined to behave prosocially in diverse ways and across diverse opportunities. Personal predispositions to behave altruistically are not the only contributors to altruistic action, however. Certain situational factors that can fluctuate from moment to moment also affect children's prosocial tendencies. We shall consider four classes of such variables: the presence of bystanders when an opportunity for altruism arises, the child's mood, how the child's work or play environment is structured, and characteristics of the potential recipient of the altruistic behavior.

The Presence of Bystanders

In a celebrated case that occurred in New York City in the 1960s, a woman, Kitty Genovese, was knifed to death in the street while 38 witnesses remained at their apartment windows watching the murder without answering the woman's cries for help or even calling the police. Horrified by the mass indifference, several psychologists decided to study factors that inhibit intervention by people who could help in such emergencies, but do not. One possibility is that the presence of inactive bystanders significantly affects the probability of helping. In other words, the knowledge that somebody else could be helping but is not may contribute to the spread of freezing reactions among group members in emergency situations. In some early experiments on this question, adult subjects who heard a female confederate in an adjoining room apparently fall and hurt her ankle or feign an epileptic fit were indeed far more likely to rush into the next room to rescue her if they had been waiting in a room alone rather than in a room containing other individuals who failed to register concern (Darley & Latane, 1968; Latane & Rodin, 1969). In a developmental study, Staub (1970) gave children of different ages an opportunity to rescue a child who had presumably fallen and hurt herself. Children were tested either alone or in the presence of a partner. The inhibiting effect of bystanders was found to begin in the mid-elementary years.

Why should bystanders reduce rescue attempts? Possibly, inactive bystanders serve as models of lack of concern. It is also likely that a group situation diffuses responsibility, thereby making people feel that they are unlikely to be personally blamed for not intervening.

Mood

People's moods are surprisingly powerful determinants of their inclinations to behave altruistically. In general, positive moods increase altruism. The situation with negative moods is more complex, with negative moods sometimes increasing altruism and sometimes decreasing it. We shall examine the effects of positive and negative moods separately.

Positive Moods A variety of experiences that should make people feel happy have been shown to enhance altruistic tendencies in both children and adults. Children who are asked to think up and dwell on something

that makes them happy—like eating ice cream or getting a nice present—are more likely to share money they have been given than children who have been asked to think neutral thoughts (Moore, Underwood, & Rosenhan, 1973; Rosenhan, Underwood, & Moore, 1974). When adults read statements describing happy moods, they volunteer to serve more hours as subjects in an experiment that involves receiving noxious stimulation (Aderman, 1972). Experiencing success at a game or a task enhances both donating and helping (Berkowitz & Connor, 1966; Isen, 1970). College students who unexpectedly receive cookies while studying in the library, who discover a dime in a phone booth, or who receive a surprise gift packet of stationery are more willing to perform helpful acts like making a phone call for someone or mailing a stamped letter they happen to find (Isen, Clark, & Schwartz, 1976; Isen & Levin, 1972; Levin & Isen, 1975). Even good weather can make a difference. The more the sun shines, the more adults will donate their time as research subjects and the larger the tip they will leave a waitress in a restaurant (Cunningham, 1979).

Clearly, good moods produce a "warm glow of good will." But why? Perhaps happiness increases the individual's self-perceptions of competence and goodness, and this increases the individual's fear of guilt for not behaving altruistically. Or maybe good moods increase people's optimism and confidence about their own welfare, freeing them to be more responsive to the needs of others. Although it is uncertain just what causes positive moods to heighten altruism, children and adults who are successful, popular, emotionally secure, self-confident, and happy are more likely to behave altruistically than people lacking these characteristics (Hoffman, 1977a).

We should note, however, one exception to the rule that positive moods facilitate altruism. When people are asked to imagine someone other than themselves having a good time (e.g., on a vacation in Hawaii), they behave less altruistically than if they are in a neutral mood. Perhaps happiness that derives from contemplating another's good fortune becomes tainted with a jealousy that reduces one's inclinations to help (Rosenhan, Salovey, & Hargis, 1981).

Negative Moods The effects that bad moods—feeling depressed, guilty, or like a failure—have on altruism often depend on the age of the individual. Typically, bad moods depress altruism in children through the elementary-school years. For example, children who are asked to think up and dwell on sad events (e.g., falling down and skinning a knee, not getting invited to a birthday party) usually share less than children asked to think neutral thoughts (Cialdini & Kenrick, 1976; Moore et al., 1973; Rosenhan et al., 1974). The usual interpretation of this finding is that the unhappy children are self-therapeutically trying to cheer themselves up by hanging onto as many of their assets as possible.

There are some exceptions to the rule that sadness decreases altruism in children, however. If the children are tested for altruism in the presence of an adult (or can expect social reinforcement for donating), then sad children may actually donate more than neutral-mood children (Isen, Horn, & Rosenhan, 1973; Kenrick, Baumann, & Cialdini, 1979; Staub, 1968). The theory here is that sadness motivates children to perform actions that will alleviate their sadness and sad children are believed to donate especially large amounts when adults are around because they expect the adults' praise to reduce their depression (Kenrick et al., 1979). Also, if children are asked to dwell on another person's sadness rather than their own, their altruistic tendencies may increase rather than diminish (Barnett, King, & Howard, 1979). Focusing on another individual's misfortune and sadness may arouse empathy, which increases altruism.

In adults, negative moods usually increase altruism. Instructions to contemplate sad events increase adults' donating (Cialdini &

Kenrick, 1976). Guilt, too, promotes helping: Subjects are more likely to volunteer to help another if they have previously given electric shocks to someone (Carlsmith & Gross, 1969) or if they have inconvenienced someone (Freedman, Wallington, & Bless, 1967).

Why do negative moods gradually reverse their effects on altruism with age? There are at least two possibilities. First, with age people are more likely to internalize the norm that helping others is intrinsically desirable. Thus, adults more than children should anticipate feeling good about themselves when they help. Adults may help others when in a bad mood because they expect their feelings of pride and self-satisfaction to cancel out their negative mood (Cialdini & Kenrick, 1976). Second, when asked to think sad thoughts, adults may think of another person's problems, while children think of their own misfortune. Thus thinking sad thoughts arouses empathy in adults but self-preoccupation in children. Interestingly, when adults are asked specifically to focus on their own distress, sadness decreases altruism, just as it does in children (Thompson, Cowan, & Rosenhan, 1980).

The Work and Play Environment

A critical factor influencing the rate of prosocial exchanges among members of a group of children is whether the group is structured for cooperative or competitive interaction. When children are working for shared goals or rewards, altruism is more common than when children are competing for individual prizes (Bryan, 1975; Cook & Stingle, 1974; Nelson & Madsen, 1969). For example, when adults tell children who are working on a project together that they will all share a reward for their efforts, the children engage in more friendly conversation, share more with each other, help each other, praise other group members more, brag less, and put each other down less often, than when the children are told that only one child will be awarded a prize (Stendler, Damrin, & Haines, 1951).

Children who participate in cooperative ventures are also more likely to generalize the pleasant, prosocial manner of interaction that they have learned from such experiences to new interpersonal situations (Barnett & Bryan, 1974; Bryant, 1977; McGuire & Thomas, 1975).

In a classic study of the effects of competition among peer groups, Sherif, Harvey, White, Hood, and Sherif (1961) divided boys at a summer camp into two groups for daily sports competitions. The degree of viciousness between the two groups became so drastic, generalizing into every aspect of camp life, that the authors were motivated to find some strategy that would restore peace. Having the groups work cooperatively toward a common goal (e.g., restoring the water supply to the camp) was successful.

It is clear then that cooperation facilitates and competition impedes prosocial development. In its emphasis on mutual gain, cooperation probably promotes a perception of oneself as a member of a group. This may cause reactions that benefit others as well as oneself. Competitive activity probably fosters a preoccupation with battling and self-concern, which inhibit thinking about others' needs. Teachers and parents are well advised to reward children contingently for group rather than individual accomplishments if they desire to create considerate children (Bryan, 1975).

Other structural variables besides cooperation and competition influence altruism. The more rigidly structured the activities and movements of children in a classroom, the less prosocial behavior the children are likely to show (Huston-Stein, Friedrich-Cofer, & Susman, 1977). It seems that if a classroom is highly structured, children focus attention on themselves as they attend to their independent tasks. Of course, it is unlikely that classrooms that are chaotic, noisy, and crowded will be conducive to altruism either. Further study of the activities at school and home that assist or impede prosocial development is needed.

Are city people more or less altruistic than country folk? Research with adults reveals some interesting findings. The incidence of spontaneous acts of helping in natural settings (e.g., helping a woman stand after she has fallen) is lower in urban than in rural areas (Rushton, 1980). Probably, in the city a number of environmental factors conspire to reduce altruism—the presence of inactive bystanders, distraction from competing sights and sounds, norms of "minding one's own business," lack of familiarity with the victim, and so on. However, when city-reared people are compared with country-reared people in a standardized laboratory test of readiness to rescue a distressed other, the city people do better (Weiner, 1976). Thus, once they are freed of the inhibitors of altruism that prevail in their natural environments, city people show higher degrees of altruism. The intriguing question is why. Does growing up in the city broaden people's conceptions of the in-group? Do country dwellers consider it more inappropriate to try to aid a stranger?

Characteristics of the Recipient

Children tend to be more generous, helpful, and complimentary with their friends and children of similar social class, sex, and background than they are with less familiar others (Krebs, 1970; Newcomb, Brady, & Hartup, 1979; Staub & Sherk, 1970). Children are especially likely to behave generously toward a friend if they fear that their relationship is threatened, and if they view their generosity as a means of restoring their friendship (Staub & Noerenberg, 1981).

There is an exception to the rule that children are more generous to friends than nonfriends, however. Sometimes boys are less helpful toward close male friends than toward strangers or mere acquaintances, especially if they fear that helping the friend will put them at a disadvantage relative to the friend. For example, a boy may be reluctant to share a tool or a resource with a close friend if he fears that doing so will allow the friend to build or make something better than what the first boy possesses. It seems that close male friendships often involve a strong element of competition, and when boys believe that helping another will reduce their own status compared to the friend's, they may inhibit helping (Berndt, 1981a, 1981b; Staub & Noerenberg, 1981).

We should also note that children sometimes are less generous or helpful toward other children of a similar age than they are toward children who are of a different age, especially children who are younger than themselves. Naturalistic observations of children's play groups suggest that there is more prosocial behavior when there is some mix in the children's ages than when the children are all of a similar age (Hartup, 1979; Whiting & Whiting, 1975). In mixed-age interactions, there is more nurturance, protectiveness, and cooperation; there is less competition. Also, in mixed-age groups disputes tend to be settled less through overt aggression than through dominance-submission relations (the children can tell in advance who is likely to win a fight, so arguments are settled quickly without fighting, usually in favor of the more dominant member).

For a unique look at the question of whether people are more likely to behave altruistically toward same-sex or toward other-sex recipients, Davis, Rainey, and Brock (1976) invented a "pleasure machine." College students were instructed to reward a confederate for making correct responses on a learning task by choosing to press (for each correct response) 1 of 10 buttons that presumably delivered varying intensities of pleasurable vibrations—to a recipient's buttocks. The major finding was that subjects tended to administer more pleasure to opposite-sex recipients than to same-sex recipients. However, if the recipient was an especially attractive person or emitted enthusiastic verbal responses to the vibrations, less pleasure was given opposite-sex than same-sex partners. Possibly, an attractive or responsive cross-sex recipient added sexual

overtones to the situation, and subjects may have felt that excessive pleasuring to an opposite sex partner might appear to be too forthright for an initial encounter.

In the course of growing up, children learn rules about what kinds of people are and are not appropriate to help. For example, people are supposed to come to the aid of those who have previously helped them, who really need assistance, who do not deserve their misfortune, and so on. In the next section we take a look at the norms children learn and whether these norms influence their altruistic behavior.

SOCIAL COGNITION AND PROSOCIAL BEHAVIOR

Here we examine relationships between what goes on in children's minds and their altruistic behavior. A number of social-cognitive factors are implicated in altruism: the degree to which children internalize society's norms of appropriate conduct in the form of personal standards, the sophistication of the criteria children use to justify prosocial action or inaction (moral reasoning), the inferences and evaluations children make about another's plight and its causes (role taking), and the degree to which behaving altruistically is important to the child's self-concept. We shall consider each of these factors.

Children's Understanding and Use of Norms

According to social learning theory, children abstract rules of appropriate conduct from a variety of social learning experiences, including what they hear people preach, how they see others behave, and how they are disciplined for their own behavior. Once children discern how people like themselves are supposed to act, they often internalize the rules in the form of personal standards, coming to reward themselves for living up to their standards, but punishing themselves when they fall short of them. That children do learn that altruism is a behavior worthy of self-praise is evident in a study by Masters and Pisarowicz (1975): Children rewarded themselves more for performing a tedious task if they believed their behavior was benefiting another child than if they had no knowledge of the altruistic effect of their behavior. Children also learn more subtle rules governing altruism—rules saying when an altruistic response is called for, and when it is not. We shall have a look at the relationship of some of these norms to altruistic behavior.

The Norm of Social Responsibility According to some psychologists, a norm of social responsibility, or the idea that help should be given to others on the basis of their need or dependency regardless of the likelihood of external reward for such help, often motivates altruism (Berkowitz & Daniels, 1964). Some acts of altruism do seem at least partly motivated by an acceptance of this norm. Adults, for example, are more likely to help recipients who really need help than they are people who are less in need (Krebs, 1970). As children get older, they increasingly verbalize an acceptance of the norm of social responsibility. However, simply being aware of the norm is not always enough to guarantee real-life helping (Peterson, 1980). If a potential recipient's need is not salient enough to arouse children's empathy or if incentives for nonaltruistic behavior exist in the situation, even children well aware of the norm may avoid altruism.

The Norm of Deserving According to Long and Lerner (1974), people like to believe that "People get what they deserve" because it reassures them that the world is a fair and predictable place. This motive, sometimes called the "just world motive," presumably causes people to try to ensure that resources and help are distributed fairly. Indeed, children (and adults) are more charitable to recipients who do not deserve their plight than they are to recipients who bring their misfortune on themselves (Barnett, 1975; Miller &

Smith, 1977). Students, for example, are less likely to say that they would loan their class notes to a classmate who had skipped class to go to the beach than to a classmate who had developed an eye problem and was unable to attend class (Weiner, 1980).

Also in line with the justice motive is the finding that children who unexpectedly and undeservedly receive a windfall of assets (perhaps by being overpaid for carrying out some task) often try to redistribute their wealth by sharing it with others (Long & Lerner, 1974; Miller & Smith, 1977; see also Olejnik, 1976). The reverse situation also confirms the justice motive: Children who receive less than their fair share of resources often react stingily on subsequent tests of altruism, as if trying to right the balance (Masters, 1971; Miller & Smith, 1977).

The Norm of Reciprocity The norm of reciprocity is the rule that people should help, and should not injure, those who have helped them (Gouldner, 1960). Children usually become aware of this norm around the time they begin school (Berndt, 1979b). Studies show that children and adults do return favors (Dreman, 1976; Peterson, 1980). For example, the more prior help a teenage subject received from a partner in completing a puzzle, the more help the subject was likely to give the partner (Cox, 1974). Several factors influence the likelihood of reciprocating help (Krebs, 1970). These include the need state of the original donor (if a donor gives away something he or she really needs, the chances of later reciprocal helping from the recipient are increased), the resources of the original donor (a donor who gives from a limited resource supply is more likely to be helped later), and the motives of the original donor (if a donor is sincere and gives of his or her own free will, the chance of reciprocity is increased).

Because the norm of reciprocity implies that one's favors should be returned, helping or giving may sometimes be prompted by external considerations, such as expectations of future reciprocity or the desire to form new reciprocal relationships, rather than by an unselfish desire to help. Studies do show that people give to those from whom they stand to gain. These tendencies are stronger among the sons of "entrepreneurial" fathers, or self-made businessmen, than among the children of working-class men or other middle-class men whose profession is traditionally of a less competitive nature (Berkowitz & Friedman, 1967; Dreman, 1976; Dreman & Greenbaum, 1973). Of course, if a recipient becomes suspicious that a benefactor is deliberately trying to indebt him or her, the likelihood of reciprocal altruism diminishes (Dreman, 1976; Lazarowitz, Stephan, & Friedman, 1976).

Norms of Distributive Justice (Equity vs. Equality)   Norms of distributive justice are the rules people use when they are asked to divide rewards among members of a group who have been working on a task but have contributed in different degrees to the task's completion. For example, a child may be asked to work with another child pasting stickers onto boards or sorting blocks into containers. The experimenter arranges things so that one child fills 15 containers with blocks and the other child only 5. Each subject is then asked to divide a pool of money or candy between him- or herself and the other worker in any way that he or she wishes. Of interest is the rule used by the children to divide the rewards. Do the children selfishly grab all or most of the rewards for themselves? Do the children divide the rewards carefully on the basis of each member's relative input (a norm of *equity*) or simply give each member the same amount (a norm of *equality*)? Do the norms of distribution children employ change with age?

Children younger than 4 or 5 tend to act in ignorance of any norms of distributive justice. When asked to divide rewards, they simply take for themselves the greater proportion no matter what the contributions they or their partners have made (Lane & Coon, 1972; Masters, 1971; Nelson & Dweck, 1977).

If any norm is operating, it is one of self-interest.

By kindergarten or first grade, self-interest distributions are relatively rare. Instead, children now spontaneously employ one of two norms in their distributions: the norm of equity or the norm of equality (sometimes called the norm of *parity*). Children who divide rewards in proportion to each member's contribution are assumed to be using an equity norm; children who divide the rewards equally among members are assumed to be using an equality norm.

Distributions based on equity and equality norms replace those based on self-interest for both social and cognitive reasons. Children gradually realize that acting on self-interest is frowned on, and thus they are motivated to employ a more socially acceptable norm. Of course, children must be able to count and halve before they can use the norm of equality, and they have to be able to weigh simultaneously the relative inputs of contributors before they can divide on the basis of equity (Enright, Franklin, & Manheim, 1980; Hook & Cook, 1979; Lane & Coon, 1972; Larsen & Kellogg, 1974; Peterson, Peterson, & McDonald, 1975; Tompkins & Olejnik, 1978).

By first grade, most children have acquired the capacity to employ both equity and equality norms. The really interesting question, however, concerns what makes children decide between using an equity or an equality norm when faced with an opportunity to divide rewards. Several social variables operating in the particular situation seem to influence which norm children choose to employ. First, when children are told that they are a "team" working for a common goal, equality distributions increase and equity distributions decrease (Barnett & Andrews, 1977; Lerner, 1974). Second, if children are led to believe that they will have future social interactions with other group members, equality distributions increase (Graziano, Brody, & Bernstein, 1980; Shapiro, 1975). Third, children told that they are "supervisors" are more likely to use equity distributions (Streater & Chertkoff, 1976). A fourth factor is that boys show more concern with equity and girls with equality, probably because of boys' greater socialization for competitive, instrumental behavior and girls' socialization for concern with group welfare and desire to comfort those less successful than themselves (Barnett & Andrews, 1977; Leventhal, Popp, & Sawyer, 1973). Females also tend to underpay themselves (Callahan-Levy & Messe, 1979). Finally, the amount of the child's own contribution makes a difference: The less a child's own contribution, the more likely he or she is to divide rewards equally (Streater & Chertkoff, 1976). Although self-interest may gradually give way to norms of equity and equality, it no doubt remains a potent force in children's distributive justice.

Comment on Norms   There is little question that children rapidly do become aware of norms of social responsibility, deserving, reciprocity, equity, and equality. They also learn that it is good to behave in accordance with such norms (Bryan & Walbek, 1970; Masters & Pisarowicz, 1975). However, there are problems when it comes to invoking norms as explanations of altruistic behavior.

First, it is often difficult to identify a single norm as the basis for the performance of a given altruistic act. For example, a child may give to a person in need, apparently acting in accordance with the norm of social responsibility; however, the child may not act out of a desire to follow the rule that one should help needy others, but because he or she expects that the recipient will one day reciprocate. Second, altruistic acts that appear to reflect an altruism norm may reflect something other than the operation of a norm: Children may help needy others because helping reduces their empathic emotional distress rather than because of a norm of social responsibility; being overpaid may enhance children's altruism because it puts them in a good mood, not because it activates a justice motive; or children may repay favors

not because of a norm of reciprocity but because the original donor has modeled an act of altruism. Finally, Hoffman (1975b) suggests that many helpful acts, especially those in emergency situations, seem to be more impulsively and spontaneously initiated than the operation of norms would suggest.

Before concluding that norms function as independent causes of behavior, it would seem necessary to show that the degree to which people endorse a specific norm (measured perhaps by paper-and-pencil tests) predicts how much they actually behave in accordance with that norm (in situations where alternative, nonnormative explanations for behaving altruistically can be ruled out). So far, attempts at this have not been successful (Bryan, 1975; Bryan & Walbek, 1970).

Moral Reasoning and Altruism

What factors do children consider when deciding whether it is right or wrong to offer help, and do these considerations relate to their altruistic behavior? Eisenberg-Berg has studied the development of children's "prosocial moral reasoning." In one revealing experiment, children first heard stories in which a central character had to decide whether or not to help someone else when the altruistic act would be performed at personal cost. Then the children had to indicate whether the character should help or not and, more important, they had to give reasons for their decisions. Here is an example of a story used with preschoolers (Eisenberg-Berg & Hand, 1979):

> One day a girl named Mary was going to a friend's birthday party. On her way, she saw a girl who had fallen down and hurt her leg. The girl asked Mary to go to her house and get her parents so that the parents could come and take her to a doctor. But if Mary did run and get the child's parents, she would be late to the birthday party and miss the ice cream, cake, and all the games.
>
> What should Mary do? Why?

Preschoolers' and elementary-school children's reasoning is frequently hedonistic ("I like birthday cake, so Mary should go to the party"), stereotyped ("It's nice to help"), or approval-oriented ("Mary's mother would want her to help"), but it does also often refer to the recipient's needs ("Mary should help because the girl's leg hurts"). As children get older, their reasoning becomes increasingly needs-oriented and begins to reflect the internalization of more general rules ("If everyone helps, we'd all be better off") (Bar-Tal, Raviv, & Leiser, 1980; Eisenberg-Berg, 1979a; Eisenberg-Berg & Hand, 1979).

Do children who employ the more developmentally sophisticated reasoning methods to support their decisions actually behave more altruistically? Yes, and this relationship between altruistic reasoning and altruistic behavior is present from a surprisingly early age. Eisenberg-Berg and Hand (1979), for instance, found that preschoolers who base their decisions on the needs of a recipient rather than on their own hedonistic desires engage in more spontaneous sharing with their peers in the natural preschool environment. Possibly, children who justify altruism by referring to another's needs are responding more empathically, and, as we shall see, empathy correlates positively with prosocial action.

Empathy and Role Taking

Empathy involves reacting to another person's situation or display of emotion with the same emotion as the other is experiencing. A child who feels sad when another is sad, angry when another is angry, happy when another is happy, and so on, is said to be responding empathically. Empathy should be distinguished from role taking. Role taking involves accurately comprehending what another is feeling, thinking, or perceiving, but it does not necessarily entail actually feeling the same way as the other person. One can realize another is angry, for example, without personally experiencing the anger. Both empathy and role taking, however, are other-oriented capacities, and both have been implicated in altruism.

Empathy How does empathy develop? A capacity for empathy may be partly innate, and primitive empathy reactions, such as a baby crying in response to another baby crying, are evident quite early in life (Hoffman, 1975b; 1981). But social learning experiences are important, too. Learning theorists (Aronfreed, 1968; Bandura, 1977) suggest that children will learn to react empathically to expressive cues in others if they frequently *share* emotional experiences with other people. If two children frequently experience happiness or sadness at the same time, then signs of happiness or sadness in one child should, by classical conditioning, acquire the capacity to arouse a corresponding emotional state in the other. Experiments support this reasoning (Aronfreed, 1968; Midlarsky & Bryan, 1967). And, if shared social experiences are important, then one might predict that socially deprived individuals will be less likely to react empathically. An animal experiment confirms this: Monkeys isolated for their first year of life fail to show the normal quickening of heart rate when they see another monkey in distress (Miller, Caul, & Mirsky, 1967). Boys who have developed a close friendship with another boy are more altruistic, possibly because they have had more opportunities for sharing pleasant and unpleasant experiences with another (Mannarino, 1976). Parents should be able to strengthen children's empathic responding if, when disciplining their children for causing another's distress, they draw their children's attention to the other's distress while at the same time scolding the child (Maccoby, 1980).

Are people who score high on tests of empathy more altruistic? One would predict that this is so. Empathic people should be motivated to perform responses that cause happiness or relieve distress in another person because doing so will make him feel better, too.

The strength of the expected empathy-altruism link increases with age. Preschool children who report feeling happy or sad when they hear stories or see slides depicting these emotions in other people (high-empathy children) sometimes do score high on measures of prosocial behavior, such as cooperation (Marcus, Telleen, & Roke, 1979), absence of competition (Barnett, Matthews, & Howard, 1979), sharing, and helping (Buckley, Siegel, & Ness, 1979). However, other studies find empathic preschoolers to be less prosocial (Eisenberg-Berg & Lennon, 1980) and more aggressive (Feshbach & Feshbach, 1969; Murphy, 1937) than their less empathic peers. Reasons for the confusing findings are not at all clear and are currently a subject of much investigation. Inconsistencies in the way empathy is measured may be especially important.

Among older individuals, empathy-altruism relationships are more consistently positive. In one study, first-grade boys who reported being afraid when they heard someone fall and crash more speedily initiated a rescue or called for help (Weissbrod, 1976). High-school boys who scored high on an empathy questionnaire by endorsing such statements as, "It makes me sad to see a lonely stranger in a group," volunteered to serve more hours in a dull experiment (Eisenberg-Berg & Mussen, 1978). University men who reacted physiologically to the sight of pain faked by an experimental confederate were subsequently more likely to sacrifice money or take an electric shock in order to help another, particularly if the men perceived themselves as similar to the confederate in interests and personality (Krebs, 1975).

Role Taking   In Chapter 5, we discussed at length how children gradually outgrow their egocentrism (confusing their own perspective on a situation with that of others) and become more skilled at accurately inferring what other people are thinking, feeling, and perceiving. It makes sense to think that children who can place themselves in a po-

tential recipient's shoes, and can accurately decipher the factors responsible for the other's misfortune, will be better equipped to intervene on the other's behalf.

From an early age, role taking skills relate positively to prosocial behavior. Youngsters who are cooperative, generous, and helpful do well at tasks that require them to choose a picture that correctly depicts the emotion experienced by a story character, to rotate a display of plastic figures so that they can see the same view as a doll with a different perspective, to communicate to a peer in a way that takes the peer's viewpoint into account, and to consider a story character's motives and intentions when asked to judge the goodness or badness of the character's actions (Buckley et al., 1979; Dreman, 1976; Johnson, 1975; Rubin & Schneider, 1973). Furthermore, providing children with practice in role taking can increase their altruistic tendencies. For example, children who were required to act out in skits how each of several story characters was reacting to a situation were later more likely to share with a needy other (Iannotti, 1978).

Hoffman's Theory: Altruism is Motivated by a Combination of Empathy and Role Taking   According to Hoffman (1975b), both empathy and skill in role taking are necessary to motivate altruism. An empathically aroused person will take little altruistic action unless he or she realizes that it is another person's situation that is causing the emotional arousal. Similarly, taking the perspective of another will not be very effective unless one personalizes the other's reaction, imagining how it would feel to be in the same situation. It is people who are not only emotionally aroused but who also know what is causing the arousal and how to alleviate it that are most motivated and capable of taking altruistic action.

Hoffman believes that empathy is present as early as infancy, though it increases with age and social learning experiences. Systematic age changes in children's role taking capacities, however, place limits on their ability to act altruistically and are associated with age changes in the way children try to express altruism when empathically distressed. Hoffman outlines four stages in the development of altruism.

In the first stage, corresponding roughly to the first year of life, infants are believed unable to differentiate themselves from others. Consequently, although infants may react with some empathic distress to another's cries, they fail to realize that the cause of their distress lies with the other. Thus, they try only to comfort themselves, as by sucking their thumb, and ignore the distressed other.

The second stage, occurring between the ages of 1 and 2, is marked by the attainment of person permanence, or the knowledge that others exist as independent entities. However, when children of this age become empathically distressed, they experience confusion over the cause of the upset, wondering whether it originates within themselves or with someone else. Not knowing for sure the cause of the upset, the children take little realistic action to alleviate it. Consequently, they may try to comfort the other person in ways in which they themselves have been comforted, as by offering their teddy bear or kissing the distressed person.

Sometime between the ages of 2 and 3, children realize that the cause of empathic distress lies with another. Thus the child tries to locate and terminate the condition hurting the other person. At this stage, however, children can respond empathically only when they are in the immediate presence of a distressed other; they do not become empathically aroused by imagining how someone who is not in their immediate presence may be suffering.

Finally, when children are between 6 and 9 years of age, they realize that other people lead lives apart from the occasions on which the children observe them. In other words, children now know that even when others are not in sight, they are behaving, thinking, and feeling in response to their own unique circumstances. Now empathy can be aroused simply by imagining that another is suffering. If a child's mental representation of another's plight falls short of some minimal standard of well-being, sympathetic distress is aroused, which can lead the child to take altruistic action—either preventive or corrective—even in the physical absence of the person in danger.

Hoffman's basic hypothesis—that it is the joint occurrence of empathic reaction and mature role taking that motivates altruism—is plausible and intuitively appealing, but validation of Hoffman's stages must await further research. One recent study with adults, however, lends support to some of Hoffman's ideas. Gaertner and Dovidio (1977) found that adults were most likely to rescue a woman who had fallen and hurt herself if they not only had an empathic reaction (assessed by a quickened heart rate) but also perceived their distress to be caused by the woman's injury. In contrast, subjects who were aroused by the woman's fall, but who were led to believe that their arousal was caused by a drug they had taken prior to the experiment, were less altruistic. Thus empathy combined with a correct causal attribution of the distress (a component of role taking) led to the greatest acts of altruism.

Self-Perceptions

Students of altruism have tended to emphasize knowledge of others' feelings and thoughts (empathy and role taking) as important ingredients of altruism, but recent research shows that knowledge of the self also figures in one's concern for others (Grusec & Redler, 1980). Children who learn to value altruistic action, to regard it as essential for their self-esteem, and to have confidence in their ability to perform the actions that will alleviate another's plight should behave more altruistically.

We have already noted that children who are told by adults that they are intrinsically motivated to behave cooperatively or generously do behave more prosocially than children who have not received such motivation

(Grusec & Redler, 1980; Jensen & Moore, 1977). Possibly, when children hear good things about themselves, they come to believe the information, and the attributions thus become part of their conceptions of themselves. These children may then strive to perform altruistic behavior when given the opportunity because they fear guilt and self-criticism for not living up to their expectations.

Helping often requires doses of self-confidence and courage, too. Understandably, children who are given the opportunity to rescue a distressed other often show signs of being afraid. They may fear that what happened to the distressed person will befall them also, or they may fear embarrassment for themselves or for the person they are trying to help. In one study, for example, preschool children who were given an opportunity to rescue showed approach-avoidance behavior, as if unsure about what to do: The children sometimes started in the direction of the distress cues, but then ran back to their seats (Yarrow et al., 1976). It is not surprising, then, that a moderate degree of courageousness, outgoingness, willingness to take risks, and even aggression are frequently associated with children's propensities to give aid (Barrett & Yarrow, 1977; Bryan, 1975; Friedrich & Stein, 1975; Yarrow et al., 1976). Even adults, if they are worried about their own safety, are likely to display signs of uncertainty in rescue situations (Wilson, 1976). Clearly, as we stressed earlier, an important aspect of socialization involves deliberately giving children practice in altruistic action, so that the children develop the skills and the confidence needed to take positive prosocial action when necessary.

SUMMARY

Alarmed by evidence that American children are singularly deficient in cooperating, sharing, helping, and showing respect and concern for other people, psychologists have turned to the study of factors that cultivate and undermine prosocial development. Prosocial behavior may be considered a form of moral behavior, but it involves special other-oriented skills and capacities (the tendency to empathize with others' suffering, knowledge of what is causing another's plight and how it might be alleviated, and so on) that many other varieties of morality do not.

How well do the various theories of altruism fare? The trait-theory prediction that stable individual differences exist among children regarding the tendency to behave prosocially across situations and in different ways (in other words, that it is meaningful to say that some children are in a "high-altruistic" category and others are in a "low-altruistic" category) receives modest support. The fact that there is some cross-situational consistency in displays of altruism, however, does not negate the fact that momentary situational factors also exert a strong influence on altruistic behavior. Unfortunately, trait theory has little to say about how prosocial traits develop or fail to develop.

Conditioning theorists apply principles of operant and classical conditioning to explain prosocial development. They suggest, for example, that altruism can be instrumentally conditioned by social reinforcement and that empathic reactions result from a classical conditioning process (with a distressed other's pain cues serving as conditioned stimuli, eliciting a similar reaction in the observer). Though their predictions are supported, the conditioning theorists neglect the well-documented influence of cognitive factors in prosocial behavior.

Social learning theorists argue that children's altruistic behavior, like most forms of social behavior, is under cognitive control. Children are thought to generate rules about the appropriateness of various forms of prosocial action in various situations (e.g., "You are supposed to share your toys with children who don't have any and don't have the money to buy any"). Children are believed to form their rules on the basis of a wide variety of direct and vicarious social learning experiences, including the verbal instructions and reasoning they have heard from adults, the disciplinary pressures they have experienced when they are expected to behave prosocially, and the degree to which they have seen others practice altruism. Once children generate rules of conduct, they often internalize the rules into "personal standards," coming to fear self-criticism for not performing altruistic actions when their rules call for it and to expect feelings of pride for adhering to their rules of self-sacrifice. There is strong support for the social learning hypothesis that socialization pressures and altruistic modeling influence children's internalization of altruistic dispositions.

The cognitive-developmentalists' view that altruistic development proceeds via a fixed sequence of discrete stages has few data to recommend it. However, these theorists have pointed to one crucial social-cognitive skill that plays a major role in altruistic expression: role taking. Children who can break away from their own egocentric perspective on a situation to consider a potential recipient's needs and wants are more inclined to behave altruistically.

There appears to be a relationship between child-rearing practices and prosocial development. Parental warmth and responsiveness to children's needs facilitate altruism (so long as the warmth does not take the form of noncontingently indulging children with favors). Parents can foster altruistic habits by demanding prosocial behavior from their offspring and refusing to tolerate nonaltruistic action. Simply preaching platitudes such as "It is good to give" is usually ineffective in eliciting altruism, but providing children with justifications for requiring altruistic action (e.g., by employing victim-centered inductive reasoning) is very helpful. Praising children when they cooperate, share, or help, and verbally attributing prosocial motivation to them are also recommended socialization practices.

Observing aggressive models undermines children's altruism, whereas seeing examples of helpfulness strengthens it. Parents, teach-

ers, peers, and television characters can all be effective as altruistic models. Altruistic modeling is effective because it helps children acquire standards of acceptable conduct and because it helps children see that helping can produce positive benefits for the helper as well as the recipient.

Fluctuating situational circumstances can dramatically influence children's prosocial tendencies. For instance, people are less likely to attempt a rescue if they are among a number of inactive bystanders, probably because the bystanders diffuse responsibility and serve as models of inaction. The moods of individuals make a difference, too: Good moods create a "warm glow of good will" that increases altruism in both children and adults; bad moods tend to depress altruism in young children, but promote it by adulthood. Teachers and parents can increase children's prosocial interactions if they structure the children's work and play environments to stress cooperation rather than competition. Children tend to be more altruistic toward their friends than toward strangers. Also, there is more helping, nurturing, sharing, and cooperating among children playing in mixed-age groups than among children who are playing with others who are very close in age. Homogeneity in age seems to elicit competition.

Psychologists are studying links between social cognition and prosocial behavior. Children learn a number of norms governing prosocial action. They learn that it is good to help needy others (the norm of social responsibility), that help should be given to people according to whether they deserve their misfortune (the norm of deserving), that it is good to return favors (the norm of reciprocity), and that rewards should be divided fairly among members of a working group (the norms of equality and equity). Although most children learn these rules, there is some question as to whether children who endorse the norms most strongly actually are the most altruistic.

Children who justify their recommendation that a story character behave altruistically by pointing to the needs of the recipient tend to be more altruistic than children who are preoccupied with their own needs and wants. A capacity for empathy (responding emotionally to another's expression of emotion) and also for role taking (accurately inferring the nature and causes of another person's feelings and thoughts) relates positively to prosocial behavior. Children who are confident in their ability to act effectively on another's behalf and who consider themselves to be altruistically motivated tend to act more altruistically when the opportunity arises.

9
Sex Differences and Sex Typing

Males and females differ psychologically as well as biologically. As a group, for example, boys are more aggressive, more interested in consorting with their peers, and more proficient at mathematics than girls; girls are more nurturant, more interested in interacting with adults or playing alone, and more interested in art and music than boys. Furthermore, within each sex there exist marked individual differences in the degree to which children display the behaviors that are typically associated with their own sex rather than the other sex. One boy may be especially aggressive, show a strong preference for the company of his peers over that of adults, and so on, whereas another boy may show a less "masculine" and more "feminine" pattern of interests and behaviors. In this chapter, we summarize what we know about differences between the sexes in personality and social behavior. We also try to evaluate various the-

oretical explanations of the *sex-typing* process. Sex typing, also known as *sex-role development*, is the process whereby children come to acquire the behaviors, attitudes, interests, emotional reactions, and motives that are culturally defined as appropriate for members of their sex.

We begin the chapter with a summary of sex differences in personality and social behavior. Some of our conclusions will confirm the stereotypes that many of us hold about sex differences. For example, boys are indeed the more noncompliant and defiant sex. But other conclusions may be surprising and shatter some of our myths. Girls, for example, cannot simply be pegged as the more sociable, more dependent, and more conforming of the two sexes. In fact, there are numerous situations where boys are more sociable and conforming than girls.

The discussion of sex differences is followed by a review of major theories of sex typing. We first discuss trait theory, paying particular attention to the ways in which researchers conceptualize and measure masculinity and femininity. We then review the Freudian, the social learning, and the cognitive-developmental approaches to understanding sex-role development. We illustrate how biological, cognitive, and social learning factors all interact to influence a child's sex typing.

Next we consider in more detail the cognitive bases of sex typing. How do children come to know what sex they are? How do children learn what is expected behavior for the two sexes? Do children's ideas about their own sex and about what is expected from members of their sex influence their adoption of sex-linked attitudes and attributes?

Despite the trend toward more egalitarian sex roles in contemporary society, children still face considerable pressures to conform to culturally prescribed sex roles. Parents play a major role in this pressuring process, but readers may be surprised at the degree to which teachers, playmates, and even the television set also help socialize children toward traditional sex roles.

Finally, we consider whether customary sex roles are appropriate today. Traditionally, it has been thought that a strong preference for same-sex activities and interests contributes to one's psychological adjustment and well-being. Several contemporary psychologists are questioning this concept, wondering whether individuals and society might not be better off if children were socialized to be a little more *androgynous,* which means a blend of the masculine and the feminine.

SEX DIFFERENCES

Here we briefly review sex differences in play patterns, peer relations, parent-child relations, and scholastic achievement. An important point to bear in mind is that most sex differences represent very small, though statistically significant, differences between the group means for males and females. Variability within each sex is usually large, with the distributions for the two sexes overlapping to a high degree. Thus, for example, although boys on the average do better than girls on tests of mathematical aptitude, there are many girls who score higher than the male average.

We should add that sex differences are not the same thing as *sex stereotypes.* Stereotypes are people's *beliefs* about differences between the sexes, and they often bear little relation to real sex differences. We shall certainly discuss sex stereotypes later, for they undoubtedly play a role in the sex-typing process, but for now we concentrate on real, not imagined, differences between the sexes. Also, we must emphasize that our discussion focuses on sex differences as they exist in American society. Not all the differences we discuss would be expected to hold up across other cultures.

Play Patterns and Peer Relations

Sex differences in the objects and activities children prefer are present from a surprisingly early age. For example, 1-year-old boys prefer robots to stuffed animals, whereas the reverse is true of baby girls (Jacklin, Maccoby, & Dick, 1973). The exact toy qualities (e.g., softness, manipulativeness, number of moving parts, presence or absence of a face) that are responsible for this early difference are unknown. By the time children are 3 or 4 years old, the list of sex differences in toy and activity preferences expands dramatically, with boys preferring airplanes, balls, blocks, cube puzzles, motors, logs, tinker toys, cooties, trucks, and wagons, and girls preferring crayons and coloring, doll play, kitchen activities, musical instruments, painting, playing records, sewing, and telephoning (Connor & Serbin, 1977).

Recently, researchers have turned to the study of sex differences in fantasy and imagination. Although stereotypes suggest girls to be the more fanciful sex, the evidence indicates otherwise (Harper & Sanders, 1975;

Johnson & Ershler, 1981; Lott, 1978; Sanders & Harper, 1976). Nursery-school boys score higher on most measures of symbolic and dramatic play, which involves pretending to be another person (or an animal or a machine), or using an object to represent something it isn't (e.g., pretending a stick is a rifle); girls do not engage in pretend play as frequently as boys and are more often onlookers or take part in constructive parallel play, such as cutting out figures alongside another girl who is doing the same thing. However, there is one type of symbolic play girls perform more than boys. This is the enactment of everyday complementary social roles, such as playing mother and baby or teacher and pupil. When children are interviewed about their daydreams, boys cite more active-heroic themes; girls daydream more about playing house. Girls' daydreams are more emotionally charged than boys', with girls more often reporting themes involving intense happiness, sadness, and fear of harm and punishment (Rosenfeld, Huesmann, Eron, & Torney-Purta, 1982).

In their play with peers, children segregate themselves by sex: Girls play with girls and boys with boys. This striking feature of children's play is apparent by the time children are 2 or 3 years of age and continues through elementary school (Freedman, 1977; Strayer, 1977). In a study designed to get a closer look at same-sex and mixed-sex interaction in young children, Jacklin and Maccoby (1978) paired 33-month-old children with a child of either the same or the opposite sex and then observed the children during a short play session. When a boy was paired with a boy or a girl with a girl, levels of social interaction were high. Much of the social behavior was friendly (e.g., offering a toy, accepting an offer, and smiling at one's partner), but some of it was negative (e.g., grabbing, pushing, hitting and resisting the other's request). However, in mixed-sex dyads, interaction was low, with girls tending to withdraw into passivity and boys playing, but tending to ignore the girls. Girls sometimes criticized the boys, but the

boys simply ignored them. The authors suggested that there is something about boys' behavior that tends to scare other children. Little girls respond to this "something" by withdrawing and staying away. Little boys may also be frightened by each other, but they also find each other exciting and attractive. Thus boy-boy interactions are more a mix of aroused interest and approach combined with wariness and occasional withdrawal.

All-girl groups function differently from all-boy groups. DiPietro (1981) invited 4-year-olds to come in groups of either three girls or three boys to play in a mobile trailer equipped with a mattress for jumping, a ball, a pillow, and a Bobo doll. The all-girl groups tended to structure their interactions through self-generated rules and suggestions (e.g., "Let's take turns with the ball"). Interaction tended to be verbal and to center around the toys. Interaction in the boy groups was marked by exuberant physical contact with one another and with the toys. There was more unrestrained "rough-and-tumble" play or mock fighting. DiPietro advanced a *signal-response meshing* hypothesis to describe the boys' rough-and-tumble play. Specifically, boys may send and interpret certain cues as signals of interest in rough-and-tumble play. For example, a boy who playfully attempts to take a toy away from another seems to be sending the signal that "I want to play-fight." Other boys seem primed to respond to such overtures with the expected rough-housing response.

Occasionally, researchers have tried to break up the rigid patterns of sex-segregated play in young children, perhaps with the help of teachers who encourage and reward children for playing in mixed-sex groups (Bianchi & Bakeman, 1978; Serbin, Tonick, & Sternglanz, 1977). The philosophy has been that mixed-sex play helps children develop more enlightened, egalitarian conceptions of sex roles. Though behavior modification programs aimed to increase mixed-sex play sometimes work as long as the researchers' reinforcement contingencies are in effect, once the contingencies are discontinued, the children quickly return to sex-segregated play. The pull for same-sex play is very strong.

Boys may be characterized as more peer-oriented and as more interested in outdoor play than girls (Lott, 1978; Roper & Hinde, 1978). At school, boys are more gregarious, more likely to seek the company of other children, and usually elect to play outside at recess and lunch, often roaming the playground in groups or engaged in some other group activity. Girls enjoy their peers and the outdoors, too, but they are more likely than boys to remain indoors to play alone or interact with the teacher, and, if they go outdoors, they are less concerned about hooking themselves up to a larger group. A similar situation holds true at home. After school and on the weekends, boys spend more time outdoors and with their peers; girls are more content to remain inside, perhaps talking to a parent, watching television, or playing quietly in their rooms.

Boys and girls develop different patterns of friendships during childhood. Boys tend to develop more friendships than girls, but their relationships tend to be more superficial than those of girls—girls tend to form deeper relationships, but have fewer friends overall. This has led Waldrop and Halverson (1975) to characterize boys' friendships as "extensive" and girls' as "intensive."

Is the stereotype of girls as the more dependent sex accurate? There is no simple answer to this question. Since girls seek the proximity of adults more than boys, we might conclude that they are more adult-dependent. Furthermore, since girls develop deeper friendships with their peers than boys, we might expect them to be more dependent on specific friends for emotional support. However, boys are more eager to affiliate with their peers and are more concerned about conforming to the attitudes of their peer group than are girls. So in this sense, boys are more dependent than girls.

Perhaps the best-documented sex differences lie in the area of aggression. From 2 or 3 years of age, boys more often serve as the

aggressors as well as the victims of aggression. (See Chapter 7 for an in-depth review of this sex difference.)

Are girls more altruistic than boys? Studies have not reliably shown females to be more generous or helpful than males, though the studies that do report a sex difference usually favor females. In one study, for example, girls were more responsive to a request to collect craft materials for children in the hospital (Shigetomi, Hartmann, & Gelfand, 1981). Girls do tend to avoid games and activities that produce differential rewards or outcomes for the participants (e.g., one winner and one loser), preferring instead situations that allow all participants to share equally in available rewards (Ahlgren & Johnson, 1979; Barnett & Andrews, 1977; Knight & Kagan, 1981). It may be that girls are more motivated to avoid seeing someone hurt or disadvantaged, since girls have stronger empathic reactions to the distress of others than boys (Hoffman, 1977b).

Females of all ages take a stronger interest in, and are more nurturant of, infants and younger children than are males. When an infant is placed in a crib at the back of a classroom or in a waiting room at a research center and people's reactions to the infant are unobtrusively observed, females are more likely than males to approach the infant, look at him or her, and respond to the infant's bids for attention (Berman, Monda, & Myerscough, 1977; Feldman & Nash, 1978; Feldman, Nash, & Cutrona, 1977). In a study designed to determine whether females are biologically "wired" for greater nurturance, Frodi and Lamb (1978) recorded men's and women's physiological reactions to an infant's smiles and cries. When the infant smiled, women did not show greater heart rate deceleration (a response believed to reflect a positive expression of interest). Further, when the infant cried, women did not show greater sweating, heart rate acceleration, or increases in blood pressure. This suggested that a crying infant is no more alarming (physiologically) to women than to men. Thus the study hinted that greater female nurturance is not biologically rooted.

Parent-Child Relations

Girls may be off to a slight headstart in forming attachment bonds to their mothers. Infant girls smile more, talk earlier, are more responsive to their mothers' verbalizations, and show a greater preference for looking at human faces than do infant boys; these early positive overtures are reciprocated by mothers who show somewhat more interest in interacting with their infant daughters than their infant sons (Gunnar & Donahue, 1980; Hutt, 1977; Moss, 1967). But these early sex differences are slight and probably do not contribute to a major sex difference in the attachment process. Boys and girls follow a similar timetable in forming specific attachments—recognizing familiar caregivers at 2 or 3 months, showing a strong preference for specific caregivers around 6 months. Furthermore, the proportions of infants classified as "securely attached" or "insecurely attached" (see Chapter 2) do not differ by sex. It is true that girls eventually come to be somewhat more adult-oriented than boys, but it is unlikely that this greater adult-orientation is a direct outgrowth of stronger attachment bonds in girls in infancy.

As stereotyped as it sounds, boys are harder to raise than girls! This is apparent as early as infancy. Male infants are more irritable, fussier, and more insistent in their demands for their mothers' attention. Martin (1981) observed 10-month-olds while their mothers filled out a questionnaire in a waiting room. Boys were especially unwilling to accept withdrawal of the mother's attention, escalating the intensity of their demands if mother did not respond. Maccoby (1980) reports that 12-month-old boys, when observed in a waiting room with their fathers, were likely to get into mischief—climbing on furniture, pulling at curtains, and handling ashtrays, vases, and other valuable objects. One provocative hypothesis is that young

boys have a stronger need for a sense of control over their environments than do girls and therefore that boys react more adversely when their feelings of mastery are threatened. In some revealing experiments, Gunnar (1980) found that when 1-year-old boys were prevented from controlling a frightening toy (e.g., a cymbal-clashing monkey), many of the boys became very upset, crying and, in fact, becoming so distressed that the session had to be terminated. Such reactions were not observed in girls. Further evidence for the hypothesis that boys have a need for control comes from studies showing that boys whose mothers ignore their sons' bids for attention are less well developed cognitively and socially than boys whose mothers provide high levels of contingent responsiveness. For example, studies reveal that infant boys who are cooperative, curious, and self-reliant have mothers who are responsive to their sons' bids for attention, but who are also careful not to disturb their sons when the boys do not seek contact with their mothers (Martin, 1981; Martin, Maccoby, & Jacklin, 1981). Boys whose mothers ignore their sons' bids are more likely to develop frustrated, coercive, aggressive styles of interaction, trying to force their mothers to give them their way.

Girls, in contrast, do not appear to share the need for control and contingent responsiveness that boys do. Although contingent responsiveness may foster secure attachments in girls to their mothers, just as it does in boys (see Chapter 2), its absence does not lead to the same behavior problems in girls as it does in boys. That is, girls lacking in maternal contingent responsiveness do not become cognitively inept or uncooperative and aggressive. In fact, it has been suggested that a crucial ingredient for the establishment of independence and self-reliance in girls is not contingent responsiveness but rather a style of "abrasive intrusiveness" (Baumrind, 1979; Martin, 1981; Martin et al., 1981). These researchers have shown that competent preschool girls tend to have mothers who actually intrude on their daughters' freedom. We have commented that girls tend to play indoors and alone more than boys. It seems that mothers who intrude on their daughters' passivity to suggest an activity and then push their daughters into performing the activity are helping nudge their daughters out of the nest to become more exploratory and self-reliant. In sum, the child-rearing qualities making for competent young boys and girls may differ: Boys may require supportive, cooperative, contingent responsiveness; girls, however, may benefit from being challenged and treated abrasively, and they may need to be forced into action.

Despite the finding that contingent maternal responsiveness may help build cooperation in sons, the fact remains that boys are less likely to cooperate with their parents. Boys are more likely to balk when asked to change what they are doing, and they more often express indignation when asked to do routine chores like making their beds or clearing the dinner table. The result is that boys get into more battles of will with their parents. It should not be surprising, then, that parents end up using harsher disciplinary measures, especially physical punishment, with their sons than with their daughters (Hoffman & Saltzstein, 1967; Zussman, 1978). Also interesting is that parents use more inductive reasoning with their daughters than with their sons.

Parents tend to become more involved in child-rearing when their child is of their own sex. Mothers imitate, talk to, and play with their infant daughters more than with their sons. Fathers show more interest in their sons: They make more trips to the hospital to visit their newborn if it is a boy than if it is a girl, and they engage their sons in play more often, especially physical games, than they do their daughters (Cherry & Lewis, 1976; Clarke-Stewart, 1973; Moss, 1967; Parke, 1978; Thoman, Leiderman, & Olson, 1972). The special interest parents show their same-sex offspring may enhance the parents' attractiveness to their children, making it more likely that the children will seek their parents

out as companions and role models. There is an interesting twist to the story of greater parental interest in same-sex children, however: Parents tend to be stricter and more punitive with children of their own sex (Baumrind, 1973; Noller, 1980; Rothbart & Maccoby, 1966). For whatever reasons, there is some truth to the tale that fathers are more indulgent and permissive toward their daughters, and mothers toward their sons.

A final point on sex differences in parent-child relations is that boys are more vulnerable to breakdowns in the family system than girls. Hetherington, Cox, and Cox (1979) found that boys show more noncompliant, aggressive, and antisocial behaviors following divorce than do girls. Also, Block, Block, and Morrison (1981) found that when the parents in intact homes do not agree on child-rearing values, and send confusing and contradictory messages to their children, boys' development suffers more than girls'. Boys, but not girls, from such homes are rated lower on resourcefulness, acceptance of responsibility for one's actions and feelings, and intellectual functioning. The exact reasons for the sex difference in response to marital discord are unknown. It may be that harmony between the parents creates a more structured, predictable, and controllable environment, and, as we have seen, a loss of controllability is more devastating for boys than for girls. It could also be that boys require firmer disciplinary control. When parents divorce or disagree on child-rearing practices, it is probably much harder to furnish boys with the degree of firmness and consistent discipline they need.

Scholastic Achievement

A sex difference with tremendous social consequences lies in the area of academic achievement. In elementary school, girls do better than boys: They score higher on standardized achievement tests and their teachers give them better grades. But by the time children are in high school, the tables have turned: Across a broad array of subjects, but especially in mathematics and science-related courses, boys outperform girls. High-school girls tend to have low expectations for success in school, they tend to avoid enrolling in math and science courses, and, when they do, they typically receive lower grades than boys. Surveys of adults who have achieved eminence in their fields consistently reveal women to be underrepresented, again especially in the science areas (Deaux, 1976; Maccoby & Jacklin, 1974; Tyler, 1965).

What psychological processes account for the reversal in the achievement pattern for the two sexes over the school years? One possibility, advanced by Horner (1972), is that girls develop a "fear of success" as they enter puberty and realize that achievement is incompatible with the female sex role. Recent research shows that, beginning in adolescence, girls sometimes do avoid doing well in experimental achievement situations if doing well means competing and winning against a boy on a task that boys are "supposed" to do better at, such as math problems (Condry & Dyer, 1977; Entwisle, 1972; Krauss, 1977; Peplau, 1976; Romer, 1975; Stein & Bailey, 1973; Tresemer, 1974; Zuckerman & Wheeler, 1975).

Another popular hypothesis is that boys and girls develop different attributional styles in achievement situations, or ways of explaining their successes and failures, that cause poorer female achievement. Some researchers have proposed that when girls fail in an achievement situation, they tend to attribute their failure to a lack of ability (Dweck & Bush, 1976; Dweck, Davidson, Nelson, & Enna, 1978). Because a lack of ability is something the girls feel they can do little about, they are likely to give up in the face of failure, develop lower expectations for success in the future, and eventually even avoid situations in which failure is a possible outcome. In contrast, boys generate less devastating explanations for their failures. Boys are more likely to attribute their failures simply to a lack of effort or else blame their failures on external

factors, such as bad luck, the difficulty of the task, or a personality conflict with the teacher. None of these latter attributions is as debilitating as thinking that one lacks the ability to do the work. In Chapter 3 we reviewed Dweck's research suggesting that the ways teachers criticize children for their mistakes in the classroom help create these sex differences in attributions.

Deaux (1976) proposes that once girls develop low self-perceptions of ability, their low expectations of success and high avoidance of achievement situations are maintained. Research has shown that when people develop low expectations for success, they interpret their subsequent failures as further signs of their low ability. But equally bad, they attribute any successes they have to good luck. Thus failures reinforce girls' lack of confidence, and successes fail to bolster their optimism. In contrast, when people expect to succeed, they interpret success as confirming their high ability and write off their failures as due to bad luck. Boys expect to succeed, so failures do not daunt them and successes simply reinforce their sense of high ability, thereby strengthening their achievement motivation even more.

THE CONSTRUCTS OF MASCULINITY AND FEMININITY

How do psychologists conceptualize and measure people's "masculinity" and "femininity"? Here we review some popular methods for assessing individual children's sex typing. Then we raise the issue of whether masculinity and femininity are best considered as one dimension or two.

Assessment of Sex Typing

Masculinity and femininity can be assessed at several levels of psychological depth. At one level, the terms masculinity and femininity can be used to describe the degree to which people overtly display the behaviors that are more typical of one sex than the other. In this case, an individual's surface behavior is the criterion for determining the person's sex typing. At the other extreme, masculinity and femininity can refer to people's unconscious or semi-conscious identification with, or basic feelings of compatibility with, one sex role rather than the other. At this level, assessment of masculinity and femininity requires delving deeper into the person's psyche. Psychologists have devised ways to assess sex typing at surface levels, at deep levels, and at in-between levels (e.g., Biller & Borstelmann, 1967; Lynn, 1969). We shall review some of the more popular strategies, beginning with surface levels of assessment and ending with deeper levels.

Behaviorally oriented psychologists regard children's overt enactment of sex-linked activities as the most objective criterion of sex typing. Determining children's sex typing from their overt behavior, however, is no easy feat and usually requires observing children for considerable periods of time. In a fine study, Connor and Serbin (1977) observed children in a nursery school over several weeks, carefully checking off the frequencies with which children of each sex participated in various activities (doll play, building with blocks, etc.). The authors determined an empirically derived key of male-preferred and female-preferred activities, and the sex typing of individual children was inferred from how much the children preferred male-versus female-type activities. In other studies, parents or teachers have simply been asked to estimate how much they have observed children to participate in boy- and girl-type activities (Bates & Bentler, 1973; Bates, Bentler, & Thompson, 1973).

A second way of assessing sex typing is by soliciting subjects' verbal preferences for boy-type and girl-type activities (e.g., Fling & Manosevitz, 1972). Children can simply be asked how much they would like to play with airplanes, pretend to cook dinner, play outdoors, read quietly inside, and so on, and their responses are then evaluated to determine

their masculinity and femininity. Notice that it is possible for a child to want to behave like members of a particular sex yet not actually do so, perhaps because of lack of skill (e.g., a boy may want to participate in boy-type activities, but lack what it takes to play baseball, be aggressive, etc.).

Third, sex typing can be assessed in terms of self-perceived possession of masculine and feminine attributes. Several questionnaires have been designed for use with adults in which respondents indicate how much they believe they possess various attributes (e.g., gentleness, independence, nurturance, and assertiveness). The adjectives have previously been judged to be more typical and/or more desirable for one sex than the other (Bem, 1974; Orlofsky, 1981; Spence, Helmreich, & Stapp, 1975). Recently, Hall and Halberstadt (1980) developed a similar test for use with elementary school children.

Psychologists are also interested in studying children's deeper levels of acceptance of and satisfaction with their sex role. A boy may strive to enact male-type behaviors, perhaps in order to gain societal approval, yet down deep actually feel some discomfort over being a boy and maybe even wish he were a girl. This underlying feminine identification or orientation may not be entirely conscious to the boy. How is this aspect of sex typing measured? One strategy is to use a projective test. Brown (1956) developed what he called the "It Scale." In this test, children are shown a drawing of a stick figure, named "It." The figure is drawn so as to look neither definitely male nor definitely female (though in subsequent research, "It" has been shown actually to look a little more male than female). Children are asked to select various sex-linked activities and toys that they think "It" would prefer. For example, children say whether "It" would prefer to play with a doll or a truck, with a highchair or a rifle, and to dress up as an Indian princess or an Indian chief. The assumption is that children project their own sex-role identification onto "It," making choices for "It" that they would really want for themselves. There is some debate over exactly what the "It Scale" taps (Dickstein & Seymour, 1977; Edelbrock & Sugawara, 1978; Fling & Manosevitz, 1972), but the test remains a popular one.

When the same children have been tested on several dimensions of sex typing and their scores intercorrelated, usually the correlations turn out to be low or nonsignificant. (Fling & Manosevitz, 1972; Hall & Halberstadt, 1980; Orlofsky, 1981; Schau, Kahn, Diepold, & Cherry, 1980; Storms, 1979). Thus it seems safe to say that for a great many children, sizable discrepancies can exist among the various levels of sex typing.

Masculinity and Femininity: One Dimension or Two?

Thus far we have spoken of masculinity and femininity in the traditional way: as opposite ends of a single continuum. A number of psychologists have recently taken issue with the conceptualization of masculinity and femininity as bipolar opposites, arguing that the presence in an individual of attributes typical of or desirable for one sex does not necessarily imply the absence of qualities characteristic of the opposite sex (Bem, 1974; 1977; Spence et al., 1975). After all, is it not possible for a person to be interested in both athletics and music, to be both aggressive and nurturant, and to be both dependent and independent, at different times and under different circumstances?

Bem, Spence, and their colleagues see masculinity and femininity as separate, orthogonal dimensions. That is, an individual's location on one dimension is believed to be independent of the person's location on the other dimension. One popular method for locating a person's position in the two-dimensional space created by these dimensions is Bem's (1974, 1977) Sex Role Inventory. On this test, respondents rate themselves on a list of 40 sex-typed adjectives (e.g., self-reliant, athletic, tender, flatterable). Two scores are then computed, one for the person's average

self-rating on the masculine adjectives and one for the person's average self-rating on the feminine adjectives. Then the individual is placed into one of four categories, depending on the configuration of his or her scores on the two scales. Have a look at Figure 9–1. People who rate themselves high on feminine attributes and low on masculine attributes are categorized as "feminine sex-typed"; people with the reverse pattern are labeled "masculine sex-typed"; people with low scores on both dimensions are called "undifferentiated"; and people who perceive themselves as possessing both masculine and feminine characteristics receive the label of "androgynous." Bem believes that androgynous individuals, who see themselves possessing attributes of both sexes, are most flexible and adaptable, being unencumbered in their thinking and behavior by rigid sex-role stereotypes. For example, Bem claims, these people feel free to be compassionate when the situation calls for it, and yet they can also act assertively when necessary. The separation of masculinity and femininity into two dimensions and the introduction of the concept of psycholog-

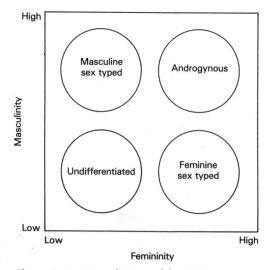

Figure 9–1 Masculinity and femininity as orthogonal dimensions and the locations of four personality types within this framework.

ical androgyny are important advances, which we shall more closely examine later in the chapter.

THEORIES OF SEX TYPING

We shall briefly consider five theoretical perspectives on sex typing: trait theory, Freudian theory, social learning theory, cognitive-developmental theory, and the biological viewpoint.

Trait Theory

Trait theorists have little to say about the development of sex typing, but they have had considerable impact on the kinds of predictions psychologists make about sex-typed behavior. First, trait theorists conceive of people as possessing underlying dispositions or motives that produce cross-situational consistencies in behavior. The model proposed by Bem (1977), which we previously reviewed, however, suggests that people might differ from one another in terms of how much they display consistency in sex-typed behavior across situations. According to Bem's conceptualization, people who are sex-typed as either masculine or feminine are considered to possess a trait of sex typing that leads them to display a good deal of conformity to a particular sex role across situations. However, people who are categorized as androgynous or undifferentiated are not thought to possess a trait that pushes for behavior consistent with a given sex role across diverse circumstances. Not being concerned with monitoring their behavior to make sure it conforms to a given sex role, these latter individuals should display both masculine and feminine behaviors. At a later point in this chapter, we shall see that children do develop different degrees of concern for monitoring their behavior in terms of a given sex role. Thus, as Bem suggests, some children seem to possess a masculine or feminine trait that pushes for consistency across situations, whereas other children do not.

A second prediction offered by trait theorists is that individuals retain their relative degree of sex typing over time. We shall briefly consider the evidence for stability in sex typing here.

Kagan and Moss (1962) reported positive correlations between children's sex typing in middle childhood (ages 6 to 10 years) and their sex typing 20 years later. Boys who were interested in competitive games, sports, gross motor activities, and mechanics were also sex typed in their interests as adults. Similarly, girls who were interested in sewing, cooking, reading, and noncompetitive games favored feminine activities in their adult years. In another longitudinal study, Tyler (1964) found that girls who displayed masculine play and activity interests in the first grade were most likely to be career-oriented as adults.

There are complications, however, when trying to assess the longitudinal stability of sex typing. For one thing, as people develop, they change in the way that they express the masculine and feminine sides of their personalities. Kagan and Moss (1962) found evidence of this in their longitudinal study. Although boys who were aggressive in childhood grew up to be directly aggressive in adulthood, girls who were aggressive in youth changed in the way that they expressed their aggressiveness as they got older: They were not openly aggressive as adults but instead they became more intellectually competitive and developed more masculine interests. Kagan and Moss also found that although girls who were dependent on adults in childhood continued to be directly dependent as adults, boys who were dependent and passive in childhood tended not to be dependent in adulthood; the boys did, however, tend to be relatively noncompetitive and sexually apprehensive as adults. Thus children may maintain cross-sex-typed motives, yet change in the way they express them as they get older.

A provocative idea is that a person's sex typing is not a trait that is fixed for life but rather fluctuates with the person's life circumstances, especially the person's stage in his or her life cycle. Consider some of the various stages into which life can be divided: childhood, adolescence, single adulthood, cohabitation, married-childless, anticipation of first child, young parenthood, mature parenthood, empty-nest period, grandparenthood. Clearly, even adulthood is a period of continuous change, a series of transitions from one life situation to another, each involving distinct tasks and the need to redefine attitudes and behaviors (Feldman, Biringen, & Nash, 1981). When people at various life stages have been tested for sex-role behaviors or self-perceptions, some interesting findings emerge. For example, cohabiting adults, regardless of sex, tend to behave in a more masculine than feminine manner. Also, parenthood for young married couples brings a sharp divergence in sex roles between the male and the female, presumably because the male grows more concerned with fulfilling his role as breadwinner and the female with her role as nurturant caregiver (Abrahams, Feldman, & Nash, 1978). An interesting trend is that as adults grow older, they become less sex typed and more androgynous, with, for example, men perceiving themselves as increasingly expressive and nurturant, and women viewing themselves as more autonomous (Feldman, et al., 1981). In an observational study of adults' behavior toward an infant in a waiting room situation, grandfathers were more nurturant toward the infant than men at earlier stages of the life cycle (Feldman & Nash, 1979). Of course, evidence for a trend toward androgyny with age does not mean that people become more like the opposite sex in every respect; as women mature, for example, they do not perceive themselves as becoming athletic or as assuming positions of leadership more frequently than they did when they were younger (Hyde & Phillis, 1979). The main point of this discussion is that an individual's sex typing is not a fixed entity that emerges full-blown and unchangeable in early or middle childhood. Sex typing undergoes changes throughout adolescence and adulthood—it is a continuous process.

Freudian Theory and Its Derivatives

Freud stressed identification with the same-sex parent as the mechanism of sex-role development. According to Freud, both boys and girls initially identify with their mother, since it is she who constitutes the child's major source of biological and emotional satisfaction. At about 3 to 5 years of age, aggressive or Oedipal identification is thought to begin. The child presumably experiences incestuous feelings toward the opposite-sex parent, but fears violent retaliation from the jealous same-sex parent. Specifically, boys are thought to fear castration and girls to fear a symbolic reenactment of the act that they believe made them girls—that "castrated" them—in the first place. Consequently, the children defensively identify with the same-sex parent. Girls strengthen their identification with their mothers, which intensifies their femininity; boys shift their identification to their fathers, which signals the beginning of their masculine development and the abandonment of their femininity. Freud also thought that the motivation for parental identification (and thus sex typing) was stronger in boys than in girls since, anatomically speaking, boys have more to lose than girls.

Few psychologists today buy Freud's theory as it was originally stated, partly because the evidence for his central notion of defensive identification with the aggressor is so scanty. Recall from Chapter 4 that children are far more likely to imitate warm models or socially powerful models—those who control resources desired by the children—than they are to imitate threatening persons with whom they have developed rivalrous relationships.

Nevertheless, a number of contemporary theorists still assign parental identification a major role in the sex-typing process, though they concede that it is the parents' warmth and social power rather than their hostility that make their children identify with them (e.g., Hetherington, 1967; Mussen & Distler, 1959). In this chapter, we shall review evidence that is consistent with the notion that children's sex typing is partially determined through identification with the same-sex parent. For example, masculine boys tend to have fathers whom they perceive as affectionate and powerful (though no similar relationship holds for girls and their mothers). However, the role of parental identification in sex typing has probably been exaggerated. Parents probably influence their children's sex typing more by rewarding sex-appropriate behavior than by modeling it. Moreover, the peer group, the media, and societal pressures contribute to sex typing. Freud ignored these important extrafamilial influences.

Social Learning Theory

According to social learning theory (Bandura, 1977; Mischel, 1970), sex typing is the product of a variety of learning experiences that the child has with his or her social environment. Socializing agents, including the child's parents, teachers, and peers, are thought to prompt and selectively reinforce sex-typed behaviors. Thus parents buy their children sex-appropriate toys and reward their children for playing with them; they discourage their children's participation in cross-sex activities; and they help their children learn to discriminate sex-appropriate and sex-inappropriate activities by labeling activities as "only for girls" or "just for boys."

According to the theory, an important way in which children learn what behaviors are appropriate for the two sexes is by observation. By watching parents, siblings, teachers, playmates, television characters, and other classes of models, children acquire a vast repertoire of new response patterns. For example, from watching their peers, most nursery schoolers soon learn new varieties of aggression, new ways of playing with certain

toys, and so on. After observing the behaviors, children may try to imitate them, especially if they look like fun, but many of the behaviors are simply stored in children's minds in symbolic form, ready to help guide enactment of the behaviors if children later choose to perform them. At the same time as children are learning new behavior patterns, they are also learning that some of the behaviors are more appropriate for one sex than the other. One way children learn this is by simply observing that the two sexes differ in the frequency with which they perform various responses: Boys aggress more than girls, girls play dress-up more than boys, and so on. Another way children discern the sex-appropriateness of an activity is by witnessing the differential consequences children of the two sexes receive for performing behaviors. When children see their teachers and peers laugh at boys for playing house, but accept this behavior in girls, they are likely to encode the behavior as girl-appropriate.

Thus through direct experience and observational learning, children gradually form conceptions of the kinds of behaviors that are expected of the two sexes. Furthermore, although children learn the behaviors that are appropriate for both sexes, they come to perform same-sex activities and to inhibit opposite-sex activities. Part of the motivation for this sex-typing process lies in external realities—the presence of parents, siblings, peers, and so on who are ready to reward or ridicule. But part of the motivation for sex typing is internal. As children learn that society expects or demands certain behaviors from them, they come to realize that it would be to their advantage to regulate their behavior to conform to these standards. The boy who knows his peers will be distressed if he picks up a doll will learn to say to himself "No, don't do that—find something else to play with" as he reaches for a doll. He may feel relief and eventually even pride when he turns to a boy-appropriate alternative that he knows will be approved of by others. In other words, external social sanctions teach children that sex is an important dimension on which to regulate their behavior. This leads children to institute contingencies of self-direction and self-evaluation, so that children come to feel upset with themselves when they perform strongly discouraged cross-sex behavior, and to feel pride and a sense of accomplishment when they select and master a sex-appropriate activity. As we shall see in this chapter, a great deal of what we know about sex-role development can be summarized by invoking these principles of social learning theory.

Cognitive-Developmental Theory

According to Kohlberg's (1966, 1969) cognitive-developmental theory, sex typing is a consequence of stagelike advances in the child's cognitive functioning. Until the child is roughly 6 or 7 years old, the child is presumed to be functioning at Piaget's preoperational stage of intellectual development. During this stage, little sex-role development is thought to take place. As we noted when discussing the cognitive-developmental theory of imitation in Chapter 4, the preoperational child is thought to derive a sense of competence and mastery from seeking out and imitating older, powerful, and more competent models (e.g., parents and television superheroes), but sex is not yet thought to be a major dimension influencing children's selection and imitation of models.

Things change as children enter the concrete operational stage. At this juncture, Kohlberg suggests, children begin to shift in their conceptions of what will make them competent and give them a sense of self-esteem. Earlier, being similar to stronger and powerful others made children feel proud, but now notions of *class membership* become paramount in motivating children's behavior. As children enter the concrete operational stage, they learn that the contents of their social world can be divided into various categories (i.e., adults vs. children, males vs. females, our team vs. your team, etc.). Furthermore, children come to realize that they belong to one

or more of these classes, and, once they do, they seek ardently to become exemplary members of those groups. In his theory of sex typing, Kohlberg assigns great importance to the child's attainment of gender constancy, or the child's firm realization that he or she is a boy or a girl and will remain so throughout life. Once the child attains gender constancy, he or she is motivated to look for differences between the sexes and to emulate the same-sex role. This is because the child's self-esteem rests on perceiving him- or herself to be similar to a class of same-sex individuals.

In certain respects, the social learning and cognitive-developmental theories of sex typing are very similar. In both theories, sex typing is viewed as the product of a "self-socialization" process in which children constantly strive to discern what behaviors are appropriate for the two sexes and try to emulate behaviors associated with their own sex.

But the two theories differ in three important ways. First, in contrast to social learning theory, Kohlberg claims that children must attain gender constancy before much significant sex typing can take place. The validity of this assertion is in doubt. As we shall see, children reveal considerable sex typing long before they establish firm gender constancy, although it is true that once they do attain gender constancy, the sex-typing process takes on extra speed. Second, in Kohlberg's theory the motivation for sex typing is entirely intrinsic: Innate strivings for competence in interaction with cognitive development provide the impetus for sex-role development. Social learning theorists, in contrast, argue that internal processes of self-regulation and external incentives (e.g., pressures from parents, peers, etc.) work together to fuel the sex-typing process. Finally, cognitive-developmental theory has a harder time than social learning theory explaining individual differences in sex typing. According to Kohlberg's theory, the cognitive factors that motivate sex typing are presumed to operate in all children in roughly the same manner; the theory cannot explain why one girl adopts a feminine identity while another girl develops androgynously. Social learning theory, on the other hand, holds that individual differences in sex typing are a reflection of varying degrees of social pressure children experience for conforming to sex roles.

Biological Bases of Sex Differences

It seems probable that some psychological sex differences have a basis that is, at least in part, rooted in biology. Several lines of evidence converge to suggest this. First, prenatal development is rather more complicated in male infants, and this may have important consequences for sex differences. Male fetuses begin as female fetuses, but have to undergo transformations to become male, whereas female fetuses simply persist in their initial female pattern of development. The extra steps required in male development may provide greater opportunity for things to go awry or may weaken the organism in ways that are apparent only long after birth. Indeed, males are more likely to develop defects and are more vulnerable to disease and stress both before and after birth. The male's XY sex chromosome make-up also makes it more likely that genetic defects will be revealed in males than in females, whose XX pattern affords more protection. If a gene that causes a certain disease is located on one of the females's X chromosomes, there is a good chance that the female will carry a corresponding gene on her second X chromosome that will prevent the first gene from causing ill-effects. For the male, however, defective genetic material on either chromosome cannot be corrected by healthier genetic material on the other. In sum, from a genetic perspective, the male sex is the weaker.

A biological basis for sex differences is also supported by the fact that certain differences are apparent very early in life, before there has been much opportunity for learning to occur. As we noted, for example, infant girls are more socially responsive, whereas infant boys are more irritable and fussy (Hutt, 1977; Phillips, King, & Dubois, 1978), and greater

male noncompliance and aggression are evident early in development, too (Maccoby & Jacklin, 1980).

Third, sex hormones may play a role in sex differences. When female monkeys are given doses of male hormones (either while still developing in their mothers' uteruses or in infancy), they reveal a variety of "masculine" social behaviors in adolescence (Young, Goy, & Phoenix, 1964). Compared to normal females, they are more aggressive and issue more threats to other animals. They are also less afraid of the threats of others. They display mounting actions, engage in rough-and-tumble play, and try to ascend the male dominance hierarchy. Occasionally, a female human fetus for some reason receives an overdose of male hormones while still developing in the mother's uterus. As children, these girls reveal some behaviors that are strikingly similar to those displayed by androgenized female monkeys—tomboyishness, interest in vigorous athletic activities, assertiveness, attempts to establish themselves in male hierarchies (but without concern for their standing among females), and a lack of interest in traditional female activities. They show great interest in establishing careers and they begin to date late, though they are not homosexual (Money & Ehrhardt, 1972). Possibly, prenatal hormonal influences establish different neural patterns in boys than in girls, which cause children and adults of the two sexes to respond differently to certain social stimuli later in life.

Fourth, there are cross-cultural regularities in certain sex differences. Males almost always are more aggressive and are more likely to serve in the breadwinner role, whereas women more often take the role of nurturant homemaker. Nevertheless, there are divergences from these stereotypes. Margaret Mead (1935) reported a study of sex roles in three primitive tribes. In one, both men and women were passive, cooperative, and unassertive. In the second, both sexes were cruel and restrictive. In the third, there was a reversal of the usual trend, with men displaying social sensitivity and interests in arts and crafts and women being more aggressive and acting as the decision makers. Thus, if there exist constitutionally based sex differences in social behavior, they can be considerably modified by cultural forces.

Despite these clues for the importance of biology, the principle that biology and experience interact to effect sex differences and sex typing bears repeating. If, for instance, girls are by nature more attentive when their parents reason with them, the parents may increase their use of inductive reasoning with their daughters; this should help make the girls more empathic and altruistic as well as less aggressive than boys. It no longer makes sense to argue that sex differences are "primarily due to biology" or "primarily due to learning." Instead, we need to chart the nature-nurture interplays that create significant differences between the sexes.

COGNITIVE BASES OF SEX TYPING

Social learning theorists and cognitive-developmental theorists alike regard the sex typing process as, at least in part, a process of self-socialization guided by cognitive factors. Children must learn that the world is divided into two sexes and that they belong to one of these sexes. They must learn the behaviors that are expected of males and females, and they must feel motivated to perform behaviors that they associate with their own sex role. Some children learn these lessons exceptionally well; these children develop extreme concerns about monitoring their behavior in terms of its appropriateness for their sex role. For other, more androgynous, children, the sex-appropriateness of a situation or an activity is not a salient dimension organizing and guiding their behavior.

We begin this section by discussing how children come to think of themselves as boys or girls and eventually acquire gender constancy. Then we discuss how children learn about expected patterns of behavior for the two sexes and how these stereotypes influence children's perception and interpretation

of their worlds. Finally, we focus directly on the evidence for self-socialization of sex roles: Do children, in fact, become sex typed because they are trying to match their behavior to what they conceive to be appropriate for their sex?

Gender Constancy

Stages in Attainment of Gender Constancy Kohlberg (1966, 1969) used the term *gender constancy* to refer to the concept that a person's sex is a permanent attribute that is tied to underlying biological properties (i.e., the person's genitals and genetic constitution) and does not depend on surface characteristics such as the person's hair length, style of clothing, choice of play activities, and so on. Recall that, according to cognitive-developmental theory, up until around age 7 children are thought to be at the preoperational stage, and up to that time their problem with perceptual centration causes them to make judgments about people solely in terms of salient superficial qualities. However, once children reach the concrete operational stage, they begin to conserve, or realize that certain underlying properties of objects can remain the same despite changes in the surface appearance of the object. Gender constancy is a form of conservation.

Studies of the development of gender constancy show that gender constancy does not emerge full-blown around age 7 but rather unfolds gradually in a series of stages, typically beginning when the child is about 2 years old and continuing until the child is 7 or 8 years old (e.g., Slaby & Frey, 1975). In fact, it is possible to identify four discrete levels of understanding on the path to gender constancy. From least to most mature, these are called the identity, stability, motivation, and consistency components of gender constancy (Eaton & Von Bargen, 1981; Ruble, Balaban, & Cooper, 1981).

The earliest form of gender self-understanding is *gender identity,* or the simple ability to label oneself as a boy or a girl. When children are asked, "Are you a boy or a girl?"

or are asked to place a Polaroid picture of themselves into a pile of either male or female photographs (Thompson, 1975), they usually respond correctly by the time they are $2\frac{1}{2}$ years old.

Next comes *gender stability*, or the recognition that gender remains permanent over time. This aspect of gender constancy is assessed by asking questions such as, "When you grow up, will you be a mommy or a daddy?"

The third level of understanding, which deals with the *motivation* component of gender constancy, is based on the belief that gender cannot change, even if a person wishes to change. This is usually assessed by asking children, "If you really wanted to be a girl (boy), could you be?"

Finally, around age 6 or 7, children attain *gender consistency*, or the knowledge that gender is invariant despite changes in activity, dress, or appearance. Again, a child's level of understanding can be determined by asking certain questions. For example, a young boy may be asked the following: "If you played with dolls, what would you be?"; or, "If you had your hair styled like this (the boy is shown a drawing of a girl with her hair styled in a definitely feminine way), what would you be?"

Sometimes children are asked not only to give answers to questions like these but also to furnish explanations for their answers. Interestingly, although 5- and 6-year-old children sometimes answer the constancy questions correctly, their explanations fail to reveal the knowledge that gender constancy is rooted in biological unalterables. In fact, many children fail to cite genitals as the reason for gender constancy until they reach 8 or 9 years of age (Emmerich, Goldman, Kirsh, & Sharabany, 1977; McConaghy, 1979).

Determinants of Gender Constancy
How do children learn what sex they are? Maccoby (1980) suggests children learn to label themselves appropriately simply because their parents tell them they belong to one sex or the other. But the more refined aspects of gender constancy probably depend on more than simple labeling. In part, children may learn through their own experiences that their sex remains unchanged across time and across changes in surface appearance and behavior. The older children get, the longer they have known themselves to be consistently male or female. Most children at least occasionally play with opposite-sex toys or dress up as an opposite-sex person, and, when they do, they can see that their sex does not change. This may help them realize that their underlying maleness or femaleness remains constant across changes in their behavior and appearance.

Intelligence is associated with gender constancy: Brighter children progress through the phases of gender constancy faster than less intelligent children (Gouze & Nadelman, 1980). However, attempts to tie gender constancy development to success on Piagetian tests of physical conservation (of volume, area, etc.) have not met with much success (LaVoie & Andrews, 1975; Marcus & Overton, 1978). It does not seem that gender constancy and physical conservation are simply two reflections of an identical underlying thought structure.

The more advanced a child is in gender constancy development, the harder it is to get the child to change his or her gender identity, if a change is required. Occasionally, children are assigned to the incorrect sex at birth. This can occur in cases of genital abnormalities that lead the delivering physician and the parents to mistake one sex for the other. Specifically, a child who is genetically female may be born with an enlarged clitoris resembling a penis, or a genetic male may be born with his penis and testicles tucked inside. If misassignment of sex occurs, the child will of course be reared, until the mistake is discovered, as a member of the opposite sex. If the error is discovered by the time the child is 3 years old, the child usually accepts reassignment to the correct sex rather easily. But beyond that age, as gender constancy sets in, it becomes extraordinarily difficult to get children to switch their gender identities. In such cases, it may be necessary to initiate a sex-change process surgically (Money & Ehrhardt, 1972).

Before children can deliberately strive to emulate a role, they must learn what that role entails. Hence we turn now to the question of how children acquire sex-role stereotypes, or develop beliefs about the behaviors that are appropriate and inappropriate for the two sexes.

Acquiring Sex-Role Stereotypes

Developmental Trends in Acquisition of Sex-Role Stereotypes Two-year-olds show little awareness that certain activities or toys are more closely associated with one sex than the other (Blakemore, LaRue, & Olejnik, 1979). However, by the time children are 3 or 4, considerable awareness of sex stereotypes is evident. Kuhn, Nash, and Brucken (1978), for example, found that 3-year-olds were likely to choose a male doll to have said things like "I can hit you" and a female doll to have made statements like "I like to play dolls."

The process of learning sex stereotypes begins early, but continues for years. Young children's knowledge of sex roles is limited and tends to focus on concrete behavioral differences between the sexes (e.g., toy play preferences); perceived differences in subtler personality traits between the sexes (e.g., that males are "adventurous" and females are "dreamy") take longer to learn (Best, Williams, Cloud, Davis, Robertson, Edwards, Giles, & Fowles, 1977). By the time children are in high school, they have even learned sex-stereotyped ways of explaining the behavior of the two sexes, especially in achievement situations. For example, people tend to explain success by a male actor in terms of high ability or high effort, but to attribute success by a female actor to good luck (Bird & Williams, 1980; Deaux, 1976).

Preschool and early-elementary-school children hold rather rigid stereotypes: Doc-

tors *must* be male and nurses *must* be female, for example. But as children develop, their stereotypes relax and become more egalitarian. They realize that many activities are not exclusively male or exclusively female, but are possible for both sexes, though perhaps still more typical of one sex than the other (Garrett, Ein, & Tremaine, 1977; Marantz & Mansfield, 1977; Meyer, 1980). Urberg (1979) found that adults held less rigid stereotypes than high-school students. Possibly the shift toward androgyny in adulthood that we mentioned earlier is related to this relaxation in sex-role stereotypes.

Determinants of Sex-Role Stereotypes Sex-role stereotypes are acquired mainly through observational learning. Remember that from an early age children segregate themselves by sex, preferring to engage in sex-linked activities with others of their sex (e.g., girls playing dress-up together, or boys building block towers together). It is no surprise that children learn to associate certain behaviors with certain sexes. Even neutral (non-sex-typed) activities can take on a sex-role meaning if children see the activity preferred by one sex more than the other. In a study by Perry and Bussey (1979), 8- and 9-year-olds watched while eight adults (four men and four women) indicated their preferences among objects (e.g., whether they would prefer an apple or a pear, or a pencil or an eraser). When an object was consistently chosen by all four members of one sex and rejected by all four adults of the other sex, the children came to view the item as more appropriate for the former sex than for the latter. Thus children notice differences in the frequencies with which males and females, as groups, endorse various activities and encode the actions as male- or female-appropriate in their minds. Probably, children's playmates, television heroes, parents, and teachers all serve as models of sex-role learning. The more consistently an activity is performed by diverse models of one sex, the more children will see it as sex typed. Since the process of acquiring sex-role stereotypes involves skill in perceptual discrimination and categorization of information, it is not surprising that children with high IQ scores show the greatest awareness of sex stereotypes (Edelbrock & Sugawara, 1978; Kohlberg, 1969; Mischel, 1970).

Impact of Sex-Role Stereotypes on Social Information Processing Stereotyping is a normal cognitive process. Without being able to group and subsume pieces of information into meaningful categories, the human organism would be overwhelmed by disorganized data. Stereotypes can also help people generate appropriate responses to situations. For example, a child buying a Christmas present for a 7-year-old male cousin he has never met may rely on his knowledge of sex-stereotyped preferences (e.g., that young boys prefer toy racing cars to dolls) when selecting the gift. But because stereotypes can lead us to ascribe qualities to people on the basis of their group membership rather than on the basis of their individual needs and wishes, mistakes can occur. Stereotypes can also be self-perpetuating.

Stereotypes are schemas, or cognitive representations of experiences. Sex-role schemas take the form of "Boys are supposed to . . ." and "Girls are supposed to . . ." rules. Once people develop schemas about the ways things are supposed to operate, their perception and memory of events related to those schemas are affected. Most important, people are likely to encode and remember information that is consistent with their schemas, and they are prone to ignore or forget material that is incongruent with their beliefs (Martin & Halverson, 1981). A study by Koblinsky, Cruse, and Sugawara (1978) illustrates how this principle applies to sex-role stereotypes. Fifth graders heard stories that described male and female characters performing both sex-appropriate and sex-inappropriate behaviors. Later, when recalling the content of the stories, the children remembered masculine behaviors performed by a male character and feminine behaviors performed by a female character better than they

recalled feminine behaviors displayed by a male or masculine behaviors displayed by a female.

Equally important, because of sex-role schemas, people sometimes remember events differently from the way they actually happened. When Cordua, McGraw, and Drabman (1979) showed 5- and 6-year-olds a short movie depicting a male nurse or a female doctor, the children reported after the film that the nurse had been female and the doctor had been male! Children have a particularly hard time remembering a male actor performing a traditionally female activity, probably because the taboos against cross-sex behavior are stronger for males (Cordua et al., 1979; Liben & Signorella, 1980).

Can Self-Socialization Theory Explain Early Sex Typing?

Both cognitive-developmental and social learning theorists believe that once children know what sex they are, they strive to incorporate behaviors and attributes they perceive to be appropriate for their sex role into their own personalities and social repertoires, thereby becoming sex typed. Although this process of self-socialization—an active, conscious attempt to match one's behavior to stereotypes—may assist the sex-typing process as children enter grade school, it probably is inadequate as an explanation of the origins of sex typing in the preschool period. The main reason for this conclusion is that a great deal of sex typing occurs *before* the child acquires either a firm notion of his or her gender identity or a knowledge of sex differences. Since gender constancy and acquisition of sex-role stereotypes follow rather than precede early sex typing, they could hardly be considered its causes. We shall briefly cite the evidence for this conclusion.

Children show considerable sex typing in toy and activity preferences by the time they are 2 years old (Blakemore et al., 1979; Etaugh, Collins, & Gerson, 1975). But both gender constancy and knowledge of sex-role stereotypes come later. As we reviewed earlier, the higher levels of gender constancy are not attained until at least 5 or 6 years of age. Of course, it is possible to argue that the highest levels of gender constancy are not necessary for self-socialization of sex typing—that perhaps the attainment of gender identity, or the simple knowledge that one is a boy or a girl, is enough. In fact, this has occasionally been suggested, by both cognitive-developmental and social learning theorists. For example, in a revised cognitive-developmental position, Ullian (1976) proposed that sex typing before full gender constancy may represent the mistaken belief by young children that one must do same-sex things or else lose one's gender and become a member of the opposite sex! Within a social learning theory perspective, full attainment of gender constancy is also not necessary for sex typing. According to this perspective, sex typing results from children's knowledge that they are male or female and are subject to the same expectations and reinforcement contingencies as others of their own sex (Bandura, 1969b; Bussey & Perry, 1976).

But even if theorists are agreed, for whatever reasons, that full gender constancy is not necessary for sex typing, there are still grounds for rejecting the hypothesis that early sex typing results from attempts to socialize the self to conceptions of same-sex-appropriate behavior. This is because children reveal a knowledge of sex-role stereotypes only after they have already displayed considerable sex typing in their interests and activities. One group of researchers found that although 2-year-old boys strongly preferred boys' toys, not one of the boys could identify the toys as being more appropriate for boys than for girls (Blakemore et al., 1979). In another intriguing study, Eisenberg, Murray, and Hite (1982) approached 3- and 4-year-old children in the nursery school as the children initiated sex-typed activities (went to the dress-up corner, to the sand box, etc.) and asked them why they had chosen the activities they did. The children did not justify their behavior on the basis of its appropriateness for their sex. Instead, when explaining their choice of toy,

children referred mainly to what they thought the toy could do (e.g., "You can wash her hair," or "You can roll it") or to specific characteristics of the toy (e.g., "It's a pretty color"). In sum, there is little evidence that self-socialization to same-sex standards plays much of a role in the origination of sex typing during the preschool years.

If self-socialization to same-sex stereotypes does not account for early sex typing, then what does? Biological predispositions for certain kinds of toys or activities may contribute. Parents may also be furnishing their children sex-typed toys and rewarding their play with them. Sex-segregated play with peers provides further opportunities for practicing certain activities and exercising certain interests. As children practice their sex-typed activities and are rewarded by their same-sex peers for doing so, their feelings of competence at the activities should grow. Children like to do what they think they can do best (Bandura, 1981). Early sex typing may have little to do with conscious attempts to adhere to sex stereotypes.

The preceding discussion does not imply that self-socialization of sex typing does not occur. It almost assuredly does, but probably not much before children enter grade school. Once children are 5 or 6 years old there is more evidence that children's concepts about their own gender and their knowledge of sex-role stereotypes actively influence the sex-typing process. For example, children who score at the higher stages of gender constancy prefer to watch a same-sex actor rather than an opposite-sex actor on a television set (Slaby & Frey, 1975). Other researchers showed 4- to 6-year-olds a specially made television commercial that depicted either two boys or two girls playing with a new toy (Ruble et al., 1981). Afterwards, when the subjects were given a chance to play with the toy, high gender-constancy children played with the toy if the children in the commercial had been of their sex, but avoided the toy if the actors had been of the opposite sex. Low gender-constancy children played with the toy regardless of the actors' sex. By 8 or 9 years, children—especially boys—display strong tendencies to imitate actions they have discerned to be appropriate for members of their sex (Perry & Bussey, 1979). In sum, though neither gender constancy nor knowledge of sex-role stereotypes is necessary for early sex typing, both factors play a part in the sex-typing process in the elementary-school years.

Gender Schema Theory: The Psychology of the Highly Sex-Typed Person

All normal children eventually reach mature gender constancy and realize that there are different behavioral prescriptions for the two sexes, yet there still exist considerable individual differences within each sex in sex typing. One approach to understanding these differences is in terms of Bem's gender schema theory. In Bem's view, people differ in the extent to which gender becomes a salient dimension of the self. Self-schemas are mental summaries or constructions of past behavior that allow people to understand their own experience and to organize a wide range of information about themselves (Markus, Crane, Bernstein, & Siladi, 1982). Highly sex-typed individuals, suggests Bem, are *gender schematic* because, for them, gender is a salient factor influencing how they perceive, interpret, and react to social stimuli. Androgynous people are *gender aschematic,* because, unlike sex-typed people, they are not constantly on the alert for the sex-role implications of a situation or various courses of action.

As Bem predicts, highly sex-typed children and adults do possess a greater readiness to process information in terms of its relation to gender than their more androgynous counterparts. For example, sex-typed individuals have a stronger tendency to classify things as masculine or feminine. In one study, sex-typed and androgynous adults were presented with a list of 61 words, including some with masculine and some with feminine connotations (e.g., trousers, bikini, hurling, and blushing), and then were asked to recall the words; the sex-typed subjects more often grouped the words by gender than did the androgynous subjects (Bem, 1981). Kail and Levine (1976) found that 7- and 10-year-old girls, identified as highly sex-typed individuals on the basis of their toy preferences, were more likely to encode words in memory along a masculinity-femininity dimension than were their less sex-typed peers. In a study by Perry and Perry (1975), when children were shown a movie depicting a man and a woman doing various things with objects and then were asked to recall what the adults did, children previously identified as highly sex-typed recalled more of what the same-sex model did than of what the adult of the opposite sex did. Thus it does appear that highly sex-typed people possess a salient gender schema. We might expect self-socialization of sex roles to be stronger in these individuals than in more androgynous, gender aschematic people.

We have proposed that the concept of self-socialization helps explain the sex-typing process as children enter the school years, if not before. We have also stressed that children differ considerably in the strength of their concern over conforming to culturally prescribed sex roles. Thus far, however, we have said very little about what motivates sex typing. What provides the impetus for self-socialization and why do some children worry about this process more than others? According to social learning theory, the family, the school, the peer group, and other socializing agencies not only teach children sex roles but also pressure children to conform to these roles. In the next section we review the evidence regarding social influences on sex typing.

SOCIAL INFLUENCES ON SEX-ROLE DEVELOPMENT

Family Influences on Sex Typing

Parents as Tutors of Sex Roles Many parents structure their children's activities in ways that give birth to sex differences. Rheingold and Cook (1975) went into the homes of children under 6 years of age and took detailed notes on how the parents had furnished the children's bedrooms. Boys' rooms contained more vehicles, depots, machines, army equipment and soldiers, animal furnishings, education-art materials, spatial-temporal toys, and sports equipment. Girls' rooms contained more dolls (especially girl and baby dolls), and floral-patterned, ruffled furnishings (e.g., floral bedspreads with lace trimming). Note that boys were provided with a wider variety of toys and that their toys were ones that directed the boys' attention to activities away from home—toward sports, cars, animals, and the military. Girls' toys directed their attention to keeping house and caring for children.

A look at the household chores assigned to boys and girls confirms the belief that parents channel their children into traditional sex roles. Girls are assigned tasks usually performed by the mother—dishes, beds, and dusting. Boys are asked to help with chores typically carried out by the father, such as taking out the garbage and washing the car. Although assignment of household tasks by sex has decreased over the last 2 decades, it is still substantial (L. Hoffman, 1977).

Not only do parents actively solicit sex-appropriate behavior, but they reward it when it occurs; they also punish cross-sex activity (Langlois & Downs, 1980). In a home observation study of parents and their toddlers, Fagot (1978a) found that parents reinforced (with smiles, attention, and praise) their daughters more than their sons for dancing, dressing up, playing with dolls, asking for help, and simply following the parents around the house, but they rewarded their boys more than their girls for playing with blocks. Parents criticized their girls more than their boys for manipulating objects, running, jumping, and climbing, but they rebuked their boys more for playing with dolls, asking for help, or volunteering their help. Corter and Bow (1976) found that mothers smile more at their infant daughters than at their infant sons

when their children are inactive, but when the children get involved in manipulating a toy, mothers smile more at their sons than their daughters. Apparently, parents like to see their sons doing things with their environments. What causes the differential treatment of children by sex? Parents may fear for their children's adjustment and acceptance by others if the children do not live up to cultural stereotypes for their sex. Parents may also fear for their own embarrassment at having reared a "deficiently" sex-typed child.

Adults' selection of activities for children is influenced by the stereotypes the adults hold about sex-appropriate behavior. In several studies, adults have been introduced to an infant or young child, told the child is either male or female (the child's real sex is not obvious), and then given an opportunity to interest the child in toys that are available. Adults do try to interest a "girl" in feminine play (e.g., nurturant play with a doll and bottle) and a "boy" in masculine play (e.g., tricycle riding and playing ball). Not surprisingly, it is those adults who most strongly endorse traditional sex roles that are the most active in directing children into sex-appropriate activities (Bell & Carver, 1980; Frisch, 1977; Smith & Lloyd, 1978). Children younger than 2 or 3 years of age may be too naive to socialize themselves to conform to sex stereotypes, but their parents are doing a good job of it for them!

Sometimes stereotypes cause parents to place different interpretations on the behavior of their sons and their daughters, and, if these different interpretations are communicated to the children, lasting effects on the children's emotional and social development may well result. In a provocative study, Condry and Condry (1976) showed adults a videotape of an infant who was displaying reactions to a variety of stimuli, including a jack-in-the-box, a loud noise, and a teddy bear. Half the adults were told that the infant was a girl; the other half were told it was a boy. The adults had to indicate what emotion they thought the infant was experiencing at various points during the tape. When the infant was shown the jack-in-the-box, the infant displayed a moderate amount of arousal that was neither clearly positive nor clearly negative. The interesting finding was that the way the adults interpreted this ambiguous emotional reaction depended on the sex they thought the child was: If told the infant was a girl, the adults tended to perceive the arousal as *fear*; if told it was a boy, they interpreted it as *anger*. One can imagine the consequences if parents tend to react to their daughters' ambiguous emotions by giving comfort and solace, saying, "You're afraid, dear," but tend to react to similar emotional expression in boys with impatience, perhaps angrily exclaiming, "You're just mad—now stop it!"

We have suggested that much early sex typing results from parents' pressuring their young to conform to stereotypes. But we must not lose sight of the possibility that some of the differences in the ways parents treat their sons and their daughters may be reactions to preexisting, perhaps biologically-based, sex differences in the children. Bell and Carver (1980) found that, regardless of an infant's sex, adults tend to give a quiet infant feminine toys to play with and give a vocally active infant masculine toys to play with. If, for biological reasons, more girls happen to be quiet than boys, we would expect parents to furnish more feminine toys for their daughters.

A number of studies also have found that parents tend to show more "respect" for their sons than their daughters. Parents are quicker to respond to demanding-type, fussy behavior from their baby boys than from their baby girls (Feiring & Lewis, 1979; Goldberg & Lewis, 1969; Hutt, 1977; Moss, 1967); they are more likely to retrieve a distressed male infant than a distressed female infant (Corter & Bow, 1976); they are more prone to stop feeding a baby boy than a baby girl if the infant spits up or coughs (Parke & Sawin, 1981); they put up with more insolence from their sons than from their daughters (Hoffman & Saltzstein, 1967); and they interrupt the speech of girls more often than they interrupt their boys (Greif, 1979). One interpretation is that, because of their stereotypic ideals, parents value boys more or believe boys are worthy of more respect. But we should remember that when children do not get their way, or feel they are losing control over a situation, boys tend to make life far more miserable for their parents than girls do. Maybe boys do a better job than girls of training their parents to respond when they fuss. In sum, parents treat boys and girls differently, in part because parents want their children to conform to cultural stereotypes, but also because boys and girls demand different sorts of treatment.

Parents as Models of Sex-Role Behavior Social learning and cognitive-developmental theorists believe that the presence of an adult male and an adult female in the home can help sharpen children's conceptions of sex-role behavior, especially if the parents conform to cultural stereotypes for their sex. By giving children a clearer picture of what is required of them if they want to become like others of their sex, the parents can thus assist their children in the process of self-socialization, which we discussed earlier. But neither the social learning theorists nor the cognitive-developmentalists believe that parents serve as uniquely important models for the sex typing of children. Youngsters are thought to base their notions of sex-appropriate behavior on observations of many examples of each sex, both within and outside of the home.

As we have previously mentioned, Freud assigned identification with the same-sex parent a primary role in the sex-typing process. Though there is no evidence that sex typing results from identification with a same-sex parent perceived by the child to be a hostile rival for the opposite-sex parent's affection, there is some evidence that parental identification does influence sex typing. In Chapter 4, we concluded that two variables strengthening children's imitation of an adult are the adult's warmth and perceived power.

There is substantial evidence that masculine boys have fathers who are both affectionate and powerful—these men love their sons and enjoy their company, are dominant over their wives in making family decisions, and control rewards and punishments available to the boys (Hetherington, 1967; Mussen & Rutherford, 1963; Payne & Mussen, 1956). Perhaps affectionate fathers are most likely to take the time to participate with their sons in masculine activities.

Curiously, despite the strong relationship between boys' masculinity and their fathers' personalities, there is very little evidence for a parallel relationship between mothers and daughters. In fact, as we shall see later, paternal personality characteristics influence girls' sex typing more than the mothers' personalities.

In support of the influential role of the father on boys' sex typing is the finding that boys from father-absent homes engage in more feminine play and develop feminine interest patterns, are less aggressive, more dependent, and engage in fewer contact sports (Bach, 1946; Burton, 1972; Drake & McDougall, 1977; Hetherington, 1966; Lynn & Sawrey, 1959; Sears, 1951). Father-absent boys also score lower in school achievement tests and are deficient in general intelligence; they also display reversals in the usual male pattern of superiority of spatial/quantitative skills over verbal skills (Blanchard & Biller, 1971; Carlsmith, 1964; Shinn, 1978). In addition, their general social and emotional adjustment is rated lower by their teachers (LeCorgne & Laosa, 1976).

Recently, maternal employment has been implicated as a factor in children's sex role development, especially for girls. Daughters of working mothers have more flexible ideas concerning the roles of the sexes: They believe that both men and women go to work and earn money, make important decisions, take care of children, do the dishes, and do housework. They perceive women as more competitive, more competent, and less easily hurt emotionally. They report more enjoyment at getting into fights and their teachers rate them as less quiet and less restrained. Of significance is the fact that daughters of working mothers are more likely to nominate their mother as the person they would most want to be if they had their choice of being anyone in the world. Such findings suggest that not only do these girls develop more egalitarian views of sex roles, but that they value and will try to emulate their mothers' independence (Marantz & Mansfield, 1977; Miller, 1975).

The Special Role of the Father   In a provocative perspective on sex-role development, Johnson (1963, 1977) has proposed that fathers play a uniquely important role in the sex-typing process. According to Johnson, fathers show great discrepancies in the ways that they treat their sons as compared to their daughters. Johnson argues that mothers treat their sons and daughters rather alike, but that fathers develop distinctly different styles of interaction with their male and female children, which lead the children to develop masculine and feminine traits. Johnson proposes that fathers interact with sons in a demanding and critical manner, insisting that the boys display traditionally masculine behaviors and shun feminine ones. On the other hand, fathers teach daughters how to be feminine by interacting with them in a warmly indulgent, protective, and mildly flirtatious way. It is primarily the heterosexual aspect of femininity—how to relate to members of the opposite sex—that Johnson believes girls learn through interactions with their fathers. Johnson suggests that by interacting with their daughters as interested males who protect them from outside males, fathers treat their daughters like "sex objects" and teach them how to be "little ladies." Thus the father socializes both boys and girls toward independence, but in different ways—boys toward instrumental competence in the male peer group and girls toward eventual establishment of an expressive role within a new family context.

One might take issue with some of Johnson's reasons for why fathers and not mothers differentiate between the sexes to such an extent. For example, Johnson argues that there are stronger taboos on mother-son incest than on father-daughter incest, and the stronger mother-son taboos prevent mothers from "flirting" with sons the way that fathers do with daughters. Nevertheless, there is considerable evidence that fathers are, as a group, far more concerned about socializing sex-appropriate behavior in their children than are mothers.

Stronger sex discrimination by fathers is visible even when their children are infants. When parents are asked to rate their 1-day-old babies, fathers of boys proudly report their babies to be firmer, larger-featured, stronger, better coordinated, more alert, and hardier than do the fathers of daughters; fathers of girls see their offspring as softer, finer-featured, awkward, inattentive, weaker, and delicate. Mothers' ratings are far less influenced by the sex of their child (Rubin, Provenzano, & Luria, 1974). Earlier we discussed a study by Condry and Condry (1976) in which adult men and women were found to interpret moderate distress in a male infant as anger, but to interpret the same reaction in a female infant as fear. A sidelight of this study was that the discrimination by sex was stronger for men than for women.

Men are more likely than women to judge certain behaviors as definitely more appropriate for boys and other activities as definitely more appropriate for girls (Fagot, 1973). At home, fathers, more than mothers, actively reward children for play that is considered appropriate to their sex and punish play that is considered inappropriate (Fagot, 1978a; Lansky, 1967). In a laboratory study, Langlois and Downs (1980) gave children instructions to play with same-sex and cross-sex toys and then sent in their mothers or fathers. Fathers were particularly pleased when their children played with same-sex toys and became especially upset when their children engaged in cross-sex play.

A variety of findings supports Johnson's hunch that girls learn to relate to males in part by interacting with a loving, masculine father who enjoys his daughter's femininity. When observed saying goodbye to their children at day-care centers, fathers kissed, hugged, and cuddled their daughters more than their sons; mothers were equally demonstrative toward their sons and their daughters (Noller, 1978). Girls who score high on feminine sex typing tend to have fathers who are masculine and assertive, yet affectionate and approving of feminine behavior in their daughters (Hetherington, 1967; Mussen & Rutherford, 1963). Young women who describe their fathers as affectionate, sympathetic, and interested in them have the strongest expectations to marry and have a family (Johnson, 1977). In fact, women who describe their fathers as having invested a less serious or dependable interest in them report more difficulty in achieving orgasm (Fisher, 1973).

If fathers play a special role in establishing heterosexual aspects of their daughters' femininity, then girls who have lost their fathers might show unusual patterns of relating to males. Hetherington (1972) observed the behavior of father-absent and father-present adolescent girls at a mixed-sex recreation center as well as during an interview with a male experimenter. The effects of father absence were dramatic, but they depended, too, on whether the absence was due to divorce or death. Daughters of divorcees seemed overly anxious for masculine attention, displaying exceptionally assertive behavior with boys and men. For example, they asked boys to dance and assumed relaxed, almost provocative postures when interviewed by a male researcher. By comparison, the daughters of widows seemed shy, sexually anxious, and uncomfortable around males. They tended to be the "wall flowers" at dances, and they assumed tighter, more inhibited and distant stances when talking to male interviewers. The behavior of father-present girls generally fell somewhere between these two extremes. Hetherington speculated that divorced women may communicate to their daughters an aggressive, embittered attitude toward men, whereas widows may idealize their lost spouses, making their daughters feel that no other men are as worthy as the deceased husbands/fathers.

The extreme effects of father absence observed by Hetherington may be limited to adolescence. Hainline and Feig (1978) found only a single difference in the heterosexual attitudes of adult women who had lost their fathers through either death or divorce in childhood: Daughters of widows more strongly disapproved of premarital sex than daughters of divorcees.

Why do men perpetuate sex roles more ardently than women? Is it because, as some people have stated, men are concerned with maintaining the power and status advantages they currently enjoy? Maybe so, in part, but another explanation is that men are simply transmitting to others the stronger pressure they themselves have experienced for conforming to the culturally prescribed male sex role. Boys are more highly sex-typed than girls (Brown, 1956; Faulkender, 1980; Kleinke & Nicholson, 1979; Marcus & Overton, 1978), partly because cross-sex play is punished more severely in boys, both by their parents and their playmates (Fagot, 1977; Fling & Manosevitz, 1972). Consequently, boys more actively self-socialize themselves to sex roles: As compared to girls, they more easily accept cultural stereotypes for sex-appropriate behavior (Best et al., 1977; Edelbrock & Sugawara, 1978; Garrett et al., 1977), and they show a stronger preference for attending to and imitating same-sex models (Abramovitch & Grusec, 1978; Grusec & Brinker, 1972; Slaby & Frey, 1975; Wolf, 1973, 1975). Is it any wonder that males are also more concerned about socializing others to traditional roles?

Sibling Influences Having a sibling of the same sex might increase a child's sex typing: The children might model same-sex behaviors for each other and practice same-sex activities together. Having an opposite-sex sibling, on the other hand, might increase children's exposure to cross-sex activities, making the children more androgynous. In support of such a notion, several studies have found that children's sex-typing scores are more feminine if they have a sister, but more masculine if they have a brother (Brim, 1958; Koch, 1956a, 1956b; Sutton-Smith, Roberts, & Rosenberg, 1964; Sutton-Smith & Rosenberg, 1970). Also, father-absent boys are not as likely to show reduced masculine sex typing if they have a brother—especially an older brother (Biller, 1968; Santrock, 1970; Wohlford, Santrock, Berger, & Liberman, 1971).

But the evidence is not clear-cut. Several theorists have proposed that when two siblings are of the same sex, the children may strive harder to establish their own independent identities. This may lead them to cultivate personality traits that are different from those they perceive in their same-sex sibling. This is sometimes called a *contrast hypothesis* or a *role diversification hypothesis* of sibling development. If this hypothesis has merit, we might expect children with same-sex siblings to be less sex typed than children with opposite-sex siblings. Several investigators have reported just such a pattern (Grotevant, 1978; Schachter, Shore, Feldman-Rotman, Marquis, & Campbell, 1976; Tauber, 1979). Obviously, no conclusive statement about sibling effects on sex typing can be offered at this point.

Peer and Teacher Influences Children's playmates and teachers share in training sex roles. A considerable amount of sex-role learning occurs in the context of sex-segregated play. Playing together with others of the same sex allows children to learn and practice same-sex activities. Indeed, Eisenberg-Berg, Boothby, and Matson (1979) found that the most feminine nursery schoolers were those who interacted mostly with girls; the most masculine children preferred the company of male peers.

Preschool children reward sex-appropriate

and punish sex-inappropriate behavior. Fagot (1977) found that nursery schoolers reward boys for activities like hammering and playing in the sandbox, but reward girls for playing in the kitchen, playing with dolls, and dressing up. Children are critical, sometimes downright scandalized, when they discover a child—especially a boy—engaged in cross-sex behavior (Fagot, 1977; Langlois & Downs, 1980). Peer-dispensed rewards and punishments actually influence the behavior of children a great deal. Lamb and Roopnarine (1979) found that when 3-year-olds were criticized by their peers for engaging in a cross-sex activity, they quickly shifted what they were doing; when they were rewarded for sex-appropriate play, they continued at it longer than usual. From an early age, peers guide each other into sex-typed play.

Nursery-school teachers also reward sex-appropriate play and discourage cross-sex play, although they do not discriminate by sex as much as the peer group does. In fact, many teachers, at least at the preschool level, show a bias in the direction of eliciting and reinforcing feminine behaviors from both boys and girls (Etaugh, Collins, & Gerson, 1975; Fagot, 1977; Fagot & Patterson, 1969). Furthermore, unlike the peer group, teachers do not reject boys with feminine interests.

The tendency for teachers to encourage feminine behavior seems to increase with their experience as teachers. Inexperienced teachers of either sex reinforce children for behavior appropriate for each child's sex, but as they gain experience in the classroom, teachers become more interested in trying to preserve peace and order and in promoting the kinds of attributes they perceive as necessary for success in school. It so happens that many of these attributes and behaviors are of a feminine nature. The conflict young boys feel as their peers try to socialize them toward masculinity and their teachers toward femininity may contribute to boys' early dislike of and poorer achievement in school (Etaugh & Hughes, 1975; Fagot, 1978b, 1981; Levitin & Channie, 1972).

School books also influence sex typing. In children's books, boys do more active, important, and interesting things. Females, on the other hand, tend to be passive, dependent, ineffectual people who either serve the males or else get rescued by them; rarely are they shown outside the home, active in a professional capacity. Flerx, Fidler, and Rogers (1976) found that exposing children to specially written stories in which adult characters of both sexes performed traditionally sex-typed activities (e.g., both men and women went to work, took part in child care, etc.) helped break children of their rigid beliefs that certain activities are appropriate for only one sex or the other. Our previous discussion of the effects of stereotypes on the processing of social information, however, would lead us to predict that exposure to counter-stereo-typed material would have to be frequent and massive in order to have much of an impact on children's beliefs. This is because children tend to ignore information that challenges their beliefs or else they distort the information to fit their preconceptions.

Influence of Television

Television, like children's fiction, portrays sex roles in stereotypic ways. Men are more often depicted as constructive, aggressive, and evil. Women characters more often defer to others, get into trouble for displaying initiative, use unrealistic styles of influence over others (especially magic), and have little influence over the course of events (Sternglanz & Serbin, 1974). It is no surprise that children who watch a great deal of television display more stereotyped toy and activity preferences than children who watch little television (Frueh & McGhee, 1975).

Television is potentially a powerful medium for making children's conceptions of appropriate behavior for the sexes more egalitarian. Davidson, Yasuna, and Tower (1979) found that when 5- and 6-year-olds were shown a cartoon depicting characters in nontraditional roles (e.g., two knowledgeable girls helping some boys build a clubhouse), the children's stereotypes became less conventional. Considering the large amount of television viewing in which children engage, television would seem to be a promising candidate for liberating children's sex-role stereotypes.

ARE TRADITIONAL ROLES APPROPRIATE TODAY?

For many years the assumption has been that strong sex typing is healthy. Perhaps this began with Freud, who maintained that a strong identification with the masculine or feminine role was essential for normal development. However, this assumption is under attack today (Lamb & Urberg, 1978). Foremost among the critics of this position is Bem (1975, 1981), who argues that slavish adherence to a given sex role produces the gender schematic individual who is so concerned about behaving in sex-appropriate ways that he or she fails to display a traditionally cross-sex attribute even when it would be beneficial to do so. We shall now take a closer look at Bem's proposition and the evidence that supports it.

Androgyny: New Standard of Sex-Role Maturity?

Parsons (1955) used the terms "instrumental" and "expressive" to refer, respectively, to the traditional masculine and feminine roles in our society. The masculine role is instrumental because it involves decision making, leadership, achievement outside the family, competitiveness, and serving in the breadwinner role. The feminine role is expressive because it entails emotionality, kindness, concern for interpersonal harmony, and an orientation toward caring for others in the home. Androgyny theorists, such as Bem (1975), suggest that sex-typed people feel comfortable performing behaviors consistent with one of these two roles, but that they have tremendous difficulty displaying behav-

iors congruent with the other role, even when it would be to their advantage. Androgynous people, in contrast, feel freer to display either instrumental or expressive behavior, as the situation calls for it (see also Spence, Helmreich, & Stapp, 1975).

In an early test of her theory, Bem (1975) asked men and women who had been classified as masculine, feminine, or androgynous (on the basis of Bem's Sex Role Inventory) to participate in situations calling for either traditionally masculine or traditionally feminine behavior. The test for masculine behavior involved pressuring the subject to change his or her opinions and measuring how firmly the subject stood his or her ground. The test for feminine behavior involved asking the subject to look after a kitten for several minutes and measuring the subject's nurturant play with the animal. The hypothesis was that androgynous individuals would perform equally well in both situations, in the sense that they would display feminine nurturance when the situation required it and masculine independence when that was required, but that sex-typed subjects would be able to display only one or the other sort of behavior—whichever was consistent with their sex role. Results were consistent with Bem's hypothesis: Androgynous adults "passed" both tests, while sex-typed adults "flunked" one or both of them.

Sometimes the thought of doing something cross-sex-typed makes sex-typed people feel so uncomfortable that they avoid doing it even though it would bring them financial rewards. Bem and Lenney (1976) gave androgynous, masculine, and feminine adults opportunities to engage in a variety of masculine activities (e.g., oiling the squeaky lid of a tool box and baiting a fishing line) and feminine behaviors (e.g., ironing napkins and filling a baby bottle). The adults were promised different sums of money for performing the jobs. Subjects sex typed as either masculine or feminine more often avoided cross-sex activities, even when the cross-sex activity led to more money than performing a same-sex job.

Masculine men show the greatest preference for gender-congruent tasks (Helmreich, Spence, & Holahan, 1979).

Traditionally, the instrumental male role and expressive female role have been thought of as complementary and compatible. But would the man who is "all business" and the woman who is "all feeling" really be a good match for each other? In an interesting study, Ickes and Barnes (1978) paired previously unacquainted adults for a get-acquainted session. The adults had previously taken Bem's Sex Role Inventory. The main finding was that mixed-sex dyads composed of a masculine male and a feminine female actually got along less well together than mixed-sex dyads in which at least one member was androgynous. Recall Jacklin and Maccoby's (1978) finding that when 33-month-olds were paired for a play session with an opposite-sex child, the children tended to put each other off. Maybe highly sex-typed adults have never outgrown their early discomfort at communicating with opposite-sex people!

Do androgynous adults make better parents? As one might expect, fathers who score as androgynous participate in routine caregiving and play with their children more than masculine sex-typed fathers do (Russell, 1978). But Baumrind (1982) has cautioned that we must not jump to the conclusion that androgyny is highly desirable in parents. We have seen throughout this book that a parenting style of high affection plus firm enforcement of maturity demands is associated with a variety of measures of social competence in children—friendliness, popularity, altruism, taking responsibility, self-reliance, and self-direction. Baumrind reports that androgynous mothers are less nurturant and androgynous fathers are less firm than their more sex-typed counterparts. Furthermore, the children of androgynous parents are rated as somewhat less competent than the children of sex-typed parents. Whether the presence of androgynous parents *per se* is detrimental to children's development or whether androgynous parents are, for whatever reasons,

deficient in critical aspects of child-rearing (e.g., less consistent in enforcement of sanctions, less affectionate, use inductive reasoning less often, or are more permissive) is a question that remains for future researchers to answer.

Are androgynous people happier, better adjusted, and more appreciated by other people? To answer this, we need to look at the data for males and females separately.

During childhood, there are few signs that being androgynous is more beneficial to boys' adjustment than is being sex typed as masculine. Through adolescence, masculine boys enjoy more self-esteem and popularity with their peers and teachers than do boys with apparent feminine components to their personalities (Hall & Halberstadt, 1980; Massad, 1981; Mussen, 1962). However, in adulthood the addition of feminine attributes to men's personalities (e.g., nurturance, concern for the well-being of others) boosts their self-esteem as well as their popularity with other adults (Major, Carnevale, & Deaux, 1981). We must emphasize that it is the addition of feminine traits, not the substitution of feminine traits for masculine ones, that is desirable. In other words, it is the ability to engage confidently in both instrumental and expressive behaviors, as the situation demands, that is desirable—not a feminizing or toning down of one's masculine potential.

Feminine girls are rated as more socially mature by their teachers than their more androgynous and masculine counterparts (Hall & Halberstadt, 1980). However, there are signs that the possession of masculine traits is also of benefit to females, in both childhood and adulthood, in critical ways. Girls who see themselves in exclusively feminine terms have poorer self-concepts, are less well accepted by their peers, and have more difficulty achieving in mathematics (Hall & Halberstadt, 1980; Massad, 1981). In adulthood, women who perceive themselves as possessing desirable masculine traits enjoy more self-esteem, report fewer neurotic symptoms, and are perceived as better adjusted by other adults (Heilbrun, 1981; Helmreich, Spence, & Holahan, 1979; Major et al., 1981; Spence, Helmreich, & Holahan, 1979). Thus for both sexes there seems to be some advantage to incorporating qualities of the opposite sex into one's own personality, though the advantage of doing this may be seen earlier in girls than in boys.

While there are apparent advantages of androgyny, we must point out that mental health and adjustment are more strongly associated with high masculinity than with high femininity. Individuals of either sex who are categorized as highly feminine are more at risk for low self-esteem and poor social adjustment than are people categorized as highly masculine (Bem, 1975; Major et al., 1981). Is there something about femininity that actually causes this? In our next section we shall examine this question.

The Female's Double Bind

Although females are expected to conform to cultural stereotypes for the female sex role, society places less value on feminine behavior. It is instructive to note some of the differences in the attributes adults assign to men and women. When adults are asked to nominate qualities that describe men and women, they say that men are more assertive, independent, dominant, competitive, ambitious, stable, confident, coarse, disorderly, objective, competent, logical, and sexually active; females are said to be more sensitive, warm, expressive, appreciative, gentle, rattle-brained, complaining, fickle, loving, supportive, poised, and sexually inhibited (Broverman, Vogel, Broverman, Clarkson, & Rosenkrantz, 1972). But are these two sets of traits equally valued? In a revealing study, a group of clinical psychologists were presented with a list of personality attributes and asked to pick attributes that they thought were essential for "the healthy man," "the healthy woman," and "the healthy adult" (Broverman et al., 1972). The attributes the clinicians ascribed to the healthy man and to

the healthy adult did not differ. For example, the psychologists thought both the healthy man and the healthy adult should be competent, mature, logical, and independent. However, there were huge gaps between the clinicians' description of the healthy woman and their description of the healthy adult. In fact, some of the attributes ascribed to the healthy woman (e.g., supportive, receptive, and refined) could be considered antagonistic to what the clinicians considered essential for the healthy adult. Thus women in our society can't win: if they adopt behaviors specified for the healthy adult, they risk being labeled "unfeminine"; if they adopt feminine behaviors, they risk being thought of as "immature."

The message that traditional female traits are undervalued is not lost on the developing female. Although very young preschool girls are similar to boys in valuing activities appropriate for their own sex more than cross-sex activities (Kuhn et al., 1978), over the elementary-school years girls show a steady decrease in own-gender pride (Zalk & Katz, 1978) and even come to belittle such traditionally feminine prosocial qualities as considerateness, helpfulness, appreciation of art and music, and creativity (Connor & Serbin, 1978; Hall & Halberstadt, 1980). By adulthood, females as well as males assign more favorable evaluations to male traits than to female traits (Rosenkrantz, Vogel, Bee, Broverman, & Broverman, 1968). Perhaps the frustration females so often experience is due to this contradiction between their desire to be both feminine and also competent and valued (Broverman et al., 1972), and is one reason why more women report signs of maladjustment (Tyler, 1965).

What might be done to correct this injustice? Of course, traditional sex roles are changing in some important respects. For example, more and more women are seeking fulfillment in careers, and advances in contraceptive methods have given women the opportunity to exert more control over their lives. Given this trend, we might wonder whether parents who socialize girls according to the traditional feminine roles are doing them a disservice. Providing girls with opportunities traditionally more available or acceptable for boys is obviously one possible route to correcting the imbalance. But not everyone agrees that this is the best route. Socializing girls to be like boys may have some bad effects as well; perhaps it would increase the level of aggression and competitiveness in society. Eron (1980) has suggested that instead of offering girls opportunities traditionally reserved for boys, it may be better to socialize boys in the same way that girls have been socialized. This means that if parents take pains to socialize boys like girls—avoiding the use of harsh physical punishment, employing inductive reasoning, and so on—then parents will foster in boys the socially positive, tender, cooperative, nurturant, and sensitive qualities that are antithetical to aggressive behavior. Possibly, socializing children for the sex roles of tomorrow should involve some of both strategies: broadening opportunities outside the home for females, and preparing males to share in the responsibilities of homemaking and child care, and to be more compassionate.

But in the meantime, how do parents who wish to prepare their children for egalitarian sex roles do it in such a way that their children develop a firm and comfortable gender identity? Can a parent who wants his or her son to grow up to be compassionate and gentle also expect the son to take pride in being male? And how does a parent communicate to his or her daughter a belief that career commitment is not incompatible with femininity? Lamb (1979) speculates that the responsibility for taking care of these problems may lie primarily with the father. We have seen that in many ways fathers are especially effective at instilling in their children a sense of masculinity or femininity. If fathers are able to foster desirable cross-sex attributes and interests in their children, yet at the same time reassure their children that such behaviors do not threaten the integrity of the children's gender identity, then per-

haps more children will be able to develop some degree of androgyny without confusion over their gender identity.

SUMMARY

Sex typing, the process by which children come to acquire the behaviors, attitudes, and feelings that are more commonly associated with one sex than with the other, is also known as sex-role development. Indeed, there are many differences between the sexes in personality and social behavior which can be attributed to their sex-role development. Boys and girls differ in play preferences, in peer relations, in interactions with their parents, and in scholastic achievement. Some of the sex differences confirm our stereotypes (e.g., boys are more aggressive than girls). However, some widely held stereotypes are myths. Girls, for example, cannot simply be characterized as the more dependent sex.

Masculinity and femininity can be conceptualized and assessed at several levels of psychological depth. For example, sex typing can be assessed in terms of how much a person overtly displays behaviors associated with a particular sex role, or, at a deeper level, in terms of how much a person subconsciously identifies with or feels more comfortable with one sex role rather than the other. It is currently preferable to consider masculinity and femininity not as polar opposites of a single dimension but as independent dimensions. People who feel free to perform both masculine and feminine behaviors, though of course at different times and under different circumstances, are considered androgynous.

Different views on sex typing are offered, including the trait, Freudian, social learning, cognitive-developmental, and biological perspectives. Trait theorists are not concerned with explaining the development of sex typing, but they expect people to display cross-situational consistencies in sex-typed behavior according to how much they possess masculine or feminine traits. Some children, who are labeled gender schematic because they monitor their behavior to make sure it conforms to a particular sex role, do show considerable cross-situational consistency in sex-typed behavior; more androgynous, gender aschematic children show more situational specificity in sex-typed behavior. Children tend to maintain their degree of masculinity or femininity as they approach adulthood, but life circumstances place demands on people that can alter their degree of sex typing. As men become grandfathers, for example, they become more androgynous.

Freud's theory that sex typing results primarily from the child's aggressive identification with the same-sex parent has little evidence to support it. Boys and girls almost certainly do learn some aspects of the male and female roles by observing their parents' actions, but it is doubtful that sex typing in either sex is primarily founded on a powerful wish to become like the same-sex parent.

Social learning theorists argue that a variety of socializing agents—parents, teachers, peers, and even television characters—contribute to sex typing by prompting, modeling, and selectively rewarding sex-appropriate behavior. According to this view, children of both sexes cognitively acquire the behavior patterns appropriate for both sexes (mainly through observational learning), but they prefer to perform behaviors they discern as appropriate for their own sex role. In part, children prefer to perform same-sex-appropriate activities because they expect external reward for doing so (as well as censure for behaving in cross-sex fashion), but sex typing eventually also comes under the control of internal self-regulatory processes. Once children discern standards of sex-appropriate and sex-inappropriate behavior, they find it works to their advantage to monitor their own behavior to conform to these standards. In other words, to make sure that their behavior conforms to cultural expectations, children direct themselves to behave in same-sex-appropriate fashion, praise themselves for

doing so, and criticize themselves for deviating from these prescriptions.

According to cognitive-developmental theory, as children reach the stage of concrete operations and understand notions of classification, they firmly establish their realization that they belong to a category of same-sex individuals, and they delight in perceiving themselves to be similar to others of this category. This process of matching one's behavior to standards discerned to be appropriate to one's sex is not thought to progress very far until the child attains gender constancy, or the knowledge that gender is an underlying biological property that remains invariant across time and changes in surface appearance (e.g., clothing, hairstyle, toy play, etc.). Cognitive-developmental theorists see little need for external social pressures in fueling the sex-typing process; sex-role development is intrinsically motivated simply by the feelings of self-esteem that result from perceiving oneself to be similar to a class of same-sex others.

Both social learning and cognitive-developmental theorists believe that sex typing is in part a result of self-socialization in which children first acquire a knowledge of sex-role stereotypes, or conceptions of appropriate behavior for the two sexes, and then actively seek to incorporate aspects of the same-sex role into their personalities and behavior. However, sex typing in the first 2 or 3 years of life is probably not dependent on conscious attempts to match one's behavior to conceptions of same-sex appropriate behavior. This is because young children show considerable sex typing in their toy and activity preferences before they realize that certain behaviors are more appropriate for boys and certain activities are more appropriate for girls. Also, contrary to the cognitive-developmental perspective, much sex typing occurs before gender constancy is developed in children. Actually, factors other than self-socialization—perhaps biological factors or the direct eliciting of sex-appropriate behavior by parents or peers—must account for the earliest manifestations of sex typing. However, in the elementary-school years, deliberate self-socializing to sex-role standards probably does occur.

Evidence is increasing that biological factors (genetics, hormones, neurology, muscularity, and temperament) contribute to certain sex differences. Future theorists should pay serious attention to how biology, social learning, and cognition interact to produce sex differences and sex typing.

As social learning theorists predict, much of the impetus for sex typing comes from external social sources, such as the child's parents, siblings, teachers, playmates, and the television set. Parents furnish their children with sex-appropriate toys, reward their play with them, and punish their play with cross-sex toys. Fathers play a more active role than mothers in transmitting traditional sex roles to children. Fathers believe more strongly than mothers that the two sexes should be different, and fathers go to greater lengths to solicit and reward sex-appropriate play and to punish cross-sex activity. Although fathers seem particularly distressed when their sons engage in cross-sex behavior, they also assume an active role in establishing their daughters' femininity, and particularly a feminine style of interacting with males. Perhaps fathers are more concerned than mothers about perpetuating sex roles because as children boys are subjected to substantially stronger pressures to conform to sex-role stereotypes than are girls. This may lead more boys than girls to grow up to be gender schematic, or primed to monitor and react to situations and people in terms of sex-role-appropriateness.

Children's teachers and peers are also tutors of sex roles, rewarding same-sex and punishing cross-sex behavior. The media, including children's books and television, likewise tend to depict the sexes in ways that help confirm stereotypic beliefs that the sexes are supposed to display distinctly different personality attributes, pursue different career paths, and so on.

As more women adopt traditionally masculine roles (e.g., pursue careers) and as more men assume a greater share of traditionally feminine responsibilities (e.g., child care and homemaking), the question of whether traditional sex roles will remain adaptive and appropriate is a legitimate one. There already is evidence that highly gender schematic individuals experience some difficulty and discomfort when called upon to perform a behavior traditionally associated with the opposite sex. Hence some psychologists have argued that the androgynous individual should be the new ideal. The evidence does suggest that adults who accept both masculine and feminine qualities in themselves enjoy more self-esteem as well as more respect from others, as compared to adults who deny the possession of cross-sex attributes. Interestingly, though, the possession of many masculine qualities is more related to psychological health than the possession of many feminine traits. If we assume that some degree of androgyny is desirable for tomorrow's adults, how should we socialize today's children? Should we encourage girls to be like boys, boys to be like girls, or some combination of both? How do we help children feel comfortable engaging in cross-sex behavior yet still feel secure and happy with their biologically assigned gender? Since fathers play such a powerful role in instilling a sense of masculinity or femininity in their children, they may be most valuable in helping children to feel content with their own gender while helping them to feel free to participate in cross-sex behavior when it would benefit them and others.

10 Peer Relations

In this chapter, we discuss children's relationships with their peers. A child's peers may be thought of as the child's social equals—other children who interact with the child at a similar level of complexity and who usually, but not necessarily, are similar in age to the child. For many years the peer group was neglected in accounts of socialization. Perhaps this was due to the influence of psychoanalytic theory, which held that the family is the major, if not exclusive, influence on the child's development. But times have changed. New theories have sprung up, theories that assign the peer group a prominent role in the socialization process. Furthermore, changes in modern society—such as increases in the employment of women with children—have meant that children are spending more and more time in the company of their peers and are doing so at earlier and earlier ages. These developments demand that the role of the peer group in the socialization process be taken seriously.

We shall begin with an overview of three theoretical perspectives on the influence of the peer group: ethological theory, cognitive-developmental theory, and social learning theory. While important differences exist among these theories, all share the conviction that peers are powerful forces in socialization. Moreover, all three theories assume that peers make unique contributions to socialization. In other words, peers are thought to teach and prepare each other for later life in ways that adults do not. Theorists have suggested, for example, that it is only through interaction with the peer group that children learn how to dominate, how to protect, how to assume responsibility, how to reciprocate, how to appreciate another's viewpoint, and how to arrive at realistic estimates of their own competencies and other personal attributes.

After summarizing theories of peer influence, we trace the young child's gradual integration into the peer group. Infants are interested in and influenced by their peers from a surprisingly early age. And once children familiarize themselves with a playmate or two, they spend a considerable amount of time engaged in social play. We shall describe children's play, tell how play changes with age, and speculate as to the purposes play serves in children's social and cognitive development.

Much of the chapter is devoted to the growth of social competence—children's acquisition of the skills necessary for making and sustaining friendships and for being accepted into the peer group. Rejected and isolated children usually want to make friends, but often simply do not know how to initiate and sustain mutually satisfying interactions with other children. Thankfully, recent research has identified some of the specific deficits in the social repertoires of such children, and researchers have developed techniques for teaching "fringe" children the skills necessary for effective social interaction. We shall describe progress in this area.

Much of children's interaction with their peers takes place in larger groups, such as play groups or clubs. When children join together in a group, what determines who will be the leader and who will be the followers? What factors influence group cohesiveness? How does the peer group control its members? What do children learn from group interaction? These are some of the questions we examine in our final section on group formation and dynamics.

THEORIES OF PEER RELATIONS

Ethological Theory

Ethologists emphasize that certain patterns of social interaction have evolved because they have had survival value for the species. Remember the case of mother-infant attachment. Ethologists point out that attachment bonds have evolved because they help infants develop social responsiveness to other members of the species, because they assist infants in exploration of the environment, and because they help infants survive until they are able to move on their own. But increasingly the peer group, too, is being recognized as serving important adaptive functions. Ethologists believe that peer contacts are essential for the acquisition of certain social skills necessary for competent functioning at maturity. The peer group is thought to provide children with opportunities to learn how to make friends, to learn and practice rules of reciprocity, and to learn to express certain behaviors (e.g., dominance, aggression, and sexual interest) in ways that are socially acceptable. In short, the peer group is believed to provide training for the assumption of adult social roles.

Perhaps the finest illustration of the critical role that peer contact can play in development comes from research on monkeys reared under varying degrees of peer accessibility. Based on comparisons of monkeys reared with and without peers, Suomi and Harlow (1978) proposed that peer play may be the most important behavior that young monkeys can develop. These authors argue that peer play provides the basis for the development and perfection of almost all appropriate adult monkey behavior. To provide some flavor for why Suomi and Harlow feel this way, we shall summarize some of their observations.

Under normal laboratory rearing conditions, infant monkeys have contact not only with their mothers but also with other young monkeys. Although the social interaction of infants for the first few weeks of life is primarily centered on their mothers, infants soon come to show an interest in exploring, approaching, and eventually playing with their peers. Importantly, in the beginning, these playful contacts are gentle and positive; in fact, the mutual pleasure and comfort the young monkeys derive from one another's company lead them to form strong attachment bonds to each other. Thus regular playmates seek each other out, come to enjoy each other's company, and even derive emotional security from each other when their mothers are not nearby.

Shortly after young monkeys have developed positive emotional ties to one another, aggression emerges in the monkeys' repertoires. Suomi and Harlow argue that aggression—threatening, biting, wrestling, and chasing—is probably biologically determined. However, the manner in which aggression is integrated into the behavioral system of monkeys is highly dependent on the nature of their social environment. For monkeys who have formed positive peer ties, aggression is gradually integrated into existing patterns of nonserious social play. Aggressive contacts do become very rough—incorporating vigorous wrestling, threats, and harmless biting—but the aggression is not destructive and rarely results in physical injury to the participants. In essence, the monkeys are learning to make sure that the aggression they direct toward friendly peers is playful and nonserious. In contrast, serious aggression is reserved for strangers. This outcome is clearly adaptive. Intragroup aggression is hardly conducive to perpetuation of the species, and out-group aggression can serve an adaptive function because the environment contains predators as well as competitors for resources. The important point is that positive peer attachments and peer play help young monkeys learn to avoid hurting their friends and to aggress only when it is adaptive to do so.

If, as we have been suggesting, early peer contact is essential for the adaptive patterning of certain response systems, such as aggression, then animals reared without opportunities for peer contact should be inadequately socialized. To find out, Suomi and Harlow (1978) compared the social development of monkeys reared under three different rearing conditions: a mother-only condition (infants were reared with their mothers, but were not permitted contact with peers), a peers-only condition (infants were separated from their mothers at birth and reared in groups of peers), and a total isolation condition (infants were reared alone). Comparison of the three groups of animals as they matured indicated that mothers and peers affect infant response systems in different ways.

Infants in the mother-only condition developed relatively normal attachments to their mothers—sucking, clinging, and using the mother as a secure base for exploration were common. But, as might be expected, the emergence of aggression posed a problem for these infants. Lacking a peer affectional base, they were not ready for it. When these animals were later joined with a larger community of monkeys, their aggression was inappropriate. They were hyperaggressive and not good playmates. They foolishly attacked larger, dominant monkeys, and they aggressed inappropriately against younger, defenseless animals—something almost never seen in normally reared animals. The animals tended to be social isolates and avoided social play.

Infants reared in the peers-only condition also had problems. Lacking a mother to suck and clasp, the infants developed excessive self-stimulating behavior. The infants were timid and easily frightened, presumably because they lacked a secure maternal home base from which to explore and adapt themselves to novelty. However, the infants did cling to each other and eventually social play emerged. The infants had little difficulty integrating aggression, and, like normals, they learned to minimize aggression toward friends, but to attack strangers vigorously. As they reached sexual maturity, few disturbances in sexual behavior were apparent. Males knew how to approach and mount females; females knew how to attract males.

Monkeys reared in total isolation suffered far more serious difficulties. We reviewed some of their problems when we discussed the effects of maternal deprivation in Chapter 2—extreme withdrawal, rocking and self-clasping, inappropriate aggression, and sexual incompetence. The main point we are making here is that the peer group serves the socialization process, at least in monkeys, in ways that mothers do not.

Ethologists studying human children (e.g., Blurton-Jones, 1972) have also pointed to the adaptive functions that the peer group serves in socialization. We shall see in this chapter, for example, that groups of children, like groups of young monkeys, form dominance hierarchies; once group members know each person's place in the hierarchy, within-group aggression is minimized. When disputes arise, children can exchange signals of dominance and submission that remind each other of their places in the hierarchy. For example, when two children squabble, the more dominant member's threatening gestures and facial expression remind the less dominant member of who is likely to win if they come to blows; the less dominant child acknowledges probable defeat with a submissive signal, thus bringing the episode to an end before a physical fight ensues. In this way, overt intragroup aggression is minimized. In addition to learning how to cope with stronger and weaker others, the peer group helps children learn how to nurture, to protect, to teach, and to assume responsibility (Hartup, 1980). In sum, the ethological view is that, over the course of evolution, certain patterns of peer interaction have survived because they help prepare the young for effective and productive functioning in maturity.

Cognitive-Developmental Theory

In theorizing about the importance of peers in the socialization process, cognitive-developmental theorists (Kohlberg, 1969; Piaget, 1932, 1951) stress that peer contacts provide children with opportunities for sharpening their social-cognitive skills. The improvements in social-cognitive functioning that derive from peer contact presumably allow children to interact with people in increasingly sophisticated ways.

For their first few years, children interact mainly with adults, and especially their parents. According to cognitive-developmental theory, this adult orientation places serious restrictions on children's social-cognitive functioning. When children are limited to interacting with authority figures whose orders they must unquestioningly obey, the children gain little practice in social reasoning. The children develop a style of accepting the rewards, punishments, and decisions meted out by their parents at face value, without understanding that there might exist social considerations, such as other people's feelings and rights, that justify the demands that parents place on their children. Children's unilateral respect for adult authority causes them to turn automatically to adults when they want the answer to a question, when they want a dispute settled, and so on. In the process, children develop an engrained habit of looking no further than external adult authority for the answers to life's problems and questions.

The following incident, witnessed by one of the authors, illustrates what Piaget meant by young children's tendency to settle disputes by appealing to adult authority. Elizabeth and Leya, both in early elementary school, were playing a card game, when the following dialogue ensued:

ELIZABETH   If you have a yellow card you have
to play it.
LEYA   No, I don't. If I have a yellow one I can
play it if I want to but I don't have to.
ELIZABETH   Yes, you do.
LEYA   No, I don't.
ELIZABETH   Yes, you do.
LEYA   No, I don't.
ELIZABETH   **ASK MY MOTHER!**

End of discussion. Leya played a yellow card, and the girls continued the game without further bickering.

Piaget considered young children's unilateral respect for external adult authority to be so powerful that he held it responsible for locking children into the preoperational stage of cognitive development. Piaget maintained that the central limitation of preoperational children's thinking is perceptual centration, or their tendency to focus attention on salient external aspects of a stimulus when trying to solve a problem involving the stimulus. This problem with centration can be seen in many aspects of the young children's social-cognitive functioning. One such aspect is that young children tend to base their moral judgments of others on external considerations (e.g., whether the actor has caused some objective damage that might anger an adult) rather than on subjective factors (e.g., whether the actor intended to perform a good act or a harmful one). Piaget believed such limitations were reflections of centration brought on by children's habit of relying on external authority for solutions to problems.

Piaget assigned the peer group a critical role in helping children outgrow some of these early deficiencies. The theory is that in the course of interacting with their peers, children encounter differences of opinion and conflicts, but, being among equals, the children cannot always simply appeal to an adult authority to resolve their disputes. In consequence, the children are left to try to resolve the difficulty themselves. Settling a dispute effectively usually involves a solution that takes into account the independent and divergent needs of the various parties involved. Hence when children resolve conflicts by themselves, they are forced into perceiving other people's thoughts, feelings, and desires, and they learn to appreciate the independent viewpoints of others. Many parents apparently agree with Piaget's notion that practice in conflict resolution promotes social-cognitive growth, for they make a point of telling quarreling children to settle matters for themselves.

Thus, as a consequence of sustained peer interaction, children are believed to outgrow their preoperational centration and to move into the stage of concrete operations. This is thought to occur roughly around the time children begin grade school. Children are now believed capable of basing their moral judgments on subjective factors such as an actor's intentions and of conceptualizing and reacting to people in terms of their hidden motives and dispositions rather than strictly in terms of their surface behavior and characteristics. Piaget hypothesized that the peer group must play a major role in instigating these developments; adults, by virtue of their superior social status, simply cannot.

Kohlberg (1969) takes a slightly different view from Piaget. While agreeing that peer interaction typically offers children excellent opportunities for taking the role of the other and thus contributes to social-cognitive growth, Kohlberg believes that adults, too, can provide children with opportunities to practice role taking. Many adults do engage children in discussion and debate, encouraging children both to state their own views and to appreciate the views of others. Regardless of whether peers are unique contributors to social-cognitive growth, however, or whether adults play a part as well, the cognitive-developmentalists' main thesis is clear: Peer contacts provide children with opportunities for expanding their social-cognitive skills; these improvements in social cognition help children interact with others in increasingly sophisticated ways.

Social Learning Theory

In social learning theory (Bandura, 1969b, 1977), peers play a vital role in teaching children new modes of behavior, in imparting information to children about what forms of behavior are expected or appropriate under various circumstances, and in setting standards against which children can assess and evaluate their own personalities and competencies. Peers influence the developing child according to the same laws of social learning as do the child's parents, teachers, television heroes, and other classes of socializing agents. However, the content of what children learn from their peers is often very different from what they learn from adults. Furthermore, there are occasions when children deliberately seek out their peers rather than adults for certain kinds of social information. If children want to guage their skill at a sport or their popularity, for example, they turn to their peer group for answers. We shall briefly elaborate on some of these points.

According to social learning theory, much of social behavior is under the control of cognitively represented response-outcome contingency rules. Children generate mental rules linking social behaviors to their consequences (praise, criticism) and they guide their behavior according to these rules. Peers are an influential source for contingency rule learning. Much of this learning is vicariously mediated, i.e., occurs through the observation of other children's behavior and the consequences other children receive for performing various responses. By observing the actions of their peers, children learn and remember many brand new response patterns (e.g., new ways of getting the teacher's attention, of taking a toy away from a playmate, or of throwing a ball), but, equally important, children also learn rules linking behaviors to performer attributes, situational circumstances, and social consequences. A child may discern, for example, that girls tend to be praised for playing with dolls in the pre-

school, whereas boys do not. Furthermore, when deciding how to behave themselves, children tend to follow the response-outcome guidelines which they have learned apply to children who are similar to themselves. This is because children learn that society expects them to behave like others of their own sex, age, and so on. Thus boys tend to regulate their behavior according to the rules that govern the behavior of other boys in their society, and girls come to follow the response-outcome guidelines for girls.

Peers serve not only as models but also as agents of reinforcement and punishment. Thus, in part, children's response-outcome rules are learned through the direct consequences they themselves receive from their peers for performing various responses. A boy who unwittingly plays with dolls may be laughed at and thereafter may avoid doll play and certain other girl-preferred activities.

According to social learning theory, much behavior is under the control of internal self-regulation as well as external consequences. Once children abstract guidelines of appropriate conduct for themselves, they begin to pressure themselves into conforming to these guidelines. In the process, they experience pride when their behavior matches their standards, and they criticize themselves when they fall short of their standards. The intensity of a child's self-reward or self-punishment following an act is governed by a variety of factors, but one important factor is *social comparison*, or the child's assessment of how well his or her performance compares to that of other children. Children experience the most pride and self-esteem when their performance exceeds that of their peers; they are most dejected when comparisons are unfavorable.

Social learning theory also regards children's perceptions of their capabilities (or their perceptions of self-efficacy) as critical determinants of the activities children will choose to undertake and persist at mastering (Bandura, 1981). A girl who is confident of her swimming ability, but terrified of failing mathematics, will be more likely to enroll in a swimming class than a mathematics course. Children's perceptions of self-efficacy are influenced by several factors (see Chapter 5), but one of the most important of these is social comparison. Bandura proposes that when children wish to estimate their competence at an activity they tend to compare their performance at the activity to that of their peers, especially children who are similar or slightly higher in ability than themselves. If children want to know how good they are at tennis, they select their agemates for comparison; they would not choose either younger children or a professional tennis player. Furthermore, children can learn new skills and overcome behavioral deficits through observing the step-by-step performance by a competent peer model—especially a similar peer. We shall see in this chapter, for example, that peer models can teach children new social skills and help them overcome irrational fears.

EARLY PEER CONTACTS

The Baby Party Technique

To study peer interactions in infancy, investigators usually arrange a "baby party." Two or more mothers and their infants are invited to a research laboratory, the mothers are seated on cushions on the floor, and the infants are allowed to crawl and interact freely. Sometimes the room is furnished with toys, which, as we shall see, can play a crucial role in facilitating infant-infant interaction.

Results of such investigations have revealed a number of interesting findings. Young infants are neither afraid of nor disinterested in their peers. Most of the contacts infants have with one another are positive and mutually rewarding rather than characterized by aggressive struggles over toys or other self-centered behavior. Furthermore, recent research shows that infants contribute to one another's cognitive and social develop-

ment in ways that adults do not. We shall now take a closer look at some of these findings.

The Nature of Infant-Infant Interaction

Peer interaction has not been studied extensively in infants under 6 months of age, but it is clear that by 6 months infants can and do direct social behaviors toward one another. Vandell, Wilson, and Buchanan (1980) found that 6-month-olds spent considerable time exchanging social signals with an infant partner. For example, infants often took turns vocalizing to each other. However, the social sequences were simple and usually brief, two-unit exchanges in which one child acted and the second child responded.

As infants get older, they participate in more interaction sequences with a partner and engage in fewer isolated nonsocial actions. Their social interaction sequences become more complex. By the time they are 1 year old, infants are making numerous social overtures and are synchronizing their movements, resulting in lengthy chains of interaction (Holmberg, 1980; Vandell et al., 1980). Much infant-infant social behavior can be characterized as *turntaking contingent responses*. The infants may mimic one another, and they may take turns performing an action with a toy. Infants also may participate in short sequences involving complementary actions: One child may offer a toy and the other child take it, or one child may play the chaser and the other the chased (Finkelstein, Dent, Gallacher, & Ramey, 1978; Mueller & Lucas, 1975). Between their first and second birthdays, infants add another feature to their interactions: role switching. Now two children playing the chaser and the chased, for example, may switch roles during their interaction (Brenner & Mueller, 1982).

Although much of infant-infant interaction is motoric and centered around a toy or other object, the predominant modes of infant interaction are distal: Vocalizing, looking, and smiling are the most common responses. In fact, it is vocalizing that most reliably triggers a reaction from an infant playmate (Eckerman, Whatley, & Kutz, 1975; Vandell et al., 1980).

So strong is infant interest in peer interaction that from an early age (8 or 9 months) infants prefer to interact with peers rather than with their mothers, at least in the relaxed, nonthreatening atmosphere of a baby party. This preference for peer over mother increases as the infants get older (Becker, 1977; Eckerman et al., 1975). Infants behave somewhat differently toward their mothers and a peer, too. They are more likely to look at and vocalize to a peer, but more likely to touch their mothers (Vandell et al., 1980).

In Chapter 2, when discussing infants' reactions to strangers, we noted that infants' initial reactions to nonthreatening strange adults (i.e., adults who behave naturally and approach the infant at a comfortable pace) are often a blend of wariness and distal-affiliative behavior. The infants may stare soberly, frown, and occasionally glance away (the fear/wariness system), but at the same time try to engage the stranger in distal interaction by occasionally vocalizing, smiling, and looking (the affiliative system). Infants' reactions to novel peers are also frequently a blend of wariness and affiliation (e.g., Jacobson, 1980), but the affiliative system assumes ascendance over wariness more quickly with peer strangers than with adult strangers. Furthermore, only rarely do infants display the full-fledged fear reaction to a peer that they sometimes do to a strange adult. The important point is that infants' interest in their peers is strong and positive, though it may be a little cautious at the start.

The Importance of Toys

Significantly, most early peer interactions center around toys, which seem somehow to serve as "topics of conversation" or catalysts for interaction (Eckerman & Whatley, 1977; Mueller & Brenner, 1977). When toys are removed from a baby party, the infants grow more irritable, spend more time with their mothers, and engage in less synchronous play with each other. When toys are present, infants simultaneously manipulate them, exchange them, and show them to each other. Nothing seems to make a toy more interesting than its use by another child.

Some researchers have suggested that early peer interaction is nonsocial and object-centered—that infants may focus their attention on a common toy, but are oblivious to each other as social partners (Mueller & Lucas, 1975). This characterization seems erroneous, because infants vocalize, smile, and look at each other at very young ages even when there are no toys or objects to manipulate (Jacobson, 1981; Vandell et al., 1980). Nevertheless, even if toys are not essential for early social interaction, it is clear that they facilitate it. Joint manipulation of a toy provides a context in which children learn to share, reciprocate, take turns, communicate, and integrate their own responses with those of a partner. In fact, so crucial is shared toy play for sustained social interaction among infants, that Eckerman, Whatley, and McGehee (1979) believe that showing interest in a toy manipulated by another child should be considered a basic social skill of the 1-year-old.

The Benefits of Early Peer Interaction

Is early peer interaction beneficial? In a revealing study, Rubenstein and Howes (1976) compared the play of 18-month-olds on days when they were at home with their mothers with days when they were visited by a familiar infant playmate. The main discovery was that the peer stimulated the children toward more mature behaviors. Without the peer, children manipulated objects and toys mainly by mouthing or passively touching them, but with the peer, children did more unusual and creative things with objects. The children also engaged in more interactive games, imitations, and offers of toys when a peer was present than when they were with their mothers.

It is not surprising, then, that infants who have had several weeks or months of experience interacting with one or more peers show greater complexity and coordination in their peer interactions, and are more relaxed and sociable when meeting new peers, than children with less prior peer experience (Becker, 1977; Howes, 1980; Lieberman, 1977; Mueller & Brenner, 1977).

Individual Differences in Infant Social Style

Though, as we have described, most infants enjoy interacting with their peers, there exist considerable individual differences among infants in style of interacting socially. Furthermore, these stylistic differences influence the degree of acceptance infants receive from their peers. Lee (1973) observed distinct behavioral differences between the most and least popular members of a play group containing infants who ranged in age from 8 to 10 months. The most sought-after infant was one who made relatively few social initiations, but who made his overtures nonaggressively by looking at or slowly approaching another infant; he was also quick to reciprocate the initiations of his peers. The least-preferred infant was rather asocial, but when he did initiate interactions, he tended to be aggressive, perhaps grabbing a toy away from another child; he ignored the overtures of others or responded inappropriately to them, and he selfishly engaged in sustained interactions only when he had initiated them. In part, these early stylistic differences may reflect biologically based differences in temperament. It is also likely, however, as we shall discuss later in this chapter, that children's styles of interaction are influenced by the relationships they have established with their parents.

PLAY: ITS NATURE AND FUNCTIONS

Play is difficult to define, but most would agree that play is nonserious activity in which children structure their behavior in idiosyn-cratic ways that are not necessarily related to reality. We have already seen that when two infants are paired with one another, play is a likely outcome, especially if toys are available to facilitate playful interaction. Here we describe the development of play more fully. Play takes numerous forms. It can occur when the child is alone or in the company of other children. It can involve the simple motor manipulation of an object or complex fanciful sequences in which children pretend they are someone else and let objects represent other things. Certain forms of play are more mature than others. Some forms of play are highly associated with advanced cognitive development and social competence, whereas other varieties of play are more common in children whose social adjustment and intellectual development are less optimal. Because a great many children fail to engage in the forms of play that are beneficial, researchers are striving to develop ways of teaching children how to enjoy these kinds of play.

Smilansky's Cognitive Play Categories

Smilansky (1968) identified four types of children's play that differ in terms of the cognitive activity they involve. The four types of play differ in frequency as a function of age, but each type follows an inverted-U shape developmental function. In other words, each play type begins with a low frequency, rises to some peak level, and then reduces to a low frequency again. The four types of play can be ordered from least to most mature in terms of the age at which they peak. *Functional play* is defined as simple repetitive muscle movements performed with or without an object, such as shaking a rattle, jumping up and down, or bouncing a ball; it begins in the first year and peaks between 2 and 3 years of age. *Constructive play* is the manipulation of objects with the intention of constructing something, such as a cut-and-paste activity; children pursue this form of play in the second year, peaking at 3 to 4 years. Smilansky's third type of play is called *pretend play*, and involves letting an object or person symbolize a thing or person it is not; it is also known as dramatic or symbolic play, and begins in the second year, but reaches its optimal level at 6 to 7 years. Finally, children engage in *games with rules* (e.g., checkers, Old Maid). Children typically start playing games with rules in the preschool years, but do so to the greatest extent at 10 to 11 years. The four types should not be considered "stages" of play development, because most children are interested in two or more kinds of play at any given point in their development. Even a 10-year-old, for example, is likely to engage in some functional, some constructive, and some pretend play as well as show interest in games with rules. However, as children get older, they are involved with the more mature varieties with increasing frequency, and the less mature forms become less important.

Developmental Changes in Pretend Play Even well into the elementary-school years, the bulk of most children's play time is spent in functional and constructive play; pretend play typically occupies a small percentage of the child's play time. Nevertheless, because dramatic play may be the most important for the child's cognitive and social development, it has become the most extensively studied form of play. Pretend play can take many forms, including treating inanimate objects as animate, performing everyday activities in the absence of the necessary props, performing actions usually done by someone else, terminating action sequences before their customary end points, and substituting one object for another (Fein, 1981; McCune-Nicolich, 1981). In her review of the pretend play literature, Fein (1981) points out that pretend play undergoes several interesting changes as children develop.

First, pretend play changes from being exclusively self-referenced to being other-referenced as well (e.g., Fenson & Ramsay, 1980). The earliest pretend actions, which usually occur around 1 year of age, are "self-referenced" in that the child pretends to engage the self in some everyday activity (e.g.,

pretends to be eating, pretends to go to sleep). Eventually pretend sequences become less egocentric, with the child pretending that someone else is engaged in an activity (e.g., pretending that a doll is going to sleep).

Second, young children are heavily dependent on concrete props for pretend activities—they cannot perform pretend actions with imaginary props. Jackowitz and Watson (1980) tell of a young boy who, when asked to pretend he was drinking, searched the floor until he found a piece of lint to serve as a cup. Young children also have trouble letting an object that has its own distinct use serve as a symbolic representation of another object. For example, young children have a terrible time if asked to pretend that a pair of scissors is a comb—to them, scissors are for cutting (Pederson, Rook-Green, and Elder, 1981). But children quickly become more flexible with age, and by 4 years some children have even generated an imaginary companion.

Third, pretend play progresses from the solitary to the social (Rubin, Watson, & Jambor, 1978). Between the ages of 3 and 5, children sharply reduce the amount of dramatic play they perform alone while at preschool. In other words, dramatic play gradually becomes confined to the presence of other children, at least in the school setting.

Fourth, the fantasy roles children enact become progressively less familiar with age (Garvey & Berndt, 1977). For example, 3-year-olds pretend to be mother, baby, or some other familiar figure, but 5-year-olds can pretend to take on roles they have never witnessed or experienced first hand (e.g., Superman or a robber).

Correlates of Pretend Play Though preschoolers engage in far more functional and constructive play than pretend play, those who do display relatively high levels of pretend play enjoy social advantages over their less imaginative and fanciful peers. Children who engage in the most dramatic play are more popular with their peers, more patient, more cooperative, friendlier, and score higher on tests that rate the ability to imagine what other people are thinking and feeling (Fein, 1981; Rubin & Maioni, 1975). Pretend play is also conducive to prosocial behavior. While children are engaged in dramatic play, they show a good deal of sharing, positive emotions, and concentration; aggression and other negative behaviors are infrequent (Freyberg, 1973; Smilansky, 1968).

While pretend play is the form of play most positively correlated with social competence, functional play is the type of play most negatively correlated with social competence. Preschool children who spend much time engaged in simple repetitive motor movements tend to be the least liked by their peers and are relatively lacking in social skills (Rubin & Maioni, 1975).

In addition to enhancing social skills, high levels of pretend play have also been associated with advanced cognitive development. Preschoolers who engage in the most dramatic play are brighter and score higher on tests of spatial relations and classification skills (Rubin & Maioni, 1975; Rubin et al., 1978).

There is a strong association between preschoolers' pretend play and their family background. Disadvantaged preschoolers from lower-class homes show substantially less constructive and pretend play (as well as more functional play) than do their middle-class counterparts (Rubin, Maioni, & Hornung, 1976; Smilansky, 1968; Udwin & Shmukler, 1981). Perhaps there is less opportunity and space for peaceful practice of pretend play in lower-class homes (Singer, 1973), but the degree of emotional security in the home may influence pretend play, too. Matas, Arend, and Sroufe (1978) found that children who were judged to be securely attached to their mothers at 18 months engaged in more pretend play at 24 months than children who were judged to be anxiously attached at 18 months. Breakdowns in the family system may also interfere with pretend play. Hetherington, Cox, and Cox (1979) found preschool children of divorced parents to be

more rigid in their imaginative play than children from intact homes: Children in the divorced sample adopted fewer different characters in their play, were less likely to use play objects in novel ways, engaged in less overall fantasy, and were preoccupied with acting out aggressive themes. Finally, Fein (1981) notes that children who receive the most attention from their parents, especially their fathers, and children who watch relatively little television engage in more pretend play.

Encouraging Pretend Play Working on the assumption that pretend play helps cause social and cognitive competence, several investigators have set out to develop ways of teaching children how to enjoy the world of make-believe. For example, adults have introduced toys conducive to dramatic role playing (such as medical kits and firefighters' hats) into children's play, or have encouraged children to act out roles from fairy tales. Results are encouraging. When children undergo a series of sessions designed to produce pretend play, they improve in cooperation, role taking, intelligence, creativity, the ability to differentiate fantasy from reality, and the ability to use fantasy to distract themselves from thinking about tempting but prohibited activities (Burns & Brainerd, 1979; Dansky, 1980; Johnson, 1976; Saltz, Dixon, & Johnson, 1977). Fantasy training programs are most effective if children must act out stories rather than simply listen to adults read them, and if the stories involve fantasies and roles remote from reality (Saltz et al., 1977).

Parten's Social Participation Play Categories

In a classic article published many years ago, Parten (1932) proposed that preschool children's play progresses in a series of three stages. The stages varied along a dimension of involvement with other children. From least to most mature, these stages were: *solitary play* (the child is unoccupied, watches other children play, or plays alone); *parallel play* (the child engages in an activity also being performed by a close neighbor, such as playing with clay alongside another child also playing with clay); and *group play* (the child plays with at least one other child). We might note that these categories are largely independent of Smilansky's categories. In other words, children may engage in functional, constructive, or pretend play alone, in parallel with another child, or in a group.

Data collected subsequent to Parten's study indicate that Parten's three types of play should not be thought of as stages (Smith, 1978). Over the preschool years, solitary and parallel play decrease in frequency and group play increases, but most children—even children well into elementary school—show a blend of all three varieties. Furthermore, contemporary work on Parten's categories indicates that all three forms of play have a place in the mature child's play repertoire. We shall review some recent research on solitary and parallel play.

Solitary Play: Not Necessarily Bad Children who play only by themselves will be disadvantaged. They will have little opportunity to acquire and practice the social skills that come through social interaction. However playing by oneself is not necessarily bad. In fact, it has been argued that children who supplement their group play with occasional periods of solitary play, and who know how to make good use of their time when playing alone, are more flexible and competent than their peers who feel compelled always to play in the company of others. Furthermore, studies of what children are doing when they are playing alone indicate that most solitary play is mature and involves activities adults would like to encourage in children. Solitary play typically involves goal-directed activity, including play with construction toys; arts and crafts; large muscle activities; and challenging educational materials, such as puzzles and workbooks (Moore, Evertson, & Brophy, 1974; Roper & Hinde, 1978; Rubin et al., 1976, 1978; Smith, 1978).

Rubin (1982) stresses that it is not just children's rate of solitary play but rather what the children are doing while alone that is important for their development. If children are wasting their time while alone—if they are unoccupied or are doing something that is better done in a group—then high rates of solitary play may be detrimental for the children's development. But if children are spending their time alone wisely, then solitary play may be beneficial. In an excellent study, Rubin investigated whether socially competent preschoolers spent their solitary play time differently from their less competent peers. Social competence was assessed by a variety of measures, including popularity with the peer group, role taking ability, and ability to generate solutions to hypothetical interpersonal problems. Rubin used Smilansky's categories to classify the content of children's solitary play. Findings revealed that when a child was engaged in solitary play, the more time he or she devoted to constructive play, the higher the child scored on the measures of competence. On the other hand, the more time a child spent engaged in either functional or dramatic play when he or she was alone, the lower the child scored on the tests of social competence. Constructive play is an efficient use of solitary time, whereas functional play is not. The negative association between solitary-dramatic play and competence is especially interesting, because we concluded earlier that pretend play is beneficial for children. Apparently, by the time children are 4 years old, solitary pretend play in the preschool setting is inappropriate. That is, competent preschoolers are saving pretend play for group interaction, at least while they are at school. In any case, *how* a child spends his or her time alone may be more diagnostic of social competence than simply the amount of time the child spends alone.

Uses and Abuses of Parallel Play Children who spend large amounts of their time at preschool engaged in parallel play are less mature and less socially competent than children whose use of parallel play is more moderate (Howes, 1980; Johnson, Ershler, & Bell, 1980; Rubin et al., 1976). However, it would be wrong to conclude that all parallel play is undesirable. Rubin (1982) reports that the frequency of parallel *constructive* play correlates positively with measures of social competence. Working on a project (e.g., cutting-and-pasting, making something out of clay, or building a tinkertoy) alongside another child who is working on a similar activity is an efficient and educational use of time. But spending long periods of time standing next to and copying another child's motor movements without a constructive goal in sight (functional parallel play) is not the sign of a mature child.

Apart from parallel constructive play, there is another healthy use of parallel play for children. When a child wishes to join the play activity of one or more other children, one highly successful way of achieving entry into the play group involves coming alongside the other children, doing what they are doing for a while, and eventually blending into the group. When used in this way, as a brief prologue to interaction, parallel play is not a sign of immaturity (Bakeman & Brownlee, 1980). In fact, the use of parallel play to initiate interaction may be considered a social skill.

Importance of a Balanced Play Diet   We have suggested that solitary, parallel, and group play are all important, as long as they are used in the right circumstances. It would be a mistake for teachers to encourage one type of play, such as group play, to the exclusion of the others. With this in mind, some preschools are designed deliberately to encourage a variety of play activities. Vandenberg (1981) reports on one such school, which contained two playrooms—a "large muscle" room (equipped with a jungle gym, two slides, tumbling mats, and large blocks) and a "fine motor" room (equipped with tables and chairs, paper, pencils, paints, crayons, scissors, and paste). More group play occurred in

the large muscle room, and more parallel and solitary play occurred in the fine motor room.

Occasionally, teachers might encourage children who tend to gravitate to one kind of play environment to diversify their play patterns. For example, in Vandenberg's (1981) study, children who tested as more egocentric and less cognitively mature tended to be attracted to the fine motor room. Teachers of such children might occasionally encourage these children to try the more social atmosphere engendered by the large muscle room.

Having a diversity of play settings also caters to sex differences in play interests. Boys are more interested in group play than girls, and girls engage in more solitary play than boys (see Chapter 9). Furthermore, girls sometimes show their most sophisticated and creative forms of play when they are alone, whereas boys tend to be most creative when playing with a peer (Cohen & Tomlinson-Keasey, 1980). Teachers might encourage children to try new forms and settings for play. Also, they should be aware that not all children profit from the same types of play.

The Functions of Play

Why has play evolved? What adaptive purpose does it serve? We have already touched on a number of ways in which play benefits the child's development, but it is useful to review these and to consider still other functions of play.

First, play provides children with opportunities to learn rules of reciprocity in social interaction and to sharpen their communicative and other social-cognitive skills.

Second, play helps children learn socially acceptable ways of expressing their emotions. Many emotions can be overwhelming to children. By acting out exaggerated hate, love, joy, sadness, and other emotions in a safe, playful context, children become familiar with emotions, bring them under their control, and make them less threatening. For example, by engaging in rough-and-tumble play and mock fighting with their peers, children explore the acceptable limits of aggressive behavior and learn the conditions under which aggression is appropriate or inappropriate.

Third, play—and more specifically, pretend play—furthers children's cognitive development. Pretending should help train children's thought processes to be less dependent on immediate environmental stimuli, it should facilitate children's understanding of what symbols are and can do, and it should make it easier for children, as they mature, to imagine, create, and solve problems symbolically (Piaget, 1926; Vygotsky, 1934).

Fourth, play teaches children subroutines of action that can later be applied to solve problems or enact adult social roles (Bruner, 1972; Smith & Dutton, 1979; Vandenberg, 1978). Functional and constructive play expand children's repertoires of sensorimotor schemas and familiarize children with materials and spatial relationships that may come in handy at some later time—for example, for carpenters or for engineers. Similarly, pretending to be mother or father to a doll may make it easier for children to assume the parenting role in later life.

Finally, play provides a context in which children establish lasting, mutually satisfying friendships with their peers. In part, children are attracted to one another precisely because of their mutual interest in play. Thus play facilitates children's transition from the family to the peer group. Even in adulthood, play can contribute to the formation of deep, new affectional bonds. For example, many couples first meet at the bridge table, on the dance floor, or on the golf course.

If play is so vital, why does it diminish as children get older? Piaget (1926) theorized that children's development of logic eventually leads them to reject play as incompatible with reality. Singer (1973), on the other hand, proposes that play never ends, but instead is internalized, stimulating people's imagination and fantasy lives as they get older. At present, we do not know exactly why active play becomes less important as children mature, or if it changes form, as Singer has suggested. But we do know that children who do not take advantage of their prerogative to play in youth are embarking on adolescence at a relative disadvantage to their peers.

THE GROWTH OF FRIENDSHIPS

As children develop, they become acquainted with an increasing number of other children, but most children eventually develop special relationships with one or more specific peers with whom they enjoy a mutually satisfying relationship—*friendship*. The toddler seeks out a specific other child with whom to enjoy constructive and pretend play; the grade schooler enjoys having a particular playmate come on weekends for "sleep-overs"; and the adolescent searches for satisfaction in a relationship with a member of the opposite sex. It is difficult to say precisely what constitutes a friend, in part because, as we shall see, children of different ages expect rather different things from their friends. Here we describe factors influencing children's friendship selections and tell how friendships influence children's social development.

Determinants of Children's Friendship Selections

Freud and Dann (1951) describe a rather dramatic example of friendship in childhood. These authors encountered a group of six German-Jewish infants who had been placed together for several years in an institution after losing their parents in World War II. During their years together, the children developed intense, protective attachments to one another. In fact, they became so attached that they refused to separate for even brief periods and became hostile and destructive toward adults who threatened to disturb their group. When one child was separated from the others because of illness, the others became severely depressed and negativistic, remaining so until the group was reunited. The children's interactions, among themselves, were characterized by a good deal of sharing and helping; antisocial behavior, such as jealousy and competition, was virtually nonexistent. They found it nearly impossible to accept adults or other children, though they eventually did.

Of course, the Freud and Dann study describes an unusual case of friendship formation. Lacking parental attachment figures, the infants turned to one another for emotional security. The motivation for most children's friendships is not as extreme as this, but the study illustrates the intensity that peer friendship bonds can attain.

What forms the basis for most children's friendships? Do opposites attract? Or do children tend to become friends with children who are similar to themselves? The latter seems closer to the truth. Children usually make friends with children of similar age, sex, race, degree of sociability, interests, and values (Asher, Gottman, & Oden, 1977; Hartup, 1979; Singleton & Asher, 1979). In fact, when children do make friends with a dissimilar other (e.g., a cross-sex peer), the relationship tends to be unstable or short-lived (Gronlund, 1959).

The qualities that children seek in a friend vary with age. In several investigations, children have been asked to tell what they want from a friend (Bigelow, 1977; Bigelow & LaGaipa, 1975; Hayes, 1978; Reisman & Shorr, 1978). On the basis of children's answers, Bigelow (1977) proposes that children's friendship expectations fall into three stages. The first stage lasts through the early elementary-school years and is called a *reward-cost stage*. To children of this age, the ideal friend is someone who is useful and a source of pleasure—someone who is easily accessible (e.g., lives next door), has nice toys, joins the child in play, and is entertaining. But we should not form the impression that young children's friendships are entirely selfish or "all take and no give." Even preschool children form reciprocal, mutually satisfying friendships in which each member both is rewarded by *and* rewards the other at a high rate (Hayes, Gershman, & Bolin, 1980; Masters & Furman, 1981).

In mid-elementary school, children enter a *normative stage* in which shared values and rules become important. Children at this stage stress that mutual acceptance, admiration, and loyalty are important for friendship. The children acknowledge that friends are supposed to help each other, and they also express confidence that their friends will be satisfied by how much help they receive (Berndt, 1981a).

In adolescence, children enter an *empathic stage*. Perhaps for the first time, children really begin to care about what happens to a friend. In their descriptions of friends, children now stress mutual understanding, self-disclosure, and intimacy. However, they still expect their friends to be useful to them (Reisman & Shorr, 1978).

We have noted that children tend to form stable friendships with similar others, so it is not surprising that most children's friendships tend to be with same-sex peers. As children develop into adolescents, they become more likely to establish close relationships with opposite-sex peers as well. Contrary to popular thought, however, the onset of dating is less related to biological sexual maturation than it is to peer pressure (Dornbusch, Carlsmith, Gross, Martin, Jennings, Rosenberg, & Duke, 1981).

Intimacy is an important dimension of friendship, but the degree of intimacy children experience in their friendships changes with age and with the sexual composition of the friendship. In a study of 480 children in the fifth, seventh, ninth, and eleventh grades, Sharabany, Gershoni, and Hofman (1981) studied age trends in the depth of intimacy with same- and opposite-sex friends. Children were first asked to name a close same-sex or opposite-sex friend, and then to respond to the Sharabany Intimacy Scale, a questionnaire designed to assess the degree of intimacy a person feels for a friend. The scale includes items designed to tap eight aspects of intimacy: frank spontaneity, sensitivity to

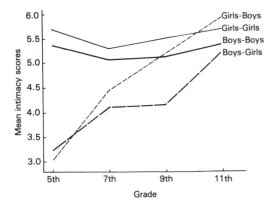

Figure 10–1 Mean intimacy scores according to grade and type of friendship (boys referring to boys; boys referring to girls; girls referring to girls; girls referring to boys) (From Sharabany, Gershoni, and Hofman, 1981). Copyright 1981 by the American Psychological Association. Reprinted by permission of the author.

what the other is thinking and feeling, attachment, exclusiveness of the relationship, giving and sharing, imposing and taking, common activities, and trust and loyalty. Children's intimacy scores as a function of age and type of friendship are plotted in Figure 10–1. Several aspects of the data are noteworthy. Notice that same-sex friendships involve a high level of intimacy right across the age span. In fact, from an early age, same-sex friendships appear to be as intimate as the opposite-sex friendships that eventually emerge. This corroborates Sullivan's (1953) theory that intimacy is not something that is reserved for opposite-sex friendships but rather is an important ingredient of the same-sex friendships that precede opposite-sex relationships. Intimacy in opposite-sex friendships develops between the fifth and eleventh grades, but notice that girls report high intimacy in opposite-sex friendships earlier than boys do. In fact, at all ages, girls report more intimacy in their friendships than boys.

Differences in Social Interaction Between Friends and Nonfriends

If friendships truly are, as children claim, special relationships, then friends ought to behave differently toward one another than toward mere acquaintances. Observational studies of social interaction between friends and nonfriends bear this out. Doyle, Con-

nolly, and Rivest (1980) compared toddlers' interaction when with a friend versus when with a less familiar playmate. With the friend, children engaged in more social interaction and in more sophisticated forms of play, especially dramatic play. There was more communication, more seeking of attention, more asking of questions, more leading (e.g., making suggestions for play), more displays of affection, and less passive watching. Among older children, too, social interaction is more lively and is more frequently characterized by positive exchanges in groups of friends than among nonfriends (Foot, Chapman, & Smith, 1977; Lewis, Young, Brooks, & Michalson, 1975; Masters & Furman, 1981; Newcomb, Brady, & Hartup, 1979). Interactions with friends, then, should promote the development of social skills.

Are friends more altruistic toward one another than toward nonfriends? One might expect so, but the answer is not so simple. Berndt (1981b) asked kindergarten through fourth-grade children to predict how much they would help either a friend or a nonfriend in hypothetical situations in which a child required assistance. Girls said they would help the friend more than the nonfriend, but boys indicated that they would give the friend and nonfriend equal amounts of help. The children were also given a behavioral test of helping a friend and a nonfriend. Children were paired with either a friend or an acquaintance and taken to a room at the school. Each of the two children was asked to complete a color-by-numbers design, and the children were told that whoever colored more in the time allotted would win a prize. The hitch, however, was that some of the crayons were limited, so that the children had to share them. The main question was whether children shared more when their partner was a friend or when their partner was a nonfriend. Girls shared equally with their friends and nonfriends, but boys actually shared less with their friends than the nonfriends. Berndt surmised that one ingredient of friendship between boys is competition, with boys simply not wanting their male friends to outdo them in competitive situations.

In another study, Berndt (1981a) arranged the experimental situation so that a noncompetitive outcome was an option: Children were told that they could each get the same amount of money if they colored equal portions of their designs. In this situation, both boys and girls shared more with a friend than with a nonfriend partner. Sharing among friends, then, depends on sex as well as whether the situation is structured for competition or cooperation.

In this section we briefly sketched some factors influencing children's friendships, but we neglected to discuss the important role that children's social skills play in the establishment and maintenance of friendships. Some children know how to begin relationships and keep them going; other children simply do not. In the next section we shall examine the development of social skills and discuss what it means to be a socially competent child.

DEVELOPMENT OF SOCIAL COMPETENCE

On the Meaning of Social Competence

What is Social Competence? Socially competent children possess the skills necessary to achieve the social goals they desire:

They know how to make friends, how to influence a playmate, how to solicit information, and so on, and they know how to accomplish these goals in socially acceptable ways. Most children want to make friends with their peers. Hence the social skills necessary to initiate and sustain friendships constitute an important part of social competence. Many children simply lack the necessary skills to make friends and, as a result, are forgotten, left out, or isolated. In this section we focus on describing the social skills that help children enter into meaningful relationships with their peers.

We must emphasize that social competence is not the same thing as having a high rate of social interaction. Some children can be very active socially, yet be aggressive or obnoxious; others can have a low rate of interaction, yet be quite competent and agreeable when they do enter into a relationship with another child. The quality or skillfulness of a child's interaction is more important to social competence than the child's overall rate of interaction (Asher, Markell, & Hymel, 1981; Peery, 1979).

Sociometric Assessment of Competence How do researchers identify socially competent children? Most investigators assume that a child's popularity among his or her peers is a good index of the child's social competence. The argument is that a child could not have won the acceptance and respect of his or her peers without possessing the skills necessary to win friends and sustain social interaction with other children in acceptable ways. Hence most researchers employ some sort of sociometric analysis of popularity when trying to assess competence. One popular technique is a peer nomination method. Each child in a class is asked to nominate two, or perhaps three, children whom he or she is friends with, enjoys playing with, and would invite to a birthday party (or something similar). To determine rejected children, children may also be asked to nominate peers whom they definitely do not like. Sometimes children are asked to look at photographs of all their classmates before they respond, to make sure that they don't forget anybody. Each child's score is determined by the number of classmates who nominate the child. Another technique is a peer rating method. In this method, children rate every other member of their class on likability, perhaps using a 3-point scale.

The two methods—peer nominations and peer ratings—yield somewhat different information (Gresham, 1981; Singleton & Asher, 1979). Nominations probably are an index of how many friendships a child has established; ratings probably indicate how generally acceptable a child is to his or her peers. Thus a child who is rated as acceptable by the peer group may actually have no friends. If friendship making is the object of study, then investigators ought probably to use a nomination method.

On the Importance of being Popular Before we begin the discussion of the components of social competence, we might ask whether it really is important for a child to be popular with his or her peers. Won't children who are shy, anxious, isolated, or rejected by their peers outgrow their difficulties and eventually mature into well-adjusted and socially accepted members of society? Of course, many children who are deficient in certain social skills do eventually overcome their difficulties. But the more important point is that many unpopular children do *not* spontaneously shake their difficulties as they develop. In particular, children who are actively rejected by their peers in grade school—especially children who are rejected because of problems with aggression and other antisocial behavior—stand an above-average risk of dropping out of school, of becoming delinquent, of being diagnosed neurotic or psychotic, and of even committing suicide (Cowen, Pederson, Babigan, Izzo, & Trost, 1973; Kohn & Clausen, 1955; Roff, Sells, & Golden, 1972; Stengel, 1971).

A Social Skills Approach to Conceptualizing Social Competence

To the extent that socially incompetent children are lacking in the skills necessary to form the relationships they want, they will be unhappy. Thus it would seem worthwhile to dissect social competence, determine its components, and develop ways of teaching children desirable social skills.

Asher, Renshaw and Hymel (1982) point out that socially competent children are skilled in at least three areas: at initiating interactions with their peers, at maintaining ongoing interactions, and at resolving interpersonal conflicts. We shall discuss how competent children differ from their less socially skilled counterparts in each of these domains.

Skill in Initiating Social Interaction Popular children initiate new relationships and social interactions more gracefully than less popular children. Gottman, Gonso, and Rasmussen (1975) asked popular and unpopular children to role play the friendship-making process, by pretending the experimenter was a new child at school whom they wanted to befriend. Popular children played the scene better. Compared to less popular children, they greeted their new "friend" more (e.g., "Hi. What's your name?"), asked more appropriate questions (e.g., "What do you like to play?"), gave more information (e.g., "I like baseball"), and more often tried to include the friend in their activities (e.g., "Wanna play soccer at recess?").

In addition to knowing how to make new friends, competent children do a better job of gaining entry into ongoing play groups. When several children are playing and another child tries to join them, often the children who are playing resist or reject the newcomer. Competent children are more adept at gaining entry without rejection. They tend to utilize a technique that involves approaching their peers, quietly observing their activities, and waiting for a natural break to occur, at which time they begin behaving the way the peers are behaving (Asher et al., 1982; Corsaro, 1981). Thus they integrate themselves in a nondisruptive way.

In a careful look at children's entry into peer groups, Putallaz and Gottman (1981) asked popular and unpopular children to enter a room in which two children were already playing a card game, and observed how the children attempted to join the group. Unpopular children were more likely to call attention to themselves by talking about themselves, introducing new topics of conversation, and even disagreeing with what the other children were saying and doing. These strategies did not go over well, and the children were often ignored or rejected. In contrast, popular children adopted the framework of the group and integrated themselves more unobtrusively into the conversation and activity of the group. Putallaz and Gottman provide an example in which one unpopular child (Terry) disrupted the ongoing focus of the group by making irrelevant comments about the game, the room, and even the table:

JANET   Okay, I want this one again.
TERRY   This is fun, ain't it?
JANET (to Vera)   Do you want this one again?
VERA   I want this one.
TERRY   This is a nice room, ain't it?
JANET (to Vera)   You can have this one. Here.
TERRY   This is a nice table, ain't it?
JANET (to Terry)   Pick your one.

Competent children are more confident of their friendship-making ability than less popular children. Thus they are more persistent when trying to make a new friend. Some children tend to give up trying to make a new friend or join a play group if their initial attempt fails. Goetz and Dweck (1980) found that children who were most likely to quit trying to make a friend when their initial attempt was rebuffed were children who held themselves and their friendship-making ability in low esteem (e.g., "I just can't make

friends"). Competent children, who are more confident of their social prowess, keep trying to make a friend, even if they don't always succeed.

Skill in Maintaining Interaction   Competent children sustain the relationships and interactions they have begun more successfully than less popular children. In general, competent children have a more prosocial style of interaction than their less competent peers (Asher et al., 1982). Popular preschool children are skilled in rewarding other children. They smile at, attend to, approve of, comply with, imitate, and share their toys and activities with other children more often than less popular children do (Hartup, Glazer, & Charlesworth, 1967). The willingness to reward others is important, for it signals to other children that a child who displays this trait can be counted on to cooperate, to be a good sport, and to comply reasonably often with others' suggestions (Asher et al., 1982). Unpopular children not only reward their peers less often but also have unusual ideas about what constitutes helpful behavior. Ladd and Oden (1979) showed popular and unpopular grade-school children cartoons depicting a child being teased by peers, being yelled at by a peer, and having a schoolwork problem. They then asked the children to suggest ways of helping the child in need. Unpopular children came up with more bizarre suggestions.

Expertise in a variety of social-cognitive skills is also associated with social competence. Compared to their less popular peers, competent children have better-developed communication skills. They are better speakers, in that they are careful to adjust their messages to include the information their listeners need, and they edit out ambiguities from their speech before speaking. They are also better listeners, in that they are attentive, ask appropriate questions, and inform a speaker when his or her message is ambiguous (Asher et al., 1977; Deutsch, 1974b; Gottman et al., 1975; Rubin, 1972). Popular children are better at perspective taking, or at surmising what a peer is thinking or feeling (Jennings, 1975). In addition, these children are more aware of the friendship patterns among their peers (Krantz, 1982) and are more accurate at estimating their own and their peers' statuses in the peer status hierarchy (Goslin, 1962). Finally, competent children have a more sophisticated understanding of morality. When judging an actor's behavior as right or wrong, they are more concerned with whether the action violates a principle of mutual respect among people for the rights and welfare of others than simply with whether the action brings external reward or punishment for the actor (Enright & Sutterfield, 1980). All these advantages in social cognition help the competent child interact with others in ways that encourage friendship and acceptance.

Skill in Interpersonal Problem Analysis
Competent children settle disputes more effectively than less popular children. As children age, their disputes tend to revolve around different issues. Preschoolers' conflicts tend to center on possession of a toy or other object; older children argue over what activity to engage in, which children to be with, and who is to blame for some negative event (Asher et al., 1982). To handle such disputes effectively, children must possess some measure of assertiveness and persuasiveness, but they also need to recognize the importance of taking turns and sharing (Asher, 1978). Popular children tend to apply social norms and rules when settling disputes. (For example, a popular child may reason: "We played that last time. Now it's my turn to decide. One person isn't supposed to decide all the time.") In the Putallaz and Gottman (1981) study, pairs of either popular or unpopular children were observed while playing a word game. Popular children disagreed less with each other than unpopular children, but when popular children did disagree, they tended to cite a general rule for their disa-

greement and then provided an acceptable alternative action for the other child. Here is an example of a popular child's use of a rule following disagreement:

> "No, you ain't. You ain't supposed . . . you ain't supposed to use this first. You're supposed to pick one of these."

In contrast, unpopular children would typically explain their disagreement by giving a reason very specifically related to the previous act of the other child, without providing an alternative action for that child. For example:

> "No. Can't say 'bank' again (after the child had used the word bank on a previous turn of the game)."

Thus far we have summarized the correlates of peer competence in preschool and grade-school children. A study by Ford (1982) indicates that many of the skills we have suggested as important for competence in childhood are also important for social success in high school. Ford obtained estimates of social competence in ninth and twelfth graders by asking their peers and teachers to nominate students whom they thought would be particularly good at handling each of a series of challenging social situations. Students selected as competent were found on a series of questionnaires to assign high priorities to achieving interpersonal goals (such as getting along with their parents, having close friends, and helping people with their problems), and they confidently described themselves as possessing the interpersonal resources to accomplish their goals. They also scored high on the ability to empathize with the feelings of others, the ability to generate new ways to attain their goals, and the tendency to consider the behavioral consequences of various courses of action when planning their behavior. This study indicates that there is continuity in the correlates of social competence as children develop into adolescents.

Family Influences on Social Competence

The kinds of relationships children enjoy at home with their families influence their competence in the peer group. Ainsworth (1979) and Sroufe (1979) hypothesize that infants and toddlers who are secure in their attachments to their parents should be more likely than insecurely attached infants to embark confidently on new relationships beyond the family, because secure infants know that they can always return home for reassurance or to be comforted. Furthermore, secure parent-child attachments should provide a context in which children learn patterns of reciprocity and mutual concern that they can generalize to their interactions with peers. This hypothesis has, in fact, been confirmed. Compared to insecurely attached children, securely attached children show more leadership and skill in social interactions. They more often seek out, and are sought out by, other children (Easterbrooks & Lamb, 1979; Waters, Wippman, & Sroufe, 1979). They are less aggressive, more reciprocal, more helpful, and more sympathetic to peer distress (Lieberman, 1977; Pastor, 1981). In addition, securely attached children are more creative at resolving conflicts (Arend, Gove, & Sroufe, 1979; Pastor, 1981). On the other hand, boys from broken homes, who may be assumed to be experiencing some insecurity, are more likely to play by themselves and with younger children than boys from intact homes (Hetherington et al., 1979). In sum, security in the home increases the child's freedom to explore new relationships and fosters competence in the peer group.

Parental discipline is also associated with peer competence. Parents who insist that their children comply with their requests for mature and independent behavior, who are warm and affectionate, and who prefer inductive reasoning over power assertive discipline tend to have children who are self-reliant, self-controlled, explorative, and well-liked by their peers (Baumrind, 1973; Elkins, 1958; Winder & Rau, 1963). George and Main (1979) found that toddlers who were physically abused by their parents at home tended to be assaultive toward their peers and hostile toward their caregivers in day care—qualities we have already noted to cause peer rejection.

Finally, we might note a correlation between birth order and peer popularity. Although first-born and only children are more active and assertive with their peers than later-born children (Snow, Jacklin, & Maccoby, 1981), later-born children are more popular and egalitarian and less demanding and jealous in their peer relations (Exner & Sutton-Smith, 1970; Miller & Maruyama, 1976; Schachter, 1964). Possibly, later-borns must develop powers of negotiation, compromise, and tolerance in order to obtain their share of resources in the home, whereas first-borns get accustomed to simply taking whatever they want.

Teaching Children Social Competence

Most techniques for improving children's social competence and popularity fall into one of three categories: shaping, modeling, and social skills coaching.

Shaping Shaping is a technique sometimes used to increase the rate of social interaction in extremely withdrawn, isolated children. The technique involves rewarding children (with attention, praise, etc.) for approaching and interacting with other children. Sometimes a *successive approximations* procedure is used, in which the child is first rewarded for making a desired response that may be fairly far removed from the desired end product (perhaps just looking toward a group of interacting peers), but the criterion for reward is gradually raised so that reinforcement becomes contingent on successively closer approximations to the desired degree of interaction (O'Connor, 1972). A variation on the theme is to reward a child's peers for approaching and interacting with the isolated child, rather than vice-versa (Strain & Timm, 1974). Shaping procedures tend to be tedious and their effectiveness short-lived (Combs & Slaby, 1977). Shaping is best reserved for use in conjunction with other training techniques, such as social skills coaching.

Modeling   Modeling is another technique typically used to increase social participation in withdrawn children. For example, O'Connor (1969, 1972) showed preschool isolates a 23-minute film depicting 11 episodes in which a shy, isolated peer model approached other groups of children. The situations were graduated from low-threat (e.g., sharing a toy with two other children) to high-threat (e.g., joining a group of highly active children who are gleefully tossing play equipment around the room). Compared to isolates who viewed a nontherapeutic control film, isolates who saw O'Connor's therapeutic film (or a similar one) have shown lasting gains in social approach (Evers & Schwarz, 1973; Evers-Pasquale & Sherman, 1975; Jakibchuk & Smeriglio, 1976; Keller & Carlson, 1974; O'Connor, 1969; 1972). Therapeutic modeling is most effective if the model is similar to the observing child (i.e., appears to be shy at the beginning of the film) and if the movie is accompanied by narration calling the child's attention to the model's behavior and its underlying purposes and consequences (Asher et al., 1982).

Although shaping and modeling are sometimes effective in increasing isolated children's rates of interaction, we should bear in mind that isolated children are not always the ones most in need of therapeutic intervention. Many children selected as isolates do have one or two friends and are not lacking in the skills required to initiate and sustain friendships; they simply choose to interact with others less than their more active peers. Perhaps it is children who are actively rejected by their peers or who have failed to establish any friendships at all that are most in need of therapeutic intervention (Asher et al., 1981; Conger & Keane, 1981). Furthermore, for these children, training in the specific social skills necessary to make friends and to sustain harmonious interactions may be what is required, not training designed simply to increase the children's overall rate of interaction.

Coaching   Social skills coaching involves telling or showing children how to enact a specific social skill, providing children with opportunities to practice the skill, and giving children feedback with suggestions for improving their use of the skill (Asher et al., 1977). A study by Ladd (1981) illustrates the benefits of social skills training. Third graders who received low ratings from their classmates on the question "How much do you like to play with this person in school?" served as subjects. The children were assigned to one of three conditions: a social skills training condition, an attention control group (children received the same amount of attention from the researchers as the first group, but received no social skills training), or a no-treatment control. Children in the first condition received eight 45–50 minute training sessions that focused on teaching the children three specific skills: asking appropriate questions of peers, leading peers (offering useful suggestions and directions), and offering supportive statements to peers. During the training sessions, the children were taught the skills and were also taught to be sensitive to the effects their use of the skills had on other children. The children were encouraged to practice the skills during both regular interactions with their peers and specially arranged practice sessions with a peer partner. Ladd provides an example from his basic training script that illustrates how the children were taught to ask positive questions:

> INSTRUCTOR   To begin, I'd like to talk with you about an idea that might make a game more fun to play and help you get to know other kids while you are playing. One way you can make a game fun and get to know other kids is to ask questions that are positive. Okay, (child's name), if you were playing a game

with some kids what is a way that you might ask a question that's positive?

CHILD   How do you play this game?

INSTRUCTOR   Good, that's a positive question. Now, what do you think another person might say or do if you said that?

CHILD   Probably tell me the rules . . . give some directions.

INSTRUCTOR   Yes, something like that might happen. Okay, now, what would be an example of a question that isn't positive?

CHILD   Ahh. . . . Can't you do anything right?

INSTRUCTOR   Yes, that would be a question that isn't positive. What do you think another person might say or do if you said that?

CHILD   They'd probably get mad . . . maybe tell you to get lost.

INSTRUCTOR   Yes, I guess something like that could happen . . . . (After completing this procedure with each child) . . . Okay, now let's try to play this game together. We will begin by . . . . While we play this game I would like you to try out asking questions that are positive . . . . (As the children play) How could I find out if (child's name) likes this game? Show me how you'd do it . . . . (Child's name), what is a question you have about this game? . . . (etc.).

CHILD   Do you think this is a fun game?

PEER   Yeah, kinda. How 'bout you?

INSTRUCTOR   Good (children's names), those are positive questions.

Assessments of the children's use of social skills in naturalistic peer interaction were taken both before and after the training sessions. Children in the treatment condition increased their frequency of asking appropriate questions and leading their peers. The frequency of supportive statements was too low to analyze. Moreover, when the children were given another sociometric test of peer acceptance after training was concluded, the training children showed significant gains in popularity, whereas children in the two control groups did not. These gains in popularity were still evident on a final follow-up test of popularity administered 4 weeks later.

Other skills besides asking questions and making leading suggestions have been fostered in unpopular or isolated children and have been found to produce increases in peer acceptance or interaction. These include learning to dispense positive social reinforcers, such as smiles and compliments (Cooke & Apolloni, 1976; Crowder, 1975; Kirby & Toler, 1970; Oden & Asher, 1977; Wahler, 1967); assertiveness, such as making good eye contact, speaking audibly, and saying "No" politely but firmly (Bornstein, Bellack, & Hersen, 1977); and cooperating, sharing, taking turns, listening, and communicating with another's needs in mind (Gottman, Gonso, & Schuler, 1976; Oden & Asher, 1977). Coaching of social skills appears to be a promising method for helping socially handicapped children acquire the skills it takes to participate effectively.

Some Other Correlates of Peer Popularity

Apart from social skills, a number of other personal qualities affect children's chances of acceptance by the peer group. Perhaps one of the most unfair facts of life is that children's first names affect their popularity. Children with unusual or funny-sounding names receive lower sociometric scores (Bruning & Husa, 1972). Whether the peer group rejects children with such names or whether parents who assign their children odd names also fail to provide a social learning environment conducive to the development of social skills is a matter for future research.

Another unjust correlate of popularity is physical attractiveness: Physically unattractive children suffer in peer acceptance (Cavior & Dokecki, 1973; Dion, 1972; Kleck, Richardson, & Ronald, 1974; Langlois & Stephan, 1977; Lerner & Lerner, 1977). When asked to choose pictures of children to exemplify negative qualities like "He hits me without a good reason" or "He's scary," even preschoolers select photos of children rated by independent judges as unattractive (Dion,

1973). Why might this be? Perhaps children's stereotypes about what attractive and unattractive people's personalities are supposed to be like attract them to good-looking peers and repel them from ugly peers. After all, as Langlois and Downs (1979) point out, children learn that Cinderella is beautiful, good, and kind, while her stepsisters are ugly, wicked, selfish, and cruel.

One revealing fact, however, is that unattractive children actually behave in a more disagreeable way than their more attractive classmates. Langlois and Downs (1979) took behavioral observations of interactions of 5-year-olds whose photographs had been rated for attractiveness by adults unfamiliar with the children. Unattractive children were more aggressive and tended to play in an active, boisterous manner with masculine toys. Perhaps a self-fulfilling prophecy helps turn physically unattractive children into socially unattractive children. If, because of their stereotypes about ugly people, children expect their unattractive peers to be aversive, then unattractive children may experience rejection and frustration, lose self-esteem, and actually become less attractive playmates.

Physically handicapped and overweight children also suffer in popularity (Lerner, 1972). In one study, children preferred, from most to least, photos of the following: a normal child, a child with crutches and a brace, a child in a wheelchair, a child with a hand missing, a child with facial disfiguration, and an obese child (Richardson, Goodman, Hastorf, & Dornbusch, 1961). Children may be most repelled by the obese child because they suspect that this child simply lacks self-control (Lerner & Korn, 1972).

Rate of physical maturation is also implicated in peer acceptance in adolescence (Jones & Bayley, 1950). Early maturing boys enjoy somewhat more prestige and popularity in adolescence than boys who are slow to mature. The boys who mature later than average are rated as less attractive, more childish, more restless, bossier, more talkative,

and more attention-seeking. They are also underrepresented in student offices and athletics. Maturation rate is less consistently associated with peer acceptance in girls.

Finally, children are more attracted to peers who are academically competent (Green, Forehand, Beck, & Vosk, 1980) and to peers who are hardworking and likely to contribute productively to group efforts (Levine, Snyder, & Mendez-Caratini, 1982).

PEER GROUP DYNAMICS

One of the most striking aspects of children's social behavior is that children tend to interact in groups. Groups may be thought of as collections of interacting people who share a common goal, motive, or interest. We have already discussed one kind of children's group—friendships. We noted there exist considerable individual differences among children in friendship patterns, and we discussed the interpersonal skills needed by children to make and keep a friend. But children spend much of their time interacting in groups composed of children who are not necessarily their close friends. Several children may play together in the sandbox, team up to play cops and robbers, or form a chess club without necessarily being bosom buddies. In this section we take a closer look at the formation, structure, and functioning of children's groups. Our level of analysis will be at the group rather than the individual level. Thus, for example, we will be concerned with factors that make a group stick together rather than with what makes an individual child an effective or ineffective member of the group.

Group Formation

The Bases for Children's Groups   Shared goals are the catalyst for group formation. For young children, common play goals are the main thing attracting children to one another for group interaction. Even 1- and 2-year-old children break themselves up into smaller play groups at day care: Some children play in the building blocks corner, some play dress-up, and so on. By the time children are 3 or 4, they band together in groups with a "we" identity that clearly sets them apart from other groups (e.g., playing cowboys and Indians). Shared play activities continue to be important as children get older, but organized school activities, athletics, clubs, and lessons also begin to be bases for group formation (Hartup, 1970).

As we noted in the last chapter, segregation by sex is a striking feature of children's groups: Boys play with boys and girls with girls. The particular goals underlying group activity depend on age and social class as well as sex, however. Lower-class adolescent boys, for example, often group together deliberately to escape adult supervision, whereas upper-class girls meet to enjoy slumber parties or to patronize high-class restaurants (Phelps & Horrocks, 1958). In adolescence, participation in groups composed of both boys and girls increases—the two sexes share such activities as dances and double-dates.

The Emergence of Status Hierarchies
Researchers have observed children's play groups in their formative stages, as when a group of young children begin preschool together or when children go to summer camp. Certain regularities in group formation and structure have emerged from these studies. When a group forms, the children usually develop a status hierarchy or "pecking order." Even nursery schoolers form dominance hierarchies, and their hierarchies are based on toughness, or the children's relative abilities to dominate each other in conflict situations (Freedman, 1977; Omark & Edelman, 1975, 1976; Strayer & Strayer, 1976; Zivin, 1977). Hierarchies usually gel after an initial period in which children resolve disputes through overt aggression. For example, for the first few weeks of nursery school, children test each other's limits, with many disputes ac-

tually coming to blows and resulting in one winner and one loser. Hierarchies result from this process, as children come to learn who can beat whom. Positions in the hierarchy are transitive: If A is dominant over B and B is dominant over C, then A is dominant over C (Sluckin & Smith, 1977; Strayer & Strayer, 1976). The first positions to become stabilized are the highest- and lowest-ranking ones. This is called *anchoring*. Gradually, the in-between ranks become filled, though they tend to remain less stable than the extremes (Sherif & Sherif, 1964). Once children know each other's rank, overt aggression declines. This is because disputes tend to be settled in the dominant member's favor before the children actually come to blows.

Although hierarchies exist in preschool groups, preschoolers tend not to be very good judges of each other's positions in the hierarchy. In fact, when asked the question, "Who's the toughest kid in your class?" boy preschoolers tend to answer with an egotistical and excited "Me!" Girls are less excited by the question. By first grade, children's verbal reports of who occupies which position in the hierarchy correspond closely to behavioral observation. We might add that the higher positions in the hierarchy tend to be occupied by boys.

Savin-Williams (1979) examined dominance hierarchies in groups of adolescents attending summer camp. Camp counselors took detailed notes on the adolescents' daily behavior. For both sexes, compared to other group members, dominant members were found to be biologically more mature; to possess more athletic ability (strength, speed, and coordination); and to possess skills of group leadership (assertiveness and self-assurance). There were several sex differences in the ways dominance was asserted. Boy leaders were more likely to assert themselves physically, to argue with others, and to displace cabin-mates; girls were more apt to recognize the status of others, to give unsolicited advice and information, and to shun and ignore others. The adolescents tended to make friends with people close to their own dominance rank. In fact, 80 percent of friendships were with individuals of an immediately adjacent rank. Over time, the dominance hierarchy became more established. When shifts in ranks did occur, they tended to occur between two adjacently ranked members.

The Functions of Hierarchies Savin-Williams (1979) notes that dominance hierarchies may serve several functions. First, as we already noted, dominance hierarchies help reduce within-group aggression. As with Suomi and Harlow's monkeys, once children establish a ritualized, nonaggressive way of settling disputes (e.g., the more dominant member makes a threatening gesture and the more submissive member submits without a contest), serious aggression becomes reserved for outsiders.

Second, dominance hierarchies engender a division of labor. Members with low status tend to occupy worker roles, performing tasks decided on by higher-ranking members (Savin-Williams, 1976). Communication and attention tend to be directed toward the leader of the group, especially in more cohesive and smoothly functioning groups (Abramovitch & Grusec, 1978; Freedman, 1977).

Third, dominance hierarchies help distribute scarce resources. This does not mean, though, that hierarchies ensure that resources are shared equally among all members. On the contrary, high-ranking members tend to help themselves to desirable resources! In Savin-Williams' summer camp study (1979), dominant adolescents "frequently ate the bigger piece of cake at mealtimes, sat where they wanted to during discussions, and slept in the preferred sleeping sites during camp-outs (near the fire)—all scarce resources at summer camp" (p. 934).

Finally, by making children aware of their places among their peers, dominance hierarchies help members in the process of identity formation. High-status individuals may benefit from the added prestige and attention they command. This may enhance their self-esteem and their conception of themselves as socially competent. But more subordinate individuals may also benefit from the dominance hierarchy. As Savin-Williams (1979) points out, many last-ranked members identify with the group's goals and accept their low status as a way of life. For these individuals, not making decisions or being responsible for others may be a preferred pattern of behavior. Finding acceptance for this preference from one's peers may help consolidate the low-ranking member's self-esteem.

Influences on Group Cohesiveness

Dominance hierarchies contribute to smooth group functioning and efficiency because of the attention structure and division of labor they promote. But group cohesiveness and success depend on a variety of other factors as well. These include leadership style, whether the group is structured for competition or cooperation, and the amount of prior experience the group members have had in cooperative peer interaction. We shall discuss each of these factors in turn.

Leadership Style Groups headed by either authoritarian leaders (who take an arbitrary, "Do this because I say so" approach to leading) or laissez-faire leaders (who lay down few rules and allow a free-for-all to develop) are characterized by more friction and aggressive interactions than groups headed by democratic leaders (who implement rules agreed on by the majority). Furthermore, in the most harmonious groups, group members direct a high proportion of attention and communication toward their highest-status members. In fact, when members increase their communication to lower-ranking members, it may mark the beginning of factionalization (Hartup, 1970).

Competitive and Cooperative Structure Intragroup competition undermines harmonious and effective group functioning. When resources are scarce and group members are in competition for them, members work less well together. For example, Aiello, Nicosia, and Thompson (1979) found that when children play under crowded conditions with few toys available, they become not only more aggressive but also more fearful and more likely to withdraw into solitary activity.

How a group divides the fruits of its labor is a potent influence on group cohesion. For example, when groups are asked to build block towers with the promise that rewards will be shared equally among all members, the groups perform more efficiently than when they are informed that rewards will be dispensed to members in proportion to their individual contributions. Not only do the former groups build taller towers, but they develop better divisions of labor. For example, two children may quickly place the blocks on the tower while a third straightens the tower and warns the builders when the tower becomes too high or unstable (Brownell & Hartup, 1981; French, Brownell, Graziano, & Hartup, 1977; Graziano, French, Brownell, Hartup, 1976). Members of cooperating groups also enjoy their experiences more and report liking each other more than members of competing groups (Crockenberg, Bryant, & Wilce, 1976).

Although intragroup competition undermines group solidarity, intergroup competition sometimes strengthens the cohesiveness of the competing groups. When one group is pitted against another, children tend to develop a sharp differentiation between the "in-group" and the "out-group." The feeling of belonging to the in-group is enhanced, but often at the expense of increased hostility toward members of the out-group. The classic demonstration of this effect is the field experiment conducted by Sherif, Harvey, White, Hood, and Sherif (1961). To explore the consequences of between-group competition, these researchers arranged for two groups of children attending summer camp to develop a rivalrous relationship. Actually, simply assigning the children to two separate cabins and giving each of the groups a dis-tinct name served the authors' purpose quite well, leading to spontaneous acts of inter-group competition (e.g., athletic challenges) and hostilities. In fact, the mutual antago-nism quickly became so intense that the investigators felt obliged to seek some way of reducing it. Putting the two groups of children together for social events failed miserably in promoting positive relationships between the two groups; in fact, this served simply to spark more hostilities. However, when the investigators asked the two groups to work cooperatively on achieving goals that benefited both groups—including working together to restore a blocked water supply to the camp, pooling money to rent a movie, and using a rope to start the food supply truck—intergroup hostilities finally diminished.

Cooperative Peer-Rearing: Effects of Growing up in Israeli Kibbutzim Children reared in Israeli kibbutzim enjoy especially congenial peer relations. In a kibbutz, children spend the entire day in the company of agemates. They eat, sleep, go to classes, work on the garden, and engage in recreational activities together. In fact, there is little opportunity for escape or even privacy. If they shirk work responsibilities, bully other children, or disrupt the group for any reason, the peer group applies powerful sanctions. Education in the kibbutz focuses on cooperation, responsibility, and dedication to selfless work for the collective good and downplays conventional academic achievement and mobility aspirations (Devereux, Shouval, Bronfenbrenner, Rodgers, Kav-Venaki, Kiely, & Karson, 1974).

Compared to family-reared city children in Israel, kibbutz children perceive their peers as more supportive and more ready to help with each other's problems and schoolwork (Avgar, Bronfenbrenner, & Henderson, 1977). Furthermore, behavioral observations reveal that kibbutz children behave more cooperatively and less competitively than their more conventionally reared city counterparts. Shapira and Madsen (1974) compared kibbutz- and city-reared children's behavior on the Madsen cooperation board, a game that allows a player either to try to maximize his or her own rewards at the expense of another player or to work out a cooperative, turntaking strategy with another player so that rewards are earned and shared by both players. Kibbutz children cooperated more than city children, who often engaged in unrestrained tugs-of-war over the resources. Shapira and Madsen speculated that the kibbutz experience teaches children to trust each other. City children often remarked that they considered a turntaking strategy but did not use it for fear the other child would not reciprocate.

Mechanisms of Peer Influence

How do children who are interacting in a group influence each other? Here we consider several of the more important ways in which groups regulate their members and teach individual children new social habits and skills.

Reward and Punishment From an early age, children control each other partly through the social consequences, or the contingent rewards and punishments, they exchange. Children tend to repeat behaviors their peers approve of, and they learn to inhibit actions that their peers discourage. Observations of nursery schoolers reveal that a variety of peer consequences serves as positive reinforcers (Charlesworth & Hartup, 1967; Furman & Masters, 1980). These include praising, smiling, joining another's play, showing interest in another's play, submitting to another's request, and sharing one's own resources. Similarly, a variety of consequences serves as punishers. These include ridicule, refusal to comply with a child's request, complaining to the teacher about a child, and ignoring or walking away from a child. In Chapter 7, we saw that young children can strengthen or weaken each other's aggressive habits depending on how they react to instances of peer aggression. For ex-

ample, nursery schoolers strengthen a peer's aggressive tendencies if they respond to an aggressive attack by submitting, by crying, or by assuming a defensive posture; they decrease a peer's aggressive habits if they react by fighting back or by telling the teacher (Patterson, Littman, & Bricker, 1967). Also, in the last chapter we noted that the peer group is a powerful molder of sex-typed habits in children, responding positively when children perform behaviors deemed appropriate for their sex and and disapproving when children behave sex-inappropriately (Fagot, 1977; Lamb, Easterbrooks, & Holden, 1980). Numerous social behaviors are influenced by peer sanctions.

A striking feature of children's peer interactions is the high degree of reciprocity that exists between the way a child treats his or her peers and the way that child is treated by his or her peers. Children who are pleasant and interested in their peers receive a high degree of reinforcement in return; unpleasant or unappreciative children tend to be treated negatively by their peers (Charlesworth & Hartup, 1967; Kohn, 1966). Leiter (1977) found that young children who initiate interactions in a friendly fashion tend to elicit compliance and smiles from other children; children who try to begin interactions in a demanding, aversive way elicit unpleasant reactions in return. Thus patterns of peer reward and punishment help teach children the "golden rule" of social interactions: What one gives, one gets back.

Modeling Children cognitively acquire many new social behaviors through observational learning—by watching the actions of their peers and by coding, organizing, and storing these actions in their minds in symbolic form. Furthermore, by observing who performs the behaviors, the situational contexts in which the behaviors occur, and the social consequences the responses invite, children formulate rules about the behaviors that are permissible or impermissible for certain kinds of children in certain situations

(Bandura, 1977). For example, when children see a model perform a novel aggressive act and then receive reinforcement for it (perhaps the victim gives the aggressor what he or she wants), they not only symbolically encode the aggressive act in memory but also may very well perform the behavior themselves when an appropriate opportunity arises (Bandura, 1965). Likewise, after seeing peers punished for misbehaving, children are likely to avoid similar misbehavior themselves (Walters & Parke, 1964). Children also learn the behaviors that are expected from members of their sex and from members of the opposite sex by observing differences in the frequencies with which male and female peers perform various activities (Perry and Bussey, 1979).

Which of their peers do children choose to imitate the most? One factor influencing children's choice of peer models is perceived similarity to the model: Children prefer to imitate other children whom they perceive to be similar to themselves. Thus children prefer to imitate same-sex rather than opposite-sex peers, they are more likely to emulate same-age children than children who are much younger or much older than themselves, and so on (Kohlberg, 1969; Bussey & Perry, 1976). This is because children learn that they are expected to behave like others who are similar to themselves.

Children are also more likely to imitate the dominant members of their groups than they are to imitate the more submissive, lower-status members (Abramovitch & Grusec, 1978). Sometimes a "ripple effect" occurs in which a group leader is the first to react to an external threat or stimulus, and then the leader's reaction is imitated in down-the-line fashion by lower-ranking members of the hierarchy. For example, in field studies of aggression in which cottages of delinquent boys are shown violent movies, the most dominant boys are typically the first to display aggressive reactions to the movies. Then the aggression spreads contagiously to the less dominant and less popular cottage-mates (Leyens, Camino, Parke, & Berkowitz, 1975).

Imitation is a mechanism of group conformity, but it is also a social skill. The more dominant and socially successful members of children's groups know how to use imitation to win friends and influence people. Group leaders not only are imitated the most, but they also do the most imitating of other children (Abramovitch & Grusec, 1978). Dominant children seem to know that other children enjoy being imitated and that they can gain influence over other children by imitating them. Children are flattered when they are imitated by a peer, especially an older, more skilled, or more competent peer. Indeed, when imitated by a peer, children increase their liking of the peer and they tend to imitate the peer in return (Thelen, Dollinger, & Roberts, 1975; Thelen, Miller, Fehrenbach, Frautschi, & Fishbein, 1980). Dominant children exploit this rule of reciprocity in imitation, knowing how to ingratiate children and bring them under their influence by imitating them first. Also, as we noted earlier in the chapter, socially skilled children use imitation to integrate themselves into a play group they wish to join. When competent children want to join the play of other children, they minimize their chances of being rejected by the other children by quietly coming alongside them and imitating them (Asher et al., 1982; Grusec & Abramovitch, 1982).

Social Comparison When discussing the development of identity and self-concept in Chapter 5, we noted that children often reach conclusions about their personalities and competencies by comparing their actions and accomplishments with those of similar others—a process known as social comparison. If most of a child's peers swim faster than the child, the child will infer that he or she is a poor swimmer; if most of a child's peers contribute less of their allowance to the March of Dimes, the child will infer that he or she is a fairly altruistic person; and so on. Children as young as 3 and 4 years compare themselves to their peers (Mosatche & Bragonier, 1981), though children become increasingly sophisticated in the kinds of inferences they draw from social comparisons as they get older (Eisert & Kahle, 1982; Ruble, Boggiano, Feldman, & Loebl, 1980; Spear & Armstrong, 1978).

Which Children Conform the Most to Peer Pressure?   To measure a child's susceptibility to peer pressure, investigators typically employ a situation in which children answer questions after they have heard several of their peers, who are serving as confederates of the researcher, give incorrect answers to the questions. The extent to which a child distorts his or her answers to match those of the peer confederates is taken as an index of the child's conformity to the peer group. Children who reveal an exaggerated tendency to conform in such situations tend to have low self-esteem and to be rather anxious and submissive (Hartup, 1970). They also tend to define morally correct behavior rather simplistically as any behavior that meets the approval of other people rather than as behavior that conforms to universal principles of mutual respect and responsibility (Saltzstein, Diamond, & Belenky, 1972).

Do girls conform more than boys? Girls do tend to conform more than boys in standard situations, as described above, but if the experiment is introduced as a test of achievement motivation, then boys conform more than girls do (Patel & Gordon, 1960; Sampson & Hancock, 1967). Furthermore, it would be incorrect to suggest that in most situations girls are more conforming to peer pressure than boys. In fact, as we concluded in the last chapter, boys are actually considerably more worried about conforming to their peer group and gaining peer approval than girls. For example, boys consort more with their peers than do girls, who are more often content to play alone or interact with adults (Lott, 1978), and boys show a stronger preference for im-

itating other boys than girls do for imitating other girls (Perry & Bussey, 1979; Siman, 1977). Researchers also have observed that boys get more upset and are more likely to alter their behavior when told that they are doing poorly at something their peers are good at (Spear & Armstrong, 1978). Finally, boys are more likely than girls to say that they would go along with their peers if the peers wanted to engage in mischief that involves breaking an adult rule (Bixenstine, DeCorte, & Bixenstine, 1976). In short, boys are more conforming to their peer groups than girls.

Does the Peer Group Work at Cross-Purposes with Adult Values?   Adolescence is often characterized as a period when children become disenchanted with adult values and rules and begin to shift their allegiance to the peer group. How accurate is this picture?

To get a look at age trends in children's conformity to adult and peer pressure, Berndt (1979a) asked children in the third through twelfth grades to rate how much they would yield to adult or peer pressure in a variety of hypothetical situations. In some situations peers were described as trying to lure the children into misbehaving. Here is an example:

> You are with a couple of your best friends on Halloween. They're going to soap windows, but you're not sure whether you should or not. Your friends say you should, because there's no way you could get caught. What would you *really* do?

In other situations, peers or adults were described as trying to persuade the children to participate in a prosocial act (e.g., to help a sibling with homework) or a neutral act (e.g., to go bowling with them).

Results indicated that conformity to adult pressure decreased steadily between the third and twelfth grades. Conformity to peer pressure, on the other hand, followed a curvilinear trend, beginning at a low level in the third grade, increasing to reach a peak at ninth grade, and then falling off. Thus midadolescence was the period of greatest parent-peer conflict. Berndt suggests that the peak opposition between parent and peer pressure at ninth grade may be partly due to the fact that adolescents at this age are particularly likely to join their peers in mischief, something almost certain to provoke arguments with parents. Children of this age also quarrel with their parents about how much time is spent with family and friends. Furthermore, it is about this time that adolescents experience something of a crisis of confidence in adults, becoming disillusioned with adult wisdom, good will, and fair-mindedness (Bixenstine et al., 1976; Spear & Armstrong, 1978). But for most adolescents the turmoil is short-lived. As Berndt's data reveal, by the end of high school, peer conformity decreases, adolescents begin to accept conventional standards for behavior, and their relationships with their parents improve.

Although conformity to adult values decreases and conformity to peer pressure increases as children enter adolescence, we must be careful not to exaggerate the degree of parent-peer conflict. For most children, adolescence is not a period of stormy conflict between parent and peer values. In fact, peer values and parent values more often reinforce than oppose each other. As Hartup (1970) notes, adolescents usually select friends whose values, for the most part, are compatible with their parents' values. Of course, some adolescents, especially those from homes lacking in parental warmth and support, essentially repudiate the family in favor of the peer group. Researchers also report that adolescents who perceive their parents—and especially their fathers—as vulnerable, weak, and possessing many shortcomings are the most likely to become disillusioned with adults and join a peer subculture (Bixenstine et al., 1976).

Instead of viewing the parent versus peer issue as a contest in which one source of influence comes to dominate the other, Brittain (1963) argues that the relative influence of peers and adults varies with situations and

behaviors. Brittain found, for example, that adolescents turn to their parents when they want advice about future aspirations and academic matters, but they turn to their peer group for information about their popularity, social status, and personal identity.

In line with Brittain's approach, several researchers are looking at the relative influence of parents and peer group on adolescents' adoption of specific behaviors, such as smoking and drinking. Although many parents might like to think that their adolescents' drinking is due to the negative influence of the peer group, the fact is that many children who drink are imitating their parents' drinking habits. Bacon and Jones (1968) found that many adolescents begin drinking at home with their parents and follow the rules of alcohol consumption that their parents model. Middle- and upper-class adolescents drink more than their working-class counterparts. In a study of the relative influence of peers and parents on children's smoking, Krosnick and Judd (1982) found that parents and peers were roughly equally important influences on the smoking behavior of preadolescents (11-year-olds). However, by the time children were adolescents (14-year-olds), children's smoking was more strongly determined by whether or not one's friends smoked than by parental attitude or behavior.

Thus far we have described the results of research carried out in the United States, but it is important to bear in mind that the degree of conflict children experience between parent and peer pressures is culture-dependent. In the United States the school and peer group are both expected to share in the socialization of children, so it is not surprising that the peer group is a powerful force in socialization. In Europe, on the other hand, there is a sharper division of responsibilities between the home and the school, with the home assuming primary responsibility for social development and the school assuming responsibility for academic training, but not for socialization. Thus it is not surprising that, compared to their American counterparts,

Swiss children rely less on their peers and more on their parents for advice (Boehm, 1957).

In Russia, children's contacts with their peers are deliberately engineered so that the peer group assists in transmitting traditional adult values to children (Bronfenbrenner, 1970). This is especially true of Russian boarding schools, where the entire peer group is punished if a single child breaks an adult rule and the whole group is rewarded when an individual child excels. The rewards and punishments are administered publicly, bringing pride or shame to the entire group. This system of group rewards and punishments quickly causes the children to pressure one another into conforming to the adult values. To improve the efficiency of the system even further, members of the peer group are assigned by adults to monitor, evaluate, and report on each other's behavior. A positive consequence of this system is that when children see a peer falling behind in schoolwork or breaking a rule, they spontaneously come to the aid of, or give advice to, the child. Under these circumstances, it is not surprising that Soviet children are far less likely than their American counterparts to state that they would engage in mischievous behavior if tempted by their peers to do so (Bronfenbrenner, 1970).

In Russia, then, the peer group is used to transmit the status quo in adult values. Israel, however, provides a good example of a country in which the peer group is expected to act as a medium of cultural change rather than continuity. In Israel, childhood is thought of as a time of mischief and adventure that prepares the young citizen for an adult role emphasizing self-confidence, independence, and a break with tradition. This is true even in the kibbutzim (Devereux et al., 1974). Israeli children in fact are proud to announce that they will break an adult rule if their peers suggest it—a situation exactly opposite to that in Russia (Shouval, Kav Venaki, Bronfenbrenner, Devereux, & Kiely, 1975).

In sum, there is no fixed relationship be-

tween parent and peer values. In some cultures the peer group pressures children away from traditional adult values (e.g., Israel) and in some cultures the peer group is exploited to transmit adult values (e.g., Russia).

Benefits of Interaction With Different-Age Peers

We have seen that contact between children of a similar age plays a vital role in social development. It is with equals that children learn to negotiate settlements to disputes based on principles of fairness and compromise rather than arbitrary dimensions such as physical strength; it is with equals that children are forced to come to grips with their position in the dominance hierarchy; and it is with equals that children exercise social comparison to reach conclusions about the sort of people they are. But it would be wrong to give the impression that children benefit only from interactions with children of their own age. In fact, most children have a good deal of contact with children who differ from them in age by several years, and these mixed-age contacts enrich the children's social development in unique ways.

Hartup (1980) and Konner (1975) point out that, in the effort to educate children for an industrialized society, modern society requires children to spend more time in contact with same-age peers (e.g., in the school classroom) than has been the case in the past. In more primitive hunter-gatherer societies, peer interaction typically took place in mixed-age groups comprised of infants, children, and adolescents. For example, in certain Kenyan tribes, where mothers assume major agricultural responsibilities, children are assigned the duty of infant care.

Although it may be true that mixed-age contacts are less prevalent now than centuries ago, it would be wrong to conclude that mixed-age interaction has been entirely supplanted by same-age contacts. Ellis, Rogoff, and Cromer (1981) observed American children between the ages of 1 and 12 both at home and outside in the neighborhood to determine the proportion of free time that children spend with same-age and different-age companions. The authors found that children were about equally likely to play with a child who differed from them by at least 2 years as they were to play with a child who differed from them by less than 1 year.

What do children learn from interacting with children who are older or younger than themselves? A number of studies suggest that mixed-age play may be especially conducive to the development of prosocial behavior. Specifically, when children interact in mixed-age groups, there is more nurturance, sharing, helping, cooperation, and protectiveness, and there is less aggression and competition, than when children play in same-age groups (Hartup, 1979; Konner, 1975; Murphy, 1937; Whiting & Whiting, 1975). Also, when preschool children play in classes composed of children of several ages, there is less parallel play and more interactive and solitary play than when children are all of a similar age (Goldman, 1981; Reuter & Yunik, 1973). Mixed-age interaction also helps children, especially the older members of the group, acquire skills of leadership and assertiveness. For example, when children are teamed up with younger children for work on a project, they become more directive and assume more responsibility for initiating and sustaining group activity (Graziano et al., 1976).

A dramatic illustration of the benefits of interaction with a younger peer comes from Harlow's efforts to rehabilitate isolated and depressed monkeys. As we noted earlier in this chapter, Harlow discovered that placing baby rhesus monkeys in social isolation for 6 months after birth causes the monkeys to become severely withdrawn and depressed. Reasoning that transferring the depressed monkeys to a cage containing a normal monkey might help the isolates acquire social skills and overcome their depression, Harlow, Dodsworth, and Harlow (1965) caged some isolates for several weeks with either an adult or a same-age peer (a normal 6-month-old).

The results were disastrous. The isolates were attacked, did not reciprocate the attacks, and remained withdrawn and victimized. Then Suomi and Harlow (1972) tried placing the isolates in cages with *younger*, 3-month-old peers. The results were dramatic and positive. At first, the young peer "therapists" clung to their isolate cagemates, preventing the isolates from engaging in stereotyped depressive activities like rocking, huddling, and self-clasping. Being younger and smaller, the peer therapists were not aggressive toward the isolates. Gradually, with the therapists' interest and help, the isolates began to move about the cage, explore, and play. After several months of being housed with their young therapists, the isolates' social deficits were eradicated. Similarly impressive effects have been reported for monkeys reared for a whole year in isolation and then given therapy with 2-month-old therapists (Novak & Harlow, 1975). Figure 10–2 shows a younger peer therapist clinging to an isolate "client" at the beginning of rehabilitation therapy.

Recently, Furman, Rahe, and Hartup (1979) extended some of the principles of Harlow's innovative form of therapy to socially isolated human children. Initially, the researchers combed day-care centers to find a sample of 24 children whose rates of social interaction were exceptionally low. A third of these children were then given 10 20-minute play sessions with a peer "therapist" who was 12–20 months younger; another third were given play sessions with a same-age peer; and a final third received no treatment. When the children were later observed for social interaction in their day-care centers, both experimental groups of children showed improvement in social interaction. However, gains were most marked among children in the younger-therapist group, who nearly doubled their pretreatment interaction rates. They especially increased their rates of praising, greeting, cooperating, smiling, laughing, giving, reassuring, and protecting other children.

Why is therapy with a younger peer so ef-

Figure 10-2 A younger peer "therapist" monkey clings to a depressed, isolate monkey at start of rehabilitation therapy. (Photo courtesy of Steve Suomi and the University of Wisconsin Primate Laboratory.)

fective for withdrawn children and monkeys? Possibly, interaction with a younger peer constitutes a gentle introduction into social intercourse, allowing withdrawn and frightened children gradually to build up self-confidence as they establish patterns of nonthreatening, mutually reinforcing interaction. Or maybe therapy with a younger peer works because the withdrawn child can assume some degree of leadership over another child. The isolate can behave directively and assertively and can see these efforts reinforced in the form of compliance from the younger peer. It is worth noting that successfully rehabilitated monkeys are in fact ones who do successfully dominate their therapists—who displace

them from shelves, ledges, and desired objects, and who direct aggressive responses toward them (Novak & Harlow, 1975). In fact, when a peer therapist is temperamentally too assertive to allow an isolate to dominate, therapy is not very successful (Furman et al., 1979).

Though children can clearly benefit from interaction with younger peers, we must not overlook the other side of the coin—that children can gain from interacting with others who are older and more skilled than themselves. Perhaps one of the most important opportunities for interaction with older individuals comes during adolescence in the form of employment. Adolescents who work not only learn to fulfill the obligations of the adult work world but also earn a degree of financial independence that speeds the process of separation from the family. A number of contemporary social critics have portrayed work experience as a potentially positive influence on adolescents, and propose that adolescents be encouraged (or even obliged) to supplement school with work (e.g., President's Science Advisory Committee, 1973).

But is work an unmitigated blessing for adolescents? Research on this topic suggests not. Investigators have found that part-time employment during high school has costs as well as benefits to adolescent development (Greenberger, Steinberg, & Vaux, 1981; Steinberg, Greenberger, Garduque, Ruggiero, & Vaux, 1982). Benefits include improvement in self-management skills: After a work experience, adolescents report becoming more punctual, dependable, persistent, capable of resisting distraction, and self-reliant. Furthermore, working adolescents, especially boys, are less likely than their nonworking peers to report symptoms of psychological distress (feelings of nervousness, depression, and upset) and physical ailments (headaches, stomach aches, illness, fatigue, and injury).

However, the more hours adolescents work and the more stressful their jobs are (e.g., adverse working conditions or little opportunity for advancement), the more they are absent from school and the more they report using cigarettes, alcohol, and marijuana. Although, as we noted, working facilitates the development of personal responsibility, it does not promote the development of social responsibility: Adolescents who work show no more concern for others or social tolerance (willingness to interact with people of varying social and ethnic backgrounds) than their nonworking peers. Furthermore, working fosters some negative work-related attitudes. Research shows that working adolescents are more cynical about the intrinsic value of work, are more accepting of unethical business practices, and are more materialistic. Finally, working diminishes the adolescent's involvement in school, family, and peer interaction: Working adolescents enjoy school less, spend less time on their homework, and participate less in extracurricular activities. Also, working girls (but not boys) report a loss in family closeness, and working adolescents report a loss of emotional closeness with their friends. These findings prompted Steinberg and his associates (1982) to conclude:

> One of the developmental tasks of adolescence is to begin the process of detachment from the institutions of childhood. It is tempting, therefore, to view such movement as part of the natural transition to more adult interests, roles, and responsibilities. However, it is also possible that for some young people, immersion in the work place may occur before they cease to need what the school, family, and peer group have to offer. We raise seriously the question of whether 15- and 16-year-olds who commit 20–25 hours weekly to a part-time job may be missing out on important socialization and learning experiences that occur in other settings. (p. 394)

Thus, the work experience may promote the development of autonomy and self-reliance and contribute to the continuity between adolescence and adulthood, but these benefits may come at the expense of a reduced impact of other central socialization agencies on adolescents at a critical point in their development.

SUMMARY

Three theories—ethological, cognitive-developmental, and social learning—assign peer contact a major role in socialization. All three theories hold that children teach each other things that parents, teachers, and other socializing agents do not. Ethologists stress that peer contacts are essential for the adaptive patterning of certain response systems, such as aggression. For example, monkeys who enjoy normal peer relations while growing up learn to reserve serious aggression for strangers, whereas monkeys deprived of early peer contact attack friends as well as enemies. Cognitive-developmental theorists believe that peer contacts promote gains in social cognition (such as the loss of egocentrism and the ability to appreciate others' viewpoints), and that these gains allow the child to behave and interact in increasingly mature ways. According to social learning theory, peers play a vital role in teaching children new modes of behavior, in imparting information to children about what forms of behavior are expected or appropriate under various circumstances, and in setting standards against which children assess and evaluate their own personalities and competencies.

Children's interest in their peers begins at a few months of age. When babies are allowed to interact with each other in a relaxed situation (with mothers present), they in fact show more interest in each other than in their mothers. Their interactions tend to be positive and reciprocal rather than characterized by strife. As infants get older, their behavior with a playmate becomes more complex. Early opportunities for peer interaction may aid the infant's cognitive and social development, because infants tend to be more creative and competent when playing with a peer, and infants who have had plenty of peer experience adjust more smoothly when entering new peer groups (e.g., at day care) and making new friends.

Children spend considerable amounts of

time in play, which can be defined as self-structured, nonserious activity that often bears little relationship to reality. Certain kinds of play are more mature than others, and certain forms may be more important for children's social and cognitive development than others. Play probably serves several functions, including teaching children rules of social interaction (e.g., how to take turns and reciprocate favors), helping children learn to control the expression of powerful emotions and motives, furthering children's symbolic capacities, teaching children subroutines of action that can later be used to solve problems and enact social roles, and helping children establish a friendship with one or more peers.

Though children become acquainted with a great many other children as they get older, most children develop friendships with one or more than one other child. Most friends are similar to one another in terms of age, sex, and play interests. Children change in what they say they want from a friend as they get older. Preschoolers want friends who are accessible and rewarding; elementary-school children want friends who share their values and rules; and adolescents look for mutual understanding and intimacy in friendship. Friends tend to help and cooperate more with each other than with nonfriends, though boy-boy friendships are often also characterized by a fierce competition. Friendships help children learn trust, and they promote the development of social skills.

Some children are more socially competent than other children. The socially competent child is one who possesses the skills necessary to achieve the social goals he or she desires—making a friend, asking a question, influencing a playmate, and so on—and who can do so in socially acceptable ways. To identify competent children, investigators usually employ a sociometric test of peer popularity. The rationale is that a child could not have won the acceptance and respect of his or her peers without possessing the skills necessary to win friends and sustain successful social interaction. Because unpopular (less competent) children are at risk for a variety of psychological problems, researchers are attempting to identify the specific social skills possessed by competent children, so that the skills necessary for successful social interaction can be taught to less competent children. Compared to unpopular children, competent children are better at initiating interaction, better at sustaining interaction, and better at resolving interpersonal conflicts. These skills have been successfully taught to less popular children by a variety of techniques, including shaping, modeling, and coaching. Children acquire social competence largely through interaction with peers, but the sorts of relationships children establish with their family members at home also influence their popularity among their peers.

Children tend to interact in groups, and researchers note certain regularities in the dynamics of children's groups. Common goals (e.g., shared play interests) are what bring children together. In the early stages of group formation, children test out each other's strengths and weaknesses and eventually a fairly stable dominance hierarchy, or pecking order, emerges. Hierarchies serve several adaptive functions, including reducing intragroup aggression, engendering a division of labor, distributing scarce resources, and helping individual members learn to be effective leaders or gracious followers. Several factors influence group harmony and effectiveness, including leadership style, whether the group is structured for competition or cooperation, and the degree to which group members have previously experienced positive contacts with peers, as on a kibbutz. Groups control individual members by serving as models of behavior, by administering sanctions, and by serving as standards for social comparison. Adolescence is a time when conformity to the peer group becomes especially important to children and when many children, for a while at least, become disillusioned with adult wisdom and good will. But for most adolescents, the clash between parent and peer values is not severe. Adolescents tend to turn to their parents for advice and for information on certain issues (e.g., academic aspirations) and to their peers for input on certain other concerns (e.g., status identity issues).

While there are many benefits associated with interacting with peers of a similar age, children also have contact with and benefit from interaction with peers who are considerably younger or older than themselves. Interacting with younger children, for example, teaches children responsibility, nurturance, assertiveness, and skills of leadership. Children also learn and benefit from interaction with people who are older and more competent than themselves; for example, adolescents learn self-management skills when they join the adult work force. There is some concern, however, that the reduction in contact with family and friends that usually results when adolescents join the work force may not be beneficial.

References

ABRAHAMS, B., FELDMAN, S. S., & NASH, S. C. Sex role self-concept and sex role attitudes: Enduring personality characteristics or adaptations to changing life situations? *Developmental Psychology*, 1978, *14*, 393–400.

ABRAMOVITCH, R. Children's recognition of situational aspects of facial expression. *Child Development*, 1977, *48*, 459–463.

ABRAMOVITCH, R., & GRUSEC, J. E. Peer imitation in a natural setting. *Child Development*, 1978, *49*, 60–65.

ADAMS, R. E., & PASSMAN, R. H. Effects of visual and auditory aspects of mothers and strangers on the play and exploration of children. *Developmental Psychology*, 1979, *15*, 269–274.

ADERMAN, D. Elation, depression, and helping behavior. *Journal of Personality and Social Psychology*, 1972, *24*, 91–101.

AHLGREN, A., & JOHNSON, D. W. Sex differences in cooperative and competitive attitudes from the 2nd through the 12th grades. *Developmental Psychology*, 1979, *15*, 45–49.

AIELLO, J. R., NICOSIA, G., & THOMPSON, D. E. Physiological, social and behavioral consequences of crowding on children and adolescents. *Child Development*, 1979, *50*, 195–202.

AINSWORTH, M. D. S. The development of infant-mother attachment. In B. M. Caldwell & H. N. Ricciuti (Eds.), *Review of child development research* (Vol. 3). Chicago: University of Chicago Press, 1973.

AINSWORTH, M. D. S. Infant-mother attachment. *American Psychologist*, 1979, *34*, 932–937.

AINSWORTH, M. D. S., & BELL, S. Attachment, exploration, and separation: Illustrated by the behavior of one-year-olds in a strange situation. *Child Development*, 1970, *41*, 49–67.

AINSWORTH, M. D. S., BELL, S. M., & STAYTON, D. J. Individual differences in the development of some attachment behaviors. *Merrill-Palmer Quarterly*, 1972, *18*, 123–143.

AINSWORTH, M. D. S., & WITTIG, D. S. Attachment and exploratory behavior of one year olds in a strange situation. In B. M. Foss (Ed.), *Deter-*

minants of infant behavior (Vol. 4). London: Methuen, 1969.

ALLEN, M. K., & LIEBERT, R. M. Effects of live and symbolic deviant modeling cues on adoption of a previously learned standard. *Journal of Personality and Social Psychology*, 1969, *11*, 253–260.

ALLINSMITH, W. Moral standards: II. The learning of moral standards. In D. R. Miller & G. E. Swanson (Eds.), *Inner conflict and defense*. New York: Holt, Rinehart & Winston, 1960.

ALLPORT, G. W. Traits revisited. *American Psychologist*, 1966, *21*, 1–10.

AMIR, Y. The role of intergroup contact in change of prejudice and ethnic relations. In P. A. Katz (Ed.), *Towards the elimination of racism*. New York: Pergamon Press, 1976.

ANCHOR, K. N., & CROSS, H. J. Maladaptive aggression, moral perspective, and the socialization process. *Journal of Personality and Social Psychology*, 1974, *30*, 163–168.

ANDERSON, C. W., NAGLE, R. J., ROBERTS, W. A., & SMITH, J. W. Attachment to substitute caregivers as a function of center quality and caregiver involvement. *Child Development*, 1981, *52*, 53–61.

ANDERSON, R., MANOOGIAN, S. T., & REZNICK, J. S. The undermining and enhancing of intrinsic motivation in preschool children. *Journal of Personality and Social Psychology*, 1976, *34*, 915–922.

ARCO, C. M. B., & MCCLUSKEY, K. A. "A change of pace": An investigation of the salience of maternal temporal style in mother-infant play. *Child Development*, 1981, *52*, 941–949.

AREND, R., GOVE, F. L., & SROUFE, L. A. Continuity of individual adaptation from infancy to kindergarten: A predictive study of ego-resiliency and curiosity in preschoolers. *Child Development*, 1979, *50*, 950–959.

ARMSBY, R. E. A reexamination of the development of moral judgments in children. *Child Development*, 1971, *42*, 1241–1248.

ARONFREED, J. The origin of self-criticism. *Psychological Review*, 1964, *71*, 193–218.

ARONFREED, J. *Conduct and conscience: The socialization of internalized control over behavior*. New York: Academic Press, 1968.

ARONFREED, J., CUTICK, R. A., & FAGEN, S. A. Cognitive structure, punishment, and nurturance in the experimental induction of self-criticism. *Child Development*, 1963, *34*, 281–294.

ASCIONE, F. R. The effects of continuous nurturance and nurturance withdrawal on children's behavior: A partial replication. *Child Development*, 1975, *46*, 790–795.

ASHER, S. R. Children's peer relations. In M. E. Lamb (Ed.), *Social and personality development*. New York: Holt, Rinehart & Winston, 1978.

ASHER, S. R., GOTTMAN, J. M., & ODEN, S. L. Children's friendships in school settings. In E. M. Hetherington & R. D. Parke (Eds.), *Contemporary readings in child psychology*. New York: McGraw-Hill, 1977.

ASHER, S. R., MARKELL, R. A., & HYMEL, S. Identifying children at risk in peer relations: A critique of the rate-of-interaction approach to assessment. *Child Development*, 1981, *52*, 1239–1245.

ASHER, S. R., RENSHAW, P. D., & HYMEL, S. Peer relations and the development of social skills. In S. G. Moore (Ed.), *The young child: Reviews of research* (Vol. 3). Washington, D.C.: National Association for the Education of Young Children, 1982.

AUSTIN, V. D., RUBLE, D. N., & TRABASSO, T. Recall and order effects as factors in children's moral judgments. *Child Development*, 1977, *48*, 470–474.

AVGAR, A., BRONFENBRENNER, V., & HENDERSON, C. R. Socialization practices of parents, teachers, and peers in Israel: Kibbutz, moshav, and city. *Child Development*, 1977, *48*, 1219–1227.

BABAD, E. Y. Person specificity of the "social deprivation-satiation effect." *Developmental Psychology*, 1972, *6*, 210–213.

BABAD, E. Y. Effects of informational input on the "social deprivation-satiation effect." *Journal of Personality and Social Psychology*, 1973, *27*, 1–15.

BABAD, E. Y., & WEISZ, P. Effectiveness of social reinforcement as a function of contingent and noncontingent satiation. *Journal of Experimental Child Psychology*, 1977, *24*, 406–414.

BACH, G. R. Father-fantasies and father-typing in father-separated children. *Child Development*, 1946, *17*, 63–80.

BACHRACH, R., HUESMANN, L. R., & PETERSON, R. A. The relation between locus of control and the development of moral judgment. *Child Development*, 1977, *48*, 1340–1352.

BACON, M., & JONES, M. B. *Teenage drinking*. New York: Thomas Y. Crowell, 1968.

BAER, D. M., PETERSON, R. F., & SHERMAN, J. A. The development of imitation by reinforcing behavioral similarity to a model. *Journal of the Experimental Analysis of Behavior,* 1967, *10,* 405–416.

BAER, D. M., & SHERMAN, J. A. Reinforcement control of generalized imitation in young children. *Journal of Experimental Child Psychology,* 1964, *1,* 37–49.

BAKEMAN, R., & BROWN, J. V. Early interaction: Consequences for social and mental development at three years. *Child Development,* 1980, *51,* 437–447.

BAKEMAN, R., & BROWNLEE, J. R. The strategic use of parallel play: A sequential analysis. *Child Development,* 1980, *51,* 873–878.

BALDWIN, A. L. *Theories of child development.* New York: John Wiley, 1967.

BALDWIN, C. P., & BALDWIN, A. L. Children's judgments of kindness. *Child Development,* 1970, *41,* 29–47.

BALL, S., & BOGATZ, G. A. Summative research of Sesame Street: Implications for the study of preschool children. In A. D. Pick (Ed.), *Minnesota symposium on child psychology,* (Vol. 6). Minneapolis: University of Minnesota Press, 1972.

BALL, S., & BOGATZ, G. A. *Reading with television: An evaluation of The Electric Company.* Princeton, N.J.: Educational Testing Service, 1973.

BALTES, P. B., & SCHAIE, K. W. (Eds.), *Life-span developmental psychology: Personality and socialization.* New York: Academic Press, 1973.

BANDURA, A. Influence of models' reinforcement contingencies on the acquisition of imitative responses. *Journal of Personality and Social Psychology,* 1965, *1,* 589–595.

BANDURA, A. *Principles of behavior modification.* New York: Holt, Rinehart & Winston, 1969.(a)

BANDURA, A. Social learning theory of identificatory processes. In D. A. Goslin (Ed.), *Handbook of socialization theory and research.* Chicago: Rand McNally, 1969.(b)

BANDURA, A. *Aggression: A social learning analysis.* Englewood Cliffs, N.J.: Prentice-Hall, 1973.

BANDURA, A. *Social learning theory.* Englewood Cliffs, N.J.: Prentice-Hall, 1977.

BANDURA, A. On paradigms and recycled ideologies. *Cognitive Therapy and Research,* 1978, *2,* 79–103.(a)

BANDURA, A. The self system in reciprocal determinism. *American Psychologist,* 1978, *33,* 344–358.(b)

BANDURA, A. Psychological mechanisms of aggres-

sion. In M. von Cranach, K. Foppa, W. Lepenies, and D. Ploog (Eds.), *Human ethology: Claims and limits of a new discipline.* Cambridge: Cambridge University Press, 1979.

BANDURA, A. Self-referent thought: A developmental analysis of self-efficacy. In J. H. Flavell & L. D. Ross (Eds.), *Social cognitive development: Frontiers and possible futures.* Cambridge: Cambridge University Press, 1981.

BANDURA, A., & BARAB, P. G. Conditions governing nonreinforced imitation. *Developmental Psychology,* 1971, *5,* 244–255.

BANDURA, A., GRUSEC, J. E., & MENLOVE, F. L. Observational learning as a function of symbolization and incentive set. *Child Development,* 1966, *37,* 499–506.

BANDURA, A., GRUSEC, J. E., & MENLOVE, F. L. Vicarious extinction of avoidance behavior. *Journal of Personality and Social Psychology,* 1967, *5,* 16–23.

BANDURA, A., & HUSTON, A. C. Identification as a process of incidental learning. *Journal of Abnormal and Social Psychology,* 1961, *63,* 311–318.

BANDURA, A., & JEFFERY, R. W. Role of symbolic coding and rehearsal processes in observational learning. *Journal of Personality and Social Psychology,* 1973, *26,* 122–130.

BANDURA, A., & KUPERS, C. J. The transmission of patterns of self-reinforcement through modeling. *Journal of Abnormal and Social Psychology,* 1964, *69,* 1–9.

BANDURA, A., & MCDONALD, F. J. The influence of social reinforcement and the behavior of models in shaping children's moral judgments. *Journal of Abnormal and Social Psychology,* 1963, *67,* 274–281.

BANDURA, A., & MENLOVE, F. L. Factors determining vicarious extinction of avoidance behavior through symbolic modeling. *Journal of Personality and Social Psychology,* 1968, *8,* 99–108.

BANDURA, A., & PERLOFF, B. Relative efficacy of self-monitored and externally imposed reinforcement systems. *Journal of Personality and Social Psychology,* 1967, *7,* 111–116.

BANDURA, A., ROSS, D., & ROSS, S. A. Transmission of aggression through imitation of aggressive models. *Journal of Abnormal and Social Psychology,* 1961, *63,* 575–582.

BANDURA, A., ROSS, D., & ROSS, S. A. A comparative test of the status envy, social power, and secondary reinforcement theories of identificatory learning. *Journal of Abnormal and Social Psychology*, 1963, 67, 527–534.(a)

BANDURA, A., ROSS, D., & ROSS, S. A. Imitation of film-mediated aggressive models. *Journal of Abnormal and Social Psychology*, 1963, 66, 3–11. (b)

BANDURA, A., & WALTERS, R. H. *Adolescent aggression*. New York: Ronald Press, 1959.

BANDURA, A., & WALTERS, R. H. Aggression. In H. W. Stevenson (Ed.), *Child Psychology*. Chicago: National Society for the Study of Education, 1963.(a)

BANDURA, A., & WALTERS, R. H. *Social learning and personality development*. New York: Holt, Rinehart & Winston, 1963.(b)

BANKS, W. C. White preference in blacks: A paradigm in search of a phenomenon. *Psychological Bulletin*, 1976, 83, 1179–1186.

BANKS, W. C., MCQUATER, G. V., & ROSS, J. A. On the importance of white preference and the comparative difference of blacks and others: Reply to Williams and Morland. *Psychological Bulletin*, 1979, 86, 33–36.

BANKS, W. C., & ROMPF, W. J. Evaluative bias and preference behavior in black and white children. *Child Development*, 1973, 44, 776–783.

BARENBOIM, C. Developmental changes in the interpersonal cognitive system from middle childhood to adolescence. *Child Development*, 1977, 48, 1467–1474.

BARENBOIM, C. The development of person perception in childhood and adolescence: From behavioral comparisons to psychological constructs to psychological comparisons. *Child Development*, 1981, 52, 129–144.

BARKER, R. G., DEMBO, T., & LEWIN, K. Frustration and regression: An experiment with young children. *University of Iowa Studies in Child Welfare*, 1941, 18, 1–314.

BARNETT, M. A. Effects of competition and relative deservedness of the other's fate on children's generosity. *Developmental Psychology*, 1975, 11, 665–666.

BARNETT, M. A., & ANDREWS, J. A. Sex differences in children's reward allocation under competitive and cooperative instructional sets. *Developmental Psychology*, 1977, 13, 85–86.

BARNETT, M. A., & BRYAN, J. H. Effects of competition with outcome feedback on children's helping behavior. *Developmental Psychology*, 1974, 10, 838–842.

BARNETT, M. A., KING, L. M., & HOWARD, J. A. Inducing affect about self or other: Effects on generosity in children. *Developmental Psychology*, 1979, 15, 164–167.

BARNETT, M. A., MATTHEWS, K. A., & HOWARD, J. A. Relationship between competitiveness and empathy in 6- and 7-year olds. *Developmental Psychology*, 1979, 15, 221–222.

BARON, R. A. Aggression as a function of magnitude of victims' pain cues, level of prior anger arousal, and aggressor-victim similarity. *Journal of Personality and Social Psychology*, 1971, 18, 48–54. (a)

BARON, R. A. Magnitude of victim's pain cues and level of prior anger arousal as determinants of adult aggressive behavior. *Journal of Personality and Social Psychology*, 1971, 17, 236–243. (b)

BARON, R. A. Aggression as a function of victim's pain cues, level of prior anger arousal, and exposure to an aggressive model. *Journal of Personality and Social Psychology*, 1974, 29, 117–124.

BARRERA, M. E., & MAURER, D. The perception of facial expressions by the three-month-old. *Child Development*, 1981, 52, 203–206.

BARRETT, D. E., & YARROW, M. R. Prosocial behavior, social inferential ability, and assertiveness in children. *Child Development*, 1977, 48, 475–481.

BAR-TAL, D., RAVIV, A., & LEISER, T. The development of altruistic behavior: Empirical evidence. *Developmental Psychology*, 1980, 16, 516–524.

BATES, J. E. Effects of a child's imitation versus nonimitation on adults' verbal and nonverbal positivity. *Journal of Personality and Social Psychology*, 1975, 31, 840–851.

BATES, J. E., & BENTLER, P. M. Play activities of normal and effeminate boys. *Developmental Psychology*, 1973, 9, 20–27.

BATES, J. E., BENTLER, P. M. & THOMPSON, S. K. Measurement of deviant gender development in boys. *Child Development*, 1973, 44, 591–598.

BATES, J. E., FREELAND, C. A., & LOUNSBURY, M. L. Measure of infant difficultness. *Child Development*, 1979, 50, 794–803.

BATESON, M. C. Mother-infant exchanges: The epigenesis of conversational interaction. *Annals of the New York Academy of Sciences*, 1975, 263, 101–113.

BAUMRIND, D. Child care practices anteceding three patterns of preschool behavior. *Genetic Psychology Monographs*, 1967, 75, 43–88.

BAUMRIND, D. The development of instrumental competence through socialization. In A. D. Pick

(Ed.), *Minnesota symposia on child psychology* (Vol. 7). Minneapolis: University of Minnesota Press, 1973.

BAUMRIND, D. *Sex-related socialization effects.* Paper presented at the biennial meeting of the Society for Research in Child Development, San Francisco, March 1979.

BAUMRIND, D. Are androgynous individuals more effective persons and parents? *Child Development*, 1982, 53, 44–75.

BEAMAN, A. L., KLENTZ, B., DIENER, E., & SVANUM, S. Self-awareness and transgression in children: Two field studies. *Journal of Personality and Social Psychology*, 1979, 37, 1835–1846.

BEARISON, D. J., & CASSEL, T. Z. Cognitive decentration and social codes: Communicative effectiveness in young children from differing family contexts. *Developmental Psychology*, 1975, 11, 29–36.

BEARISON, D. J., & ISAACS, L. Production deficiency in children's moral judgments. *Developmental Psychology*, 1975, 11, 732–737.

BECKER, J. M. T. A learning analysis of the development of peer-oriented behavior in nine-month-old infants. *Developmental Psychology*, 1977, 13, 481–491.

BECKER, W. C. Consequences of different kinds of parental discipline. In M. L. Hoffman & L. W. Hoffman (Eds.), *Review of child development research* (Vol. 1). New York: Russell Sage Foundation, 1964.

BELL, N. J., & CARVER, W. A reevaluation of gender label effects: Expectant mothers' responses to infants. *Child Development*, 1980, 51, 925–927.

BELL, R. Q. A reinterpretation of the direction of effects in studies of socialization. *Psychological Review*, 1968, 75, 81–95.

BELL, R. Q. Parent, child, and reciprocal influences. *American Psychologist*, 1979, 34, 821–826.

BELL, R. Q., & HARPER, L. V. *The effect of children on parents.* Hillsdale, N.J.: Erlbaum, 1977.

BELL, S. M. The development of the concept of the object as related to infant-mother attachment. *Child Development*, 1970, 41, 291–311.

BELL, S. M., & AINSWORTH, M. D. S. Infant crying and maternal responsiveness. *Child Development*, 1972, 43, 1171–1190.

BELSKY, J. Mother-father-infant interaction: A naturalistic observational study. *Developmental Psychology*, 1979, 15, 601–607.

BELSKY, J. Child maltreatment: An ecological integration. *American Psychologist*, 1980, 35, 320–335.

BELSKY, J., & STEINBERG, L. D. The effects of day care: A critical review. *Child Development*, 1978, 49, 929–949.

BEM, D. J. Self-perception theory. In L. Berkowitz (Ed.), *Advances in experimental social psychology* (Vol. 6). New York: Academic Press, 1972.

BEM, D. J., & ALLEN, A. On predicting some of the people some of the time: The search for cross-situational consistencies in behavior. *Psychological Review*, 1974, 81, 506–520.

BEM, S. L. The measurement of psychological androgyny. *Journal of Consulting and Clinical Psychology*, 1974, 42, 155–162.

BEM, S. L. Sex role adaptability: One consequence of psychological androgyny. *Journal of Personality and Social Psychology*, 1975, 31, 634–643.

BEM, S. L. On the utility of alternative procedures for assessing psychological androgyny. *Journal of Consulting and Clinical Psychology*, 1977, 45, 196–205.

BEM, S. L. Gender schema theory: A cognitive account of sex typing. *Psychological Review*, 1981, 88, 354–364.

BEM, S. L., & LENNEY, E. Sex typing and the avoidance of cross-sex behavior. *Journal of Personality and Social Psychology*, 1976, 33, 48–54.

BERKOWITZ, L. The contagion of violence: An S-R mediational analysis of some effects of observed aggression. In W. J. Arnold & M. M. Page (Eds.), *Nebraska symposium on motivation.* Lincoln: University of Nebraska Press, 1970.

BERKOWITZ, L. Control of aggression. In B. M. Caldwell & H. Ricciuti (Eds.), *Review of child development research*, (Vol. 3). New York: Russell Sage Foundation, 1973.

BERKOWITZ, L. Some determinants of impulsive aggression: Role of mediated associations with reinforcement for aggression. *Psychological Review*, 1974, 81, 165–176.

BERKOWITZ, L., & CONNOR, W. H. Success, failure, and social responsibility. *Journal of Personality and Social Psychology*, 1966, 4, 664–669.

BERKOWITZ, L., & DANIELS, L. Affecting the salience of the social responsibility norm: Effects of past help on the response to dependency relationships. *Journal of Abnormal and Social Psychology*, 1964, 68, 275–281.

BERKOWITZ, L., & FRIEDMAN, P. Some social class differences in helping behavior. *Journal of Personality and Social Psychology*, 1967, 5, 217–224.

BERMAN, P. W., MONDA, L. C., & MYERSCOUGH, R. P.

Sex differences in young children's responses to an infant: An observation within a day-care setting. *Child Development,* 1977, 48, 711–715.

BERNDT, T. J. The effect of reciprocity norms on moral judgment and causal attribution. *Child Development,* 1977, 48, 1322–1330.

BERNDT, T. J. Developmental changes in conformity to peers and parents. *Developmental Psychology,* 1979, 15, 608–616. (a)

BERNDT, T. J. Lack of acceptance of reciprocity norms in preschool children. *Developmental Psychology,* 1979, 15, 662–663. (b)

BERNDT, T. J. Age changes and changes over time in prosocial intentions and behavior between friends. *Developmental Psychology,* 1981, 17, 408–416.(a)

BERNDT, T. J. Effects of friendship on prosocial intentions and behavior. *Child Development,* 1981, 52, 636–643.(b)

BERNDT, T. J., & BERNDT, E. G. Children's use of motives and intentionality in person perception and moral judgment. *Child Development,* 1975, 46, 904–912.

BERNSTEIN, A. C., & COWAN, P. A. Children's concepts of how people get babies. *Child Development,* 1975, 46, 77–91.

BERTENTHAL, B. I., & FISCHER, K. W. Development of self-recognition in the infant. *Developmental Psychology,* 1978, 14, 44–50.

BEST, D. L., WILLIAMS, J. E., CLOUD, J. M., DAVIS, S. W., ROBERTSON, L. S., EDWARDS, J. R., GILES, H., & FOWLES, J. Development of sex-trait stereotypes among young children in the United States, England, and Ireland. *Child Development,* 1977, 48, 1375–1384.

BETTELHEIM, B. Individual and mass behavior in extreme situations. *Journal of Abnormal and Social Psychology,* 1943, 38, 417–452.

BEVAN, D., DAVES, W. & LEVY, G. W. The relation of castration, androgen therapy, and pre-test fighting experience to competitive aggression in male C57BL/10 mice. *Animal Behavior,* 1960, 8, 6–12.

BIALER, I. Conceptualization of success and failure in mentally retarded and normal children. *Journal of Personality,* 1961, 29, 303–320.

BIANCHI, B. D., & BAKEMAN, R. Sex-typed affiliation preferences observed in preschoolers: Traditional and open school differences. *Child Development,* 1978, 49, 910–912.

BIGELOW, B. J. Children's friendship expectations: A cognitive developmental study. *Child Development,* 1977, 48, 246–253.

BIGELOW, B. J., & LA GAIPA, J. J. Children's written descriptions of friendship: A multidimensional analysis. *Developmental Psychology,* 1975, 11, 857–858.

BIJOU, S. W., & BAER, D. M. *Child development* (Vol. 1). New York: Appleton-Century-Crofts, 1965.

BILLER, H. B. A multi-aspect investigation of masculine development in kindergarten age boys. *Genetic Psychology Monographs,* 1968, 76, 89–139.

BILLER, H. B., & BORSTELMANN, L. J. Masculine development: An integrated review. *Merrill-Palmer Quarterly,* 1967, 13, 253–294.

BILLMAN, J., & MCDEVITT, S. C. Convergence of parent and observer ratings of temperament with observations of peer interaction in nursery school. *Child Development,* 1980, 51, 395–400.

BIRD, A. M., & WILLIAMS, J. M. A developmental-attributional analysis of sex role stereotypes for sport performance. *Developmental Psychology,* 1980, 16, 319–322.

BIXENSTINE, V. E., DECORTE, M. S., & BIXENSTINE, B. A. Conformity to peer-sponsored misconduct at four grade levels. *Developmental Psychology,* 1976, 12, 226–236.

BLAKEMORE, J. E. O., LARUE, A. A., & OLEJNIK, A. B. Sex-appropriate toy preferences and the ability to conceptualize toys as sex-role related. *Developmental Psychology,* 1979, 15, 339–340.

BLANCHARD, M., & MAIN, M. Avoidance of the attachment figure and social-emotional adjustment in day-care infants. *Developmental Psychology,* 1979, 15, 445–446.

BLANCHARD, R. W., & BILLER, H. B. Father availability and academic performance among third grade boys. *Developmental Psychology,* 1971, 4, 301–305.

BLEHAR, M. Anxious attachment and defensive reactions associated with day care. *Child Development,* 1974, 45, 683–692.

BLEHAR, M. C., LIEBERMAN, A. F., & AINSWORTH, M. D. S. Early face-to-face interaction and its relation to later infant-mother attachment. *Child Development,* 1977, 48, 182–194.

BLOCK, J. *Lives through time.* Berkeley, Ca.: Bancroft Books, 1971.

BLOCK, J. H., BLOCK, J., & MORRISON, A. Parental agreement-disagreement on childrearing orientations and gender-related personality correlates in children. *Child Development,* 1981, 52, 965–974.

BLOOM, K. Evaluation of infant vocal conditioning. *Journal of Experimental Child Psychology,* 1979, 27, 60–70.

BLURTON-JONES, N. (Ed.). *Ethological studies of child behavior.* Cambridge: Cambridge University Press, 1972.

BOEHM, L. The development of independence: A comparative study. *Child Development,* 1957, 28, 85–92.

BOGATZ, G. A., & BALL, S. *The second year of Sesame Street: A continuing evaluation.* Princeton, N.J.: Educational Testing Service, 1971.

BOGGIANO, A. K., & RUBLE, D. N. Competence and the overjustification effect: A developmental study. *Journal of Personality and Social Psychology,* 1979, 37, 1462–1468.

BORKE, H. Interpersonal perception of young children: Egocentrism or empathy? *Developmental Psychology,* 1971, 5, 263–269.

BORKE, H. The development of empathy in Chinese and American children between three and six years of age: A cross-culture study. *Developmental Psychology,* 1973, 9, 102–108.

BORNSTEIN, M. R., BELLACK, A. S., & HERSEN, M. Social-skills training for unassertive children: A multiple-baseline analysis. *Journal of Applied Behavior Analysis,* 1977, 10, 183–195.

BOSWELL, D. A., & WILLIAMS, J. E. Correlates of race and color bias among preschool children. *Psychological Reports,* 1975, 36, 147–154.

BOWERS, K. S. Situationism in psychology: An analysis and a critique. *Psychological Review,* 1973, 80, 307–336.

BOWLBY, J. *Attachment and loss* (Vol. 1). New York: Basic Books, 1969.

BOYANOWSKY, E. O., NEWTSON, D., & WALSTER, E. Film preferences following a murder. *Communications Research,* 1974, 1, 32–43.

BRACKBILL, Y. Extinction of the smiling response in infants as a function of reinforcement schedule. *Child Development,* 1958, 29, 115–124.

BRENNER, J., & MUELLER, E. Shared meaning in boy toddlers' peer relations. *Child Development,* 1982, 53, 380–391.

BRETHERTON, I., & AINSWORTH, M. D. S. Responses of one-year-olds to a stranger in a strange situation. In M. Lewis & L. A. Rosenblum (Eds.), *The origins of fear.* New York: John Wiley, 1974.

BRIM, O. G. Family structure and sex role learning by children: A further analysis of Helen Koch's data. *Sociometry,* 1958, 21, 1–16.

BRITTAIN, C. V. Adolescent choices and parent-peer cross-pressures. *American Sociological Review,* 1963, 28, 385–391.

BRODY, G. H., & HENDERSON, R. W. Effects of multiple model variations and rationale provision on the moral judgments and explanations of young children. *Child Development,* 1977, 48, 1117–1120.

BRODZINSKY, D. M., MESSER, S. B., & TEW, J. D. Sex differences in children's expression and control of fantasy and overt aggression. *Child Development,* 1979, 50, 372–379.

BRONFENBRENNER, U. *Two worlds of childhood: U.S. and U.S.S.R.* New York: Russell Sage Foundation, 1970.

BRONFENBRENNER, U. Toward an experimental ecology of human development. *American Psychologist,* 1977, 32, 513–531.

BRONFENBRENNER, U. Contexts of child rearing: Problems and prospects. *American Psychologist,* 1979, 34, 844–850.

BRONSON, G. Aversive reactions to strangers: A dual process interpretation. *Child Development,* 1978, 49, 495–499.

BROOKS-GUNN, J., & LEWIS, M. Infant social perception: Responses to pictures of parents and strangers. *Developmental Psychology,* 1981, 17, 647–649.

BROVERMAN, I. K., VOGEL, S. R., BROVERMAN, D. M., CLARKSON, F. E., & ROSENKRANTZ, P. S. Sex role stereotypes: A current appraisal. *Journal of Social Issues,* 1972, 28, 59–78.

BROWN, D. G. Sex role preference in young children. *Psychological Monographs,* 1956, 70, (14, Whole No. 421).

BROWN, I., JR., & INOUYE, D. K. Learned helplessness through modeling: The role of perceived similarity in competence. *Journal of Personality and Social Psychology,* 1978, 36, 900–908.

BROWN, P., & ELLIOT, R. Control of aggression in a nursery school class. *Journal of Experimental Child Psychology,* 1965, 2, 103–107.

BROWNELL, C. A., & HARTUP, W. W. Indeterminate and sequential goal structures in relation to task performance in children's small groups. *Child Development,* 1981, 52, 651–659.

BRUNER, J. S. Nature and uses of immaturity. *American Psychologist,* 1972, 27, 687–708.

BRUNING, J. L., & HUSA, F. T. Given names and stereotyping. *Developing Psychology,* 1972, 7, 91.

BRYAN, J. H. Model affect and children's imitative behavior. *Child Development,* 1971, 42, 2061–2065.

BRYAN, J. H. Children's cooperation and helping behaviors. In E. M. Hetherington (Ed.), *Review of child development research* (Vol. 5). Chicago: The University of Chicago Press, 1975.

BRYAN, J. H., & LONDON, P. Altruistic behavior by

children. *Psychological Bulletin*, 1970, 73, 200–211.

BRYAN, J. H., & WALBEK, N. H. Preaching and practicing generosity: Children's actions and reactions. *Child Development*, 1970, *41*, 329–353.

BRYANT, B. K. The effects of the interpersonal context of evaluation on self- and other-enhancement behavior. *Child Development*, 1977, *48*, 885–892.

BRYANT, B. K., & CROCKENBERG, S. B. Correlates and dimensions of prosocial behavior: A study of female siblings with their mothers. *Child Development*, 1980, *51*, 529–544.

BUCHANAN, J. P., & THOMPSON, S. K. A quantitative methodology to examine the development of moral judgment. *Child Development*, 1973, *44*, 186–189.

BUCKLEY, N., SIEGEL, L. S., & NESS, S. Egocentrism, empathy, and altruistic behavior in young children. *Developmental Psychology*, 1979, *15*, 329–330.

BUEHLER, R. E., PATTERSON, G. R., & FURNISS, J. M. The reinforcement of behavior in institutional settings. *Behavior Research and Therapy*, 1966, *4*, 157–167.

BUFFORD, R. K. Discrimination and instructions as factors in the control of nonreinforced imitation. *Journal of Experimental Child Psychology*, 1971, *12*, 35–50.

BULLOCK, D., & MERRILL, L. The impact of personal preference on consistency through time: The case of aggression. *Child Development*, 1980, *51*, 808–814.

BURNS, N., & CAVEY, L. Age differences in empathic ability among children. *Canadian Journal of Psychology*, 1957, *11*, 227–230.

BURNS, S. M., & BRAINERD, C. J. Effects of constructive and dramatic play on perspective taking in very young children. *Developmental Psychology*, 1979, *15*, 512–521.

BURTON, R. V. Cross-sex identity in Barbados. *Developmental Psychology*, 1972, *6*, 365–374.

BURTON, R. V. The generality of honesty reconsidered. *Psychological Review*, 1963, *70*, 481–499.

BUSS, A. H. *The psychology of aggression*. New York: John Wiley, 1961.

BUSS, A. H., & PLOMIN, R. *A temperament theory of personality development*. New York: John Wiley, 1975.

BUSS, D. M., BLOCK, J. H., & BLOCK, J. Preschool activity level: Personality correlates and developmental implications. *Child Development*, 1980, *51*, 401–408.

BUSSEY, K., & PERRY, D. G. Sharing reinforcement contingencies with a model: A social-learning analysis of similarity effects in imitation research. *Journal of Personality and Social Psychology*, 1976, 34, 1168–1176.

BUSSEY, K., & PERRY, D. G. The imitation of resistance to deviation: Conclusive evidence for an elusive effect. *Developmental Psychology*, 1977, *13*, 438–443.

CAIRNS, R. B. Development, maintenance, and extinction of social attachment behavior in sheep. *Journal of Comparative and Physiological Psychology*, 1966, *62*, 298–306.

CAIRNS, R. B. The information properties of verbal and nonverbal events. *Journal of Personality and Social Psychology*, 1967, *5*, 353–357.

CAIRNS, R. B. Meaning and attention as determinants of social reinforcer effectiveness. *Child Development*, 1970, *41*, 1067–1082.

CAIRNS, R. B. The ontogeny and phylogeny of social interactions. In M. Hahn and E. C. Simmel (Eds.), *Evolution of communicative behaviors*. New York: Academic Press, 1976.

CAIRNS, R. B. (Ed.) *The analysis of social interactions*. Hillsdale, N.J.: Erlbaum, 1979. (a)

CAIRNS, R. B. *Social development: The origins and plasticity of interchanges*. San Francisco: W. H. Freeman & Company Publishers, 1979. (b)

CALDWELL, B. M. The effects of infant care. In M. L. Hoffman & L. W. Hoffman (Eds.), *Review of child development research* (Vol. 1). Chicago: University of Chicago Press, 1964.

CALLAHAN-LEVY, C. M., & MESSE, L. A. Sex differences in the allocation of pay. *Journal of Personality and Social Psychology*, 1979, 37, 433–446.

CAMP, B. W. Verbal mediation in young aggressive boys. *Journal of Abnormal Psychology*, 1977, 86, 145–153.

CAMPOS, J. J., EMDE, R. N., GAENSBAUER, T., & HENDERSON, C. Cardiac and behavioral interrelationships in the reactions of infants to strangers. *Developmental Psychology*, 1975, *11*, 589–601.

CANTOR, G. N. Use of a conflict paradigm to study race awareness in children. *Child Development*, 1972, 43, 1437–1442.

CANTOR, G. N., & PATERNITE, C. E. A follow-up study of race awareness using a conflict paradigm. *Child Development*, 1973, 44, 859–861.

CANTOR, N. L., & GELFAND, D. M. Effects of responsiveness and sex of children on adults' behavior. *Child Development*, 1977, 48, 232–238.

CAPLAN, P. J. Beyond the box score: A boundary condition for sex differences in aggression and achievement striving. In B. A. Maher (Ed.), *Progress in Experimental Personality Research* (Vol. 9). New York: Academic Press, 1979.

CARLSMITH, J. M., & GROSS, A. E. Some effects of guilt on compliance. *Journal of Personality and Social Psychology*, 1969, *11*, 232–239.

CARLSMITH, L. Effect of early father absence on scholastic aptitude. *Harvard Educational Review*, 1964, *34*, 3–21.

CARR, S. J., DABBS, J. M., JR., & CARR, T. S. Mother-infant attachment: The importance of the mother's visual field. *Child Development*, 1975, *46*, 331–338.

CATTELL, R. B. *Personality and motivation: Structure and measurement.* Yonkers-on-Hudson: World Book, 1957.

CAVIOR, N., & DOKECKI, P. R. Physical attractiveness, perceived attitude similarity, and academic achievement as contributors to interpersonal attraction among adolescents. *Developmental Psychology*, 1973, *9*, 44–54.

CHANDLER, M. J. Egocentrism and antisocial behavior: The assessment and training of social perspective-taking skills. *Developmental Psychology*, 1973, *9*, 321–332.

CHANDLER, M. J., GREENSPAN, S., & BARENBOIM, C. Judgments of intentionality in response to videotaped and verbally presented moral dilemmas: The medium is the message. *Child Development*, 1973, *44*, 315–320.

CHARLESWORTH, R., & HARTUP, W. W. Positive social reinforcement in the nursery school peer group. *Child Development*, 1967, *38*, 993–1002.

CHARTIER, G. M., & WEISS, R. L. Comparative test of positive control, negative control, and social power theories of identificatory learning in disadvantaged children. *Journal of Personality and Social Psychology*, 1974, *29*, 724–730.

CHERRY, L., & LEWIS, M. Mothers and two-year-olds: A study of sex-differentiated aspects of verbal interaction. *Developmental Psychology*, 1976, *12*, 278–282.

CHEYNE, J. A. Effects on imitation of different reinforcement combinations to a model. *Journal of Experimental Child Psychology*, 1971, *12*, 258–269.

CHEYNE, J. A., GOYECHE, J. R., & WALTERS, R. H. Attention, anxiety, and rules in resistance-to-deviation in children. *Journal of Experimental Child Psychology*, 1969, *8*, 127–139.

CHOMSKY, N. *Language and mind.* New York: Harcourt Brace Jovanovich, Inc., 1968.

CIALDINI, R. B., & KENRICK, D. T. Altruism as hedonism: A social developmental perspective on the relationship of negative mood state and helping. *Journal of Personality and Social Psychology*, 1976, *34*, 907–914.

CLARK, A., HOCEVAR, D., & DEMBO, M. H. The role of cognitive development in children's explanations and preferences for skin color. *Developmental Psychology*, 1980, *16*, 332–339.

CLARKE-STEWART, K. A. Interactions between mothers and their young children. *Monographs of the Society for Research in Child Development*, 1973, *38*, (Whole No. 153).

CLARKE-STEWART, K. A. And daddy makes three: The father's impact on mother and young child. *Child Development*, 1978, *49*, 466–478.

CLARKE-STEWART, K. A., & HEVEY, C. M. Longitudinal relations in repeated observations of mother-child interaction from 1 to 2½ years. *Developmental Psychology*, 1981, *17*, 127–145.

CLARKE-STEWART, K. A., UMEH, B. J., SNOW, M. E., & PEDERSON, J. A. Development and prediction of children's sociability from 1 to 2½ years. *Developmental Psychology*, 1980, *16*, 290–302.

CLARKE-STEWART, K. A., VANDERSTOEP, L. P., & KILLIAN, G. A. Analysis and replication of mother-child relations at two years of age. *Child Development*, 1979, *50*, 777–793.

CLINE, V. B., CROFT, R. G., & COURRIER, S. Desensitization of children to television violence. *Journal of Personality and Social Psychology*, 1973, *27*, 360–365.

COATES, B., ANDERSON, E. P., & HARTUP, W. W. Interrelations in the attachment behavior of human infants. *Developmental Psychology*, 1972, *6*, 218–230.

COATES, B., & HARTUP, W. W. Age and verbalization in observational learning. *Developmental Psychology*, 1969, *1*, 556–562.

COATES, B., PUSSER, H. E., & GOODMAN, I. The influence of "Sesame Street" and "Mister Rogers' Neighborhood" on children's social behavior in the preschool. *Child Development*, 1976, *47*, 138–144.

COCHRAN, M. M., & BRASSARD, J. A. Child development and personal social networks. *Child Development*, 1979, *50*, 601–616.

COHEN, L. J. The operational definition of human attachment. *Psychological Bulletin*, 1974, *81*, 207–217.

COHEN, N. L., & TOMLINSON-KEASEY, C. The effects of peers and mothers on toddlers' play. *Child Development*, 1980, *51*, 921–924.

COIE, J. D., & PENNINGTON, B. F. Children's perceptions of deviance and disorder. *Child Development*, 1976, *47*, 407–413.

COLLINS, W. A. Effects of temporal separation between motivation, aggression, and consequences: A developmental study. *Developmental Psychology*, 1973, 8, 215–221.

COLLINS, W. A., BERNDT, T. J., & HESS, V. L. Observational learning of motives and consequences for television aggression: A developmental study. *Child Development*, 1974, 45, 799–802.

COMBS, M. L., & SLABY, D. A. Social-skills training with children. In B. B. Lahey & A. E. Kazdin (Eds.), *Advances in clinical child psychology* (Vol. 1). New York: Plenum, 1977.

CONDRY, J. Enemies of exploration: Self-initiated versus other-initiated learning. *Journal of Personality and Social Psychology*, 1977, 35, 459–477.

CONDRY, J., & CHAMBERS, J. Intrinsic motivation and the process of learning. In D. Grune & M. Lepper (Eds.), *The hidden costs of rewards*. Hillsdale, N.J.: Erlbaum, 1982.

CONDRY, J. & CONDRY, S. Sex differences: A study of the eye of the beholder. *Child Development*, 1976, 47, 812–819.

CONDRY, J. C. & DYER, S. L. Behavioral and fantasy measures of fear of success in children. *Child Development*, 1977, 48, 1417–1425.

CONGER, J. C., & KEANE, S. P. Social skills intervention in the treatment of isolated or withdrawn children. *Psychological Bulletin*, 1981, 90, 478–495.

CONNOR, J. M., & SERBIN, L. A. Behaviorally based masculine- and feminine-activity-preference scales for preschoolers: Correlates with other classroom behaviors and cognitive tests. *Child Development*, 1977, 48, 1411–1416.

CONNOR, J. M., & SERBIN, L. A. Children's responses to stories with male and female characters. *Sex Roles*, 1978, 4, 637–645.

COOK, H., & STINGLE, S. Cooperative behavior in children. *Psychological Bulletin*, 1974, 81, 918–933.

COOK, N. C. *Attachment and object permanence in infancy: A short-term longitudinal study.* Unpublished doctoral dissertation, University of Minnesota, 1972.

COOK, S. W. A comment on the ethical issues involved in West, Gunn, and Chernicky's "Ubiquitous Watergate: An attributional analysis." *Journal of Personality and Social Psychology*, 1975, 32, 66–68.

COOKE, T., & APOLLONI, T. Developing positive social-emotional behaviors: A study of training and generalization effects. *Journal of Applied Behavior Analysis*, 1976, 9, 65–78.

COOLEY, C. H. *Human nature and the social order.* New York: Scribner's, 1902.

COOPERSMITH, S. *The antecedents of self-esteem.* San Francisco: W. H. Freeman & Company Publishers, 1967.

CORDUA, G. D., MCGRAW, K. O., & DRABMAN, R. S. Doctor or nurse: Children's perception of sex typed occupations. *Child Development*, 1979, 50, 590–593.

CORSARO, W. A. Friendship in the nursery school: Social organization in a peer environment. In S. R. Asher & J. M. Gottman (Eds.), *The development of children's friendships.* New York: Cambridge University Press, 1981.

CORTER, C. M. The nature of the mother's absence and the infant's response to brief separations. *Developmental Psychology*, 1976, 12, 428–434.

CORTER, C., & BOW, J. The mother's response to separation as a function of her infant's sex and vocal distress. *Child Development*, 1976, 47, 872–876.

COSTANZO, P. R., COIE, J. D., GRUMET, J. F., & FARNILL, D. A reexamination of the effects of intent and consequence on children's moral judgments. *Child Development*, 1973, 44, 154–161.

COWAN, P. A., LANGER, J., HEAVENRICH, J., & NATHANSON, M. Social learning and Piaget's cognitive theory of moral development. *Journal of Personality and Social Psychology*, 1969, 11, 261–274.

COWEN, E. L., PEDERSON, A., BABIGAN, H., IZZO, L. D., & TROST, M. A. Long-term follow-up of early detected vulnerable children. *Journal of Consulting and Clinical Psychology*, 1973, 41, 438–446.

COX, N. Prior help, ego development, and helping behavior. *Child Development*, 1974, 45, 594–603.

CRANDALL, V. C., KATKOVSKY, W., & CRANDALL, V. J. Children's beliefs in their own control of reinforcement in intellectual-achievement situations. *Child Development*, 1965, 36, 91–109.

CROCKENBERG, S. B. Infant irritability, mother responsiveness, and social support influences on the security of infant-mother attachment. *Child Development*, 1981, 52, 857–865.

CROCKENBERG, S. B., BRYANT, B. K., & WILCE, L. S. The effects of cooperatively and competitively structured learning environments on inter- and intrapersonal behavior. *Child Development*, 1976, 47, 386–396.

CROWDER, J. Teaching elementary school children the application of principles and techniques of applied behavior analysis. Paper presented at the Ninth Annual Convention of Association for Advancement of Behavior Therapy, San Francisco, Ca., December 1975.

CROWLEY, P. M. Effect of training upon objectivity of moral judgment in grade-school children. *Journal of Personality and Social Psychology,* 1968, 8, 228–232.

CUMMINGS, E. M. Caregiver stability and day care. *Developmental Psychology,* 1980, 16, 31–37.

CUNNINGHAM, C. E., & BARKLEY, R. A. The interactions of normal and hyperactive children with their mothers in free play and structured tasks. *Child Development,* 1979, 50, 217–224.

CUNNINGHAM, M. R. Weather, mood, and helping behavior: Quasi experiments with the sunshine Samaritan. *Journal of Personality and Social Psychology,* 1979, 37, 1947–1956.

CUTRONA, C. E., & FESHBACH, S. Cognitive and behavioral correlates of children's differential use of social information. *Child Development,* 1979, 50, 1036–1042.

DAMON, W. *The social world of the child.* San Francisco: Jossey-Bass, 1977.

DANSKY, J. L. Make-believe: A mediator of the relationship between play and associative fluency. *Child Development,* 1980, 51, 576–579.

DARLEY, J. M., KLOSSON, E. C., & ZANNA, M. P. Intentions and their contexts in the moral judgments of children and adults. *Child Development,* 1978, 49, 66–74.

DARLEY, J. M., & LATANE, B. Bystander intervention in emergencies: Diffusion of responsibility. *Journal of Personality and Social Psychology,* 1968, 8, 377–383.

DARWIN, C. *The expression of the emotions in man and animals.* London: John Murray, 1872.

DAVIDSON, E. S., YASUNA, A., & TOWER, A. The effects of television cartoons on sex-role stereotyping in young girls. *Child Development,* 1979, 50, 597–600.

DAVIS, D., RAINEY, H. G., & BROCK, T. C. Interpersonal physical pleasuring: Effects of sex combinations, recipient attributes, and anticipated future interaction. *Journal of Personality and Social Psychology,* 1976, 33, 89–106.

DAVITZ, J. The effects of previous training on post-frustration behavior. *Journal of Abnormal and Social Psychology,* 1952, 47, 309–315.

DEAUX, K. Sex: A perspective on the attribution process. In J. H. Harvey, W. J. Ickes, & R. F. Kidd (Eds.), *New directions in attribution research* (Vol. 1). Hillsdale, N.J.: Erlbaum, 1976.

DEBOER, M. M., & BOXER, A. M. Signal functions of infant facial expression and gaze direction during mother-infant face-to-face play. *Child Development,* 1979, 50, 1215–1218.

DENGERINK, H. A., & MYERS, J. T. The effects of failure and depression on subsequent aggression. *Journal of Personality and Social Psychology,* 1977, 35, 88–96.

DEUTSCH, F. Female preschoolers' perceptions of affective responses and interpersonal behavior in videotaped episodes. *Developmental Psychology,* 1974, 10, 733–740. (a)

DEUTSCH, F. Observational and sociometric measures of peer popularity and their relationship to egocentric communication in female preschoolers. *Developmental Psychology,* 1974, 10, 745–747. (b)

DEUTSCH, F. Effects of sex of subject and story character on preschoolers' perceptions of affective responses and intrapersonal behavior in story sequences. *Developmental Psychology,* 1975, 11, 112–113.

DEVEREUX, E. C., SHOUVAL, R., BRONFENBRENNER, U., RODGERS, R. R., KAV-VENAKI, S., KIELY, E., & KARSON, E. Socialization practices of parents, teachers, and peers in Israel: The kibbutz versus the city. *Child Development,* 1974, 45, 269–281.

DICKSTEIN, E. B., & SEYMOUR, M. W. Effect of the addition of neutral items on IT Scale scores. *Developmental Psychology,* 1977, 13, 79–80.

DIENER, E., FRASER, S. C., BEAMAN, A. L., & KELEM, R. T. Effects of deindividuation variables on stealing among Halloween trick-or-treaters. *Journal of Personality and Social Psychology,* 1976, 33, 178–183.

DIENSTBIER, R. A., HILLMAN, D., LEHNHOFF, J. H., HILLMAN, J., & VALKENAAR, M. C. An emotion-attribution approach to moral behavior: Interfacing cognitive and avoidance theories of moral development. *Psychological Review,* 1975, 82, 299–315.

DION, K. K. Physical attractiveness and evaluation of children's transgressions. *Journal of Personality and Social Psychology,* 1972, 24, 207–213.

DION, K. K. Young children's stereotyping of facial attractiveness. *Developmental Psychology,* 1973, 9, 183–188.

DIPIETRO, J. A. Rough and tumble play: A function of gender. *Developmental Psychology,* 1981, 17, 50–58.

DIVITTO, B., & MCARTHUR, L. Z. Developmental differences in the use of distinctiveness, consensus, and consistency information for making causal attributions. *Developmental Psychology,* 1978, 14, 474–482.

DIX, T., & GRUSEC, J. E. Parental influence techniques: An attributional analysis. Unpublished manuscript, University of Toronto, 1982.

DLUGOKINSKI, E. L., & FIRESTONE, I. J. Other centeredness and susceptibility to charitable appeals: Effects of perceived discipline. *Developmental Psychology*, 1974, *10*, 21–28.

DODGE, K. A. Social cognition and children's aggressive behavior. *Child Development*, 1980, *51*, 162–170.

DODGE, K. A. Social information processing variables in the development of aggression and altruism in children. Paper presented at the Society for Research in Child Development and Foundation for Child Development Conference on Aggression and Altruism, Bethesda, Maryland, 1982.

DODGE, K. A., & FRAME, C. L. Social cognitive biases and deficits in aggressive boys. *Child Development*, 1982, *53*, 620–635.

DOKE, L. A., & RISLEY, T. R. Some discriminative properties of race and sex for children from an all-Negro neighborhood. *Child Development*, 1972, *43*, 677–681.

DOLLARD, J., DOOB, L., MILLER, N. E., MOWRER, O. H., & SEARS, R. R. *Frustration and aggression*. New Haven: Yale University Press, 1939.

DOLLARD, J., & MILLER, N. E. *Personality and psychotherapy*. New York: McGraw-Hill, 1950.

DOLLINGER, S. J., & THELEN, M. H. Overjustification and children's intrinsic motivation: Comparative effects of four rewards. *Journal of Personality and Social Psychology*, 1978, *36*, 1259–1269.

DONNERSTEIN, E., & WILSON, D. W. Effects of noise and perceived control on ongoing and subsequent aggressive behavior. *Journal of Personality and Social Psychology*, 1976, *34*, 774–781.

DONOVAN, W. L. Maternal learned helplessness and physiologic response to infant crying. *Journal of Personality and Social Psychology*, 1981, *40*, 919–926.

DONOVAN, W. L., & LEAVITT, L. A. Early cognitive development and its relation to maternal physiologic and behavioral responsiveness. *Child Development*, 1978, *49*, 1251–1254.

DOOB, A. N., & WOOD, L. Catharsis and aggression: The effects of annoyance and retaliation on aggressive behavior. *Journal of Personality and Social Psychology*, 1972, *22*, 156–162.

DORNBUSCH, S. M., CARLSMITH, J. M., GROSS, R. T., MARTIN, J. A., JENNINGS, D., ROSENBERG, A., & DUKE, P. Sexual development, age, and dating: A comparison of biological and social influences upon one set of behaviors. *Child Development*, 1981, *52*, 179–185.

DOYLE, A., CONNOLLY, J., & RIVEST, L. The effect of playmate familiarity on the social interactions of young children. *Child Development*, 1980, *51*, 217–223.

DRABMAN, R. S., SPITALNIK, R., & O'LEARY, K. D. Teaching self-control to disruptive children. *Journal of Abnormal Psychology*, 1973, *82*, 10–16.

DRABMAN, R. S., & THOMAS, M. H. Does media violence increase children's tolerance of real-life aggression? *Developmental Psychology*, 1974, *10*, 418–421.

DRAKE, C. T., & MCDOUGALL, D. Effects of the absence of a father and other male models on the development of boys' sex roles. *Developmental Psychology*, 1977, *13*, 537–538.

DREMAN, S. B. Sharing behavior in Israeli school-children: Cognitive and social learning factors. *Child Development*, 1976, *47*, 186–194.

DREMAN, S. B., & GREENBAUM, C. W. Altruism or reciprocity: Sharing behavior in Israeli kindergarten children. *Child Development*, 1973, *44*, 61–68.

DWECK, C. S., & BUSH, E. S. Sex differences in learned helplessness: I. Differential debilitation with peer and adult evaluators. *Developmental Psychology*, 1976, *12*, 147–156.

DWECK, C. S., DAVIDSON, W., NELSON, S., & ENNA, B. Sex differences in learned helplessness: II. The contingencies of evaluative feedback in the classroom and III. An experimental analysis. *Developmental Psychology*, 1978, *14*, 268–276.

DWECK, C. S., & REPPUCCI, N. D. Learned helplessness and reinforcement responsibility in children. *Journal of Personality and Social Psychology*, 1973, *25*, 109–116.

DYCK, R. J., & RULE, B. G. Effect on retaliation of causal attributions concerning attack. *Journal of Personality and Social Psychology*, 1978, *36*, 521–529.

EASTERBROOKS, M. A., & LAMB, M. E. The relationship between quality of infant-mother attachment and infant competence in initial encounters with peers. *Child Development*, 1979, *50*, 380–387.

EATON, W. O., & VON BARGEN, D. V. Asynchronous development of gender understanding in preschool children. *Child Development*, 1981, 1020–1027.

EBERHARD, M. T. W. The evolution of social behavior by kin selection. *The Quarterly Review of Biology,* 1975, *50,* 1-33.

ECKERMAN, C. O., & WHATLEY, J. L. Toys and social interaction between infant peers. *Child Development,* 1977, *48,* 1645-1658.

ECKERMAN, C. O., WHATLEY, J. L., & KUTZ, S. L. Growth of social play with peers during the second year of life. *Developmental Psychology,* 1975, *11,* 42-49.

ECKERMAN, C. O., WHATLEY, J. L., & MCGEHEE, L. J. Approaching and contacting the object another manipulates: A social skill of the 1-year-old. *Developmental Psychology,* 1979, *15,* 585-593.

EDELBROCK, C., & SUGAWARA, A. I. Acquisition of sex-typed preferences in preschool-aged children. *Developmental Psychology,* 1978, *14,* 614-623.

EGELAND, B., & SROUFE, L. A. Attachment and early maltreatment. *Child Development,* 1981, *52,* 44-52.

EISENBERG, L. School phobia: A study in the communication of anxiety. *American Journal of Psychiatry,* 1958, *114,* 712-718.

EISENBERG, N., MURRAY, E., & HITE, T. Children's reasoning regarding sex-typed toy choices. *Child Development,* 1982, *53,* 81-86.

EISENBERG-BERG, N. Development of children's prosocial moral judgment. *Developmental Psychology,* 1979, *15,* 128-137. (a)

EISENBERG-BERG, N. Relationship of prosocial moral reasoning to altruism, political liberalism, and intelligence. *Developmental Psychology,* 1979, *15,* 87-89. (b)

EISENBERG-BERG, N., BOOTHBY, R., & MATSON, T. Correlates of preschool girls' feminine and masculine toy preferences. *Developmental Psychology,* 1979, *15,* 354-355.

EISENBERG-BERG, N., & GEISHEKER, E. Content of preachings and power of the model/preacher: The effect on children's generosity. *Developmental Psychology,* 1979, *15,* 168-175.

EISENBERG-BERG, N., & HAND, M. The relationship of preschoolers' reasoning about prosocial moral conflicts to prosocial behavior. *Child Development,* 1979, *50,* 356-363.

EISENBERG-BERG, N., & LENNON, R. Altruism and the assessment of empathy in the preschool years. *Child Development,* 1980, *51,* 552-557.

EISENBERG-BERG, N., & MUSSEN, P. Empathy and moral development in adolescence. *Developmental Psychology,* 1978, *14,* 185-186.

EISENBERGER, R., KAPLAN, R. M., & SINGER, R. D. Decremental and nondecremental effects of

noncontingent social approval. *Journal of Personality and Social Psychology,* 1974, *30,* 716-722.

EISERT, D. C., & KAHLE, L. R. Self-evaluation and social comparison of physical and role change during adolescence: A longitudinal analysis. *Child Development,* 1982, *53,* 98-104.

EKEHAMMAR, B. Interactionism in psychology from a historical perspective. *Psychological Bulletin,* 1974, *81,* 1026-1048.

ELKIND, D., & DABEK, R. F. Personal injury and property damage in the moral judgments of children. *Child Development,* 1977, *48,* 518-522.

ELKINS, D. Some factors related to the choice status of ninety eighth-grade children in a school society. *Genetic Psychology Monographs,* 1958, *58,* 207-272.

ELLIS, S., ROGOFF, B., & CROMER, C. C. Age segregation in children's social interactions. *Developmental Psychology,* 1981, *17,* 399-407.

EMMERICH, W., GOLDMAN, K. S., KIRSH, B., & SHARABANY, R. Evidence for a transitional phase in the development of gender constancy. *Child Development,* 1977, *48,* 930-936.

ENDLER, N. S., & MAGNUSSON, D. Toward an interactional psychology of personality. *Psychological Bulletin,* 1976, *83,* 956-974.

ENRIGHT, R. D., FRANKLIN, C. C., & MANHEIM, L. A. Children's distributive justice reasoning: A standardized and objective scale. *Developmental Psychology,* 1980, *16,* 193-202.

ENRIGHT, R. D., & SUTTERFIELD, S. J. An ecological validation of social cognitive development. *Child Development,* 1980, *51,* 156-161.

ENTWISLE, D. R. To dispel fantasies about fantasy-based measures of achievement motivation. *Psychological Bulletin,* 1972, *77,* 377-391.

ENZLE, M. E., & LOOK, S. C. Self versus other reward administration and the overjustification effect. Unpublished manuscript, University of Alberta, 1980.

ERIKSON, E. H. *Identity and the life cycle.* New York: International Universities Press, 1959.

ERON, L. D. Relationship of T.V. viewing habits and aggressive behavior in children. *Journal of Abnormal and Social Psychology,* 1963, *67,* 193-196.

ERON, L. D. Prescription for reduction of aggression. *American Psychologist,* 1980, *35,* 244-252.

ERON, L. D., LEFKOWITZ, M. M., HUESMANN, L. R., & WALDER, L. O. Does television violence cause aggression? *American Psychologist,* 1972, *27,* 253-263.

ERWIN, J., & KUHN, D. Development of children's

understanding of the multiple determination underlying human behavior. *Developmental Psychology*, 1979, *15*, 352–353.

ETAUGH, C., COLLINS, G., & GERSON, A. Reinforcement of sex-typical behaviors of two-year-old children in a nursery school setting. *Developmental Psychology*, 1975, *11*, 255.

ETAUGH, C., & HUGHES, V. Teachers' evaluations of sex-typed behaviors in children: The role of teacher sex and school setting. *Developmental Psychology*, 1975, *11*, 394–395.

EVERS, W. L., & SCHWARZ, J. C. Modifying social withdrawal in preschoolers: The effects of filmed modeling and teacher reinforcement. *Journal of Abnormal Child Psychology*, 1973, *1*, 248–256.

EVERS-PASQUALE, W., & SHERMAN, M. The reward value of peers. *Journal of Abnormal Child Psychology*, 1975, *3*, 179–189.

EXNER, J. E., & SUTTON-SMITH, B. Birth order and hierarchical versus innovative role requirements. *Journal of Personality*, 1970, *38*, 581–587.

EYSENCK, H. J. *The dynamics of anxiety and hysteria.* New York: Praeger, 1957.

FAGOT, B. I. Sex-related stereotyping of toddlers' behavior. *Developmental Psychology*, 1973, *9*, 429.

FAGOT, B. I. Consequences of moderate cross-gender behavior in preschool children. *Child Development*, 1977, *48*, 902–907.

FAGOT, B. I. The influence of sex of child on parental reactions to toddler children. *Child Development*, 1978, *49*, 459–465. (a)

FAGOT, B. I. Reinforcing contingencies for sex-role behaviors: Effects of experience with children. *Child Development*, 1978, *49*, 30–36. (b)

FAGOT, B. I. Male and female teachers: Do they treat boys and girls differently? *Sex Roles*, 1981, *7*, 263–271.

FAGOT, B. I., & PATTERSON, G. R. An in vivo analysis of reinforcing contingencies for sex-role behaviors in the preschool child. *Developmental Psychology*, 1969, *1*, 562–568.

FANTZ, R. L., FAGAN, J. F., III, & MIRANDA, S. B. Early visual selectivity. In L. B. Cohen & P. Salapatek (Eds.), *Infant perception: From sensation to cognition* (Vol. 1). New York: Academic Press, 1975.

FAREL, A. M. Effects of preferred maternal roles, maternal employment, and sociodemographic status on school adjustment and competence. *Child Development*, 1980, *51*, 1179–1186.

FARRAN, D., & RAMEY, C. Infant day care and at-tachment behaviors toward mothers and teachers. *Child Development*, 1977, *48*, 1228–1239.

FAULKENDER, P. J. Categorical habituation with sex-typed toy stimuli in older and younger preschoolers. *Child Development*, 1980, *51*, 515–519.

FAUST, D., & ARBUTHNOT, J. Relationship between moral and Piagetian reasoning and the effectiveness of moral education. *Developmental Psychology*, 1978, *14*, 435–436.

FEFFER, M. The cognitive implications of role-taking behavior. *Journal of Personality*, 1959, *27*, 152–168.

FEIN, G. G. The effect of chronological age and model reward on imitative behavior. *Developmental Psychology*, 1973, *9*, 283–289.

FEIN, G. G. Pretend play in childhood: An integrative review. *Child Development*, 1981, *52*, 1095–1118.

FEINGOLD, B. D., & MAHONEY, M. J. Reinforcement effects on intrinsic interest: Undermining the overjustification hypothesis. *Behavior Therapy*, 1975, *6*, 367–377.

FEINMAN, S., & ENTWISLE, D. R. Children's ability to recognize other children's faces. *Child Development*, 1976, *47*, 506–510.

FEIRING, C., & LEWIS, M. Sex and age differences in young children's reactions to frustration: A further look at the Goldberg and Lewis subjects. *Child Development*, 1979, *50*, 848–853.

FELDMAN, N. S., KLOSSON, E. C., PARSONS, J. E., RHOLES, W. S., & RUBLE, D. N. Order of information presentation and children's moral judgments. *Child Development*, 1976, *47*, 556–559.

FELDMAN, S. S., BIRINGEN, Z. C., & NASH, S. C. Fluctuations of sex-related self-attributions as a function of stage of family life cycle. *Developmental Psychology*, 1981, *17*, 24–25.

FELDMAN, S. S., & INGHAM, M. E. Attachment behavior: A validation study in two age groups. *Child Development*, 1975, *46*, 319–330.

FELDMAN, S. S., & NASH, S. C. Interest in babies during young adulthood. *Child Development*, 1978, *49*, 617–622.

FELDMAN, S. S. & NASH, S. C. Sex differences in responsiveness to babies among mature adults. *Developmental Psychology*, 1979, *15*, 430–436.

FELDMAN, S. S., NASH, S. C., & CUTRONA, C. The influence of age and sex on responsiveness to babies. *Developmental Psychology*, 1977, *13*, 675–676.

FENIGSTEIN, A. Does aggression cause a preference for viewing media violence? *Journal of Person-

ality and Social Psychology, 1979, *37,* 2307–2317.

FENSON, L., & RAMSAY, D. S. Decentration and integration of the child's play in the second year. *Child Development,* 1980, *51,* 171–178.

FERGUSON, T. J., & RULE, B. G. Effects of inferential set, outcome severity, and basis for responsibility on children's evaluations of aggressive acts. *Developmental Psychology,* 1980, *16,* 141–146.

FESHBACH, N. D., & FESHBACH, S. The relationship between empathy and aggression in two age groups. *Developmental Psychology,* 1969, *1,* 102–107.

FESHBACH, N. D., & ROE, K. Empathy in six and seven year olds. *Child Development,* 1968, *39,* 133–145.

FESHBACH, S. The catharsis hypothesis and some consequences of interaction with aggressive and neutral play objects. *Journal of Personality,* 1956, *24,* 449–462.

FESHBACH, S. The function of aggression and the regulation of aggressive drive. *Psychological Review,* 1964, *71,* 257–272.

FESHBACH, S. Aggression. In P. Mussen (Ed.), *Carmichael's manual of child psychology.* New York: John Wiley, 1970.

FESTINGER, L. A theory of social comparison processes. *Human Relations,* 1954, *7,* 117–140.

FIELD, T. Interaction behaviors of primary versus secondary caretaker fathers. *Developmental Psychology,* 1978, *14,* 183–184.

FIELD, T. M., WIDMAYER, S. M., STRINGER, S., & IGNATOFF, E. Teenage, lower-class, black mothers and their preterm infants: An intervention and developmental follow-up. *Child Development,* 1980, *51,* 426–436.

FINKELSTEIN, N. W., DENT, C., GALLACHER, K., & RAMEY, C. T. Social behavior of infants and toddlers in a day-care environment. *Developmental Psychology,* 1978, *14,* 257–262.

FISCHER, W. F. Sharing in preschool children as a function of amount and type of reinforcement. *Genetic Psychology Monographs,* 1963, *68,* 215–245.

FISHER, S. *The female orgasm: Psychology, physiology, fantasy.* New York: Basic Books, 1973.

FITZ, D. A renewed look at Miller's conflict theory of aggression displacement. *Journal of Personality and Social Psychology,* 1976, *33,* 725–732.

FLAVELL, J. H. *Cognitive development.* Englewood Cliffs, N.J.: Prentice-Hall, 1977.

FLEENER, D. E. Experimental production of infant maternal attachment behaviors. *Proceedings of the 81st Annual Convention of the American Psychological Association,* 1973, *8,* 57–58.

FLERX, V. C., FIDLER, D. S., & ROGERS, R. W. Sex role stereotypes: Developmental aspects and early intervention. *Child Development,* 1976, *47,* 998–1007.

FLING, S. & MANOSEVITZ, M. Sex typing in nursery school children's play interests. *Developmental Psychology,* 1972, *7,* 146–152.

FOOT, H. C., CHAPMAN, A. J., & SMITH, J. R. Friendship and social responsiveness in boys and girls. *Journal of Personality and Social Psychology,* 1977, *35,* 401–411.

FORD, M. E. The construct validity of egocentrism. *Psychological Bulletin,* 1979, *86,* 1169–1188.

FORD, M. E. Social cognition and social competence in adolescence. *Developmental Psychology,* 1982, *18,* 323–340.

FOREHAND, R., & SCARBORO, M. E. An analysis of children's oppositional behavior. *Journal of Abnormal Child Psychology,* 1975, *3,* 27–31.

FOUTS, G., & LIIKANEN, P. The effects of age and developmental level on imitation in children. *Child Development,* 1975, *46,* 555–558.

FOUTS, G. T., WALDNER, D. N., & WATSON, M. W. Effects of being imitated and counterimitated on the behavior of preschool children. *Child Development,* 1976, *47,* 172–177.

FRAIBERG, S. The development of human attachments in blind and sighted infants. In E. M. Hetherington and R. D. Parke (Eds.), *Contemporary readings in child psychology.* New York: McGraw-Hill, 1981.

FREEDMAN, D. G. The development of social hierarchies. In E. M. Hetherington & R. D. Parke (Eds.), *Contemporary readings in child psychology.* New York: McGraw-Hill, 1977.

FREEDMAN, D. G., & KELLER, B. Inheritance of behavior in infants. *Science,* 1963, *140,* 196–198.

FREEDMAN, J. L., WALLINGTON, A., & BLESS, E. Compliance without pressure: The effect of guilt. *Journal of Personality and Social Psychology,* 1967, *7,* 117–124.

FRENCH, D. C., BROWNELL, C. A., GRAZIANO, W. G., & HARTUP, W. W. Effects of cooperative, competitive, and individualistic sets on performance in children's groups. *Journal of Experimental Child Psychology,* 1977, *24,* 1–10.

FREUD, A., & DANN, S. An experiment in group upbringing. In *The psychoanalytic study of the child* (Vol. 6). New York: International Universities Press, 1951.

FREUD, S. An outline of psychoanalysis. In J. Strachey (Ed.), *The standard edition of the complete psychological works of Sigmund Freud* (Vol. 23). London: Hogarth Press, 1964. (Originally published, 1940).

FREYBERG, J. T. Increasing the imaginative play of urban disadvantaged kindergarten children through systematic training. In J. L. Singer (Ed.), *The child's world of make believe: Experimental studies of imaginative play*. New York: Academic Press, 1973.

FRIEDRICH, L. K., & STEIN, A. H. Aggressive and prosocial television programs and the natural behavior of preschool children. *Monographs of the Society for Research in Child Development*, 1973, 38, (4, Serial No. 151), 1–64.

FRIEDRICH, L. K., & STEIN, A. H. Prosocial television and young children: The effects of verbal labeling and role playing on learning and behavior. *Child Development*, 1975, 46. 27–38.

FRIEDRICH-COFER, L. K., HUSTON-STEIN, A., KIPNIS, D. M., SUSMAN, E. J., & CLEWETT, A. S. Environmental enhancement of prosocial television content: Effects on interpersonal behavior, imaginative play, and self-regulation in a natural setting. *Developmental Psychology*, 1979, 15, 637–646.

FRISCH, H. L. Sex stereotypes in adult-infant play. *Child Development*, 1977, 48, 1671–1675.

FRODI, A. M., & LAMB, M. E. Sex differences in responsiveness to infants: A developmental study of physiological and behavioral responses. *Child Development*, 1978, 49, 1182–1188.

FRODI, A. M., & LAMB, M. E. Child abusers' responses to infant smiles and cries. *Child Development*, 1980, 51, 238–241.

FRODI, A. M., LAMB, M. E., LEAVITT, L. A., DONOVAN, W. L., NEFF, C., & SHERRY, D. Fathers' and mothers' responses to the faces and cries of normal and premature infants. *Developmental Psychology*, 1978, 14, 490–498.

FRODI, A., MACAULAY, J., & THOME, P. R. Are women always less aggressive than men? A review of the experimental literature. *Psychological Bulletin*, 1977, 84, 634–660.

FROMMER, E. A., & O'SHEA, G. The importance of childhood experience in relation to problems of marriage and family-building. *British Journal of Psychiatry*, 1973, 123, 157–160.

FRUEH, T., & MCGHEE, P. E. Traditional sex role development and amount of time spent watching television. *Developmental Psychology*, 1975, 11, 109.

FRY, P. S. Affect and resistance to temptation. *Developmental Psychology*, 1975, 11, 466–472.

FRY, P. S. Success, failure, and resistance to temptation. *Developmental Psychology*, 1977, 13, 519–520.

FULLARD, W., & REILING, A. M. An investigation of Lorenz's "babyness." *Child Development*, 1976, 47, 1191–1193.

FURMAN, W., & MASTERS, J. C. Affective consequences of social reinforcement, punishment, and neutral behavior. *Developmental Psychology*, 1980, 16, 100–104.

FURMAN, W., RAHE, D. F., & HARTUP, W. W. Rehabilitation of socially withdrawn preschool children through mixed-age and same-age socialization. *Child Development*, 1979, 50, 915–922.

GAERTNER, S. L., & DOVIDIO, J. F. The subtlety of white racism, arousal, and helping behavior. *Journal of Personality and Social Psychology*, 1977, 35, 691–707.

GALST, J. P. Television food commercials and pronutritional public service announcements as determinants of young children's snack choices. *Child Development*, 1980, 51, 935–938.

GARBARINO, J., & SHERMAN, D. High-risk neighborhoods and high-risk families: The human ecology of child maltreatment. *Child Development*, 1980, 51, 188–198.

GARRETT, C. S., EIN, P. L., & TREMAINE, L. The development of gender stereotyping of adult occupations in elementary school children. *Child Development*, 1977, 48, 507–512.

GARVEY, C., & BERNDT, R. Organization of pretend play. *Catalogue of Selected Documents in Psychology*, 1977, 7, 1589.

GEEN, R. G., & QUANTY, M. B. The catharsis hypothesis of aggression: An evaluation of an hypothesis. In L. Berkowitz (Ed.), *Advances in experimental social psychology* (Vol. 10). New York: Academic Press, 1977.

GEEN, R. G., & STONNER, D. Context effects in observed violence. *Journal of Personality and Social Psychology*, 1973, 25, 145–150.

GELFAND, D. M., HARTMANN, D. P., CROMER, C. C., SMITH, C. L., & PAGE, B. C. The effects of instructional prompts and praise on children's donation rates. *Child Development*, 1975, 46, 980–983.

GELFAND, D. M., HARTMANN, D. P., LAMB, A. K., SMITH, C. L., MAHAN, M. A., & PAUL, S. C. The effects of adult models and described alternatives on children's choice of behavior management techniques. *Child Development*, 1974, *45*, 585–593.

GEORGE, C., & MAIN, M. Social interactions of young abused children: Approach, avoidance, and aggression. *Child Development*, 1979, *50*, 306–318.

GERBNER, G., & GROSS, L. Living with television: The violence profile. *Journal of Communication*, 1976, *26*, 173–199.

GERST, M. S. Symbolic coding processes in observational learning. *Journal of Personality and Social Psychology*, 1971, *19*, 7–17.

GEWIRTZ, J. L. The course of infant smiling in four child-rearing environments in Israel. In B. M. Foss (Ed.), *Determinants of infant behaviour* (Vol. 3). London: Methuen, 1965.

GEWIRTZ, J. L. Mechanisms of social learning: Some roles of stimulation and behavior in early human development. In D. A. Goslin (Ed.), *Handbook of socialization theory and research*. Chicago: Rand McNally, 1969.

GEWIRTZ, J. L., & BAER, D. M. Deprivation and satiation of social reinforcers as drive conditions. *Journal of Abnormal and Social Psychology*, 1958, *57*, 165–172. (a)

GEWIRTZ, J. L., & BAER, D. M. The effect of brief social deprivation on behaviors for a social reinforcer. *Journal of Abnormal and Social Psychology*, 1958, *56*, 49–56. (b)

GEWIRTZ, J. L., & BOYD, E. F. Does maternal responding imply reduced infant crying? A critique of the 1972 Bell and Ainsworth report. *Child Development*, 1977, *48*, 1200–1207.

GEWIRTZ, J. L., & STINGLE, K. C. The learning of generalized imitation as the basis for identification. *Psychological Review*, 1968, *75*, 374–397.

GINSBURG, H. J., POLLMAN, V. A., & WAUSON, M. S. An ethological analysis of nonverbal inhibitors of aggressive behavior in male elementary school children. *Developmental Psychology*, 1977, *13*, 417–418.

GLUECK, S., & GLUECK, E. T. *Unraveling juvenile delinquency*. Cambridge, Mass.: Harvard University Press, 1950.

GOETZ, T. E., & DWECK, C. S. Learned helplessness in social situations. *Journal of Personality and Social Psychology*, 1980, *39*, 246–255.

GOLDBERG, S., & LEWIS, M. Play behavior in the year-old infant: Early sex differences. *Child Development*, 1969, *40*, 21–31.

GOLDFARB, W. Effects of early institutional care on adolescent personality. *Journal of Experimental Education*, 1943, *12*, 106–129.

GOLDMAN, J. A. Social participation of preschool children in same- versus mixed-age groups. *Child Development*, 1981, *52*, 644–650.

GOODENOUGH, F. L. *Anger in young children*. Minneapolis: University of Minnesota Press, 1931.

GORN, G. J., GOLDBERG, M. E., & KANUNGO, R. N. The role of educational television in changing the intergroup attitudes of children. *Child Development*, 1976, *47*, 277–280.

GOSLIN, D. A. Accuracy of self-perception and social acceptance. *Sociometry*, 1962, *25*, 283–289.

GOTTLIEB, D. E., TAYLOR, S. E., & RUDERMAN, A. Cognitive bases of children's moral judgments. *Developmental Psychology*, 1977, *13*, 547–556.

GOTTMAN, J. M. Detecting cyclicity in social interaction. *Psychological Bulletin*, 1979, *86*, 338–348.

GOTTMAN, J., GONSO, J., & RASMUSSEN, B. Social interaction, social competence, and friendship in children. *Child Development*, 1975, *46*, 709–718.

GOTTMAN, J., GONSO, J., & SCHULER, P. Teaching social skills to isolated children. *Journal of Abnormal Child Psychology*, 1976, *4*, 179–197.

GOULDNER, A. The norm of reciprocity: A preliminary statement. *American Sociological Review*, 1960, *25*, 161–178.

GOUZE, K. R., & NADELMAN, L. Constancy of gender identity for self and others between the ages of three and seven. *Child Development*, 1980, *51*, 275–278.

GOVE, F. L., & KEATING, D. P. Empathic role-taking precursors. *Developmental Psychology*, 1979, *15*, 549–600.

GRAHAM, F., & CLIFTON, R. Heart-rate change as a component of the orienting response. *Psychological Bulletin*, 1966, *65*, 305–320.

GRAZIANO, W. G., BRODY, G. H., & BERNSTEIN, S. Effects of information about future interaction and peer's motivation on peer reward allocations. *Developmental Psychology*, 1980, *16*, 475–482.

GRAZIANO, W., FRENCH, D., BROWNELL, C., & HARTUP, W. W. Peer interaction in same- and mixed-age triads in relation to chronological age and incentive condition. *Child Development*, 1976, *47*, 707–714.

GREEN, K. D., FOREHAND, R., BECK, S. J., & VOSK, B. An assessment of the relationship among measures of children's social competence and children's academic achievement. *Child Development*, 1980, *51*, 1149–1156.

GREEN, S. K. Causal attribution of emotion in kindergarten children. *Developmental Psychology,* 1977, *13,* 533–534.

GREENBERG, D. J., HILLMAN, D., & GRICE, D. Infant and stranger variables related to stranger anxiety in the first year of life. *Developmental Psychology,* 1973, *9,* 207–212.

GREENBERG, M. T., & MARVIN, R. S. Reactions of preschool children to an adult stranger: A behavioral systems approach. *Child Development,* 1982, *53,* 481–490.

GREENBERGER, E., STEINBERG, L. D., & VAUX, A. Adolescents who work: Health and behavioral consequences of job stress. *Developmental Psychology,* 1981, *17,* 691–703.

GREIF, E. B. Sex differences in parent-child conversations: Who interrupts whom. Paper presented at the meeting of the Society for Research in Child Development, San Francisco, 1979.

GRESHAM, F. M. Validity of social skills measures for assessing social competence in low-status children: A multivariate investigation. *Developmental Psychology,* 1981, *17,* 390–398.

GROCH, A. S. Joking and appreciation of humor in nursery school children. *Child Development,* 1974, *45,* 1098–1102.

GRONLUND, N. E. *Sociometry in the classroom.* New York: Harper & Row, Pub., 1959.

GROSS, L. The real world of television. *Today's Education,* 1974, *63,* 86–92.

GROSS, M. D. Violence associated with organic brain disease. In J. Fawcett (Ed.), *Dynamics of violence.* Chicago: American Medical Association, 1972, 85–91.

GROSSMAN, K., THANE, K., & GROSSMAN, K. E. Maternal tactual contact of the newborn after various postpartum conditions of mother-infant contact. *Developmental Psychology,* 1981, *17,* 158–169.

GROTEVANT, H. D. Sibling constellations and sex typing of interests in adolescence. *Child Development,* 1978, *49,* 540–542.

GRUSEC, J. E. Power and the internalization of self-denial. *Child Development,* 1971, *42,* 93–105.

GRUSEC, J. E. Demand characteristics of the modeling experiment: Altruism as a function of age and aggression. *Journal of Personality and Social Psychology,* 1972, *22,* 139–148.

GRUSEC, J. E. Effects of co-observer evaluations on imitation: A developmental study. *Developmental Psychology,* 1973, *8,* 141.

GRUSEC, J. E., & ABRAMOVITCH, R. Imitation of peers and adults in a natural setting: A functional analysis. *Child Development,* 1982, *53,* 636–642.

GRUSEC, J. E., & BRINKER, D. B., JR. Reinforcement for imitation as a social learning determinant with implications for sex-role development. *Journal of Personality and Social Psychology,* 1972, *21,* 149–158.

GRUSEC, J. E., & EZRIN, S. A. Techniques of punishment and the development of self-criticism. *Child Development,* 1972, *43,* 1273–1288.

GRUSEC, J. E., & KUCZYNSKI, L. Teaching children to punish themselves and effects on subsequent compliance. *Child Development,* 1977, *48,* 1296–1300.

GRUSEC, J. E., & KUCZYNSKI, L. Direction of effect in socialization: A comparison of the parent's versus the child's behavior as determinants of disciplinary techniques. *Developmental Psychology,* 1980, *16,* 1–9.

GRUSEC, J. E., KUCZYNSKI, L., RUSHTON, J. P., & SIMUTIS, Z. M. Modeling, direct instruction, and attributions: Effects on altruism. *Developmental Psychology,* 1978, *14,* 51–57.

GRUSEC, J. E., KUCZYNSKI, L., RUSHTON, J. P., & SIMUTIS, Z. M. Learning resistance to temptation through observation. *Developmental Psychology,* 1979, *15,* 233–240.

GRUSEC, J. E., & MISCHEL, W. Model's characteristics as determinants of social learning. *Journal of Personality and Social Psychology,* 1966, *4,* 211–215.

GRUSEC, J. E., & REDLER, E. Attribution, reinforcement, and altruism: A developmental analysis. *Developmental Psychology,* 1980, *16,* 525–534.

GRUSEC, J. E., SAAS-KORTSAAK, P., & SIMUTIS, Z. M. The role of example and moral exhortation in the training of altruism. *Child Development,* 1978, *49,* 920–923.

GRUSEC, J. E., & SKUBISKI, S. L. Model nurturance, demand characteristics of the modeling experiment, and altruism. *Journal of Personality and Social Psychology,* 1970, *14,* 352–359.

GUILFORD, J. P. *Personality.* New York: McGraw-Hill, 1959.

GUNNAR, M. R. Control, warning signals, and distress in infancy. *Developmental Psychology,* 1980, *16,* 281–289.

GUNNAR, M. R., & DONAHUE, M. Sex differences in social responsiveness between six months and twelve months. *Child Development,* 1980, *51,* 262–265.

GUNNAR-VONGNECHTEN, M. R. Changing a frightening toy into a pleasant toy by allowing the infant to control its actions. *Developmental Psychology,* 1978, *14,* 157–162.

HAAN, N., SMITH, M. B., & BLOCK, J. Moral reasoning

of young adults: Political-social behavior, family background, and personality correlates. *Journal of Personality and Social Psychology*, 1968, *10*, 183–201.

HAINLINE, L., & FEIG, E. The correlates of childhood father absence in college-aged women. *Child Development*, 1978, *49*, 37–42.

HALL, C. S., & LINDZEY, G. *Theories of personality.* New York: John Wiley, 1970.

HALL, J. A., & HALBERSTADT, A. G. Masculinity and femininity in children: Development of the Children's Personal Attributes Questionnaire. *Developmental Psychology*, 1980, *16*, 270–280.

HAPKIEWICZ, W. G., & RODEN, A. H. The effect of aggressive cartoons on children's interpersonal play. *Child Development*, 1971, *42*, 1583–1585.

HARLOW, H. F., DODSWORTH, R. O., & HARLOW, M. K. Total social isolation in monkeys. *Proceedings of the National Academy of Sciences*, 1965, *54*, 90–96.

HARLOW, H. F., & ZIMMERMAN, R. R. Affectional responses in the infant monkey. *Science*, 1959, *130*, 421–432.

HARPER, L. V., & SANDERS, K. M. Preschool children's use of space: Sex differences in outdoor play. *Developmental Psychology*, 1975, *11*, 119.

HARRIS, B. Developmental differences in the attribution of responsibility. *Developmental Psychology*, 1977, *13*, 257–265.

HARTER, S. Pleasure derived by children from cognitive challenge and mastery. *Child Development*, 1974, *45*, 661–669.

HARTER, S. The effects of social reinforcement and task difficulty level on the pleasure derived by normal and retarded children from cognitive challenge and mastery. *Journal of Experimental Child Psychology*, 1977, *24*, 476–494.

HARTER, S. Pleasure derived from challenge and the effects of receiving grades on children's difficulty level choices. *Child Development*, 1978, *49*, 788–799.

HARTIG, M., & KANFER, F. H. The role of verbal self-instructions in children's resistance to temptation. *Journal of Personality and Social Psychology*, 1973, *25*, 259–267.

HARTMANN, D. P. Influence of symbolically modeled instrumental aggression and pain cues on aggressive behavior. *Journal of Personality and Social Psychology*, 1969, *11*, 280–288.

HARTSHORNE, H., & MAY, M. S. *Studies in the nature of character* (Vol. 1): *Studies in self-control.* New York: Macmillan, 1929.

HARTUP, W. W. Nurturance and nurturance-withdrawal in relation to the dependency behavior of preschool children. *Child Development*, 1958, *29*, 191–201.

HARTUP, W. W. Peer interaction and social organization. In P. H. Mussen (Ed.), *Carmichael's manual of child psychology* (Vol. 2). New York: John Wiley, 1970.

HARTUP, W. W. Aggression in childhood: Developmental perspectives. *American Psychologist*, 1974, *29*, 336–341.

HARTUP, W. W. Current issues in social development. Paper presented at the biennial meeting of the Society for Research in Child Development, San Francisco, 1979.

HARTUP, W. W. Children and their friends. In H. McGurk (Ed.), *Child social development.* London: Methuen, 1980.

HARTUP, W. W., & COATES, B. Imitation of a peer as a function of reinforcement from the peer group and rewardingness of the model. *Child Development*, 1967, *38*, 1003–1016.

HARTUP, W. W., GLAZER, J. A., & CHARLESWORTH, R. Peer reinforcement and sociometric status. *Child Development*, 1967, *38*, 1017–1024.

HARVEY, S. E., & LIEBERT, R. M. Abstraction, inference, and acceptance in children's processing of an adult model's moral judgments. *Developmental Psychology*, 1979, *15*, 552–558.

HAUGAN, G. M., & MCINTIRE, R. Comparisons of vocal imitation, tactile stimulation, and food as reinforcers for infant vocalizations. *Developmental Psychology*, 1972, *6*, 201–209.

HAY, D. F. Cooperative interactions and sharing between very young children and their parents. *Developmental Psychology*, 1979, *15*, 647–653.

HAY, D. F. Multiple functions of proximity seeking in infancy. *Child Development*, 1980, *51*, 636–645.

HAYES, D. S. Cognitive bases for liking and disliking among preschool children. *Child Development*, 1978, *49*, 906–909.

HAYES, D. S., & BIRNBAUM, D. W. Preschoolers' retention of televised events: Is a picture worth a thousand words? *Developmental Psychology*, 1980, *16*, 410–416.

HAYES, D. S., GERSHMAN, E., & BOLIN, L. J. Friends and enemies: Cognitive bases for preschool children's unilateral and reciprocal relationships. *Child Development*, 1980, *51*, 1276–1279.

HAYES, L. A., & WATSON, J. S. Neonatal imitation: Fact or artifact? *Developmental Psychology*, 1981, *17*, 655–660.

HEBB, D. O. On the nature of fear. *Psychological Review*, 1946, *53*, 259–276.

HEBBLE, P. W. The development of elementary

school children's judgment of intent. *Child Development*, 1971, 42, 1203–1215.

HEIDER, F. *The psychology of interpersonal relations.* New York: John Wiley, 1958.

HEILBRUN, A. B., JR. Gender differences in the functional linkage between androgyny, social cognition, and competence. *Journal of Personality and Social Psychology*, 1981, 41, 1106–1118.

HELMREICH, R. L., SPENCE, J. T., & HOLAHAN, C. K. Psychological androgyny and sex role flexibility: A test of two hypotheses. *Journal of Personality and Social Psychology*, 1979, 37, 1631–1644.

HENSHEL, A. The relationship between values and behavior: A developmental hypothesis. *Child Development*, 1971, 42, 1997–2007.

HERBERT, E. W., GELFAND, D. M., & HARTMANN, D. P. Imitation and self-esteem as determinants of self-critical behavior. *Child Development*, 1969, 40, 421–430.

HESS, E. H. The conditions limiting critical age of imprinting. *Journal of Comparative and Physiological Psychology*, 1959, 52, 515–518.

HESS, R. D., & SHIPMAN, V. C. Cognitive elements in maternal behavior. In J. P. Hill (Ed.), *Minnesota symposium on child psychology*, (Vol. 1). Minneapolis: University of Minnesota Press, 1967.

HETHERINGTON, E. M. Effects of paternal absence on sex-typed behaviors in Negro and white preadolescent males. *Journal of Personality and Social Psychology*, 1966, 4, 87–91.

HETHERINGTON, E. M. The effects of familial variables on sex typing, on parent-child similarity, and on imitation in children. In J. P. Hill (Ed.), *Minnesota symposia on child psychology* (Vol. 1). Minneapolis: University of Minnesota Press, 1967.

HETHERINGTON, E. M. Effects of father absence on personality development in adolescent daughters. *Developmental Psychology*, 1972, 7, 313–326.

HETHERINGTON, E. M. Divorce: A child's perspective. *American Psychologist*, 1979, 34, 851–858.

HETHERINGTON, E. M., COX, M., & COX, R. Beyond father absence: Conceptualization of effects of divorce: In E. M. Hetherington & R. D. Parke (Eds.), *Contemporary readings in child psychology*. New York: McGraw-Hill, 1977.

HETHERINGTON, E. M., COX, M., & COX, R. Family interaction and the social, emotional, and cognitive development of preschool children following divorce. Paper presented at the biennial meeting of the Society for Research in Child Development, San Francisco, 1979.

HETHERINGTON, E. M., & FRANKIE, G. Effects of parental dominance, warmth, and conflict on imitation in children. *Journal of Personality and Social Psychology*, 1967, 6, 119–125.

HETHERINGTON, E. M., & MARTIN, B. Family interaction and psychopathology in children. In H. C. Quay & J. S. Werry (Eds.), *Psychopathological disorders of childhood*. New York: John Wiley, 1972.

HICKS, D. J. Imitation and retention of film-mediated aggressive peer and adult models. *Journal of Personality and Social Psychology*, 1965, 2, 97–100.

HICKS, D. J. Effects of co-observer's sanctions and adult presence on imitative aggression. *Child Development*, 1968, 39, 303–309.

HICKS, D. J. Girls' attitudes toward modeled behaviors and the content of imitative private play. *Child Development*, 1971, 42, 139–147.

HILL, W. F. Learning theory and the acquisition of values. *Psychological Review*, 1960, 67, 317–331.

HINDE, R. A., & STEVENSON-HINDE, J. *Constraints on learning: Limitations and predispositions.* New York: Academic Press, 1973.

HOCK, E. Working and nonworking mothers with infants: Perceptions of their careers, their infants' needs, and satisfaction with mothering. *Developmental Psychology*, 1978, 14, 37–43.

HOFFMAN, L. W. Changes in family roles, socialization, and sex differences. *American Psychologist*, 1977, 32, 644–657.

HOFFMAN, L. W. Maternal employment: 1979. *American Psychologist*, 1979, 34, 859–865.

HOFFMAN, M. L. Parent discipline and the child's consideration for others. *Child Development*, 1963, 34, 573–588.

HOFFMAN, M. L. Conscience, personality and socialization techniques. *Human Development*, 1970, 13, 90–126. (a)

HOFFMAN, M. L. Moral development. In P. H. Mussen (Ed.), *Carmichael's manual of child psychology*. New York: John Wiley, 1970. (b)

HOFFMAN, M. L. Father absence and conscience development. *Developmental Psychology*, 1971, 4, 400–406. (a)

HOFFMAN, M. L. Identification and conscience development. *Child Development*, 1971, 42, 1071–1082. (b)

HOFFMAN, M. L. Altruistic behavior and the parent-child relationship. *Journal of Personality and Social Psychology*, 1975, 31, 937–943. (a)

HOFFMAN, M. L. Developmental synthesis of affect and cognition and its implications for altruistic motivation. *Developmental Psychology*, 1975, 11, 607–622. (b)

HOFFMAN, M. L. Moral internalization: Current theory and research. In L. Berkowitz (Ed.), *Advances in experimental social psychology* (Vol. 10). New York: Academic Press, 1977. (a)

HOFFMAN, M. L. Sex differences in empathy and related behaviors. *Psychological Bulletin*, 1977, 84, 712–722. (b)

HOFFMAN, M. L. Is altruism part of human nature? *Journal of Personality and Social Psychology*, 1981, 40, 121–137.

HOFFMAN, M. L., & SALTZSTEIN, H. D. Parent discipline and the child's moral development. *Journal of Personality and Social Psychology*, 1967, 5, 45–57.

HOKANSON, J. E., & EDELMAN, R. Effects of three social responses on vascular processes. *Journal of Personality and Social Psychology*, 1966, 3, 442–447.

HOLLENBECK, A. R., & SLABY, R. G. Infant visual and vocal responses to television. *Child Development*, 1979, 50, 41–45.

HOLLOS, M. Logical operations and role-taking abilities in two cultures: Norway and Hungary. *Child Development*, 1975, 46, 638–649.

HOLMBERG, M. C. The development of social interchange patterns from 12 to 42 months. *Child Development*, 1980, 51, 448–456.

HOLSTEIN, C. B. Irreversible, stepwise sequence in the development of moral judgment: A longitudinal study of males and females. *Child Development*, 1976, 47, 51–61.

HONESS, T. Self-reference in children's descriptions of peers: Egocentricity or collaboration? *Child Development*, 1980, 51, 476–480.

HOOK, J. G., & COOK, T. D. Equity theory and the cognitive ability of children. *Psychological Bulletin*, 1979, 86, 429–445.

HORNER, M. S. Toward an understanding of achievement motivation. *Journal of Social Issues*, 1972, 28, 156–176.

HOWES, C. Peer play scale as an index of complexity of peer interaction. *Developmental Psychology*, 1980, 16, 371–372.

HUDSON, L. M. On the coherence of role-taking abilities: An alternative to correlational analysis. *Child Development*, 1978, 49, 223–227.

HUSTON-STEIN, A., FRIEDRICH-COFER, L., & SUSMAN, E. J. The relation of classroom structure to social behavior, imaginative play, and self-regulation of economically disadvantaged children. *Child Development*, 1977, 48, 908–916.

HUTT, C. Sex differences in human development. In E. M. Hetherington & R. D. Parke (Eds.), *Contemporary readings in child psychology*. New York: McGraw-Hill, 1977.

HYDE, J. S., & PHILLIS, D. E. Androgyny across the life span. *Developmental Psychology*, 1979, 15, 334–336.

IANNOTTI, R. J. Effect of role-taking experiences on role taking, empathy, altruism, and aggression. *Developmental Psychology*, 1978, 14, 119–124.

ICKES, W. J., & BARNES, R. D. Boys and girls together—and alienated: On enacting stereotyped sex roles in mixed-sex dyads. *Journal of Personality and Social Psychology*, 1978, 36, 669–683.

IMAMOGLU, E. O. Children's awareness and usage of intention cues. *Child Development*, 1975, 46, 39–45.

ISEN, A. M. Success, failure, attention, and reaction to others: The warm glow of success. *Journal of Personality and Social Psychology*, 1970, 15, 294–301.

ISEN, A. M., CLARK, M., & SCHWARTZ, M. F. Duration of the effect of good mood on helping: "Footprints on the sands of time." *Journal of Personality and Social Psychology*, 1976, 34, 385–393.

ISEN, A. M., HORN, N., & ROSENHAN, D. L. Effects of success and failure on children's generosity. *Journal of Personality and Social Psychology*, 1973, 27, 239–247.

ISEN, A. M., & LEVIN, P. F. Effect of feeling good on helping: Cookies and kindness. *Journal of Personality and Social Psychology*, 1972, 21, 384–388.

ISRAEL, A. C., & BROWN, M. S. Effects of directiveness of instructions and surveillance on the production and persistence of children's donations. *Journal of Experimental Child Psychology*, 1979, 27, 250–261.

JACKLIN, C. N., & MACCOBY, E. E. Social behavior at thirty-three months in same-sex dyads. *Child Development*, 1978, 49, 557–569.

JACKLIN, C. N., MACCOBY, E. E. & DICK, A. E. Barrier behavior and toy preference: Sex differences (and their absence) in the year-old child. *Child Development*, 1973, 44, 196–200.

JACKOWITZ, E. R., & WATSON, M. W. Development of object transformations in early pretend play. *Developmental Psychology*, 1980, 16, 543–549.

JACOBSON, J. L. Cognitive determinants of wariness toward unfamiliar peers. *Developmental Psychology*, 1980, 16, 347–354.

JACOBSON, J. L. The role of inanimate objects in early peer interaction. *Child Development*, 1981, 52, 618–626.

JAKIBCHUK, Z., & SMERIGLIO, V. L. The influence of symbolic modeling on the social behavior of preschool children with low levels of social responsiveness. *Child Development*, 1976, *47*, 838–841.

JAMES, W. *The principles of psychology.* New York: Holt, Rinehart & Winston, 1896.

JENNINGS, K. D. People versus object orientation, social behavior, and intellectual abilities in preschool children. *Developmental Psychology*, 1975, *11*, 511–519.

JENSEN, L., & HUGHSTON, K. The effect of training children to make moral judgments that are independent of sanctions. *Developmental Psychology*, 1971, *5*, 367.

JENSEN, R. E., & MOORE, S. G. The effect of attribute statements on cooperativeness and competitiveness in school-age boys. *Child Development*, 1977, *48*, 305–307.

JERSILD, A. T., & MARKEY, F. V. Conflicts between preschool children. *Child Development Monographs*, 1935.

JOHNSON, D. W. Affective perspective taking and cooperative predisposition. *Developmental Psychology*, 1975, *11*, 869–870.

JOHNSON, J. E. Relations of divergent thinking and intelligence test scores with social and nonsocial make-believe play of preschool children. *Child Development*, 1976, *47*, 1200–1203.

JOHNSON, J. E., & ERSHLER, J. Developmental trends in preschool play as a function of classroom program and child gender. *Child Development*, 1981, *52*, 995–1004.

JOHNSON, J. E., ERSHLER, J., & BELL, C. Play behavior in a discovery-based and a formal-education preschool program. *Child Development*, 1980, *51*, 271–274.

JOHNSON, M. M. Sex role learning in the nuclear family. *Child Development*, 1963, *34*, 319–333.

JOHNSON, M. M. Fathers, mothers, and sex typing. In E. M. Hetherington & R. D. Parke (Eds.), *Contemporary readings in child psychology.* New York: McGraw-Hill, 1977.

JONES, E. E., & NISBETT, R. E. The actor and the observer: Divergent perceptions of the causes of behavior. In E. E. Jones, D. E. Kanouse, H. H. Kelley, R. E. Nisbett, S. Valins, & B. Weiner (Eds.), *Attribution: Perceiving the causes of behavior.* Morristown, N.J.: General Learning Press, 1972.

JONES, M. C., & BAYLEY, N. Physical maturing among boys as related to behavior. *Journal of Educational Psychology*, 1950, *41*, 129–148.

KAADA, B. Brain mechanisms related to aggressive behavior. In D. C. Clemente and D. B. Lindsley (Eds.), *Aggression and defense.* Berkeley: University of California Press, 1967.

KAGAN, J. *Change and continuity in infancy.* New York: John Wiley, 1971. (a)

KAGAN, J. *Understanding children.* New York: Harcourt Brace Jovanovich, Inc., 1971. (b)

KAGAN, J. Emergent themes in human development. *American Scientist*, 1976, *64*, 186–196.

KAGAN, J., KEARSLEY, R. B., & ZELAZO, P. R. *Infancy: Its place in human development.* Cambridge, Mass.: Harvard University Press, 1978.

KAGAN, J., & MOSS, H. A. *Birth to maturity: A study in psychological development.* New York: John Wiley, 1962.

KAIL, R. V., & LEVINE, L. E. Encoding processes and sex-role preferences. *Journal of Experimental Child Psychology*, 1976, *21*, 256–263.

KALTENBACH, K., WEINRAUB, M., & FULLARD, W. Infant wariness toward strangers reconsidered: Infants' and mothers' reactions to unfamiliar persons. *Child Development*, 1980, *51*, 1197–1202.

KANFER, F. H., & DUERFELDT, P. H. Age, class standing, and commitment as determinants of cheating in children. *Child Development*, 1968, *39*, 545–557.

KANFER, F. H., & ZICH, J. Self-control training: The effects of external control on children's resistance to temptation. *Developmental Psychology*, 1974, *10*, 108–115.

KARABENICK, J. D., & HELLER, K. A. A developmental study of effort and ability attributions. *Developmental Psychology*, 1976, *12*, 559–560.

KARGER, R. H. Synchrony in mother-infant interactions. *Child Development*, 1979, *50*, 882–885.

KARNIOL, R. Children's use of intention cues in evaluating behavior. *Psychological Bulletin*, 1978, *85*, 76–85.

KARNIOL, R. A conceptual analysis of immanent justice responses in children. *Child Development*, 1980, *51*, 118–130.

KARNIOL, R., & ROSS, M. The development of causal attributions in social perception. *Journal of Personality and Social Psychology*, 1976, *34*, 455–464.

KARNIOL, R., & ROSS, M. The effect of performance-relevant and performance-irrelevant rewards on children's intrinsic motivation. *Child Development*, 1977, *48*, 482–487.

KARNIOL, R., & ROSS, M. Children's use of a causal attribution schema and the inference of manipulative intentions. *Child Development*, 1979, *50*, 463–468.

KATZ, P. A. Perception of racial cues in preschool children: A new look. *Developmental Psychology*, 1973, *8*, 295–299. (a)

KATZ, P. A. Stimulus predifferentiation and modification of children's racial attitudes. *Child Development*, 1973, *44*, 232–237. (b)

KATZ, P. A., & SEAVEY, C. Labels and children's perceptions of faces. *Child Development*, 1973, *44*, 770–775.

KATZ, P. A., SOHN, M., & ZALK, S. R. Perceptual concomitants of racial attitudes in urban grade-school children. *Developmental Psychology*, 1975, *11*, 135–144.

KATZ, P. A., & ZALK, S. R. Modification of children's racial attitudes. *Developmental Psychology*, 1978, *14*, 447–461.

KATZ, P. A., & ZIGLER, E. Self-image disparity: A developmental approach. *Journal of Personality and Social Psychology*, 1967, *5*, 186–195.

KATZ, P. A., ZIGLER, E., & ZALK, S. R. Children's self-image disparity: The effects of age, maladjustment, and action-thought orientation. *Developmental Psychology*, 1975, *11*, 546–550.

KATZ, R. C. Interactions between the facilitative and inhibitory effects of a punishing stimulus in the control of children's hitting behavior. *Child Development*, 1971, *42*, 1433–1446.

KAUFMAN, I. C., & ROSENBLUM, L. A. Depression in infant monkeys separated from their mothers. *Science*, 1967, *155*, 1030–1031.

KEASEY, C. B. Social participation as a factor in the moral development of preadolescents. *Developmental Psychology*, 1971, *5*, 216–220.

KEASEY, C. B. Experimentally induced changes in moral opinions and reasoning. *Journal of Personality and Social Psychology*, 1973, *26*, 30–38.

KEASEY, C. B. The influence of opinion agreement and quality of supportive reasoning in the evaluation of moral judgments. *Journal of Personality and Social Psychology*, 1974, *30*, 477–482.

KELLER, B. B., & BELL, R. Q. Child effects on adults' method of eliciting altruistic behavior. *Child Development*, 1979, *50*, 1004–1009.

KELLER, M. F., & CARLSON, P. M. The use of symbolic modeling to promote social skills in preschool children with low levels of social responsiveness. *Child Development*, 1974, *45*, 912–919.

KELLEY, H. H. The process of causal attribution. *American Psychologist*, 1973, *28*, 107–128.

KENNY, D. T. *An experimental test of the catharsis theory of aggression.* Unpublished doctoral dissertation, University of Washington, 1952.

KENRICK, D. T., BAUMANN, D. J., & CIALDINI, R. B. A step in the socialization of altruism as hedonism: Effects of negative mood on children's generosity under public and private conditions.

Journal of Personality and Social Psychology, 1979, *37*, 747–755.

KENRICK, D. T., & STRINGFIELD, D. O. Personality traits and the eye of the beholder: Crossing some traditional philosophical boundaries in the search for consistency in all of the people. *Psychological Review*, 1980, *87*, 88–104.

KIRBY, F. D., & TOLER, H. C. Modification of preschool isolate behavior: A case study. *Journal of Applied Behavior Analysis*, 1970, *3*, 309–314.

KISTER, M. C., & PATTERSON, C. J. Children's conceptions of the causes of illness: Understanding of contagion and use of immanent justice. *Child Development*, 1980, *51*, 839–846.

KLAUS, M. H., & KENNELL, J. H. *Maternal-infant bonding.* St. Louis: C. V. Mosby, 1976.

KLECK, R. E., RICHARDSON, S. A., & RONALD, L. Physical appearance cues and interpersonal attraction in children. *Child Development*, 1974, *45*, 305–310.

KLEINKE, C. L., & NICHOLSON, T. A. Black and white children's awareness of de facto race and sex differences. *Developmental Psychology*, 1979, *15*, 84–86.

KNIGHT, G. P., & KAGAN, S. Apparent sex differences in cooperation-competition: A function of individualism. *Developmental Psychology*, 1981, *17*, 783–790.

KOBLINSKY, S. G., CRUSE, D. F., & SUGAWARA, A. I. Sex role stereotypes and children's memory for story content. *Child Development*, 1978, *49*, 452–458.

KOCH, H. Attitudes of young children toward their peers as related to certain characteristics of their siblings. *Psychological Monographs*, 1956, *70*, (19, Whole No. 426). (a)

KOCH, H. Sissiness and tomboyishness in relation to sibling characteristics. *Journal of Genetic Psychology*, 1956, *88*, 231–244. (b)

KOHLBERG, L. A cognitive-developmental analysis of children's sex role concepts and attitudes. In E. Maccoby (Ed.), *The development of sex difference.* Stanford, Ca.: Stanford University Press, 1966.

KOHLBERG, L. Stage and sequence: The cognitive-developmental approach to socialization. In D. A. Goslin (Ed.), *Handbook of socialization theory and research.* Chicago: Rand McNally, 1969.

KOHLBERG, L., & KRAMER, R. B. Continuities and discontinuities in childhood and adult moral development. *Human Development*, 1969, *12*, 93–120.

KOHLBERG, L., & ZIGLER, E. The impact of cognitive maturity on the development of sex-role attitudes in the years 4–8. *Genetic Psychology Monographs*, 1967, 75, 84–165.

KOHN, M. The child as a determinant of his peers' approach to him. *Journal of Genetic Psychology*, 1966, 109, 91–100.

KOHN, M., & CLAUSEN, J. Social isolation and schizophrenia. *American Sociological Review*, 1955, 20, 265–273.

KONECNI, V. J. Annoyance, type and duration of postannoyance activity, and aggression: The "cathartic effect." *Journal of Experimental Psychology: General*, 1975, 104, 76–102.

KONECNI, V. J., & EBBESEN, E. B. Disinhibition versus the cathartic effect: Artifact and substance. *Journal of Personality and Social Psychology*, 1976, 34, 352–365.

KONNER, M. Relations among infants and juveniles in comparative perspective. In M. Lewis & L. Rosenblum (Eds.), *Friendship and peer relations*. New York: John Wiley, 1975.

KOOCHER, G. P. Childhood, death, and cognitive development. *Developmental Psychology*, 1973, 9, 369–375.

KRANTZ, M. Sociometric awareness, social participation, and perceived popularity in preschool children. *Child Development*, 1982, 53, 376–379.

KRASNER, L., & ULLMANN, L. P. (Eds.). *Research in behavior modification*. New York: Holt, Rinehart & Winston, 1965.

KRAUSS, I. K. Some situational determinants of competitive performance on sex-stereotyped tasks. *Developmental Psychology*, 1977, 13, 473–480.

KREBS, D. L. Altruism: An examination of the concept and a review of the literature. *Psychological Bulletin*, 1970, 73, 258–302.

KREBS, D. Empathy and altruism. *Journal of Personality and Social Psychology*, 1975, 32, 1134–1146.

KROSNICK, J. A., & JUDD, C. M. Transitions in social influence at adolescence: Who induces cigarette smoking? *Developmental Psychology*, 1982, 18, 359–368.

KUHN, D. Short-term longitudinal evidence for the sequentiality of Kohlberg's early stages of moral judgments. *Developmental Psychology*, 1976, 12, 162–166.

KUHN, D., NASH, S. C., & BRUCKEN, L. Sex role concepts of two- and three-year-olds. *Child Development*, 1978, 49, 445–451.

KUHN, D., & PHELPS, H. The development of children's comprehension of causal direction. *Child Development*, 1976, 47, 248–251.

KUHN, M. H. Self attitudes by age, sex, and professional training. *Physiological Quarterly*, 1960, 1, 39–55.

KUN, A. Development of the magnitude-covariation and compensation schemata in ability and effort attributions of performance. *Child Development*, 1977, 48, 862–873.

KUN, A. Evidence of preschoolers' understanding of causal direction in extended causal sequences. *Child Development*, 1978, 49, 218–222.

KUNCE, J. T., & THELEN, M. H. Modeled standards of self-reward and observer performance. *Developmental Psychology*, 1972, 7, 153–156.

KURDEK, L. A. Convergent validation of perspective taking: A one year follow-up. *Developmental Psychology*, 1977, 13, 172–173.

KURDEK, L. A., & RODGON, M. M. Perceptual, cognitive, and affective perspective taking in kindergarten through sixth-grade children. *Developmental Psychology*, 1975, 11, 643–650.

KURTINES, W., & GREIF, E. B. The development of moral thought: Review and evaluation of Kohlberg's approach. *Psychological Bulletin*, 1974, 81, 453–470.

LADD, G. W. Effectiveness of a social learning method for enhancing children's social interaction and peer acceptance. *Child Development*, 1981, 52, 171–178.

LADD, G. W., & ODEN, S. The relationship between peer acceptance and children's ideas about helpfulness. *Child Development*, 1979, 50, 402–408.

LAMB, M. E. Effects of stress and cohort on mother- and father-infant interaction. *Developmental Psychology*, 1976, 12, 435–443. (a)

LAMB, M. E. (Ed.). *The role of the father in child development*. New York: John Wiley, 1976. (b)

LAMB, M. E. Twelve-month-olds and their parents: Interaction in a laboratory playroom. *Developmental Psychology*, 1976, 12, 237–244. (c)

LAMB, M. E. The development of mother-infant and father-infant attachments in the second year of life. *Developmental Psychology*, 1977, 13, 637–648. (a)

LAMB, M. E. Father-infant and mother-infant interaction in the first year of life. *Child Development*, 1977, 48, 167–181. (b)

LAMB, M. E. Paternal influences and the father's role. *American Psychologist*, 1979, 34, 938–943.

LAMB, M. E., EASTERBROOKS, M. A., & HOLDEN, G. W. Reinforcement and punishment among preschoolers: Characteristics, effects, and correlates. *Child Development*, 1980, 51, 1230–1236.

LAMB, M. E., FRODI, A. M., HWANG, C., FRODI, M., & STEINBERG, J. Mother- and father-interaction involving play and holding in traditional and nontraditional Swedish families. *Developmental Psychology*, 1982, *18*, 215–221.

LAMB, M. E., & ROOPNARINE, J. L. Peer influences on sex-role development in preschoolers. *Child Development*, 1979, *50*, 1219–1222.

LAMB, M. E., & URBERG, K. A. The development of gender role and gender identity. In M. E. Lamb (Ed.), *Social and personality development*. New York: Holt, Rinehart & Winston, 1978.

LANE, I., & COON, R. Reward allocation in preschool children. *Child Development*, 1972, *43*, 1382–1389.

LANGLOIS, J. H., & DOWNS, A. C. Peer relations as a function of physical attractiveness: The eye of the beholder or behavioral reality? *Child Development*, 1979, *50*, 409–418.

LANGLOIS, J. H., & DOWNS, A. C. Mothers, fathers, and peers as socialization agents of sex-typed play behaviors in young children. *Child Development*, 1980, *51*, 1237–1247.

LANGLOIS, J. H., & STEPHAN, C. The effects of physical attractiveness and ethnicity on children's behavioral attributions and peer preferences. *Child Development*, 1977, *48*, 1694–1698.

LANSKY, L. M. The family structure also affects the model: Sex role attitudes in parents of preschool children. *Merrill-Palmer Quarterly*, 1967, *13*, 139–150.

LARSEN, G. Y., & KELLOGG, J. A developmental study of the relation between conservation and sharing behavior. *Child Development*, 1974, *45*, 849–851.

LARSON, S., & KURDEK, L. A. Intratask and intertask consistency of moral judgment indices in first-, third-, and fifth-grade children. *Developmental Psychology*, 1979, *15*, 462–463.

LATANE, B., & RODIN, J. A lady in distress: Inhibiting effects of friends and strangers on bystander intervention. *Journal of Experimental Social Psychology*, 1969, *5*, 189–203.

LAVOIE, J. C. Cognitive determinants of resistance to deviation in seven-, nine-, and eleven-year-old children of low and high maturity of moral judgment. *Developmental Psychology*, 1974, *10*, 393–403.

LAVOIE, J. C., & ANDREWS, R. Cognitive determinants of gender identity and constancy. Paper presented at the meeting of the American Psychological Association, 1975.

LAZAROWITZ, R., STEPHAN, W. G., & FRIEDMAN, S. T. Effects of moral justifications and moral rea-

soning on altruism. *Developmental Psychology*, 1976, *12*, 353–354.

LEAHY, R. L. Developmental trends in qualified inferences and descriptions of self and others. *Developmental Psychology*, 1976, *12*, 546–547.

LEAHY, R. L. Development of conceptions of prosocial behavior: Information affecting rewards given for altruism and kindness. *Developmental Psychology*, 1979, *15*, 34–37.

LEAHY, R. L., & HUARD, C. Role taking and self-image disparity in children. *Developmental Psychology*, 1976, *12*, 504–508.

LECORGNE, L. L., & LAOSA, L. M. Father absence in low-income Mexican-American families: Children's social adjustment and conceptual differentiation of sex role attributes. *Developmental Psychology*, 1976, *12*, 470–471.

LEE, L. C. Social encounters of infants: The beginnings of popularity. Paper presented at the biennial meeting of the International Society for the Study of Behavioral Development, Ann Arbor, Michigan, 1973.

LEIFER, A. D., COLLINS, W. A., GROSS, B. M., TAYLOR, P. H., ANDREWS, L., & BLACKMER, E. R. Developmental aspects of variables relevant to observational learning. *Child Development*, 1971, *42*, 1509–1516.

LEIFER, A. D., LEIDERMAN, P. H., BARNETT, C. R., & WILLIAMS, J. A. Effects of mother-infant separation on maternal attachment behavior. *Child Development*, 1972, *43*, 1203–1218.

LEITER, M. P. A study of reciprocity in preschool play groups. *Child Development*, 1977, *48*, 1288–1295.

LEON, M. Pheromonal mediation of maternal behavior. In T. Alloway, P. Pliner, & L. Krames (Eds.), *Attachment behavior* (Vol. 3). New York: Plenum, 1977.

LEPPER, M. R. Dissonance, self-perception, and honesty in children. *Journal of Personality and Social Psychology*, 1973, *25*, 65–74.

LEPPER, M. R. Intrinsic and extrinsic motivation in children: Detrimental effects of superfluous social controls. In W. A. Collins (Ed.), *Minnesota Symposia on Child Psychology* (Vol. 14). Minneapolis: University of Minnesota Press, 1981.

LEPPER, M. R., & GILOVICH, T. Accentuating the positive: Eliciting generalized compliance from children through activity-oriented requests. *Journal of Personality and Social Psychology*, 1982, *42*, 248–259.

LEPPER, M. R., GREENE, D., & NISBETT, R. E. Undermining children's intrinsic interest with extrinsic reward: A test of the "overjustification" hypothesis. *Journal of Personality and Social Psychology,* 1973, *28,* 129–137.

LEPPER, M. R., SAGOTSKY, G., & MAILER, J. Generalization and persistence of effects of exposure to self-reinforcement models. *Child Development,* 1975, *46,* 618–630.

LERNER, M. J. The justice motive: "Equity" and "parity" among children. *Journal of Personality and Social Psychology,* 1974, *29,* 539–550.

LERNER, R. M. "Richness" analyses of body build stereotype development. *Developmental Psychology,* 1972, *7,* 219.

LERNER, R. M., & KORN, S. J. The development of body-build stereotypes in males. *Child Development,* 1972, *43,* 908–920.

LERNER, R. M., & LERNER, J. V. Effects of age, sex, and physical attractiveness on child-peer relations, academic performance, and elementary school adjustment. *Developmental Psychology,* 1977, *13,* 585–590.

LEVENTHAL, G. S., POPP, A. L., & SAWYER, L. Equity or equality in children's allocation of reward to other persons? *Child Development,* 1973, *44,* 753–763.

LEVIN, P. F., & ISEN, A. M. Further studies on the effect of feeling good on helping. *Sociometry,* 1975, *38,* 141–147.

LEVINE, C. Role-taking standpoint and adolescent usage of Kohlberg's conventional stages of moral reasoning. *Journal of Personality and Social Psychology,* 1976, *34,* 41–46.

LEVINE, F. M., & FASNACHT, G. Token rewards may lead to token learning. *American Psychologist,* 1974, *29,* 817–820.

LEVINE, J. M., SNYDER, H. N., & MENDEZ-CARATINI, G. Task performance and interpersonal attraction in children. *Child Development,* 1982, *53,* 359–371.

LEVITIN, T. E., & CHANNIE, J. D. Responses of female primary school teachers to sex-typed behaviors in male and female children. *Child Development,* 1972, *43,* 1309–1316.

LEVITT, M. J. Contingent feedback, familiarization, and infant affect: How a stranger becomes a friend. *Developmental Psychology,* 1980, *16,* 425–432.

LEWIS, M., & BROOKS, J. Self, other and fear: Infants' reactions to people. In M. Lewis & L. A. Rosenblum (Eds.), *The origins of fear.* New York: John Wiley, 1974.

LEWIS, M., & BROOKS-GUNN, J. Self, other, and fear: The reaction of infants to people. In E. M.

Hetherington & R. D. Parke (Eds.), *Contemporary readings in child psychology.* New York: McGraw-Hill, 1981.

LEWIS, M., & GOLDBERG, S. Perceptual-cognitive development in infancy: A generalized expectancy model as a function of mother-infant interaction. *Merrill-Palmer Quarterly,* 1969, *15,* 81–100.

LEWIS, M., YOUNG, S., BROOKS, J., & MICHALSON, L. The beginning of friendship. In M. Lewis & L. A. Rosenblum (Eds.), *Friendship and peer relations.* New York: John Wiley, 1975.

LEYENS, J., CAMINO, L., PARKE, R. D., & BERKOWITZ, L. Effects of movie violence on aggression in a field setting as a function of group dominance and cohesion. *Journal of Personality and Social Psychology,* 1975, *32,* 346–360.

LIBEN, L. S., & SIGNORELLA, M. L. Gender-related schemata and constructive memory in children. *Child Development,* 1980, *51,* 11–18.

LIEBERMAN, A. F. Preschoolers' competence with a peer: Relations with attachment and peer experience. *Child Development,* 1977, *48,* 1277–1287.

LIEBERT, R. M., & ALLEN, M. K. Effects of rule structure and reward magnitude on the acquisition and adoption of self-reward criteria. *Psychological Reports,* 1967, *21,* 445–452.

LIEBERT, R. M., & BARON, R. A. Some immediate effects of televised violence on children's behavior. *Developmental Psychology,* 1972, *6,* 469–475.

LIEBERT, R. M., & FERNANDEZ, L. E. Effects of vicarious consequences on imitative performance. *Child Development,* 1970, *41,* 847–852.

LITTENBERG, R., TULKIN, S. R., & KAGAN, J. Cognitive components of separation anxiety. *Developmental Psychology,* 1971, *4,* 387–388.

LIVESLEY, W. J., & BROMLEY, D. B. *Person perception in childhood and adolescence.* London: Wiley, 1973.

LOEB, R. C. Concomitants of boys' locus of control examined in parent-child interactions. *Developmental Psychology,* 1975, *11,* 353–358.

LONDERVILLE, S., & MAIN, M. Security of attachment, compliance, and maternal training methods in the second year of life. *Developmental Psychology,* 1981, *17,* 289–299.

LONG, G. T., & LERNER, M. J. Deserving, the "personal contract," and altruistic behavior by children. *Journal of Personality and Social Psychology,* 1974, *29,* 551–556.

LONGSTRETH, L. E. Revisiting Skeels' final study: A

critique. *Developmental Psychology*, 1981, *17*, 620–625.

LOOFT, W. R. Egocentrism and social interaction across the life span. *Psychological Bulletin*, 1972, 78, 73–92.

LORENZ, K. Z. *On aggression.* New York: Harcourt Brace Jovanovich, 1966.

LOTT, B. Behavioral concordance with sex role ideology related to play areas, creativity, and parental sex typing. *Journal of Personality and Social Psychology*, 1978, 36, 1087–1100.

LOVAAS, O. I. Interaction between verbal and nonverbal behavior. *Child Development*, 1961, 32, 329–336.

LYNN, D. B. *Parental and sex-role identification: A theoretical formulation.* Berkeley, Ca.: McCutchan, 1969.

LYNN, D. B., & SAWREY, W. L. The effects of father absence on Norwegian boys and girls. *Journal of Abnormal and Social Psychology*, 1959, 59, 258–262.

LYTTON, H. Observation studies of parent-child interaction: A methodological review. *Child Development*, 1971, 42, 651–684.

LYTTON, H. Do parents create, or respond to, differences in twins? *Developmental Psychology*, 1977, 13, 456–459.

LYTTON, H. Disciplinary encounters between young boys and their mothers and fathers: Is there a contingency system? *Developmental Psychology*, 1979, 15, 256–268.

LYTTON, H., CONWAY, D., & SAUVE, R. The impact of twinship on parent-child interaction. *Journal of Personality and Social Psychology*, 1977, 35, 97–107.

LYTTON H., & ZWIRNER, W. Compliance and its controlling stimuli observed in a natural setting. *Developmental Psychology*, 1975, 11, 769–779.

MAAS, E., MARECEK, J., & TRAVERS, J. R. Children's conceptions of disordered behavior. *Child Development*, 1978, 49, 146–154.

MACCOBY, E. E. Role-taking in childhood and its consequences for social learning. *Child Development*, 1959, 30, 239–252.

MACCOBY, E. E. *Social development: Psychological growth and the parent-child relationship.* New York: Harcourt Brace Jovanovich, 1980.

MACCOBY, E. E., & JACKLIN, C. N. *The psychology of sex differences.* Stanford, Ca.: Stanford University Press, 1974.

MACCOBY, E. E., & JACKLIN, C. N. Sex differences in aggression: A rejoinder and reprise. *Child Development*, 1980, 51, 964–980.

MACDONALD, N. W., & SILVERMAN, I. W. Smiling and laughter in infants as a function of level of arousal and cognitive evaluation. *Developmental Psychology*, 1978, 14, 235–241.

MADSEN, M. S., & SHAPIRA, A. Cooperative and competitive behavior of urban Afro-American, Anglo-American, Mexican-American, and Mexican village children. *Developmental Psychology*, 1970, 3, 16–20.

MAIER, S. F., SELIGMAN, M. E. P., & SOLOMON, R. L. Pavlovian fear conditioning and learned helplessness: Effects on escape and avoidance behavior of (a) the CS-UCS contingency and (b) the independence of voluntary responding. In B. A. Campbell, & R. M. Church (Eds.), *Punishment and aversive behavior.* New York: Appleton-Century-Crofts, 1969.

MAIN, M., TOMASINI, L., & TOLAN, W. Differences among mothers of infants judged to differ in security. *Developmental Psychology*, 1979, 15, 472–473.

MAIN, M., & WESTON, D. R. The quality of the toddler's relationship to mother and to father: Related to conflict behavior and the readiness to establish new relationships. *Child Development*, 1981, 52, 932–940.

MAITLAND, K. A., & GOLDMAN, J. R. Moral judgment as a function of peer group interaction. *Journal of Personality and Social Psychology*, 1974, 30, 699–704.

MAJOR, B., CARNEVALE, P. J. D., & DEAUX, K. A different perspective on androgyny: Evaluations of masculine and feminine personality characteristics. *Journal of Personality and Social Psychology*, 1981, 41, 988–1001.

MALLICK, S. K., & MCCANDLESS, B. R. A study of catharsis of aggression. *Journal of Personality and Social Psychology*, 1966, 4, 591–596.

MANNARINO, A. P. Friendship patterns and altruistic behavior in preadolescent males. *Developmental Psychology*, 1976, 12, 555–556.

MARANTZ, S. A., & MANSFIELD, A. F. Maternal employment and the development of sex-role stereotyping in five- to eleven-year-old girls. *Child Development*, 1977, 48, 668–673.

MARCUS, D. E., & OVERTON, W. F. The development of cognitive gender constancy and sex role preferences. *Child Development*, 1978, 49, 434–444.

MARCUS, R. F., TELLEEN, S., & ROKE, E. J. Relation between cooperation and empathy in young children. *Developmental Psychology*, 1979, 15, 346–347.

MARKUS, H., CRANE, M., BERNSTEIN, S., & SILADI, M.

Self-schemas and gender. *Journal of Personality and Social Psychology*, 1982, *42*, 38–50.

MARSH, D. T., SERAFICA, F. C., & BARENBOIM, C. Effect of perspective-taking training on interpersonal problem solving. *Child Development*, 1980, *51*, 140–145.

MARTIN, B. Parent-child relations. In F. D. Horowitz (Ed.), *Review of child development research* (Vol. 4). Chicago: University of Chicago Press, 1975.

MARTIN, C. L., & HALVERSON, C. F., JR. A schematic processing model of sex typing and stereotyping in children. *Child Development*, 1981, *52*, 1119–1134.

MARTIN, J. A. The control of imitative and nonimitative behaviors in severely retarded children through "generalized-instruction following." *Journal of Experimental Child Psychology*, 1971, *11*, 390–400.

MARTIN, J. A. A longitudinal study of the consequences of early mother-infant interaction: A microanalytic approach. *Monographs of the Society for Research in Child Development*, 1981, *46*. (3, Serial No. 190).

MARTIN, J. A., MACCOBY, E. E., & JACKLIN, C. N. Mothers' responsiveness to interactive bidding and nonbidding in boys and girls. *Child Development*, 1981, *52*, 1064–1067.

MASSAD, C. M. Sex role identity and adjustment during adolescence. *Child Development*, 1981, *52*, 1290–1298.

MASTERS, J. C. Effects of social comparison upon children's self-reinforcement and altruism toward competitors and friends. *Developmental Psychology*, 1971, *5*, 64–72.

MASTERS, J. C., & FURMAN, W. Popularity, individual friendship selection, and specific peer interaction among children. *Developmental Psychology*, 1981, *17*, 344–350.

MASTERS, J. C., FURMAN, W., & BARDEN, R. C. Effects of achievement standards, tangible rewards, and self-dispensed achievement evaluations on children's task mastery. *Child Development*, 1977, *48*, 217–224.

MASTERS, J. C., & PISAROWICZ, P. A. Self-reinforcement and generosity following two types of altruistic behavior. *Child Development*, 1975, *46*, 313–318.

MASTERS, J. C., & SANTROCK, J. W. Studies in the self-regulation of behavior: Effects of contingent cognitive and affective events. *Developmental Psychology*, 1976, *12*, 334–348.

MASTERS, J. C., & WELLMAN, H. M. The study of human infant attachment: A procedural critique. *Psychological Bulletin*, 1974, *81*, 218–237.

MATAS, L., AREND, R. A., & SROUFE, L. A. Continuity of adaptation in the second year: The relationship between quality of attachment and later competence. *Child Development*, 1978, *49*, 547–556.

MATTHEWS, K. A. Caregiver-child interactions and the Type A coronary-prone behavior pattern. *Child Development*, 1977, *48*, 1752–1756.

MAURER, A. Corporal punishment. *American Psychologist*, 1974, *29*, 614–626.

MAURER, D., & SALAPATEK, P. Developmental changes in the scanning of faces by young infants. *Child Development*, 1976, *47*, 523–527.

MCCALL, R. B. Challenges to a science of developmental psychology. *Child Development*, 1977, *48*, 333–344.

MCCALL, R. B., PARKE, R. D., & KAVANAUGH, R. D. Imitation of live and televised models by children one to three years of age. *Monographs of the Society for Research in Child Development*, 1977, *42* (Whole No. 173).

MCCONAGHY, M. J. Gender permanence and the genital basis of gender: Stages in the development of constancy of gender identity. *Child Development*, 1979, *50*, 1223–1226.

MCCORD, J. Some childrearing antecedents of criminal behavior in adult men. *Journal of Personality and Social Psychology*, 1979, *37*, 1477–1486.

MCCUNE-NICOLICH, L. Toward symbolic functioning: Structure of early pretend games and potential parallels with language. *Child Development*, 1981, *52*, 785–797.

MCGHEE, P. E. Development of children's ability to create the joking relationship. *Child Development*, 1974, *45*, 552–556.

MCGHEE, P. E. Children's appreciation of humor: A test of the cognitive congruency principle. *Child Development*, 1976, *47*, 420–426.

MCGUIRE, J. M., & THOMAS, M. H. Effects of sex, competence, and competition on sharing behavior in children. *Journal of Personality and Social Psychology*, 1975, *32*, 490–494.

MCMAINS, M. J., & LIEBERT, R. M. Influence of discrepancies between successively modeled self-reward criteria on the adoption of a self-imposed standard. *Journal of Personality and Social Psychology*, 1968, *8*, 166–171.

MEAD, G. H. *Mind, self, and society*. Chicago: University of Chicago Press, 1934.

MEAD, M. *Sex and temperament in three primitive societies*. New York: Morrow, 1935.

MEICHENBAUM, D. Examination of model characteristics in reducing avoidance behavior. *Journal of Personality and Social Psychology*, 1971, *17*, 298–307.

MEICHENBAUM, D., & GOODMAN, J. Training impulsive children to talk to themselves: A means of developing self-control. *Journal of Abnormal Psychology*, 1971, *77*, 115–126.

MELAMED, B., & SIEGEL, L. Reduction of anxiety in children facing hospitalization and surgery by use of filmed modeling. *Journal of Consulting and Clinical Psychology*, 1975, *43*, 511–521.

MELTZOFF, A. D., & MOORE, M. K. Imitation of facial and manual gestures by human neonates. *Science*, 1977, *198*, 75–78.

MEYER, B. The development of girls' sex-role attitudes. *Child Development*, 1980, *51*, 508–514.

MEYER, T. P. Effects of viewing justified and unjustified real film violence on aggressive behavior. *Journal of Personality and Social Psychology*, 1972, *23*, 21–29.

MIDLARSKY, E., & BRYAN, J. H. Training charity in children. *Journal of Personality and Social Psychology*, 1967, *5*, 408–415.

MIDLARSKY, E., BRYAN, J. H., & BRICKMAN, P. Aversive approval: Interactive effects of modeling and reinforcement on altruistic behavior. *Child Development*, 1973, *44*, 321–328.

MILLAR, W. S. Operant acquisition of social behaviors in infancy: Basic problems and constraints. In H. W. Reese (Ed.), *Advances in child development and behavior* (Vol. 11). New York: Academic Press, 1976.

MILLER, D. T., & KARNIOL, R. Coping strategies and attentional mechanisms in self-imposed delay situations. *Journal of Personality and Social Psychology*, 1976, *34*, 310–316. (a)

MILLER, D. T., & KARNIOL, R. The role of rewards in externally and self-imposed delay of gratification. *Journal of Personality and Social Psychology*, 1976, *33*, 594–600. (b)

MILLER, D. T., & SMITH, J. The effect of own deservingness and deservingness of others on children's helping behavior. *Child Development*, 1977, *48*, 617–620.

MILLER, D. T., WEINSTEIN, S. M., & KARNIOL, R. Effects of age and self-verbalization on children's ability to delay gratification. *Developmental Psychology*, 1978, *4*, 569–570.

MILLER, N. E. Theory and experiment relating psychoanalytic displacement to stimulus-response generalization. *Journal of Abnormal and Social Psychology*, 1948, *43*, 155–178.

MILLER, N., & MARUYAMA, G. Ordinal position and peer popularity. *Journal of Personality and Social Psychology*, 1976, *33*, 123–131.

MILLER, R. E., CAUL, W. F., & MIRSKY, I. F., Communication of affects between feral and socially isolated monkeys. *Journal of Personality and Social Psychology*, 1967, *7*, 231–239.

MILLER, R. L., BRICKHARDT, P., & BOLEN, D. Attribution versus persuasion as a means for modifying behavior. *Journal of Personality and Social Psychology*, 1975, *31*, 430–441.

MILLER, R. S., & MORRIS, W. N. The effects of being imitated on children's responses in a marble-dropping task. *Child Development*, 1974, *45*, 1103–1107.

MILLER, S. M. Effects of maternal employment on sex role perception, interests, and self-esteem in kindergarten girls. *Developmental Psychology*, 1975, *11*, 405–406.

MILLIONES, J. Relationships between perceived child temperament and maternal behaviors. *Child Development*, 1978, *49*, 1255–1257.

MISCHEL, W. *Personality and assessment.* New York: John Wiley, 1968.

MISCHEL, W. Sex typing and socialization. In P. H. Mussen (Ed.), *Carmichael's manual of child psychology* (Vol. 2). New York: John Wiley, 1970.

MISCHEL, W. *Introduction to personality.* New York: Holt, Rinehart & Winston, 1971.

MISCHEL, W. Toward a cognitive social learning reconceptualization of personality. *Psychological Review*, 1973, *80*, 252–283.

MISCHEL, W. Processes in delay of gratification. In L. Berkowitz (Ed.), *Advances in experimental social psychology* (Vol. 7). New York: Academic Press, 1974.

MISCHEL, W. On the interface of cognition and personality: Beyond the person-situation debate. *American Psychologist*, 1979, *34*, 740–754.

MISCHEL, W., & BAKER, N. Cognitive appraisals and transformations in delay behavior. *Journal of Personality and Social Psychology*, 1975, *31*, 254–261.

MISCHEL, W., & PATTERSON, C. J. Substantive and structural elements of effective plans for self-control. *Journal of Personality and Social Psychology*, 1976, *34*, 942–950.

MOIR, D. J. Egocentrism and the emergence of conventional morality in preadolescent girls. *Child Development*, 1974, *45*, 299–304.

MONEY, J., & EHRHARDT, A. *Man and woman, boy and girl.* Baltimore: Johns Hopkins University Press, 1972.

MONSON, T. C. The impact of methodology on the conclusions about the relationship between dispositions and behavior. Paper presented at the Midwestern Psychological Association meeting in Minneapolis, 1982.

MOORE, B. S., BARON, R. M., & BYRNE, D. V. The informativeness and frequency of presentation of a social stimulus as determinants of its efficacy as a reinforcer. *Journal of Experimental Child Psychology*, 1980, 29, 519–528.

MOORE, B. S., CLYBURN, A., & UNDERWOOD, B. The role of affect in delay of gratification. *Child Development*, 1976, 47, 273–276.

MOORE, B. S., MISCHEL, W., & ZEISS, A. Comparative effects of the reward stimulus and its cognitive representation in voluntary delay. *Journal of Personality and Social Psychology*, 1976, 34, 419–424.

MOORE, B. S., UNDERWOOD, B., & ROSENHAN, D. L. Affect and altruism. *Developmental Psychology*, 1973, 8, 99–104.

MOORE, N. V., EVERTSON, C. M., & BROPHY, J. E. Solitary play: Some functional reconsiderations. *Developmental Psychology*, 1974, 10, 830–834.

MORAN, J. J., & JONIAK, A. J. Effect of language on preference for responses to a moral dilemma. *Developmental Psychology*, 1979, 15, 337–338.

MORGAN, G. A., & RICCIUTI, H. N. Infants' responses to strangers during the first year. In B. M. Foss (Ed.), *Determinants of infant behavior, IV*. London: Methuen, 1969.

MORRIS, E. K., & REDD, W. H. Children's performance and social preference for positive, negative, and mixed adult-child interactions. *Child Development*, 1975, 46, 525–531.

MOSATCHE, H. S., & BRAGONIER, P. An observational study of social comparison in preschoolers. *Child Development*, 1981, 52, 376–378.

MOSKOWITZ, D., SCHWARZ, J., & CORSINI, D. Initiating day care at three years of age: Effects on attachment. *Child Development*, 1977, 48, 1271–1276.

MOSS, H. A. Sex, age, and state as determinants of mother-infant interaction. *Merrill-Palmer Quarterly*, 1967, 13, 19–36.

MOWRER, O. H. *Learning theory and personality dynamics*. New York: Ronald Press, 1950.

MUELLER, E., & BRENNER, J. The origins of social skills and interaction among playgroup toddlers. *Child Development*, 1977, 48, 854–861.

MUELLER, E., & LUCAS, T. A developmental analysis of peer interaction among toddlers. In M. Lewis & L. A. Rosenblum (Eds.), *Friendship and peer relations*. New York: John Wiley, 1975.

MULHERN, R. K., JR., & PASSMAN, R. H. The child's behavioral pattern as a determinant of maternal punitiveness. *Child Development*, 1979, 50, 815–820.

MURPHY, L. B. *Social behavior and child personality: An exploratory study of some roots of sympathy*. New York: Columbia University Press, 1937.

MURRAY, A. D. Infant crying as an elicitor of parental behavior: An examination of two models. *Psychological Bulletin*, 1979, 86, 191–215.

MUSSEN, P. H. Long-term consequents of masculinity of interests in adolescence. *Journal of Consulting Psychology*, 1962, 26, 435–440.

MUSSEN, P. H., & DISTLER, L. Masculinity, identification and father-son relationships. *Journal of Abnormal and Social Psychology*, 1959, 59, 350–356.

MUSSEN, P. H., & JONES, M. C. Self-conceptions, motivations, and interpersonal attitudes of late and early maturing boys. *Child Development*, 1957, 28, 243–256.

MUSSEN, P. H., & RUTHERFORD, E. Effects of aggressive cartoons on children's aggressive play. *Journal of Abnormal and Social Psychology*, 1961, 2, 461–464.

MUSSEN, P. H., & RUTHERFORD, E. Parent-child relations and parental personality in relation to young children's sex-role preferences. *Child Development*, 1963, 34, 489–507.

MUSTE, M. J., & SHARP, D. F. Some influential factors in the determination of aggressive behavior in preschool children. *Child Development*, 1947, 18, 11–28.

NADELMAN, L. Sex identity in American children: Memory, knowledge, and preference tests. *Developmental Psychology*, 1974, 10, 413–417.

NAHIR, H. T., & YUSSEN, S. R. The performance of kibbutz- and city-reared Israeli children on two role-taking tasks. *Developmental Psychology*, 1977, 13, 450–455.

NELSON, L. & MADSEN, M. Cooperation and competition in 4-year-olds as a function of reward contingency and subcultures. *Developmental Psychology*, 1969, 1, 340–344.

NELSON, S. A., & DWECK, C. S. Motivation and competence as determinants of young children's reward allocation. *Developmental Psychology*, 1977, 13, 192–197.

NEWCOMB, A. F., BRADY, J. E., & HARTUP, W. W. Friendship and incentive condition as determinants of children's task-oriented social behavior. *Child Development*, 1979, 50, 878–881.

NICHOLLS, J. G. Development of causal attributions and evaluative responses to success and failure in Maori and Pakeha children. *Developmental Psychology*, 1978, *14*, 687–688.

NOLLER, P. Sex differences in the socialization of affectionate expression. *Developmental Psychology*, 1978, *14*, 317–319.

NOLLER, P. Cross-gender effect in two-child families. *Developmental Psychology*, 1980, *16*, 159–160.

NOVAK, M. A. Social recovery of monkeys isolated for the first year of life: II. Long-term assessment. *Developmental Psychology*, 1979, *15*, 50–61.

NOVAK, M. A., & HARLOW, H. F. Social recovery of monkeys isolated for the first year of life: I. Rehabilitation and therapy. *Developmental Psychology*, 1975, *11*, 453–465.

NOWICKI, S., & STRICKLAND, B. A locus of control scale for children. *Journal of Consulting and Clinical Psychology*, 1973, *40*, 148–154.

NUMMEDAL, S. G., & BASS, S. C. Effects of the salience of intention and consequence on children's moral judgments. *Developmental Psychology*, 1976, *12*, 475–476.

O'CONNOR, R. D. Modification of social withdrawal through symbolic modeling. *Journal of Applied Behavior Analysis*, 1969, *2*, 15–22.

O'CONNOR, R. D. The relative efficacy of modeling, shaping, and the combined procedures for the modification of social withdrawal. *Journal of Abnormal Psychology*, 1972, *79*, 327–334.

ODEN, S., & ASHER, S. R. Coaching children in social skills and friendship making. *Child Development*, 1977, *48*, 495–506.

O'LEARY, K. D., & DRABMAN, R. Token reinforcement programs in the classroom: A review. *Psychological Bulletin*, 1971, *75*, 379–398.

OLEJNIK, A. B. The effects of reward-deservedness on children's sharing. *Child Development*, 1976, *47*, 380–385.

OLEJNIK, A. B., & MCKINNEY, J. P. Parental value orientation and generosity in children. *Developmental Psychology*, 1973, *8*, 311.

OLIVER, P. R., ACKER, L. E., & OLIVER, D. D. Effects of reinforcement histories of compliance and non-compliance on nonreinforced imitation. *Journal of Experimental Child Psychology*, 1977, *23*, 180–190.

OLWEUS, D. Aggression and peer acceptance in adolescent boys: Two short-term longitudinal studies of ratings. *Child Development*, 1977, *48*, 1301–1313.

OLWEUS, D. Stability of aggressive reaction patterns in males: A review. *Psychological Bulletin*, 1979, *86*, 852–875.

OLWEUS, D. Familial and temperamental determinants of aggressive behavior in adolescent boys: A causal analysis. *Developmental Psychology*, 1980, *16*, 644–660.

OMARK, D. R., & EDELMAN, M. S. A comparison of status hierarchies in young children: An ethological approach. *Social Sciences Information*, 1975, *14*, 87–107.

OMARK, D. R., & EDELMAN, M. S. The development of attention structures in young children. In M. R. A. Chance & R. Larsen (Eds.), *The social structures of attention*. New York: John Wiley, 1976.

ORLOFSKY, J. L. Relationship between sex role attitudes and personality traits and the Sex Role Behavior Scale-1: A new measure of masculine and feminine role behaviors and interests. *Journal of Personality and Social Psychology*, 1981, *40*, 927–940.

PAPOUSEK, H., & PAPOUSEK, M. Mothering and the cognitive head-start: Psychobiological considerations. In H. R. Schaffer (Ed.), *Studies in mother-infant interaction*. London: Academic Press, 1977.

PARIS, S. G., & CAIRNS, R. B. An experimental and ethological analysis of social reinforcement with retarded children. *Child Development*, 1972, *43*, 717–729.

PARKE, R. D. Effectiveness of punishment as an interaction of intensity, timing, agent nurturance, and cognitive structuring. *Child Development*, 1969, *40*, 213–236.

PARKE, R. D. The role of punishment in the socialization process. In R. A. Hoppe, G. A. Milton, & E. C. Simmel (Eds.), *Early experiences and the processes of socialization*. New York: Academic Press, 1970.

PARKE, R. D. Rules, roles, and resistance to deviation: Recent advances in punishment, discipline, and self-control. In A. D. Pick (Ed.), *Minnesota symposium on child psychology* (Vol. 8). Minneapolis: University of Minnesota Press, 1974.

PARKE, R. D. Perspectives on father-infant interaction. In J. D. Osofsky (Ed.), *Handbook of infancy*. New York: John Wiley, 1978.

PARKE, R. D. Interactional designs. In R. B. Cairns (Ed.), *The analysis of social interactions: Method, issues, and illustrations*. Hillsdale, N.J.: Erlbaum, 1979.

PARKE, R. D., BERKOWITZ, L., LEYENS, J. P., WEST, S. G., & SEBASTIAN, R. J. Some effects of violent and nonviolent movies on the behavior of juvenile delinquents. In L. Berkowitz (Ed.), *Advances in experimental social psychology* (Vol. 10). New York: Academic Press, 1977.

PARKE, R. D., & COLLMER, C. W. Child abuse: An interdisciplinary analysis. In E. M. Hetherington (Ed.), *Review of child development research* (Vol. 5). Chicago: University of Chicago Press, 1975.

PARKE, R. D., & SAWIN, D. B. Infant characteristics and behavior as elicitors of maternal and paternal responsibility in the newborn period. Paper presented at the biannual meeting of the Society for Research in Child Development, Denver, April, 1975.

PARKE, R. D., & SAWIN, D. B. Father-infant interaction in the newborn period: A re-evaluation of some current myths. In E. M. Hetherington & R. D. Parke (Eds.), *Contemporary readings in child psychology.* New York: McGraw-Hill, 1981.

PARKE, R. D., SAWIN, D. B., & KRELING, B. The effect of child feedback on adult disciplinary choices. Unpublished manuscript, Fels Research Institute, 1974.

PARKE, R. D., & WALTERS, R. H. Some factors determining the efficacy of punishment for inducing response inhibition. *Monographs of the Society for Research in Child Development,* 1967, 32, (Whole No. 109).

PARSONS, T. Family structure and the socialization of the child. In T. Parsons & R. F. Bales (Eds.), *Family socialization and interaction process.* Glencoe, Ill.: Free Press, 1955.

PARTEN, M. B. Social participation among preschool children. *Journal of Abnormal and Social Psychology,* 1932, 27, 243–269.

PARTON, D. A. Learning to imitate in infancy. *Child Development,* 1976, 47, 14–31.

PASSMAN, R. H. Arousal reducing properties of attachment objects: Testing the functional limits of the security blanket relative to the mother. *Developmental Psychology,* 1976, 12, 468–469.

PASSMAN, R. H., & ERCK, T. W. Permitting maternal contact through vision alone: Films of mothers for promoting play and locomotion. *Developmental Psychology,* 1978, 14, 512–516.

PASSMAN, R. H., & WEISBERG, P. Mothers and blankets as agents for promoting play and exploration by young children in a novel environment: The effects of social and nonsocial attachment objects. *Developmental Psychology,* 1975, 11, 170–177.

PASTOR, D. L. The quality of mother-infant attachment and its relationship to toddlers' initial sociability with peers. *Developmental Psychology,* 1981, 17, 326–335.

PATEL, H. S., & GORDON, J. E. Some personal and situational determinants of yielding to influence. *Journal of Abnormal and Social Psychology,* 1960, 61, 411–418.

PATTERSON, A. H. Hostility catharsis: A naturalistic quasi-experiment. Paper presented at the meeting of the American Psychological Association, New Orleans, September 1974.

PATTERSON, C. J., & CARTER, D. B. Attentional determinants of children's self-control in waiting and working situations. *Child Development,* 1979, 50, 272–275.

PATTERSON, C. J., & MISCHEL, W. Effects of temptation-inhibiting and task-facilitating plans on self-control. *Journal of Personality and Social Psychology,* 1976, 33, 209–217.

PATTERSON, G. R. A basis for identifying stimuli which control behaviors in natural settings. *Child Development,* 1974, 45, 900–911.

PATTERSON, G. R. The aggressive child: Victim and architect of a coercive system. In L. A. Hamerlynck, L. C. Handy, & E. J. Mash (Eds.), *Behavior modification and families. I. Theory and research.* New York: Brunner-Mazel, 1976.

PATTERSON, G. R., & COBB, J. A. A dyadic analysis of "aggressive" behaviors. In J. P. Hill (Ed.), *Minnesota symposium on child psychology* (Vol. 5). Minneapolis: University of Minnesota Press, 1971.

PATTERSON, G. R., LITTMAN, R. A., & BRICKER, W. Assertive behavior in children: A step toward a theory of aggression. *Monographs of the Society for Research in Child Development,* 1967, 32 (5, Whole No. 113).

PATTERSON, G. R., & REID, J. B. Reciprocity and coercion: Two facets of social systems. In C. Neuringer & J. L. Michael (Eds.), *Behavior modification in clinical psychology.* New York: Appleton-Century-Crofts, 1970.

PAYNE, D. E., & MUSSEN, P. H. Parent-child relations and father identification among adolescent boys. *Journal of Abnormal and Social Psychology,* 1956, 52, 358–362.

PAYNE, F. D. Children's prosocial conduct in structured situations and as viewed by others: Consistency, convergence, and relationships with person variables. *Child Development,* 1980, 51, 1252–1259.

PEDERSEN, F. A., & ROBSON, K. S. Father participation in infancy. *American Journal of Orthopsychiatry,* 1969, 39, 466–472.

PEDERSON, D. R., ROOK-GREEN, A., & ELDER, J. L. The role of action in the development of pretend play in young children. *Developmental Psychology*, 1981, *17*, 756–759.

PEERY, J. C. Popular, amiable, isolated, rejected: A reconceptualization of sociometric status in preschool children. *Child Development*, 1979, *50*, 1231–1234.

PEERY, J. C. Neonate-adult head movement: No and Yes revisited. *Developmental Psychology*, 1980, *16*, 245–250.

PEEVERS, B. H., & SECORD, P. F. Developmental changes in attribution of descriptive concepts of persons. *Journal of Personality and Social Psychology*, 1973, *27*, 120–128.

PEPLAU, L. A. Impact of fear of success and sex-role attitudes on women's competitive achievement. *Journal of Personality and Social Psychology*, 1976, *34*, 561–568.

PERCIVAL, P., & HAVILAND, J. M. Consistency and retribution in children's immanent justice decisions. *Developmental Psychology*, 1978, *14*, 132–136.

PERRY, D. G., & BUSSEY, K. Self-reinforcement in high- and low-aggressive boys following acts of aggression. *Child Development*, 1977, *48*, 653–658.

PERRY, D. G., & BUSSEY, K. The social learning theory of sex differences: Imitation is alive and well. *Journal of Personality and Social Psychology*, 1979, *37*, 1699–1712.

PERRY, D. G., BUSSEY, K., & FREIBERG, K. Impact of adults' appeals for sharing on the development of altruistic dispositions in children. *Journal of Experimental Child Psychology*, 1981, *32*, 127–138.

PERRY, D. G., BUSSEY, K., & PERRY, L. C. Factors influencing the imitation of resistance to deviation. *Developmental Psychology*, 1975, *11*, 724–731.

PERRY, D. G., BUSSEY, K., & REDMAN, J. Reward-induced decreased play effects: Reattribution of motivation, competing responses, or avoiding frustration? *Child Development*, 1977, *48*, 1369–1374.

PERRY, D. G., & GARROW, H. The "social deprivation-satiation effect": An outcome of frequency or perceived contingency? *Developmental Psychology*, 1975, *11*, 681–688.

PERRY, D. G., & PARKE, R. D. Punishment and alternative response training as determinants of response inhibition in children. *Genetic Psychology Monographs*, 1975, *91*, 257–279.

PERRY, D. G., & PERRY, L. C. Denial of suffering in the victim as a stimulus to violence in aggressive boys. *Child Development*, 1974, *45*, 55–62.

PERRY, D. G., & PERRY, L. C. Observational learning in children: Effects of sex of model and subject's sex role behavior. *Journal of Personality and Social Psychology*, 1975, *31*, 1083–1088.

PERRY, D. G., & PERRY, L. C. A note on the effects of prior anger arousal and winning or losing a competition on aggressive behavior in boys. *Journal of Child Psychology and Psychiatry*, 1976, *17*, 145–149.

PERRY, D. G., PERRY, L. C., BUSSEY, K., ENGLISH, D., & ARNOLD, G. Processes of attribution and children's self-punishment following misbehavior. *Child Development*, 1980, *51*, 545–551.

PERVIN, L. A. A free-response description approach to the analysis of personality-situation interaction. *Journal of Personality and Social Psychology*, 1976, *34*, 465–474.

PETERSON, C., PETERSON, J., & FINLEY, N. Conflict and moral judgment. *Developmental Psychology*, 1974, *10*, 65–69.

PETERSON, C., PETERSON, J., & MCDONALD, N. Factors affecting reward allocation by preschool children. *Child Development*, 1975, *46*, 942–947.

PETERSON, L. Developmental changes in verbal and behavioral sensitivity to cues of social norms of altruism. *Child Development*, 1980, *51*, 830–838.

PETERSON, L., HARTMANN, D. P., & GELFAND, D. M. Developmental changes in the effects of dependency and reciprocity cues on children's moral judgments and donation rates. *Child Development*, 1977, *48*, 1331–1339.

PETERSON, R. A. Aggression as a function of expected retaliation and aggression level of target and aggressor. *Developmental Psychology*, 1971, *5*, 161–166.

PETERSON, R. F., MERWIN, M. R., MOYER, T. J., & WHITEHURST, G. J. Generalized imitation: The effects of experimenter absence, differential reinforcement, and stimulus complexity. *Journal of Experimental Child Psychology*, 1971, *12*, 114–128.

PETERSON, R. F., & WHITEHURST, G. J. A variable influencing the performance of generalized imitative behaviors. *Journal of Applied Behavior Analysis*, 1971, *4*, 1–9.

PHELPS, H. R., & HORROCKS, J. E. Factors influencing informal groups of adolescents. *Child Development*, 1958, *29*, 69–86.

PHILLIPS, D. A., & ZIGLER, E. Children's self-image disparity: Effects of age, socioeconomic status, ethnicity, and gender. *Journal of Personality and Social Psychology,* 1980, *39,* 689–700.

PHILLIPS, S., KING, S., & DUBOIS, L. Spontaneous activities of female versus male newborns. *Child Development,* 1978, *49,* 590–597.

PIAGET, J. *The language and thought of the child.* London: Rutledge & Kegan Paul, 1926.

PIAGET, J. *The moral judgment of the child.* London: Kegan, Paul, Trench, & Trubner, 1932.

PIAGET, J. *Play, dreams, and imitation in childhood.* New York: W. W. Norton & Co., Inc., 1951.

PIAGET, J., & INHELDER, B. *The child's conception of space.* London: Routledge & Kegan Paul, 1956.

PICHE, G. L., MICHLIN, M. L., RUBIN, D. L., & JOHNSON, F. L. Relationships between fourth graders' performances on selected role-taking tasks and referential communication accuracy tasks. *Child Development,* 1975, *46,* 965–969.

PIEN, D., & ROTHBART, M. K. Incongruity and resolution in children's humor: A reexamination. *Child Development,* 1976, *47,* 966–971.

PLOMIN, R., & ROWE, D. C. Genetic and environmental etiology of social behavior in infancy. *Developmental Psychology,* 1979, *15,* 62–72.

PORTNOY, F. C., & SIMMONS, C. H. Day care and attachment. *Child Development,* 1978, *49,* 239–242.

PRENTICE, N. M., & FATHMAN, R. E. Joking riddles: A developmental index of children's humor. *Developmental Psychology,* 1975, *11,* 210–216.

PRESBIE, R. J., & COITEUX, P. F. Learning to be generous or stingy: Imitation of sharing behavior as a function of model generosity and vicarious reinforcement. *Child Development,* 1971, *42,* 1033–1038.

President's Science Advisory Committee. *Youth: Transition to Adulthood.* Chicago: University of Chicago Press, 1973.

PUTALLAZ, M., & GOTTMAN, J. M. An interactional model of children's entry into peer groups. *Child Development,* 1981, *52,* 986–994.

RAGOZIN, A. Attachment behavior of day-care children: Naturalistic and laboratory observations. *Child Development,* 1980, *51,* 409–415.

RANSEN, D. L. The mediation of reward-induced motivation decrements in early and middle childhood: A template matching approach. *Journal of Personality and Social Psychology,* 1980, *39,* 1088–1100.

RAUSCH, H. Interaction sequences. *Journal of Personality and Social Psychology,* 1965, *2,* 487–499.

REDD, W. H., MORRIS, E. K., & MARTIN, J. A. Effects of positive and negative adult-child interactions on children's social preference. *Journal of Experimental Child Psychology,* 1975, *19,* 153–164.

REISMAN, J. M., & SHORR, S. I. Friendship claims and expectations among children and adults. *Child Development,* 1978, *49,* 913–916.

REISS, S., & SUSHINSKY, L. W. Overjustification, competing responses, and the acquisition of intrinsic interest. *Journal of Personality and Social Psychology,* 1975, *31,* 1116–1125.

REST, J. R. The hierarchical nature of moral judgment: A study of patterns of comprehension and preference of moral stages. *Journal of Personality,* 1973, *41,* 86–109.

REST, J. R., DAVISON, M. L., & ROBBINS, S. Age trends in judging moral issues: A review of cross-sectional, longitudinal, and sequential studies of the Defining Issues Test. *Child Development,* 1978, *49,* 263–279.

REST, J. R., TURIEL, E., & KOHLBERG, L. Level of moral development as a determinant of preference and comprehension of moral judgments made by others. *Journal of Personality,* 1969, *37,* 225–252.

REUTER, J., & YUNIK, G. Social interaction in nursery schools. *Developmental Psychology,* 1973, *9,* 319–325.

RHEINGOLD, H. L., & BAYLEY, N. The later effects of an experimental modification of mothering. *Child Development,* 1959, *30,* 363–372.

RHEINGOLD, H. L., & COOK, K. V. The content of boys' and girls' rooms as an index of parents' behavior. *Child Development,* 1975, *46,* 459–463.

RHEINGOLD, H. L., & ECKERMAN, C. O. The infant separates himself from his mother. *Science,* 1970, *168,* 78–83.

RHEINGOLD, H. L., GEWIRTZ, J. L., & ROSS, H. W. Social conditioning of vocalizations in the infant. *Journal of Comparative and Physiological Psychology,* 1959, *52,* 68–73.

RHEINGOLD, H. L., HAY, D. F., & WEST, M. J. Sharing in the second year of life. *Child Development,* 1976, *47,* 1148–1158.

RICCIUTI, H. Fear and development of social attachments in the first year of life. In M. Lewis and L. A. Rosenblum (Eds.), *The origins of human behavior: Fear.* New York: John Wiley, 1974.

RICE, M. E., & GRUSEC, J. E. Saying and doing: Effects on observer performance. *Journal of Per-

sonality and Social Psychology, 1975, 32, 584–593.

RICHARD, B. A., & DODGE, K. A. Social maladjustment and problem solving in school-aged children. *Journal of Consulting and Clinical Psychology*, 1982, 50, 226–233.

RICHARDSON, S. A., GOODMAN, N., HASTORF, A. H., & DORNBUSCH, S. M. Cultural uniformity in reaction to physical disabilities. *American Sociological Review*, 1961, 26, 241–247.

RINKOFF, R. F., & CORTER, C. M. Effects of setting and maternal accessibility on the infant's response to brief separation. *Child Development*, 1980, 51, 603–606.

ROBSON, K. S., & MOSS, H. A. Patterns and determinants of maternal attachment. *Journal of Pediatrics*, 1970, 77, 976–985.

ROCHA, R. F., & ROGERS, R. W. Ares and Babbitt in the classroom: Effects of competition and reward on children's aggression. *Journal of Personality and Social Psychology*, 1976, 33, 588–593.

RODE, S. S., CHANG, P., FISCH, R. O., & SROUFE, L. A. Attachment patterns of infants separated at birth. *Developmental Psychology*, 1981, 17, 188–191.

ROE, K. V. Infants' mother-stranger discrimination at 3 months as a predictor of cognitive development at 3 and 5 years. *Developmental Psychology*, 1978, 14, 191–192.

ROEDELL, W. C., & SLABY, R. G. The role of distal and proximal interaction in infant social preference formation. *Developmental Psychology*, 1977, 13, 266–273.

ROFF, M., SELLS, S. B., & GOLDEN, M. M. *Social adjustment and personality development in children.* Minneapolis: University of Minnesota Press, 1972.

ROMER, N. The motive to avoid success and its effects on performance in school-age males and females. *Developmental Psychology*, 1975, 11, 689–699.

ROPER, R., & HINDE, R. A. Social behavior in a play group: Consistency and complexity. *Child Development*, 1978, 49, 570–579.

ROSENBACH, D., CROCKETT, W. H., & WAPNER, S. Developmental level, emotional involvement, and the resolution of inconsistency in impression formation. *Developmental Psychology*, 1973, 8, 120–130.

ROSENFELD, E., HUESMANN, L. R., ERON, L. D., & TORNEY-PURTA, J. V. Measuring patterns of fantasy behavior in children. *Journal of Personality and Social Psychology*, 1982, 42, 347–366.

ROSENFIELD, A. G. Visiting in the intensive care nursery. *Child Development*, 1980, 51, 939–941.

ROSENHAN, D. L. Some origins of concern for others. In P. H. Mussen, J. Langer, & M. Covington (Eds.), *Trends and issues in developmental psychology.* New York: Holt, Rinehart & Winston, 1969.

ROSENHAN, D. L., SALOVEY, P., & HARGIS, K. The joys of helping: Focus of attention mediates the impact of positive affect on altruism. *Journal of Personality and Social Psychology*, 1981, 40, 899–905.

ROSENHAN, D. L., UNDERWOOD, B., & MOORE, B. Affect mediates self-gratification and altruism. *Journal of Personality and Social Psychology*, 1974, 30, 546–552.

ROSENHAN, D. L., & WHITE, G. M. Observation and rehearsal as determinants of prosocial behavior. *Journal of Personality and Social Psychology*, 1967, 5, 424–431.

ROSENKOETTER, L. I. Resistance to temptation: Inhibitory and disinhibitory effects of models. *Developmental Psychology*, 1973, 8, 80–84.

ROSENKRANTZ, P., VOGEL, S., BEE, H., BROVERMAN, I., & BROVERMAN, D. Sex-role stereotypes and self-concepts in college students. *Journal of Consulting and Clinical Psychology*, 1968, 32, 287–295.

ROSENTHAL, M. K. Vocal dialogues in the neonatal period. *Developmental Psychology*, 1982, 18, 17–21.

ROSENTHAL, T. L., & BANDURA, A. Psychological modeling: Theory and practice. In S. L. Garfield & A. E. Bergin (Eds.), *Handbook of psychotherapy and behavior change.* New York: John Wiley, 1978.

ROSENTHAL, T. L., & ZIMMERMAN, B. J. *Social learning and cognition.* New York: Academic Press, 1978.

ROSS, H. S., & GOLDMAN, B. D. Infants' sociability toward strangers. *Child Development*, 1977, 48, 638–642.

ROSS, L. The intuitive psychologist and his shortcomings: Distortions in the attribution process. In L. Berkowitz (Ed.), *Advances in experimental social psychology* (Vol. 10). New York: Academic Press, 1977.

ROTHBART, M. K. Laughter in young children. *Psychological Bulletin*, 1973, 80, 247–256.

ROTHBART, M. K. Measurement of temperament in

infancy. *Child Development*, 1981, *52*, 569–578.

ROTHBART, M. K., & MACCOBY, E. E. Parents' differential reactions to sons and daughters. *Journal of Personality and Social Psychology*, 1966, *4*, 237–243.

ROTTER, J. B. Generalized expectancies for internal versus external control of reinforcement. *Psychological Monographs*, 1966, *80*, (1, Whole No. 609).

RUBENSTEIN, J., & HOWES, C. The effects of peers on toddler interaction with mother and toys. *Child Development*, 1976, *47*, 597–605.

RUBENSTEIN, J. L., & HOWES, C. Caregiving and infant behavior in day care and in homes. *Developmental Psychology*, 1979, *15*, 1–24.

RUBIN, J. Z., PROVENZANO, F. J., & LURIA, Z. The eye of the beholder: Parents' views on sex of newborns. *American Journal of Orthopsychiatry*, 1974, *43*, 720–731.

RUBIN, K. H. Relationship between egocentric communication and popularity among peers. *Developmental Psychology*, 1972, *7*, 364.

RUBIN, K. H. Egocentrism in childhood: A unitary construct? *Child Development*, 1973, *44*, 102–110.

RUBIN, K. H. Role taking in childhood: Some methodological considerations. *Child Development*, 1978, *49*, 428–433.

RUBIN, K. H. Nonsocial play in preschoolers: Necessarily evil? *Child Development*, 1982, *53*, 651–657.

RUBIN, K. H., & MAIONI, T. L. Play preference and its relationship to egocentrism, popularity, and classification skills in preschoolers. *Merrill-Palmer Quarterly*, 1975, *25*, 171–179.

RUBIN, K. H., MAIONI, T. L., & HORNUNG, M. Free play behaviors in middle- and lower-class preschoolers: Parten and Piaget revisited. *Child Development*, 1976, *47*, 414–419.

RUBIN, K.H., & SCHNEIDER, F. W. The relationship between moral judgment, egocentrism, and altruistic behavior. *Child Development*, 1973, *44*, 661–665.

RUBIN, K. H., & TROTTER, K. T. Kohlberg's Moral Judgment Scale: Methodological considerations. *Developmental Psychology*, 1977, *13*, 535–536.

RUBIN, K. H., WATSON, K. S., & JAMBOR, T. W. Free-play behaviors in preschool and kindergarten children. *Child Development*, 1978, *49*, 534–536.

RUBLE, D. N., BALABAN, T., & COOPER, J. Gender constancy and the effects of sex-typed televised toy commercials. *Child Development*, 1981, *52*, 667–673.

RUBLE, D. N., BOGGIANO, A. K., FELDMAN, N. S., & LOEBL, J. H. Developmental analysis of the role of social comparison in self-evaluation. *Developmental Psychology*, 1980, *16*, 105–115.

RUBLE, D. N., PARSONS, J. E., & ROSS, J. Self-evaluative response of children in an achievement setting. *Child Development*, 1976, *47*, 990–997.

RULE, B. G. The hostile and instrumental functions of human aggression. In W. W. Hartup & J. de Wit (Eds.), *Determinants and origins of aggressive behaviors.* The Hague: Mouton, 1974.

RULE, B. G., & DUKER, P. The effect of intentions and consequences on children's evaluations of aggressors. *Journal of Personality and Social Psychology*, 1973, *27*, 184–189.

RULE, B. G., FERGUSON, T. J., & NESDALE, A. R. Emotional arousal, anger and aggression: The misattribution issue. In P. Pliner, L. Kramis, & K. Blankstein (Eds.), *Perception of emotion in self and others. Advances in the Study of Communication and Affect* (Vol. 4). New York: Plenum Press, 1978.

RULE, B. G., & NESDALE, A. R. Emotional arousal and aggressive behavior. *Psychological Bulletin*, 1976, *83*, 851–863.

RULE, B. G., NESDALE, A. R., & MCARA, M. J. Children's reactions to information about the intentions underlying an aggressive act. *Child Development*, 1974, *45*, 794–798.

RUSHTON, J. P. Generosity in children: Immediate and long-term effects of modeling, preaching, and moral judgment. *Journal of Personality and Social Psychology*, 1975, *31*, 459–466.

RUSHTON, J. P. Socialization and the altruistic behavior of children. *Psychological Bulletin*, 1976, *83*, 898–913.

RUSHTON, J. P. *Altruism, socialization, and society.* Englewood Cliffs, N.J.: Prentice-Hall, 1980.

RUSSELL, G. The father role and its relation to masculinity, femininity, and androgyny. *Child Development*, 1978, *49*, 1174–1181.

RUTHERFORD, E., & MUSSEN, P. Generosity in nursery school boys. *Child Development*, 1968, *39*, 755–765.

RUTTER, M. Maternal deprivation, 1972–1978: New findings, new concepts, new approaches. *Child Development*, 1979, *50*, 283–305.

RYBASH, J. M., & ROODIN, P. A. A reinterpretation of the effects of videotape and verbal presentation modes on children's moral judgments. *Child Development*, 1978, *49*, 228–230.

RYBASH, J. M., SEWALL, M. B., ROODIN, P. A., & SULLIVAN, L. Effects of age of transgressor, damage and type of presentation on kindergarten children's moral judgments. *Developmental Psychology*, 1975, *11*, 874.

SAGAR, H. A., & SCHOFIELD, J. W. Racial and behavioral cues in black and white children's perceptions of ambiguously aggressive acts. *Journal of Personality and Social Psychology*, 1980, *39*, 590–598.

SALATAS, H., & FLAVELL, J. H. Perspective taking: The development of two components of knowledge. *Child Development*, 1976, *47*, 103–109.

SALILI, F., MAEHR, M. L., & GILLMORE, G. Achievement and morality: A cross-cultural analysis of causal attribution and evaluation. *Journal of Personality and Social Psychology*, 1976, *33*, 327–337.

SALTZ, E., DIXON, D., & JOHNSON, J. Training disadvantaged preschoolers on various fantasy activities: Effects on cognitive functioning and impulse control. *Child Development*, 1977, *48*, 367–380.

SALTZ, E., & JOHNSON, J. Training for thematic-fantasy play in culturally disadvantaged children: Preliminary results. *Journal of Educational Psychology*, 1974, *66*, 623–630.

SALTZSTEIN, H. D., DIAMOND, R. M., & BELENKY, M. Moral judgment level and conformity behavior. *Developmental Psychology*, 1972, *7*, 327–336.

SALTZSTEIN, H. D., SANVITALE, D., & SUPRANER, A. Social influence on children's standards for judging criminal culpability. *Developmental Psychology*, 1978, *14*, 125–131.

SAMEROFF, A. J., & CAVANAUGH, P. Learning in infancy: A developmental perspective. In J. D. Osofsky (Ed.), *Handbook of infant development*. New York: John Wiley, 1979.

SAMPSON, E. E., & HANCOCK, T. An examination of the relationship between ordinal position, personality, and conformity: An extension, replication, and partial verification. *Journal of Personality and Social Psychology*, 1967, *5*, 398–407.

SAMUELS, H. R. The effect of an older sibling on infant locomotor exploration of a new environment. *Child Development*, 1980, *51*, 607–609.

SANDERS, K. M., & HARPER, L. V. Free-play fantasy behavior in preschool children: Relations among gender, age, season, and location. *Child Development*, 1976, *47*, 1182–1185.

SANTROCK, J. W. Paternal absence, sex typing, and identification. *Developmental Psychology*, 1970, *2*, 264–272.

SANTROCK, J. W. Father absence, perceived maternal behavior, and moral development in boys. *Child Development*, 1975, *46*, 753–757.

SARNOFF, I. Identification with the aggressor: Some personality correlates of anti-Semitism among Jews. *Journal of Personality*, 1951, *20*, 199–218.

SAVIN-WILLIAMS, R. C. An ethological study of dominance formation maintenance in a group of human adolescents. *Child Development*, 1976, *47*, 972–979.

SAVIN-WILLIAMS, R. C. Dominance hierarchies in groups of early adolescents. *Child Development*, 1979, *50*, 923–935.

SAWIN, D. B., & PARKE, R. D. Development of self-verbalized control of resistance to deviation. *Developmental Psychology*, 1979, *15*, 120–127.

SCHACHTER, F. F. Toddlers with employed mothers. *Child Development*, 1981, *52*, 958–964.

SCHACHTER, F. F., SHORE, E., FELDMAN-ROTMAN, S., MARQUIS, R. E., & CAMPBELL, S. Sibling deidentification. *Developmental Psychology*, 1976, *12*, 418–427.

SCHACHTER, S. Birth order and sociometric status. *Journal of Abnormal and Social Psychology*, 1964, *68*, 453–456.

SCHAEFER, E. S. A circumplex model for maternal behavior. *Journal of Abnormal and Social Psychology*, 1959, *59*, 226–235.

SCHAFFER, H. R. *The growth of sociability*. Baltimore: Penguin Books, 1971.

SCHAFFER, H. R., & CROOK, C. K. Maternal control techniques in a directed play situation. *Child Development*, 1979, *50*, 989–996.

SCHAFFER, H. R., & CROOK, C. K. Child compliance and maternal control techniques. *Developmental Psychology*, 1980, *16*, 54–61.

SCHAFFER, H. R., & EMERSON, P. E. The development of social attachments in infancy. *Monographs of the Society for Research in Child Development*, 1964, *29* (3, Whole No. 94).

SCHAFFER, H. R., GREENWOOD, A., & PARRY, M. H. The onset of wariness. *Child Development*, 1972, *43*, 165–175.

SCHAU, C. G., KAHN, L., DIEPOLD, J. H., & CHERRY, F. The relationship of parental expectations and preschool children's verbal sex typing to their sex-typed toy play behavior. *Child Development*, 1980, *51*, 266–270.

SCHLEIFER, M., & DOUGLAS, V. I. Effects of training on the moral judgment of young children. *Journal of Personality and Social Psychology*, 1973, 28, 62–68.

SCHLESINGER, H. The impact of deafness on the life style. In J. M. Stack (Ed.), *The special child*. New York: Human Sciences Press, 1980.

SCHUBERT, J. B., BRADLEY-JOHNSON, S., & NUTTAL, J. Mother-infant communication and maternal employment. *Child Development*, 1980, 51, 246–249.

SCHWARZ, J. C. *Social and emotional effects of day care: A review of recent research*. Paper presented to an interdisciplinary study group sponsored by the Society for Research in Child Development at Michigan, October, 1975.

SEARS, P. S. Doll play aggression in normal young children: Influence of sex, age, sibling status, father's absence. *Psychological Monographs*, 1951, 65 (6, Whole No. 323).

SEARS, R. R., MACCOBY, E. E., & LEVIN, H. *Patterns of child rearing*. Evanston, Ill.: Row-Peterson, 1957.

SEARS, R. R., RAU, L., & ALPERT, R. *Identification and child rearing*. Stanford, Ca.: Stanford University Press, 1965.

SEASHORE, M. J., LEIFER, A. D., BARNETT, C. R., & LEIDERMAN, P. H. The effects of denial of early mother-infant interaction on maternal self-confidence. *Journal of Personality and Social Psychology*. 1973, 26, 369–378.

SEDLAK, A. J. Developmental differences in understanding plans and evaluating actors. *Child Development*, 1979, 50, 536–560.

SELIGMAN, M. E. P. On the generality of the laws of learning. *Psychological Review*, 1970, 77, 406–418.

SELIGMAN, M. E. P. *Helplessness: On depression, development, and death*. San Francisco: W. H. Freeman & Company Publishers, 1975.

SELMAN, R. L. The relation of role taking to the development of moral judgment in children. *Child Development*, 1971, 42, 79–91.

SELMAN, R. Social-cognitive understanding: A guide to educational and clinical practice. In T. Lickona (Ed.), *Moral development and behavior*. New York: Holt, Rinehart, & Winston, 1976.

SERBIN, L. A., TONICK, I. J., & STERNGLANZ, S. H. Shaping cooperative cross-sex play. *Child Development*, 1977, 48, 924–929.

SHAKLEE, H. Development in inferences of ability and task difficulty. *Child Development*, 1976, 47, 1051–1057.

SHANAB, M. E., & YAHYA, K. A. A behavioral study of obedience in children. *Journal of Personality and Social Psychology*, 1977, 35, 530–536.

SHANTZ, C. U. The development of social cognition. In E. M. Hetherington (Ed.), *Review of child development research* (Vol. 5). Chicago: University of Chicago Press, 1975.

SHANTZ, D. W., & PENTZ, T. Situational effects on justifiableness of aggression at three age levels. *Child Development*, 1972, 43, 274–281.

SHANTZ, D. W., & VOYDANOFF, D. A. Situational effects on retaliatory aggression at three age levels. *Child Development*, 1973, 44, 149–153.

SHAPIRA, A., & MADSEN, M. C. Between- and within-group cooperation and competition among kibbutz and nonkibbutz children. *Developmental Psychology*, 1974, 10, 140–145.

SHAPIRO, E. G. Effect of expectations of future interaction on reward allocations in dyads: Equity or equality. *Journal of Personality and Social Psychology*, 1975, 31, 873–880.

SHARABANY, R., GERSHONI, R., & HOFMAN, J. E. Girlfriend, boyfriend: Age and sex differences in intimate friendship. *Developmental Psychology*, 1981, 17, 800–808.

SHATZ, M., & GELMAN, R. The development of communication skills: Modifications in the speech of young children as a function of listener. *Monographs of the Society for Research in Child Development*, 38, (5, Serial No. 152).

SHERIF, M., HARVEY, O. J., WHITE, B. J., HOOD, W. R., & SHERIF, C. W. *Intergroup conflict and cooperation: The Robbers Cave experiment*. Norman: University of Oklahoma Press, 1961.

SHERIF, M., & SHERIF, C. W. *Reference groups*. New York: Harper & Row, Pub., 1964.

SHERMAN, L. W. An ecological study of group glee in small groups of children. *Child Development*, 1975, 46, 53–61.

SHIGETOMI, C. C., HARTMANN, D. P., & GELFAND, D. M. Sex differences in children's altruistic behavior and reputations for helpfulness. *Developmental Psychology*, 1981, 17, 434–437.

SHINN, M. Father absence and children's cognitive development. *Psychological Bulletin*, 1978, 85, 295–324.

SHOUVAL, R., KAV VENAKI, S., BRONFENBRENNER, U., DEVEREUX, E. C., & KIELY, E. Anomalous reactions to social pressure of Israeli and Soviet children raised in family versus collective settings. *Journal of Personality and Social Psychology*, 1975, 32, 477–489.

SHULTZ, T. R. Development of the appreciation of

riddles. *Child Development,* 1974, *45,* 100–105.

SHULTZ, T. R., & BUTKOWSKY, I. Young children's use of the schema for multiple sufficient causes in the attribution of real and hypothetical behavior. *Child Development,* 1977, *48,* 464–469.

SHULTZ, T. R., & HORIBE, F. Development of the appreciation of verbal jokes. *Developmental Psychology,* 1974, *10,* 13–20.

SHULTZ, T. R., & MENDELSON, R. The use of covariation as a principle of causal analysis. *Child Development,* 1975, *46,* 394–399.

SHULTZ, T. R., & RAVINSKY, F. B. Similarity as a principle of causal inference. *Child Development,* 1977, *48,* 1552–1558.

SIEGLER, R. S. The effects of simple necessity and sufficiency relationships on children's causal inferences. *Child Development,* 1976, *47,* 1058–1063.

SIEGLER, R. S., & LIEBERT, R. M. Effects of contiguity, regularity and age on children's causal inferences. *Developmental Psychology,* 1974, *10,* 574–579.

SIMON, M. L. Application of a new model of peer group influence to naturally existing adolescent friendship groups. *Child Development,* 1977, *48,* 270–274.

SINGER, J. L. (Ed.). *The child's world of make-believe.* New York: John Wiley, 1973.

SINGLETON, L. C., & ASHER, S. R. Racial integration and children's peer preferences: An investigation of developmental and cohort differences. *Child Development,* 1979, *50,* 936–941.

SKARIN, K., & MOELY, B. E. Altruistic behavior: An analysis of age and sex differences. *Child Development,* 1976, *47,* 1159–1165.

SKEELS, H. Adult status of children with contrasting early life experiences. *Monographs of the Society for Research in Child Development,* 1966, *31,* No. 3.

SKINNER, B. F. *Science and human behavior.* New York: Macmillan, 1953.

SLABY, R. G., & CROWLEY, C. G. Modification of cooperation and aggression through teacher attention to children's speech. *Journal of Experimental Child Psychology,* 1977, *23,* 442–458.

SLABY, R. G., & FREY, K. S. Development of gender constancy and selective attention to same-sex models. *Child Development,* 1975, *46,* 849–856.

SLABY, R. G., & QUARFOTH, G. R. Effects of television on the developing child. In B. W. Camp (Ed.), *Advances in behavioral pediatrics* (Vol. 1). Greenwich, Conn.: Johnson Associates, 1980.

SLUCKIN, A. M., & SMITH, P. K. Two approaches to the concept of dominance in preschool children. *Child Development,* 1977, *48,* 917–923.

SMILANSKY, S. *The effects of sociodramatic play on disadvantaged preschool children.* New York: John Wiley, 1968.

SMITH, C., & LLOYD, B. Maternal Behavior and Perceived sex of infant: Revisited. *Child Development,* 1978, *49,* 1263–1265.

SMITH, C. L., GELFAND, D. M., HARTMANN, D. P., & PARTLOW, M. E. Y. Children's causal attributions regarding help giving. *Child Development,* 1979, *50,* 203–210.

SMITH, M. C. Children's use of the multiple sufficient cause schema in social perception. *Journal of Personality and Social Psychology,* 1975, *32,* 737–747.

SMITH, M. C. Cognizing the behavior stream: The recognition of intentional action. *Child Development,* 1978, *49,* 736–743.

SMITH, P. K. A longitudinal study of social participation in preschool children: Solitary and parallel play reexamined. *Developmental Psychology,* 1978, *14,* 517–523.

SMITH, P. K., & DUTTON, S. Play and training in direct and innovative problem solving. *Child Development,* 1979, *50,* 830–836.

SMITH, T. W., & PITTMAN, T. S. Reward, distraction, and the overjustification effect. *Journal of Personality and Social Psychology,* 1978, *36,* 565–572.

SNOW, M. E., JACKLIN, C. N., & MACCOBY, E. E. Birth-order differences in peer sociability at thirty-three months. *Child Development,* 1981, *52,* 589–595.

SNYDER, M. Self-monitoring processes. In L. Berkowitz (Ed.) *Advances in experimental social psychology.* (Vol. 12). New York: Academic Press, 1979.

SONTAG, L. W., BAKER, C. T., & NELSEN, V. L. Mental growth and personality: A longitudinal study. *Monographs of the Society for Research in Child Development,* 1958, *23,* (No. 68), 1–143.

SORCE, J. F., & EMDE, R. N. Mother's presence is not enough: Effect of emotional availability on infant exploration. *Developmental Psychology,* 1981, *17,* 737–745.

SPEAR, P. S., & ARMSTRONG, S. Effects of performance expectancies created by peer comparison as related to social reinforcement, task difficulty, and age of child. *Journal of Experimental Child Psychology,* 1978, *25,* 254–266.

SPELKE, E., ZELAZO, P., KAGAN, J., & KOTELCHUCK, M.

Father interaction and separation protest. *Developmental Psychology*, 1973, 9, 83–90.

SPENCE, J. T. Verbal reinforcement combinations and concept-identification learning: The role of nonreinforcement. *Journal of Experimental Psychology*, 1970, 85, 321–329.

SPENCE, J. T., HELMREICH, R. L., & HOLAHAN, C. K. Negative and positive components of psychological masculinity and femininity and their relationships to self-reports of neurotic and acting out behaviors. *Journal of Personality and Social Psychology*, 1979, 37, 1673–1682.

SPENCE, J. T., HELMREICH, R., & STAPP, J. Ratings of self and peers on sex role attributes and their relation to self-esteem and conceptions of masculinity and femininity. *Journal of Personality and Social Psychology*, 1975, 32, 29–39.

SPENCER, M. B., & HOROWITZ, F. D. Effects of systematic social and token reinforcement on the modification of racial and color concept attitudes in black and white preschool children. *Developmental Psychology*, 1973, 9, 246–254.

SPENCER-BOOTH, Y., & HINDE, R. A. Effects of brief separations from mothers on behaviour of rhesus monkeys 6–24 months later. *Journal of Child Psychology and Psychiatry*, 1971, 12, 157–172.

SPIVACK, G., & SHURE, M. B. *Social adjustment of young children: A cognitive approach to solving real-life problems.* San Francisco: Jossey-Bass, 1974.

SPRAFKIN, J. N., LIEBERT, R. M., & POULOS, R. W. Effects of a prosocial televised example on children's helping. *Journal of Experimental Child Psychology*, 1975, 20, 119–126.

SROUFE, L. A. Wariness of strangers and the study of infant development. *Child Development*, 1977, 48, 731–746.

SROUFE, L. A. The coherence of individual development: Early care, attachment, and subsequent developmental issues. *American Psychologist*, 1979, 34, 834–841.

SROUFE, L. A., & WATERS, E. The ontogenis of smiling and laughter: A perspective on the organization of development in infancy. *Psychological Review*, 1976, 83, 172–189.

SROUFE, L. A., & WATERS, E. Attachment as an organizational construct. *Child Development*, 1977, 48, 1184–1199.

SROUFE, L. A., WATERS, E., & MATAS, L. Contextual determinants of infant affective response. In M. Lewis & L. Rosenblum (Eds.), *The origins of fear.* New York: John Wiley, 1974.

STACY, M., DEARDEN, R., PILL, R., & ROBINSON, D. Hospitals, children, and their families. London: Routledge & Kegan Paul, 1970.

STAUB, E. *The effects of success and failure on children's sharing behavior.* Paper presented at the meeting of the Eastern Psychological Association, Washington, D.C., April 1968.

STAUB, E. A child in distress: The influence of age and number of witnesses on children's attempts to help. *Journal of Personality and Social Psychology*, 1970, 14, 130–141.

STAUB, E. A child in distress: The influence of nurturance and modeling on children's attempts to help. *Developmental Psychology*, 1971, 5, 124–132. (a)

STAUB, E. Helping a person in distress: The influence of implicit and explicit "rules" of conduct on children and adults. *Journal of Personality and Social Psychology*, 1971, 17, 137–144. (b)

STAUB, E. The use of role playing and induction in children's learning of helping and sharing behavior. *Child Development*, 1971, 42, 805–816. (c)

STAUB, E., & NOERENBERG, H. Property rights, deservingness, reciprocity, friendship: The transactional character of children's sharing behavior. *Journal of Personality and Social Psychology*, 1981, 40, 271–289.

STAUB, E., & SHERK, L. Need for approval, children's sharing behavior, and reciprocity in sharing. *Child Development*, 1970, 41, 243–252.

STAYTON, D. J., AINSWORTH, M. D. S., & MAIN, M. B. The development of separation behavior in the first year of life: Protest, following and greeting. *Developmental Psychology*, 1973, 9, 213–225.

STEIN, A. H. Imitation of resistance to temptation. *Child Development*, 1967, 38, 157–169.

STEIN, A. H., & BAILEY, M. M. The socialization of achievement motivation in females. *Psychological Bulletin*, 1973, 80, 345–366.

STEIN, A. H., & FRIEDRICH, L. K. Impact of television on children youth. In E. M. Hetherington (Ed.), *Review of child development research* (Vol. 5). Chicago: University of Chicago Press, 1975.

STEINBERG, L. D., GREENBERGER, E., GARDUQUE, L., RUGGIERO, M., & VAUX, A. Effects of working on adolescent development. *Developmental Psychology*, 1982, 18, 385–395.

STEINMAN, W. M. Generalized imitation and the discrimination hypothesis. *Journal of Experimental Child Psychology*, 1970, 10, 79–99.

STEINMAN, W. M., & BOYCE, K. D. Generalized imitation as a function of discrimination difficulty and choice. *Journal of Experimental Child Psychology*, 1971, *11*, 251–265.

STENDLER, C. B., DAMRIN, D., & HAINES, A. C. Studies in cooperation and competition: The effects of working for group and individual rewards on the social climate of children's groups. *Journal of Genetic Psychology*, 1951, *79*, 173–198.

STENGEL, E. *Suicide and attempted suicide*. Middlesex: Penguin, 1971.

STEPHAN, W. G. School desegregation: An evaluation of predictions made in Brown v. board of education. *Psychological Bulletin*, 1978, *85*, 217–238.

STERN, D. N. The goal and structure of mother-infant play. *Journal of the American Academy of Child Psychiatry*, 1974, *13*, 403–421.

STERNGLANZ, S. H. & SERBIN, L. A. Sex role stereotyping in children's television programs. *Developmental Psychology*, 1974, *10*, 710–715.

STEUER, F. B., APPLEFIELD, J. M., & SMITH, R. Televised aggression and the interpersonal aggression of preschool children. *Journal of Experimental Child Psychology*, 1971, *11*, 442–447.

STEVENS-LONG, J. The effect of behavioral context on some aspects of adults' disciplinary practice and affect. *Child Development*, 1973, *44*, 476–484.

STEVENSON, H. W., & STEWART, E. C. A developmental study of racial awareness in young children. *Child Development*, 1958, *29*, 399–409.

STIPEK, D. J., & WEISZ, J. R. Perceived personal control and academic achievement. *Review of Educational Research*, 1981, *51*, 101–137.

STORMS, M. D. Sex role identity and its relationships to sex role attributes and sex role stereotypes. *Journal of Personality and Social Psychology*, 1979, *37*, 1779–1789.

STRAIN, P., & TIMM, M. An experimental analysis of social interaction between a behaviorally disordered preschool child and her classroom peers. *Journal of Applied Behavior Analysis*, 1974, *4*, 583–590.

STRAYER, F. F. Peer attachment and affiliative subgroups. In F. F. Strayer (Ed.), *Ethological perspectives on preschool social organization*. Memo de Recherche #5, Université du Quebec, A Montreal, Department of Psychologie, Avril 1977.

STRAYER, F. F., & STRAYER, J. An ethological analysis of social agonism and dominance relations among preschool children. *Child Development*, 1976, *47*, 980–989.

STREATER, A. L., & CHERTKOFF, J. M. Distribution of rewards in a triad: A developmental test of equity theory. *Child Development*, 1976, *47*, 800–805.

SULLIVAN, H. S. *The interpersonal theory of psychiatry*. New York: W. W. Norton & Co., Inc., 1953.

SULS, J., GUTKIN, D., & KALLE, R. J. The role of intentions, damage, and social consequences in the moral judgments of children. *Child Development*, 1979, *50*, 874–877.

SULS, J., & KALLE, R. J. Intention, damage, and age of transgressor as determinants of children's moral judgments. *Child Development*, 1978, *49*, 1270–1273.

SULS, J., & KALLE, R. J. Children's moral judgments as a function of intention, damage, and an actor's physical harm. *Developmental Psychology*, 1979, *15*, 93–94.

SUOMI, S. J., & HARLOW, H. F. Social rehabilitation of isolate-reared monkeys. *Developmental Psychology*, 1972, *6*, 487–496.

SUOMI, S. J., & HARLOW, H. F. Early experience and social development in rhesus monkeys. In M. E. Lamb (Ed.), *Social and personality development*. New York: Holt, Rinehart, & Winston, 1978.

SURBER, C. F. Developmental processes in social inference: Averaging of intentions and consequences in moral judgment. *Developmental Psychology*, 1977, *13*, 654–665.

SUTTON-SMITH, B., ROBERTS, J. M., & ROSENBERG, B. G. Sibling association and role involvement. *Merrill-Palmer Quarterly*, 1964, *10*, 25–38.

SUTTON-SMITH, B., & ROSENBERG, B. G. *The sibling*. New York: Holt, Rinehart & Winston, 1970.

SVEJDA, M. J., CAMPOS, J. J., & EMDE, R. N. Mother-infant "bonding": Failure to generalize. *Child Development*, 1980, *51*, 775–779.

TAUBER, M. A. Sex differences in parent-child interaction styles during a free-play session. *Child Development*, 1979, *50*, 981–988.

TEYBER, E. C., MESSE, L. A., & STOLLAK, G. E. Adult responses to child communications. *Child Development*, 1977, *48*, 1577–1582.

THELEN, M. H., DOLLINGER, S. J., & ROBERTS, M. C. On being imitated: Its effects on attraction and reciprocal imitation. *Journal of Personality and Social Psychology*. 1975, *31*, 467–472.

THELEN, M. H., FRAUTSCHI, N. M., FEHRENBACH, P. A., & KIRKLAND, K. Imitation in the interest of social influence. *Developmental Psychology*, 1978, *14*, 429–430.

THELEN, M. H., & KIRKLAND, K. D. On status and being imitated: Effects on reciprocal imitation and attraction. *Journal of Personality and Social Psychology,* 1976, 33, 691–697.

THELEN, M. H., MILLER, D. J. FEHRENBACH, P. A., FRAUTSCHI, N. M., & FISHBEIN, M. D. Imitation during play as a means of social influence. *Child Development,* 1980, *51,* 918–920.

THELEN, M. H., PAUL, S. C., & DOLLINGER, S. J. Response uncertainty and imitation: The interactive effects of age and task options. *Journal of Research in Personality,* 1978, *12,* 370–380.

THOMAN, E. B., KORNER, A. F., & BEASON-WILLIAMS, L. Modification of responsiveness to maternal realization in the neonate. *Child Development,* 1977, 48, 563–569.

THOMAN, E. B., LEIDERMAN, P. H., & OLSON, J. P. Neonate-mother interactions during breast feeding. *Developmental Psychology,* 1972, 6, 110–118.

THOMAS, A., CHESS, S., & BIRCH, H. G. *Temperament and behavior disorders in children.* New York: New York University Press, 1968.

THOMAS, M. H., HORTON, R. W., LIPPINCOTT, E. C., & DRABMAN, R. S. Desensitization to portrayals of real-life aggression as a function of exposure to television violence. *Journal of Personality and Social Psychology,* 1977, 35, 430–458.

THOMPSON, R. A., LAMB, M. E., & ESTES, D. Stability of infant-mother attachment and its relationship to changing life circumstances in an unselected middle-class sample. *Child Development,* 1982, 53, 144–148.

THOMPSON, S. K. Gender labels and early sex role development. *Child Development,* 1975, 46, 339–347.

THOMPSON, W. C., COWAN, C. L., & ROSENHAN, D. L. Focus of attention mediates the impact of negative affect on altruism. *Journal of Personality and Social Psychology,* 1980, 38, 291–300.

TIEGER, T. On the biological basis of sex differences in aggression. *Child Development,* 1980, 51, 943–963.

TINBERGEN, N. *The study of instinct.* London: Oxford University Press, 1951.

TINBERGEN, N. *The animal in its world: Explorations of an ethologist.* London: Allen & Unwin, 1972.

TOMLINSON-KEASEY, C., & KEASEY, C. B. The mediating role of cognitive development in moral judgment. *Child Development,* 1974, 45, 291–298.

TOMPKINS, B. M., & OLEJNIK, A. B. Children's reward allocations: The impact of situational and cognitive factors. *Child Development,* 1978, 49, 526–529.

TONER, I. J., LEWIS, B. C., & GRIBBLE, C. M. Evaluative verbalization and delay maintenance behavior in children. *Journal of Experimental Child Psychology,* 1979, 28, 205–210.

TONER, I. J., MOORE, L. P., & EMMONS, B. A. The effect of being labeled on subsequent self-control in children. *Child Development,* 1980, *51,* 618–621.

TONER, I. J., & SMITH, R. A. Age and overt verbalization in delay-maintenance behavior in children. *Journal of Experimental Child Psychology,* 1977, 24, 123–128.

TRACY, R. L., & AINSWORTH, M. D. S. Maternal affectionate behavior and infant-mother attachment patterns. *Child Development,* 1981, 52, 1341–1343.

TRESEMER, D. Fear of success: Popular but unproven. *Psychology Today,* 1974, 7, 82–85.

TRIVERS, R. L. The evolution of reciprocal altruism. *The Quarterly Review of Biology,* 1971, 46, 35–57.

TRONICK, E., ALS, H., ADAMSON, L., WISE, S., & BRAZELTON, T. B. The infant's response to entrapment between contradictory messages in face-to-face interaction. *Journal of the American Academy of Child Psychiatry,* 1978, *17,* 1–13.

TULVING, E. Episodic and semantic memory. In E. Tulving and W. Donaldson (Eds.), *Organization of memory.* New York: Academic Press, 1972.

TURIEL, E. An experimental test of the sequentiality of developmental stages in the child's moral judgments. *Journal of Personality and Social Psychology,* 1966, 3, 611–618.

TURNER, C. W., & GOLDSMITH, D. Effects of toy guns and airplanes on children's antisocial free play behavior. *Journal of Experimental Child Psychology,* 1976, *21,* 303–315.

TURNURE, C. Cognitive development and role-taking ability in boys and girls from 7 to 12. *Developmental Psychology,* 1975, *11,* 202–209.

TYLER, L. E. The antecedents of two varieties of interest pattern. *Genetic Psychology Monographs,* 1964, 70, 177–227.

TYLER, L. E. *The psychology of human differences.* New York: Appleton-Century-Crofts, 1965.

UDWIN, O., & SHMUKLER, D. The influence of sociocultural, economic, and home background factors on children's ability to engage in imaginative play. *Developmental Psychology,* 1981, *17,* 66–72.

UNDERWOOD, B., & MOORE, B. S. Sources of behavioral consistency. *Journal of Personality and Social Psychology,* 1981, 40, 780–785.

ULLIAN, D. Z. The development of conceptions of masculinity and femininity. In B. Lloyd & J. Ascher (Eds.), *Exploring sex differences*. London: Academic Press, 1976.

URANOWITZ, S. W. Helping and self-attributions: A field experiment. *Journal of Personality and Social Psychology*, 1975, *31*, 852–854.

URBAIN, E. S., & KENDALL, P. C. Review of social-cognitive problem-solving interventions with children. *Psychological Bulletin*, 1980, *88*, 109–143.

URBERG, K. A. Sex role conceptualizations in adolescents and adults. *Developmental Psychology*, 1979, *15*, 90–92.

URBERG, K. A., & DOCHERTY, E. M. Development of role-taking skills in young children. *Developmental Psychology*, 1976, *12*, 198–203.

VANDELL, D. L. Effects of a playgroup experience on mother-son and father-son interaction. *Developmental Psychology*, 1979, *15*, 379–385.

VANDELL, D. L., WILSON, K. S., & BUCHANAN, N. R. Peer interaction in the first year of life: An examination of its structure, content, and sensitivity to toys. *Child Development*, 1980, *51*, 481–488.

VANDENBERG, B. Play and development from an ethological perspective. *American Psychologist*, 1978, *33*, 724–738.

VANDENBERG, B. Environmental and cognitive factors in social play. *Journal of Experimental Child Psychology*, 1981, *31*, 169–175.

VAUGHN, B., EGELAND, B., SROUFE, L. A., & WATERS, E. Individual differences in infant-mother attachment at twelve and eighteen months: Stability and change in families under stress. *Child Development*, 1979, *50*, 971–975.

VAUGHN, B. E., GOVE, F. L., & EGELAND, B. The relationship between out-of-home care and the quality of infant-mother attachment in an economically disadvantaged population. *Child Development*, 1980, *51*, 1203–1214.

VERNON, D. T. A. Modeling and birth order in responses to painful stimuli. *Journal of Personality and Social Psychology*, 1974, *29*, 794–799.

VYGOTSKY, L. S. *Thought and language*. Cambridge, Mass.: M.I.T. Press, 1934.

WAHLER, R.G. Child-child interactions in free field settings: Some experimental analyses. *Journal of Experimental Child Psychology*, 1967, *5*, 278–293.

WALDFOGEL, S. The development, meaning, and management of school phobia. *American Journal of Orthopsychiatry*, 1957, *27*, 754–780.

WALDROP, M. F., & HALVERSON, C. F., JR. Intensive and extensive peer behavior: Longitudinal and cross-sectional analyses. *Child Development*, 1975, *46*, 19–26.

WALKER, L. J. Cognitive and perspective-taking prerequisites for moral development. *Child Development*, 1980, *51*, 131–139.

WALKER, L. J., & RICHARDS, B. S. Stimulating transitions in moral reasoning as a function of stage of cognitive development. *Developmental Psychology*, 1979, *15*, 95–103.

WALSTER, E. Assignment of responsibility for an accident. *Journal of Personality and Social Psychology*, 1966, *3*, 73–79.

WALTERS, G. C., & GRUSEC, J. E. *Punishment*. San Francisco: W. H. Freeman & Company Publishers, 1977.

WALTERS, R. H., & BROWN, M. Studies of reinforcement of aggression: III: Transfer of responses to an interpersonal situation. *Child Development*, 1963, *34*, 563–571.

WALTERS, R. H., & DEMKOW, L. Timing of punishment as a determinant of response inhibition. *Child Development*, 1963, *34*, 207–214.

WALTERS, R. H., & PARKE, R. D. Influence of response consequences to a social model on resistance to deviation. *Journal of Experimental Child Psychology*, 1964, *1*, 269–280.

WALTERS, R. H., & PARKE, R. D. The role of distance receptors in the development of social responsiveness. In L. Lipsitt & C. Spiker (Eds.), *Advances in child development and behavior* (Vol. 2). New York: Academic Press, 1965.

WALTERS, R. H., & PARKE, R. D. The influence of punishment and related disciplinary techniques on the social behavior of children: Theory and empirical findings. In B. A. Maher (Ed.), *Progress in experimental personality research* (Vol. 4). New York: Academic Press, 1967.

WARREN, V. L., & CAIRNS, R. B. Social reinforcement satiation: An outcome of frequency or ambiguity? *Journal of Experimental Child Psychology*, 1972, *13*, 249–260.

WATERS, E. The reliability and stability of individual differences in infant-mother attachment. *Child Development*, 1978, *49*, 483–494.

WATERS, E., MATAS, L., & SROUFE, L. A. Infants' reactions to an approaching stranger: Description, validation, and functional significance of wariness. *Child Development*, 1975, *46*, 348–356.

WATERS, E., VAUGHN, B. E., & EGELAND, R. R. Individual differences in infant-mother attachment relationships at age one: Antecedents in neonatal behavior in an urban, economically disadvantaged sample. *Child Development,* 1980, *51,* 208-216.

WATERS, E., WIPPMAN, J., & SROUFE, L. A. Attachment, positive affect, and competence in the peer group: Two studies in construct validation. *Child Development,* 1979, *50,* 821-829.

WATSON, D. The actor and the observer: How are their perceptions of causality divergent? *Psychological Bulletin,* 1982, *92,* 682-700.

WATSON, J. S., HAYES, L. A., VIETZE, P., & BECKER, J. Discriminative infant smiling to orientations of talking faces of mother and stranger. *Journal of Experimental Child Psychology,* 1979, *28,* 92-99.

WATSON, J. S., & RAMEY, C. T. Reactions to responsive contingent stimulation in early infancy. *Merrill-Palmer Quarterly,* 1972, *18,* 219-227.

WEINER, B. A theory of motivation for some classroom experiences. *Journal of Educational Psychology,* 1979, *71,* 3-25.

WEINER, B. May I borrow your class notes? An attributional analysis of judgments of help giving in an achievement-related context. *Journal of Educational Psychology,* 1980, *72,* 676-681.

WEINER, B., & PETER, N. A cognitive-developmental analysis of achievement and moral judgments. *Developmental Psychology,* 1973, *9,* 290-309.

WEINER, F. H. Altruism, ambiance and action: The effects of rural and urban rearing on helping behavior. *Journal of Personality and Social Psychology,* 1976, *34,* 112-124.

WEINER, H. R. & DUBANOSKI, R. A. Resistance to extinction as a function of self- or externally determined schedules of reinforcement. *Journal of Personality and Social Psychology,* 1975, *31,* 905-910.

WEINRAUB, M., & FRANKEL, J. Sex differences in parent-infant interaction during free play, departure, and separation. *Child Development,* 1977, *48,* 1240-1249.

WEINRAUB, M., & LEWIS, M. The determinants of children's responses to separation. *Monographs of the Society for Research in Child Development,* 1977, *42,* (3, Serial No. 172).

WEINRAUB, M., & PUTNEY, E. The effects of height on infants' social responses to unfamiliar persons. *Child Development,* 1978, *49,* 598-603.

WEISBERG, P. Social and nonsocial conditioning of infant vocalizations. *Child Development,* 1963, *34,* 377-388.

WEISS, R. F., BUCHANAN, W., ALSTATT, L., & LOMBARDO, J. P. Altruism is rewarding. *Science,* 1971, *171,* 1262-1263.

WEISSBROD, C. S. Noncontingent warmth induction, cognitive style, and children's imitative donation and rescue effort behaviors. *Journal of Personality and Social Psychology,* 1976, *34,* 274-281.

WEISSBROD, C. S. The impact of warmth and instructions on donation. *Child Development,* 1980, *51,* 279-281.

WEISZ, J. R. Transcontextual validity in developmental research. *Child Development,* 1978, *49,* 1-12.

WELLS, D., & SHULTZ, T. R. Developmental distinctions between behavior and judgment in the operation of the discounting principle. *Child Development,* 1980, *51,* 1307-1310.

WEST, H. Early peer-group interaction and role-taking skills: An investigation of Israeli children. *Child Development,* 1974, *45,* 1118-1121.

WEST, S. G., GUNN, S. P., & CHERNICKY, P. Ubiquitous Watergate: An attributional analysis. *Journal of Personality and Social Psychology,* 1975, *32,* 55-65.

WHITE, C. B., BUSHNELL, N., & REGNEMER, J. L. Moral development in Bahamian school children: A 3-year examination of Kohlberg's stages of moral development. *Developmental Psychology,* 1978, *14,* 58-65.

WHITE, E., ELSOM, B., & PRAWAT, R. Children's conceptions of death. *Child Development,* 1978, *49,* 307-310.

WHITE, G. M. Immediate and deferred effects of model observation and guided and unguided rehearsal on donation and stealing. *Journal of Personality and Social Psychology,* 1972, *21,* 139-148.

WHITE, G. M., & BURNAM, M. A. Socially cued altruism: Effects of modeling, instructions, and age on public and private donations. *Child Development,* 1975, *46,* 559-563.

WHITEHURST, G. J., & SONNENSCHEIN, S. The development of communication: Attribute variation leads to contrast failure. *Journal of Experimental Child Psychology,* 1978, *25,* 490-504.

WHITEMAN, M., BROOK, J. S., & GORDON, A. S. Children's motivational perception as related to the instrumentality and effect of action. *Developmental Psychology,* 1974, *10,* 929-935.

WHITING, B. B., & WHITING, J. W. M. *Children of six cultures: A psychocultural analysis.* Cambridge, Mass.: Harvard University Press, 1975.

WHITING, J. W. M. Resource mediation and learning by identification. In I. Iscoe & H. W. Stevenson (Eds.), *Personality development in children.* Austin: University of Texas Press, 1960.

WHITT, J. K., & PRENTICE, N. M. Cognitive processes in the development of children's enjoyment and comprehension of joking riddles. *Developmental Psychology*, 1977, *13*, 129–136.

WILLIAMS, J. E., BOSWELL, D. A., & BEST, D. L. Evaluative responses of preschool children to the colors white and black. *Child Development*, 1975, *46*, 501–508.

WILLIAMS, J. E., & MORLAND, J. K. Comment on Bank's "White preference in blacks: A paradigm in search of a phenomenon." *Psychological Bulletin*, 1979, *86*, 28–32.

WILSON, E. O. *Sociobiology.* Cambridge, Mass.: Harvard University Press, 1975.

WILSON, J. P. Motivation, modeling, and altruism: A person x situation analysis. *Journal of Personality and Social Psychology*, 1976, *34*, 1078–1086.

WINDER, C. L., & RAU, L. Parental attitudes associated with social deviance in preadolescent boys. *Journal of Abnormal Social Psychology*, 1963, *64*, 418–424.

WINSTON, A. S., & REDD, W. H. Instructional control as a function of adult presence and competing reinforcement contingencies. *Child Development*, 1976, *47*, 264–268.

WOHLFORD, P., SANTROCK, J. W., BERGER, S. E., & LIBERMAN, D. Older brothers' influence on sex-typed, aggressive, and dependent behavior in father-absent children. *Developmental Psychology*, 1971, *4*, 124–134.

WOLF, T. M. Effects of live modeled sex-inappropriate play behavior in a naturalistic setting. *Developmental Psychology*, 1973, *9*, 120–123.

WOLF, T. M. Response consequences to televised modeled sex-inappropriate play behavior. *Journal of Genetic Psychology*, 1975, *127*, 35–44.

WOLFF, P. H. Observations on the early development of smiling. In B. M. Foss (Ed.), *Determinants of infant behavior* (Vol. 2). New York: John Wiley, 1963.

WOLFF, P. H. The natural history of crying and other vocalizations in early infancy. In B. M. Foss (Ed.), *Determinants of infant behavior* (Vol. 4). London: Methuen, 1969.

WOLKIND, S., HALL, F., & PAWLBY, S. Individual differences in mothering behaviour: A combined epidemiological and observational approach. In P. J. Graham (Ed.), *Epidemiological approaches in child psychiatry*. London: Academic Press, 1977.

WRIGHT, M. E. The influence of frustration upon the social relations of young children. *Character and Personality*, 1943, *12*, 111–112.

YALISOVE, D. The effect of riddle structure on children's comprehension of riddles. *Developmental Psychology*, 1978, *14*, 173–180.

YARROW, L. J., & GOODWIN, M. S. The immediate impact of separation reactions of infants to a change in mother figures. In L. J. Stone, H. T. Smith, & L. B. Murphy (Eds.), *The competent infant*. New York: Basic Books, 1973.

YARROW, L. J., GOODWIN, M. S., MANHEIMER, H., & MILOWE, I. D. Infancy experience and cognitive and personality development at ten years. In L. J. Stone, H. T. Smith, & L. B. Murphy (Eds.), *The competent infant*. New York: Basic Books, 1973.

YARROW, M. R., & CAMPBELL, J. D. Person perception in children. *Merrill-Palmer Quarterly of Behavior and Development*, 1963, *9*, 57–72.

YARROW, M. R., SCOTT, P. M., & WAXLER, C. Z. Learning concern for others. *Developmental Psychology*, 1973, *8*, 240–260.

YARROW, M. R., WAXLER, C. Z., BARRETT, D., DARBY, J., KING, R., PICKETT, M., & SMITH, M. Dimensions and correlates of prosocial behavior in young children. *Child Development*, 1976, *47*, 118–125.

YARROW, M. R., WAXLER, C. Z., & SCOTT, P. M. Child effects on adult behavior. *Developmental Psychology*, 1971, *5*, 300–311.

YATES, B. T., & MISCHEL, W. Young children's preferred attentional strategies for delaying gratification. *Journal of Personality and Social Psychology*, 1979, *37*, 286–300.

YOUNG, W. C., GOY, R. W., & PHOENIX, C. H. Hormones and sexual behavior. *Science*, 1964, *143*, 212–218.

YUSSEN, S. R. Determinants of visual attention and recall in observational learning by preschoolers and second graders. *Developmental Psychology*, 1974, *10*, 93–100.

YUSSEN, S. R., & LEVY, V. M., JR. Developmental changes in predicting one's own span of short-term memory. *Journal of Experimental Child Psychology*, 1975, *19*, 502–508.

ZAHN-WAXLER, C., RADKE-YARROW, M., & BRADY-SMITH, J. Perspective-taking and prosocial behavior. *Developmental Psychology*, 1977, *13*, 87–88.

ZAHN-WAXLER, C., RADKE-YARROW, M., & KING, R. A. Childrearing and children's prosocial initiations toward victims of distress. *Child Development*, 1979, *50*, 319–330.

ZALK, S. R., & KATZ, P. A. Gender attitudes in children. *Sex Roles*, 1978, *4*, 349–357.

ZIGLER, E., LEVINE, J., & GOULD, L. Cognitive processes in the development of children's appreciation of humor. *Child Development*, 1966, *37*, 507–518.

ZIGLER, E., LEVINE, J., & GOULD, L. Cognitive challenge as a factor in children's humor appreciation. *Journal of Personality and Social Psychology*, 1967, *6*, 332–336.

ZIMMERMAN, B. J., & ROSENTHAL, T. L. Observational learning of rule governed behavior by children. *Psychological Bulletin*, 1974, *81*, 29–42.

ZIVIN, G. On becoming subtle: Age and social rank changes in the use of a facial gesture. *Child Development*, 1977, *48*, 1314–1321.

ZUCKERMAN, M., & WHEELER, L. To dispel fantasies about the fantasy-based measure of fear of success. *Psychological Bulletin*, 1975, *82*, 932–946.

ZUSSMAN, J. U. Relationship of demographic factors to parental discipline techniques. *Developmental Psychology*, 1978, *14*, 685–686.

Author Index

Menlove, F. L., 126, 133
Merrill, L., 8, 202
Merwin, M. R., 120
Messe, L. A., 102, 255
Messer, S. B., 228
Meyer, B., 278
Meyer, T. P., 223
Michalson, L., 309
Michlin, M. L., 159
Midlarsky, E., 247, 256
Millar, W. S., 47
Miller, D. J., 129, 322
Miller, D. T., 193, 253
Miller, N., 314
Miller, N. E., 198, 214
Miller, R. E., 256
Miller, R. L., 97, 191
Miller, R. S., 129
Miller, S. M., 284
Milliones, J., 59, 67, 102
Milowe, I. D., 63
Miranda, S. B., 46
Mirsky, I. F., 256
Mischel, W., 7, 9, 11, 126, 140, 166, 191–193, 211, 273, 279
Moely, B. E., 242
Moir, D. J., 180
Monda, L. C., 265
Money, J., 275, 278
Monson, T. C., 8
Moore, B. S., 7, 96, 193–194, 249–250
Moore, L. P., 191
Moore, M. K., 117
Moore, N. V., 305
Moore, S. G., 97, 191, 245, 259
Moran, J. J., 179
Morgan, G. A., 72–73
Morland, J. K., 150
Morris, E. K., 86
Morris, W. N., 129
Morrison, A., 267
Mosatche, H. S., 148, 323
Moskowitz, D., 65
Moss, H. A., 67, 201, 266–267, 271, 283
Mowrer, O. H., 113–114, 198
Moyer, T. J., 120
Mueller, E., 129, 300–302
Mulhern, R. K., Jr., 103
Murphy, L. B., 257, 326
Murray, A. D., 45
Murray, E., 280
Mussen, P. H., 208, 212, 221, 237, 241, 246, 257, 273, 284–285, 289

Muste, M. J., 201
Myers, J. T., 211
Myerscough, R. P., 265

Nadelman, L., 277
Nagle, R. J., 65
Nahir, H. T., 162
Nash, S. C., 265, 272, 278
Nathanson, M., 180
Neff, C., 68
Nelsen, V. L., 21
Nelson, L., 250
Nelson, S., 88, 268
Nelson, S. A., 254
Nesdale, A. R., 154, 175, 200, 212, 226
Ness, S., 257
Newcomb, A. F., 251, 309
Newtson, D., 224
Nicholls, J. G., 157
Nicholson, T. A., 286
Nicosia, G., 320
Nisbett, R. E., 93, 142, 156, 181
Noerenberg, H., 251–252
Noller, P., 267, 285
Novak, M. A., 62, 326–327
Nowicki, S., 145
Nummedal, S. G., 175
Nuttal, J., 65

O'Connor, R. D., 27, 314–315
Oden, S., 308, 312, 316
O'Leary, K. D., 93, 232
Olejnik, A. B., 98, 242, 253–254, 278
Oliver, D. D., 120
Oliver, P. R., 120
Olson, J. P., 267
Olweus, D., 201, 217, 219
Omark, D. R., 318
Orlofsky, J. L., 269–270
O'Shea, G., 68
Overton, W. F., 277, 286

Page, B. C., 244
Papousek, H., 117
Papousek, M., 117
Paris, S. G., 88, 96
Parke, R. D., 26–27, 47, 53, 67–71, 83–84, 86, 89, 92, 103–104, 117, 189, 193, 222, 267, 283, 322
Parry, M. H., 71
Parsons, J. E., 175, 186
Parsons, T., 115, 288
Parten, M. B., 304–307

Subject Index